北京大学中国语言学研究中心

早期北京话珍稀文献集成

主编 刘云

——西人北京话教科书汇编

分卷主编 翟赟 郭利霞 陈颖

语言自迩集

[英] 威妥玛 编著

卷一

北京大学出版社
PEKING UNIVERSITY PRESS

图书在版编目(CIP)数据

语言自迩集：全二册 /（英）威妥玛编著. —影印本. —北京：北京大学出版社，2017.9
（早期北京话珍本典籍校释与研究）
ISBN 978-7-301-28674-6

Ⅰ.①语… Ⅱ.①威… Ⅲ.①北京话—汉语史—史料 ②北京话—对外汉语教学—研究资料 Ⅳ.①H172.1

中国版本图书馆CIP数据核字（2017）第214841号

书　　名	语言自迩集（卷一、卷二）（影印本）
	YUYAN ZI ER JI
著作责任者	［英］威妥玛　编著
责任编辑	崔　蕊　任　蕾
标准书号	ISBN 978-7-301-28674-6
出版发行	北京大学出版社
地　　址	北京市海淀区成府路205号　100871
网　　址	http://www.pup.cn　　新浪微博：@北京大学出版社
电子信箱	zpup@pup.cn
电　　话	邮购部 62752015　发行部 62750672　编辑部 62754144
印 刷 者	北京虎彩文化传播有限公司
经 销 者	新华书店
	720毫米×1020毫米　16开本　43.25印张　313千字
	2017年9月第1版　2018年10月第2次印刷
定　　价	168.00元（全二册）

未经许可，不得以任何方式复制或抄袭本书之部分或全部内容。
版权所有，侵权必究
举报电话：010-62752024　电子信箱：fd@pup.pku.edu.cn
图书如有印装质量问题，请与出版部联系，电话：010-62756370

会的关系提供了很好的素材。

　　了解历史才能更好地把握未来。新中国成立后，北京不仅是全国的政治中心，而且是全国的文化和科研中心，新的北京话和京味文化或正在形成。什么是老北京京味文化的精华？如何传承这些精华？为把握新的地域文化形成的规律，为传承地域文化的精华，必须对过去的地域文化的特色及其形成过程进行细致的研究和理性的分析。而近几十年来，各种新的传媒形式不断涌现，外来西方文化和国内其他地域文化的冲击越来越强烈，北京地区人口流动日趋频繁，老北京人逐渐分散，老北京话已几近消失。清代以来各个重要历史时期早期北京话语料的保护整理和研究迫在眉睫。

　　"早期北京话珍本典籍校释与研究（暨早期北京话文献数字化工程）"是北京大学中国语言学研究中心研究成果，由"早期北京话珍稀文献集成""早期北京话数据库"和"早期北京话研究书系"三部分组成。"集成"收录从清中叶到民国末年反映早期北京话面貌的珍稀文献并对内容加以整理，"数据库"为研究者分析语料提供便利，"研究书系"是在上述文献和数据库基础上对早期北京话的集中研究，反映了当前相关研究的最新进展。

　　本丛书可以为语言学、历史学、社会学、民俗学、文化学等多方面的研究提供素材。

　　愿本丛书的出版为中华优秀文化的传承做出贡献！

王洪君、郭锐、刘云
2016年10月

总　序

　　语言是文化的重要组成部分，也是文化的载体。语言中有历史。

　　多元一体的中华文化，体现在我国丰富的民族文化和地域文化及其语言和方言之中。

　　北京是辽金元明清五代国都（辽时为陪都），千余年来，逐渐成为中华民族所公认的政治中心。北方多个少数民族文化与汉文化在这里碰撞、融合，产生出以汉文化为主体的、带有民族文化风味的特色文化。

　　现今的北京话是我国汉语方言和地域文化中极具特色的一支，它与辽金元明四代的北京话是否有直接继承关系还不是十分清楚。但可以肯定的是，它与清代以来旗人语言文化与汉人语言文化的彼此交融有直接关系。再往前追溯，旗人与汉人语言文化的接触与交融在入关前已经十分深刻。本丛书收集整理的这些语料直接反映了清代以来北京话、京味文化的发展变化。

　　早期北京话有独特的历史传承和文化底蕴，于中华文化、历史有特别的意义。

　　一者，这一时期的北京历经满汉双语共存、双语互协而新生出的汉语方言——北京话，她最终成为我国民族共同语（普通话）的基础方言。这一过程是中华多元一体文化自然形成的诸过程之一，对于了解形成中华文化多元一体关系的具体进程有重要的价值。

　　二者，清代以来，北京曾历经数次重要的社会变动：清王朝的逐渐孱弱、八国联军的入侵、帝制覆灭和民国建立及其伴随的满汉关系变化、各路军阀的来来往往、日本侵略者的占领，等等。在这些不同的社会环境下，北京人的构成有无重要变化？北京话和京味文化是否有变化？进一步地，地域方言和文化与自身的传承性或发展性有着什么样的关系？与社会变迁有着什么样的关系？清代以至民国时期早期北京话的语料为研究语言文化自身传承性与社

"早期北京话珍稀文献集成"序

清民两代是北京话走向成熟的关键阶段。从汉语史的角度看，这是一个承前启后的重要时期，而成熟后的北京话又开始为当代汉民族共同语——普通话源源不断地提供着养分。蒋绍愚先生对此有着深刻的认识："特别是清初到19世纪末这一段的汉语，虽然按分期来说是属于现代汉语而不属于近代汉语，但这一段的语言（语法，尤其是词汇）和'五四'以后的语言（通常所说的'现代汉语'就是指'五四'以后的语言）还有若干不同，研究这一段语言对于研究近代汉语是如何发展到'五四'以后的语言是很有价值的。"（《近代汉语研究概要》，北京大学出版社，2005年）然而国内的早期北京话研究并不尽如人意，在重视程度和材料发掘力度上都要落后于日本同行。自1876年至1945年间，日本汉语教学的目的语转向当时的北京话，因此留下了大批的北京话教材，这为其早期北京话研究提供了材料支撑。作为日本北京话研究的奠基者，太田辰夫先生非常重视新语料的发掘，很早就利用了《小额》《北京》等京味儿小说材料。这种治学理念得到了很好的传承，之后，日本陆续影印出版了《中国语学资料丛刊》《中国语教本类集成》《清民语料》等资料汇编，给研究带来了便利。

新材料的发掘是学术研究的源头活水。陈寅恪《〈敦煌劫余录〉序》有云："一时代之学术，必有其新材料与新问题。取用此材料，以研求问题，则为此时代学术之新潮流。"我们的研究要想取得突破，必须打破材料桎梏。在具体思路上，一方面要拓展视野，关注"异族之故书"，深度利用好朝鲜、日本、泰西诸国作者所主导编纂的早期北京话教本；另一方面，更要利用本土优势，在"吾国之旧籍"中深入挖掘，官话正音教本、满汉合璧教本、京味儿小说、曲艺剧本等新类型语料大有文章可做。在明确了思路之后，我们从2004年开始了前期的准备工作，在北京大学中国语言学研究中心的大力支持下,早期北京话的挖掘整理工作于2007年正式启动。本次推出的"早期北京话珍稀文献集成"是阶段性成果之一,总体设计上"取异族之故书与吾国之旧籍互相补正",共分"日本北京话教科书汇编""朝鲜日据时期汉语会话书汇编""西人北京话教科书汇编""清代满汉合璧文献萃编""清代官话正音文献""十全福""清末民初京味儿小说书系""清末民初京味儿时评书系"八个系列,胪列如下:

"日本北京话教科书汇编"于日本早期北京话会话书、综合教科书、改编读物和风俗纪闻读物中精选出《燕京妇语》《四声联珠》《华语跬步》《官话指南》《改订官话指南》《亚细亚言语集》《京华事略》《北京纪闻》《北京风土编》《北京风俗问答》《北京事情》《伊苏普喻言》《搜奇新编》《今古奇观》等二十余部作品。这些教材是日本早期北京话教学活动的缩影,也是研究早期北京方言、民俗、史地问题的宝贵资料。本系列的编纂得到了日本学界的大力帮助。冰野善宽、内田庆市、太田斋、鳟泽彰夫诸先生在书影拍摄方面给予了诸多帮助。书中日语例言、日语小引的翻译得到了竹越孝先生的悉心指导,在此深表谢忱。

"朝鲜日据时期汉语会话书汇编"由韩国著名汉学家朴在渊教授和金雅瑛博士校注,收入《改正增补汉语独学》《修正独习汉语指南》《高等官话华语精选》《官话华语教范》《速修汉语自通》《速修汉语大成》《无先生速修中国语自通》《官话标准:短期速修中国语自通》《中语大全》《"内鲜满"最速成中国语自通》等十余部日据时期(1910年至1945年)朝鲜教材。这批教材既是对《老乞大》《朴通事》的传承,又深受日本早期北京话教学活动的影响。在中韩语言史、文化史研究中,日据时期是近现代过渡的重要时期,这些资料具有多方面的研究价值。

"西人北京话教科书汇编"收录了《语言自迩集》《官话类编》等十余部西人主编教材。这些西方作者多受过语言学训练,他们用印欧语的眼光考量汉语,解释汉语语法现象,设计记音符号系统,对早期北京话语音、词汇、语法面貌的描写要比本土文献更为精准。感谢郭锐老师提供了《官话类编》《北京话语音读本》和《汉语口语初级读本》的底本,《寻津录》、《语言自迩集》(第一版、第二版)、《汉英北京官话词汇》、《华语入门》等底本由北京大学图书馆特藏部提供，谨致谢忱。《华英文义津逮》《言语声片》为笔者从海外购回，其中最为珍贵的是老舍先生在伦敦东方学院执教期间，与英国学者共同编写的教材——《言语声片》。教材共分两卷：第一卷为英文卷，用英语讲授汉语，用音标标注课文的读音；第二卷为汉字卷。《言语声片》采用先用英语导入，再学习汉字的教学方法讲授汉语口语，是世界上第一部有声汉语教材。书中汉字均由老舍先生亲笔书写，全书由老舍先生录音，共十六张唱片，京韵十足，殊为珍贵。

上述三类"异族之故书"经江蓝生、张卫东、汪维辉、张美兰、李无未、王顺洪、张西平、鲁健骥、王澧华诸先生介绍，已经进入学界视野，对北京话研究和对外汉语教学史研究产生了很大的推动作用。我们希望将更多的域外经典北京话教本引入进来，考虑到日本卷和朝鲜卷中很多抄本字迹潦草，难以辨认，而刻本、印本中也存在着大量的异体字和俗字，重排点校注释的出版形式更利于研究者利用，这也是前文"深度利用"的含义所在。

对"吾国之旧籍"挖掘整理的成果，则体现在下面五个系列中：

"清代满汉合璧文献萃编"收入《清文启蒙》《清话问答四十条》《清文指要》《续编兼汉清文指要》《庸言知旨》《满汉成语对待》《清文接字》《重刻清文虚字指南编》等十余部经典满汉合璧文献。入关以后，在汉语这一强势语言的影响下，熟习满语的满人越来越少，故雍正以降，出现了一批用当时的北京话注释翻译的满语会话书和语法书。这批教科书的目的本是教授旗人学习满语，却无意中成为了早期北京话的珍贵记录。"清代满汉合璧文献萃编"首次对这批文献进行了大规模整理，不仅对北京话溯源和满汉语言接触研究具有重要意义，也将为满语研究和满语教学创造极大便利。由于底本多为善本古籍，研究者不易见到，在北京大学图书馆古籍部和日本神户外国语大学竹越孝教授的大力协助下，"萃编"将以重排点校加影印的形式出版。

"清代官话正音文献"收入《正音撮要》（高静亭著）和《正音咀华》（莎彝尊著）两种代表著作。雍正六年(1728)，雍正谕令福建、广东两省推行官话，福建为此还专门设立了正音书馆。这一"正音"运动的直接影响就是以《正音撮要》和《正音咀华》为代表的一批官话正音教材的问世。这些书的作者或为旗人，或寓居京城多年，书中保留着大量北京话词汇和口语材料，具有极高的研究价值。沈国威先生和侯兴泉先生对底本搜集助力良多，特此致谢。

《十全福》是北京大学图书馆藏《程砚秋玉霜簃戏曲珍本》之一种，为同治元年陈金雀抄本。陈晓博士发现该传奇虽为崑腔戏，念白却多为京话，较为罕见。

以上三个系列均为古籍，且不乏善本，研究者不容易接触到，因此我们提供了影印全文。总体来说，由于言文不一，清代的本土北京话语料数量较少。而到了清末民初，风气渐开，情况有了很大变化。彭翼仲、文实权、蔡友梅等一批北京爱国知识分子通过开办白话报来"开启民智""改良社会"。著名爱国报人彭翼仲在《京话日报》的发刊词中这样写道："本报为输进文明、改良风俗，以开通社会多数人之智识为宗旨。故通幅概用京话，以浅显之笔，达朴实之理，纪紧要之事，务令雅俗共赏，妇稚咸宜。"在当时北京白话报刊的诸多栏目中，最受市民欢迎的当属京味儿小说连载和《益世余谭》之类的评论栏目，语言极为地道。

"清末民初京味儿小说书系"首次对以蔡友梅、冷佛、徐剑胆、儒丐、勋锐为代表的晚清民国京味儿作家群及作品进行系统挖掘和整理，从千余部京味儿小说中萃取代表作家的代表作品，并加以点校注释。该作家群活跃于清末民初，以报纸为阵地，以小说为工具，开展了一场轰轰烈烈的底层启蒙运动，为新文化运动的兴起打下了一定的群众基础，他们的作品对老舍等京味儿小说大家的创作产生了积极影响。本系列的问世亦将为文学史和思想史研究提供议题。于润琦、方梅、陈清茹、雷晓彤诸先生为本系列提供了部分底本或馆藏线索，首都图书馆历史文献阅览室、天津图书馆、国家图书馆提供了极大便利，谨致谢意！

"清末民初京味儿时评书系"则收入《益世余谭》和《益世余墨》，均系著名京味儿小说家蔡友梅在民初报章上发表的专栏时评，由日本岐阜圣德学园大学刘一之教授、矢野贺子教授校注。

这一时期存世的报载北京话语料口语化程度高，且总量庞大，但发掘和整理却殊为不易，称得上"珍稀"二字。一方面，由于报载小说等栏目的流行，外地作者也加入了京味儿小说创作行列，五花八门的笔名背后还需考证作者是否为京籍，以蔡友梅为例，其真名为蔡松龄，查明的笔名还有损、损公、退化、亦我、梅蒐、老梅、今睿等。另一方面，这些作者的作品多为急就章，文字错讹很多，并且鲜有单行本存世，老报纸残损老化的情况日益严重，整理的难度可想而知。

上述八个系列在某种程度上填补了相关领域的空白。由于各个系列在内容、体例、出版年代和出版形式上都存在较大的差异，我们在整理时借鉴《朝鲜时代汉语教科书丛刊续编》《〈清文指要〉汇校与语言研究》等语言类古籍的整理体例，结合各个系列自身特点和读者需求，灵活制定体例。"清末民初京味儿小说书系"和"清末民初京味儿时评书系"年代较近，读者群体更为广泛，经过多方调研和反复讨论，我们决定在整理时使用简体横排的形式，尽可能同时满足专业研究者和普通读者的需求。"清代满汉合璧文献萃编""清代官话正音文献"等系列整理时则采用繁体。"早期北京话珍稀文献集成"总计六十余册，总字数近千万字，称得上是工程浩大，由于我们能力有限，体例和校注中难免会有疏漏，加之受客观条件所限，一些拟定的重要书目本次无法收入，还望读者多多谅解。

"早期北京话珍稀文献集成"可以说是中日韩三国学者通力合作的结晶，得到了方方面面的帮助，我们还要感谢陆俭明、马真、蒋绍愚、江蓝生、崔希亮、方梅、张美兰、陈前瑞、赵日新、陈跃红、徐大军、张世方、李明、邓如冰、王强、陈保新诸先生的大力支持，感谢北京大学图书馆的协助以及萧群书记的热心协调。"集成"的编纂队伍以青年学者为主，经验不足，两位丛书总主编倾注了大量心血。王洪君老师不仅在经费和资料上提供保障，还积极扶掖新进，"我们搭台，你们年轻人唱戏"的话语令人倍感温暖和鼓舞。郭锐老师在经费和人员上也予以了大力支持，不仅对体例制定、底本选定等具体工作进行了细致指导，还无私地将自己发现的新材料和新课题与大家分享，令人钦佩。"集成"能够顺利出版还要特别感谢国家出版基金规划管理办公室的支持以及北京大学出版社王明舟社长、张凤珠副总编的精心策划，感谢汉语编辑室杜若明、邓晓霞、张弘泓、宋立文等老师所付出的辛劳。需要感谢的师友还有很多，在此一并致以诚挚的谢意。

"上穷碧落下黄泉，动手动脚找东西"，我们不奢望引领"时代学术之新潮流",惟愿能给研究者带来一些便利,免去一些奔波之苦,这也是我们向所有关心帮助过"早期北京话珍稀文献集成"的人士致以的最诚挚的谢意。

刘 云

2015年6月23日

于对外经贸大学求索楼

2016年4月19日

改定于润泽公馆

导　读

张卫东

一、威妥玛与《语言自迩集》及其版本

威妥玛（Thomas Francis Wade，1818—1895），曾就读剑桥大学。1841年随英军来华，学习北京话和粤语。1843年任香港英国殖民当局中文翻译、香港最高法院粤语翻译。1847年退伍，任英国驻华商务监督署汉文副使。1853年任英国驻上海副领事。1854年被委任为上海海关第一任外国税务司。1855年任驻华公使馆汉文正使。1861年任英国驻华使馆参赞、中文秘书，负责海外雇员的汉语教学，期间研发了威妥玛式拼音，编著了汉语口语课本《寻津录》《语言自迩集》等。1871年升任驻华公使。1882年卸任回国，将他的四千多册中文藏书捐予剑桥大学。1888年成为剑桥大学首任汉学教授。威妥玛23岁来中国，64岁卸任回国。1852年曾因疟疾回国治疗，次年返回上海。除去这一年，他在中国生活了整整40年。

《寻津录》（*Hsin Ching Lu*，1859），是威妥玛在香港编著出版的第一部汉语教材，对北京话口语语音、词汇以及语法特点进行了一次试验性探索，因而被他反复强调这是一部"试验手册"（*Book of Experiments*）。第一册为课本，第二册是一份84页的《北京话字音表》。全书两册共170页。第一次推出了威妥玛制订的拉丁字母表音法及其拼音方案。该方案精准记录了北京官话声韵调特点：27个声母，39个韵母，4个声调，共397个音节，反映了北京话见、精组细音声母腭化，尖团合流，疑微两母消失并入零声母，四

呼俱全，入声调和入声韵消失等时代特征。到《语言自迩集》，音节数量由397个增加到420个。此后，这个方案被普遍用来拼写中国的人名、地名等专有词语，一般称为威妥玛式拼音。清末至1958年汉语拼音方案公布前，中国和国际上流行的就是这个中文拼音方案。

《语言自迩集》（以下简称《自迩集》）先后出了三个版本：1867年第一版，1886年第二版，1903年节略版。

1867年第一版《序言》中，威妥玛这样表明其编著宗旨：

> 笔者的一项职责，就是指导英国驻中国领事馆招募人员学习汉语；……它的基本功能是帮助领事馆的学员打好自己的基础，用最少的时间学会这个国家的官话口语，并且还要学会这种官话的书面语，不论它是书本上的、公文信件上的，抑或具有公众性质的文献资料中的官话。

威妥玛进一步介绍其编著体例与内容安排：

> 本书主要分为两大部分，分别称为"口语（Colloquial）系列"和"公文（Documentary）系列"。书名所用的"自迩集"（TZǓ ÊRH CHI），也许译成"循序渐进的课程"（Progressive Course）更妥。中国经典云"行远必自迩"，千里之行，始于足下。两部分课程称为"集"，其一属于资料汇编，冠以"语言"二字以示区别，所收的词汇与短语都是口语的；而另一集收的是"公文"，属书面语、公文课程。
> ……
> 本系列的第一章讲"发音"（Pronunciation）；第二章讲"部首"（The Radicals），即常用汉字的书写构件；第三、四、五、六章是

练习，有些是这一种类型，有些是另一种类型，是通行于各大都市衙门的口语（the oral language），直接称之为"北京话"（the Peking Dialect）；第七章是一套练习，用以举例说明北京话里声调的影响；第八章及最后的"勘误与补遗"，称之为"词类章"（Chapter on the Parts of Speech），讨论汉语口语在某些条件下——即便不是全部——类似我们用语法术语所描述的同类现象。

第一版《自迩集》（不含书面语教材《文件自迩集》），一共四卷。第一卷即"口语系列"，共分八章。第二卷是口语系列的答案（Key）。第三卷是《平仄编》（新版《北京音节总表》，威妥玛对他的表音方案做了修订，包括增加iai韵和uo韵，增加了23个音节，令《北京音节总表》中的音节数达至420个）。第四卷是《汉字习写法》，为汉字书写练习配套教程。

19年之后，即1886年，《自迩集》出了第二版。此时威妥玛已经68岁，卸任回国4年了。这一版分三卷。第一卷仍是"口语系列"的八章。第二卷是第三、四、五、六、七、八章中文课文的标音、英译和注释，并随课文进程相应附加了1080条字词释义和用法示例，相当于一部小型辞典。第三卷是四个附录：

附录一"（英文）词语汇编（第二卷第三、四、五、六章）"；

附录二"汉字引得（第二卷第二、三、四、五、六、七章，以部首为序）"；

附录三"北京话音节表、北京话字音表、异读字表"；

附录四"汉字书写练习"。

跟第一版比较，主要的改动是，在中文课文旁边都加了英文译文，每一个汉译英练习之后都附加了英译汉练习，并呈上了英文答案。由"北京话声调方面的高级权威"禧在明（Walter Hillier）先生"细心地校正了新版前七章里每个词的声调符号"；将"问答章之十"即"一段关于语言的句法结构的对话"删除了，换上了"他自己写的一段对话"，因为"不止一个认真的初学者抱怨说，原来的那段让人吃不消"。"原来的那段"，话题从汉字部首、汉字结构、口音、反切、"音母"记音、"京话字音的定数"（不论声调"共总四百一十多"），直到《清文指要》《清汉合璧》和"我们这儿说话的神气、层次、句法呀"，共77条，2200多字，确实"让人吃不消"。另一个较大的改动，就是原来的第五章即"续散语（十八章）"全部删除，将原来的第六章"谈论篇"提为第五章，增加了"践约传"为第六章。这些是《第二版序言》提到的改动，而大量的未曾提及的改动，是在中文课文里数不胜数的细微修改、加注、标音和润色等。例如第一版"散语章四十之七"：

12—17条：这屋里很黑，拏一盏灯来。有人拏了那盏灯去。桌子上的那腊灯谁拏了去了？是我给厨子拏过去了。厨房里没有火。饭锅是煮饭的，锅盖就是饭锅的盖儿。茶碗、茶盅都可以有盖儿。酒杯、酒盅子这两个东西不大很分。

第二版"散语章·练习七"（Exercise VII）相应的话条就有不少改动：

7.4 这屋里黑了，快拿灯来。桌子上的那腊灯是谁拏了去了？是我给厨子拏过去了。厨房的火弄①上还没著②呢。

注：①弄 lung^2，参见163。

②著 chao^2，在这里不是助动词，跟练习5.1中的不同，而是一个独立的动词，表示燃烧。

7.5 饭锅 fan^4–kuo^1 是煮饭的，锅盖 kuo^1–kai^4 就是饭锅的盖儿。茶碗

ch'a² wan³茶盅ch'a²chung¹也有有盖儿kai-'rh的。

注：也有yeh yu，也可以有；有盖儿的yu kai-'rh ti，有盖子的东西。

7.6 酒杯chiu³ pei¹酒盅子chiu³ chung¹-tzǔ这两个东西不大很分，可也分得出来①，本是酒杯比酒盅儿大②。

注：①分得出来fên tê ch'u lai，可以用"区别"（distinguished）或"能区分"（distinguishable）替代；动词的语气和时态完全由上下文决定。回答问题时，"你分得出来分不出来？"（Can（or do）you distinguish or not？）"分得出来。"（I can（or do）distinguish）跟我们说的话一样，用陈述语气现在时态。

②本pên³，实际上，参见120；是shih⁴，事实上。在这个意义上，"本pên³"是各种副词性结构中的一个成分。

第二版此类修改几乎遍布全书，但目标只是一个，就是从语音、词汇和语法各方面努力记好当时的北京话，记好说话时的语境、神气、语态，向学生准确地介绍当时的北京话，让学生学到真正地道的北京话。这一努力，使得第二版"口语系列"的篇幅大增，是第一版的两倍多。

1903年出版的第三版，是《自迩集》的节略版。这年，威妥玛已去世8年。《第三（节略）版出版者序言》（Publishers' Preface to Third (Abridged) Edition）交代：

以节略的方式再版威妥玛的伟大著作，是采纳了禧在明（Walter Hillier）先生的建议。他是1886年第二版的合作者，也是威妥玛先生的遗嘱执行人。

这篇1903年4月写于上海的《序言》，执笔者应该是禧在明本人。他在《序言》中介绍说：1886年以来，又出了许多汉语口语的新课本。英国公使馆里译员学生课程中，《自迩集》的许多课文已被替换。《谈论篇》和《秀才求婚》多年前就放弃了。而《自迩集》的初衷，是用来教领事馆学生的——至少眼下还是如此——只印出那些章节来继续做他们的课本。现在重版所包含的只是第一章到第四章，即：关于发音和部首的介绍，以及随后的散语章和问答章。在主管当局看来，学习北京话口语的学生以这四部分为入门，即可成功。

《序言》强调："对于威妥玛的表音系统，赞成的，反对的，都已经说了许多，写了许多。对于这场旷日持久的争论，我们已经不想再多说什么了，除非有初学者请求。就是说，要记住，这是唯一的拉丁字系统，它传播流布甚广，并获得持久的成功。"

以上三个版本，都是正版。历史上还曾出现过"盗版"。锺少华先生曾寄来一封短信："近日翻出家中一本（仅一本）《自迩集》，发现与你书上的个别翻译不同，故复印两页寄上，请核对。"从复印件看，是木刻版，小开本，每页竖排9行，每行24字。共30页，全是"问答十章"的。其中一页，是"问答章之七"的第63条至80条。经核对，是1867年第一版的"盗版"，而且是一"精致盗版"，因为从这一页看，除了未标条目，竟未错一字：

你这个人竟是打听！小儿原是在户部。他不是单住么？他这会儿单搬出去了。请问他住在甚么地方儿？他是在交民巷，西头儿路北里。他是在交民巷住么？真是！你疑惑作甚么？我估摸是城外头住的。离衙门那们远，不行，你怎么估摸着是城外头呢？昨儿日头落，碰见他的车，在琉璃厂。那有这个话？他昨儿晚上在我这儿来着。车是他的，他却没在车上。他没在车上，你怎么知道车是他的？车上坐着个老婆子，他说是孟大爷的车。老婆子抱着个孩子么？不错，是个七八岁的小孩子。必是我那小孙子。嗳？那早晚儿那儿去？老爷放心，有点儿事情。

这一节，第二、三两版的文字完全相同，跟第一版的不同之处有（第一版//第二、三版）：

1. 他是在交民巷，西头儿路北里。//他在交民巷，西头儿路北。
2. 真是！你疑惑作甚么？//真的阿！你疑惑作甚么？
3. 我估摸是城外头住的。//我估摸是在城外头住的。
4. 离衙门那们远，……//离衙门那么远，……
5. 那有这个话？//那'儿有这个话？
6. 嗳？那早晚儿那儿去？//嗳？那早晚儿那'儿去？

共有六七处的变动。从5和6两条追到第一版（正版）可知："那'儿"（哪儿）的这种写法，威妥玛编第一版的时候，确实还没发明出来。这个"那'儿"（哪儿）可以看作《自迩集》第一版跟二、三版版本辨识的标志之一。

锺少华先生不同意称之为"盗版"。"也许是威妥玛同意的呢？"这个本子前面残毁若干页，不见辑者姓名，亦不见序跋之类的文字，无法作进一步的讨论。2017年9月13日，笔者终于在国家图书馆文津街古籍馆得见又一册清末铅印本《语言自迩集》。此本原封面不存，修补之蓝色封皮左侧外贴白纸条，楷书"语言自迩集"，书名上顶书双行"习官话用"四小字。扉页单书"语言自迩集"五字。正文55页（现代标法110页），全汉文。每单面竖排14行，每行31字。全书只取1886年《语言自迩集》第二版的第三章（散语章）和第四章（问答章）的中文课文。前40页为"散语章"的四十练习及其答案，后15页是"问答章"之一至十。行文上，除"得děi""那nǎ"不作"得'""那'"（未被辑者接受？），其余皆与1886年第二版同。

从这种"盗版"的接连出现还可以推知：一、《自迩集》第一版刊出不久，中国民间便有人"盗印"了它的中文课文用以教外国人学汉语；二、民间对这种汉语教材的认可；三、民间的这种对外汉语教学，当时规模应该已经不小，方使这种教材有了相当的市场，否则，书商是不会下本儿冒险刊印的。

以前，我们只知道《自迩集》是那个时代英美人学汉语普遍使用的课本，是日本人改学北京话时的唯一依托，也曾引起朝鲜人和俄国人的注意和转抄、模仿，却未见有中国人翻印与使用这套课本的报道。现在，这类"盗版"的发现，让我们可以确信：这套课本在清末民初中国民间的对外汉语教学中曾扮演过重要角色，发挥过积极作用。

《自迩集》之所以能够获得如此成功，取决于威妥玛非凡的努力，取决于跟威妥玛同心同德、长期合作的中外学者团队。

威妥玛1841年来华，当年便投身汉语的学习，以近乎神奇的速度学会了粤语并应聘出任了香港最高法院的粤语翻译。与此同时，他一刻不停地开始学习北京话，不久便成为观察与研究汉语、对中国官话特别是北京话有独到见地的一流汉语语言学家。他的身边逐渐形成了一个高水平的中外学者团队。团队中的中国学者，为首的是生于北京的一位学者，威妥玛尊称为"老师"："我的老师应龙田（Ying Lung-t'ien）"，"一位受过良好教育的北京人，一位令人钦佩的发音人"。从他们在香港相遇，直到1861年应龙田去世，他们没有分开过，包括1852年威妥玛因疟疾回国治疗一年，1853年调任上海，应龙田都跟威妥玛在一起，参与《寻津录》和《自迩集》的编撰工作。威妥玛先后请过数十位中国老师和中国朋友帮忙（有资料显示他曾"从北京引进大量老师到香港"），其中还有一位留下姓名的，叫于子彬（Yü

Tzǔ-pin），一位满族学者。威氏非常尊重中国老师，并作为自己的一条为人原则："我的为人是，我不能让自己相信我对汉语的认识会跟我的中国老师一样好。"他对于中国老师和中国朋友提供的帮助，绝不贪天功为己有，只要一有机会就真诚地表示敬意与谢意：

正如我在《寻津录》（*Hsin Ching Lu*）或称"试验手册"（*Book of Experiments*）中——我的字母表1859年第一次在那里发表——解释的，在北京话的口语中，这个声调（按，第五声即入声）已不复存在（the non-existence any longer），而第一次唤起我注意的是应龙田（Ying Lung-t'ien），一位受过良好教育的北京人，一位令人钦佩的发音人，他已为我自行重新整理了一份词汇表，其中的调类是实际使用的。他的表中，所有第五声都并入第二声，而一年之后我住进北京的时候，我发现应龙田是对的。我听过一位非常有资格的鉴定专家表态说，他的声调分类"无懈可击"。

凡他认为对于学习口语并非必不可少的词语，全部删去，将剩余的部分重新归类，保留原来的声母和韵母，作为检索音节的类目，但是，对于大量词语的语音做了订正，有些是改变了发音或者声调，有些则是二者都改了，并且彻底清除了第五声即所谓入声（re-entering tone）。我发现，他对声韵和声调两方面的判断，在整个七年中经受住了考验，被认为大体正确。对于一个人讲话所需词语数量，他的限制比较严格，这是很了不起的，因为他自己的用语，跟他选定的语汇一样丰富讲究。他1861年去世。为了弥补他所提供的字表之不足，从一个比他分析过的大得多的词汇表里进行独立的选择，从那时起已由另一些本地助手为我做起来了。

二、《语言自迩集》是现代汉语普通话零公里里程碑

《自迩集》问世后,在汉学界引发了一场不小的论争。论争涉及两个方面,一方面涉及表音法方案或某些章节内容的编排,另一方面的争论是关乎官话标准音、关乎北京话历史地位的。

表音法方案方面,威妥玛说:"我认为,它被反对的主要有三项。"即浊擦音 j(日母)、ang 韵中的主要元音 a 和"儿"êrh 音的描写。用拉丁文字母描写北京话的这几个音确非易事,对于那些熟悉西语西文而略知北京话的汉学家们,更各有不同的体验和自以为是的表音方案。威妥玛在这方面遭遇的反对,多数是学术范围的,即使争论不休,也算是正常的。这方面的一些争论旷日持久,莫衷一是,再争亦无益,所以,威妥玛在《第二版序言》作了最后申述后便宣布:"此后,我要跟这个讨论告别了。"

而另一方面涉及的,却是一个大问题——关乎北京话历史地位的论争。《自迩集》问世之前,汉语官话史上刚刚经历了一场大变革,这场大变革催生了《自迩集》,而《自迩集》的面世,又引发了一场大论战。

《寻津录》《自迩集》以北京话作为教学目标语言,这在西人编著的汉语教科书中是第一次。此事曾轰动一时,与其说是引发一场大论战,还不如说是旷日持久的讥讽、责难与围攻。威妥玛曾回顾说:"……1859年我出版的初级读物《寻津录》一书……这个系统并没有被普遍接受,然而对它表示异议的,通常来自那些在本书出版之前开始研究的人;任何初学者,只要他采用这个系统并得到帮助,这种异议与声讨就会出现。"

"那些在本书出版之前开始研究的人"是些什么人呢?他们研究的是什么?他们是早先抵达中国的西方人,将南京官话作为研究对象并成为"颇负盛名的汉学家","因有这种特殊造诣而十分骄傲""独占鳌头"的权威。

他们认定南京官话才是"帝国官话"（kuan hua of the Empire），并为它付出了毕生时间与精力。他们看不到或不承认"帝国官话"已经由南京官话转为北京官话。于是他们将《自迩集》采用的这个系统讥讽为"公使馆汉语"（Legation Chinese），对于《自迩集》承认第五声即入声在北京话所代表的"帝国官话"里已经消失（the disappearance），汉学权威卫三畏博士"最近已断然提出抗议"。

"这种异议与声讨"即起因于"帝国官话"代表点的转变。以研究南京官话起家的汉学权威们看不到或者说是不愿意承认这种转变，有些人更恼羞成怒。他们不像日本学界那样平静地顺应了这种转变。专攻日本汉语教育史的六角恒广教授说：

> 那时候可以说，不仅在北京，即使在世界上，北京官话的教科书，除威妥玛的这本《语言自迩集》以外，再也没有了。明治九年（1876）9月，日本的汉语教学，从官方到民间，同时由南京话转向北京话。威妥玛的《语言自迩集》第一版便成了此时日本汉语教育唯一可用的教材。1879年日本出版的北京官话课本《亚细亚言语集》，即以《语言自迩集》为蓝本。

威妥玛这样介绍当时的"官话"和"帝国官话"：

> "官话"作为口语媒介，不只是属于官吏和知识阶层，而且属于近五分之四的帝国民众。在如此辽阔的地域，伴随它的必是多种多样的方言（dialects）。艾约瑟先生，谁也不如他那么勤奋地去探究过这些不同方言的规则与界线。他把官话划分为三个主要系统：南方官话（the southern mandarin）、北方官话（the northern mandarin）和西部官话（the

western mandarin），他以南京、北京和成都——四川省省会，分别代表各个官话系统的标准。他认为南京官话（Nanking mandarin）在更大的范围被理解，尽管后者更为时髦；可是他又承认那些想说帝国官廷语言的人一定要学习北京话，而净化了它的土音的北京话，就是公认的"帝国官话"。

"官话""分为三个主要系统"，"南京、北京和成都""分别代表各个官话系统的标准"。在官话全国通语形成之前，它们就是官话的三个"准通语"，皆属一方之"权威方言"。

通过自己的学习与独立研究，威妥玛较早地认识到这一点：

> 选择并确定一种话（a dialect），这大约是20年前的事，其次就是建立表音法。那时没人把北京话作为写作对象，而各种表音法都声称描写的是南方官话——诸如马礼逊博士（Dr. Morrison）（即第一部汉英辞典的编纂者）、麦都思博士（Dr. Medhurst）和卫三畏博士（Dr. Wells Williams）等人——他们对于本地话系统的描写，远不是无懈可击的。对于马礼逊表音法，有人主张把它看作官话表音法，艾约瑟先生根本否定任何这类主张。他说："马礼逊正在编撰他的很有实用价值的音节辞典（syllabic dictionary），却没有意识到他所列的音根本不是官话音，而是已经废弃不用的发音。"麦都思博士作了一些修订以求完善的表音法，几乎是马礼逊博士表音法的翻版；他辩解说，我没把它当作最好的，却因为它是最知名的。我相信，卫三畏博士正跟辞典编纂者的儿子、很有造诣的马儒翰先生（Mr. John Robert Morrison）合作，重订《音节辞典》（the Syllabic Dictionary）的语音系统，但是迄今只涉及了拼写方式。因而，这种表音法最后虽说更匀称整齐，但在我看来，似乎并不

比第一种更臻精确。

这场论争意味着，大约是1850年前后，北京音才获得官话正音的地位，成为"帝国官话"的代表。北京音获得官话全国通语地位，意味着历史已步入"以北京音为标准音"的现代汉语普通话阶段。正是在这个意义上说：《自迩集》是现代汉语普通话零公里里程碑。

而看不到这种变化的还有另一种表现：1950年代，权威学者就坚持说："至少六百年来北京音一直是官话正音。"真的"至少六百年来北京音一直是官话正音"吗？（张卫东，1998）这是近现代汉语史理论架构上的一个基本问题。《自迩集》的问世，标志着北京音成为"官话正音"即现代普通话标准音（"净化了它的土音的北京话"），自1850年至今不过160多年。对于中国语言学界承认北京音成为官话正音"至今不过160多年"这一点的难度，看来一点儿也不亚于160年前那些汉学权威们承认南京音已经让位于北京音的难度。

三、《语言自迩集》是19世纪中期北京话的描写语言学巨著

《自迩集》的初衷，是为学生编一部学习"帝国官话"即清末北京官话的课本，不期然成了北京话描写语言学的经典巨著。2001年版《语言自迩集：19世纪中期的北京话》的《译序》说："本译稿采用的是1886年的第二版。这是目前能见到的唯一的本子，从二版序言推知，也是最好的本子。这部三卷本的汉语课本，共一千一百余页，容量极大。百余年前的这部北京话描写语言学巨著，在中国现代语言学史上，可能拥有多项'第一'。"商务印书馆前副总编辑李思敬先生曾说："这部书可列为语言学经典。"今天，我们仍然认为，这种评价，殊不过分。

《自迩集》采用描写语言学的视角、方法和手段，全方位地精确考察、

记录北京话的语音、词汇、语法，力图"拥有本地人说话的自然气质"，"符合语言习惯"。不仅有共时平面的描写，还有历时的比较和历史的探讨。如此一来，《自迩集》就成了迄今所能见到的19世纪中期北京话最为珍贵富饶的语料库。《自迩集》作为汉语教材，有许多值得今日借鉴的地方。而作为百余年前的北京话描写语言学巨著、一个半世纪前的北京话大型语料库，已往的研究只能算初步，未来尚需我们从语音、词汇、语法各方面进行更系统深入的研究与讨论。

（一）语音

有了《自迩集》记录在案的大量可靠的记音资料，我们就可以把北京话元、明、清、民国至今诸如《蒙古字韵》《老乞大谚解》《朴通事谚解》《自迩集》《国音字典》《现代汉语词典》等标音文献系联成一条长链，将北京话六七百年的语音演变史，形成一个可以目睹其演变过程的历史。这一求证过程与结果，又逆向证明了《自迩集》所提供的北京话资料之可信与可靠。

近代官话语音演变是一个相当长的历史过程，各方言区的演变也往往是不同步的，先后发生格局性音变，通过交际实践而互动，诸如轻重唇分化、全浊清化、重韵合流、浊上变去、入声舒化等，相继普遍发生，并被吸纳、集中。这种吸纳与集中发生在哪里，跟各权威方言的表现相关。例如"入声舒化"在北系官话区和南系官话北缘普遍发生，南京音则"顽强地"保留入声，就失去了做全国通语的一个砝码。近代官话史上最后一波格局性音变，即从《中原音韵》时代先后发生的三组入声韵和一组阳声韵为代表的文白异读的消变，被谁拒绝，为谁吸纳，便是关键：

第一组，宕江二摄铎药觉三韵萧豪歌戈两韵并收。北系变萧豪，南系变歌戈，属北系官话的北京音形成部分字萧豪歌戈两韵并收，而以南京音为代表的南系官话坚持歌戈而拒绝萧豪。这组两韵并收经过一系列持续变化，终于在《伍伦全备谚解》（1709）之后、《自迩集》（1867）之前，萧豪韵优势和文读音地位让位于歌戈韵。这一音变结果，被北京音吸纳，被南京音和大部分南方官话拒绝（其北缘受北京音影响接纳了少数萧豪韵异读）（张卫东，2010）。

第二组，通摄屋浊二韵鱼模尤侯两韵并收。南、北同变鱼模，以武汉为代表的部分西部官话（含上江官话和西南、西北官话）变尤侯，北系官话吸纳了部分字的尤侯读法，属北系官话的北京音形成部分字鱼模尤侯两韵并收，赖南北合力鱼模韵读法始终保持着正音地位，部分字尤侯韵读法虽然"反客为主"获得正音地位，但始终维持在不足一成的低水平。而以南京音为代表的南系官话坚持鱼模而拒绝尤侯。北京音再获晋级全国通语的又一筹码（张卫东，2012）。

第三组，《中原音韵》之后出现的曾梗二摄德陌麦三韵洪音皆来歌戈两韵并收。这些字《中原音韵》归皆来、《蒙古字韵》归佳韵（与皆来同），《西儒耳目资》归第二摄e"入声甚"，相当于歌戈。从明代中叶《翻译老乞大》（1517）可知，这种"两韵并收"已经出现：脉（左韵-aiω，右韵-e），北德色瀞克黑伯百栢珀帛白窄核（左韵- ŭiω，右韵-e），客隔（左韵- ŭiω，右韵-ie），国或（左韵-uiω，右韵-ue）；少数字左右音都是皆来韵：摘（左韵- ŭiω，右韵-ai），得特肋尅剋（左韵- ŭiω，右韵- ŭi），忒（左韵- ŭiω，开口；右韵-ui，合口）。德陌麦三韵洪音，从今方言现状看，北系官话变皆来，南系官话变歌戈，北京音在北系官话变皆来的基础上吸纳南系官话歌戈韵读法，形成皆来歌戈两韵并收。南系官话的北缘（济南、西安等）多变为-ei韵，这可能是北系官话皆来韵影响所致，也可能是其自身机制所致，无论怎样，是给北系官话变皆来增加了砝码。南系官话的大部分坚持歌戈读法至今。在争当通语的"较量"中这一波的"输"与"赢"亦无需赘言。（张卫东，2016）

第四组，曾梗通三摄阳声韵重组形成[əŋ、iŋ、uŋ、yŋ]一套韵母。《中原音韵》东钟庚青两韵并收，实际上就是中古曾梗通三摄阳声韵重新组合全过程的发端，300年之后，通过《西儒耳目资》可见这种"重组运动"在南方官话已有表现。在《老》《朴》等朝鲜谚解文献中，这种运动持续着，通摄"风缝蜂"等轻唇字直到《老七》（1745）方有松动："缝蜂"二字右音变"庚青"（-一ㅇ，即-uŋ），左音不变（-ㅜㅇ，即-uŋ），而"风"到《老A》（1795）仍不变（左右音皆-ㅜㅇ，即-uŋ）。威妥玛也一直关注着这个情况。在《语言自迩集》第一章《发音》中，他不无兴奋地报告说：

> ên, êng两个韵母是被用来替代声母f, m, p音节中的un, ung的。这种情况最先见于在广东出版的教广东人学官话的本地课本。人们发现，这种演变已被北京人完全认可了。上个世纪满洲人的发音还是fung, mung, 不过也经常是fên, mên, pên。

按，最后一句原文疑有阙，全文应该是"上个世纪满洲人的发音还是fun, mun, pun; fung, mung, pung, 不过也经常是fên, mên, pên; fêng, mêng, pêng"。就是说，上个世纪满洲人（北京内城人口主体）发音已是-un/-ên, -ung/-êng"两韵并收"。"风、梦"等字，通摄帮组最后几个仍读合口-ung韵的字终于有了开口-êng韵异读，由fung, mung, pung变为fêng, mêng, pêng！他异常兴奋，是因为早在编写《寻津录》（1859）时，他已注意到的"这种演变"，终于被广东出版的官话课本证实了，表明"被北京人完全认可了"，涉及现代汉民族共同语的最后一个格局性的音变终于完成了。（张卫东，2013）

这四组音变，皆属格局性音系变化，是近代官话史上南、北、西各大区域权威方言相互激荡、叠加、约定俗成的结果，不是任何主观意志的"认定"与"取舍"。这四组音系变化的历史是客观的、物质的，可知，可察，可量化分析，量变到质变，行迹可循，规则可现，绝不是"没有规范的"，更不"可能因人而异"。这一波格局性音系变化，具有区别不同质的阶段的标志性，跟"入派三声""浊音清化"等普遍的历史音变意义完全不同。而北京音系吸纳了近代发生的各项重要的音系变化，特别是这最后一波格局性音系变化，体现了最大的包容性，从而成为区别于其他各区域权威方言的特点之一。

至此，一个"现代汉民族共同语形成之层级模式"浮现在眼前：近代官话的长期演变发展，逐渐形成了南、北、西三大区系，并在各自区域形成了权威方言——南京话、北京话、成都话三个"准通语"。以金尼阁《西儒耳目资》、马礼逊《华英字典》为代表的明清来华传教士所记，是以南京音为标准音的南部准通语；而朝鲜谚解《老》《朴》系列所记，是以北京音为标准音的北部准通语。明代南部准通语影响大些，入清以后北部准通语地位持续上升，在新的政治、经济、文化条件下的社会交流交往，促使近代官话进一步演变发展，并产生了形成全国通语的需要与可能。北京话，以其得天独厚的社会条件、语言条件，加上它的包容性，终于获得了全国通语的地位。

现代汉语的标准音是北京音。当我们这么说的时候，"北京音"指的是有着上述形成史的19世纪中后期的北京音，是已晋级为现代汉民族共同语标准音的北京音；它已不只是北系官话的代表，它的基础方言已扩展为广义的"北方官话"（北系官话+南系官话+西部官话）。这是"现代汉语"题中应有之义，反映现代北京音跟各官话方言的新型关系，是北京音能够成为现代汉民族共同语标准音的语言学基础。据我们目前的考察，这一切，最早地、全面地、如实地反映在应运而生的威妥玛《自迩集》中。威妥玛《自迩集》无可争议地、当之无愧地成为近代官话史终结、现代汉语史开启的标志性文献，实乃历史必然。

(二) 词汇

《自迩集》的词汇量极大，借以进行那个时代北京话词汇的共时研究是很方便的。细心的读者会发现，书中还有许多材料可以引导人们拓展新的研究领域。例如，《自迩集》里常见一种说法：某字"不见于字典"，某字"不被字典所承认""未被字典所承认""本地字典不承认它"，或者某音、某义、某个用法"不见于本地字典""本地字典不认可"，等等。

这里所说的"字典""本地字典"，看来就是《康熙字典》。所说"不见于字典"的各字，确为《康熙字典》未收的字。有的字收了，或音、义有所不同，甚至相反。例如：

（1）傻sha^3，本指精明的家伙，但口语所指却正好相反。

《康熙字典》：傻，《广韵》沙瓦切，《集韵》《韵会》数瓦切，并沙上声。轻慧貌。《韵笺逸字》傻音洒。《韵会》傻俏不仁。

（2）懞懂mêng^2-tung^3，失去了知觉，失礼了，不合时宜：懞mêng，健忘的，愚笨的；懂tung，亦有大体相同的意思；"懂tung"的第二个义项的意思是"理解、明白"，但不被本地字典所承认。

《康熙字典》：懂，《正韵》多动切，音董，懵懂，心乱也。

（3）抿著嘴儿min^3 cho tsui，合拢嘴唇；各字典不承认"抿"的这个意思。

《康熙字典》：抿，《集韵》眉贫切，撋字省文。《说文》抚也。一曰摹也。

（4）篮lan^2，一般比"筐子"小点儿，虽然字典上说得正相反。

《康熙字典》：篮，《正韵》卢监切，并音蓝，大笼筐也。

从一些小注还能看到某些字词定形的曲折过程，例如今"崭新"一词，就几经周折：斩新chan^3 hsin^1，新制的，刚刚切下来的湛chan^4，本书第一版用了这个字，卫三畏的字典（Williams's Dictionary）也收了这个字，但中国字典给的是前一个读音chan³。

《自迩集》对这方面的观察是很敏感的，并且不厌其烦地记录下来，这是在引导学生学会观察、认识和把握活的动态，因而是地道的北京话。而客观上就给我们留下了词汇及其相关用字新陈代谢的实录。让我们再看一些例子（"不见于本地字典"仍指《康熙字典》）：

（1）傢chia¹，这个字不见于本地字典。

（2）伙huo³，也不见于本地字典；二字合成"傢伙chia¹-huo³"一词，指各种各样的厨具。随便儿说，小型武器也可以叫"傢伙chia¹-huo³"；如梭标，步枪，或任何随身用具。

（3）噗嗤p'u¹ ch'ih¹，发笑的声音；前一个字不见于字典。

（4）惦tien⁴，想念着；惦记tien chi，出于好意地记挂着某人。字典里没有"惦tien"字。

（5）嘟哝tu¹ nang¹，轻声低语……"嘟tu"字不见于字典。

《国音字典》嘟、哝二字单立：嘟ㄉㄨ都阴， 状声字。哝ㄋㄨㄥ农阳，哝哝，多言而声细，如"群司兮哝哝"，见《楚辞》。《现汉》【嘟囔】dū·nang，【嘟哝】dū·nong，音近义同。

（6）账chang⁴，账单；账目。这个字是"帐chang⁴"的讹体；本地字典不承认它；然而，却用得非常普遍，已经取代了正体"帐"。

（7）愣lêng⁴，发呆；这个字，字典不承认。

《国音字典》：愣㊀ㄌㄥ冷去 ①呆貌。②卤莽貌。③率意而行……㊁ㄌㄥ棱阴，愣儿，犹言呆子……。《现汉》单音lèng，义同㊀。

（8）虼蚤ko⁴-tsao³，或读tsao¹，蚤目昆虫：虼ko，字典不承认的字；蚤 tsao，书面语单用。

《国音字典》：虼ㄍㄜ各去（入），虼蚤，虫名，即蚤。语音似ㄍㄜ·ㄗㄠ。

（9）镣铐liao⁴ k'ao⁴，脚镣……铐k'ao，铐在脚上的，通常叫"脚镣"；"铐"字，未被字典所承认。

《国音字典》：铐，考去，手铐，械手之刑具。

（10）炸cha⁴，是未被本地字典认可的字，由火huo（火烛）乍cha（突然）构成；炸炮cha p'ao，炸弹；炸开，爆炸。

《国音字典》：炸㊀ㄓㄚ乍去①谓火力爆发。②激怒，如"他听了登时炸了"。③喧噪哄散。㊁ㄓㄚ札阳（人）谓以油煎食物。

《自迩集》也"参与"了造字。它自创了两个"字"：那'（na³）、得'（tei³）。当时表what、where、anywhere的新词na³，表must的tei³，一时都找不到合适的汉字，只得借用旧有的、音义有些关联的"那"和"得"加修饰符号，创造出"中西合璧"的"那'"与"得'"。其实，这不能算严格意义上的"汉字"。后来，假借了音义都不同的"哪"取代了"那'"，假借了音义确有关联的"得"取代了"得'"。得，曾摄德韵字，在入声消失过程中变化出te和tei二音，即"两韵并收"，是合乎历史音变规律的，以"得"取代"得'"，实为回归原点。

这类情况，正与现代汉语新语素、复音词大量涌现相关。

《康熙字典》，据中华书局影印本出版说明，"依据明代《字汇》《正字通》两书加以增订"，成书于1717年。其所"增"者，在很大程度上反映了明中至清中二百年间官话语用情况的发展变化。例如心部五画"怎"字下将"始见"于《五音集韵》对"怎"的解释全文录入后，加"按"曰：

此字《广韵》《集韵》皆未收，唯韩孝彦《五音集韵》收之。今时扬州人读"争"上声，吴人读"尊"上声，金陵人读"津"上声，河南人读如"楂"，各从乡音而分也。

《自迩集》异读字表：怎tsên³｜tsêng³。

练习十六介绍说：怎tsên³，如何，什么，在北京口语里总是随个"么mo¹"（23）说"怎么"，而且韵母里的n听不到了，双音节的发音变成了tsêm³-mo，重音在第一个音节。

这是北京音。而异读"怎tsêng³"可能是语流音变的结果，也可能是"扬州人读'争'上声"叠加于北京话的。

再如近指代词"这"。《康熙字典》辵部七画"這"：

> 《广韵》鱼变切，《集韵》牛堰切，并音彦。《玉篇》迎也。《正字通》周礼有"掌訝"，主迎。訝，古作"這"。毛晃曰：凡称"此箇"为"者箇"。俗多改用"這"字。這，乃迎也。

《康熙字典》简要回顾"這"的音韵训诂史，正确地指出：近代汉语近指代词"這"是假借古字而音"者"。《自迩集》异读字表列出6个异读音：这chai⁴｜chê⁴，chei⁴，tsê⁴，tsên⁴，tsêng⁴，完全不睬其"迎這"之古音古义。《国音字典》近指代词"这"的两个音，跟其中chê⁴、chei⁴二音相同。（《国音字典》㈠ㄓㄜ 宅去（入），此，如"三十六峰犹不见，况伊如燕這身材"……按古用"者"作"此"字义，唐以后用"這"者始多。㈡ㄓㄟ 近指，盖"这一"之合。㈢ㄧㄢ 雁去，迎也，见《玉篇》。）而余下的4个异读除了chai⁴，另外3个：tsê⁴，可能来自没有卷舌音的方言区，叠加于北京话；tsên⁴、tsêng⁴，则见于语流音变。

从1717年到1867年，即从《康熙字典》到《自迩集》的150年，正是北京话从近代演进到现代的最后关键阶段。入声的阴声化，全浊声母的清化，尖团音的混一，异读的大量出现，量词、代词、助词、介词、叹词等各系统的成长与完善化，表述方式的改变与词法、句法结构的适应性变化等等，呈现出语音、词汇、语法、文字全面的大变化或细小微调并存的更新大局面。文字是语言的书写工具。语言与文字，于社会平稳发展时期，一般是大体平衡的。文字一般会随语言的演进发生适应性的新陈代谢。第一性的"语"，第二性的"文"，二者同步互动发展，达至大体平衡，这是最理想的。然而，文字的创新往往滞后，跟不上语音、词汇的发展变化。特别是语言剧烈变动期间，"语"与"文"的平衡不仅会被打破，甚至会严重失衡。这种时候，在"新词"面前，读书人往往会自认"不会写"。然而从总体上说，民间却不会那么消极。言语交际的需要往往促成新字新词率先于民间诞生。民间造字自古亦然。但是，教习语文的课本，能像《自迩集》这样大胆、自然地启用民间造字与新词，却是极少见的。这样做，丝毫不存猎奇与哗众取宠之意，完全是为了让学生能学到地道的、即时鲜活的北京话。这样的教学取向，使得《自迩集》在成为当时最好的汉语课本的同时，也成为那个时代北京话语用状况的敏锐观察与忠实记录。

（三）语法

威妥玛多次声明，《自迩集》是作为教材编纂的，没把它当作一本语法书来写。然而，这并非意味着《自迩集》只讲语音、词汇而不讲语法。在1867年《第一版序言》里，威妥玛用了相当的篇幅讨论和比较中西语文、语法的同与不同，克服重重困难（"没有一套共同的语法术语"）陈述其汉语语法观。威妥玛的汉语语法观极具学术价值。

在语法方面，对于汉语跟英语的同异，威妥玛的表述清晰明确、一语中的，表现得冷静而客观，请看《第一版序言》中的几段话（下画线为笔者所加）：

> 外国语言学家告诉我们，语法（Grammar），作为言语科学（the Science of Words），可分为语源学（Etymology）和句法（Syntax）两部分；而语源学规律又再分为屈折的和派生的（the laws of Inflexion and of

Derivation）。<u>汉语服从这个规定，但只是有限度地服从</u>。在派生规律（derivation）方面，它的语源学有<u>些</u>地方跟其他语言有某些共同点；而在屈折规律（inflexion）方面，它没有语源学。

他注意到汉语"字""词"的关系：

> 至于派生规律，汉语所有单个词（single words）的词源在很大程度上是可知的，因为在书面语中它们每一个都有其典型（representative），罕有例外；而<u>这</u>些典型形态被不太准确地称为"汉字"。

他敏锐地发现：汉语语法的核心就在于"汉语词的多功能性"：

> 至于语源学的另一分支，即屈折变化方面，我再重复一遍，汉语语法完全不允许它占有一席之地；汉语词的多功能性（the versatility）——如果可以这样称呼的话，即汉语中对于这么多的词语（尤其是我们倾向于称之为名词和动词的词）有共通性，<u>在有广泛差别的语法功能的可容性方面达到如此程度</u>：任何把语言权威性地划分到像我们语言中"词性"的范畴里去的努力，都将枉费心机。而且，我们语言中的词类分析当然得有它们相对应的汉语说法，且不管能否对它们作词类分析；<u>在所有别的语言中用屈折变化生效而产生的大部分结果所需的那些方法，汉语自身也拥有，</u>否则汉语就不成其为一种语言。汉语并不打乱它的词语系统，也不是要把它的各部分——不论是现存的还是过时的——都合并到词语系统中去，从而实现我们用格、数、语气、时态、语态等术语或诸如此类的东西所表述的情况。<u>汉语通过词语的句法处理，几乎达到了这些现存的限定所能实现的一切，几乎全部保持了词</u>

语在别处整体或独立运用的能力。

他敏锐地察觉到"汉语词的多功能性",没有跌进"词无定类"的泥淖;他科学地论断"在所有别的语言中用屈折变化生效而产生的大部分结果所需的那些方法,汉语自身也拥有","汉语通过词语的句法处理,几乎达到了这些现存的限定所能实现的一切",从而深刻地揭示了汉语的内在机制和语法特征。这些话说得何等好啊!一百多年前,一个接受欧洲语言学严格训练的西方人,来到东方研究汉语,竟无一丝"生搬硬套"的味道。这跟早期留洋的不少中国人对自己母语所作的"生吞活剥"式的分析,形成鲜明对照。

原书第二卷之第八章"词类章"与第一卷之第八章"言语例略"内容大体相同。后者为中文课文,分13段,无段名;前者为英语译文和注释,亦分13段,各有段名,借用西方语言学的概念,讨论当时北京话口语的语法。威妥玛强调"该章不是讲语法,也没当语法来写"。这13节没有以西语语法的框框套汉语,没有机械地"对照"与"类比";所得汉语词类10种,跟我们今天的词类分析十分接近,而其中的某些成果,例如对量词的认识与表述,中国学者直到20世纪50年代初才达到同一水平。(何九盈,2008)

第八章"绪论"(Introductory Observations)首先肯定:"天下各国的话,没有全不相同的地方儿。是人心里的意思发出来,随势自然分好些神气(character of expression: 神气shên ch'i, gait, air, attitude)。"这是"文字语言的总例(a general law which affects all language, written or spoken),是中外各国人情自然相同之理"。随后,威妥玛借用中国传统的"死字""活字""实字""虚字"之说,揭示"汉语词的多功能性"的存在:

至于那个"死字""活字"不同,就是"你""钱"这两个字是"死"的,那"要"字一个字是"活"的。然而那"要"字,才说是"活字"，在此处固然是"活"的，别处也能够当"死"的用。比如"其要在速ch'i yao tsai su（要点是从速）"这一句，那"要yao"字、"速su"字可不是"死字"么？再问这一句里头，"活字"没有么？就是那"在tsai"字必算是"活字"。又考这些字里"虚""实"之分，就是那"其ch'i""在tsai"这俩字，虽然各有正义，在这儿仍算是"虚字"。

中国有些学者已经通过自己独立研究走上同一条路，可谓殊途同归。范晓接替胡裕树主持修订的《现代汉语》1995年重订本已改弦易辙，距离"汉语词的多功能性"仅一步之遥了。而北京大学早在20世纪60年代已经迈出这一步。朱德熙先生1985年的《语法答问》抓住"汉语自己的特点"，在中国第一次推出"汉语词的多功能性"的概念，并强调"这件事不但影响我们对整个词类问题的看法，而且还关系到对句法结构的看法"：

> 有的汉语语法书所以会走上这条路（按，指"词无定类"），根本的原因是受了印欧语法观念的束缚，看不见汉语自己的特点，不知道汉语的名词、动词、形容词都是"多功能"的，不像印欧语那样，一种词类只跟一种语法成分对应。（7页）
>
> 汉语词类没有这种形态标记，不管放在什么语法位置上，形式都一样，这就造成词类多功能的现象。另外一方面，由于汉语动词没有限定形式与非限定形式（不定形式和分词形式）的对立，这就造成了词组和句子构造上的一致性。（9页）
>
> 在印欧语里，词类和句法成分之间有一种简单的一一对应关系。大致说来，动词跟谓语对应，名词跟主宾语对应，形容词跟定语对应，副词跟状语对应……（而就汉语而言）动词和形容词既能做谓语，又能做主宾

语。做主宾语的时候，还是动词、形容词，并没有改变性质。这是汉语区别于印欧语的一个非常重要的特点。说它重要，因为这件事不但影响我们对整个词类问题的看法，而且还关系到对句法结构的看法。（5—6页）

在这方面，启功先生的《汉语现象论丛》、王宁先生的《汉语现象和汉语语言学》在20世纪90年代初也都迈出了这一步，并用"螺丝钉""不干胶""多面体"等来形容"汉语词的多功能性"，十分形象：

  词是一种多面功能的零件：譬如一个螺丝钉，可以左右旋转，也可以钻进、退出，更可用锤钳直接钉入或拔掉。例如"衣"和"食"，作为名词，是衣服、食物；作为动词则是穿衣的"穿"、吃饭的"吃"。所以可以说"解衣衣我，推食食我"。如果说"衣我食我"，即是"给我衣穿，给我饭吃"。那么这句中的"衣""食"二字即同时各具有动、名两种性质。（启功，1997：10）

  像英语、俄语这些种语言，一个词像一根小铁钩，一边有环，一边带钩，这个钩钩进那个环，连成一条就是一句话。钩和环得对合适了，大钩穿不进小环，大环挂不牢小钩，词的自由结合度很小，错了一点就被判为语法错误。可汉语的词像一个多面体，每面抹的都是不干胶，面面都能接，而且用点心都可以接得严丝合缝。比如回文诗，干脆结成一个圈儿，从哪儿都能念。这虽是文字游戏，可难道不启发人去想汉语的特点吗？（王宁，1996：39-40）

参考文献

何九盈（2008）《中国现代语言学史》，商务印书馆，北京。

启　功（1997）《汉语现象论丛》，中华书局，北京。

王　宁（1996）汉语现象和汉语语言学，载于《汉语现象问题讨论论文集》，文物出版社，北京。

张卫东（1998）北京音系何时成为汉语官话标准音，《深圳大学学报（人文社科版）》第4期。

张卫东（2010）论《中原音韵》的萧豪歌戈"两韵并收"，《语言学论丛》第四十一辑，商务印书馆，北京。

张卫东（2012）论《中原音韵》的鱼模尤侯"两韵并收"，载于早稻田大学文学部《中国语学研究·开篇》VOL.31。

张卫东（2013）论《中原音韵》东钟庚青之"两韵并收"，《语言学论丛》第四十八辑，商务印书馆，北京。

张卫东（2016）曾梗二摄德职陌麦韵入声洪音字的"两韵并收"——基于《老朴》等标音文献的考察，《语言学论丛》第五十三辑，商务印书馆，北京。

朱德熙（1985）《语法答问》，商务印书馆，北京。

集遍自言語
Yü-yen Tzŭ-erh Chi,

A PROGRESSIVE COURSE

DESIGNED TO ASSIST THE STUDENT OF

COLLOQUIAL CHINESE,

AS SPOKEN IN THE CAPITAL AND THE METROPOLITAN DEPARTMENT;

In Eight Parts;

WITH KEY, SYLLABARY, AND WRITING EXERCISES;

BY

THOMAS FRANCIS WADE C.B.

SECRETARY TO H.B.M. LEGATION AT PEKING.

LONDON:
TRÜBNER & CO., 60, PATERNOSTER ROW.

MDCCCLXVII.

PREFACE.

"What Chinese is it that you want to learn, Sir?" asked the first sinologue of established reputation that I consulted; "there is the language of the ancient classics, and the language of more modern books, and the language of official documents, and the epistolary language, and the spoken language, of which there are numerous dialects; now which Chinese is it that you wish to begin with?" The learned gentleman was one of a very small number, who, at the time the Treaty of Nanking was signed, monopolised the credit of an acquaintance with the language, and, in the pride of this exceptional eminence, he was by no means averse to mystification of the uninitiated. Still, without doubt, the question with which he began and ended is the first that must be answered by any one who aspires to learn Chinese, or professes to teach it; what does either mean by Chinese, divided as it is into written and spoken, and subdivided as the written and spoken languages are, the former by its variety of styles, the latter by more dialectic differences than the most advanced scholar is as yet in a position to define.

The answer must depend upon the vocation of the enquirer. Is he a philologist, pure and simple, or a merchant who wishes for direct intercourse, orally or in writing, with his native constituents, or a missionary whose object is the propagation of spiritual truth, or an official interpreter whose duties, as an international agent, will continue, until such time as the Chinese become competent to interpret and translate for themselves, scarcely inferior to the duties of the missionary in importance?

The business of the writer is with aspirants of the last mentioned class. It is one of his duties to direct the studies of the gentlemen destined to recruit the ranks of Her Majesty's Consular Service in China, and although the work now submitted to the public will not perhaps be esteemed valueless by either the missionary or the merchant who may use it, its primary object is to assist the Consular Student in grounding himself with the least possible loss of time in the spoken government language of this country, and in the written government language as it is read, either in books, or in official correspondence, or in documents in any sense of a public character.

The work is in two principal divisions, respectively denominated Colloquial and Documentary Series. The words TZŬ ERH CHI which recur in the title of both may be fairly translated Progressive Course. To go far, says a Chinese classic,* we must start *tzŭ erh*, from what is near. The two courses are *chi*, collections of matter, of which that distinguished by the prefix *yŭ-yen*, words and phrases, is the colloquial, the other, being a collection of *wên-chien*, written papers, the documentary course.

---

* The CHUNG YUNG, Rule of the Mean, or avoidance of extremes, the second of the Four Books known as Confucian, the bible of Chinese morality, contains the following passage:—

自 *tzŭ* 高 *kao*, 如 *ju* 邇 *erh*; 必 *pi* 行 *hsing* 辟 *pi* 之 *chih* 君 *Chun*
卑 *pi*. 必 *pi* 登 *têng* 辟 *pi* 自 *tzŭ* 遠 *yuan* 如 *ju* 道 *tao*, 子 *tzŭ*

"The way [in wisdom] of the *chun tzŭ*, model man, is as that of the traveller, who to go far must start from what is near; or of him that climbs, who to go high must start from what is low." Whoever would be a proficient, must begin with what is elementary.

PREFACE.

The first, that contained in the present volume, is the only one of the two that is legitimately denominated progressive. This does lead the scholar *tzŭ erh*, from what is near, to no inconsiderable distance in the spoken language, and if he have the patience thoroughly to master the text of it before venturing on the documentary series, he will have so familiarised himself with the form and meaning of written words as greatly to lessen his difficulties as a translator. Beyond this the colloquial is not an introduction to the documentary series, nor can any one of the sixteen parts of the latter be said to be an introduction to any other part; the term series, therefore, as applied to the volume of documents, is in some sort a misnomer. But this is unimportant. That collection of papers fairly answers the end proposed, which is to set before the student in bold type and properly punctuated, a number of specimens of Chinese documentary composition. A Key or Commentary, now in course of preparation, will accompany the course, and may possibly be followed by a translation of the whole of the papers contained in it.

Our immediate affair is the Colloquial Series, which occupies the volume before us. In the Appendices are repeated all the words that have been met with in the Chinese text, in the order in which they first occur. The Key forms an additional volume; the Syllabary, of which more will be said by-and-bye, another; and the Writing Course, another. The student is recommended to keep these four volumes separate.

The first part of the Series is devoted to Pronunciation, the second, headed the Radicals, to the construction of the written words ordinarily known as Chinese characters. The third, fourth, fifth, and sixth, are exercises, some in one shape, some in another, in the oral language of the metropolitan department, styled for brevity the Peking Dialect; the seventh is a set of exercises designed to illustrate the influence of the Tones upon the dialect in question; the eighth and last, entitled a Chapter on the Parts of Speech, is a talk in colloquial Chinese upon certain, though by no means upon the whole, of those conditions that are the equivalents in Chinese of such as we describe by the term grammatical. Something farther will be said regarding this last part elsewhere, which will explain to the reader the occasion of this cautious periphrasis.

The order of the Colloquial Series has been dictated by the following considerations. The persons whose requirements it is the primary object of its compilation to satisfy are, as I have said above, Consular Students, to whom the knowledge of the written is not less indispensable than that of the oral language. They have to learn not only to talk, but to translate from and into written Chinese. Their foremost duty is beyond doubt application to the spoken language; not because there devolves upon the interpreter a heavier responsibility as a speaker than as a translator; on the contrary, an error in the *litera scripta* may be unquestionably of the greater significance; but because it is established by experience that, while the difficulties of the written language give way perceptibly before a sustained effort to surmount them, even comparative proficiency in speaking is not to be achieved by adults of average aptitude, unless the dialect to be spoken is specially and diligently laboured at while the ear is fresh. On the other hand, it has been admitted by some of the very few foreigners who have limited themselves to the acquisition of a dialect phonetically, and some of the best speakers have so limited themselves, that the difficulties of the written language, when they did at last turn to it, appeared doubly disheartening. Why this should be so, it is needless here to enquire; the data on which either of the above conclusions is based are not abundant; but they suffice, in my opinion, to justify the recom-

PREFACE.

mendation that while, for a given time, he accept improvement in speaking as his chief obligation, the student should nevertheless allow himself to consider no word or phrase added to his vocabulary, of the written form of which he is not assured. He is not at all engaged by this injunction to the study of Chinese composition, between the idiom of which, no matter in which of its departments, and that of the colloquial language, no matter in which of its dialects, there are notable diversities; but he is called upon to examine, with his eyes, the constitution of every word or phrase that he is committing to memory. This conceded, that the eye is so far to assist the ear, it follows that his first step must be to acquaint himself with the construction of written words. He cannot do this until he is familiar with the Radicals, and accordingly a list of these, with translation, illustrations, and test tables, is supplied him in Part II. These are the indices under which all words are classed by modern Chinese lexicographers; many of them are themselves independent words used both in speech and writing; some are used in writing alone; some are obsolete symbols; but whether words or symbols, they must of course be retained each by a name or sound, and as every sound has to be represented by a combination of the letters of foreign alphabets, a consideration of the orthographic system employed to this end must of necessity precede the study of the Radicals, and the system here employed is therefore assigned a place under the head of Pronunciation in Part I.

The question of Pronunciation, it will there be seen, is divided into Sound, Tone, and Rhythm. The two last are all-important, and have been farther treated of with some detail in the prefatory pages of the Key to Part VII. The first, which should rather have been described as Orthography, is of less consequence by much. No orthography that professes to reproduce the syllabic sounds of a Chinese dialect is at the best more than an approximation. Neither vowels nor consonants, even when their defectiveness has been relieved by diacritic marks, are equal to the whole duty imposed upon them. Still, the learner, having made choice of a dialect, would soon find himself embarrassed, if he tried to make way without any orthographic system at all, and his confusion of both sounds and tones would certainly be augmented, if, while still in his apprenticeship, he attempted the fabrication of a system, in preference to adopting the work of an older hand. Students using the present work are, of course, left no option as to dialect or orthographic system. The system it provides, except that, to include certain occasional varieties, the number of syllables in it has been raised from 397 to 420, is almost the same as that contained in the HSIN CHING LU, an elementary work published by me in 1859. This system has been by no means universally approved, and although the objections taken to it have come generally from those who had commenced their studies before its appearance, it will be to the advantage of any beginner who may use it, that these objections should be declared and combated *in limine*. But before going farther into this question, it may be as well to explain why the particular dialect here set before him has been selected.

Some standard was necessary. Scarcely any stranger can have heard the spoken language of China mentioned without observing that one form of it is alluded to as the Mandarin Dialect. This is the *kuan 'hua*; properly translated, the oral language of government. The word *kuan*, an official, has been europeanised through the Portuguese as *mandarin*, and this term has become, as Mr. Edkins remarks,[*]

---

[*] Grammar of the Chinese Colloquial Language, commonly called the Mandarin Dialect, by the Revd. Joseph Edkins. Shanghai, 1864. 2nd Edition, page 7.

PREFACE.

too convenient an equivalent for *kuan* to be lightly abandoned; but the word *dialect* is misleading; for the *kuan 'hua* is the colloquial medium not only of the official and educated classes, but of nearly four-fifths of the people of the empire. In so vast an area, however, it follows that there must be a vast variety of dialects. Mr. Edkins, than whom no one has more diligently explored the laws and limits of these differences, divides the *kuan 'hua* into three principal systems, the southern, the northern, and the western, of which, he makes Nanking, Peking, and Ch'êng-tu, the capital of the province of Ssŭ Ch'uan, respectively the standards. The Nanking mandarin, he observes, is more widely understood, than that of Peking, although the latter is more fashionable, but he admits that "the Peking dialect must be studied by those who would speak the language of the imperial court, and what is, when purified of its localisms, the accredited *kuan 'hua* of the empire."

The opinion here cited but confirms a conclusion long since arrived at by myself, to wit, that Pekinese is the dialect an official interpreter ought to learn. Since the establishment of foreign legations with their corps of students at Peking, it has become next to impossible that any other should take precedence. When, in due time, the beginner's services are required at the Yamên of Foreign Affairs, he finds that the language he has been learning is that spoken by the chief officers of the Imperial Government. Meanwhile, his teachers, servants, and nine-tenths of the people he comes in contact with, naturally speak nothing else. Lastly, whether it be the fact or not that the peculiarities of Pekinese are, as it is alleged, by degrees invading all other dialects of the mandarin, the student may rest assured that if he speak Pekinese *well*, he will have no difficulty in understanding or being understood by any mandarin-speaking native whose dialect is not a flagrant divergence from the standard under which it would be enrolled by the geographer or the philologist. I have seen one interpreter who was really a proficient in Pekinese, as intelligible at Hankow as in the capital; I have known another, who was reputed to speak a local dialect of mandarin with fluency, unable to communicate with any mandarin but one whom circumstances had made familiar with the particular dialect he spoke.

This point, the selection of a dialect, decided, now some twenty years ago, the next step was the construction of an orthography. No one at the time had written on Pekinese, and the orthographies professing to represent the southern mandarin, those of Dr. Morrison, compiler of the first dictionary in Chinese and English, Dr. Medhurst, and Dr. Wells Williams, were far from unassailable representatives of the native system they professed to reproduce. To the first, Mr. Edkins goes so far as to deny all claim to be regarded as a mandarin orthography. "Morrison," says he, "in preparing his very useful syllabic dictionary, was not aware that the sounds he followed were not Mandarin at all, but an obsolete pronunciation." Dr. Medhurst, with some modifications for the better, nearly copied Dr. Morrison's orthography; not, he says, as being the best, but because it was the best known. Dr. Williams, working, I believe, in concert with the lexicographer's accomplished son, Mr. John Robert Morrison, recast the system of the Syllabic Dictionary, but only so far as the mode of spelling is concerned. The last orthography, consequently, though more symmetrical, is, in my opinion, hardly nearer accuracy than the first.* The only sinologue of standing who spoke the Peking mandarin was

---

* I should be sorry were it to appear that I spoke without sufficient respect for the labours of Dr. Morrison. It is impossible, as Mr. Meadows has remarked, not to feel a sort of gratitude to one who has so abridged the toil of the student. Dr. Wells Williams, the most industrious of sinologues, has nearly ready for the press a dictionary, which, as it will be an improvement upon his very useful work published some ten years ago, will be a notable addition to the materials for an education in Chinese.

PREFACE.

Mr. Robert Thom. By his advice that dialect had been studied, and with great success, by Mr. Thomas Meadows, and to the latter gentleman I was indebted not only for a right direction at starting, but for much assistance which there was at the time no one else within reach to afford. His Desultory Notes appeared shortly after, and to the chapters in that work relating to the language and administration of China, I am bound to acknowledge my obligations. These Notes contain, I believe, the first published scheme of a Pekinese orthography, but while admitting in general the justice of the author's appreciation of the characteristics of the dialect, I did not as a rule subscribe to his method of representing those characteristics; and, although it was in the main due to Mr. Meadows's suggestions that I got upon the right track, I am not, on reflection, aware of having adopted any thing from his system but the initial *hs;* of which more in the proper place.

My difficulty, when I first tried to form a list of syllables, was this, that no native work contained a syllabic system at all to be relied on. If you want to speak Cantonese as it is spoken in Canton, you can buy a vocabulary that will keep you perfectly straight, so far as sound is concerned. The Chinese have a rude expedient which it is an abuse of terms to call spelling, by which a native who is more or less lettered can divine the sound of a new written word once he has found it. The written word *p'ao*, for instance, tells him the initial sound of a certain word; the written word *t'ien*, below *p'ao*, supplies the final; and amalgamation of *p'ao* and *t'ien*, gives him *p'ien*. The Canton vocabulary is divided into chapters according to the Tones, and the initials being arranged after a predetermined order, and the terminals, also in a fixed order, under every initial, the word sought is looked for under its terminal. The process of course involves some preliminary acquaintance with the Chinese written language. Other dialects besides Cantonese have similar standard vocabularies; there are some for various shades of the mandarin; there are also phrase books with elaborate orthographic systems for instructing outsiders, at all events Cantonese, in mandarin pronunciation; but the latter I found to possess almost all two serious defects; the mandarin they attempted to reproduce was both in idiom and sound an antiquated dialect; and the initial and final sounds combined in them to effect an imitation of the mandarin syllable, still presenting themselves to the provincial student as unmutilated syllables of the dialect he had been accustomed to speak, neither adequately informed the eye, nor confirmed the ear.

It was not till 1855, when I had been making and re-making orthographies for some eight years, that a native author brought out a fair approximation to a Peking sound-table. This was published at Canton; but my teacher YING LUNG-T'IEN had already of his own motion compiled for me an index of words, which, after reducing the syllables to alphabetic order, I eventually appended to the HSIN CHING LU as the Peking Syllabary. His base was an old edition of the *Wu Fang Yüan Yin*, Sounds in the general language of the empire according to their Rhymes; a vocabulary with a most limited exegesis, but comprising some 10,000 authorised characters, that is, written words, arranged in five Tone divisions (see Part I, page 6), the words in each division being classed with reference to twelve initials and twenty finals in a prescribed order. Having struck out of this all words that he thought unavailable for colloquial purposes, he re-classed the remainder, retaining the primitive initials and finals as indices of syllabic categories, but changing either the Sound or Tone, or both, of a large number of words, and entirely suppressing the 5th or re-entering Tone. His judgments both on Sound and Tone, I have found, during the seven years his table has been on trial, to be generally held correct.

PREFACE.

His measure of the number of words that should suffice a speaker has proved somewhat restricted, and this is remarkable, for his own stock of phraseology was as copious as it was elegant. He died in 1861, and to supply what was defective in his list, an independent selection has since been made for me, by other native assistants, from a much larger vocabulary than that which he had dissected. The revised collection being then incorporated in the original Syllabary, a fresh copy of this and its Appendix was carefully prepared for the press under the superintendence of Mr. Charles Bismarck, Chinese Secretary of the Prussian Legation, a scholar of much promise whether as a speaker or translator. The new Appendix is entirely the work of his hand.

The value of the Syllabary, practically, is this. The eye and the ear, it will be borne in mind, are so to work together that no word is to be considered in the student's possession, until he shall have assured himself of its written form. The written form, or character, (see Part II, page 13,) consists of two parts, the Radical, which vaguely indicates the sense of the word, the Phonetic which vaguely indicates its sound. When his teacher uses a word unknown to the student, the latter, by referring to the Syllabary, (and after a very short acquaintance with the orthography his ear will guide him to the right syllable,) will find under that syllable not only the word he seeks in its proper tone-class, and printed in its authorised form, but grouped as near as may be on the same line with it, all words of the same Sound which have also the same Phonetic. His comparison of these, his observations of the difference between their Radicals, and the difference or identity of their Tones, will do much to impress the word sought, with all its incidents, form, sound, and tone, upon the memory. In the absence of his teacher, again, he will find his recollection of the characters he ought to know, in general strengthened, and, particularly, his knowledge of the Tones confirmed, by reference to the Syllabary, while the distinction between Sounds and Tones common to the same words, is taught or recalled to him by the Appendix.

The method of spelling resorted to in this work, I have said above, has been more or less attacked. Accuracy being impossible, I have inclined to the combinations that seemed to me to reproduce most simply the Syllabic Sounds without indifference to the exigencies of the Tone-scale; and for the sake both of printer and student I have always, where I could, employed alphabetic symbols in preference to diacritic marks. Thus the *i* as in *ship*, is shortened in *chih*, *shih*, by the *h*, which succeeds it, instead of being written *ĭ*. Neither *chĭ* nor *chih* will be pronounced correctly without the information that must accompany any orthographic system, but it appears to me that the alphabetic method has the advantage of simplicity. The vowel *u* in the various diphthongs in which it figures, is preferred to *w*, because, as the Tone Exercises in Part VII will shew, the emphasis falls, under some Tones, on the *u*, under others, on the vowel or vowels coming after it. The syllable *yu*, under some Tones, reads like *yo* in *yore*, but it is elsewhere incontestably *yu*, and we want *yo* as a distinct sound for the syllable *yo* as in *yonder*. So with *iu*, in the the syllables *liu*, *miu*, *niu*. These, under some Tones, are nearly *leyeu*, *meyeu*, *neyeu*, but under the second Tone, the student will find that he requires, if I may call it so, the more monosyllabic sound of *liu*. For like reasons I prefer *ui* to *uei*. The sound which is, to my ear, *er* in *perch*, or *ur* in *murrain*, Mr. Edkins writes *rĭ*; I have preferred *erh*. The initial *j* is intended to approach the sound of *s* in *fusion*, *z* in *brazier*, the French *j* in *jaune*. If the organs exercised in the pronunciation of this consonant be closely watched, it will no doubt appear that it is preceded by something like *r* or *er*; but not so markedly as to call for special indication. A speaker softening the *j* as

PREFACE.

in French, will be as surely understood when he says *ju jo*, as if he strives to utter a modification of *ru ro;* indeed with greater certainty than if he makes this latter effort. Lastly, there is the initial *hs,* which some complain is liable to confusion with *sh.* The aspirate precedes the sibilant; if the first *i* in *hissing* be dropped, you retain very exactly the Chinese syllable *hsing.* Rules cannot go far in such matters. The ear must advise itself by practice.*

On the sounds which I write *ssŭ*, *tzŭ*, and *tz'ŭ*, it is scarcely necessary to discourse. The vowels in these syllables defy a European alphabet more obstinately than any we have to deal with. Dr. Morrison's *sze* was changed by Dr. Williams to *sz'*. I used this for many years, but a tendency I noticed in some speakers to pronounce the syllable *sizz*, determined me to restore the vowel. Mr. Edkins writes *st*, which is neither better nor worse than *ssŭ*, or, as it read in the old Syllabary, *szŭ*. The vowel that *ĭ* or *ŭ* is supposed to stand for does not exist in our system, and, represent it by what letter we will, some diacritic mark is indispensable.

For practical purposes the beginner, having at his side of course a native instructor,—no orthography, however scientific, will teach him to pronounce without one,—will find, I believe, the illustrations that accompany the orthography in Part I, with the farther observations prefixed to the Key of Part VII, amply sufficient to regulate his ear. Until some more ambitious dictionary than any as yet published by a foreigner, overbears the distinctions taken by existing controversialists, controversy on the subject of syllabification will continue. The notes attached to the different parts of this course will enable the beginner to dispense almost entirely with a dictionary, and I would advise him, for the time being, to take what they tell him upon trust, and until he shall have reached a point considerably beyond their limits, to refrain from theorising in the matter either of sense or of sound.

---

* This initial *hs*, as the Sound Table will shew, is only met with before the vowel sounds of the Italian *i* or the French *u*, and the syllables beginning with it have a history of their own which claims a passing remark. Many of the words now pronounced *hsi*, were some years ago *hi*, many others *si;* similarly, words now pronounced *hsu*, were some of them *hu* and some *su*. In very modern mandarin vocabularies, these syllabic distinctions are preserved. The fusion of them is variously accounted for. While the Peking Syllabary was undergoing revision, I was urged by my friend Mr. Edkins to admit into my orthography some change that might serve as an index of the original sound in the case of words differing as above, and had the work been of a lexicographic character, I would have adopted the suggestion. Nothing could be easier than to mark all words that have been HI, as H^{s}I, and all that have been SI, as ^{H}SI; so with *hsu* and *su*; and to the philologist this recognition of pedigree might be of a certain value; but the syllable to be learned by the student of the colloquial language in this dialect, whether he express it by *hsi*, *hsu*, or otherwise, is still a sound common to all the words classed under it by the native speakers who compiled the syllabaries; the change would have involved a double tabular arrangement under all the syllables concerned, and it is to be doubted whether the beginner would not have been rather confused than advantaged by having what is now become, practically, but one category of sound, subdivided into two. If I live to publish a vocabulary, (not of Pekinese, but of Mandarin in general,) for which I have been for some years collecting materials, the peculiarity will not be left unnoticed.

The initial *ch* is common before all the vowels, but wherever it precedes the above vowel sounds *i* or *u*, it has been, and in other dialects still is, either *k* or *ts*. Thus *kiang*, and *tsiang*, are now both pronounced by a Pekinese, *chiang;* *kin* and *tsin* have both become *chin*. With some speakers, the articulation will sometimes vacillate between *ch* and *ts*, in these sounds, but the *ch* as a rule predominates, and you never hear the *k* hard. It is an instance of the caprice of these dialectic peculiarities that in the adjoining department of Tien-tsin, *ch* is *ts* even before *a;* the word *ch'a*, tea, is *ts'a*. At Shanghai, it is something like *dzó;* at Foochow, *t'a;* at Amoy *t'i*, (our *tea;*) and at Canton, again *ch'a*.

PREFACE.

The notice on the third page of the Key will enable any one to proceed with Part III who has fairly worked up the Test Tables in Part II, and then onward to the end of Part VI. The principle of instruction in all these, especially in Part III, is, to a certain extent, that which the methods of Ahn and Ollendorf have popularised in Europe. To a certain extent only. All specimens of these methods that I have examined, it is true, at once introduce the pupil to a certain stock of words and sentences; but the order of their lessons is regulated by that of the divisions of ordinary European grammars. They begin with the Article, decline the Noun, conjugate the Verb, and so on. I shall have to refer again to the absence of inflectional mechanism in Chinese, and the consequent impossibility of legislating as in other tongues for its etymology. Suffice it here to say, that preliminary investigation of etymological laws aids us less in this than perhaps in any language; the sooner we plunge into phraseology the better. The Forty Exercises of Part III were prepared two years ago, at first with fifty characters in the vocabulary column placed on the right of each. A gentleman of above average proficiency in certain European languages, whom chance made the *corpus vile* of the experiment, remonstrated against the magnitude of this task as excessive for a tiro. The vocabulary was accordingly reduced, and after four revisions, the Exercises were left as they now are. The progress of the Consular Students who have used them in manuscript, is fair guarantee of their utility as elementary lessons.

The Ten Dialogues of Part IV, which come next, were dictated by me to a remarkably good teacher of the spoken language, who of course corrected my idiom as he took them down. The matter of most of them is trivial enough, but they give the interpreter some idea of a very troublesome portion of his duties, namely, the cross-examination of an unwilling witness. It was with this object that they were composed.

The Dialogues are followed by the Eighteen Sections, the term section being chosen for no reason but to distinguish the divisions of this Part V from those of the foregoing parts and of the next succeeding one. The phrases contained in each of its eighteen pages are a portion of a larger collection written out years ago by YING LUNG-T'IEN. I printed the Chinese text of this with a few additions of my own in 1860. Finding them in some favor with those who have used them, I have retained all but my own contributions to the original stock, or such phrases in the latter as are explained in other parts of this work, and now republish them as a sort of continuation of Part III. The contents of that part are in Chinese styled *San Yü*, detached phrases; those of the fifth part are *Hsü San Yu*, a supplement to those phrases. The intermediate Dialogues are *Wên Ta Chang*, question and answer chapters, and the papers which follow in Part VI, are *T'an Lun P'ien*, or chapters of chat, for distinction's sake entitled The Hundred Lessons. These last are nearly the whole of a native work compiled some two centuries since to teach the Manchus Chinese, and the Chinese Manchu, a copy of which was brought southward in 1851 by the Abbé Huc. Its phraseology, which was here and there too bookish, having been thoroughly revised by YING LUNG-T'IEN, I printed it with what is now reduced to the *Hsü San Yü*; but it has since been carefully retouched more than once by competent natives.

The Sections and Lessons of the two last parts possess the advantage of being the spontaneous composition of native speakers. As such they are of course more incontestably idiomatic than the Exercises and Dialogues of Parts III and IV.

The words *Lien-hsi Yen Shan P'ing-Tsê Pien*, which form the Chinese title of Part VII, will

PREFACE.

translate freely as Exercises in the Tone System of Peking, and the prefecture in which it stands. Of the Exercises themselves it is unnecessary to say much more than that, from the very commencement, the student will do well to have a portion of them read over and over again to him daily by his teacher, whom he should try to follow *vivâ voce*. This will be to many a very irksome operation, and the Exercises are all translated in order that the learner may be spared the dulness of attending to the sound of words in complete ignorance of their sense; but their chief end is to drill him thoroughly in the nature and law of the Tones, and although, if he retain their meanings, he will find a large share of these a useful addition to his vocabulary, he should be more anxious to acquire from them a just notion of the rules and practice of accentuation which they are intended to illustrate. His command of speech will be every day receiving accessions from the earlier portions of the Series, on which he will naturally bestow the greater share of his attention. The Key to this Part will inform him of the plan of these Tone Exercises, which are in the order of the syllables alphabetically arrayed in the Sound Table appended to Part I.

He is at the same time specially invited to observe the principle on which the Chinese notes appended to the characters that act as Syllabic indices in this Part are constructed.

The *tzŭ*, written words of the Chinese language, as observed in Part I, are some thousands, while the *yin*, sounds, by which the *tzŭ* are called, are but a few hundreds, in number. Many of the *tzŭ* will never be met with in the oral language, but whether the student be engaged on the oral language or the written, his instructor will be constantly making reference, by its *yin*, to such or such a *tzŭ*; and inasmuch as, under many of the sounds, a number of *tzŭ* are known not only by one *yin*, syllabic sound, but often by the same *shêng*, intonation, of that sound, the confusion between the *tzŭ* alluded to and other homophonous *tzŭ*, unless the written form of the first be before the hearer's eye, may be imagined. The difficulty is fairly met by the Chinese practice of recalling the dissyllabic or polysyllabic combination in which the *tzŭ* spoken of most commonly plays a part. Just as in English, if it be necessary to particularise whether by a certain sound we mean *wright*, *write*, *right*, or *rite*, we make our meaning clear by a context that shews whether the syllable uttered is that in ship*wright*, to *write* letters, *right* and left, or *rite* of baptism, so a Chinese will explain that the *ai* he is speaking of, is the *ai* in *ai-ch'iu*, to implore, in *ch'ên-ai*, dust, in *kao ai*, tall and short, or in *ai-hsi*, to love; but homophony being, in his language, as much the rule as in ours it is the exception, he is very constantly obliged to fall back on this expedient.

The moral of this digression is that when studying Chinese, oral or written, the student should always endeavour to connect a newly discovered monosyllable with its best known associate; if his teacher be worth anything he will always be ready with this when called upon; and then, never forgetting that, in a large majority of instances, the *tzŭ*, no matter with what others they may combine, preserve their capability of employment as independent monosyllables or in distinct alliances, he will find the difficulties presented by the acquisition of a *primâ facie* monosyllabic language considerably diminished. The dialogue which closes the Supplement of Part VIII is an illustration of the difficulty in question, and the expedient proposed to remove it.

And now to come to the Eighth and last Part of this Series, and its supplement. In the memorandum appended to the Table of Contents for the guidance of the student, he will see that this Supplement is the first thing that he is to look at; not, as he might lawfully suppose, because Chinese text is

PREFACE.

read from what with us is the latter end of the book, but because the text of the Supplement contains a certain number of words and phrases which are among the first that he will require to use. It was an after-thought, or its matter might easily have been worked into the earlier Exercises of Part III. As regards Part VIII itself, after what has been said above on the subject of grammatical analysis, the introduction of a chapter purporting to treat of the Parts of Speech in Chinese may be thought an inconsistency. The reader is requested to hear in mind that the chapter is not, and does not assume to be, a grammar. It is no more than the result of an experiment which there has not been time to elaborate; of an attempt to set before the student some of the chief contrasts and analogies in the grammatical conditions of inflected English and uninflected Chinese.

The foreign linguist tells us that Grammar, as the Science of Words, is divisible into Etymology and Syntax, and that Etymology again subdivides itself into the laws of Inflection and of Derivation. The Chinese language yields but a qualified submission to this decree. In the sense of *derivation* its Etymology has something in common with that of other tongues; in the sense of *inflection* it has no etymology.

As to Derivation, the pedigree of all single words in Chinese is to a certain point accessible, for the single words have, with rare exceptions, each one its representative in the written language, and these representative forms, called with some confusion Chinese characters, are invariably made up of two elements known to foreign sinologues as the Radical and the Phonetic. The Radical indicates the category of *sense*, the Phonetic the category of *sound*, to which any word belongs. Neither Radical nor Phonetic, it is true, is in all cases such an index of sense or sound as to ensure prompt recognition of either; for although there has never been in Chinese that fusion of parts that has so obliterated the primitive features of other languages, the monosyllabic sound has been in many instances modified in the course of time, and both Radicals and Phonetics, but especially the latter, there is reason believe, have on occasion been corruptly exchanged. Still, the native dictionaries supply us with information fairly satisfying as regards the hereditary descent of some thousands of the single words constantly met with. In what we may call polysyllabic combinations, the work is apparently easier, because each syllable is a word in its original integrity, and we are at first sight led to infer that explaining the separate parts we can explain the whole. But it is far from being always evident how, its ancient or its more modern signification considered, the word claiming attention has come to play the part it does as the confederate of the word or words to which we now see it allied. The sense in which the compound is used, both colloquially and in writing, is frequently to be arrived at only by referring to the text of the classical work in which it first appears, or of the historian or other later writer who has applied the classical quotation after a fashion of his own ; and interpretation of the polysyllabic compound by as it were a sub-translation of its component parts, will often be as utterly misleading as an explanation of the epithet Shakesperian based on the hypothesis that the words *shake* and *spear* contain the secret of its meaning.

It is essential, therefore, that, while examining each member of a compound apart, for without this examination the single word will not be retained in his memory, the student should be on the watch against temptation too eagerly to adopt what may seem the self-evident conclusion deducible from his analysis. This caution is not wholly valueless with reference to any of the polysyllabic languages, where it is but seldom that the compound retains its parts so unmodified as to force upon us

PREFACE.

the recollection of their independent significations; but it is doubly necessary in Chinese, because, from the relation of the spoken and written languages, no one syllable of a compound ever presents itself in any other form than what belongs to it when it is employed as an a independent monosyllable. Experience of the danger to which a vicious process of etymological investigation exposes the translator, must be my excuse for occupying so much space with the subject.

As to the other branch of Etymology, namely Inflection, it cannot, I repeat, be allowed to have a place in Chinese grammar at all; and the versatility, if it be lawful to call it so, of the Chinese word, the capacity common to so many words (especially to those that we are wont to call nouns and verbs,) for grammatical services so widely differing, is such that any attempt to divide the language authoritatively into the categories known to us as Parts of Speech would be futile. Still, our Parts of Speech must of course have their equivalents in Chinese, whether we are able to categorise them as Parts of Speech or not; nor could Chinese be a language unless it possessed within itself the means of producing most of the results effected in all other tongues by inflection. It does not break off portions of its words or incorporate in them fragments of words, extant or obsolete, for the purpose of indicating the conditions we describe by the terms Case, Number, Mood, Tense, Voice, or the like; but it achieves nearly as much as these modifications can effect by a syntactic disposition of words, all extant, and almost all universally retaining their power to employ themselves integrally and independently elsewhere.

Now, for speculative purposes there are various treatises on Mandarin grammar, which may be perused with profit by the more advanced student; in particular those by M. Bazin and Mr. Edkins; but I have no faith in these, or in any Grammar that I have examined, as helps, *in the beginning*, towards acquisition of the spoken language. It occurred to me, nevertheless, shortly after I had put my hand to the elementary course now published, that if this were accompanied by a collection of examples that should give some notion, as I have said above, of the contrasts and analogies of the two languages, it might avail to remove some of the stumbling-blocks common to beginners in either, without committing them to the bondage of rules fashioned too strictly after our European pattern; and taking the simplest school grammar I could find, I went through its etymology with the able teacher before mentioned, translating the examples to him *vivâ voce*, and expounding to the best of my ability the rules and definitions these examples were intended to illustrate. Our embarrassment was a grammatical nomenclature; for as China does not as yet possess the science of grammar, she is of course very ill found in its terminology; and the reader will see to what straits the would-be grammarian is reduced in describing, for instance, the Case of the Noun. The teacher, thus inoculated, suggested sundry amplifications and curtailments as we read on, and the text finally approved being submitted to another learned native, he pronounced it to be a *Yen Yü Li Lüo*, or Summary of the Laws of Phraseology, by which somewhat pretentious designation it is accordingly distinguished in the Tzŭ Erh Chi. The experiment was pursued so desultorily, and the Chapter on the Parts of Speech, as I prefer to call it, is so crude and incomplete a production, that I am scarcely willing to expose it to the criticism of the majority who, notwithstanding the modesty of this title, can scarce fail to be as little pleased with it as its author. To the beginner, for all that, and it is for the beginner that the colloquial course is intended, its text and notes will prove of a certain value; not the least this, that its matter and method will together provide both his Chinese teacher and himself with a means of adding largely to the kind

PREFACE.

of information which the chapter does not profess more than partially to supply. The memorandum before mentioned will shew how I think he will best turn its contents to account.

The whole Colloquial Series has been either written or rewritten in the last two years, and it has been printed with the Documentary Series at Shanghai in the last few months. The fact that five presses, scarce any of them accustomed or adapted to the execution of printing on a grand scale, have been employed at the same time upon the volumes now issued, must be my excuse for the long list of errata appended to some of them. The errors noticed would have been more numerous but for the friendly offices of Messrs. Mowat and Jamieson, Consular Assistants stationed at Shanghai. The former gentleman bids fair to become an authority upon the Tone System. I am indebted to him for calling my attention to a grave oversight in the construction of the 3rd Tone Exercises in Part VII, and it is to his accuracy and diligence that the present correctness of the Key to that Part is mainly to be ascribed.

If I do not wind up as is the wont of diffident writers, with a depreciation of the merits of my work, it is not because I am blind to its imperfections. Still, these admitted, a campaign extending over about a quarter of a century encourages me to believe that the Series will be of no small assistance to the interpretorial wants which it is more particularly designed to relieve. The collection of elementary matter it contains will put any student of ordinary aptitude and application in possession of a very respectable acquaintance with the oral language in one twelve-month from the day he arrives at Peking. The course is far from exhaustive, but the speaker who can pass in it will find himself in a position of which he need not be ashamed. Let him give it a fair chance for at least his first eighteen months, and above all let him abstain during that period from exploration of any shorter path to perfection that he may imagine he has discovered; from all original attempts at systematisation. There is much about the written language to lure a novice from what he may not unnaturally regard as the less serious, because it appears the less formidable, undertaking. A man with a quick ear may fancy that, working at written texts with a native instructor, the verbal explanations of the latter will bring him the habit of speech without any special consecration of his powers to its acquirement, and his progress in reading is so much more evident, and as such so flattering to his self-love, that he may easily persuade himself to prefer the labour that seems to promise the more immediate remuneration of his pains. There can be no greater error. If he yield to the temptation, if he neglect the spoken language for the written during his noviciate, he will repent his mistake throughout the whole of his career. Even when his acquaintance with the colloquial course before him shall have satisfied a competent examiner, he must not by any means look upon the oral language as a thing that will now take care of itself. All that the course professes to give him is a respectable foundation. To fit himself for the higher duties of his calling, he must considerably enlarge his range. For this purpose, he can draw on no better source than popular fictions of the country. The dialogue and descriptions, under proper guidance, will enrich his vocabulary, and he will gather from both a knowledge of Chinese thought and character, which, restricted as difference of habits makes our intercourse with this people, is no where else more pleasantly or usefully supplied. In Chinese, of all languages, it is an economy of time to consult a good translation, and the student may safely trust to Sir John Davis's version of The Fortunate Union, or to those of *Les Deux Cousines* and *Les Jeunes Filles Lettrées* recently published by M. Stanislas Julien,

PREFACE.

the greatest of living sinologues. But, translated or untranslated, the novel should be read with a native sufficiently learned to explain the allusions in it, and to guard his pupil against too ready adoption of its phrases as colloquial. A fair proportion of them of course are colloquial, but deeply as the vulgar tongue of China is rooted in her literature, there is much in such works as we are speaking of that is far too classical for every day use, and the random employment of quasi-Johnsonian phraseology would be to a native hearer as astounding as Sir Walter Scott's visitors are stated to have thought his resuscitation of Froissart. This rock avoided, the future interpreter should remember that improvement in its form is scarcely less a duty than augmentation of his vocabulary.

It is in no spirit of academical purism that I make this observation. It is justified by the peculiar circumstances which render the relations of the foreign and Chinese official so far from satisfactory. The latter, rising from the educated class which is in reality the governing class of this empire, is a man thoroughly conversant with the philosophy, history, law, and polite literature of his own country, and there is nothing that more confirms him in the stubborn immobility which so baffles the foreign agent, than his conviction that it is impossible for that barbarian to rise to the level of Chinese education. The discussion of affairs may often be conducted, I grant, in Chinese little better than the French of Arthur Pendennis, without any perceptible prejudice to the interests immediately at stake; but I hold that the foreign agent is responsible for something more than a mere hand-to-mouth despatch of his daily business. It is essential to the interests of China and of foreign nations alike, that the governing class should be brought to amend its erroneous estimate of foreign men and foreign things. His opportunities of influencing it are not numerous, but with the exception of the foreign agent, there is no one who possesses any opportunity of influencing the governing class at all. Beginning as late as most of us begin, it would be hardly possible, were it desirable, that we should traverse the enormous field in which a lettered Chinese is so at home, but it is by no means an extravagant ambition that our speech should become sufficiently polished to disabuse the learned man of his belief that we are incapable of cultivation; and it lies, I say, almost exclusively with the foreign official to commence the removal of this impression. I had hoped to bring out this year a short history of China, which might have served to introduce the Student Interpreter to that higher style of language to which I conceive it incumbent upon him to strive to advance; but this, with some other enterprises projected on his behalf, must wait. Pending their maturity, I commend to his patient attention the humbler phraseology of this elementary course.

SHANGHAI, 16th May, 1867.

CONTENTS OF THE TZŬ ERH CHI.

CONTENTS OF THE TZŬ ERH CHI. Colloquial Series.

		PAGE
I. Pronunciation.		
	Sound or Orthography	1
	Tone	6
	Rhythm	7
	Sound Table	8
II. The Radicals		13
	General Table	15
	Abbreviations	23
	Test Table I.	25
	Test Table II.	26
	Test Table III.	27
	Exercise in the Colloquial Radicals	28
III. San Yu Chang, The Forty Exercises		31
IV. Wên-Ta Chang, The Ten Dialogues		from 109 to 74
V. Hsu San Yü, The Eighteen Sections		112
VI. T'an-Lun P'ien, The Hundred Lessons		from 214 to 132
VII. Lien-hsi Yen Shan P'ing Tsê Pien, The Tone Exercises		219
VIII. Yen Yü Li Lüo, The Chapter on the Parts of Speech		from 288 to 245
	Supplement	289
	APPENDICES containing all characters in Parts III, IV, V, VI, and VII.	

CONTENTS OF THE KEY TO THE TZŬ ERH CHI.

		PAGE
Observations on the Use of the Key to Parts III, IV, V, and VI.		3
Translation of Part III.		4
Table of Weights, Measures, &c.		84
Notes on Part III.		85
Translation and Notes of Part IV.		105
Do. do. Part V.		141
Do. do. Part VI.	(second series of pages.)	1
Do. do. Part VII.		57
Do. do. Part VIII.		101
Errata of the Colloquial Series, Key, Syllabary, and Writing Exercises		133

TZŬ ERH CHI. Colloquial Series.

1. Tables of the Corrections and Additions required in the Tzŭ Erh Chi, the Appendices, the Key, the Syllabary, and the Writing Exercises, will be found at the end of the Key, and the Student's first care should be to amend the text throughout.
2. He should observe also that the order of the pages of the Key has been broken at the end of Part V. It recommences with page 1 of Part VI.
3. Having secured a teacher, he should have the Sound Table given on page 8 read over to him, carefully noting the value of the vowels and consonants employed in the orthography, as explained on pages 3–6.
4. He should at once get up the Supplement commencing on page 289. The text is in columns ranging from right to left on each page, with the orthography of every character placed to its right. The numbers will shew him the order of the sentences, and will guide him through the English version which he will find on the last pages of the Key. The phrases in this Supplement are of the simplest kind, and with the exception of those in the conversation with the teacher at the close of it, he had better learn them *by ear*, without troubling himself to retain the characters in which they are written. A servant of moderate education would be able to read them to him.
5. There is nothing to prevent him at the same time studying the Radicals. He will find on page 13 sufficient information as to the course he is to pursue with these.
6. To retain them he should write them out, and to avoid a false direction, he had better copy them as he finds them in the Writing Exercises, of which they form the first part. His teacher will shew him how they must be traced, and while he forms his hand by the practice, the interval that he devotes to it will relieve both eye and ear.
7. As soon as he is fairly familiar with the Tables and Exercises on pages 25–28, he will proceed to Part III. Page 3 of the Key renders farther direction unnecessary regarding the use of this or the succeeding parts to the end of Part VI. He should keep to the Writing Exercises as far as they carry him, and when these are ended, he should have slips copied for him in a large hand from the Appendices, which will always serve him as a sort of test table of his knowledge of the characters in the course.
8. From the moment he has read Part I, he should, for at least an hour a day, have read to him a portion of the Tone Exercises in Part VII. He will see that the Key supplies him with a full translation of these; but, as I have observed in the Preface, he need not at first regard the Tone Exercises as a contribution to his vocabulary. In the orthography there given, the tone of every syllable is marked in the manner explained in Part I, page 7; these tone marks will assist his ear, and he must patiently repeat what his teacher will read aloud to him, till the latter pronounces his intonation correct. When he comes to Part III, he should not only watch his teacher's intonation of the single words, combined words, and short sentences, but he should continually invite his criticism as well as that of other teachers. His attention is at the same time particularly called to the observations on page 57 of the Key to Part VII, regarding the rhythm of short sentences or other polysyllabic combinations. Until he has finished Part III, he need not trouble himself with the Syllabary, but thenceforth it should be frequently consulted, and the difference in Breathing should be as carefully noted as that in Tone. See remarks on page 6 of Part I.
9. I should recommend that the English version of Part VIII be read through as soon as the student is ready to go on with Part III. The translation which accompanies this in the Key, and the Notes commencing on page 85 of it, will tell him almost all he can require to know about the Exercises in this Part; but he will soon begin to apply what he learns from these in conversation with his teacher, and the text of Part VIII, especially from page 105 to the end, will often stand him in the stead of a vocabulary.

MEMORANDUM FOR THE GUIDANCE OF THE STUDENT.

More careful examination of the Chinese text of Part VIII may be deferred until he has accomplished the Ten Dialogues. He will then find himself able to read all the short dialogues illustrative of the Verb, Adverb, &c.

10. As to general directions :—I have insisted much in the Preface upon the danger of being seduced from the spoken by the attractions of the written language. The student must equally guard against a temptation to abandon the more fatiguing for the easier parts of the Colloquial Series. A man of average aptitude and power of work should be able to pass in the Forty Exercises in three months. He will then know by sight the written forms of some 1,200 words, the Radicals included. There are not 300 new words in the Ten Dialogues, and he will fly through these consequently in a few days; but I should urge him to read them some eight or ten times before he goes farther. Proceeding next to the Eighteen Sections, he will find these, though full of fresh matter, comparatively unattractive; but, if he get them up so as to pass in them, he will be repaid both by the improvement of his idiom, and large increase of his store of words. The part, moreover, is of no great length. Part VI contains several dialogues, and these, and of course, similarly, the dialogues of Part IV, will be best turned to account by having them read aloud by two teachers. As the student goes through either of these Parts with notes and translation, he should engage one of his colleagues to combine with him in this *vivâ voce* exercise. The value of listening is scarcely enough appreciated in any language. The learner is generally too anxious to begin to talk.

Finally, let the more eager beware of over zeal at starting, and let all, as far as in them lies, have fixed hours for the different sections of their work. They are proposing to themselves, primarily, the acquisition of the oral language, and, subsidiarily, such acquaintance with its written forms as will enable them to recognise those they have met in reading, and to reproduce them in writing. For the time being, the last object is of the less consequence; the more important is the first; but if the student is to use this course, the first is scarcely separable from the second. The relative quickness of the eye and ear is so different in different persons, that proportions of work to be assigned to either must be left to the individual. He should early decide which it is incumbent on him to use the more; learning by his teacher's repetition of the text, if his ear is slow; reperusing the text, if he finds that the characters slip from his memory. Under any circumstances, let him, as soon as possible, lay down a rule for the division of his time; so much for reading, so much for writing, so much for exercise of the ear, whether listening or conversing, and for some months to come let him be slow to disturb his rule. There is no language of which the acquirement is so forwarded by method as the Chinese, be the memory quick or slow.

These remarks, he will bear in mind, refer exclusively to the Colloquial Series. When he is ready for the Documentary Series, the Key to that Series will give him some hints regarding his course of study as a translator.

PART I. PRONUNCIATION.

TZŬ ERH CHI.

COLLOQUIAL SERIES.

PART I. PRONUNCIATION.

PART II. RADICALS.

PART I. PRONUNCIATION.

In order to correctness of Pronunciation in Chinese, three conditions must be satisfied; there must be accuracy of Sound, of Tone, and of Rhythm.

Of these three conditions accuracy of Sound, as considered with reference to the expression of it, syllabically or alphabetically, is the least important. We run less chance of being misunderstood if we say *lan* for *nan*, for instance, provided that we preserve the correct tone, than if we were to say *nan*[2] when we should have said *nan*[1].

Still, we must have a distinct idea of the syllable we are to pronounce, and as Chinese furnishes, in comparison with our alphabets, nothing but the most imperfect aid to the end in view, we are forced to supply the deficiency by combinations of our own alphabetic symbols, sometimes at the rate of their prescriptive values, sometimes reinforcing them by diacritic marks, or arbitrarily constraining them to do a duty for which there is little precedent.

1. **Sound.** The values assigned to the letters of the alphabet employed in the spelling of the syllables given below are here considered independently of *tone*; but the syllable has been spelt generally in the form that appeared to approach nearest to an adequate representation of the spoken *sound*, and at the same time to admit, without change of the letters composing it, of an application to it of the inflections proper to a change of *tone*.

Vowels and Dipthongal Sounds.

a ; the *a* in *father* ; when pronounced singly, in particular after words terminating in vowel sounds, slightly nasalised, as though preceded by *'ng*.
ai ; nearly our sound *aye*, but better represented by the Italian *ai*, in *hái*, *amái*,
ao ; the Italian *ao* in *Aosta*, *Aorno* ; but not unfrequently inclining to *á-oo*, the Italian *au* in *cauto*.
e ; in *eh*, *en*, as in *yet*, *lens*.
ei ; nearly *ey* in *grey*, *whey*, but with greater distinctness of the vowels as in the Italian *lei*, *contei*.
ê ; nearest approached in English by the vowel sound in *earth*, in *perch*, or in any word where *e* is followed by *r*, and a consonant not *r* ; as in *lurk*. Singly, or as an initial, it has the nasal prefix *'ng* stronger than the syllable *a*.
i ; the foregoing *ê* followed enclitically by *y*. Strike out the *n* from the word *money*, and you have the syllable *mêi*. If the syllable *nêi* exist at all, which some Chinese dispute, the *êi* is most apparent in *nêi*.
êrh ; the *urr*, in *burr*, *purr*.
i ; as a single syllable, or as a final, the vowel sound in *ease*, *tree* ; in *ih*, *in*, *ing*, shortened as in *chick*, *chin*, *thing*.
ia ; with the vowels distinct ; not *ya*, but as in the Italian *piazza*, *Maria*. In some syllables terminating in *ia*, *iang*, *iao*, the *ia* is, in certain tones almost *éa* or *eyah*. This is oftener observable where the initial is *l*, *m*, or *n* ; but even with these the usage is capricious.
iai ; the *iaj* in the Italian *veechiaja*.
iao ; the vowels as in *ia* and *ao*, with the terminal peculiarity of the latter. This sound is also modified by the *tones*.
ie ; with the vowels distinct, as in the Italian *siesta*, *niente*. The *i* is modified, as in case of *ia*, under similar circumstances ; that is, in certain tones *ie*, inclines to become *éé*, or *eyeh*, often making *lien*, *nien*, almost *leyen*, *neyen*.

TZŬ ERH CHI. **Colloquial Series.**

io; shorter than the Italian *io*; more nearly the French *io* in *pioche*.

iu; as a final, nearly *eeyew* or *eeoo*, at all times longer than our *ew*. Thus *chiu* is not *chew*, but rather *chyew*, and the tone may even make the vowel sounds more distinct. In the syllables *liu*, *niu*, the *i* is affected as in *ia*, *ie*, they become almost *leyew*, *neyew*. In *chiung*, *hsiung*, (the only syllables ending in consonants into which I have introduced *iu*,) it must be admitted that in most instances, though not in all, the *iung*, is rather *eeyŏng*, than *eeyoong*; the *ŏ*, representing *o* in *roll*.

o; something between the vowel sound in *awe*, *paw*, and that in *roll*, *toll*. When single, it commences with a slight consonantal sound, part nasal and part guttural, which the *'ng* inadequately expresses, and is inflected at the close as if an *a*, or *ah*, were appended to it. The Tones seriously modify this syllable. As a final the power of the vowel remains the same, with the same terminal inflection, and not altogether divested of the guttural peculiarity which it is not within the compass of our alphabet to reproduce. Let the reader, as an experiment, try to pronounce *lo*, as, *law*, prolonging the *aw* in his throat.

ou; in reality *êŏ*, the vowel-sounds in *burrow*, when all the consonants are withdrawn; in English, nearest the *ou* in *round*, *loud*.

ŭ; when uttered alone, as it is at times for *yu*, or when a final, nearest the vowel-sound in the French *eût*, *tu*. In *un* it is not so long as in the French *une*, but nearer the *un*, in the German *Munchen*.

ŭa; occurs only in the final *uan*, which in some tones is *uen*; the *u* as above, but the *a* much flatter than in the final *an*, nearer the *an* in *antic*.

ŭe; the *u* as above, the *e* as in *eh*, the vowel sounds in the French *tu es*, represent this combination perfectly.

uo; a disputed sound, used, if at all, interchangeably with *io* in certain syllables.

u; when single, (as at times instead of *wu*,) and when a final, the *oo*, in *too*; in *un* and *ung*, it is shorter, as in the Italian *punto*, *lungo*. In the latter final it vacillates between *ung* and *ŏng*; being nasalised at the close so as to produce a sound between the French *long* and *longue*.

ua; as we pronounce it in Juan; nearly *ooa*, which in many instances contracts to *wa*. In the finals *uan*, *uang*, it is also sometimes *ŏa*, or *oá*, as the Tones may rule.

uai; as in the Italian *guai*, the above sound *ua*, with the *i* in *ai* appended to it; the *u* subject to the same changes as in *ua*.

uei; the *u* as in *ua*, *uai*, often in value *w*; the *ei* as in *ei* final; the vowel sounds in the French *jouer* answer fairly to *uei*.

uê; the *u* as in *ua*; the *ê* as explained before. It is found only in the final *uên*, which sounds as if written *ú-ŭn*, frequently *wên*, or *wun*. It is in many cases difficult to distinguish *uên* from *un*.

ui; the *u* as above, followed enclitically by *i*, as if *oo-y*; the vowel sounds in *screwy*; more enclitic than in the French *Louis*, or the Italian *lui*.

uo; the *u* as above; the *o* as in *lone*; the Italian *uo* in *fuori*; often *wo*, and, at times, nearly *ŏŏ*.

ŭ; between the *i* in *bit* and the *u* in *shut*; only found with the initials *ss*, *tz*, *tz‘*, which it follows from the throat, almost as if the speaker were guilty of a slight eructation. We have no vowel sound that fairly represents it.

Consonantal Sounds.

ch; before any of the above finals except *ih*, simply as in *chair*, *chip*; before *ih*, it is softened to *dj*; *chih*, being in many cases pronounced *djih*.

ch‘; a strong breathing intervening between the initial *ch* and the vowel sound, but without reduplicating the latter. Drop the first vowel in *chàhá*, or the italicised letters in *much-harm*, and the *ch-ha* remaining will give a fair idea of the syllable *ch‘a*. This may also be obtained if we contrast the smooth syllable *cha* with *tcha*; the breathing becoming apparent in the greater effort needed to utter the latter syllable. The *ch‘* does sometimes soften like the unaspirated *ch* before *ih*, but much more rarely.

f; as in *farm*.

‘h; as the *ch*, in the Scotch *loch*; the *ch* of the Welch and Gaelic.

PART I. PRONUNCIATION.

hs; a slight aspirate preceding and modifying the sibilant, which is, however, the stronger of the two consonants. To pronounce *hsing*, let the reader try to drop the first *i* in *hissing*. He will exaggerate both the aspirate and the sibilant, but the experiment will give him a clear idea of the process. The aspiration is effected by closing the middle of the tongue upon the back of the palate, before the tip of the tongue is raised for the sibilation. It differs from *sh*, although this difference is less observable before the dipthongs *ia, ie*.

j; most nearly the French *j* in *jaune*; our *s*, in *fusion*, or *z* in *brazier*, are the nearest imitation of which our alphabet admits.

k; as *c* in *car*, *k* in *king*, but when following other sounds, often softened to *g* in *go, gate*. In the word *ko*, for instance, the Numerative (see EXERC. I, note), proper to many nouns, when this is preceded by *ua*, that, or *chê*, this, the *k* is softened; the two syllables being pronounced almost *nago, chêgo*.

k'; the aspirate as in *ch'*. Drop the italicised letters in *kick-hard* and you will have *k'a*.

l; as in English.

m; as in English.

n; as in English.

'ng, a consonantal sound of partly nasal and partly guttural influence upon the vowels it precedes. To produce *'nga*, take the italicised consonants in the French mo*n galant*; for *'ngai*, in mo*n gaillard*; for *'ngo* in so*n gosier*. It is never so evident in a syllable pronounced by itself, as when following another syllable that terminates in a vowel, or in *n*.

p; as in English.

p'; the aspirate as in *ch', k'*. Observe the manner in which an Irishman pronounces *p*arty, *p*arliament; or drop the italicised letters in *s*lap-hard, and you will retain *p'a*.

s; as in English.

sh; as in English.

ss; *ssŭ* is the only syllable in which this initial is found. The object of employing *ss* is to fix attention on the peculiar vowel sound *ŭ*, which, as stated above, it is so hard to reproduce.

t; as in English.

t'; as in *k', p'*, &c. Observe an Irishman's pronunciation of *t* in *tenor, torment*; or drop the italics in *h*it-hard, and you have *t'a*.

ts; as in *jetsam, catsup*, after another word, often softened to *ds* in *gladsome*.

ts'; the aspirate intervening as in *ch*, and other initials. Let the reader drop the italicised letter in *b*ets-hard, and he will retain *ts'a*

tz; is employed to mark the peculiarity of the final *ŭ*, but is hardly of greater power than *ts*.

tz', like *ts'* above. This and the preceding initial are, like *ss*, only used before the *ŭ*.

w; as in English; but very faint before *u*, if indeed it exist at all.

y; as in English, but very faint before *i*, or *u*.

In the Final *ao* I have followed the Manchu spelling, against Morrison and Williams, who write *aou, áu*. This, as I have admitted, is the approximate sound in certain Tones.

The Final *eh*, used only in *yeh*, may seem unnecessarily separated from *ieh*. In my opinion the consonant *y* is sufficiently plain to authorise it, and the tone-inflection is not less practicable in the syllable *yeh* than in *ieh* So with the final *ên*.

In the Final *ê* some confusion with *o* is unavoidable. I have endeavoured to guide myself by the Manchu; but find that, although native teachers consign them to different finals, it is next to impossible, in many words, to say, whether *ê* (or *ngê*,) *chê, jê, kê, mê, tê*, or *o, cho, jo, ko, lo, mo, to*, be the correct orthography. The same is true with the aspirated *ch, k, t*, but I think that, after the aspirate in general, the *o* prevails; also, that while none of these syllables, sometimes sounded as ending in *ê*, is exempt from the changes to *o*, there are many in *o* which never change to *ê*. It will be found that some natives incline more to the one and some more to the other.

The Final *êi* is of doubtful existence even in *nêi*, which certainly ends in a sound somewhat different from the terminal of *lei, mei*. These have taken the place of *lui, mui*, the old orthography of the mandarin as spoken in the south.

TZŬ ERH CHI. **Colloquial Series.**

The Finals ên and êng were originally substituted for un and ung in syllables beginning with *f*, *m*, *p*, after the latest native works published at Canton to teach the Cantonese to talk Mandarin, and the modification has been found to be fully authorised by the Pekinese. The Manchu orthography of last century was *fung, mung*, but always *fên, mên, pên*.

The *u* in *iung, ung*, and in *ua, uai*, and other combinations, in which it figures both as *o* and *w*, has been retained nevertheless, as the vowel most certainly to be recognised in the simplest form of the *sound*, and as the most convenient for exhibiting the variation of the *tone*, without change of *syllable*, to which end, moreover, it was expedient to avoid using the initials '*hw, kw*.

Breathings

The Aspirate which intervenes between the initials *ch, k, p, t, ts, tz*, and the vowels following them, is indicated, as will have been seen above, by an inverted comma in preference to an *h*, lest the English reader following his own laws of spelling, should be led to pronounce *ph* as in *triumph, th* as in *month*, and so on; which would be a serious error. The full recognition of the aspirate's value is of the last importance; the *tones* themselves are not of more. A speaker who says *kan* when he ought to say *khan*, might as well speak of Loudon for London. The aspirate prefixed to the initial *h* is a very strong breathing, but the omission of it is not attended with the same serious consequences.

2. **Tone.** There is no subject on which it is more important to write, and none on which it is harder to avoid repeating what has been said by others.

The ideas of a Chinese are capable of expression in writing in some thousands of characters that may be used singly or in combination with each other. The sound of each of these is such that without much violence to fact we call it a monosyllable. The Chinese term this monosyllable *yin;* in no dialect known to us does the number of the *yin* exceed a few hundreds; hence great confusion to the ear, and distress to the memory, when it would distinguish between sounds, characters, or ideas, which it can only recall by an alphabetic denomination common to many. Under the *yin*, or sound, *i*, in Morrison's Dictionary there are 1165 characters differing in form and meaning. Of this *yin* there are, however, subordinate divisions, the *shêng*, which we translate Tones; keys in which the voice is pitched, and by which a variety of distinctions is effected, so delicate as to be retained only after long and anxious watching by the foreign ear, but so essential an acquisition that, until by practice his intonation be accurate, the foreign speaker is in hourly danger of making very laughable mistakes. A good deal that he says will no doubt be understood, but, whether he theorise or not on the matter, until his speech be *tonically* correct, no missionary or interpreter need imagine himself secure of being intelligible.

The term *Tone* has been so long accepted as the equivalent of the Chinese *shêng;* that it may be hardly worth while attempting to disturb the usage. It might be notwithstanding rendered with greater propriety *note*, in a musical sense, although no musical instrument to my knowledge is capable of exhibiting more than an approximation to the *shêng*. Dr. Hagel, in his folio on the Elementary Character of the Chinese Language (1801), has tried to give an idea of the *shêng* as musical notes. The attempt has been repeated, I believe, more recently, by the late Dr. Dyer, the celebrated sinologue.

The number of the *shêng* differs in different dialects. Books recognise five. In the Peking dialect there are now four; 1st, the *shang p'ing*, or upper even tone; 2nd, the *hsia p'ing*, or lower even tone; 3rd, the *shang*, or ascending tone; 4th, the *ch'u*, receding or departing tone.

In the *first* tone, the *upper even*, it may be enough to observe, the vowel sound, whether the word be pronounced quickly or slowly, proceeds without elevation or depression. One of our sinologues has not incorrectly styled it the *affirmative* tone.

In the 2nd tone, the *lower even*, the voice is jerked, much as when in English we utter words expressive of doubt and astonishment.

In the 3rd tone, the *ascending*, the sound becomes nearly as abrupt, but more resembling what with us would indicate indignation and denial.

In the 4th tone, the *receding*, the vowel sound is prolonged as it were regretfully.

The *ju*, or *entering*, an abrupt tone still recognised in studying the written language, that is to say in committing Chinese books to memory, is now ignored in the practice of the spoken language of Peking; most of the words or characters ranged under it in the vocabularies having been transferred to the 2nd tone.

PART I. PRONUNCIATION.

It is simplest, as Mr. Meadows suggests, to distinguish the Four Tones by numbers. I write the *shêng* of the syllable *pa*, accordingly, as follows :—

pa^1, pa^2, pa^3, pa^4.

The sounds of the syllables repeated in the above order form a sort of a *chime* which can only be learned by the ear, but which it is not difficult to learn. When he has caught it, the student should never hear a new phrase without taking it to pieces and satisfying himself and his teacher, word by word, of the proper tone, or note, of each. So long as his teacher declines to pass his notation as correct, so long should he carefully repeat the word or words disputed.* When absent from the teacher he will be able to fortify his ear by recurrence to the Syllabary.

There is some danger of misleading a student who has *not* caught the chime, and once he has he will dispense with all illustration. We will hazard but one parallel, for better or for worse. Let A, B, C, D, be four persons engaged in conversation, and a question be put by B regarding the fate of some one known to them all. In the four lines below, I have supposed A to assert his death in the 1st tone, B, to express his apprehension that he has been killed, in the 2nd, C, to scout this suspicion, in the 3rd, and D, to confirm it sorrowfully, in the 4th

    1.—*shang-p'ing*, A. Dead.
    2.—*hsia-p'ing*, B. *Killed?*
    3.—*shǎng*, C. No!
    4.—*ch'ü*, D. Yes!

Now in this short dialogue, or tetralogue, English speakers would ordinarily so pitch the voice as to make the whole tolerable approximation to the chime the student has to acquire. But the analogy would entirely mislead him were he not to qualify it by remembering that in the four words instanced, the voice rises and falls according to the emotion of the speaker; whereas the pitch of pa^3, pa^4, or any other syllables, is independent of any such motive. The tone of the syllable has as little relation to its sense as the note allotted to any word in most of our songs has to its meaning. The distinction next to be observed is this, that, while there is nothing to prevent the same word being allotted in different songs to any note in the scale, it is only by exception that, in Chinese speech, the place of a word in the tone-scale is ever exchanged for another. So *p'a* to fear, is always $p'a^4$, *chiao*, to teach, is at times $chiao^1$, at times $chiao^4$; for with a new meaning a word will change its Tone, sometimes, even its Sound.

As the student has been told above, however, the correct application of the Tones will only come to him by the practice of the ear, and in order to the discipline of his ear a set of Tone Exercises has been prepared in Part VII of this colloquial series. To these his attention is earnestly recommended.

3. Rhythm. What tone is to the individual sound, Rhythm is to the sentence. Like the tone, it can only be acquired from a native. The student must take careful note of the proper place of the emphasis. He must not be surprised to find the Rhythm in apparent antagonism to the Tone in some cases; especially when an adjective or adverb is formed by reduplication of a word with the enclitic particle *ti* appended; as in *sung-sung-ti*, *hsieh-hsieh-ti*, where his teacher will refuse to recognise any difference between the tones of the two *sung*, or the two *hsieh*, although, to our ear, the accent of the second differs widely from that of the first, resting in some of these polysyllabic combinations on the one, and in some, on the other syllable.

And now for the sake of securing an accurate idea of the pronunciation of each syllable, let the student carefully follow a Pekinese through the Sound Table which occupies the next four pages.

---

* To give an instance of the scrapes into which inaccuracy in the tones may betray the speaker, a gentleman, who really speaks the language well, was asking where the salt for the supply of Peking was obtained, and was told first, to his astonishment, that it was all imported by foreigners. Objecting to this, and explaining that he meant fresh salt, or the salt consumed in daily food, he was yet more astonished to hear that it was brought from the province of Ho Nan, nor was it until after some minutes' cross-examination that the Chinese addressed, detecting his error and correctly intoning the syllable, replied, "from the salines of the province of course." The foreigner had been intoning *yen* 2, the sound for, amongst others, the word *salt*, as though it were *yen* 1, the sound for, amongst others, the word *smoke*, and the Chinese had believed the first question to refer to Opium, commonly called *smoke*, and the second, in which some qualifications had been added, to refer to native tobacco.

TZŬ ERH CHI. Colloquial Series.

A	23 chi 吉	50 chou 晝	76 chung 中	94 ʻhan 寒	
1 a * 阿	24 chʻi 奇	51 chʻou 抽	77 chʻung 充	95 ʻhang 夯	
2 ai 愛	25 chia 家	52 chü 句	78 chʻuo 擢	96 hao 好	
3 an 安	26 chʻia 恰	53 chʻü 取		97 hê, hei 黑	
4 ang 昂	27 chʻiai 楷	54 chüan 捐	**E**	98 ʻhên 很	
5 ao 傲	28 chiang 江	55 chʻüan 全	79 ê * 額	99 ʻhêng 恆	
	29 chʻiang 搶	56 chüeh 絶	80 ên 恩	100 ʻho 河	
	30 chiao 交	57 chʻüch 缺	81 êng 嗶	101 ʻhou 後	
CH	31 chʻiao 巧	58 chün 君	82 êrh 兒	102 ʻhu 戶	
6 cha 乍	32 chieh 街	59 chʻün 羣		103 ʻhua 花	
7 chʻa 茶	33 chʻieh 且	60 chüo 爵	**F**	104 ʻhuai 壞	
8 chai 窄	34 chien 見	61 chʻüo 卻	83 fa 法	105 ʻhuan 換	
9 chʻai 柴	35 chʻien 欠	62 chu 主	84 fan 反	106 ʻhuang 黃	
10 chan 斬	36 chih 知	63 chʻu 出	85 fang 方	107 ʻhui 回	
11 chʻan 產	37 chʻih 尺	64 chua 抓	86 fei 非	108 {ʻhuên ʻhun} 混	
12 chang 章	38 chin 斤	65 chʻua 欻	87 fên 分	109 ʻhung 紅	
13 chʻang 唱	39 chʻin 親	66 chuai 搋	88 fêng 風	110 ʻhuo 火	
14 chao 兆	40 ching 井	67 chʻuai 膪	89 fo 佛		
15 chʻao 吵	41 chʻing 輕	68 chuan 專	90 fou 否	**HS**	
16 chê 這	42 chio 角	69 chʻuan 穿	91 fu 夫	111 hsi 西	
17 chʻê 車	43 chʻio 郤	70 chuang 牡		112 hsia 夏	
18 chei 這	44 chiu 酒	71 chʻuang 牀	**H**	113 hsiang 向	
19 chên 眞	45 chʻiu 秋	72 chui 追	92 ʻha 哈	114 hsiao 小	
20 chʻên 臣	46 chiung 窘	73 chʻui 吹	93 ʻhai 害	115 hsieh 些	
21 chêng 正	47 chʻiung 窮	74 chun 准		116 hsien 先	
22 chʻêng 成	48 cho 卓	75 chʻun 春			
	49 chʻo 綽				

* See note on page 11.

PART I. SOUND TABLE, OR LIST OF SYLLABLES.

#	syl	字	#	syl	字	#	syl	字	#	syl	字	#	syl	字
117	hsin	心	137	ju	如	158	ko, kʻo	各	182	lan	懶	207	lun	論
118	hsing	性	138	juan	輭	159	kʻo, kʻê	可	183	lang	浪	208	lung	龍
119	hsio	學	139	jui	瑞	160	kou	狗	184	lao	老			
120	hsiu	修	140	jun	潤	161	kʻou	口	185	lê	勒		**M**	
121	hsiung	兄	141	jung	絨	162	ku	古	186	lêi, lei	累	209	ma	馬
122	hsü	須				163	kʻu	苦	187	lêng	冷	210	mai	買
123	hsüan / hsüen	喧				164	kua	瓜	188	li	立	211	man	慢
124	hsüeh	雪		**K**		165	kʻua	跨	189	lia	倆	212	mang	忙
125	hsün	巡	142	ka	嘎	166	kuai	怪	190	liang	兩	213	mao	毛
126	hsüo	學	143	kʻa	卡	167	kʻuai	快	191	liao	了			
			144	kai	改	168	kuan	官	192	lieh	裂	214	mei	美
			145	kʻai	開	169	kʻuan	寬	193	lien	連	215	mên	門
	I		146	kan	甘	170	kuang	光	194	lin	林	216	mêng	夢
127	i	衣	147	kʻan	看	171	kʻuang	況	195	ling	另	217	mi	米
			148	kang	剛	172	kuei	規	196	lio	略	218	miao	苗
	J		149	kʻang	炕	173	kʻuei	愧	197	liu	留	219	mieh	滅
128	jan	染	150	kao	告	174	kuên / kun	棍	198	lo	駱	220	mien	面
129	jang	嚷	151	kʻao	考	175	kʻuên / kʻun	困	199	lou	陋	221	min	民
130	jao	繞	152	kei	給	176	kung	工	200	lü	律	222	ming	名
131	jê	熱	153	kʻei	刻	177	kʻung	孔	201	lüan	戀	223	miu	謬
132	jên	人	154	kên	根	178	kuo	果	202	lüeh	略			
133	jêng	扔	155	kʻên	肯	179	kʻuo	闊	203	lün	掄	224	mo	末
134	jih	日	156	kêng	更				204	lüo	略	225	mou	謀
135	jo	若	157	kʻêng	坑		**L**		205	lu	路	226	mu	木
136	jou	肉				180	la	拉	206	luan	亂			
						181	lai	來						

N									
227 na	那	250 nuan	暖	271 pi	必	294 sê	嗇	314 shu	書
228 nai	奶	251 nun	嫩	272 p'i	皮	295 sên	森	315 shua	刷
229 nan	男	252 nung	濃	273 piao	表	296 sêng	僧	316 shuai	衰
230 nang	囊			274 p'iao	票	297 so	索	317 shuan	拴
231 nao	鬧	O		275 pieh	別	298 sou	搜	318 shuang	雙
		253 o *		276 p'ieh	撇	299 su	素	319 shui	水
232 ńei	內	254 ou	訛偶	277 pien	扁	300 suan	筭	320 shun	順
233 nên	嫩			278 p'ien	片	301 sui	碎	321 shuo	說
234 nêng	能	P		279 pin	賓	302 sun	孫		
		255 pa	罷	280 p'in	貧	303 sung	送	SS	
235 ni	你	256 p'a	怕	281 ping	兵			322 ssŭ	絲
236 niang	娘	257 pai	拜	282 p'ing	憑				
237 niao	鳥	258 p'ai	派	283 po	波	SH		T	
238 nieh	揑	259 pan	半	284 p'o	破	304 sha	殺	323 ta	大
239 nien	念	260 p'an	盼	285 pou	不	305 shai	曬	324 t'a	他
240 nin	您	261 pang	幫	286 p'ou	剖	306 shan	山	325 tai	歹
241 ning	寧	262 p'ang	旁	287 pu	不	307 shang	賞	326 t'ai	太
242 nio	虐	263 pao	包	288 p'u	普	308 shao	少	327 tan	單
243 niu	牛	264 p'ao	跑			309 shê	舌	328 t'an	炭
244 no	挪	265 pei	北	S		310 shên	身	329 tang	當
245 nou	耨	266 p'ei	陪	289 sa	撒	311 shêng	生	330 t'ang	湯
246 nü	女	267 pên	本	290 sai	賽	312 shih	事	331 tao	道
247 nüeh	虐	268 p'ên	盆	291 san	散	313 shou	手	332 t'ao	逃
248 nüo	虐	269 pêng	迸	292 sang	桑			333 tê	得
249 nu	奴	270 p'êng	朋	293 sao	掃			334 t'ê	特
								335 tei	得

* See note on page 11.

PART I. SOUND TABLE, OR LIST OF SYLLABLES.

336 têng	等	361 tung	冬	384 tsu	祖	403 wo	我
337 t'êng	疼	362 t'ung	同	385 ts'u	粗	404 wu	武
338 ti	的			386 tsuan	攛		
339 t'i	替	**TS**		387 ts'uan	竄		
340 tiao	弔	363 tsa	雜	388 tsui	嘴	**Y**	
341 t'iao	桃	364 ts'a	擦	389 ts'ui	催	405 ya	牙
342 tieh	疊	365 tsai	在	390 tsun	尊	406 yai	涯
343 t'ieh	貼	366 ts'ai	才	391 ts'un	寸	407 yang	羊
344 tien	店	367 tsan	贊	392 tsung	宗	408 yao	要
345 t'ien	天	368 ts'an	慚	393 ts'ung	蔥	409 yeh	夜
346 ting	定	369 tsang	葬			410 yen	言
347 t'ing	聽	370 ts'ang	倉			411 yi	益
348 tiu	丢	371 tsao	早	**TZ**		412 yın	音
		372 ts'ao	草	394 tzŭ	子	413 ying	迎
349 to	多	373 tsê	則	395 tz'ŭ	次	414 yo	約
350 t'o	妥	374 ts'ê	策			415 yü	魚
351 tou	豆	375 tsei	賊	**W**		416 yüan	原
352 t'ou	頭	376 tsên	怎	396 wa	瓦	417 yüeh	月
353 tu	妒	377 ts'ên	參	397 wai	外	418 yün	雲
354 t'u	土	378 tsêng	增	398 wan	完	419 yu	有
355 tuan	短	379 ts'êng	層	399 wang	往	420 yung	用
356 t'uan	團	380 tso	作	400 wei	為		
357 tui	對	381 ts'o	錯	401 wên	文		
358 t'ui	退	382 tsou	走	402 wêng	翁		
359 tun	敦	383 ts'ou	湊				
360 t'un	吞						

NOTE.—The following sounds:—

a, ê,
ai, ên,
an, êng,
ang, o,
ao, où,

are as often pronounced *ng*a, *ng*ai, *ng*an, and so on. See the remarks on the subject on page 5, under the initial *ng*.

PART II. THE RADICALS.

We now come to the written character, which the student must, for the time, be pleased to accept as made up of two parts, its Radical, and that part which is not its Radical. The latter various sinologues have for fairly sufficient reasons agreed to term its Phonetic.

The Radicals are 214 in number. Some of them are subject to modifications which entirely change their figure. The following Table shews them arranged in 17 classes according to the number of pencil strokes in each Radical; that is, the Radicals of one stroke in the first class; those of two in the second, and so on. Before each Radical is a number marking its place in the general series, and the name of the character so numbered; after the character, its meaning, and then a number of characters, never exceeding three, which have been selected as illustrating the part that the Radical after which they stand generally plays in the composition of characters, whether in its full or its modified form. The Radicals that undergo modification are marked with an asterisk, and their modified forms are collected at the end of the great table.

The character, it has been said above, consists of its Radical and its Phonetic. Let the student turn to Radical 3, and he will see in the character given to illustrate its part in the composition, that the Radical *chu*, a point, stands on the top of it. The remainder, three horizontal strokes and a vertical one, are its Phonetic. Let him turn to the 12th Radical, *pa*, eight, and he will see that it is placed under the Phonetic in the three characters given as examples. In the examples opposite the 64th Radical, *shou*, the hand, the Radical stands in the first example, in full form, on the left of the Phonetic; in the second, in modified form, also on the left; in the third, in full form, underneath the Phonetic.

To look out a character in the Dictionaries arranged according to Radicals, it is essential, of course, in the first place to decide correctly under what Radical it is classed. This point assured, the number of strokes in the Phonetic must be accurately counted; because in the Dictionaries in question the characters under each Radical are subdivided into classes according to the number of strokes in the Phonetic. The counting of these, even where they are numerous, will not be found so formidable a task once the student becomes familiar with the Radicals; for he will observe that the Phonetic is either resolvable into other Radical characters, or, in some instances, is simply a single Radical character added to the Radical; and once he knows, as he soon will, the place of any Radical in the great table, he will recall the number of strokes composing it without the trouble of counting them. Take the third example opposite the 85th Radical, *shui*, water. The Radical itself is the abbreviated form of *s'hui*; the Phonetic resolves itself into four Radicals; the centre of the upper part is the 149th, of seven strokes; this is flanked on both sides by the 120th, of six strokes, and below is the 59th, of three strokes, making in all twenty-two strokes. In the 2nd example of the 29th Radical, the Phonetic is simply the 128th Radical; in the second example of the 75th Radical, the Phonetic is that same Radical repeated. The rule regarding the composition of the Phonetic is not strictly universal, but by the beginner may be accepted as very generally obtaining.

To assist the Student in acquiring a working knowledge of the Radicals, three Test Tables are subjoined.

The first contains all the characters chosen to illustrate the use of the Radicals in the great table, arranged in order of the number of their strokes collectively. When the student shall have examined the first thirty, or twenty, or even ten, of the Radicals in the great table, let him run down the right hand column of the test table, and try to identify the Radicals of the characters therein placed, turning to the great table for assistance, whenever his memory fails him. This will speedily acquaint him with the Radicals and the part they most commonly play.

TZŬ ERH CHI. **Colloquial Series.**

The second test table contains all the Radicals redistributed in categories of subjects, according to the meaning of each. Some are in consequence repeated. At the top of the right hand column, for instance, we have the 72nd, as the sun, followed by the 73rd, the moon; then the 72nd, again as day, followed by the 36th, as night. It is hoped that this will at the same time aid and exercise the memory; but it will not be of as great service to him as the following table, the third.

The third table exhibits the Radicals in three classes, distinguished for brevity's sake, as Colloquial, Classical, and Obsolete. The Colloquial are those which represent words used, many of them frequently, in conversation; the Classical, those not met with in conversation but found in books and writings; the Obsolete, those which, although the Dictionaries allot them a signification, are no longer employed except as Radical indices. The Colloquial Radicals are 137 in number, the Classical 30, the Obsolete 47.

The student is recommended when he shall have examined the great table sufficiently to have formed a definite idea of the nature and functions of the Radical characters arranged in it, to betake himself to the Exercise in the Colloquial Radicals which immediately follows this third test table. In this he will find a number of short combinations of words, all of them, with the exception of one or two, which are separately explained, Radical characters, arranged more or less in categories of subjects; while on the opposite page he has a translation. If he will keep to this Exercise till he really knows every character in it, he will be master of 137 of the 214 Radicals, and he will have easy victory over the remaining 77.

PART II. THE RADICALS. GENERAL TABLE.

1 Stroke.

1	yi	一	one; unity.
2	kun	丨	a stroke connecting the top with the bottom.
3	chu	丶	a point; period.
4	p'ieh	丿	a line running obliquely to the left.
5	yi	乙	a character in the time cycle of China.
6	chieh	亅	a hooked end.

2 Strokes.

7	êrh	二	two.
8	t'ou	亠	above.
9	jên	人*	man.
10	jên	儿	man.
11	ju	入	in, into; to enter.
12	pa	八	eight.
13	chiung	冂	border waste-land.
14	mi	冖	to cover over.
15	ping	冫	an icicle.
16	chi	几	a stool.
17	k'an	凵	able to contain.
18	tao	刀*	a knife; a sword.
19	li	力	strength.
20	pao	勹	to wrap round.
21	pi	匕	a spoon or scoop; weapon.
22	fang	匚	a chest.
23	hsi	匸	able to contain or conceal.
24	shih	十	ten.
25	pu	卜	to divine.
26	chieh	卩*	a joint.
27	h'an	厂	a ledge that shelters.
28	ssŭ; mou	厶	private; selfish.
29	yu	又	again.

且 乏 亂
不 乍 也 事
七 屯 主 久 九 了
亮 你 兒 兩 典
五 交 今 允 內 六 冒 冠 冬 凡 凸 凹 分 勺 北 匠 匹 千 占 危 底 去 反
井 京 來 兆 全 兵 晃 准 憑 凹 別 勁 包 匙 匪 半 卡 却 厚 參 取
湊 出 則 勒 南 原 疊

3 Strokes.

30	k'ou	口	the mouth.
31	wei	囗	able to enclose.
32	t'u	土	earth.
33	shih	士	a scholar.
34	chih	夂	to step onwards.
35	ts'ui	夊	to step slowly.
36	hsi	夕	evening.
37	ta	大	great.
38	nü	女	a female.
39	tzŭ	子	a son.
40	mien	宀	roof of a cave.
41	ts'un	寸	an inch.
42	hsiao	小	little.
43	wang	尢	bent as an ailing leg.
44	shih	尸	a corpse.
45	ch'ê	屮	sprouting; vegetation.
46	shan	山	a hill.
47	ch'uan	巛	streams.
48	kung	工	labour.
49	chi	己	self.
50	chin	巾	a napkin; head-gear.
51	kan	干	a shield; to concern.
52	yao	幺	small.
53	yen	广	roof of a house.
54	yin	廴	continued motion.
55	kong	廾	the hands folded as in salutation.
56	yi	弋	to shoot with the bow.
57	kung	弓	a bow (arcus).
58	chi	彑	pointed like a pig's-head.
59	shan	彡	streaky, like hair.
60	ch'ih	彳	to step short.

嚷 團 壞 聲
嗇 囲 墓 壺
可 回 在 壯
夏 外 太
奶 孔 官 夸 夏 外 太
夜 天 好 孫 尊 尖 就 尺 屯
峯 州 左 巷 布 平 幻 床 廷 弄 式 弔 彙 彩 往
屋 嶺 巡 巧
帳 年 店 建
弟 後

夢 奇 姓 學 寒 對
層 差 幫 幹 幾 厨
張 得

PART II. THE RADICALS. GENERAL TABLE.

4 Strokes.

61	hsin	心*	heart, mind.
62	ko	戈	a lance, spear.
63	'hu	戶	a house door.
64	shou	手*	the hand.
65	chih	支	a prop; to issue money.
66	p'u	攴*	to tap lightly.
67	wên	文	stripes or streaks; ornament as opposed to plainness; literature
68	tou	斗	Chinese bushel.
69	chin	斤	Chinese pound; an axe.
70	fang	方	square.
71	wu	无*	not.
72	jih	日	the sun, the day.
73	yüeh	曰	to speak.
74	yueh	月	the moon.
75	mu	木	wood; trees.
76	ch'ien	欠	to owe; to be wanting in.
77	chih	止	to stop (neuter).
78	tai	歹*	decayed bones of a murdered man; bad.
79	shu	殳	a quarter-staff.
80	wu; kuan	毋	do not!
81	pi	比	to compare; lay side by side.
82	mao	毛	hair, fur.
83	ch'i	气	vapour.
84	shih	氏	family from past time till now.
85	shui	水*	water.
86	'huo	火*	fire.
87	chao	爪*	claws.
88	fu	父	father.
89	yao	爻	cross wise.
90	ch'iang	爿	the radical of 91 reversed.
91	p'ien	片	a slab of wood; a slice or piece.

必成房拜　愛我扁換　慢或掌敦新　畫替朝柴　武

敀斌料斧旁旣昻更有本次正死殺毎　散斑斟斬旗　春書朋林欺步

毯氣民永炕為爺爽牀膿　河炭爵　牆　瀚然

ᒪ	92 ya	牙	the back teeth.
ᒪ	93 niu	牛*	oxen; kine.
ᒪ	94 ch'uan	犬*	the dog.

5 Strokes.

	95 yüan	玄	black.
ᒪ	96 yü	玉*	precious stones.
	97 kua	瓜	the gourd.
ᒪ	98 wa	瓦	tiles.
ᒪ	99 kan	甘	sweet.
ᒪ	100 shêng	生	to live; to produce.
ᒪ	101 yung	用	to use.
ᒪ	102 t'ien	田	fields; arable land.
ᒪ	103 p'i	疋	the bale or piece of cloth, silk, &c.
	104 ni	疒	disease.
	105 po	癶	back to back.
ᒪ	106 pai; po	白	white.
ᒪ	107 p'i	皮	skin; bark.
ᒪ	108 min	皿	covered dishes.
ᒪ	109 mu	目	the eye.
	110 mou	矛	a long lance.
ᒪ	111 shih	矢	arrows.
ᒪ	112 shih	石	stone.
ᒪ	113 ch'i; shih	示	spiritual power; revelation.
	114 jou	禸*	the print of a fox's foot.
ᒪ	115 'ho	禾	any kind of grain.
ᒪ	116 hsueh	穴	a cave in the side of a hill.
	117 li	立	to stand up, or still.

6 Strokes.

	118 chi	竹	the bamboo.
ᒪ	119 mi	米	rice uncooked.
ᒪ	120 mi; ssŭ	糸	raw silk as spun by the worm.

牲狗 特獸 牽獸 玆玻瓢瓶甚產甬男疑疼發百皺盅看矜知破祖畲秋峇站等粗紅

牽瑞辮 甜 畄 病 的 盆 盼 矩砕票 秦窮章 策絮累

璃 略 皇 盡直 短碎縶 竄豎 窶糞絲

PART II. THE RADICALS. GENERAL TABLE.

c	121 fou	缶	earthenware.				
	122 wang	网*	a fishing-net.				
d	123 yang	羊	sheep.				
	124 yü	羽	feathers.				
c	125 lao	老	old.				
b	126 êrh	而	and; but yet.				
c	127 lei	耒	the plough.				
c	128 êrh	耳	the ear.				
c	129 yu	聿	a pencil.				
c	130 jou	肉*	flesh; meat.				
b	131 ch'ên	臣	servant of the sovereign.				
c	132 tsŭ	自	self; from.				
c	133 chih	至	to come or to go; arrive at.				
c	134 chiu	臼	a stone mortar.				
c	135 shê	舌	the tongue.				
	136 ch'uan	舛	at issue; in error.				
f	137 chou	舟	ships; boats.				
c	138 kên	艮	limitation; also character in the time cycle.				
c	139 sê, shai	色	colour.				
c	140 ts'ao	艸*	plants; herbs.				
c	141 'hu	虍	the tiger's streaks.				
c	142 ch'ung; 'hui	虫	reptiles having feet.				
	143 hsieh, hsüeh	血	blood.				
	144 'hang; hsing	行	'hang, a row as of buildings; hsing, to go, to do.				
c	145 yi	衣	clothes.				
c	146 sha; hsi	西*	to cover; the west.				

7 Strokes.

c	147 chien	見	to perceive, with the eye, nose, ear, or mind.				
c	148 chio	角	horns; a corner.				
-	149 yen	言	words.				
c	150 ku	谷	a valley.				

20   TZŬ ERH CHI. Colloquial Series.

⌐	151 tou	豆	beans; a sacrificial bowl of wood.	豈	豐		
	152 shih	豕	the pig.	象			
	153 chai; ti	豸	reptiles without feet.	貌			賓
⌐	154 pei	貝	the tortoise, his shell; hence, precious.	貧	賊		
⌐	155 ch'ih	赤	flesh colour.	赦			壁
⌐	156 tsou	走	to walk or run.	起	趕		輕
⌐	157 tsu	足	the foot; enough.	跨	路		辯
⌐	158 shên	身	the body.	躬	躲		這
⌐、	159 ch'e; chu	車	vehicles; sedans.	輩	載		鄒
⌐	160 hsin	辛	bitter.	辜	辭		費
⌐	161 ch'ên	辰	{ the 5th horary period of the Chinese day, 7 to 9 o'clock A.M.; also a character in the time-cycle.	辱			量
	162 ch'o	辵*	moving and pausing.	迎	送		
⌐	163 yi	邑*	any centre of population.	那	却		
⌐	164 yu	酉	{ the 10th horary period 5 to 7 P.M.; also a character in the time-cycle.	酒	醫		
	165 ts'ai; pien	釆	to part and distinguish.	釋			鑿
⌐	166 li	里	a hamlet of 25 families; the Chinese mile.	重	野		關

8 Strokes.

⌐	167 chin	金	the metals; gold.	針	錯		陪
⌐	168 chang; ch'ang	長*	to grow; length.		間		雞
⌐	169 mên	門	a gate, a door.	開	陋		
	170 fu	阜*	a mound of earth.	阿			
	171 li; tai	隶	to reach to, arrive at.	隸			
⌐	172 chui	隹	short-tailed birds.	隻	雙		
⌐	173 yu	雨	rain.	雪	雲		
⌐	174 ch'ing	青	sky-blue.	靖	靜		
⌐	175 fei	非	negative; wrong.	靠			
⌐	176 mien	面	the face; the outside.				

9 Strokes.

	177 kê, ko	革	a hide stripped of hair; so to strip the hide, to flay.	靴	鞋
	178 wei	韋	tanned hide.	韓	
	179 chiu	韭	leeks.	韭	

PART II. THE RADICALS. GENERAL TABLE. 21

180 *yin*	音	sound.	韻	響		
181 *yeh*	頁	the head; page of a book.	頂	頭	頰	
182 *fêng*	風	wind.	颶	飄		
183 *fei*	飛	to fly as birds.				
184 *shih*	食	to eat.	飲	養	餓	
185 *shou*	首	the head.	馘	馥		
186 *hsiang*	香	fragrance.	馨			

10 Strokes.

187 *ma*	馬	the horse.	騎	驟	驚	
188 *ku*	骨	the bones.	體	髓		
189 *kao*	高	high.				
190 *piao*	髟	shaggy.	髮	鬍	鬢	
191 *tou*	鬥	to fight; to emulate.	鬧	鬭		
192 *ch'ang*	鬯	{ a sacrificial bowl of China; luxurious vegetation; contentment.	鬱			
193 *ko; li*	鬲	a sacrificial vase on crooked feet.	鬴	鬻		
194 *kuei*	鬼	spirits of the dead.	魁	魂	魔	

11 Strokes.

195 *yü*	魚	fish.	魯	鮮	鰲	
196 *niao*	鳥	birds.	鳳	鴨	鷹	
197 *lu*	鹵	natural salts.	鹹	鹽	麟	
198 *lu*	鹿	the deer species.	麒	麗		
199 *mai*	麥	wheat.	麵			
200 *ma*	麻	hemp.	麽			

12 Strokes.

201 *'huang*	黃	yellow; clay color.	黈	黏	釁	
202 *shu*	黍	millet.	黎	黛		
203 *'hei; hě*	黑	black.	點	黨		
204 *chih*	黹	embroidery.	黻	黼		

13 Strokes.

205 *mêng; min*	黽	of the frog or toad kind.	鼃	
206 *ting*	鼎	a two-eared tripod used in sacrifice.	鼐	

TZŬ ERH CHI. Colloquial Series.

207 ku   鼓   the drum, &c.   鼜   鼓

208 shu   鼠   the rat kind.

14 Strokes.

209 pi   鼻   the nose.   劓

210 ch'i   齊   arranged, in order.   斎   齊

15 Strokes.

211 ch'ih   齒   front teeth.   齡   齠

16 Strokes.

212 lung   龍   the dragon tribe.   龔   龕

213 kuei   龜   the tortoise, turtle, &c.   鼈

17 Strokes.

214 yo   龠   flutes, pipes, &c.   龢

The characters in the foregoing table, marked with an asterisk, are, some generally, some always, modified when employed as Radicals of other characters. On the opposite page are given the modifications recognised in the great Chinese Lexicon of K'ang Hsi. There are a few others allowed in manuscript, which will be acquired without great difficulty.

PART II. THE RADICALS. ABBREVIATIONS.

Rad.			changes to			
"	9 jên	人	"	亻		
"	18 tao	刀	"	刂		
"	26 chieh	卩	"	㔾		
"	43 wang	尢	"	尣	兀	
"	47 ch'uan	巛	"	巜	巛	川
"	58 ch'i	彐	"	互	彑	
"	61 hsin	心	"	忄	小	
"	64 shou	手	"	扌		
"	66 p'u	攴	"	攵		
"	71 wu	无	"	旡		
"	78 tai	歹	"	歺		
"	85 shui	水	"	氵	氺	
"	86 'huo	火	"	灬		
"	87 chao	爪	"	爫		
"	93 niu	牛	"	牜		
"	94 ch'uan	犬	"	犭		
"	96 yu	玉	"	王		
"	114 jou	禸	"	禸		
"	122 wang	网	"	四	罒	冗	冈
"	130 jou	肉	"	月		
"	140 ts'ao	艸	"	艹		
"	146 sha; hsi	襾	"	西		
"	162 ch'o	辵	"	辶		
"	163 yi	邑	"	阝		
"	168 { chang / ch'ang	長	"	镸	阝	
"	170 fu	阜	"	阝		

畫爽牽瓶甜產略票章粗累羞翎習船規訛欲貧赦這野雪頂冕壺寒尊

就幾換掌散敦斌斑替朝炊毯然為爺牽發短碎會等策粱絲書舒泉街

衙輩辜量開問雲飲罍番幹廚彙愛斟新瑞盞碎禁羣聖葬號解象賊跨

路載靖靴韭鳳亂德團墓壽夢對慢旗獸豎筴聞臺與蜜訛貌賓躱輕尉

魁魂麼璃層窗疑皺窮罷舞餓銜靠鞋颱養髮鬨黎學耨親錯靜頭鴨

稟嶺幫爵牆瓢糞磬舉艱韓鹹鮮跋黏點黻竈齋竄舊謬豐壓醫雙雞馥

騎鑒壞獸臨關韻鬍魯麒麗糯鏒鮹類瓖辨覺辭釋響飄馨鹹氂黌黨齡

蠢辯驛麾鰲齊豁聽驚龔龕龢驁體髓鬪麟豔鬢鷹灣鹽釁獸龕鬱

PART II. RADICAL TEST TABLE I.

七九丁久也凡勹千不中乏五井今六分匹反太天孔少尺屯甪且主乍
允肉冬凸凹出包北半占卡去可外左巧布平幼必本正民永交兆全匠
危回在孕奶好尖州式成有次死每百考那你兵別助却底困壯巡床
廷弄弟往我攺更步甬罕艮却阿事京來兒兩典取夜奇姓官店或
房斧昂朋林武河炕㧱狗的直知罔者服肯花虎虱衫表迎陋亮冒冠則
勁南屋巷建後扁拜春炭性玻甚皇盅看盼矜秋紅美要耐臭虐哀要
鄒重准匪厚原夏孫峯差料旁書柴殺氣特茲畱疼病矩破祖秦窖
站缺翁耕能草豈起赶躬辱酒針陪隻送湊勒匙參專巢帳張彩得斬既

TZŬ ERH CHI. RADICAL TEST TABLE II.

```
1  日月日夕風雨气
   冫水 3 鬼示卜鬯豆鼎鬲
   4 金鼓龠音 5 干支乙辛子
2  酉辰艮炙 6 金木水火土
   7 山川谷穴阜田門
   8 玉石鹵水 9 色青黃赤白黑
10 玄 人几氏自己父子女士臣
   11 身心廾手足首頁而彡耳鼻面目見面
   12 晉
13 曰口舌牙齒皮肉骨血气 力用工
   14 尸首骨卩尢疒入夂夊夂行走走隶
15 
16 彳止立食 厶歹鬥戈 生長大小長幺
   18 厂广广西口里門戶邑阜 19 衣巾
20 耑 舟車皿几匕斗白瓦缶 17 魚网牛耒糸皮革韋
   22 刀匕干戈弋弓矢矛殳
23 斤 凵勹匚匸
24 艸木竹瓜黽山 采米豆韭麥麻黍
   25 辛甘香 26 牛羊犬豕馬
27 鹿鼠鳥隹虫豸龍魚龜黽角貝
   28 羽飛爪肉采文彡虍彡 29 疋斗斤寸方長
30 丿一二八十 31 片比彐 32 旡欠足齊
   33 亠冖高彑聿 34 母又癶舛非 35 丨丶丿
```

TZŭ ERH CHI. RADICAL TEST TABLE III.

1 Colloquial.

一 二 人 入 八 刀 力 十 卜 又 口 土 士 大 女 子 小 寸 尸 山 川 工 己 巾 干 月 心 戈 戶 手
支 文 斗 斤 方 日 月 木 欠 止 歹 比 毛 氏 水 火 爪 爻 片 牙 牛 玉 瓜 瓦 甘 生 用 田 疋 白
皮 目 矢 石 禾 穴 立 竹 米 羊 羽 老 而 耳 肉 臣 自 至 舌 舛 舟 色 虫 血 行 衣 西 見 角 言
谷 豆 貝 赤 走 足 身 車 辛 辰 酉 里 金 長 門 雨 青 非 面 革 韋 音 頁 風 飛 食 首 香 馬 骨
高 鬼 魚 鳥 鹿 麥 麻 黃 黍 黑 鼎 鼓 鼠 鼻 齊 齒 龍

2 Classical.

乙 几 匕 夕 弋 无 曰 殳 母 炙 犬 玄 皿 矛 缶 耒 聿 白 艮 豕 豸 邑 阜 韋 鬯 鬲 鹵 黹 黽 龜

3 Obsolete.

一 丶 丿 亅 乚 凵 冂 冖 冫 凵 勹 匚 匸 卩 厂 厶 口 夊 夂 宀 尢 尸 廴 廾 彐 彡 彳 戈
气 爿 疒 癶 襾 肉 糸 网 艸 虍 辵 釆 隶 隹 髟 鬥 龠

28　TZŬ ERH CHI. Colloquial Series.

I. 人¹ 氏² 子³ 女⁴ 父⁵ 子⁶ 戶⁷ 口⁸ 自⁹ 巳¹⁰ 貝¹¹ 子¹² 臣¹³ 士¹⁴ 子¹⁵ 鬼¹⁶ 子 鼓 手
II. 人¹ 身² 心³ 口 手 足
III. 用 力
耳¹ 目² 牙³ 齒⁴ 口⁵ 舌⁶ 口⁷ 音⁸ 目⁹ 力¹⁰ 骨¹¹ 肉¹² 尸¹³ 首¹⁴ 骨¹⁵ 血¹⁶ 面 目 鼻 子 骨 尸 口 齒 手 心
用 力
用² 工³ 入⁴ 門⁵ 支⁶ 用⁷ 生⁸ 長⁹ 立¹⁰ 止¹¹ 甘¹² 心¹³ 辛¹⁴ 苦¹⁵ 鼎¹⁶ 舛 錯 人 力 行 走 一 齊 見 面 食 肉 革 面
IV. 大 小 子 比 父 高 老 小
行¹⁷ 文¹⁸ 食¹⁹ 壹²⁰ 土²¹ 音²² 小²³ 心²⁴ 比²⁵ 方²⁶ 齊 見 長 小 心 高 用 人
V. 手¹ 巾² 雨³ 衣 皮 衣
VI. 舟¹ 車² 車³ 馬⁴ 門 戶 瓦 面 瓦 片
VII. 刀 子
心⁴ 歹⁵ 高⁶ 大⁷ 大⁸ 臣⁹
干² 戈³ 矢⁴ 石⁵ 弓⁶ 矢⁷ 弓⁸ 刀⁹ 石
VIII. 西¹ 瓜² 禾³ 黍⁴ 米⁵ 麥⁶ 豆⁷ 角⁸ 小⁹ 麻¹⁰ 子¹¹ 竹¹² 韭¹³ 黃¹⁴ 香¹⁵ 瓜¹⁶ 肉 片
IX. 牛¹ 羊² 牛³ 馬⁴ 魚⁵ 蟲⁶ 飛 鳥 大 鹿 金 魚 長
X. 金¹ 木² 水³ 火⁴ 土⁵ 又⁶ 風⁷ 又⁸ 雨⁹
XI. 長 一 寸 八 寸
XII. 日¹
牛¹⁰ 肉¹¹ 羊¹² 肉¹³ 麂¹⁴ 肉¹⁵ 老 米 白 米 小 米 子 麥 子
蟲⁸ 西⁹ 口¹⁰ 馬¹¹ 龍¹² 爪¹³ 老¹⁴ 鼠¹⁵ 羊 皮 羽 毛 羊 毛 香 牛 皮 牛 角
田³ 土⁴ 山⁵ 水⁶ 山⁷ 川⁸ 山⁹ 谷¹⁰ 石¹¹ 穴¹² 西¹³ 方¹⁴ 欠¹⁵ 雨¹⁶ 土 子 黃 土 黑 土 雨 水
二¹ 八² 斗³ 豆⁴ 子⁵ 十⁶ 斤⁷ 一⁸ 二⁹ 疋¹⁰ 八¹¹ 十¹² 里¹³ 非¹⁴ 止¹⁵ 一¹⁶ 人¹⁷ 八¹⁸ 口¹⁹ 人²⁰ 十²¹ 口²² 人²³ 一²⁴ 方²⁵
XIII. 青¹ 白² 黑³ 白⁴ 青⁵ 黃⁶ 赤⁷ 色⁸ 黃⁹ 而¹⁰ 黑 香 色
日¹ 月² 月³ 自 辰 至 酉
XIV. 火¹ 石² 白 玉

PART II. THE RADICALS.

EXERCISE IN THE COLLOQUIAL RADICALS.

I.—1. *jên-shih*, a person from such or such a place; [*e.g.* What is he? He is a Canton man.] 2. *tzŭ nu*, sons and daughters. 3. *fu tzŭ*, father and son. 4. *'hu-k'ou*, persons in a family; *lit.* mouths in the house. 5. *tzŭ-chi*, one's-self; by oneself. 6. *pei-tzŭ*; Chinese for *beitsê*, a Manchu title of nobility. 7. *ch'ên-tzŭ*, a minister of state. 8. *shih-tzŭ*, a scholar, lettered man. 9 *Iuei-tzŭ*, a devil; term generally applied to foreigners. 10. *ku-shou*, a drummer.

II.—1. *jên shên*, a man's person, 2. *hsin-k'ou*, the breast; *lit.* the heart's mouth. 3. *shou tsu*, hand and foot; not used literally, but figuratively, of the relationship of brothers. 4. *êrh mu*, the sight and hearing, when spoken of as quick or not; a police detective. 5. *ya-ch'ih*, the teeth. 6. *k'ou shê*, altercation; *lit.* mouth and tongue. / 7. *k'ou-yin*, accent, pronunciation; *lit.* the mouth's sounds. 8. *mu li*, strength of sight. 9. *ku-jou*, bone and flesh; not literally, but figuratively of intimate relationship. 10. *shih-shou*, a corpse; *lit.* corpse and head. 11. *ku-hsueh*, bone and blood; *fig.* of intimate relationship. 12. *mien mu*, the face; *lit.* face and eyes. 13. *pi-tzŭ*, the nose. 14. *ku-shih*, a corpse; *lit.* bone and corpse. 15. *k'ou-ch'ih*; the teeth; specially with reference to dental sounds. 16. *shou-hsin*, the palm of the hand; *lit.* the hand's heart.

III.—1 *yung li*, to exert oneself; use strength. 2. *yung kung*, to work hard, use labour. 3. *ju mên*, to enter a door; not literally, but figuratively of commencing a study. 4. *chih-yung*, expenditure; *lit* what one issues and uses. 5. *shêng chang*, to be born and bred, *lit.* to be born and to grow up. 6. *li-chih*, to come to a stand, to stop. 7. *kan-hsin*, willing, *lit* with sweet or pleasant heart or mind. 8. *hsin-k'u*, affliction, trouble; *lit.* bitterness, the second character, *k'u*, which is not a Radical, has the same meaning as the first. 9. *tang ko*, the sacrificial urn taken away; *lit.* stripped off, figuratively for loss of the throne, subversion of a dynasty. 10. *ch'uan-ts'o*, error; the second character *ts'o*, which is not a Radical, means to err. 11. *jên li*, man's ability, *lit.* strength. 12. *hsing-tsou*, *lit.* to move; specially of attendance in the court or public office in which one is employed. 13. *i ch'i*, all together, *lit* in unity complete. 14. *chien mien*, to see the person, whom one has been to visit. 15. *shih jou*, to eat meat. 16. *ko mien*, to reform oneself thoroughly, *lit.* flay the face. 17. *hsing wên*, to write a despatch; *lit.* execute a composition. 18. *shih yen*, to eat one's words. 19. *t'u-yin*, a local dialect or accent. 20. *hsiao-hsin*, careful; beware! 21. *pi-fang*, for instance. *Obs., fang* is probably corruptly used for another character. 22. *ch'i hsin*, unanimous. 23. *chien chang*, to grow physically; *chien ch'ang*, to make progress intellectually. *Obs*, the verb *chien* as to feel. 24. *chien hsiao*, to be of niggardly mind. 25. *hsin kao*, of lofty aims. 26. *yung jên*, to employ people with discrimination.

IV.—1. *ta hsiao*, great and small. 2. *tzŭ pi fu kao*, the son higher, more eminent, than the father. 3. *lao hsiao*, old and young. 4. *hsin tai*, of evil disposition. 5. *kao-ta*, tall, lofty. 6. *ta ch'ên*, ministers of a certain rank.

V —1. *shou chin*, a handkerchief. 2. *yü i*, waterproof dress. 3. *p'i i*, fur-lined clothes.

VI.—1. *chou chu*, (politely,) junk or cart, land or water carriage. 2. *ch'ê ma*, or *chü ma*, carts and horses. 3. *mên-hu*, an entrance-gate; specially, a pass of importance. 4. *wa mien*, a tiled roof. 5. *wa p'ien*, a bit of tile.

VII.—1. *tao-tzŭ*, a knife. 2. *kan ko*, shield and spear, figuratively for war. 3. *shih shih*, the arrow and the stone, archery and slinging. 4 *kung shih*, bow and arrow; archery. 5. *kung, tao, shih*, bow, sword, and stone. *Obs.*, Military graduates have to prove their strength by drawing the bow, exercise with the sword, and raising the stone.

VIII.—1. *hsi kua*, water melon, *lit.* western melon. 2, *'ho shu*, rice and milet, uncut. 3. *mi mai*, rice and wheat, cut, as we say corn or grain. 4. *tou-chiao*, a bean-pod. 5. *hsiao ma-tzŭ*, cummin. 6 *chu-tzŭ*, bamboo. 7. *c'iu 'huang*, leeks, *lit.* leeks yellow, *chiu*, by itself, is generic of vegetables of the kind. 8 *hsiang kua*, melon, *lit.* scented melon. 9. *jou p'ien*, a slice or slices of meat. 10. *niu-jou*, beef. 11. *yang-jou*, mutton. 12. *lu-jou*, venison. 13. *lao mi*, old rice. 14. *pai mi*, new, *lit.* white, rice. 15. *hsiao mi-tzŭ*, oats. 16. *mai-tzŭ*, wheat.

IX.—1. *niu yang*, sheep and oxen. 2. *niu ma*, cattle and horses. 3. *yu ch'ung*, fish and reptiles. 4 *fei niao*, birds, *lit.* flying birds. 5 *ta lu*, the red, *lit* great, deer. 6 *chin yu*, gold fish. 7. *ch'ang ch'ung*, a serpent, *lit.* the long reptile. 8. *hsi-k'ou ma*, a horse from the western frontier; *lit* western mouths, *sc* frontier passes. 9. *lung chao*, dragon's claws; as in embroidery, painting; &c. 10. *lao shu*, a rat; *lit.* old rat. 11. *yang-p'i*, sheep's skin. 12. *yu-mao*, camlet; *lit.* feathers and hair. 13 *yang-mao*, wool. 14. *hsiang-niu p'i*, Russia leather; *lit.* scented cow-hide. 15. *niu-chiao*, or *niu-chio*, cow's horn.

X.—1. *chin, mu, shui, 'huo, t'u*, metal, wood, water, fire, earth; the five elements of China. 2. *yu fêng yu yu*, both wind and rain. 3 *t'ien t'u*, lands; fields. 4. *shan shui*, scenery. 5. *shan ch'uan*, hills and streams; mountain and water systems of a country. 6. *shan ku*, hill and valley. 7. *shih-hsueh*, an artificial cave or grotto. 8. *hsi-fang*, the west, *lit.* western region; used only of Buddha's land. 9. *ch'ien yu*, rain is wanting. 10. *t'u shan-tzŭ*, a mound, natural or artificial. 11. *'huang t'u*, clay. 12. *'hei t'u*, black loam; specially of the soil in Peking. 13. *yu-shui*, rain; also the name of one of the 24 periods into which the year is divided.

XI.—1. *ch'ang i ts'un*, one inch long. 2. *pa ts'un êrh*, eight inches and two [tenths]. 3. *pa tou tou-tzŭ*, eight measures of beans. 4. *shih chin mi*, ten catties of rice. 5. *i êrh p'i*, a bale or two [of cloth, silk, &c]. 6. *pa-shih-êrh li*, eighty-two *li*; something over 25 miles. 7. *fei chih i jên*, it is not only one man [that says, does, &c]. 8. *pa k'ou jên*, eight persons. 9. *shih k'ou jên*, ten persons. 10. *i fang*, a whole neighbourhood.

XII.—1 *jih jih*, daily. 2. *yüeh yueh*, monthly. 3. *tzŭ ch'ên chih yu*, from about 8 A.M. to about 5 P.M.; *ch'ên* being the fourth of the two hourly periods after midnight; *yu*, the third from noon.

XIII.—1 *ch'ing-pai*, of a sickly countenance; *lit.* blue and white. 2. *'hei-pai*, black and white; used when saying that a man is too stupid even to distinguish between these colours. 3. *ch'ing-'huang*, blue and yellow; unripe grain is said not to have reached the time when these colours mingle; the phrase is also applied to a sickly countenance. 4. *ch'ih sê*, bright scarlet, such as is used on temple walls, &c. 5. *'huang êrh 'hei*, yellow and yet black; of a sickly countenance. 6. *hsiang sê*, joss-stick colour, a pale yellow dye seen in silk, cloth, &c.

XIV.—1. *'huo shih*, a flint. 2. *pai yu*, white jade.

END OF PART II.

TZŬ ERH CHI.

COLLOQUIAL SERIES.

PART III.

THE FORTY EXERCISES.

(CHINESE TEXT.)

散語四十章之一

1. 兩三
2. 第四五六七九
3. 幾千數百萬零來多少有好些個
4. 十六,十九,二十三,四,五十七,六十八。
5. 第一,第二十七,第一千八百六十五。
6. 第一百萬零三百個,三五個,五七百個人。
7. 一百萬三十五萬五百萬零一,六百個,五十七萬六百一十七萬零二十。
8. 五萬零八十八,萬零五百零七十萬。
9. 七萬零一百九十一千,萬四千六百一十二,八千三百六十七,一萬零六一百零三。
10. 九萬八千四百零二,一千零五,四千零七十二。
11. 一百一十八,二百五十四,九百九十九萬三千。
12. 人,有好些個人,有多少人來,三萬多。
13. 數十個,幾十個,兩個,幾個,十個多,八九個,十數個,十來個,九個,二百多,五千多。
14. 肉,六斤羊肉,幾斤魚。
15. 七斗麥子,九斗米,一斗黍子。
16. 長三寸四,一身一口五斤牛。
17. 幾個牙長。
18. 幾萬里,足四萬里。
19. 有山足高二百里。

PART III. THE FORTY EXERCISES. *San Yü Chang.* 1-2.

散語四十章之二

1. 你
2. 我
3. 他
4. 偺
5. 們
6. 倆
7. 這
8. 在
9. 那
10. 兒
11. 的
12. 沒
13. 了
14. 甚
15. 麼
16. 買
17. 賣
18. 得
19. 很
20. 誰
21. 要
22. 不
23. 是
24. 東

1. 你的、我的、他的。
2. 你們、我們、他們、偺們。
3. 你們的、我們的、他們的、偺們的。
4. 我們兩個人。
5. 我們倆。
6. 偺們倆。
7. 偺們三個人。
8. 這個、那個。
9. 這兒、那兒。
10. 這麼、那麼。
11. 甚麼人。
12. 甚麼東西。
13. 那個人買東西、賣東西。
14. 那個人是個好人。
15. 他是個買賣人、賣甚麼的、賣好些個東西。
16. 我要好的、有沒有了。
17. 這個很好那個不好。
18. 有甚麼人賣甚麼東西。
19. 他是那兒的人、他不是這兒的。
20. 他們來了多少人、他們來了好些個人。
21. 我不要這個、他們要這個。
22. 這個。
23. 你們有這個東西沒有、我們不要這個東西、有多
24. 他來了沒有、他沒有來。
25. 他來了、沒有他、我們不去。
26. 這個人很好、那個人很不好。
27. 這個東西是甚麼人的、是我們的、你們有多少、這個東西有不多的。
28. 你們那兒有很好的沒有、沒有好的、你沒有很好的、我們不要了。

散語四十章之三

1. 進城
2. 家住著,
3. 街上
4. 房間
5. 屋裏
6. 開鋪
7. 關臑
8. 出去
9. 往外頭
10. 知道
11. 做過
12. 過去
13. 走著
14. 上街
15. 街上走著。
16. 往東往西。
17. 東城西城
18. 知道。
19. 做甚麼。
20. 你在那兒住,我在城裏頭。
21. 你們那
22. 你住的房子大小我住的是三間小屋子。
23. 這個房子比那個房子好多了。
24. 開了門關上臑戶,進屋裏來。
25. 外頭土大。
26. 那個人開著
27. 他在家裏做甚麼沒在家往那兒去了。你知道不知道,上街去了。
28. 那個人開著
29. 在城裏頭,東城有三個,西城有四
30. 那個鋪子裏買東西的人很多。
31. 外頭來了
32. 這個屋子沒有人住。
33. 那個鋪子是我的。
34. 他
35. 街上的人很多。

住¹房子。住²家。城³裏城外
四⁸個鋪子。關⁹門。開¹⁰臑戶出¹¹去進來。過¹²去。走¹³著上¹⁴街。街¹⁵上走著。
兒有多少房子有三十五間房子。
七個鋪子,他的鋪子是甚麼買賣開在那兒。
個,我們這兒沒有那麼大的買賣。那個鋪子裏買東西的人很多。外頭來了他
五六個人是甚麼人我不知道。這個屋子沒有人住。那個鋪子是我的。街上的人很多。
沒進來,過去往西去了,他出去做甚麼上街上買東西去了。

散語四十章之四

1. 前
2. 後
3. 叫
4. 站
5. 起
6. 躺
7. 地
8. 快
9. 慢
10. 都
11. 愛
12. 坐
13. 轎
14. 樓
15. 下
16. 回
17. 到
18. 驢
19. 騾
20. 匹
21. 輛
22. 步
23. 頂
24. 衙
25. 說

1. 躺著坐著起來站著走著步行。
2. 快走慢走。
3. 前頭後頭。
4. 回來到了。
5. 愛不愛。
6. 叫人叫人來。衙門樓上地下。
7. 一輛車一頂轎子三匹馬兩頭騾子四頭驢。
8. 他在道兒上躺著叫他起來。
9. 他在後頭走。
10. 我在樓上坐著他是地下坐著。我走得快他走得慢。我在前頭走著我是坐車來的。
11. 他是往那兒去了。
12. 他那個人回來了沒回來了。
13. 他上衙門去了。他是坐車去是坐著一頂小轎子他不愛坐車。
14. 他那個人你愛不愛他們那些人我都不愛。
15. 他買的是馬麼不是買的是騾子驢。
16. 他買這兒一匹驢子他買了多少頭買的是三頭騾子七頭驢。
17. 買馬這兒一匹都沒有驢子他買了這兒的騾子好是那兒的騾子好這兒的騾子沒有那兒的好這兒的騾子比那兒的慢那兒的騾子驢都快。

散語四十章之五

1. 眞
2. 正
3. 抄
4. 寫
5. 教
6. 學
7. 請
8. 瞧
9. 拿
10. 字
11. 典
12. 話
13. 找
14. 看
15. 先
16. 認
17. 還
18. 肯
19. 告
20. 訴
21. 呢
22. 記
23. 問
24. 騎
25. 跑

先生。[1] 教學。[2] 學生[3] 拿字典看字典。[4] 找字認字。[5] 抄寫字。[6] 找先生請先生請教。[7] 我問你請你告訴。[8] 記得不記得。[9] 口音正說話眞。[10] 看見你看見過騎著跑著你是步行兒來的是騎馬來的我是騎馬來的那匹馬跑得快。[11] 你找過先生沒有找過了。[12] 請先生教話。[13] 請先生教我。[14] 請先生。[15] 這個字你瞧過沒瞧過了。你告訴我說不記得那個字了。還有不記得的字麼那兒沒有呢。記得的少。[16] 我問你這個字你認得不認得這個字我還沒看見過呢。[17] 我請過先生教我他不肯來。請他教你甚麼請他教我們說話。[18] 你告訴我說他那個人的口音有你這麼好沒有我的口音沒有甚麼大好。他認得的字比我認得的多。[19]

散語四十章之六

1. 紙
2. 張
3. 筆
4. 管
5. 墨
6. 塊
7. 把
8. 本
9. 書
10. 念
11. 完
12. 可
13. 以
14. 給
15. 官
16. 會
17. 分
18. 聽
19. 明
20. 也
21. 懂
22. 平
23. 聲
24. 忘
25. 錯

¹一張紙,一本書,兩塊墨,五管筆。 ²官話,懂得聽見忘了 ³四聲是上平下下平上聲去聲,不錯完了,不會明白可以。 ⁴四聲都可以分得開。 ⁵我看你給我買十管筆兩塊墨。 ⁶你把那一本書拏來給我那一張紙拏給我聽見說你學官話學得很好四聲你會分不會明白有幾分不明白也有幾個字不認得。 ⁸那一本書你看完了沒有十分裏我看過八分明白不明白有幾分不明白也有幾個字不認得。 ⁹你念過多少日子的書,我念過十個月的書那書上的字都記得麽,不都記得,忘了好些個,也有記錯了的。 ¹⁰他那個人懂得官話,不懂我聽見說他不懂他認得字還認得認過四五千字,你那兒知道呢,上月我們在一塊兒看書,我叫他抄寫他可以不可以沒有甚麽不可以的。 ¹¹我問你,他的話,你聽得出來聽不出來。 ¹²你念過的書,千萬不可忘了,不錯你說得很是。

散語四十章之七

1. 炕
2. 蓆床
3. 帳鋪
4. 蓋桌椅
5. 爐燈盞
6. 隻酒杯
7. 茶碗盅
8. 廚糞飯
9. 鍋鏟勺
10. 壞
11. (continuing numbers through 24)

1. 鋪炕，一張床。
2. 帳子，蓆子鋪蓋。
3. 一張桌子，一張椅子。
4. 一盞燈，爐燈。
5. 廚房。
6. 糞飯。
7. 壞了。
8. 他在炕上鋪蓆子。
9. 我要在這張床上躺著，你
10. 那一張床上有帳子沒有。
11. 他在床上躺著，我在椅子上坐著。
12. 這屋裏很黑，拏一盞燈來。
13. 有人拏了那盞燈去。桌子上的那燈離拏了去
14. 了，是我給廚子拏過去
15. 了。廚房裏沒有火。飯鍋是煮飯用的，鍋蓋是飯鍋的
16. 蓋兒。茶碗，茶盅都可以有蓋兒。酒杯，酒盅子，這兩個東西不大很分。
17. 那屋裏
18. 那些桌子椅子都壞了。
19. 我叫你買的那茶碗你買了沒買，買過了多少個
20. 買了二十個。是在那兒買的，都是在城外頭鋪子裏買的。
21. 沒有，我們的屋裏炕上都有蓆子。

散語四十章之八

1. 傢伙
2. 攪條
3. 倒壺
4. 花瓶
5. 破
6. 收拾
7. 盤碟
8. 吃點
9. 吹滅
10. 使
11. 燒
12. 爐
13. 空
14. 滿
15. 同
16. 算
17. 碎
18.
19.
20.
21.
22.
23.
24.
25.

傢伙。[1]一條攪子一個攪子也說得。[2]一個爐子。[3]花瓶、酒瓶、酒壺、茶壺、盤子、碟子、銚子、勺子、盤子、碟子、飯碗、酒杯。[4]家裏用的東西都是傢伙。床、桌、椅、機、都是屋裏用的傢伙。[5]點燈、吹燈、燒火、滅火、倒水、[6]空壺、滿壺、壺空了、壺滿了、[7]使得破壞收拾、[8]吃飯的傢伙有刀子、銚子、勺子、盤子、碟子、飯碗、酒杯。[9]爐子有大小不同廚房做飯是爐子炕頭裏也是爐子屋裏燒火還是爐子。[10]花瓶也算是傢伙麽花瓶還可以算是傢伙。[11]那碗裏的水倒在鍋裏。[12]倒茶是也是爐子。[13]叫人把茶倒在碗裏頭。[14]那酒瓶酒壺茶壺茶碗也都是零用的傢伙。[15]你點了燈沒有我點上燈了。[16]吹燈是滅燈火滅火是滅了爐子的火。[17]你把那空的倒滿了水。[18]吹燈是滅的你一個是空的一個是滿的你倆壺裏頭有水沒有水一個是空的一個是滿[19]那花瓶是甚麼人破壞的我不知道是誰[20]快去叫人收拾使得使不得叫人收拾很使得。

散語四十章之九

1. 今年時令暖和昨天就定晝晴
2.
3.
4. 亮鐘半刻氣候冷熱雪涼颱
5.
6.
7.
8.
9.
10.
11.
12.
13.
14.
15.
16.
17.
18.
19.
20.
21.
22.
23.

[1] 前年、去年、今年、明年、後年。[2] 上月、本月、下月。[3] 前兒就是前天、昨兒、今兒、今天、明兒、明天、後兒、後天、都是那麼著。[4] 時令就是一年的四時。[5] 天氣可以分天冷天熱天凉天暖和颱風晴天下雪。[6] 時候天亮白晝黑下一會兒一點鐘雨刻半點鐘一點半鐘就是一點鐘雨刻一下鐘就是一點鐘。[7] 那人他看過二十多年的書、做過五六個月的先生。[8] 我今兒走下月可以回來。[9] 你今兒八下鐘還沒起來。[10] 前年、後年、可以說前月、後月不大很說。[11] 這兒天熱的時候兒下雨、天冷的時候兒下雪。[12] 昨兒黑下颱風天亮的時候兒很冷。[13] 他愛白晝出去騎馬黑下回家看書。[14] 昨兒黑下下雨今兒晴了天。[15] 今兒是個晴天。[16] 今年天氣暖和得很沒有去年那麼冷。[17] 我們倆到這兒好些年了。[18] 他是去年來的我是上月到的他們倆是去年來過了。

散語四十章之十

1. 更夫每夜得打罷早晚晌午嗒事情擱各樣短雲彩陰霧空
2.
3.
4.
5.
6.
7.
8.
9.
10.
11.
12.
13.
14.
15.
16.
17.
18.
19.
20.
21.
22.
23.

[1]每年、每月、每天、每日、各樣。[2]早起晌午、晚上半天下半天。[3]夜裏前半夜後半夜。[4]定更打更更夫。[5]天長天短夜長夜短。[6]多嗒工夫。[7]陰天雲彩下霧。[8]得有事情。[9]擱著罷。[10]他是早起起來、晌午街上走、晚上回家看書、到夜裏三更天就躺在炕上罷了、天天都是這麼樣。[11]各自兒就是自己一個人、這個事情得你各自各兒去、那房子就是他各自各兒住著。[12]上半天下了雨下半天就晴了。[13]前半夜還暖和後半夜冷。[14]夜裏那更夫打一更就是定更。[15]三更天就是半夜。[16]天長做事的工夫多天短沒有工夫事情得擱著罷。[17]他多嗒回來明兒可以回來。[18]那茶壺擱在那兒擱在屋裏桌子上了。[19]天上的雲彩滿了就是陰天。[20]今兒早起下得霧很大大山都瞧不見了。

散語四十章之十一

1. 怕
2. 裳
3. 件
4. 太
5. 腌
6. 臢
7. 換
8. 乾
9. 淨
10. 刷
11. 洗
12. 臉
13. 盆
14. 縫
15. 補
16. 穿
17. 鞋
18. 脫
19. 靴
20. 雙
21. 襪
22. 最
23. 溫

[1]刷洗。[2]腌臢乾淨。[3]衣裳、靴子、鞋、襪子。[4]穿上、脫下來、換上。[5]縫補。一雙靴[6]子，兩雙鞋，十雙襪子，一條手巾，八件衣裳，一個臉盆。[7]這盆水腌臢了，換乾淨的拏來我洗臉。那些衣裳腌臢拏刷子刷一刷這一件衣裳破了，叫人來縫補。你快起來穿上衣裳。[8]那一件衣裳他穿了好些日[9]子沒換呢。[10]他脫了衣裳躺著。[11]那一件衣裳他穿了好些日子沒換呢。[12]今兒個天涼你得多穿一件衣裳。[13]他是穿鞋子，他是穿著靴子來著。[14]這一條手巾腌臢擱在盆裏洗一洗。[15]你愛穿的是靴子是鞋[16]你的那皮靴子擱得日子多得刷洗[17]了。[18]你洗手是愛使涼水是愛使開水，兩樣兒都不好，涼水太涼開水太熱最[18]好的是溫和水兒。你快把這個水倒在鍋裏溫一溫。[19]那火要滅了，這水溫[20]了半天，開不了。要洗衣裳使熱水最好，刷洗靴子得使涼水。

散語四十章之十二

1. 儘
2. 摘
3. 戴
4. 撣
5. 帽
6. 砍
7. 肩
8. 汗
9. 衫
10. 單
11. 夾
12. 綿
13. 褲
14. 裁
15. 褂
16. 袖
17. 梳
18. 髮
19. 針
20. 線
21. 胰
22. 澡

綿[1]衣裳、夾衣裳、單衣裳。砍[2]肩兒、汗衫、褂子、褲子。帽[3]子、戴帽子、摘帽子。針[4]線、一個針、一條線。裁[5]縫、裁衣裳、縫衣裳。撣[6]子、撣衣裳。洗[7]澡。頭[8]髮、梳頭髮。單[9]衣裳、是就有一面兒沒有裏兒的、夾衣裳、是有裏兒有面兒的、綿衣裳、是夾衣裳中間有綿花的。砍[10]肩兒、是有前後沒袖子的那一件衣裳、汗衫是儘裏頭穿的單衣裳、褂子是儘外頭穿的衣裳、短的就叫馬褂子。這[11]一條褲子是綿的、是夾的。帽[12]子分得是小帽兒官帽兒、官帽兒裏有涼帽暖帽兩樣兒、人在街上得戴帽子、進屋裏來可以摘帽子。你[13]會針線不會、我不會、就叫一個裁縫來把我那一件汗衫補了。那[14]一件砍肩兒裁了還沒縫呢。那[15]一件破馬褂子得縫補了。拏[16]撣子撣一撣衣裳上的土。那[17]一把木梳是誰梳頭髮的。洗[18]澡是一身都洗、天天兒洗澡很好。

散語四十章之十三

1. 銀
2. 銅
3. 鐵
4. 錢
5. 吊
6. 票
7. 桿秤
8. 稱
9. 價值
10. 貴
11. 賤
12. 便宜
13. 輕
14. 重
15. 借
16. 賬
17. 該
18. 費
19. 當於
20. 好

1. 欠賬借錢該錢。
2. 賬目。
3. 花費。
4. 價值價錢。
5. 很賤不貴便宜。
6. 銀子銀子錢銅錢鐵錢票子。
7. 一兩銀子一吊錢四吊錢的票子。
8. 這個輕那個重不知道他的輕重拏秤稱一稱。
9. 他欠人的賬目不少。
10. 我借錢是我把人家的錢拏來我使我借給人使。
11. 他該我們家裏天天兒的花費不很多。
12. 花費是他過於費錢。
13. 他愛花錢好花錢都說得是把錢使了。
14. 那房子價錢不貴這一件皮袄子價值很便宜那個花瓶不值錢今年的綿花很賤。
15. 他家裏一個大錢都沒有。
16. 那當十的大錢裏頭有七分是銅的有三分是鐵的。
17. 票子是一張紙上頭寫著錢數兒買東西同銀子錢一個樣兒。
18. 金子比銀子重鐵比銀子輕。
19. 買東西要稱分兩的都得使秤。
20. 那些秤秤可以稱多少斤兩最大的可以稱三百斤。

散語四十章之十四

1. 煤炭柴麵油芝糖鹽粗細湯雞奶果菜饅喝弄端撤熟論石

麵

1. 柴火煤炭。
2. 米麵饅頭、白糖雞子兒牛奶果子。
3. 燈油香油。
4. 粗鹽細鹽。
5. 石米二百斤麵。
6. 吃飯喝湯。
7. 我昨兒買了三百斤炭、八十斤柴火、四十斤煤。
8. 燈油是豆子做的、香油是芝麻做的、燈油比香油賤。
9. 炕爐子是用煤火盆做的、都是熟茶生茶、有生的有熟的、在火上做的都是熟茶生茶是地下長出來、就可以吃得。
10. 天氣冷的時候兒煤炭用得多。
11. 盆是屋裏用的、不能做飯做水。
12. 茶是地下長出來、就可以吃得。
13. 你去給我買一隻小雞子兒、還要牛奶不要牛奶便宜我可以要幾斤、我們這兒買牛奶不論斤數兒、都是論個兒。
14. 你愛吃饅頭、愛吃飯、兩檬兒都不愛、碗論瓶買果子也不論斤、都是論個兒。
15. 我愛喝湯、愛喝甚麼湯呢、肉湯雞湯都好。
16. 你快弄飯去、飯得了就端了來。
17. 甚麼是撤了呢、你吃完了飯、都擧下去、那就是撤了。

散語四十章之十五

1. 京
2. 遠
3. 近
4. 南
5. 北
6. 路
7. 直
8. 繞
9. 河
10. 海
11. 邊
12. 深
13. 淺
14. 船
15. 客
16. 店
17. 掌
18. 櫃
19. 計
20. 受
21. 累
22. 苦
23. 乏
24. 歇
25. 連

[1] 進京、直走、繞著走、都可以。

[2] 算計道路的遠近、直走近、繞著走遠。

[3] 南邊北邊。

[4] 一隻船。

[5] 坐船、過河、走海、水深水淺。

[6] 客店掌櫃的。

[7] 辛苦、受累乏了、歇著。

[8] 你去年進京、在那兒住著、在客店裏、我聽見說城外頭客店有不很好住的、那都看掌櫃的好不好、在我說、人乏了、那兒都好、到店裏就不過歇著罷了。

[9] 你走路、愛坐車愛坐船、都是看地方兒、南邊沒有車走道兒的客人、都是坐船走河路、都是小船兒、走海的船大。

[10] 河裏的水淺、沒有海水深。

[11] 你前年坐海船不是受了累麼、不錯、是颳大風、船在山東海邊兒、上擱了淺、我們那些人辛苦得了不得。

[12] 船上吃飯、是甚麼人管、也是船家管。

[13] 算計盤費、是坐船貴、是坐車貴、坐車比坐船花的錢多、那兒車價比船價貴呢、車價貴、都是我們北邊那個車店裏的掌櫃的、也要使些個錢。

散語四十章之十六

1. 李箱
2. 包袋
3. 氊布
4. 矮駱駝
5. 牲口
6. 跟班
7. 裝帶
8. 馱
9. 追趕
10. 喚
11. 無利害
12. 春夏秋冬
13.
14.
15.
16.
17.
18.
19.
20.
21.
22.
23.
24.
25.

行李箱子包兒口袋氊子、一定布。[2] 矮牲口、駱駝馱子、跟班、[4] 裝箱子帶[5] 東西、帶牲口。追趕。[6] 太利害。[7] 春夏秋冬。[8] 行李是走道兒的客人帶的東西。[9] 箱子有皮子做的、有木頭做的、甚麽都可裝得包兒是把東西用甚麽包起來、他是拏氊子把那小箱子包起來口袋是裝零碎東西的、我們使的都是布口袋。道兒上到店裏得矮牲口。[11] 駱駝都是口外來的。牲口身上駝著[13] 東西就叫馱子、驢馱子、馬馱子都說得。你[14] 小心著行李馱子都齊了、我[16] 出門去他的跟班的是使喚的人、他叫跟班的把箱子裝在車上、那個人在那兒呢、他出去了、你[17] 快跑可以趕得上他、他早走了、怕是趕不上罷、無論趕得上趕不上追他就是了。

冬天太冷、夏天太熱、春沒有冬冷、秋沒有夏熱。

散語四十章之十七

1. 腦
2. 辮
3. 朶
4. 眼睛
5. 嘴脣
6. 鬍
7. 胳臂
8. 指甲
9. 抓
10. 腰
11. 腿
12. 壯健
13. 輭弱
14. 拉
15. 拽
16. 病
17. 疼
18. 奇怪

1. 腦袋、辮子、耳朶、眼睛、鼻子、嘴、嘴裏、脣子、鬍子、胳臂、指頭、指甲、腰腿。
2. 壯健、輭弱。
3. 拉著、拽著、拉拽、抓破、連著。
4. 有病、很疼、奇怪。
5. 人的頭裏有腦子就叫腦袋。
6. 你這個辮子得梳了。
7. 人老了耳朶聽不眞、眼睛也看不眞。
8. 那個人鼻子眼睛長得奇怪。
9. 這個人很健壯、那個人輭弱得很。
10. 你的身子有病麼沒有病、我是身子輭弱。
11. 街上那兒躺著的那個人兩腿都破了。
12. 俺們五六年沒有見你的鬍子都白了、是我的身子這幾年病得利害、走不起來。
13. 你這麼慢走是是人老了、腰腿都不好。他的舌頭有病連嘴骨子都破了。
14. 嘴裏吃東西、嘴裏說話、都說得。
15. 那女人的指甲長、把他的胳臂抓破了。
16. 我的指頭疼。
17. 拉車用甚麼牲口呢、用騾子、驢子、馬、都可以拉得。
18. 拽是說人擎手用力的拉、把那門拽住了、他拉拽著我。

PART III. THE FORTY EXERCISES. *San Yü Chang.* 17–18.   49

散語四十章之十八

1. 眉
2. 鬢
3. 顋
4. 頰
5. 巴
6. 頦
7. 脖
8. 嗓
9. 節
10. 刮
11. 剃
12. 胸
13. 背
14. 脊
15. 梁
16. 髈
17. 肚
18. 波
19. 棱
20. 踝
21. 脚
22. 體
23. 斬
24. 賊
25. 級

眉毛、鬢角兒、顋頰、下巴頦兒、鼻子眼兒、脖子、嗓子眼兒、梁背兒胸前、肚子。波棱蓋兒踝子骨骨節兒。[3]
眉毛是眉棱骨上的毛、鬢角兒是腦門子兩邊兒的頭髮。[6] 顋頰是嘴兩邊兒的肉。嘴下頭的骨頭是下巴頦兒。[8] 肩髈兒是胳臂的上頭。兩個肩髈後頭的地方兒叫脊梁背兒。[9] 波棱蓋兒是腿中間兒的骨頭節兒脚上頭的骨頭節兒、前頭叫嗓子[11]以下肚子以上。[12]胸前是脖子以下肚子以上。[13]波棱蓋兒是腿中間兒的骨頭節兒、脚上頭的骨頭節兒叫踝子骨。[14]年輕的人沒鬍子的時候兒得拏刀子刮臉。剃頭、剃的是那[15]辮子以外的短頭髮、拏住賊就斬、斬下來的腦袋就叫首級。[16]說體面人、是說那個人的行止沒有甚麼不好、說那個人長[17]得體面、是說他長得好看。他[18]那個房子蓋得體面、也說得。

散語四十章之十九

1. 君民主爵位參贊尊武兵缺額捐充謀策殺退勒索中底全姓名
2. 君上下民主子家主兒底下人。
3. 爵位參贊尊貴。
4. 官民文官武官官兵開
5. 缺補缺額數。捐官充當。官人。
6. 謀篹計策殺退。
7. 全是。
8. 民人姓名百姓。
9. 君上是百官萬民的主子家主兒是底下人的主人。
10. 君上是百官萬民的主子家主兒是底下人的主人。
11. 官民就是官長下民小民也叫百姓。
12. 爵位尊是說人做的官大說小官不算爵位比方參贊的官爵
13. 位也尊貴。管民的是文官帶兵的是武官。官兵的額數有一定的有關了
14. 缺的得補沒補的缺得找人充補。充數兒是假的沒有甚麼真本事是人是
15. 充數兒是假的沒有甚麼真本事是人是
16. 東西都說得。說民人充兵當兵那都是說他做兵。用銀子錢買官那叫捐
17. 用銀子錢買官那叫捐
18. 官。去年賊很多帶兵的大官全是謀篹不好不會定計策叫賊全跑了那賊
19. 退到河北裏見人就殺河北的官民會齊了追趕把賊全殺退了。那賊頭兒
20. 的姓名知道不知道有一個姓黃名龍是賊中的頭兒。

散語四十章之二十

1. 國
2. 章
3. 程
4. 卡
5. 倫
6. 巡
7. 察
8. 刻
9. 搜
10. 律
11. 例
12. 治
13. 理
14. 暴
15. 虐
16. 亂
17. 謬
18. 普
19. 羣
20. 耕
21. 耨
22. 囊
23. 總
24. 謂
25. 之

章程定章[1]。卡倫巡察搜拏搜察刻搜[2]。律例[3]。治亂[4]。治理道理理會。暴虐大亂太謬。普天下[7]。一羣[8]。耕耨耕田[9]。囊中[10]。名目[11]。西路那邊兒道[12]兒上有卡倫是盤察出入人的那卡倫都有一定的章程過客的行李總得搜察。城門[13]的官兵巡察是有定章也不可太刻搜。國家定[14]的律例是治理百姓的不是出於暴虐中國的道理不教而殺謂之虐。耕耨[15]是小民的本分夏天人人兒都耕田。近年[16]天下大亂是官長治理得不好是普天下百姓知道的。那塊兒的官太謬[17]不肯聽話百姓告訴他說賊快來了他總不理會全不治地方也不捜拏賊過了一會兒賊就來了殺燒得利害得很那跑了的一羣百姓[18]一齊跑著謂之一羣驟馬牛羊好些個在一塊兒也有這個一羣的名目。天下[19]治亂總在於官。

散語四十章之二十一

1. 搶奪
2. 偷
3. 逃竄
4. 散
5. 混
6. 懶惰
7. 棍
8. 扔
9. 放槍
10. 恰巧
11. 特意
12. 偶然
13. 成
14. 硬
15. 按
16. 思

搶奪偷東西。一[2]股賊。逃竄逃散。混跑混說。懶惰。一根小棍子一條槍、一桿槍裝槍放槍。扔[7]東西。恰巧[8]、特意偶然自然按著。成人成事。背[10]著人拏東西不教人知道、是偷把人家的東西硬拏了去、就是搶奪、不分夜裏白日都說得。那一股賊都逃散了。山東[12]那一股賊竄到河南去了、百姓見了賊來、都四下裏混跑。說話[13]沒有理、那筭是混說。人[14]不愛用工夫、謂之懶惰。那[15]一天有倆賊、一個拏著一條大棍子混打、有人拏著一桿槍來了、看見了那個賊混打趕著那個人、是特意來的、還是偶然來的、怕是偶然來下棍子就跑了。帶着鳥槍的那個人、是特意裝上槍拏來了的也不定。他[16]那個人很懶惰、不是成人的人、不愛念書、那兒可以成呢、人[17]不按著道兒走、就[⸺]混走。的心裏有力自然可以成事。

散語四十章之二十二

1. 凡揣摩約准否更改妥當專失神參差忙向規幹辦法胡鬧掄催
2.
3.
4.
5.
6.
7.
8.
9.
10.
11.
12.
13.
14.
15.
16.
17.
18.
19.
20.
21.
22.
23.
24.
25.

凡事大約。凡論專說。揣摩[3]。准否[4]。更改妥當。專心失神太忙參差。凡[10]做事總得有定向。

凡事辦事[7]辦理法子。胡鬧混掄。催人[9]。

定向定規。

來[11]的人是誰。我揣摩著是姓張的。大約是他。那一件事還沒有辦妥章程念書寫字都得專心也[13]

得敗，也不知道李大人准否，大約沒有甚麼更改了。

不可太忙，辦事太忙就有參差了。要幹甚麼事，先得定規立准了主意就謂[14]

之定向。幹事[15]的時候兒心裏不在那就叫失神。定安了辦事的法子就叫[16]

定規。那個[17]人有一件要事，得趕辦他一點不忙，同人催他快著些兒他不肯

聽，擎著棍子混掄，真是胡鬧。論事不能指定那就謂之凡論。說那一股賊有

幾萬，那就是賊數兒的大凡。以上這幾章是專說大股賊的多。他[20]那個人

辦理甚麼事，都辦得不安當，多有參差不齊。

散語四十章之二十三

1. 語
2. 句
3. 吵
4. 喧
5. 嚷
6. 哼
7. 阿
8. 哈
9. 嘎
10. 訛
11. 衰
12. 困
13. 極
14. 夢
15. 貌
16. 美
17. 陋
18. 摔
19. 掉
20. 擱
21. 掯
22. 窘
23. 則
24. 況
25. 且

言語一句話。吵鬧喧嚷哼阿哼的。哈哈的笑。嘎嘎的笑冷笑。訛錯。氣血衰困極了。做夢。貌美貌陋。摔了掉下來掉下去擱了掯住。地方兒窘。訛錯。一則二則況且。他的言語你懂得不懂他這麼哼阿哼的我一句話都聽不出來。他那一個人我也不愛同他說話。一則我一開口他就是哈哈的笑二則他說的話也訛錯的多況且他那個土音我聽著很費事。城門口兒的地方兒窘來往的車馬多。外頭是甚麼人喧嚷跟班的趕車的他們吵鬧呢。那老頭子氣血衰了身子困極了躺在道兒上做著夢說話那些人都嘎嘎的笑他。你看那兩個小人兒一個很貌美一個很貌陋那貌美的笑話那貌陋的那貌陋的生了氣把茶碗摔碎了有人說了他兩句他害怕就說茶碗是掉下去的掯住他的辮子要拉了他去他倒在地下把胳臂擱了。

散語四十章之二十四

1. 兆
2. 古
3. 凶
4. 祥
5. 瑞
6. 安
7. 寧
8. 順
9. 寬
10. 綽
11. 貧
12. 窮
13. 窘
14. 恆產
15. 朋友
16. 賞
17. 相幫
18. 留
19. 能
20. 丟
21. 根
22. 現

先兆吉兆凶兆祥瑞。安寧順當。寬綽貧窮很窘。恆產。好朋友。賞東西賞錢幫人銀錢。留下不能丟了。底根兒現在今日下。事情不論吉凶都有個先兆兒。事情沒來之先看見天上有甚麼可以知道日後恐怕那就謂之吉兆。家裏的錢足用的是寬綽錢太少過日子不足那謂之貧窮過日子有准進的錢那就叫做恆產。甚麼是安寧呢。比方去年河南那一塊兒下連陰雨秋天沒有收成民人甚麼都丟了人人兒窘得很地方兒鬧得大亂那就是不安寧地方官趕著賞了些米把要逃的百姓都留住了。一個朋友說俗們這些年的相好你幫我幾個錢肯不肯。他說沒有甚麼不肯真是不能我們底根兒有那些錢現在恆產沒了一個大錢都沒有連我自己也沒喫的。

散語四十章之二十五

1. 您
2. 喳
3. 親
4. 祖
5. 翁
6. 兄
7. 孫
8. 舍弟
9. 奴才
10. 迎接
11. 葬
12. 絲
13. 團
14. 絨
15. 尺
16. 貨
17. 昂
18. 替
19. 挑

您[1]。 您[2]尊重。 旁人[3]祖上老翁家兄舍弟子孫兒子孫子奴才。 喳得一聲[4]迎接[5]下葬[6]。 一團絲幾尺絨土貨[7]替我。 挑好的[8]。 昂貴[9]。 粗細[10]。 稱人您[11]是有點兒尊重人的意思您好您多喳來的就使得的老子。 旁人[12]的父親可以稱老翁。 令祖好阿令尊好阿[13]是間您祖您父親我的家祖就是我父親向人稱自己的弟兄說的是家兄舍弟稱人家的弟兄是說令兄令弟[14]。 我兒子的兒女是我的孫子孫女。 奴才就是使喚的人有是買的有不是買的還是說底下人的多。 家主兒[15]叫底下人喳得一聲是順著聽話的意思。 今兒家祖[16]回來我去迎接後兒他們老翁下葬我得幫幫他們去。 那兩團絲[17]不是你們這兒的土貨麼可不是那絨還是粗的一團是細的。 那絲[18]不是土貨請您替我挑一點兒好的近來價錢昂貴一尺不下二錢多銀子。

PART III. THE FORTY EXERCISES. *San Yü Chang.* 25-26.

散語四十章之二十六

1. 想
2. 怎麼
3. 却是
4. 睡覺
5. 相對
6. 倆人賽對賽
7. 嚐刻
8. 吞了
9. 向來
10. 疊次
11. 一斤葱
12. 草木青草苗兒老嫩桑樹林子綠森森
13. 溼了曬乾
14. 怎麼呢大家都喝酒你就睡了覺了麼
15. 你想這個錢不是他吞了却是誰我們向來沒賽過
16. 他們倆人對賽著寫字那個姓李的寫的字比你的好不好
17. 他那倆兄弟還是疊次吞人家的錢
18. 那個葱這兩天貴不分老嫩都是二百錢一斤
19. 分牛羊肉的好歹也有老嫩之說草木是生的熟的
20. 草木的總名草本的東西一出土兒叫苗兒
21. 苗子是四川東南的人分
22. 樹多謂之樹林子那桑樹林子綠森森的
23. 樹林子底下的地溼得很
24. 要把溼衣裳弄乾了得鋪在日頭地裏曬一曬曬乾了就疊起來罷

散語四十章之二十七

1. 某乍初和別素原待敦厚薄傲嫉妒慚愧絕交實憑實拜應陪

某人[1]乍見。起初原是原來平素。和我和別人待人相待。親熱厚薄敦厚刻薄傲慢待慚愧嫉妒。實在。憑他。可憑。賓客相拜。陪著正陪。

某人[1]乍見。起初原是原來平素。[2]

厚刻薄傲慢慢待慚愧嫉妒。[3]

某人[4]是不說出姓名來的人有某人嫉妒我這個好兒很刻薄我的了不得這[5]

刻薄原是嘴裏的刻薄話心裏的刻薄却是敦厚的對面兒。[6]

初乍見某人，是平素沒見過的人初次見他，多日沒見的人見了，也可以說乍[7]

他[8]和我不和和別人也不對他不分厚薄，待人都是刻薄他這個人不[9]

待人沒有不敦厚的實在沒可慚愧。他們倆起初相好近來絕了交了。他[10]

的爵位原來大待人有點兒傲慢那一天有賓客來拜他却不見他說的話也[11]

沒有一句可憑的我還要拜他去見不見憑他那兒的話呢您去理應是見我[12]

陪著您去好不好憑他慢待我可以不論。專主的是正幫同的是陪。[13]

PART III. THE FORTY EXERCISES. *San Yü Chang.* 27–28.

散語四十章之二十八

1. 裱
2. 糊
3. 匠
4. 染
5. 顏
6. 紅
7. 藍
8. 淡
9. 新
10. 舊
11. 紗
12. 氈
13. 必
14. 須
15. 光
16. 潤
17. 玻
18. 璃
19. 料
20. 擦
21. 碰
22. 裂
23. 行

1. 裱糊。
2. 匠人。
3. 一定紗、一定布、氈子。
4. 新的光潤、舊的色兒太淡,染紅的、染藍的都行。
5. 玻璃料貨。
6. 必須擦一擦。
7. 碰著碰壞了,破了,破裂裂了,碎了,破碎。
8. 窗戶紙裂了叫裱糊匠來糊上、單張紙糊在那兒是糊、雙張兒紙糊在一塊兒是裱。
9. 各行的手工人叫匠人的多、ム匠、瓦匠、鐵匠、都說得。
10. 布是綿花做的、紗是絲做的。
11. 有一塊布,有一塊紗、顏色兒舊了,必須染別的顏色,原舊的顏色兒是紅的,還可以染藍的,要染甚麼顏色,都憑人家的主意。
12. 你瞧那一定紅紗顏色兒光潤不光潤,怎麼是光潤呢?那紗原來是好紗又是新的、染得顏色兒又好看、這光潤不止於說紗說別的也行。
13. 料貨是玻璃東西的總名。
14. 我拏那個玻璃瓶來、要擦一擦、碰在桌子上、破壞了。
15. 有兩隻船相碰、這一隻壞了、那一隻破碎了。
16. 茶碗掉在地下碎了。

散語四十章之二十九

1. 剛縴
2. 再
3. 等
4. 取
5. 送
6. 落
7. 永
8. 湊
9. 挪
10. 拴
11. 套
12. 商量
13. 彀
14. 斟酌
15. 疑惑
16. 喊
17. 答應
18. 從
19. 末

剛縴[1]。等著從來從前。再來再三再四[3]。永遠[4]。末末了兒[5]。取東西、送東西[7]。落下了、挪開、湊到一塊兒。拴牲口[8]、套車。量米[9]。不彀[10]。一石[11]。斟酌[12]。商量疑惑。喊叫答應[13]。

剛縴[14]我們在這兒論起這件事來、再三的喊他過來後永遠不敢了。再三再四[16]的請他過來、他都不肯末末了兒、是我到他那邊兒去的。我們十個人[17]從前定得湊錢做買賣、後來落下了兩個人、還有把本錢取回去的、我瞧這個我也不肯再把錢送了去了。叫[18]你把箱子挪開了、怎麼挪那麼遠。這米[19]我量了不彀五石、一個單套車就拉了。不止五石、不是二套車怕拉不了。我[20]是南邊來的、從來沒坐過車、那趕車的到店裏立刻就要錢、我疑惑從來沒這個理、叫他等一等再來。

散語四十章之三十

1. 臺灣
2. 江湖
3. 流浪
4. 闊
5. 浮橋
6. 井坑
7. 衚衕
8. 巷
9. 野屯
10. 墳墓
11. 峯
12. 嶺
13. 尖
14.
15.
16.
17.
18.
19.
20.
21.

臺灣[1]。 江河湖海長江，流水順流波浪寬闊。 浮橋[3]。 一眼井，一個坑，一條衚[4]衕。 大街小巷野地屯裏墳墓。 山峯山嶺兒峯嶺。 尖兒[7]。 臺灣是中國東[8]南海裏的地方兒，南北兩頭兒山嶺兒也多也大，那峯嶺也很好看。 江河湖海是天下大水的總名兒。 俗們這兒的小河兒很窄，有浮橋就可以過去，那[11]長江之流，打西到東，湖北來的船到江西去，一路都是順流，到了江西，那兒的山水也可以。 那山峯[12]的尖兒是個個不同，山峯是高而尖的，山嶺也高，就是沒那尖[13]兒那個字眼兒甚麼刀尖筆尖尖尖都說得。 京城[14]裏沒有河水，喝的都是井水。 京城[15]的買賣大半在大街上開鋪子，衚衕小巷，都是住家兒的。 城外頭[16]沒甚麼住家兒的，就叫野地，連有墳墓的也算。 民人[17]湊到一塊住的，北邊那就叫屯。

散語四十章之三十一

1. 男
2. 爺
3. 娘
4. 幼輩
5. 頑耍
6. 蠢笨
7. 獸冒
8. 爽靜
9. 舒服
10.
11.
12.
13.
14.
15.
16.
17.
18.
19.
20.
21.
22. 艱難耐羞辱討嫌

男[1]女男人女人爺們娘兒們老爺老幼老少長輩晚輩。頑耍頑意兒耍刀。[3]獸[4]子蠢笨冒失。爽[5]快拉絲安靜熱閙。舒服欠安。艱難耐著。羞辱討人嫌。男[10]女就是爺們娘兒們賊把男女老少都殺了。是不分年高年輕的都不舒服。和祖父一輩兒的是長輩和兒孫一輩兒他[11]一家子老幼都病了的是晚輩。頑耍[13]是小人兒們弄甚麼頑意兒耍刀就是掄著刀耍是武本裏的事情。蠢笨是粗而無能的別名獸子是外面不明白的樣子某人獸得[14]很實在蠢笨都可以說得。不[15]該說的話說了不該做的事做了就是冒失。人[17]心安靜是說人心裏平定。他是個安靜人不愛熱閙。心[18]裏沒累是舒服身上欠安也謂之不舒服。日[19]子不好過是艱難總得耐著。自[20]已不體面討人嫌受了人的不好話,謂之羞辱他吞了錢受大家羞辱。

散語四十章之三十二

1. 皇宮朝廷建臨強良禁舞為匪反犯罪死黨爭鬬號靖恩赦免隨

1. 皇上朝廷。
2. 建立。
3. 皇宮。
4. 臨民臨走臨死。
5. 鼓舞。
6. 良民強暴。
7. 禁止禁地。
8. 反了為匪。賊匪死黨爭鬬。
9. 號令。
10. 地方不靖犯罪。
11. 恩典赦罪寬免難免。

皇上朝廷都說得是主子家。朝廷隨地酌情建立地方官，為臨民的官，臨[14]走是快要走的時候，臨死是就要死。有事情民人出了力，地方官賞給銀錢，臨[15]頭裏大為不靖，每有強暴兩下裏爭鬬難為良民，那官不管末了兒良民也反了。近來的官很好，把從前的事情都反過來，把那賊匪全都平了。賊匪湊[18]頭裏都算禁地，向例禁止民人不准出入。這地方[17]那是鼓舞的意思。 皇宮裏頭都算禁地，向例禁止民人不准出入。這地方[17]的多，為黨為股和賊頭兒最親近的是死黨。號令[19]是帶兵的官出的口號法令，兵不聽號令，就是犯了大罪。赦罪[20]是人犯了罪，皇上隨事酌情寬免了，那都是皇上的恩典，受恩赦罪之後，再有為匪的那實在難免死罪。

散語四十章之三十三

1. 古世
2. 孔聖
3. 儒佛
4. 廟座
5. 僧俗
6. 尙傳
7. 經楷
8. 率更
9. 濃貼
10. 牆層
11. 掛畫
12. 唱曲
13. 抽
14. 裱
15. 幾
16. 道
17. 儒
18. 和
19. 告示
20. 楷書行書草字草率墨濃
21. 早已過的時候兒是往古
22. 古來
23.
24.
25.

¹古來往古後世。²孔子聖人,聖教儒教佛爺教老子道教。³幾座廟,僧家道士念經。⁴俗家俗說俗話。⁵和尙。⁶告示。⁷楷書行書草字草率墨濃。⁸裱幾層貼在牆上掛著畫兒。⁹抽空兒唱曲。¹⁰早已過的時候兒是往古。古來¹¹有個聖人姓孔他的敎後世謂之聖敎爲中國最尊的同時還有老子的敎謂之道敎佛敎是西方僧家傳來的尊佛爺出家的是僧家俗說叫和尙尊老子出家的是道士聖敎又名儒敎儒敎裏的人叫俗家三敎的總名就是僧道儒。¹²有幾座是道士廟在那兒念經的聲兒是和人唱曲兒一個樣。¹³京城的廟多,有幾座是和尙廟,有幾座是道士廟。¹⁴牆上貼的告示寫得'用楷書那就算草率'那草字更使不得,寫楷書比寫行書墨得'濃。¹⁵我屋裏牆上掛的那一張古字今兒擎新紙裱上一層。¹⁶老弟畫得這麽好怎麽不裱上掛在屋裏呢。

散語四十章之三十四

倉庫宗考如若雜另派盼望列衆涯依戀跨捨礙彼此處偏或

1. 倉庫。
2. 米倉。
3. 銀庫。
4. 國計民生。
5. 大宗兒。
6. 如若。
7. 考察。
8. 雜亂。
9. 另派。
10. 別人。
11. 彼此處。
12. 散了。
13. 海角天涯。
14. 依戀。
15. 跨著。
16. 倉庫是米。
17. 米石銀兩是國計的大宗兒。
18. 海角天涯。
19. 出門往遠處去。
20. 人跨馬是偏在馬一旁坐著車外頭跨著是一條腿空著坐在車外邊兒。

倉[1]庫、米倉、銀庫。國[2]計民生大宗兒。如[3]若考察[4]雜亂[5]另派[6]別人彼[7]此衆人盼[8]望列位散了。此[10]處海[11]角天涯依戀[12]跨著[13]倉庫是米[14]石銀兩是國計的大宗兒米銀不足實在礙於國計民生。這[16]一件事辦得雜亂無章聽見說要另派別人不是要派是已經派過了又說派來的那一位爵位大些兒百姓盼望他來好考察衆人甚麼是衆人說的是手下的小官兒那大人考察小官兒的辦事如若雜亂那小官兒難免重辦。列[17]位是你們這些位是尊稱衆人的字眼兒衙門裏列位都散了是衆官都回去了。海[18]角天涯是說彼此相離的過遠的話頭兒。出[19]門往遠處去。臨走的時候兒難免依戀那依戀是捨不得的意思或親戚或朋友或本家都說得。人[20]跨馬是偏在馬一旁坐著車外頭跨著是一條腿空著坐在車外邊兒。

散語四十章之三十五

1. 揝
2. 灑
3. 洒
4. 掃
5. 帚
6. 砌
7. 碎
8. 狗
9. 欻
10. 修
11. 表
12. 圓
13. 扁
14. 剖
15. 寃
16. 枉
17. 迸
18. 跳
19. 造
20. 報
21. 彷
22. 彿
23. 管

揝¹ 著揝做。揝造揝報，彷彿。

水灑²了。掃地一把條帚。砌牆打碎³。一條

狗⁷ 欻一聲迸跳過去。修理⁸ 時辰表，鐘表。圓¹⁰ 的，扁¹¹ 的。剖開，分剖⁶。那

寃¹² 枉。他手裏揝著管筆，彷彿要寫甚麼。那瓦盆兒是盆兒匠做的。那¹⁵

賊揝造告示，做爲官出的。他帶著貨物揝報是行李叫卡倫察出，全收入官。擎¹⁸ 條帚來，把地掃乾淨

洒¹⁷ 字和灑字是一個字水在地下散開了，是水灑了。

了。要砌牆先得打碎。那一條狗害怕，欻一聲跳過牆去見了他的主人滿

地跳進。那²⁰ 個人打牆上進下來。我這個時辰表有點兒毛病，得找個鐘表

匠修理。若論²³ 圓扁的不同，那西瓜就是圓的，那一本書就是扁的，那個錢是

又圓又扁²¹ 的。我²⁴ 沒犯法人告我是賊，那不是我的寃枉麼，有人替我說明白

了，那就是他給我分剖了。剖²⁵ 開是用刀子破開單說西瓜不說別的。

PART III. THE FORTY EXERCISES. San Yü Chang. 35-36.

散語四十章之三十六

1. 歲
2. 紀
3. 壽
4. 因
5. 為
6. 緣
7. 故
8. 耽
9. 擱
10. 容
11. 易
12. 便
13. 勁
14. 塗
15. 喜
16. 歡
17. 惜
18. 欺
19. 哄
20. 誆
21. 騙
22. 屜

歲數兒年紀高壽。[1]因為緣故。[2]耽悞耽擱。[3]容易費事。[4]方便便宜。[5]變情。[6]對勁兒。使勁兒。[7]糊塗。[8]喜歡愛惜可惜。[9]欺哄誆騙。[10]抽屜。[11]我是年輕的他是有年紀的他多大歲數兒他有六十多歲了。[12]您高壽我今年四十五歲。[13]那一件事耽悞了是因為甚麼緣故太多不容易說。[14]這個辦法容易那個費事得很。[15]可惜那個人過於糊塗說不明白耽擱了我幾兩銀子誆騙這兩個字我懂得他欺哄人是怎麼著呢比方那一天他知道某人和他父親有交情他揑造一個字兒算是他父親要借皮袄子後來他給賣了。[16]屯裏有好些個不便宜我喜歡在京裏住。[17]我們倆彼此很對勁可惜他那個兄弟很會欺哄人去年還誆騙了我幾兩銀子誆騙這兩個字我懂得他欺哄人是怎麼著呢。[18]抽是使勁兒拉出來抽屜是桌子裏櫃子裏拉得出來的屜子。[19]把抽屜關上。[20]

散語四十章之三十七

1. 常
2. 屢
3. 公私
4. 務
5. 閒空
6. 悶慌
7. 樂
8. 煩急
9. 奉求
10. 託
11. 發信
12. 雇
13. 孩
14. 撒謊
15. 賺
16. 星所
17. 雖
18.
19.
20.
21.
22.
23.
24.
25.

平常[1]屢次。公私[2]公道。事務[3]家務。閒空兒[4]。煩悶悶得慌。奉求奉託[5][6]。您[7]打發送信。屯裏[8]。雇人[9]。孩子[10]。撒謊賺錢[11]。所以雖然[12]。那流星也[13]

是常有的、我屢次的看見過。說某事是平常多有、是說他常見的意思。公[14]事原是官事、大衆的事、也謂之公事、就是家務都可以分得公私事情、不分公私、總得按著公道辦。他在家裏閒坐悶得慌、我心裏有些煩悶。您[15]的公事雖然煩雜、心裏還樂、我有一件要事、實在累得慌、奉求您替我打算。昨兒[16]我那相好的因爲小孩子病、心裏煩悶、急要發信到屯裏、問一間託我替他雇一個人送信、我雇了一個人打發他去了、到後半天他回來說、沒有找著、我知道他是撒謊、所以不肯給錢。小價錢[17]買來的、大價錢賣、那就是賺錢、那貨是一兩銀子一斤買的、還是一兩銀子賣的、所以不能賺錢。

散語四十章之三十八

1. 承差任署習部堂司委員吏役皁隸供稟帖存稿陳案照式
2. 差使。
3. 實任,署理,署任,本任,幫辦,學習。
4. 六部堂官。平行,上司,司官,委員,書吏,書手,書班,供事,皁隸,衙役。
5. 稟帖,稟報,知會,存稿,稿底子,陳案,文書,來文,去文,照會,家信。
6. 式樣,承辦。官事不論大小都叫差使。
7. 本任的官,或是公出,或是撤任,有官替他辦事,那就是署任,和實任不同,所出的缺不大上司每派委員署理。
8. 六部的上司,都稱堂官,堂官之下,就是司官,新到衙門候補的司官為學習行走。文書所論的是公事,家信論的是私事,從下往上告報事件當用稟帖,行文的式樣不同,中外各國有事情得知會,平行的官來往用照會。
9. 京城的衙門辦稿底子不是司官辦,就是書班辦,這宗官人也叫書吏,書手,供事,是有頂子的,書班還是相同的差使。文書發了,把存稿存著,那叫陳案。
10. 衙門裏使喚的承辦零碎差使的人,總名叫衙役皁隸。

散語四十章之三十九

1. 脾性禍福命運志益活動聰願功齣辜貧抱怨寒悔善惡其餘靈
2. 性
3. 禍
4. 福
5. 命
6. 運
7. 志
8. 益
9. 活
10. 動
11. 聰
12. 願
13. 功
14. 齣
15. 辜
16. 貧
17. 抱
18. 怨
19. 寒
20. 悔
21. 善
22. 惡
23. 其
24. 餘
25. 靈

脾氣[1]、志氣、性情、性急、好性兒。

禍福[2]、命運、運氣、天命。各處處好處益處。

聰明[4]、活動、死樣。用功[5]力量。願意情願、情願意。喫齣[7]、辜貧[8]、抱怨、後悔，你性[13]

寒心。善惡[10]。其餘[11]。他脾氣好不好他性急得很，也不是不好性兒。

情愛抱怨日後難免後悔。他[12]那一件事情成了，是他的命運不關[14]

運氣都是他有志氣肯用功的好歹，也是天按着善惡的功過命定了的禍福。善人惡人處處都有，他們的好處苦[16]

處各有不等說是運氣的好歹，也是天命所定。那姓李[17]的叫他那寒心是姓李的辜貧他[16]

活的壽數長短都是天命所定。如今姓李的後悔願意相幫，他倒情願

的好處騙他的銀錢令他很喫了齣，

意喫齣不用姓李的力量。在那些人裏分其善惡內有三個是善其餘全是

惡人。聰明[19]是心裏有靈動，是蠢笨的對面活動是死樣的對面。

1. 緊
2. 預備
3. 通共
4. 合式
5. 合算除了下剩盈餘。像似不像，
6.
7.
8.
9.
10.
11.
12.
13.
14.
15.
16.
17.
18.

散語四十章之四十

著, 着
準
勢

1. 要緊緊急。預備。通共。合式。合算除了下剩盈餘。像似不像，
7. 平擱橫竪。傷心着急。馬棚。你天天兒不來，都不要緊，有緊急的事去
叫你去。你預備的那車輛都很合式。可惜他蓋的那房子不像房子的式
樣實在像馬棚兒似的住著很不合式。那房子通共多少間通共有百餘間
除了人住的下餘還有四五十間。我合算起來有一萬兩銀子的賬除了還
人之外下剩還有一二千兩銀子的盈餘。我月月兒進的錢總不敷沒有盈
餘反倒剩下些個賬目不能還過這個日子實在傷我的心彷彿天天兒着急
沒有法子。有個人放槍把他那小孩子打傷了很重。門旁邊兒的木頭是
竪的門上下的木頭是橫的。在地下平擱的東西，說橫說竪那都是隨勢酌
情的活動話。如若在面前直著的爲竪在旁面的人就以爲是橫。

END OF PART III.

THE FORTY EXERCISES.

(CHINESE TEXT.)

TZŬ ERH CHI.

COLLOQUIAL SERIES.

PART IV.

THE TEN DIALOGUES.

(CHINESE TEXT.)

一步一步的長進、那工夫不間斷、自然一個月比一個月的見強。那是必然⁷⁵的、彷彿簷溜還可以穿石呢。不錯、是因為這個、我所以把這些個淺近的給⁷⁶先生看、也不怕貽笑大方。那⁷⁷兒的話呢、登高自卑行遠自邇彼此兩國的人、互相受教、都無非是由淺以及深的這個理阿。

的叫甚麼呢。那[62]清文指要、先生看見過沒有。彷[63]彿是看見過那是清漢合璧的幾卷話倐子那部書、是不、是。是[64]那部書。那[65]一部書却老些兒漢文裏有好些個不順當的。先生說得是、因為這個我早已請過先生從新刪改了、[66]斟酌了不止一次都按着現時的說法兒改好的改名叫談論篇。這[67]就很好了、纔剛說不是還有一本正在辦着那也是本着我們這兒的成書作的麼。還[69]是談論篇的樣子、不[68]是那麼着是我和我的先生這幾個月裏零碎做的。是散話章的樣子。兩[70]樣兒都不是這一本書不是專爲我們的學生可以學貴國話就與中國人要學我們的也有點兒益處。是[71]字彙字典的樣子麼。也[72]不然貴國除了清文啟蒙之外怕沒有這樣兒的書就是清文啟蒙那個相似的地方兒也有些個得細細兒分的。依[73]您這麼說這一部書所論的想來是我們這兒說話的神氣層次句法呀。有[74]些微點兒那麼着别的不别的先把這些書做成了底下還可以有别的要續上也不定總是望着學生念了、有

音都算上阿。聲[44]可不在裏頭、竟單說音若是分聲、那有三倍多呢。不是閣[45]下算過我估摸着竟音沒有那麼些個。算得數兒不錯、您看這一篇字、是音全在上頭。這裏頭[47]似乎有幾個是重些兒的。那可不能免[48]的、是有三兩個音却是一個字的、比方那暑字不是僅有一個念法。那不錯[49]的、有諜暑有大暑、其暑字的音不同。所以[50]呢就是定那音目不能不重複的。看這音目裏、[51]都是常用的字。不錯[52]、都是話裏常用的字、弄成那些散話裏、把這些京音都羅織在題目字裏。閣下[53]很講究這音目是何所取義。那[54]是彼此兩國的口音有好些不同的、我把這京音編在散話裏頭、爲得是學生看過這個就可以練習口音不論甚麼音沒有沒閱歷過的。閣下[55]纔說的這散話章有四十章阿。不錯[56]、整是四十章。說[57]的不是先學部首後念這四十章麼。那都不拘[58]、也可以一面學部首一面看這四十章。學生[59]看熟了這四十章、還有甚麼進益的書可以看呢。還有[60]兩樣兒一本是辦妥的、一本是正在辦着。辦妥了[61]

[36] 可自然的、就瞧底下那些幾數零來、各等字、那都是望數目字連絡的、纔成小句兒、做成小句兒之後您看、就連着小句兒編成話條子、先生瞧明白了沒有。[87] 這我都明白了、就是有一件事學生不認得漢字、那兒可以知道是甚麼音、怎麼講呢。[88] 等我們刷印出書來、半篇是漢話、半篇是英話、凡是那個題目字、應該甚麼音的、都相對記出來、其餘的解法、都按着分段的次序、繙譯明白。[89] 用貴國的字記我們的口音、是按着我們的反切的理麼。[40] 我們那反切的理、有不大相同的地方兒、比貴國那反切的理細些兒、中國反切不過上下兩音湊到一塊兒、也不能很合我們那二十多個音母、不算是字單寫出來、並沒實義、不過是用他定音有四五個音母、成中國一個字音的、雖然不能個個恰對、還比貴國反切較近一點兒、那京話字音的定數兒、先生知道不知道。[41] 這一件事、我們的人沒有算過的、因爲沒有甚麼用處。[42] 那是不錯的、貴國人算那個、實在沒有甚麼益處、我却都算過、共總有四百一十多音。[43] 那是連聲帶

熟的時候兒隨時看了，可以提補他們的意思。阿閣[21]下這宗教導實在周密得很，貴國的人得這個開手的門路算計着得多少天可以記得部首也[22]看人的記性，若是聰明人半個月就可以會了，就是笨的，有一個月的工夫也沒有不行的。半個月能記得怕少罷，就是這個部首熟了之後請問還怎麼樣呢。部[24]首熟了之後，有先生幫我作的四十張散話兒。這[25]是我都聽見說過得是按着類分出字來，是不是。那[26]說按着類的理還有一點兒也不能全是按着類。怎麼[27]呢。我[28]當初的主意，是把數目你我房屋傢伙動作等類的字各歸一張，試了一試不行。有[29]甚麼不行呢。那些[30]類裏頭，竟用本類的字不能成話，總得把外字湊上纔行。這兒[31]有這頭一章請細細兒的看一看頭一行是題目凡是數目的字都在這兒。那[33]可不發罷，一、二、八、十、這些字在那兒呢。那[34]都是部首的字，學生已經看熟了，這四十章的題目裏頭不用再提。我[35]這就明白了，連部首算足了。

個字專作部首的書上也不見話裏也不說這算第三層分這三層的道理先生懂得不懂得。那都懂得。就是定過這三層之後就把那話裏頭可用的部首作成一章字眼兒教學生學習是一面學幾句話一面認得那些部首先生想好不好。[13] 好是很好一舉兩得但是二三兩層還有甚麼好學法兒閣下可以提一提。[14] 我正在要說這二三兩層通共七十八個部首既是話裏用不着怎麽能做成話裏的字眼兒呢只好選擇這些部首裏所屬的字有話裏常用的又做成一章字眼兒也有一面學話一面學部首的益處不知道先生明白這個立意不明白。[15,16] 我雖明白却不十分了然閣下手底下有這兩章可以給我看一看。[17] 就是這兩章您請看。[18] 阿是這麽着頭一章是專用頭一層部首的字連成字眼兒這二章裏頭頭一層部首的字還有那不是部首的字就是擇其歸爲二三層部首的做個榜樣這個主意很妙。[19] 那兒的話呢可是這兩章是叫人學習了還有一章是把所有的部首按義分類是爲學生學得快[20]

見⁴不錯是昨兒定規的我的敝友請先生教話您想出甚麼教的頭緒來沒
有。我們人學滿洲話有一樣兒話條子不知道貴國有這宗樣兒入手的書
沒有。⁵
話條子是有阿但是竟有英文的學生們那兒可以知道繙甚麼漢話
呢若說到漢文他們不認得字怎麼能解那個意思。⁶ 那是不錯的總得要英
漢合璧的字典察一察。察一察是必得的還是先明白部首是不是。我們
人向來沒有專學部首的理。⁷ 那是貴國的人念書的時候兒都認得的是整⁸
字不用分其原歸那一個部首細算筆畫兒這麼個累贅。閣下說得就是我⁹
們人有不認得的字也得按着部首察雖然沒有專學的那却不大很難部首
的字通共也不過二百多個不用很大費事就可以熟習。所以是我昨兒提¹⁰
的有個學話的法子是這麼着我早已把部首的字分作三層頭一層是比方¹¹
人口牛馬這宗字有一百三十六都是話裏常用的那歸一項第二層是比¹²
日犬白邑這宗字有三十個是書上有話裏所不說的另歸一項其餘四十八

解說講過一年多就自己看註子後來作了二年多的文章纔進學。阿[40]十六歲中秀才也就算早阿、是先生的天分高。那兒的話呢、那也是徼倖、後來鄉試下了多少場七八年纔中了舉人。先生[42]今年貴庚。我[43]今年三十歲。先[44]生中舉人之後這六年裏頭有甚麽公幹。沒有[45]甚麽事情前二年在家裏教書後幾年、在外頭作幕幫朋友。請問[46]令友榮任是甚麽官。是[47]山東的知縣他去年不在了、我纔回來的。先生作[48]過幕那更好了。怎麽[49]更好呢。好處[50]是這麽懞我那朋友學話之後還要學文書。可惜[51]就是這個教話沒頭緒。那[52]我倒有一個法子今兒個忙些沒空兒細說請先生明兒過來咱們再商量可以不可以。可以[53]沒有甚麽不可以的我就遵命了、明兒個幾點鐘見。明[54]兒咱們申初見罷。那[55]麽我失陪了。您請[56]。請[57]。

問答十章之十

昨[1]兒來的那蘇先生來了。請[2]進來、阿先生來了。是[3]、偺們昨兒定規的、今兒

能說些兒那看書再說。他[21]一字不懂、我從那兒教起。先生[22]是老手了、在貴國教過多少門生怎麼不能教他。我們的教學那是另有一說說話是不學而會的、至於念書、是由從小兒背念熟了的、恐怕令友不能照着我們這兒的小孩子那麼費事罷。那[24]是自然的、也可以商量一個法子、先生從多大念書。我[25]從七歲念起。先生[26]一念是先念三字經千字文麼。不[27]錯先念的是那個。貴國[28]都先念這兩個小書兒、實在有甚麼益處兒呢。三[29]字經是三個字一句、爲得是小孩子容易念、那千字文因爲沒有重字、小孩子念了、就可以認得一千字。念[30]了這個之後念甚麼呢。常[31]念的都是先念四書、後來念五經。您[32]從念四書起、到念完五經、有幾年的工夫兒。兩[33]頭兒算起來、有六七年的工夫。阿[34]那五經念完了、就是先生十四歲那一年。不[35]錯、還沒到十四歲呢。先生[36]從多大歲數兒上開講。我[37]從十二歲上纔開講。開講[38]的時候兒還是自己看註子還是聽先生的解說。我[39]一開講的時候兒、是聽先生的

問答十章之九

有先生來，要見老爺。[1]

請進來。[2] 進來了。[3] 先生請坐。[4] 請坐。[5] 先生貴姓。[6]

賤姓蘇。[7] 先生到這兒來貴幹。[8] 昨兒聽見一個相好的提說閣下要請先生。

阿必是那張先生說的。[10] 不錯，是張先生說的。[11] 張先生他告訴您是我要

我先生是我替人找先生。[13] 他沒告訴我詳細可不是閣下要請麼。不是我

要請，是一個相好的託我請。令友還是貴國的人麼。[16] 是本國的人到貴處

日子不多。[17] 旣是新來的，我們的話恐怕不懂罷。不錯，漢話一句都不懂，漢[18]

字一個也不認得。這麼着，我怎麼能教給他書呢。[19] 先生先得教他說話，話[20]

很好，又老實，又快來往進京有三四囘。那麼我可以到行裏商量商量，還有[84]

那些大箱子，運到通州的時候，僱甚麼人送進京去。老爺就可以僱小的[85]

好不好。好倒沒甚麼不好的，只怕是這麼些日子，你們行裏離不開你不容[86]

你去。可以離得開今兒打發我來，不是聽老爺的吩咐來了麼。[87]

樣呢。老爺[65]的行李有多少。就是門外頭擱着的那些東西。甚麼[67]那些大箱子也是老爺的麼。原[68]是。老爺想兩天進京恐怕不能都帶罷不但用好些個大車費錢還不能很快。那麼[70]你說還有甚麼好法子。依[71]我說老爺那個鋪蓋等項可以雇一個小車兒裝上同老爺一塊兒走。其餘上船打通州那們走。按[72]照那麼着我就坐裝行李的那輛車麼。老爺[73]再另雇一輛小車兒坐好罷。那車[74]是單套是二套。老爺[75]要快必得二套的現在的雨水大道兒不好走三套的也可以。哎[76]道兒不好走坐車不大對我的勁兒在這兒雇馬行不行。騾[77]子馬都可以雇只怕我們的鞍子老爺騎着不合式。我們[78]那兒馬身上的傢伙我都帶着呢。也[79]怕不行那馬鞍子我們的馬還可以背那籠頭卻不肯戴。籠[80]頭是甚麼呢。就[81]是牲口嘴裏的嚼子人拉的扯手都在裏頭恐怕我們的馬戴不慣與老爺有礙不如買匹外國馬倒好。外[82]國馬在天津這兒那兒可以買。可[83]以我們行裏有匹馬是我們行中夥計的要賣那馬

有是店東做掌櫃的，有是店東外請別人，替他照應買賣，做掌櫃的。就是這[54]個房錢可以望我要多少錢。那倒難說，老爺會說我們的話，可以先望他商量，看他要的價兒若很多，不妨駁他，再還他價兒。那[55]都行了，就是第二天進京還得打那麼走。[56] 早起離了河西務還是往西北去，有二十多里是到安平，還有二十多里是馬頭，從馬頭還算有二十里地，到張家灣那個老城。[57] 張家灣不是先有個小河兒麼。不是，那城是南北下裏騎着河面的老爺進[58]了南門，順着大街過了河，就出北門，那北門外頭有兩股岔道兒，往北的是上通州去，往西偏着點兒的，那就是進京的了。[59] 那離京還有多遠呢。看老爺[60]進那個門，若是城外店裏住，進沙窩門兒還算有五十多里路，若是到城裏頭，[61]走東便門，那是往北點兒多個二三里地也不算很遠。上[62]外國的公館，是進那門好。那[63]外國公館，都是在海岱門裏頭，御河橋一帶，在我說是進東便門方便些兒。很好[64]，如今我明白了。還有一件事，我走得這麼快，我的行李怎麼

一個順來、兩個都是大店、一個在街南頭兒、一個在街北頭兒。這兩個是那[36]個方便呢。若論房子吃食、都差不多南頭兒方便、北頭兒方便、那是隨老爺的意。南[38]的北的有甚麼不同相離得很遠麼。離得却不甚遠、河西務沒有這兒府[40]城那麼大地方不過是個鎮店、一條長街兩邊兒有些個鋪子甚麼的。這麼說起來、南的北的有甚麼不一樣的。沒[41]有甚麼不一樣的、是我向來在南頭兒住打京裏來的、在北頭兒住是不是。不[43]錯、老爺明白。就[44]是了、我給老爺們帶道、總是一進街就住下的時候兒多。你說[42]的那是打天津來的、到了店裏頭、叫他們弄甚麼茶好呢。老爺[45]怕沒吃過我們的茶罷。沒[46]吃過呢。阿[47]老爺還沒吃過、不如從天津做一點兒好拿的茶帶着。甚[48]麼自己帶着、到了店裏不吃他們的飯、他們願意麼。那[49]倒沒甚麼店裏還得他們的房錢。這房錢有一定的價兒麼。我[51]們人住店、差不多有一定的價兒、若是外國客人、怕那掌櫃的可以多要幾個錢。那[52]掌櫃的就是店東麼。那[53]都不定、

車馬沒甚麼那都可以攔過去。往後[19]怎麼着呢。往後[20]是這麼着離了攔渡口兒還是往大道走到離天津三十多里的那個鎮叫浦口就是頭一段兒那兒呢[22]頭一段兒不是河西務麼。河西務[23]遠多了那算是一天的道兒過了浦口之後先到楊村後到南蔡村挨晚兒的時候兒可以到河西務這些地方兒相隔大約都是三十多里地。按[24]道兒說這河西務離京還有多遠。按[25]道兒說可以算得是中間兒在那兒住一夜明兒個可以進了京。住[26]一夜是在那兒呢。貫[27]國的人向來有住店的有住廟的是[28]店裏好是廟裏好。依[29]我說是店裏方便些兒廟裏留客是格外的事情一來不定有房子沒有二來如果趕車的多和尚不願意再者丟了東西為誰是問。阿[30]店裏丟東西是店主人應管麼。原[31]是那麼着還有一說吃的喝的店裏都可以預備廟裏連廚房都沒有。沒[32]廚房廟在那兒弄飯呢。他[33]們弄的都是素菜葷的他們不能弄。阿[34]那麼不如店裏好河西務那兒還是那個店好。那[35]兒有一個富典

問答十章之八

他親自還來呢。

請[1]老爺安。好阿[2]你是甚麼人,我是英順行打發來給老爺帶路進京的,老爺定規多喒走。明兒[4]就要走。老爺[5]要走的是水路,是旱路。是[6]旱路好,是水路好。水路呢,這幾天雨大河水長了,上水的船拉着費事,再遇着北風怕爺[7]明兒動身趁着走第二天就可以到京慢着點兒第三天足可以。這[10]旱路你熟罷。哎[11]這十幾年常來往,怎麼是不熟呢。比方[12]我不用人帶道細細兒告訴我都是打那麼走,行不行。可以[13]沒甚麼不行的,老爺出了城東邊兒那個浮橋知道不知道。那個[14]知道。您[15]過了這一道橋,到熱鬧街兒那兒,再打聽第二道橋,過了第二道橋,往西北,就是進京的大道。聽見[16]說還有過河的地方,有沒有。那[17]是攔渡罷、攔渡是有。攔渡[18]是有,那車馬怎麼樣呢。

孩子麼。不[78]錯是個七八歲的小孩子。必[79]是我那小孫子、嗳、那早晚兒那兒去。老[80]爺放心有點兒事情。有[81]點兒甚麼事情呢、車驚了麼。不[82]是本來道兒不好走。那麼是車翻了麼。也[84]不然、是和對頭兒車碰了。碰[85]了老沒說開麼怎麼那早晚還在那兒。沒[86]有甚麼很利害、他從車上跳下來的時候兒把腿扭了一下兒。倒不是沒說開。就[87]是小孫子受了傷了却[88]不好。可[89]惡知道那個車是誰的不知道。就[90]是那個張爺他姪兒的。還[91]是他呀那麼送畫兒是甚麼意思呢。畫[92]兒是給你納令孫的。特[93]意兒買畫兒壓驚、是甚麼意思、是作甚麼呢。這[94]畫兒是先買的、不是特意買的。原[96]是剛纔從我們那兒買的。是[97]小孫子跟他要來着麼。不[98]是、令孫哭了。他說你別哭、我送你點兒玩意兒。就[99]是這個畫兒算玩意兒、爲甚麼不送到小兒那兒去呢。那[100]張大爺的姪兒、今兒早起到我們鋪子裏來打聽令郎的住處、我們說知道你納不知道他、他叫我們把畫兒送到府上、就是了、過兩天

多喒囬來了。甚麼⁵⁰囬來呢、他出外來着麼。他⁵¹從前不是跟官出去麼。那⁵²個我不知道是那年出去的。我⁵³記得是前年往江西去了。前年出去的、我⁵⁴從去年還見他在城裏頭。那⁵⁵都不論他給我送畫兒、是作甚麼。本⁵⁶不是給你納買的。不是給我買的、你拿來作甚麼、我萬不肯買。說甚麼買呀、錢是他給過了。你⁵⁹這個來囬的話我始終不明白。等我再告訴你幾句話。就⁶¹快說別儘自耽悞工夫兒。你⁶²納的少爺、不是在戶部有差使麼。你⁶³這個人竟是打聽小兒原是在戶部。他⁶⁴不是單住麼。他⁶⁵這會兒單搬出去了。請⁶⁶問他住在甚麼地方兒。他⁶⁷在交民巷西頭路北裏。他⁶⁸是在交民巷住麼。眞⁶⁹是、你疑惑作甚麼。我⁷⁰估摸是城外頭住的。離衙門那們遠不行、你怎麼⁷¹估摸着是城外頭呢。昨⁷²日頭落、碰見他的車在琉璃廠。那⁷³有這個話、他車⁷⁴是他的、他却沒在車上。他⁷⁵沒在車上、你怎麼知道車是他的。車⁷⁶上坐着個老婆子他說是孟大爺的車。老⁷⁷婆子抱着個昨兒晚上在我這兒來着。

不[14]是送書來了。怎[15]麼手裏拿的不是書麼。不[16]是書竟是個書套。沒[17]有書、竟送個空書套作甚麼。這[18]書套不是空的、還裝着甚麼。裝[19]着是幾張畫兒。畫兒[20]怕不是送這兒來的罷。沒[21]錯、是給這兒送來的。為[22]甚麼、我沒有買了畫兒。我[23]知道不是你納買。給[24]我買畫兒是甚麼意思。買[25]的意思你納倒有[26]別人給你納這兒來。那[27]麼為甚麼給我送了來。不[28]用打聽。到[29]底是誰給買的。那[30]堂子胡同住的張爺、你納認識不認識。張[31]爺我認識、就是他買的麼。還[32]不是他。不[33]是他、提他作甚麼。我提他有原[34]故。有原故為甚麼不說呢。你[35]納太急、囘來就明白了。你[36]這是要戲我的話、我不服。那[37]兒敢要戲你納。有[38]正經話為甚麼不說。提[39]起來話還長的話、我不服。那[40]兒敢要戲你納。就[41]是你不能說、我進去了、你去罷。噯[42]、別忙、別忙、還有話說。有[43]話就快說。他[44]那姪兒、你納認說是認得。那[45]我先告訴你了。他[46]那姪兒你納認得不認得。見[47]過一次不很熟悉。叫[48]送這個畫兒就是他。他[49]叫送來的、他我沒空兒。

話是告訴他我出了城了。他[46]若是問大人多咱回來。你[47]就說不知道多咱回來。若[48]是這麼着他若是天天兒來打聽呢。憑[49]他來多少回總不許叫他進來。我[50]想不如簡直告訴他,若打算甚麼事你轉託別人不用倚靠大人好不好。那[51]却不行,若是簡直告訴他不肯相幫,必得把所以然的話細說明白了,那更不必了。哼[52]院子裏說話,不是徐永的聲兒麼。麼[53]若是他,隨你用甚麼話推辭我是決計不見他了。我[54]是說着玩兒呢,來的是刻字匠要錢來了。叫[55]他月底再來罷。他[56]先來過兩回了。不[57]錯是有的,我應許了還錢得給。大[58]人不必費事了,我替您開發了罷。

問答十章之七

是[1]你叫門麼。是[2]我叫門。你[3]是那兒的。我[4]是城外頭來的。你[5]找誰。找[6]姓孟的。我[7]就姓孟。阿[8]你納就是孟爺。不[9]錯我姓孟,找我作甚麼。廣[10]文齋打發我來的。廣[11]文齋不是書鋪麼。不[12]錯是書鋪。叫[13]你送甚麼書來麼。

沒考過就保舉了。是個甚麼差使、是個貼寫的事情沒有一個月、就不要他了。不要[30]他、是因爲他行止不好、是因爲他沒本事。兩樣兒都不好、楷書[31]那[32]個人奇怪呀、沒有錢穿的怎麼那麼體面呢。體面[33]是甚麼體面呢、那天穿的那褂子也不怎麼樣。怎麼[34]不怎麼樣、也算是值錢的、他騎的那騾子也是很好的。我估摸[35]他是坐車來的。不是[36]坐車騎着騾子來的、那騾子十分臕壯。旣然[37]是這麼着、你旣知道他這麼靠不住、又好花錢徇庇着他、是個甚麼道理。比方[38]有人從前很享福、如今沒了路兒了、我見了他心裏怎麼能不憐恤。噯[39]怎麼憐恤他是憑你竟是有一句話可不用託我給他找甚麼事情。可惜[40]了兒的、眼看着他這個人是要要飯的。等[41]他要飯的時候兒、給他頓飯吃可以叫我保他做甚麼、我萬也不能。按[42]那天定的約他後兒來。後兒[43]他來了、你可以把我起先說的那話告訴他。告訴[44]他、大人一定不肯幫他。不是[45]那個

前一年捐的。是捐過阿、然而海賊那一案、怎麼會干涉着他的功名呢、難道他與海賊通了麼。却[14]不因為海賊、是因為走私。怎麼那個走私是叫官場中察着了。哎[15]你想一想那官役勒索的錢多、官塲中也不察照他們、有這個理麼。勒索[16]了不過三百兩銀子、也不算很多。你[17]說是不多這數兒也是應當和他們同事的、那巡船上的人、不但沒按着分兒分給同事的、他們自己留的、也是彼此相爭。大家為錢爭鬧、後來有個報了官的、是不是。就[18]是了、官既知道這件事、細究個水落石出、把老徐從重的罰了、還把他的功革[19]了。老徐[20]這個丟臉、也難怪徐永遮掩。遮掩[21]是該遮掩誰叫他張揚來着、也不用編造這些他父親因朋友受累的假話。那[22]寶在過逾虛詐。他說這個話的時候兒、我就有一半不信、我記得那李永成和他父親很熟、我心裏打着、望他打聽打聽這個人。大概[23]那姓李的說他沒有甚麽好話罷。一[24]句好話都沒有、那徐永、他是很認得、那人頭裏求他給找一個事情、他心軟了、依了

不明白。[76]一則是寡不敵衆、二則是他心裏膽虛。 膽虛是應該膽虛、到了兒怎麼樣呢。 那巡哨船早躲開了、徐永他經過那個就長了一個見識、不照前次從豐只給十兩銀子罷了。 他們[79]依不依。 那兒[80]不依呢、他們都喝的半醉了、要搜他的船也不能了、他給的不論怎麼少都可以依的。

問答十章之六

[1]那旁嵗兒的話算結了、他那年辦洋藥是甚麼人託他的、他告訴了你沒有。 [2]我不記得。 他[3]不是說是他父親叫他的麼。 [4]那我實在是不記得。 不論你記得不記得、實在是他父親叫他買的、後來他父親賠本的緣由就是因為這個。 那兒[6]呢、是他打算的不好麼。 打算得不好那一句話也可以說那洋藥出口、是往天津去的。 阿[8]在天津叫人搜出來了。 這麼着老徐的資本全丢了。 那船始終沒到天津走到[9]山東海面上叫海賊把船扣住了、丢了資本連頂戴也丢了。 他[12]原來有個功名麼、那我却不知道。 [13]是他就是

是若不給三百兩、是要全封了。這三百兩他給不給。他[58]沒有這麼些個錢、[59]沒有這麼些個錢、他還有甚麼法子辦呢。他[60]寫了個字兒叫他們跟上洋行裏取錢。奇怪[61]他們也肯要這個字兒噯、他出了這個虎口、是個便宜。還有這不算所出了虎口。怎麼呢、這巡役們要了這個字兒、又有甚麼反悔麼。不[64]是那們檪、他們大家沒商量妥的時候兒柴艇和巡船一塊往下走撞了人家灣着的兩隻船。又[65]是兩隻巡哨船麼。不[66]是關上的船、是欽差劉大人的船、一隻是他下人坐的。可笑[67]還是半夜的時候麼。怕[68]是在城裏頭公館裏底下人們還在船上樂呀唱阿的鬧呢。就是[71]那些個底下人們、到底與海關事情無干。原是[72]竟是徐永那個柴艇撞了、他們先是一驚訝、後來心定了一定兒就望他要賠補的錢。要賠補甚麼呢。賠補他[74]們受驚、賠補官船的損壞、隨便甚麼都算應賠補的。他[75]甘心受他們這個嗎、我

那時都是躉船棧房裏藏的。喫[37]的時候兒還是在外國洋行裏麼。不是[38]徐永常去的是個窰衚衕兒裏頭一個小鋪兒後頭。阿[39]這徐永也常上煙館麼眞是有甚麼老子有甚麼兒子。喫[40]的也不大很利害。阿[41]自己不喫竟是替人辦的罷就是他那個難是甚麼呢。那時煙禁未解他辦得了要出洋還是耽擱好些日子。底下出口還怎麼樣呢。那時[42]煙禁未解他把煙下在裏頭偷着出口。我[45]想上海的柴火都是進口的出口是往那兒去呢。去[46]的地方兒大概不遠那艇裝的實在是柴火少洋藥多。所以[47]出口鬧出事來了。鬧[48]出事來是這麼着那柴火艇順着水放下去抽冷子有巡船來抓住了。抓住[49]了就把這個貨封了。還沒[50]有封這些巡役們說你若不多多兒給我們錢可就要搜你的船了。巡役[51]們跟他要多少錢。他們[52]沒說數兒竟是叫他從豐。這[53]徐永他要給多少。他[54]那人糊塗說要給一百兩。一百兩那寶在從豐[55]了、那巡役們也不覺多。那兒[56]不覺多看柴火艇給一百兩銀子是沒有的說

早[12]去了世麼、他那些個兒女、却誰養活呢。他[13]女兒在他沒去世之前、就都死了、兒子單生了一個、就是這個撒謊的。那[14]怕大人是聽錯了罷。——[15]點也沒聽錯、我細細的考查過了、你不是說和徐家有層親麼。不[16]錯、我說過、這[17]四五年來你都沒見過罷。不[18]止四五年、有九年十年的光景、沒見了。就[19]是了。那[20]一時人就說他狂傲沒有甚麼那老徐在布舖作買賣、他的名聲怎麼樣。他[21]不是很愛吃煙麼。吃煙大是有的、也有點兒貪酒。却[23]原來就是你在上海遇見那徐永、他在那兒作甚麼。他[24]說是人托他辦土貨出洋。這[27]些土貨要運到那甚[25]麼土貨呢、是茶葉是湖絲、有[26]茶葉、有湖絲、有藥材。兒去。他[28]說得是往北往南我不記得。沒[31]提過辦洋藥麼。沒[29]提辦洋貨呀。他[30]巧了提過、我不記得。藥[35]一層、他還些微有點兒難處。辦[32]洋藥原有的、大人提到我纔想起來、那辦洋藥短了罷。短[34]是不短、價錢天天見長、東西還足敎買的、處處兒都是賣的。賣[35]的還是公然賣麼。也[36]不算公然

你的意思是要託我給你我個事情。老大人很這麼疼愛我、我感激的心一言難盡了。就是你今兒個來意、實在是因為這個不是。非是老大人先提起來、我實在不敢開口。很好、等我給你打算打算、請你過了十天前後兒來再說。實在是大人的揋拔、我過幾天再來請安。偺們過兩天見、請。大人請坐。

問答十章之五

龍田、那徐永再來的時候兒、你告訴他我出城去了。噯、可惜、叫他失望、他怎麼得罪了大人了。甚麼得罪呢、他那些個話通身都是假的。怎麼呢、他不是徐福慶的兒子麼。這徐福慶的兒子那却不是。他說他父親賠本不是眞的麼。賠本原是賠本、也不像他說的那麼賠本。不是像他說的那麼賠本、怎麼着呢。他賠本全是他自己糊塗、自己拋費了、沒別的。到底家裏養活的人口多。他養活家口那倒總沒有、不用提別的、那徐福慶早就不在了。

可是欠主兒硼了。　大⁵⁵人、不是那麼樣、我父親保那個朋友、跑⁵⁶了、可惡就是令尊的精神因爲這個受傷是不是　自⁵⁷然是家裏人口多、沒力量養活不免着急。你⁵⁸父親跟前你們幾個。我們弟兄四個還有三個姐妹。這⁶⁰麽多呢、未必都在家裏罷。個⁶¹個兒都在家裏。我⁶²想那姑娘都是出嫁的。本有兩個出了門子、給得都是武官、上同西路出兵都陣亡了。阿⁶⁴他們倆媳婦、就囘家來了。是⁶⁵都囘家來了、一個帶着兩個孩子、一個帶着六個孩子。噯⁶⁶那人口實在的不少、還有一個姑娘沒出門子麼。那⁶⁷倒是歲數還小呢、常愛病。常⁶⁸愛病麽是甚麽病。從⁶⁹我母親死了、他缺䘉、後來不很足壯。這⁷⁰實在可憐。你⁷²還有你們弟兄們量必可以幫着過日子。我却很願意、可惜沒個道路。是長房的不是。我⁷³排二。可⁷⁴是你大哥作甚麼呢。他⁷⁵腿脚有殘疾、甚麽都不能幹。噯⁷⁶這個光景可了不得、還有你的兄弟可怎麼樣呢。我⁷⁷父親賠本的時候兒、他們還小呢、不能栽培他們念書、他們學得還算不深。說⁷⁸來說去、

阿、那徐福慶阿、我還記得來的是他的兒子麼。不[24]錯是他的兒子。讓[25]他進來。老[26]大人讓你哪。大[27]人好。請[28]坐請坐。大[29]人請坐。請[30]坐請坐來。不錯家父名字喳[31]。 沏[32]茶來、貴姓是徐麼。賤[33]姓徐。徐福慶是你父親。徐福慶[34]是徐麼。不[35]是徐福慶。前[36]幾年我們就認識他好阿。托[37]大人的福、打發我來請大人的安[38]。叫他惦記着實勞你的駕。該[39]當的。我[40]糢糢糊糊記得他眼睛不大好、如今好了沒有。年[41]紀這麼大、眼睛還算可以。那[42]兒說到年紀歲數兒和我差不多。家[43]父今年六十九。我[44]七十一、比他大兩歲。看[45]大人這麼康健、怎[46]麼不能呢、他沒有我受的累多。我[47]父親身子能彀這麼樣、那求之不得的。大[48]人是爲國家當重任、辦事受的累多、我老子爲家業、心裏也有他的辛苦。那[48]是從前做買賣時候兒累的、如今是囘家歇着了。囘[49]家是囘家也是無可奈何。怎[50]麼呢、買賣不好麼。也[51]不竟是那們樣。怎[52]麼呢、莫不是銀錢被了窃[53]。 比丢了還可惡、所掙的錢差不多叫人都騙淨了。可[54]惜了兒這麼樣、

車價[121]你可放心罷這個茶館兒裏的事情你望他沒話麼。沒話[122]沒話請老爺給了錢小的回去了。你實在是個忠厚人哪肯擔待人的不是竟是你[123]回村兒裏告訴來順他老子他兩個兒子沒有一點兒誠實這宗樣兒的人我決不要他。

問答十章之四

龍田[1]。大人叫我作甚麼。院子[2]裏那個人是誰。那個人[3]是姓徐的。阿[4]是你認識的麼。是我陳認識[5]的。你們倆是在那兒遇見[6]的。是在上海會過的。是多咱[7]呢。前好些[8]年。你和他很有交情[9]麼。可以[10]我們本是個遠親。阿[11]有層親麼他作甚麼來了你知道不知道[12]。不知道大人要我問他麼。問他也好[13]。他說是來要見大人。來見[14]我作甚麼。他說是他父親打發他來[15]請大人的安。他那父親是作甚麼的[16]呢。從前是作買賣現在是閒住。這人[17]我所不記得是個作甚麼買賣的。西城[18]那個大布鋪大人那兒不記得。

[93]那你不用管我只要我問你甚麼你說甚麼。[94]老爺還問甚麼。[95]這個張來順是馬駒橋人麼。[96]他父親在鎭店外頭開着個菜園子。[97]這麼着這來順必是你素來認得的。[98]他小時候兒在街上玩兒我長看見他。[99]他小時候兒是老實阿是賊猾呢。[100]小的不肯說人短處。[101]不要你偏說短處,他有好處不可以說麼。[102]請老爺補還我的車錢我走了。[103]就是毆打你的是那兒的人呢。[104]是道兒上茶館裏的人。[105]離城有多遠兒。[106]就在沙窩門兒外頭。[107]是來順在那兒喝茶來着麼。[108]不是喝茶是喝酒吃東西。[109]你同他在一塊兒吃麼。[110]沒有我出去拴鞭子去了。[111]鞭子拴好就囘茶館兒了麼。[112]趕我囘來他們先跑了。[113]跑了就是騙你的車價麼。[114]不但車價連茶館兒的飯錢都沒給。[115]阿,他們跑了,茶館兒跑了,茶館兒就是望你要這個錢麼。[116]原是我不肯給,他們打了我。[117]茶館兒打你這層我有甚麼法子。[118]打不打沒甚麼要緊請老爺補還車價,我走了。[119]車價還容易,把他的工錢折給你罷了。[120]老爺可以立刻賞給叫小的囘去。

麼了。我的車錢、他那兒給過麼。是北城來的那個車麼。甚麼個北城、咱們是馬駒橋店裏的。咳、這個尚得詳細你可以小心細說。小的若有一句謊、老爺要了我的腿、都使得。你今兒甚麼時候兒起身。雞叫的時候兒、纔套車。是單套車、是二套車。是二套車、為走得快。車上就是這個來順一個坐兒麼。還有他一個同伴兒。要快是那個的主意。來順僱車來的時候兒、說若快、可以多加幾個錢。你們說明白是多少錢。說定了的是五吊錢。連他要加的錢都在裏頭。是都說在一塊兒、小的不訛人。車價還可以。是因為這個打架麼。總沒有和他打架。你不是纔說的挨了打麼。小的說挨打不是他打的。不是他是誰。有好些個人、小的不認得是誰。都是來順帶了來的伴兒麼。不是一個也沒有來順帶來的。他們是搶奪的麼。也不然曖喲說起來話長。就是話長你也得說了。請老爺補還我的錢、我走了。別忙、這件事、我還得分晰明白。不值得耽誤老爺的工夫。

也可以。阿[30]那不是來順進來了。阿[31]叫他進來、你可以去罷。老爺[32]沒有甚麼別的事使喚小的。沒[33]事、你去罷、來順。小[34]的糊塗請老爺寬恕。寶[35]在是糊塗出去為甚麼不言語。老爺[36]欠安、他們是急於和我要錢。他們[37]是誰要的是甚麼錢。那[38]天替老爺買的桌子鋪子裏要錢。那[39]鋪子不是西城麼。不[40]是鋪子在城外頭。城[41]外麼離那個門近。小[42]的城外的道兒不熟。這[43]鋪子在北邊兒在南邊兒還不知道麼。阿[44]小的想起來、在安定門外。這[45]個裏頭我有點兒不大明白。老爺[46]不明白甚麼。你[47]這個人總得說實話。小[48]的不敢撒謊。阿[49]院子裏甚麼人吵嚷。小[50]的可以出去看一看。不[51]用出去放窗戶罷。唉[52]有個人闖進來、是甚麼事情。你[53]不是趕車的、闖進來做甚麼。作[54]甚麼主呢。噯[55]哎丟了錢挨了打、求老爺伸冤。你[56]的丟錢挨打與我何干。不[57]關老爺却關老爺的底下人。我[58]那個底下人、可是那個來順麼。阿[59]不錯就是他、我頭裏沒理會。他[60]和你怎

問答十章之三

喧²進來問 老爺叫做甚麼。你³是甚麼人。小的叫來福。你姓甚麼。小⁴的姓張。你在這兒做甚麼。小的是替哥哥來替工。你哥哥是誰。小¹⁰的哥哥叫來順。是那個來順¹²。他¹³沒來、怎麼²不等我好呢。家裏¹⁶沒的的哥哥叫來順。阿¹¹、是給我看書房的那個來順麼。因¹⁴為老爺欠安他不便告假。告假、怎麼走了麼。有件很要緊的事。有甚麼要緊的事情。家母病得利害。既¹⁹這麼著、怎麼他走了、你²⁰來。他回去、是家父叫他小的來、是怕耽誤老爺這兒的工夫。請²²老爺寬恕小的哥哥快來了。阿²¹、別的先勿論、底下人出門、到底應當告假。怎²⁵麼不很遠。至多有四里地、還是東城的²⁶地方兒。就²⁷是你這個人可以去罷。小²⁸的哥哥得立刻就來。到²⁹晚晌來

長子為甚麼歸你。從前先父在的時候、家兄就管買賣。伺候令堂。原⁵⁹是因為舍弟也是在外頭作幕。阿⁵⁸、就是你在家裏

麼依着你納的主意、教我怎麼辦呢。那[32]王大人不是你的親戚麼。那[33]是我的本家。更好了、他新近不是放了巡撫了麼。[34]原是放的是河南巡撫、你納[35]還有甚麼高見。我想你若還當差使、那老大人必肯幫你。[36]你是錯了、你不知道、他向來不喜歡我。你不過這們想、甚麼是個對證。他[37]上次出外我求他帶我罷。他怎麼囘答的你。[38]他說的就是天底下沒有人、我也不要你。你不知道、他還有別的話麼。那[39]阿、他說的這麼言重、有甚麼緣故麼。他說的恨我年輕的時候兒不勤儉。唉[44]你放心罷、旣往不咎、老大人那兒還那麼恨你。[45]你不知道、他還有別的話麼。那[46]有總不肯寬宥的話麼。他說過、我無論到甚麼分兒上、再不能照應你。可[48]惜有這個好事、由兒你得不着益處。沒法子、誰叫我底根兒沒出息兒呢。[49]令尊留下的家產、專歸你一個人兒了、是還分給一家了。還有家兄舍弟、一[51]個人分了一分兒。分[52]的還是令兄的多呀。不是、是三個人均分的。留[54]下的是銀錢哪、是產業呀。有[55]現銀子、也有房子買賣。身[56]底下住房、你又不是

問答十章之二

你[1]納騎的不是我們這兒的馬麼。原是在貴處買的[2]。是誰替你買的[3]。店[4]裏那些人替我挑的。他們和你要多少錢[5]。他們要的是三十兩銀子。我看着價錢多一點沒給[6]。你[7]給了沒給呢。我[8]看着價錢多一點沒給。你[9]倒是給了多少銀子。我定規是二十二兩銀子。這[11]匹馬從前是我的。阿[12]你為甚麼賣了。因[13]為家裏沒錢、總賣了。那[14]時候有錢、買得貴。不是因為有毛病阿。一[15]點兒毛病都沒有。你[16]根兒裏多少錢買的。那[17]時候有錢、買得貴。阿[18]你那時候兒是有差使。我[19]頭裏是作衙門、到我們先父去世的時候兒擱下了、同去料理家務。哎呀[20]令尊病的日子久麼。阿[21]病了十來年呢。他[22]納這些年的病、誰照應家裏呢。雖[23]不能出門、還可以管家裏的事。令[24]尊還在世、你的差使還可以當麼。可[25]以當不可以當不定。怎[26]麼不定呢。差[27]使的得項若是多些、我還願意。你[28]從前當着賠墊麼。倒[29]沒那個、總得能多點兒總能寬綽。你[30]別怪我說你擱下的不當。那[31]

問答十章之一

您[1]貴處是那兒。敝處是天津沒領教。我[3]也是直隸人。阿[4]原來是同鄉。他[5]那一位是甚麼人。他[6]是外國人。到[7]這兒來做甚麼。我[8]不知道，你問他自己就知道。請[9]問尊駕到我們這兒做甚麼來得都是甚麼貨。我[10]是個做買賣的。您[11]帶了些甚麼貨。都[12]是東洋的油漆碎貨。是日本國。怎麼呢我聽見說過貴處出入很難。阿[13]您貴國是日本國麼。不[14]錯。我[15]頭裏却難近來解了禁好些兒。我[17]們的商民也有到過那兒的沒有。貴[18]國的商民也有。我[19]們的人怕沒在那兒，是那一省的多。多[20]一半是廣東福建的。他[21]們的買賣大小。怕[22]沒甚麼很大的。為[23]甚麼沒有本錢麼。那[24]個錢大概不很多。他[25]們沒錢往東洋去做甚麼。他[26]們多一半是跟太西國的人去的。太[27]西國帶他們有甚麼益處兒。原[28]是用他們管行作爲經手的。他[29]們和日本國的人，對勁兒不對勁兒。彼[30]此怕都有點兒異心。

PART IV.

THE TEN DIALOGUES.

(CHINESE TEXT.)

TZŬ ERH CHI.

COLLOQUIAL SERIES.

PART V.

THE EIGHTEEN SECTIONS.

(CHINESE TEXT.)

1. 他砍我。
2. 我猜是這們着。
3. 這個是了。
4. 你必定要作死。
5. 這個沒用頭。
6. 那個不對。
7. 誰這麼說的。
8. 你要說破了。
9. 穿小襖兒。
10. 牽了他來。
11. 馬上去
12. 喊孩子們來。
13. 你多嘴纔能做。
14. 辛苦了你。
15. 我餓了。
16. 你的東西都齊
17. 做甚麼。你都弄齊截了麼。
18. 跟我一塊兒去。
19. 尊大人痊愈了麼。
20. 來這兒玩
21. 這是甚麼做的。
22. 你想去竟管去。
23. 你追不上我。
24. 別搓磨他。
25. 我指頭
26. 起來讓我過去。
27. 我一個官板兒都沒有。
28. 你尋甚麼。
29. 別耽擱久了。
30. 差點兒。
31. 短點兒。
32. 別躲懶。
33. 別攪我。
34. 去幫著
35. 他已經上蘇州去了。
36. 他爹親香山住
37. 你爲甚麼這麼做。
38. 你在那兒來。
39. 今兒甚麼風兒吹了你
40. 別撒頼。
41. 改天來。
42. 除了這個都擎了去
43. 這個是該擱在這兒的。
44. 這兒是該擱這個的。
45. 貓叼著一個耗子。
46. 今兒你可回家罷。
47. 刀刺破指頭
48. 了,在樹那一邊兒。
49. 叫打雜兒的擎水來
50. 稍個信兒給某人。
51. 儘你的心
52. 今兒幾兒了。
53. 快掌燈了。
54. 你成了客了麼。
55. 你不害臊麼。
胸做,就是了。

PART V. THE EIGHTEEN SECTIONS. *Hsü San Yü.*
Section II.

1 沒羞沒臊的。 2 我也是這麼想呢。 3 別在老爺兒地裏頑兒。 4 他有件湛新的袴子。 5 快黑上來了。 6 先生許我去的麼。 7 那些個我頂喜歡這一個。 8 你你的罷。 9 我估摸著不是。 10 我不信那個。 11 這份兒是我的麼。 12 有甚麼笑頭兒。 13 沒辦安呢。 14 不拘甚麼都好。 15 鎖上那個門。 16 把孩子抱進去。 17 他仍舊不好。 18 我從來沒見過他。 19 剩得也不多了。 20 他繞剛還在這兒。 21 看樣兒還道罷了。 22 擱開點兒。 23 接頭兒另做過。 24 老是這個樣兒。 25 他有傷寒病。 26 他咳嗽得很。 27 想我幫你不想。 28 我眼睛糢糊得慌。 29 老爺兒烷眼睛。 30 你辦。 31 這時候兒別攪我。 32 你本不該這麼做。 33 跟我來溜打溜打。 34 我怕。 35 馬撒歡兒。 36 他是那一等人。 37 他是很伶俐的孩子。 38 今兒頂熱。 39 沒甚麼大用頭。 40 在這兒等我回來呢。 41 他悅悅兒上這兒來。 42 他多嚐開船。 43 別這麼冒失。 44 你要得多少半天。 45 你要去多少日子。 46 管他說去罷。 47 你要去多少日子。 48 還沒有停當麼。 49 全照著我的話做。 50 拏那個不更強麼。

續散語十八章之三

我[1]見天的喫藥。愣[2]愣兒張羅張羅。你[3]見我的硯台沒有。他[4]難過不是假粧的。他[5]盡故意兒的做的。倆搭[6]五個是多少。他[7]最愛體面揚氣。他[8]矮飽[9]他的馬了。他安排矮好他的馬了。誰[10]的不是一樣兒呢。不[11]能老是這們樣。那[12]孩子盡貪玩兒。只[13]顧自各兒多佔點兒便宜。把[14]這蛋一個一個兒拏出來。任[15]甚麼兒都不管。三[16]鼻子眼兒多出氣。你[17]蓋起新房子沒有。過[18]了一個月我纔去。他[19]有萬數兩銀子的家當兒。我[20]好容易纔明白這個意思了。你[21]成天家做甚麼。女人們梳纂。男人們打辮子。我[24]無可奈何呀。我[25]作不得主兒。我[26]不敢出主意。他[27]嬌養慣了。他[28]來這兒好幾回了。這[29]個我就見來得快了。他[30]也是老實人。你[31]愛喫石榴麼。偺[35]們頂好是幹甚麼呢。那[32]是甚麼鄉的聲兒。他[33]上船了。再沒有比這個明白了。他[35]上岸去了麼。太[37]陽平西了。太[38]陽快上來了。明[39]兒個早早兒的來。清[40]香的玫瑰花兒。你[41]多咱晚兒纔去呢。只[42]管拏就是了。

PART V. THE EIGHTEEN SECTIONS. *Hsü San Yü.*
Section IV.

你¹是誰家的妞兒。別²混擱騰東西。我³忘了上鐘弦了。跟⁴紙的似的這麼輕巧。誰⁵與你做來著。小⁶心點兒弄他。你⁷怎麼這們想起來。並⁸不是這麼樣。這⁹個大有用頭。越¹⁰多越好。我¹¹提溜不動。你¹²會浮水麼。你¹³會水麼。你¹⁴怎麼說來著。潲¹⁵的滿屋子精溼。第¹⁶二回該誰去。下¹⁷回誰要去。他¹⁸舖子在我們舖子隔壁兒。照¹⁹舊攔回那兒去。他²⁰各個兒來的芽撞。未²¹必麼。必²²定有益你的。必²³定怎麼樣兒纔好呀。不²⁴能這麼樣兒聽說罷。不²⁵能不著。再²⁶沒有不假的。左²⁷不過是你幹的。喉²⁸這是甚麼。太²⁹多嘴了。點不著。搖³⁰鈴兒是賣線的。搖³¹波浪鼓兒的。刨³²一半兒。裝³³一半兒罷。這³⁴油臨³⁵到誰了。你³⁶不肯減點兒麼。繫³⁷緊著。紮³⁸緊他。我³⁹輭弱走不⁴⁰動這麼遠。這茶忒淡了。跟⁴¹石頭這麼硬。誰⁴²肯跟他動手。別⁴³玩兒的太粗了。這⁴⁴塊地主兒是誰。活⁴⁵扣兒更容易解。礙⁴⁶你甚麼相干。這⁴⁷肉沒熬⁴⁸透。這⁴⁹肉沒燒透。別⁵⁰再上這兒來。我脚上長凍瘡了。

續散語十八章之五

熱[1]了，等他涼涼兒著。你[2]可別小心做。為[3]甚麼呆住上前兒阿。他[4]跌了個仰八腳兒。攔[5]回原處兒去。把[6]車拉後些兒。我[7]媳婦兒是他妹妹。捲起[8]這窗戶來罷。我[9]的腳麻了。各[10]式各樣兒的都有。他[11]幹事不留心。他[12]天生得又聾又啞。我[13]還不能呢，何況你。每[14]七天一個禮拜。每[15]樣兒要點兒。我[16]要造得活便纔好呢。在[17]這兒多半天了。那[18]個就保不定。你[19]起開別再碰[20]著我。這井是頂深的阿。小[21]心跌下去了。沒[22]別的能耐。你[23]起來，別擋著道兒。沒[24]有別的能處。你[25]為甚麼來得這麼遲，竟顧那一件事。這[26]陣[27]兒該當做了。別[28]聽他說瞎話。他[29]不管甚麼話兒都說。別[30]佔這們寬地方兒。儘[31]著量兒試一試。這[32]正是我想著的呀。並[33]沒有在這兒。拔[34]起這探小樹兒來。別[35]搖捏這桌子。你[36]偏著那邊兒。你[37]向著我這邊兒。他[38]是逍遙快樂的。你[39]種著多少畝地。那[40]事總別題他了。瞎[41]了一個眼。那[42]事他辦的機密。幫[43]我捽結實這繩子。幫[44]著繞結實這繩子。有[45]整千整萬的人。

PART V. THE EIGHTEEN SECTIONS. Hsü San Yü.
Section VI.

耳朵有點兒背。[1] 怕落了顏色兒。[2] 這書在那兒刷的。[3] 這書不印來賣了。[4]

這書現在不印了。[5] 向來沒別的心。[6] 打開在草頭上。[7] 這個你送的很俏皮。[8]

他全家兒敗盡了。[9] 這個可意罷。[10] 這是他最疼的兒子。[11] 他扭了腿腕子了。[12]

核兒也別扔。[13] 隨便兒就是了。[14] 這樹纔結菓子。[15] 這樹新結菓子。[16] 這個差

的真利害了。[17] 我還能辦得來麼。[18] 我再也不能受了。[19] 再也不能怒了。[20]

你見過熊麼。[21] 我寧可不去。[22] 他是頂胖大的。[23] 別這麼快。[24] 我跟他搭夥計。[25]

煎點兒下剩的羹罷。[26] 誰有銀子放賬麼。[27] 攔在樓板上。[28] 每月多少工錢。[29]

難道你給多少麼。[30] 他受罰了一兩銀子。[31] 掃了那個蛛蛛網子。[32] 切碎了他。[33]

那個我們永遠做不來的。[34] 快去你看慌了。[35] 他常丟小刀子。[36] 很像哥兒兩個。[37]

他縱孩子撒野。[38] 這孩子長得俊。[39] 漸漸兒好上來了。[40] 一回比一回好上來了。[41][42]

我叫螞蜂螫著了。[46] 他個誰頂著不是。[43] 比先頭裏的更好。[44]

越舊的更好。[45] 蠍子螫了手。[47] 跑獅馬的打扮兒。[48]

續散語十八章之七

1 打扮的整整齊齊兒的。
2 房子要脩蓋了。
3 這是該管的麼。
4 他多大財主。
5 這程子我沒見他。
6 這都不好起頭兒再做罷。
7 太寬了、綁緊點兒。
8 更要謹慎了。
9 打過了四點兒鐘了。
10 找人補這個去。
11 他心裏頭竟想發財。
12 鬬狗
13 他嘴硬、不認是他作的。
14 把這一邊兒、朝上拏著。
15 他更是老江湖了。
16 睡早覺了。
17 大夫不下藥了。
18 他又活了麼。
19 長成是這個樣兒的。
20 他們
21 那兩國打仗呢。
22 他在我們村兒裏住。
23 你種的樹、都發芽兒了。
24 水有下巴頦兒這麼深。
25 埝有脚面兒這麼深。
26 都是金子鑲成的。
27 一桃子零這一點兒。
28 屋子裏頭好些個耗子。
29 耽擱日子太多、這兒有無
30 這兒有無
31 鴉片烟是從那兒來的。
32 掛起這個來罷。
33 弄個套兒掛上他。
34 那是老樣兒的帽子。
35 怎麼這些個蚊子。
36 你會治這個病麼。
37 那些調羹短
38 了一把了。在艙底下呢。
39 還沒殼我的本兒呢。
40 這個誰上檔。
41 話不投機
42 他擋了我們了。
43 他賣這個、賺好錢呢。
44 過個門磴兒就好了。

PART V. THE EIGHTEEN SECTIONS. Hsü San Yü.
Section VIII.

1 今兒有點兒發狀。
2 倒過來再裝。
3 勤點兒攪著別叫他糊焦了。
4 不過僅殼俗們使的。
5 不論聽多少賣了他就完了。
6 這豆子沒炒麼，
7 我盡力兒幫著你幹。
8 曲曲灣灣的，走了半天。
9 你小心照應這牲口。
10 要喫個滷牲口。
11 拏鏡子照臉。
12 沒心腸幹事情。
13 用心用意的寫字。
14 他仗著甚麼餬口。
15 把這個字兒繙譯出來。
16 那都是白說。
17 那都是白饒。
18 出於情理之外。
19 也是中年的人了。
20 他該的利錢比本錢還多。
21 把事的情形告訴我。
22 明兒
23 是關餉的日子。比沒有東西強阿。
24 比窑著手兒強些兒。
25 這時候兒發了
26 大財了。這兒住伙食太貴。
27 我是外鄉人。
28 我就打發人來拏。
29 打死那個蜣蜋。
30 他們要宰一隻牛。俗們要往舟山灣一灣船。
31
32 波羅我喫怕了。
33 別發怯。
34 很不通情理的人。
35 又不通文理。
36 不過是說個笑話兒
37 管他做
38 甚麼。這個不大典，
39 鳥鎗裝了藥沒有。
40 兩樣兒、撬和著喫。
41 變了卦了。
42 言不應口。
43 他是斯文的人。
44 留下這個湊著使。
45 他是省錢的嫏兒們。

續散語十八章之九

1 說這句京話、怎麼說。2 東家有事給我做。他有發瘧子的病。這隻雞鬪不3 過那隻雞。4 這是一劑藥。5 那是犯法的。6 別吐核兒。7 他是沒禮貌的人。8 撒謊掉皮的。9 這是十足紋銀。10 臉上焦黃的。11 貪心不足。得一步進一步。12 撒謊掉皮的。13 大清早起鬧涮說。14 嘴裏說好話脚底下使絆子。滿嘴裏的瞎話、侮弄人家。15 事情辦的有邊兒了。大搖大櫚16 愛戴個高帽子。17 睜著眼兒的瞎子。18 好喫懶做的、不是東西。19 戴著老爺兒就鬧賊。20 大搖大擺21 這孩子太陶氣。22 好喫懶做的。23 戴著老爺兒就鬧賊。24 狗拏耗子多管閒事。說話不藏私。他說話不饒人兒。25 說話不藏私。26 他說話不饒人兒。27 大手大脚的、花慣了。28 辛辛苦苦的圖甚麼。29 前思後想很為難、鬧的很不像樣兒了。30 鬧的很不像樣兒了。31 見一32 樣兒會一樣兒、沒酒兒三分醉、他竟幹些個新鮮樣兒。33 他竟幹些個新鮮樣兒。34 低三兒下四的。35 拋頭露面的。錦上添花的人多、逢塲做戲的、應酬朋友們罷咧。36 錦上添花的人多。37 逢塲做戲的。38 雨溼溼39 做臉兒不做臉兒。幹事情鬼頭鬼腦的。見財起意、說話含40 幹事情鬼頭鬼腦的。41 見財起意。42 說話含43 殺生害命的。雪白的臉蛋兒。鮮紅的嘴脣兒。漆黑的頭髮。44 雪白的臉蛋兒。45 鮮紅的嘴脣兒。46 漆黑的頭髮。了衣裳了。含糊糊的。

PART V. THE EIGHTEEN SECTIONS. Hsü San Yü.
Section X.

1 碧綠的耳圈兒。2 翠藍布的大衫。3 焦黃的金鐲子。4 他穿著一件藍不藍綠不綠的。5 鹽放多了齁鹹的。6 齁臭的。7 噴香的。8 精淡的。9 齁苦的。10 訓甜的。11 齁酸的。12 怪澁的。13 粗風暴雨的天。14 晌午錯了。15 說話東拉西扯的。16 說話胡拉溜扯的。17 陰涼兒裏坐著凉快罷。18 滿嘴裏胡說八道的。19 有件事，很懸心。20 左右做人難。21 深不的，淺不的。22 輕不好，重不好。23 人不知鬼不覺的。24 二人同一心黃土變成金。25 齊心努力的幹事。26 十冬臘月的天冷。27 滑了個趔趄。28 頂高的個趔坡子。29 下坡兒容易上坡兒難。30 嘴裏的牙都活動了。31 兩隻腳，跳穩了纔好。32 晃離晃盪的站不住。33 盤著腿兒坐著，側著34 身子躺著。35 前仰兒後合的站不住。36 挐鐵通條撬開門。37 帽子沒有帽襻兒。38 挐針釘上鈕襻兒。39 馬驚了。40 冰涼的水冰的慌。41 滾熱的茶怪燙的。42 馬上43 沒見世面的人。44 眼錯不見的就沒了。45 心急腿慢總趕46 就是立刻一個樣。不上他。47 越窮越見鬼。我很佩服他。48 若要人不知除非已莫為。

SECTION XI.

續散語十八章之十一

1. 多嘴多舌的愛說話。
2. 不分青紅皁白。
3. 天寒火冷。
4. 說話眞痛快。
5. 他是光明正大的人。
6. 嘴裏混遭遇人。
7. 前不著村兒後不著店兒的地方兒。
8. 頭惛腦悶的很難受。
9. 你有點兒不懂好歹。
10. 求你好歹別說出來。
11. 眞是個滾刀肉。
12. 我橫竪不告訴人。
13. 水性楊花的。
14. 心裏頭猶預不決。
15. 兩頭兒害怕。
16. 心裏頭很不耐煩。
17. 別錯了過節兒。
18. 順情說好話耿直惹人嫌。
19. 衣冠齊楚。
20. 寄居在此地。
21. 手頭兒寬綽。
22. 心活了。
23. 說話伶牙俐齒的。
24. 有情有義。
25. 他的心眼兒好使喚。情投意合的人。
26.
27. 他是個粗魯人。
28. 他本不是個
29. 瞭涼了再喫。
30. 本來不是個好東西。
31. 前門大街走了水了。
32. 兩頭兒
33. 不見面兒的話。恐怕對出光兒來。
34. 他非骿就騙。
35. 冷不防的唬了一跳。
36. 冷冷清清的地方兒。
37. 濺了一身水。滿肚子委屈說不出來。摳癢癢兒。
38.
39.
40. 摳籃子。
41. 喫飽了、打飽呃。
42. 搋鑼播鼓。
43. 擎篩子簁簁米。酒冷了醱酒。
44.
45. 用手攄麪烙餅喫。
46. 幹事情麻利。
47. 別濶誦言兒。
48. 沒受過酸甜苦辣。

SECTION XII.

這¹廚子做東西邋遢。狗²耳朶奔拉著。趴³牆兒撓壁的、站不住。老⁴太太喫橙檳悶著。愁⁵眉不展的。大⁶處兒不算小處兒算。摸⁷摸搽搽的。欺⁸善怕惡的脾氣。轉⁹了向兒了。搖¹⁰頭幌腦的。正在氣頭兒上別惹他。這¹²事情有點兒燒頭。萬¹³事起頭兒難。裝¹⁴模做樣的不是個東西。睜¹⁵個眼兒合個眼兒。竟¹⁶拉些個老婆舌頭。劃¹⁷著花點子銀子罷咧。脚¹⁸也蹉了手也蹉了。唏¹⁹唏哈哈的笑。癟²⁰嘴子是沒牙的人。瘐²¹著一肚子氣沒地方兒生。貼²²錢買罪受。遮²³遮掩掩的、怕人家看見他。滿²⁴嘴的之乎者也。一²⁵竅不通。我²⁶是個伻漢子。反²⁷覆不定的脾氣。屠²⁸戶就是賣肉的人。筆²⁹尖兒都寫禿了。古³⁰窰的磁器。沒³¹頭髮的人就是禿子。努³²嘴兒擠眼兒。偸³³偸兒的別言語。正³⁴宿的睡不著覺。悄³⁵不聲兒的別言語。長³⁶的模樣兒很俏皮。他³⁷騎著一匹大騾驢。樹³⁸稍兒上落著個雀兒。樹³⁹根兒都叫螞蟻蛀了。白⁴⁰劾勞。滿⁴¹嘴裏告饒兒。船⁴²稍兒上坐著個柁工。大⁴³家彤兒鬧糟糕。

SECTION XIII.

續散語十八章之十三

1. 嘴裏頭吹哨子。
2. 把刀揷在鞘子裏去。
3. 身上荊棘。洗個澡就好了。
4. 造謠言。
5. 說謊話。絲毫不錯。
6. 賊咬一口入骨三分。
7. 能言快語的。
8. 各人的巧妙不同。
9. 號令嚴明。
10. 獨占鼇頭。
11. 下棋畫畫兒都有譜。
12. 步步兒留心。
13. 公的母
14. 草雞下蛋公雞打鳴兒。
15. 哥兒兩個不和睦。
16. 慕化重修。
17. 齋戒
18. 白水煮荳腐。
19. 畫符念咒眞可笑。
20. 浮頭兒的撇了他去。
21. 緊底下的。
22. 拏斧子劈柴火。
23. 臉上發了福。
24. 目覩眼見的。
25. 我最能降伏他。
26. 拏包袱包衣裳。
27. 竟做些個不要臉的事。
28. 牆上掛著四幅畫兒。
29. 我最不實
30. 當今的老佛爺。
31. 舊書裏頭有蠹魚子。
32. 堵住這個窟窿。
33. 揆情度理。
34. 首飾都是鍍金的。
35. 上吐下瀉。各省的總督就是制台。單人獨馬的。
36.
37.
38. 井台兒上有轆轤打水。
39. 獨門獨院兒的住。
40. 圖財害命的事。
41. 打了圖書沒
42. 牆上貼著一張行樂圖。
43. 兔死狐悲物傷其類。
44. 銀錢如糞土，臉面值千金。
45. 羞惱變成怒了。
46. 催了一隻大檜船。
47. 到舘子裏端兩碗滷麪。

PART V. THE EIGHTEEN SECTIONS. *Hsü San Yü.*
SECTION XIV.

績散語十八章之十四

1 千萬別受賄賂。
2 滿地下軔轆。
3 勞碌得很。
4 攀應野鹿最多。
5 鹿觭角的撅
6 揩兒。水陸平安。
7 珠寶玉器，
8 房簷兒上有蜘蛛網，
9 暫且歇歇兒。
10 近硃者赤、近墨者黑。
11 最愛喫個煮餑餑。
12 你納府上在那兒住。
13 這孩子很怐慉
14 錢鏝兒上是滿洲字。
15 幹事情顚三倒四的。
16 舐了一舌頭。
17 攀土填平了這個坑。
18 墊穩了這條桌腿兒。
19 攀手掂掂有多重
20 攀清醬沾著喫。
21 靛缸裏
22 九散膏丹都是藥。
23 手裏攀著條扁擔。
24 均攤勻散的。
25 把衣裳疊舒展了。
26 眞草隸篆四樣兒字。
27 縫縫補綻是本分事。
28 穿房入屋
29 的心慈面輭的。
30 煎湯熬藥的伺候他。
31 一文錢慾倒英雄漢。
32 川流不息
33 可著那兒都是泉水。
34 顧前不顧後的脾氣。
35 明兒給他餞行。
36 別澖
37 鏨花兒的鈕釦子。
38 黃泉路上沒老少。
39 同居各爨。
40 連竄帶跳的。
41 要個人兒舉薦穩好。
42 比神仙還舒服。
43 乾菓子鮮菓子都有。
44 嘴裏頭流黏涎子。
45 如今他都收歛了。
46 只剩了一線之路。
47 攀個針線兒來釘書。

SECTION XV.

1. 我十分羨慕他。
2. 颶颱風就是羊角風。
3. 拏刀剝了皮兒去。
4. 鞋小必得拏楦頭楦。
5. 桌子腿兒木頭鏇的。
6. 渾身都酸輭了。
7. 河底下有個漩窩。
8. 在京候選的官兒。
9. 算盤子兒打得清著呢。
10. 頭上戴的是珊瑚頂子。
11. 散了班兒了。
12. 這雨傘是多少錢一把。
13. 寃屈的受不得。
14. 一家子團圓了。
15. 拏銀子捐官竟是上檔。
16. 原本該這們著纔是。
17. 隔著院牆就看見了。
18. 別涵埋怨人家。
19. 這是你情我願的。
20. 烟燻火燎的很腌臢。
21. 頂冠束帶的。
22. 莊稼都叫大水淹了。
23. 類子裏嚥不下去。
24. 端硯出在那塊兒。
25. 俗們試演試演好不好。
26. 你替奸詐的了不得。
27. 揍胭抹粉兒的。
28. 十分討人厭。
29. 出言不遜。
30. 夢見甚麼建功
31. 眼不見嘴不饞耳不聽心不煩。
32. 大丟人。
33. 給你臉不要臉。
34. 夢見甚麼建功
35. 再別混信人家的話。
36. 耳聞不如眼見。
37. 他一點兒不關心。
38. 建功
39. 立業。寶劍贈與烈士紅粉贈與佳人。
40. 假公濟私。
41. 捲了一個鋪蓋捲兒。
42. 甘心情願替他。
43. 鰥寡孤獨的人。
44. 拏酒灌他看他喝不喝。

PART V. THE EIGHTEEN SECTIONS. *Hsü San Yü.*
SECTION XVI.

續散語十八章之十六

[1] 手裏拏著根釣魚竿兒釣魚呢。
[2] 感化他的心。
[3] 船上三枝桅杆很高。
[4] 跐拉著鞋兒。
[5] 牽腸掛肚的很難受。
[6] 說話幹事要謙恭些兒。
[7] 假粧看不見。
[8] 欠人家的還沒有還。
[9] 糧船上頭好些個拉縴的。
[10] 伸著一條腿，蹺著一條腿。
[11] 他給人家拉篷扯縴的。
[12] 搭著拳頭打人。
[13] 仗著兩個空拳頭過日子。
[14] 兵權在手。
[15] 他會打拳脚。
[16] 臉上顴骨高。
[17] 他很有權變。
[18] 殺了個雞犬不留。
[19] 勸他改邪歸正。
[20] 扇子上別落欵。
[21] 沒有犯欵。
[22] 看守著別丟了。
[23] 我有點兒憎嫌他。
[24] 搬簾子進去罷。
[25] 他爲人很險。
[26] 那是件很險的事。
[27] 連哭帶喊的叫喚。
[28] 天塌地陷。
[29] 官宦人家兒。
[30] 饅頭是沒餡兒的。
[31] 限他多少天做好了。
[32] 很懸心。
[33] 患難的朋友。
[34] 懸燈結綵很熱鬧。
[35] 關門閉戶的很冷清。
[36] 鈎搭連環的事情。
[37] 出了門兒不管換酒肉朋友柴米夫妻。
[38] 酒肉朋友柴米夫妻。
[39] 他得了一個癱瘓病。
[40] 包含著些兒。
[41] 說話含糊。
[42] 做事痛快。
[43] 他是翰林出身。
[44] 喫希罕東西，見希罕事情。
[45] 不希罕你的東西。
[46] 小漢仗兒。
[47] 滿漢酒席很講究。

SECTION XVII.

1. 再遲了、就趕不上了。
2. 我老沒有見他的面兒。
3. 遞給我那個水烟袋。
4. 喝水喝嗆了。
5. 我總摸不清這件事。
6. 穿衣裳盡鬧排子。
7. 死攏架子。
8. 一個人兒做不來。
9. 前功盡棄了。
10. 撲燈蛾兒把燈撲滅了。
11. 我避諱他。
12. 閉門思過。
13. 瞧不起他。
14. 藐視他。
15. 頂能幹的姆兒們。
16. 萬不能丟開手。
17. 這件事了不了。
18. 儘著量兒喝酒。
19. 落不出好來。
20. 我沒有很聽清楚。
21. 打了個稀糊腦子爛。
22. 把肉燉了個稀爛噴香。
23. 拙嘴体頭的不會說話。
24. 滿嘴裏混呎溷說。
25. 嘴咕。
26. 嚷甚麼嘴嘟噥甚麼。
27. 你敢强嘴我打你。
28. 性命不保。
29. 那鎮丟了鑰匙了。
30. 粗粗糯糯的一塊石頭。
31. 是個大幫手。
32. 一個巴掌拍不響。
33. 單絲不成線、孤
34. 木不成林。拏手撥擷開他。
35. 盡是白費事。
36. 白手成家。
37. 是個白丁兒。
38. 來試試誰的勁兒大。
39. 誰强誰弱。
40. 普天底下、都走偏了。
41. 說著好話就翻臉。
42. 兩口子不和氣。
43. 倒像一對雙生兒。
44. 白活了一輩子。
45. 天長日久的怎麼好。
46. 隨手兒拏別挑揀。
47. 近視眼看不清。
48. 我所認識的人有限。

PART V. THE EIGHTEEN SECTIONS. *Hsü San Yü.*
Section XVIII.

[1] 嘴碎嘮叨的，討人嫌。
[2] 他疑心太重。
[3] 骷髏肘子腫了。
[4] 要價兒還價兒。
[5] 稀鬆平常。
[6] 從頭至尾的看了一遍。
[7] 與別人不相干。
[8] 老不成材料兒了。
[9] 閱禍招非的。
[10] 正在妙齡的時候兒。
[11] 不勝其任。
[12] 矇矇亮兒就起身。
[13] 念熟了再背書。
[14] 一身不能當二役。
[15] 他是手藝人。
[16] 他是個無來由的人。
[17] 老頭子，小夥子。
[18] 天理昭彰。
[19] 誰敢擔錯兒。
[20] 做買賣賠了本兒。
[21] 眾人都信服他。
[22] 長得眉清目秀很有福氣。
[23] 相貌長得很秀氣。
[24] 文武全才的本事。
[25] 小性兒。
[26] 眼皮子淺愛小。
[27] 看不出筆跡來。
[28] 忍氣吞聲的。
[29] 這是他自己洩底。
[30] 賤貨不睬。
[31] 言聽計從的。

END OF PART V.

THE EIGHTEEN SECTIONS.

(CHINESE TEXT.)

TZŬ ERH CHI.

COLLOQUIAL SERIES.

PART VI.

THE HUNDRED LESSONS.

(CHINESE TEXT.)

使上也不巴結、只是在這上頭鑽着心兒學、眞是玷辱了滿洲咯、與其把有用的心思費在這沒用的地方兒、何不讀書呢。人往高處兒走、水往低處兒流,[3] 琵琶絃子上任憑你學到怎麼樣兒的好、卑污下賤的名兒總不能免正經官場中、能殼把彈琵琶絃子、算得本事麼。若[4] 說我的話不可信、大人們官員們裡頭、那一個是從彈琵琶絃子的出身的呀、你如今能指出來麼。

談論篇百章之一百

你¹這是怎麼說呢、天天兒喫得飽飽兒的、竟抱着琵琶弦子彈、有甚麼益處兒呢、要從此成名啊、還是要靠着這個過日子呢。咱們²幸而是滿洲、喫的是官米月間有的是錢糧、一家子頭頂着腳跐着、都是主子的、並不學正經本事、差

們裡頭、你我彼此、恭恭敬敬的、豈不好麼。他³如今來了的時候兒、動不動兒的就發豪橫、信着嘴兒混罵人、算是自己的本事啊、還是怎麼樣呢、你們瞧瞧、長得那個嘴巴骨子、臟着個大肚子、直是個傻子、還自充懂文墨的、好叫人肉麻啊、再那說話的聲兒像狗叫啊似的、人家都厭煩得不聽咯。這個⁴人若署有一點兒人心的、也該知覺咯、還腆着臉不知恥、倒像是誰喜歡他呢、越發興頭起來咯、是怎麼說呢。他⁵老子一輩子、也是漢子來着、不知道怎麼作了孽咯、養出這個賤貨兒來、噯完了、福分都叫他老子享盡了、這就是他的結果了、再想要陞騰、如何能呢。

談論篇百章之九十八

昨兒[1]個在衙門的時候兒,一點風兒都沒有,很晴的好天來着,忽然變了日頭都慘淡了,這麼着麼我就說天氣不安,要颳大風,趁着沒有颳,咱們快走罷,各人也怕是這麼樣,都散了。我剛[2]到了家就颳起來了,實在是大樹稍兒叫風摔得那個聲兒真可怕,直颳到三更天,纔略住了些兒。今兒[3]早起往這麼來的時候兒看見道兒上的人們,都是站不住,個個兒是吸吸哈哈的跑。我[4]先是順着風兒走,還好些兒,後來迎着風兒走的時候兒,那臉啊,頦啊,就像是鐵兒扎的似的,凍得疼,手指頭拘攣了,連鞭子都拏不住的,吐的唾沫沒到地兒也就凍成冰,一截兒一截兒的跌碎咯。噯呀[5]有生以來誰經過這個樣兒的冷呢。

談論篇百章之九十九

人[1]是比萬物最尊貴的,若不體好歹,不明道理,與那畜牲何異啊。就[2]是朋友

談論篇百章之九十七

再走、那兒知道、直下了一天一夜、總沒有住、到了今兒早飯後、總恍恍惚惚的、看見日頭咯、却是應時的好雨啊、想來各處兒的田地沒有不透的咯、秋天的庄稼、豈有不收成的呢。

前兒[1]黑下、好冷啊、睡夢中把我凍醒了、天一亮、我急忙起來、開開房門一瞧、原來是白亮亮的下了一地的雪。喫[2]了早飯、小晌午的時候兒、那雪飄飄颺颺的越發下起大片兒的來咯、我心裡想着沒有事、怎麼能彀得一個朋友來、說話兒也好啊。可巧[3]家下人們進來說、有客來咯、我心裡很喜歡一面兒叫收拾下酒菜兒、一面兒又叫爐了一盆子炭火、趕着請了弟兄們來、酒菜已經預備齊咯、端上來、慢慢兒的喝着酒、把簾子高高兒的捲起來、一瞧那雪景兒、比甚麼都清雅、紛紛的下着、山川樹木都是雪白、看着更高了、拏過棋來、下了兩盤、喫了晚飯點上鐙纔散了。

談論篇百章之九十六

這許多日子的連陰雨下得我心裡都熟咯、這兒也漏了、那兒也溼了、連個睡覺的地方兒都沒有、而且又是蚊子臭蟲蛇蚤叮得實在難受翻來覆去的過了亮鐘並沒有睏、把眼睛強閉着又忍了一會兒剛剛兒的恍恍惚惚的睡上來咯、正似睡不似睡的、忽然從西北上就像山崩地裂的是一個懍、响了一聲、把我陡然閒嚇醒了、過了好一會子身上還是打戰兒、心裡還是突突的跳睜開眼一瞧、屋裡所有的東西、都沒有損壞一點兒、叫人出去一看、說是街坊家的山牆叫雨淋透了倒咯、噯呀睡夢之中那兒經得起那麼大的响聲兒震哪。

昨兒清早兒起來、屋裡很黑、我疑惑是天還沒有亮呢、到院子裡一瞧、噯呀、原來是天陰的漆黑、我洗了手臉、纔要上衙門、那天一星子半點兒的下起雨來了、略等了一會兒、涮涮的响了、又坐了一坐兒、喝了盅茶的空兒忽然打了個霹雷、這雨就傾盆似的下來了、我想着這不過是一陣兒暴雨罷咧、等過了

的時候兒俗語兒說得心定自然凉若竟着會子急還能脫了麽。

談論篇百章之九十四

哎呀[1]這個樣兒的大雨你往那兒去來着快進來罷。 我[2]的一個朋友不在咯、送礩去來着今兒早起天陰陰兒的、雖然有要下雨的光景、到了晌午又是𪾢晴的天、往間裡走着的時候兒忽然一片一片的鋪開了稠雲了、我就和家裡人們說這天氣不安當、快走罷、不然咱們一定要着雨咯、正說着就涮涮的下起來咯、你台你說在漫荒野地裡可往那兒去躱呢、雨衣𧜀褂子還沒穿送當渾身都濕透咯。 無妨[3]我有衣裳拏出來你先換上、天也晚了、明兒再進城罷、我們這個僻地方兒雖然沒有甚麼好東西、家裡養的小猪子雞宰一兩隻給你喫。 嗳喫[4]還說甚麼但得這個好地方兒樓身就是便宜了、不然還怕不冒着雨兒走麼又有甚麼法子呢。

談論篇百章之九十五

談論篇百章之九十三

忙着往囘來趕。到了關裏的時候兒恍恍惚惚的、月亮都出來了、從城裏頭出去的人們、都叫快走、說掩了一扇門咯、心裏更着了急、緊加鞭子催着馬趕到了跟前兒末尾兒的、還是關在城外頭了。實在是乘輿而往、捕輿而囘。

今兒好利害呀、自從立夏之後、可以說得起是頭一天兒的熱咯、一點兒風絲兒也沒有、所有的傢伙、都是燙手兒的、熱越喝涼水越渴、沒了法兒咯、我洗了個澡、在樹底下乘了會涼兒、心裏頭纔略好了些兒嗜、這憐兒的燥熱天、別人兒都是光着脊梁坐着、還怕中暑呢、你怎麼只是低着頭寫字、是甚麼罪孽啊、不要命了麼。你這都是沒官差、白閒着的話、譬如小買賣人兒們、挑着很重的擔子、壓着肩膀伸着脖子各處兒跑着呿喝、汗流如雨的纔能瞧得百數錢兒度命、若像我這個憐兒的、奧現成兒的從從容容的寫字、他能彀麼、況且冬冷夏熱是自古至今不易之理、索性靜靜兒的耐着、或者倒有爽快

兒往下走轉過了山嘴兒一瞧那水和天的顏色兒上下一樣浩浩如銀竟無所分別實在是水清山靜。趕撐到蘆葦深的去處兒忽然聽見廟裡的鐘聲兒順着風兒悠悠楊楊的來了那時候心裡頭萬慮皆空好像水洗了似的那麼乾淨就是出了世的神仙也不過是這麼樣兒樂罷咧我們幾個人更高了興咯直喝到天亮也不覺醉也不覺乏。人生在世像這個樣兒的風清月朗的景致能彀遇着幾回若是徒然虛度了豈不可惜了兒的麼。

談論篇百章之九十二

前兒[1]我們幾個人甚麼是逛來着竟是受了罪咧出了城兒放着正經道兒不走不知道繞到那兒去了沿着路兒間着找着剛剛兒的到了閘口的跟前兒坐上船彼此說着話兒喝着酒到了東花園兒又趕回閘上來早已就日平西了。纔[2]吃完了飯我就說衆位俗們走罷跟的人都是步行兒家又離得很遠他們還說說笑笑的儘自坐着動也不動後來看見日頭快落了這纔上了馬

談論篇百章之九十一

不是麼昨兒我兄弟來了，往城外頭游玩去，約會我出城，到了曠野的地方兒，遠遠的一瞧，春景兒眞令人可愛，河沿兒上的桃花兒是鮮紅，柳枝兒是碧綠，而且樹枝兒上，各樣的雀鳥兒在那兒叫喚的實在好聽，一陣兒一陣兒的春風兒颸得草香撲鼻，水上的小船兒也是來來往往的不斷，兩岸上的游人都是三五成羣兒的逛，我們倆從小道兒上，曲曲灣灣的，走到了樹林子多的地方兒，一看也有彈的，也有唱的，也有賣茶賣酒的，而且賣活魚活蝦的都很賤，故此我們倆足足的游玩了一天，兄台可別怪我沒來約，不是瞞着你納只怕遇見和你納有不對勁兒的人哪，所以沒找你納來。

前兒[1]我們往西山裡逛去，那個樂，可說得是盡了興了，白日裡游玩的樂啊，那是不必說的了，到了黑下的時候兒更暢快。我們[2]幾個人喫了晚飯坐上船，不大的工夫兒月亮就上來了，照得如同白日一樣，慢慢兒的撐着船，順着水

肉啊,是祖宗的克食,有強讓的理麼,況且親友們來去還不迎不送呢,像這樣兒讓起來使得麼。

談論篇百章之八十九

我們[1]在關東的時候兒,天天兒打圍來着,這天我們打圍去,在草裡跑出個麅子來,我趕緊的打馬拉開弓一射,略落了點兒,後同手拔箭的空兒,只見麅子的尾巴動啊動的,一轉眼就跑過了山梁兒奔山前往上去,疾忙我緊跟着趕了去,又過了個山梁兒往山後頭去了。這麼[2]着就緊催着馬,剛剛兒的趕上一射箭,又從他頭上過去了,想不到從那邊兒來了一個鹿,纔過山梁兒往這們跑着,正中了我射的那枝箭跌倒了。彩[3]頭兒好,實在可笑正是人家說的,想不到的倒得了,若把這個話告訴別人兒說好像是撒謊的似的。

談論篇百章之九十

這[1]春天的時候兒一點兒事沒有,白開着竟在家裡坐着,很覺悶得謊啊。可[2]

談論篇百章之八十八

昨兒喫了祭神的肉就是了，又叫送背鐙的肉作甚麼。甚麼話呢，老兄台咯，是該當送的，方纔還要叫人請兄台去來着，你納是知道的，就是這幾個奴才們，宰豬的宰豬，收拾雜碎的收拾雜碎，那個都不費手呢，因爲這個纔沒有能彀打發人去請。你的事情沒有人替手兒我是知道的，還等着你請麼，因此纔約會着朋友們來喫大肉來了，我們還恐怕趕不上呢，誰想來的正是時候兒。衆位別叫主人分心，咱們就序着齒一溜兒坐下喫。兄台們請喫肉泡上湯喫。哎呀這是甚麼話呢，錯了，咱們當初有這個樣兒的規矩來着麼這個

談論篇百章之八十七

兄[1]台你這位令郎是第幾個的。這是個老生兒子。出[3]了花兒了沒有。去[4]年出得花兒。這些個都是挨肩兒的麼。都是挨肩的生了九個存了九個[6]哎[7]真是難得的兄台這不是我說句頑兒話大嫂子真能幹哪久慣會養兒子可以算得是個子孫娘娘了實在是有福的人哪。甚[8]麼福啊前生造的罪罷咧大些兒的邊好點兒這幾個小的兒每天吱兒喳兒的吵得我腦袋都疼了。世[9]上的人都是這麼樣兒又嫌多了抱怨像我們子孫稀少的人們想有一個在那兒呢叫老天爺也難了。你[10]們妞兒若不丟如今也有十幾歲了。七[11]歲上沒得若有今年十歲了。那[12]魏真是個好孩子到如今也題起他來我都替你傷心那個像貌兒言語兒比別的孩子們另外的不同見了

甚麼事呢。若是死守着舊規矩那可是在旗杆底下誤了操了大睜着眼兒就誤了那成

談論篇百章之八十六

很有理,就請通知裡頭太太們,把小兒帶進去給太太們瞧瞧彼此都合了意的時候兒再磕頭也不遲啊。

這[1]不是給女婿做的衣裳麼。 是啊[2]。 這些[3]人是做甚麼的。 他們是僱了來的裁縫們。 哎呀[5]咱們家裡的舊規矩兒你們都忘了麼,老時候兒的孩子們都會做衣裳來着,就以做棉襖論罷,鋪上棉花合上裡兒,都是大家動手翻過來的時候兒,這個縫大襟,那個打盪子,這個煞胳肢窩,那個上領條兒沿袖口兒的沿袖口兒釘鈕子的釘鈕子,不過一兩天的工夫兒就做完了,況且連帽子都是家裡做來着,若是僱人做或是買着穿,人家都從鼻子裡見笑啊。兄台[6]兒比得麼況且要娶的日子,眼看着就到了,招着指頭兒算,剛剛兒的賸了十天的話,說的雖然有理,但你只知其一,不知其二,那個老時候兒和如今一個樣的工夫,如今這麼不留空兒的叫裁縫連着夜兒做,趕得上趕不上還不定呢。

談論篇百章之八十五

吾兄[1]今兒來有甚麼見教。因[2]為有緣我們特來求親來咯、我這個孩子雖然沒有超羣的才貌奇特的本事、但只是不喫酒不賭錢、就是那些迷惑人的去處兒胡游亂走的地方兒也一點兒沒到過、若不棄嫌、老爺們就賞賜句疼愛的話兒、你往前些兒咱們叩求。老爺們[3]別、大家坐下、聽我說一句話、咱們都是老親一個樣兒的是骨肉誰不知道誰呢、但只是作夫妻這件事都是前世裡造定的緣分由不得人的、為父母的自己眼瞧着孩子們、原不過盼着能彀配個好對兒、纔把苦枒苦掖的心腸也就完了、話雖是這麼說、我還有長輩兒沒有瞧見令郎呢、再者來的太太們把我們女孩兒也瞧瞧。是[4]啊、老爺說的

兒也沒有哼、全都忍了、又坐了好一會子、看着他的光景、順着他的氣兒慢慢兒的哀求他、剛剛兒的他纔點了頭咯。你[5]想一想我的性子若是略急一點兒、你的事情就不安了。

談論篇百章之八十四

明白白兒的告訴了那個朋友咯,不承望不是他一個人兒的事,說是人多嘴肘,沒肯應承,我還要看光景再說來着,後來想了一想,說罷呀,看事情的樣子,是不能挽回了,必定強壓派着叫人家應允,使得麼。故此我回來,告訴了他個信兒,倒說我壞了他的事咯,望着我撩臉子,好叫人齣心哪,早知道這麼樣,我何必說來着,這是圖甚麼呢。

我原想你這件事情,和他說去很容易來着,誰想這宗可惡的東西,竟這麼樣兒的口緊不依,倒鬧得很費了事咯。我把咱們商量的話,告訴了他一遍,他倒沉下臉來說,我說的話是胡說,我一聽這話,氣就到了脖頸子上了,心裡說,要怎麼樣就怎麼樣罷,滿心裡要惹他一惹。後來我想了一想,自己問着自己說,你錯了,這來不是為自己的事,為的是朋友們,若是鬧起來,不耽誤了人家的事麼,容讓他些兒,又費了我甚麼了呢。任憑他儘着量兒數落我一聲

兒的遇見他不在家纔交响午,我又去了剛一進院子,就聽見上房裡頭說啊
笑的聲兒我上了台階兒悄悄的把窗戶紙兒舔破了,從窗戶眼兒裡往裡一
瞧,看見這個給那個斟酒,那個給這個囘敬,正攪在一處兒喫喝熱鬧呢,我原
想進去來着,因為有好些個不認識的朋友冲散了人家喝酒的趣兒怪不得
人意兒的,我又就抽身出來了,他們家下人看見要告訴去,我急忙擺手兒攔
住了,你可別忙,明兒我起個黑早兒和他說安當了,就完咯。

談論篇百章之八十三

誰¹情願去管他的事情來着麼,我是好好兒的在家裡坐着的人啊,不知道他
在那塊兒打聽得說我認識那個人,一連來了好幾次和我說兒台,我這件事
實實在在的仗着你納了,求我疼他一定替他說說,在屁股後頭跟着總不放
我。我²起根兒臉頓,你是深知道的人家這麼懇兒的着急跪着哀求怎麼好
意思呢叫他沒趣兒囘去呢,因為推托不開所以我纔應承了。把他的事情³

談論篇百章之八十二

人有這個理麼行又不是止又不是實在是叫我進退兩難了，怎麼能彀得一箇萬全之計纔好啊。這個事情是顯而易見的，有甚麼不得主意的地方兒呢，你若是不行，是你的造化，若是行了，你能彀堵得住誰的嘴啊，趕到吵嚷開了，人人都知道了，你那纔到了離處兒了呢，這點兒些微的小便宜兒算甚麼那正是日後的禍苗呢，有利必定有害喫了虧的時候兒後悔就晚了，若照着我的主意，你別猶豫不決的拏定主意不行，就完了，儻再遲疑不斷的拉扯住了，那就打不成米，連口袋都丟了，要出個不像事的大醜呢。

我[1]有一件事要託吾兄，只是怪難開口的，甚麼緣故呢，實在求的事情太多了，但只是不求你納除你納之外再也沒有能成全我這件事的人，因此我又煩瑣你納來咯。你[2]不是為找姓張的那件事情來了麼。是啊[3]，你納怎麼知道了。今兒[4]早起你們令郎就和我說了，喫早飯的時候兒我就去了一次，偏偏

力呢、拏着甚麼報答上天生養的恩呢。

談論篇百章之八十

作好事、是說人應該行孝悌忠信的道理、並不是竟會供神佛齋僧道、就算作好事了、比方作惡的人們、任憑怎麼樣兒的喫齋修橋補路、焉能解了他的罪惡呢、就是神佛、也不能縠降福給他啊。那喫齋的上天堂喫肉的下地獄這種㨾兒的話、都是和尙道士們、借端糊口的、豈可深信得麼、他們若不拏着這麼長那麼短的利害話嚇諕人、怎麼誆騙人的錢財呢、若叫他們盡遵着佛敎關着廟門兒天天在裏頭、靜靜兒的持齋念經、不出來化緣、要喫沒有得喫、要穿沒有得穿、叫誰養活他呢、他竟喝風過日子麼。

談論篇百章之八十一

我有一件事、特來求吾兄指敎來咯、若要行、似乎略有點兒關係的地方兒、若是中止了不行、又很可惜了兒的、現成兒的、到了嘴裡的東西不喫、平白的讓

反倒使性子摔搭人、那兒有這個情理呢、比方是你的東西、人家愛惜、你自己也不愛惜、若是不由你作主、澈底兒都拏了去、你心裏頭怎麼懊呢。昨兒[3]因爲是我肯忍你那行子的性子罷咧、若除了我、不拘是誰、也肯讓你麼好好兒的記着我這話快快兒的畋了。 你[4]若是個沒有一點兒能爲的那還又是一說、現在還是有喫有穿的、只是要占個小便宜、是個甚麼緣故呢、也不怕人家背地裏說你眼皮子淺麼。

談論篇百章之七十九

古[1]語兒說的、幼不學老何爲這個話、是特意叫人勤學不可懶惰的意思啊、說是不拘甚麼懞兒的人、學會了米粒兒大的一點兒能幹、就算得完全了一輩子的事情了、何況是好好兒的肯學、還有甚麼不能幹的、何怕不作官呢。而[2]且又是旗人喫的不愁穿的不愁不用種地不用挑擔子不用作手藝坐着喫國家的糧米、有這些個便宜、自幼兒若不努力勤學、以着甚麼本事、給主子出

談論篇百章之七十八

[1]這是個甚麽意思呢甚麽稀罕東西、每逢看見、就和人家尋、也不覺絮煩麽、實在太不體面了罷、人家臉上過不去、也給過你好些次了、你心裡還不知足麽、[2]況且給是人情、不給是本分、你必定叫人家盡其所有的、都給了你、能彀麽。

去一瞧、果然是他、直挺挺的坐着、議論不斷的、自來了總沒有住嘴兒、這樣兒那樣兒的、直說了兩頓飯的工夫兒、到了黃昏的時候兒、他纔走了。[2]漢子家又沒有甚麽事情、就在人家家裡整天家坐着說話、這也受得麽、他那個東西、不但把些個陳穀子爛芝蔴人家講究瘦了的事情儘自說、聽得人家的腦袋都疼了、還有一樣可惡的、每逢他來、不拘甚麽好啊歹啊的、還得先藏起來叫他瞧見不得、儻若叫他看見了、連問也不問、楞模着攀着就走。[3]實在他這一輩子也沒有甚麽說頭兒了、像這種樣兒的雜碎都壞盡了、就是你這麽愛便宜能彀獨自得麽。

談論篇百章之七十七

為忙着來該班兒也沒得閒一閒剛纔聽見說是他叔叔不在了是他親叔叔麼。不[2]錯是他親叔叔。你弔喪去來沒有。昨兒[4]念經我在那兒坐了一整天呢。多啥[5]出殯啊知道不知道。說是月底呢。他們的塋地在那兒。離[8]我們家的墳地很近。噯[9]若是這麼着道兒很遠哪至少說着也有四五十里地。如果你再去見了他可以替我說道惱啊等下了班兒再同着你去看看他給他道煩惱出殯之前還請你千萬給我個信兒就不能送到他墳上去也必送到城外頭了平素間我們雖沒有甚麼大來往每逢遇見的時候兒說起話兒來就很親熱況且人生在世那個不是朋友呢他這樣兒的喪事我盡個人情想來也沒有人說咱們趕着他走動的話罷。

他[1]來的時候兒我在家裡正睡覺呢猛然驚醒了一聽上房裡來了客了在那兒說話兒呢想是誰來了呢說話這麼大噪子必是那個討厭的來了罷走進

了身直走到塋上、纔到了墳上、昨兒個供了飯、奠了酒、又歇了一夜、今兒東方亮兒、就起身往囘裡走、道兒上除了打尖兒、也總沒有敢歇着、剛剛兒的趕掩城門兒的時候兒、纔進來了。在遠地方兒立墳、雖說是好、若是到了子孫們、沒有力量兒、就難按着時候兒上墳了。可不是麼舊塋地裡倒離得很近、因爲沒有地方兒葬埋人口、請了看風水的人瞧、他們都說那一塊地好、故此在那兒立了墳、略遠些、是總而言之咱們有是有的道理、沒有是沒有的道理、無論是怎麼樣兒的窨、不能彀坐車、連步行兒去、也要到墳上奠一鍾酒啊、若到了子孫們、就難定了、只看他們有出息兒、沒出息兒、就是咯、若是個沒有出息兒、不惦念上墳的子孫、就是他們住得離着墳地很近、還未必能彀燒一張紙錢呢。

談論篇百章之七十六

他們家裡誰不在了、大前兒我從那兒過、看見他家裡的人們、都穿着孝呢、因[1]

談論篇百章之七十四

昨兒往誰家去來着,囘來的那麼晚。 我是瞧咱們朋友去來着,他家住得太遠,在西城根兒底下呢,又搭着留我喫了一頓飯,故此囘來的略遲些兒。我有一件事要和你納商量,打發了幾次人去請去,你納那兒家下人們說,坐了車出去了,也沒留下話,我算計着,一定到我家裡來,誰知道等到日平西,也不見的,這幾個朋友們罷咧,瞧完了,來,算是白等了一天哪。 兄台打發找我的人沒到已前,我已經早出了門了,囘家的時候兒,小子們告訴說,老兄這兒打發了兩三次人來叫我,彼時就要來來着,因爲太晚了,又恐怕關了栅欄兒,所以今兒纔來。

談論篇百章之七十五

你前兒往莊子上上墳去來着麼。 是啊。 怎麼今兒纔囘來。 我們墳地離得很遠哪,所以當天去,不能囘來,又在那兒歇了兩夜,前兒個,頂城門兒就起

談論篇百章之七十三

我還有甚麼說得呢、那就是愛惜我兄弟了。

你[1]納往那兒去來着、我往那邊兒一個親戚家去來着、閣下順便兒到我們家裡坐坐兒罷。兄[2]台你納在這左近住麼。是啊、新近纔搬在這房子來的。若[3]是這麼着咱們住的離着卻不甚遠啊、我若是知道府上在這兒就早過來瞧來了、老兄先走。豈[4]有此理、這是我家啊、你納請上坐。我這兒坐着舒服。你[5]納這麼坐了、叫我怎麼坐呢。我[6]已經坐下了、這兒有個靠頭兒。來[7]。擎[8]火來。老[9]兄我不喫煙嘴裡長了口瘡了。若[10]是這麼着快倒茶來。兄[11]台請喫茶。老[12]弟請看飯去把現成兒的先擎了來。兄[13]台別費心、我還要往別處兒去呢。怎[14]麼了、現成兒的東西、又不是為你納預備的、隨便兒將就着喫點兒罷。兄[15]台我還是外人、已經認得府上了、敗日再來、咱們坐着說一天的話兒、今兒實在沒空兒告假了。

談論篇百章之七十二

東西、我沒喫過啊、你若這樣兒的不實誠竟是明明兒的叫我再別往你家去的意思啊。老[1]兄你怎麼纔來、我等了這麼半天了、差一點兒沒有睡着了。我[2]告訴你說、我們纔要動身往這兒來、想不到遇見個討人嫌的死肉、刺刺不休又不要緊這麼長那麼短的、只是說不完、我若沒有事絮叨些兒何妨呢、只管由他說罷咧、但只怕你等急了、沒法兒我說我們有事、明兒再說罷、這纔把他的話攔住了、不然早來都坐煩了。別[3]說太遲了來的正是時候兒、誰在這兒說呢、快放桌子想必爺們都餓了、飯哪甚麽的都簡決些兒。噯[4]兄弟你這是怎麽說呢、我[5]這有 剛的白肉就得了、又要這麼許多的菜蔬作甚麼、把我們當客待麼。你[6]這就不必過不過是一點兒心也沒有甚麼好東西啊、兄台就着喫些兒。若[7]是那們着讓了、太盛殼了、我們自家喫呢、若不喫飽也不肯放下筷子啊。

談論篇百章之七十一

這一向,你又往那兒奔波去了,遇見有空兒何不到我這兒走走呢,怎麼總不見你的面兒咯。我早要瞧兒台來着,不想叫一件旁不相干兒的事情絆住了,竟受了累了,整天家忙,那兒有點兒空兒呢,若不是今兒還不能彀脫身兒呢,今兒個摘脫,是說我有件要緊的事情撒了個謊,剛剛兒的放了我來了。你來的很好,我正悶得慌呢,想來你也可以抽點空兒來麼,咱們坐着說一天的話兒,現成兒的飯喫了去,我也不另弄別的喫的咯。但只往這兒來了,無緣無故的就這麼攪擾啊,我心裡也不安,因其這個,我就不敢常來。你怎麼這麼外道呢,咱們從幾兒分過彼此來若再隔幾天你不來,我還要預備點東西兒特請你去呢,這一頓現成兒的空飯又何足掛齒況且你的甚麼

談論篇百章之七十

兄[1]台、你聽見了麼、咱們那個饞嘴的東西、說是破敗得很困住了、襤褸成個花子樣兒、戰抖抖的披着一塊破被。那[2]趁該死的去年甚麼罪兒他沒受過、甚麼苦兒他沒喫過、但分有一點兒志氣也改悔過來了、俗語說的、窮兒來咯、還有甚麼心腸說這兒的酒好、那兒的茶好和富貴人們、一般一配的、各處兒游玩、那時候兒我就說等着到了上冬的時候兒看他怎麼樣再瞧罷咧、如今果然應了我的話了。老兄[3]話雖是這樣兒說、現在他旣落到這步田地、可當眞的瞧着叫他死麼、我心裡想着、咱們大家畧攢湊攢湊、弄點兒銀子幫幫他纔好。若[4]像這麼樣兒幫他銀子、還不是主意、怎麽說呢、他的皮氣你還不知道麼、一到了

年窄住的時候兒求到我跟前誰問他有甚麼來着他自己說他有好書你納要看我送來。像這麼懞兒的應許我後來事情完了書連提也不提了日子久沒信兒那一天我遇見他說你許給我那部書怎麼樣了誰知當面兒一問、他臉上一紅一白的只是支吾說不出甚麼緣故來咯。這一部書有甚麼稀罕啊給我不給我也不要緊竟是無故的哄人未免太討人嫌了。

談論篇百章之六十九

兄[1]台你納這麼固辭我的東西不肯留下我十分不明白你的心意還是因為我來遲了故此纔這麼樣兒待我還是因為別的呢。 素常[2]我尙且長長兒的來老家兒的好日子倒不來那怎麼是朋友呢寳在是知道晚了若是先知道應當早來纔是。 雖[3]說是有我不多沒我不少替你納待待客也好啊若論你納高親貴友送來的禮物還少麼想來是喫不了的我這點子微物兒又何足掛齒呢然而也是我一點兒孝心。那兒[4]敢必定請老人家喫呢但只略嚐點

點分兒也不肯留、必要直言奉上、雖然交朋友有規過的道理、也當看他的爲人、可勸再勸罷咧、若不這樣兒只說是個朋友、並不分親疏、那如何使得呢、方纔說的這些話、那不是好心麼、他倒心裡很不舒服、瞪着眼疑惑着說噯呀、要小心啊、保不定這是害我罷。兄[2]台、你說的這些話實在是給我治病的良藥啊、我很信服、這原是我一生的毛病兒、我豈不知道麼、就是遇見這樣兒的事情、不由的嘴就癢癢說出來、古語原有、不可與言而與之言謂之失言的話啊、從今兒起、我痛改前非罷、日後再要這麼樣兒多說話、縱使兄台往我臉上啐吐沫、我也甘心領受。

談論篇百章之六十八

好人[1]再沒有過於你了、還不住口兒的稱讚、你那個朋友太過於老實了、那混帳行子有甚麼大講究頭兒啊、斷不可提他。他[2]若有求煩人的事情、別人說甚麼話、他就照樣兒依着行、他的事情一完、把頭一轉、是人全不認得。他[3]去

談論篇百章之六十六

噯[1]世上沒有記性的人、再沒有比你過逾的了、前兒我怎麼囑咐你來着、這件事情、任憑他是誰、總不可叫人知道了、你到底兒洩漏了、咱們倆悄悄兒商量的話、如今吵嚷的處處兒沒有人沒聽見過了、他們這些人、儻若羞惱變成怒了、望咱們不依、動起手腳兒來、咱們得了甚麼便宜了麼、把好好兒的事情倒弄壞了全都是你呀。老兄[2]像你這麼樣兒怪我我真委屈現在事情已經這樣兒了、我縱然分辨個牙清口白的、你肯信麼我的心就是老天爺看得真、是我說來着不是我說來着久而自明依我的主意你先不必抱怨索性粧個不知道、看他們的動靜、依呢就依了、如果不依的時候兒、再作道理、預備也不遲啊。

談論篇百章之六十七

你啊[1]是個很好的人、心裡沒有一點渣兒、就是嘴太直、知道了人家的是非一

談論篇百章之六十五

方纔[1]我上衙門囘來、從老遠的矗得一羣人騎着馬往這邊來了、到了跟前兒、細認了一認、原是咱們舊街坊某人、穿的騎的都很體面、真是肥馬輕裘的面貌兒也大胖了、他看見我連理也沒理把臉往那們一扭望着天就過去了、彼時我就要叫住他、很很的羞辱他來、後來我想了一想、說罷啊做甚麼他理我、我就體面了麼誰那們大工夫和他計較這些個。噯[2]老兄你納不記得麼、三年以前在咱們那兒住着的時候兒那是甚麼樣兒來着很窮啊喫了早起巴結晚上的天天兒游魂似的忍着餓各處兒張羅拾着一根草都是希罕的、一天至不及也到我家兩三次不是尋這個就是要那個我的甚麼他沒喫過筷子都啞明了、如今是求不着人了、一旦之間就變了性咯、忘了舊時候兒的景況了、也不是咱們自己檯舉自己這種小人乍富的皮氣、偺們很可以不理他罷了。

談論篇百章之六十四

那[1]是個沒出息兒的東西，你怎麽瞧上他來着呢，雖是個人身子，却是牲口腸子，總是躲着他些纔好呢。你[2]把我這句話你擱在心上，他原是個無事生事的混帳行子啊，心眼子又黑，常是聽見雨兒的人家略有點兒細故，叫他聽見，他就滿處兒混嚼說張揚楊個不堪啊，把這兒的事情傳在那兒，把那兒的信兒告訴這兒，他可從中作好人兒。你[3]看我說的話信不得，你瞧不但沒有一個人兒和他相好的，若不指着他的脊梁罵他，那就是他的便宜了。嗳[4]他爺母生下這種樣兒的賤貨兒來，討人家的厭，也實在是沒德行咯。

你的話是了，一口咬定了，不肯認錯，能不叫人更生氣麽。你[3]太把我看輕咯，實在不知道你仗着甚麽能彀有這個儇兒的舉動兒，誰也不能彀了誰，誰還怕誰麽，若果然要見個高低兒很合我的式，若略打一個證兒也不是好漢子。

談論篇百章之六十三

好跟人要個嘴皮子，你有甚麼不知道的，想來又是喝醉了，你只當是沒看見沒有聽見就結了，何必理他呢。老弟[3]你不知道這樣兒輭的欺硬的怕的東西跟前若給他留點分兒他更長了價兒了他索性說我是頑兒不知不覺的話說冐失了人家或者可以原諒罷咧反倒滿臉的怒氣誰怕他不成。兄[4]台你別生氣我把這個酒鬼帶在僻靜的地方兒指着臉兒罵他一頓給你出出氣。

壞[1]了腸子咯把我輕慢得了不得，我和你說話，都不配麼動不動兒的就拏巧話兒譏誚我把自己當成甚麽咯，每日裡鼻子臉子的常在一塊兒混混，我只不說罷咧，我若說出根子來，未免又說我揭短了。你的[2]家鄉，我的住處，誰不知道誰呢，你不受人家的揉挫魆有幾天兒啊，如今賤貨兒這就和我作起足來了，是甚麼意思呢，索性說失了言兒咯，那個還可以恕得過去偏死扭着說

友們當作話把兒墶塲我這是甚麽心意呢,新近給我們孩子娶媳婦兒,我還臉上下不來,請他去來着,連一個狗也沒打發來,我所遇見的朋友都是這個薄情的,可叫我怎麽再往後結交呢。那個時候兒你還理論麽,倒很有點兒不舒服我來着。那個人說話行事很假,信不得,我沒說過麽,那個時候兒你還理論麽,倒很有點兒不舒服我來着。原是俗語兒說的知人知面不知心,他心裏頭的好歹,如何能彀知道得透澈呢,將來只得小心。那就是了,不分好歹一槪都說是很相好的使得麽。

談論篇百章之六十二

誰[1]和他說長道短了麽,本是他的話,逼着叫我說啊,瞞得住別人兒,瞞得住你麽,自從過年以來,他還走了甚麽差使麽,今兒是在那兒喝了酒了,剛一進門兒,來,就是噯呀我怎麽纔瞧見你啊,若照他那麽說,我不脫空兒的整月家替他當差使,反倒不是了麽,眞使我的氣,就到了脖脛于上了,今兒且不必論明兒再說罷。

老兄[2],不用往他較量這個,和他一般一配的爭競,做甚麽,他一味兒他也是個人罷咧,能彀不按着道理行麽,說出緣故來,你就從頭至尾的一一的分解開了,怕他能彀把你怎麽樣麽,怕殺呀,或是怕嚇了你呢。況且別人都沒動靜兒,你來不來的先這麽怕,這樣兒那樣兒的防備着,還有個漢子的味兒麽。依我勸你也放寬了心罷,他果然不依你,若和你見個高低兒還給你留情麽,你如今就是這麽懞兒的怕了,能彀乾乾淨淨兒沒事兒麽,我看起來到而今也沒個音信,想是他早已忘了,你若不信,悄悄的探聽個信兒管保你無妨無礙的呀。

談論篇百章之六十一

你[1]們很相好啊,如今怎麽了,總不登你的門檻兒了麽。我[2]不知道他,想是有誰得罪了他咯罷,不然還有一說,從前我們還好好端端的行走着來着,就是因爲一半句話上,也不犯記在心裏惱了就不往我行走了,不行走也沒甚麽要緊,怎麽背地裡還只說我這樣兒不好,那樣兒利害,所有遇見我認識的朋

談論篇百章之五十九

咱們那個朋友[1]、是遭甚麼為難的事麼、這幾天看他那個愁容滿面、無聊無賴的樣兒、是有甚麼緣故呢。不知道他素來沒一天不在街上、下雨下雪的日子、他總在家裏、除此以外是地方兒他就去逛[2]叫他在家裏白坐着、那兒坐得住呢、這一向因沒出大門兒、竟在家裡呢、昨兒我去賙他、啊[3]臉面兒還像先麼、很瘦了、竟是坐不安、睡不甯似的、我瞧着很疑惑、總要問他、可巧又來了一個親戚、把話打住了。噯呀[4]若依你這麼說、大約是叫那件事絆住心亂了、雖是那麼說、然而有經過大難、不怕小煩的話啊、他那個人從前甚麼樣兒的難事都清清楚楚兒的辦完了、這些細故又筭甚麼要緊的呢、也值得那麼愁麼。

談論篇百章之六十

你[1]太沒有經過事怯極了、有話為甚麼放在心裏、直去和他講明說開就完了、

談論篇百章之五十八

你[1]這麼寃他是甚麼道理人家恭恭敬敬的在你跟前討個主意知道就說知道不知道就說不知道罷了撒謊作甚麼儻若把人家的事情就誤了倒像你有心害他似的他若不是個可惡的人也就不怪你這麼憐兒待他我看他那個人很老實一晗就知道是個慢性子別人若是這麼欺負他咱們還當攔勸呢你反倒這樣兒的刻薄太錯了眞眞的我心裡過不去。兄台[2]你原來不知道可要叫他誆哄了啊那宗東西外面皮兒雖像愚蠢心裏却不得他那性情險惡之極你沒試過就不知道他的壞處兒了法子多圈套兒大慣會和人討憑據不論甚麼事預先拏話勾引你把你的主意套了去然後遠遠兒的觀望着聽你的空子稍微有點兒破綻跟進去就給你一個兠屁股將兄台你想這個事情原有關礙我的地方兒啊若是把徹底子的主意告訴他如何使得呢你這麼怪我我不委屈麼。

談論篇百章之五十七

兄台、你聽見了麼話頭話尾的、都是刻薄我穿的膽舊。不是我誇口、他呀還算是小孩子呢、能彀懂得甚麼這也不是他們知道的事啊、新衣裳是偶然有事情穿的罷咧、我這不過家常穿的舊些兒、何妨呢、漢子家沒有本事該當羞罷咧、穿的有甚麼關係呢、卽如我雖不穿好的、心裏頭、却比那穿好的還寬綽。甚麼緣故呢、不求告人、不欠債、這就沒有可恥的地方兒、若像他們這種年輕的人兒們、我眼角兒裡也沒有他、只知道穿鮮明衣裳搖搖擺擺的、竟充體面、能知道學漢子的本事麼、若像他們這個樣兒的、就是叫綢緞裏到底兒又有甚麼奇處兒呢。最下賤沒眼珠兒的人們、混說他體面、巴結他們罷咧、若是我說、他們不過是個掛衣裳的架子。

長兒的勸他呢、後來知道他的皮氣不能攺了、不是有出息兒的東西、何必白勞骨乏舌的勸他呢。

談論篇百章之五十六

他那個動作兒是個甚麼樣兒呢、在人家跟前兒說話、結結巴巴的、怎麼問怎麼答都不知道、畏首畏尾的、怎麼進怎麼退也不懂得、醒着倒像人家睡着了一樣的、白充個人數兒糊裡糊塗的、怎麼長來着呢、你們相好啊、略指教指教他也就好了。這個人你納沒在一塊兒長來往、還沒有深知、比這個可笑的事還多呢、和他一處兒坐下、說起話來、正說着這個、忽然想起別的來、就說那個、不然、就搭拉着嘴兒不錯眼珠兒的、瞅着你、猛然間又說出一句無頭無尾的獸話來、叫人笑斷了肚腸子啊、前兒瞧我去來着、後來臨走的時候兒、不往前直走、轉過脊梁來倒退着走、我說兄台小心門檻子、話沒說完、絆住脚了、身子往後一歪、仰着面兒跌了去咯、我急忙趕上扶住、幾幾乎沒跌倒、我還長

談論篇百章之五十五

着的老虎哄起來了，自找喫虧，這有甚麼趣兒呢，俗語兒說的，有拐棍兒不跌跤，有商量兒不失着，光你一個人兒的見識，能殼到那兒，任憑怎麼懞，我總比你長幾歲這一層，若果然是該行的，就是你心裏不願意去，我還該提撥着你催着你叫你去呢，豈有倒攔着你的情理麼。

你[1]怎麼這麼樣兒不穩重，若是體體面面兒坐着，誰說你是木雕泥塑的廢物麼，你若不言不語的，誰說你是啞吧麼，倒像在人跟前兒故意兒鬮笑兒似的，惹了這個又招那個，有甚麼樂處兒呢，你自己不覺罷咯，傍邊兒的人都受不得了，多啥遇見一個利害人喫了虧的時候兒，你纔知道有關係呢。老弟[2]你令兒的話實在是不錯，頑笑是辯嘴的由頭，久而久之生出甚麼好事來呀，若是傍不相干兒的肯這麼說得關切麼，你寡長了身量歲數兒還早呢，務必要留心啟了啊。咱們[3]沒有從那個時候過過麼，正是貪頑兒的時候兒呀，我

談論篇百章之五十四

罣礙麼、他們議論他、連咱們也稍上了、你不攔着反倒隨着他們的口氣兒說、這是甚麼意思、我心裏真有點兒不服。不是那麼着若有話、從從容容兒的說、你這麼急繃繃的、難道就算完了事咯麼、你看這兒在坐的人、都是爲你的事情來的、你只管這麼怒氣冲冲的、倒像要把誰攆出去的似的、這些人怎麼好意思坐着呢、要走罷又恐怕你臉上下不來、若在這兒多坐會兒、你又山嚷怪叫的叫喊、這就叫人進退兩難了啊、以後朋友們、還怎麼和你來往呢。

看[1]起你來、只就是嘴能幹、外面兒雖像明白、心裏却不燎亮、他不尋嗔你來、就是你的便宜、你可惹他作甚麼、好話總不聽、倒像神鬼指使的一個樣、強拗着去了、到底碰了釘子囘來咯。那該死的[2]你說他是誰、了不得、有名兒的利害人啊、從不給人留分兒、與他不相干的事、還可以略有一點兒妨碍他的地方兒、不拘是誰、蠻着勁兒、必要站住理、得了便宜纔歇手。這不是咯[3]、到底把臥

不是看財奴有愛惜銀錢不愛惜身子的理麼、都因爲前年我喫錯了藥幾幾乎沒有喪了命、到今兒想起來心裏還跳呢。如今的醫生好的離有百裏也不過挑一、其餘的只知道掙銀子錢他那兒管人家的性命死活呢。你若不信、請一個醫生來試一試、藥性他還不定懂得了沒有就大着膽子給人家治病慌慌張張的來到家裏說是診脈、其實不過使指頭混摩一囘胡哩嗎哩的、開個藥方兒拏上馬錢去了、若是好了、算是他的力量兒、若是不好、說是你的命定與他毫不相干。 我⁴這個病、我不知道麼與其奧各樣兒的藥不見效不如自己靜靜兒的養着倒好。

談論篇百章之五十三

別人¹說他與你何干呢、怎麼我這麼勸你、越勸越生氣哎、太急燥了罷、等客散了、再說罷、必定此刻要分辨明白麼。 兄台²、你說得這個話、我心裏竟聽不進去、咱們是一個船兒上的人哪、這個事也與你有點兒牽連、難道沒有一點兒

得下誰呢。話沒說完眼淚直流下來,好傷心哪,就是鐵石的人,聽了他的那個話,也沒有不慘得慌的。

談論篇百章之五十一

人若是不該死自然而然的有救星兒,他那一夜病得很沉重昏過去了,等了好一會子幾甦醒過來,我嘴裏雖然是安慰老人家說請放心無妨無妨心裏實在是沒指望兒了。誰想那老人家的福氣大病人的造化好到了第二天,另請了一個大夫治了治眼看着一天比一天的好了。前兒我去看他見他的身子雖然沒有還元兒臉上的氣色兒可轉過來了,也略長了點兒肉了,在那兒靠着枕頭喫東西呢,我說好啊大喜咯,這一塲病可不輕雖然沒死也脫了一層皮呀。他和我笑嘻嘻的說托着大家的福,如今出了災咯可大好了。

談論篇百章之五十二

你勸我喫藥,何曾不是好話,但只是我另有一個心思,若果然該當服藥,我又

這麼惦記我麼、我也沒有甚麼說的、只是記在心裏等着病好了、再磕頭道謝罷。他⁸嘴裏雖然是這麼說、身子可露出扎掙不住的樣兒來了。我們⁴就說、老弟你是個很聰明的人、不用我們多說、好好兒的養着身子、快好了罷、我們得空兒再來瞧你、說完就囘來了。

談論篇百章之五十

夏¹天的時候兒、他還可以扎掙着走來走去、近來這些日子添了病、竟躺下了、闔家子亂亂烘烘的、沒主意、老家兒們、愁得都瘦了。那²一天、我去瞧他、見他瘦得不成樣兒了、在炕上倒氣兒呢、我慢慢兒的走到他跟前兒說、你如今好了些兒麼。他³睜開眼瞧見我、把我的手緊緊的揝住說、哎、我的兄台這是我的罪呀、病到這個分兒上、大料是不能好了、我不知道麼、自從有病那個大夫沒治過、甚麼樣兒的藥沒喫過、總好了一好兒、又重落了、這是我命該如此、我並不委屈、但只惦記父母上了年紀、兄弟又小、再者親戚骨肉都在這兒、我能撂

談論篇百章之四十九

只因親戚們、昔裏昔兒的、都在這兒會齊兒、我怎麼擱下去睡呢、身子雖然強扎擇着、還在那兒陪着坐、哎、眼睛却十分受不得了、眼皮子也搭拉了、心裏也糊塗了、沒法子、等到客一散、就抓了個枕頭、穿着渾身的衣裳睡着了、直到四更天纔醒、不知道是怎麼着了點兒涼、覺着腹中膨悶渾身發燒、就像火烤的一懞、又搭上害耳朶底子、疼得連顋頰都腫了、飲食無味坐臥不安。我[3]想是停住食了、就服了一劑打藥把內裏所有好啊歹的東西、都打下來了、這心裏纔覺着鬆快些兒。

他[1]本是個弱身子、又不知道保養、過食酒色、所以氣血虧損了。如今[2]的病很延纏、昨兒我們去瞧的時候兒、他還扎擇着來到上房、和我們說、這樣兒的熱天氣、常勞動兒台們來瞧、太勞乏了、我實在不敢當、又不住的送東西、過於費心、我十分感情不盡、總還是親戚們、關心想着我、若是傍不相干兒的人、能彀

的作甚麼，總是不賭錢纔好，我必定打聽作甚麼呢。

談論篇百章之四十七

[1]我看你酒上很親，一時也離不開，貪得過逾了，每逢喝酒，必要喝得很醉，到站不住腳兒的時候兒纔算了，這不是好事啊，少喝點兒不好麼。若是[2]赴席，有喜事呢，多喝點兒還無妨，若不論有事沒事，只管掌着不離嘴的喝，生出甚麼好事來呀，不過是討女人兒厭煩，在長輩兒們跟前得不是，輕着躭誤了要緊的事情，重着要惹出大禍來咯，若說是藉着酒學了本事，長了才幹成了正經事情的，叫人家敬重那個可少啊。[3]總而言之，酒就是亂性傷身子的毒藥，任着意兒喝，萬萬使不得你若不信，照着鏡子瞧一瞧，鼻子臉都叫酒糟透了，你又不是平常的人兒，不分晝夜的這麼喝，這不是自己害了自己麼。

談論篇百章之四十八

[1]我這幾天有事，一連熬了兩夜渾身很乏，沒有勁兒。[2]昨兒晚上要早睡來着，

談論篇百章之四十六

哎[1]呀老弟你怎麼咯咱們纔隔了幾天哪這麼快韻子都白咯露出老樣兒來了你別怪我嘴直聽見說你如今上了要錢場兒了還該下許多的賬若果然是那麼着不是玩兒的呀得略收收兒纔好哪。這[2]都是沒影兒的話胡編造的你納若不信請細細兒的打聽打聽就知道了。哎[3]說的是甚麼話呢自己行的自己不知道麼看起朋友們都議論你來想必你是有點兒罷咧這要錢有甚麼捆兒若是陷進去了那是個底兒就是不犯王法也是連一個大錢膽不下都是家業弄個精光的纔撂開手這樣兒的事情我眼裏見的耳朵裏聽的離不多也有了百數個咯咱們是知己的朋友旣知道了若是不勸要相好

動幸而昨兒把所喫所喝的全吐了不然今兒也就扎掙不住了。我[4]教給你法子但只餓着肚子少少兒的喫東西若是那麼着就是些微的着點兒涼也就無妨了。

今以後叫他很很心戒了酒罷俗語兒說的主子管奴才靴子裏摸襪子他能躱到那兒去啊敀呢更好若是不敀仍舊還是這麼往醉裏喝那時候兄台重重的責罰他我就是再遇見也不管求情了。老弟你不知道他是生來不成器的東西若說喝酒就捨了命比他老子的血還親今兒饒了他我保他不能改至多一兩天不喝罷咧過了後兒必定還是照着樣兒喝。

談論篇百章之四十五

兄¹台你怎麽咯臉上刷白的冷孤丁的就瘦成這個樣兒了。老弟²你不知道因爲這幾天洵溝的味兒很不好又搭着天氣乍涼乍熱的沒準兒故此人都不能保養身子前兒喫早飯的時候兒就很涼來着一會兒的時候兒又熱起來了人人都受不得我炮燥的出了一身透汗脫了袍子要涼快涼快又喝了一碗涼茶立刻就頭疼起來了鼻子也傷了風咯嗓子也啞了身子像坐在雲彩上的一樣暈暈忽忽的不舒服。不³獨你是那樣兒我的身子也不爽快懶怠

同來那猴兒們正吵嚷呢我咳嗽了一聲走進來一齊都住了聲咯賊眉鼠眼的使眼色兒一個個的躲避着走咯今兒[2]早起剛起來該殺的們都來咯直橛兒的跪着說奴才們該死求的求磕頭的磕頭這樣兒的哀求我的氣總略平了些兒我說你們怎麼咯不好好兒的肉癢癢了罷必定叫我打一頓有甚麼便宜呢從今兒以後再要這麼着小心你們那皮肉若不結結實實的打你們也不知道怕呀說完都喳的一聲答應着出去了

談論篇百章之四十四

老弟[1]你瞧他今兒又醉了喝得成了泥咯站都站不住了我問他那個事情你告訴人家沒有他前仰兒後合的直瞪着兩眼一聲兒不言語又不是聾子啞吧爲甚麼不答言兒今兒若不把這個該殺的痛痛快快的責罰他一頓我就起個誓兒[2]台罷喲他想是忘了沒有去他的不是他不知道麼因爲這個心裏害怕不敢答言兒今兒旣然是我在這兒看着我的面上饒過這一次罷從

兒的哄着、叫他喜歡呢必定討他的厭煩作甚麼。

談論篇百章之四十二

你[1]看這種賤貨竟不是個人哪長得活脫兒的、像他老子一個儜、越瞧越討人嫌。不論[2]是到那兒、兩隻眼睛擠顧擠顧的、任甚麼兒看不見、混撞、嘴裏磕磕巴巴的、實在是漚人。正經[3]事情上、絲毫不中用、若是陶氣很能、一點兒崟兒不給、常叫他在跟前兒服侍、還好些兒、若不然、就陶氣的了不得眞是個鬧事精撂下這個、拏起那個猴兒似的一樣、嘮叨叮咕咚的不安靜。我[4]若是氣上來、眞得把他打死了纔解恨、過了氣兒又一想、可怎麼憐呢當眞的打殺他罷又怪不忍得、而且是家生子兒火棍兒短強如手撥咯遇着我有一點兒得項、或是有點兒喫喝兒的地方兒倒偏疼他些兒。

談論篇百章之四十三

昨[1]兒個、我往別處兒去的時候兒這賤奴才們、就任着意兒辯嘴吵鬧趕到我

雀兒。䴕一倒手嚕嚕的一聲飛咯我趕緊關上門剛拏住又掙脫了滿屋子裏正趕着拏的時候兒小孩子們聽見說拏住雀兒了一齊都來咯趕的拏有一個小孩子使帽子扣住了。拏他作甚麼放了罷他一定不肯打着墜毂轆兒的要沒法兒給了他咯他䴕跳跳鑽鑽的喜歡着去了。後來我說哎人家還買雀兒放生呢你

談論篇百章之四十一

兒[1]台，你納瞧這種懞兒的壞孩子可有麼別人這懞兒的勸他不過是要他好恐怕他學壞了的意思人都是這懞兒往正經本事上學很難若往壞處兒學就很容易。到[2]如今我就是說破了嘴他也不肯聽反到無精打彩的嘑着嘴撏着臉子剛䴕我心裏實在受不得動了氣很很的打了他一頓。他[3]臉上一紅和我說只是找我的錯縫子作甚麼眼淚汪汪的走了，真是個糊塗沒造化的人哪。俗語[4]兒說的眞藥苦口忠言逆耳若不是一家兒我巴不得

的一個樣兒把咱們過去的事倒像誰告訴他的算得極眞說得準對咱們的人們去的很多整天家接連不斷的命棚裏都擠滿了有這樣兒的高明人咱們何不也叫他瞧瞧去。我[2]早兒已知道了我的朋友這幾天都去過前兒我也到了那兒把我的八字兒叫他瞧了瞧爹母屬甚麼兄弟有幾個女人姓甚麼多偺得的官件件兒都算得正對絲毫也不錯的我想過去的事情雖然都應了但只未來的事怕未必能應他的話罷。雖[3]然話是這麼說咱們那兒花不了這幾百錢呢與其在家裏白坐着不如去逛一逛只當解個悶兒又有何不可呢。

談論篇百章之四十

我[1]告訴你個笑話兒剛纔我一個人兒這兒坐着看見窗戶檔兒上落着一個雀兒老爺兒照着他的影兒一跳一跳的。我[2]慢慢兒的捻手捻腳兒的走到跟前兒隔着窗戶紙兒一抓把窗戶抓了個大窟窿恰好抓住了一看是個家

談論篇百章之三十八

兄[1]台你那盤誦珠兒我說要拏去、到底沒有拏了去。甚[2]麼緣故呢。我遭遭兒來了、你都沒在家沒見你含糊着拏你的東西去有這個理麼因爲這麼着我今兒特來見你告訴了我好拏了去、你要甚麼東西合着你的意思我買了來補你的情就是鋪子裏沒有賣的我也必定想着法子各處兒尋了來給你、你心下如何。索[4]性你頭裏拏了去、倒好了。怎麼咯。丟[6]咯。噯[7]可惜了兒的菩提誦珠兒雖多像那個檛兒的却很少啊天天的拏來拏去汗溻透了很光滑了、不拏的時候兒該收在櫃子裏就好了。哎[8]也是該丟、上月我往園子裏去在排牖兒上掛着忘了沒收囘來一找那兒還有呢、連踪影兒都不見了。不知道叫誰偷了去咯。

談論篇百章之三十九

兄[1]台你可聽見麼、新近城外頭來了一個算命的、都說是很靈、就像神仙轉世

談論篇百章之三十七

你們¹對過兒的那所房子如何。你²問他作甚麼。我³有個朋友要買。那⁴個房子住不得,很凶底根兒是我們家兒住着來着,地勢很好,門面房七間,到底兒五層,住着很合懷,又乾淨,後來到了我姪兒的手裏,說廂房夥爛了,從新蓋了蓋,忽然鬼啊怪的作起祟來了,起初鬧的還好些兒,久而久之,白日裏出了聲兒咯,後來就顯了形兒,家裏的女人們動不動兒的就撞磕着嚇的了性命兒的都有,跳神也枉然,送祟也沒用,沒法兒賤賤的價兒就賣了。兄⁵台你知道麼,這都是運氣不好的緣故,若是時運旺的時候兒,就有邪祟,他也躲避着,不能害人,但是我那個朋友膽兒很小,我把這個打聽的實話告訴他就完了,買不買由他罷。

的話啊,今兒降在這兒了,忙擺了一鍾酒,禱告着祭奠了祭奠,那所着的酒立刻都滅了。這⁵是我親見的事情,你們說怪不怪。

談論篇百章之三十六

兄[1]台們提起話兒來就說鬼,我也告訴你們一件怪事,你們說的都是在古兒詞上看下來的,我這個是我親自經過的。那[2]一年,我們出城閒逛,回來的時候,看見道傍邊兒有座大墳院,房屋牆垣都破爛了,歪的倒,倒的倒,那裏頭各樣兒的樹木長得可是很深密。我[3]們說這個地方兒很涼快,咱們進去略歇一歇兒,把帶着的果子茶放下,就在墳前坐着喫喝起來了,正喫喝着的時候,鍾子裏所斟的酒忽然自己熔熔的都着了。衆[4]人看見,都嚇愣了,剛要躲着走,我一個叔叔忙擺手兒說,站住,你們別怕,頭裏時候兒,有給鄂博留謝儀戶裏跳出去了。我那朋友心裏暗想着,若果然是鬼,有拏衣裳的理麼,正想着的時候兒,那個該殺的又進來了,我那朋友就猛然起來,拏着腰刀,把他斫了一下兒,那個東西哎呀了一聲,倒在地下了。叫[5]了家下人來點上鐙一照,很可笑,原來是個賊,爲偷東西,故意兒的粧成鬼來嚇人來咯。

有個褂子的名兒就是咯毛稍兒也壞了顏色兒也變了反穿不得了。若是[10]那們等關了俸的時候兒再買件好的就是咯。哎[11]我是過了時的人了還講究甚麼樣兒呢但只燠和就是了,你們是年輕的人兒們,正在往上巴結的時候兒遇着朝會的日子穿件好的打扮打扮是該當的,我若是穿了好的不但不得樣兒,而且不舒服,況且我們武職差使上,也用不着好衣裳索性穿舊的破的倒和我們很對勁兒。

談論篇百章之三十五

我[1]有個朋友膽子很大夏天的時候兒黑下撘着窗戶睡正睡着了,覺着耳朵裏聽見有響聲兒睜開眼一瞧,大月亮底下有一個怪物臉似黄紙,眼睛裏流血渾身雪白頭髮蓬鬆着,一跳一跳的前來。我[2]那朋友在睡夢中驚醒忽然看見嚇了一大跳心裏說哎呀這就是鬼罷悄悄兒的瞧着,看他怎麼樣。那[3]鬼跳了不久的工夫兒就開開了立櫃拏出許多衣裳來,挾在胳肢窩裏從窗

談論篇百章之三十四

這件貂鼠褂子是在鋪子裏買的麼。不²是鋪子裏的,是廟上買的。多少銀子買的。你⁴猜一猜。這件⁵至不濟,也值三百兩銀子。我從二百兩上添起,添到二百五十兩他就賣了。怎麼這麼賤哪,我想從前像這樣兒的,至平常也得五百兩銀子,你看這一件,顏色兒黑,毛道兒厚又平正,而且風毛出得齊截,面子的緞子又厚,花樣兒也新鮮,又合如今的時樣兒,就是比着你的身子做,也不過這麼樣罷咧。我⁸記得你納也有一件來着。哎⁹我那個算甚麼,白

好又伶便,那種好的就是英雄少年們繫上撒袋騎着像飛鷹一般,眞可觀,你這馬是甚麼口也老了,下巴都搭拉了,腿也頓肯打前失,況且你的身子又笨,與你不大相宜呀。哎⁴可怎麼樣呢,如今已經買定了,只得將就着養活罷咧,我並沒有緊差使,又沒有甚麼遠差使,但是老實,就和我對勁兒,究竟比步行兒強啊。

河麼。不⁸是是渾河那塊兒。今年那兒的莊稼好不好。好得很,十分收成了。這¹¹奇怪咯,他們不是先說澇了,又說旱了麼。那¹²都是謠言,信不得的,別說別的,黑豆的價兒就十分便宜,十來個錢一升,這有許多年沒有這麼賤了。真¹³麼。可¹⁴不是真麼。若¹⁵是這麼着,你再打發人去的時候兒,請替我買幾石來,用多少銀子算明白了告訴我,我照着原買的價兒給你。是¹⁶啊,我看見你納槽上拴着好幾匹馬,買豆子餵是該當的,與其在咱們這兒買的價兒貴,不如在那兒帶了來,有減半兒的便宜呢。

談論篇百章之三十三

若¹買就買匹好馬,拴着看也有趣兒,費草費料的,拴着這麼匹儳頭馬,作甚麼。兄²台不知道,這匹馬昨兒率了來,我就拉到城外頭試過了,可以騎得顛得穩,跑得又快,射馬箭一點兒張裏的毛病兒都沒有,又隨手又妥當。看³起這個來,你原來不認得馬,若是好馬,骰子必定結實,耐得勞苦,園場上又熟慣兒

子還短點兒俗語兒說上山擒虎易開口告人難的話我今兒纔信了捨着臉
兒各處兒借總沒借着沒法兒找兄台來了或銀子或當頭求你納借給我點
兒等我回來的時候兒本利一併奉還幸虧你來得早若略遲些兒就趕不
上了方纔屯裏拏了幾兩銀子來還沒用呢你拏一半兒去使等喝了茶我再
稱給你我問你你這不是初次出門麽是 我告訴你些個話出遠門兒的
道理處朋友們以和爲貴待底下的官人們不必分內外都是一樣兒的疼愛
就有可以弄銀子錢的地方兒也該想着臉面要緊別手長了若是亂來於聲
名上大有關係呀 兄台說的都是金玉良言兄弟永遠記着就是咯。

談論篇百章之三十二

老弟是幾兒打屯裏來的。我到了好些日子了。老弟來了我總沒聽見說
若是聽見也早來瞧你來了。咱們住的地方兒寫遠你納又是官身子那裏
聽得見呢。我問你你們的地方在那兒。在霸州所屬的地方兒。挨着琉璃

談論篇百章之三十

¹今兒有誰來過麼。²你納出去之後有倆人來說是你納陞了官道喜來了。³誰出去答應的。⁴我在門口兒站着來說你納沒在家老爺們請到裏頭坐罷他們不肯進來囘去了。⁵都是甚麼樣兒呢。⁶一個是胖子比你納略高些兒四方臉兒連鬢鬍子暴子眼兒紫糖色兒那一個眞可笑臟得看不得一隻眼還是斜着又是糙稠麻子滿下巴鬍子咬着舌兒望我一說話我差一點兒沒有噗哧的笑了。⁷那個胖子我知道了這一個可是誰呢。⁸我問他們的姓來着每人都留下了個職名等我拏來給你納看。⁹哎呀這猴兒從那兒來你們別把他看輕了相貌雖然長得歪歪扭扭的筆底下很好心裏也有韜略兒是早已出了名的人了題起他來誰不知道呢。

談論篇百章之三十一

¹你還沒起身麼。²早晚兒就要起身了騾子行李都整理安當了只是盤纏銀

談論篇百章之二十九

[1]人生百歲不過一眨眼兒的光景把銀子錢結結實實的收着作甚麼我想這個浮生如夢的身子能彀樂幾天兒呢一恍兒就不中用了不如趁着沒有老喫點兒穿點兒若到了筋骨硬的時候兒穿呢也不成懶兒喫呢也不得味兒聽着孩子們的下巴頦兒過日子有甚麼趣兒啊只是別過逼了就是咯算計着所得的分兒樂一樂也很使得呀。[2]這個話你是知道我的事情說的呀還是揣摸着說的呢我果然是銀錢富富餘餘的樂也是應當的只是不像別人有銀錢有產業叫我拏甚麼樂呢還是賣了房子喫呢若是依你這個話行錢財兒花盡了的時候兒歎口氣就死了纔好萬一不死還有氣兒活着可怎麼樣兒過呢到那時候兒就是我求你你還理我麼

衣惜食得食你的福田能有多大呢若是這麼樣兒的不會過隄防着日子久了自己捱上了餓那時候兒纔後悔也就遲了啊

從容容的使刀一架,我們家兄的鎗尖兒齊各鐓兒的斷了一截兒去了,趕着就抽鎗沒抽迭瘸子的刀,早已放在脖子上了,我們家兄要躱叫他夾着脖子一摔,撂出好遠的去了。 因爲這麽着他很沒趣兒,我也再不學了,看起這個來,天下的能人還少麽。

談論篇百章之二十八

哎[1],你太奢侈了,各樣兒的東西上必得愛惜儉省,纔是過日子的道理呀,我若不說你,我又忍不住,若是把喫不了的飯給家下人們喫,那不好麽你竟任着意兒倒在溝眼裏是爲甚麽呢,心裏也安穩麽。 你這個人[2]只知道喫飯並不知道米的艱難種地的拉摔的受的都是甚麽樣兒的辛苦,纔到得這兒,就是一個米粒兒,也不是容易得的啊。 况且[3]咱們不能像那些個財主人家兒,喫着這個想着那個,有的是現成的銀子錢,嘴有甚麼梱兒呢,喫有甚麽盡頭兒呢,若是這麽慣了,不但折福而且要破家呀。 有年紀兒[4]的人們常說惜衣得

談論篇百章之二十七

你¹不知道這種好強、都是年輕血氣旺的緣故、等着奧過幾次虧、自然而然的就心灰了。我²這個人從前最好打把勢天天兒演習後來歇手是爲甚麼呢。我們家兄也好動勁兒慣使的是鎗就有十幾個人兒也到不了他跟前兒這樣兒的本事。這³一日在我舅舅家還遇見了一個癩子會耍刀、他們倆說要試一試本事各自拏了各自的兵器。我們家兄心裏那兒有他呢、拏起鎗來、直往他心口上就是一扎、那個癩子一點兒也不忙、從

兒尙且不着急、你先這麼催逼着、是個甚麼道理啊。不²論甚麼事情總要詳細了又詳細、得了正經主意纔可以告訴人、若像你們糊裏麻裏的不得准兒就說了、可以使得麼。我³生來的性兒就是難纏、若是事情沒得實兒強壓着頭叫我行、我斷不肯、若信我的話、就叫他等着、儻若不信、叫他求別人兒去辦罷咧、誰攔着他呢。

兒走，嘴裏雖然跟你好背地裏害得你很不輕，人若是落在他的圈套兒裏，就是一個仰面的觔斗在他手裏坑害的人可不少了屈着指頭兒算不清啊。
故此朋友們提起他來都說是可怕沒有不頭疼的。[3] 這就是俗語兒說的人心隔肚皮知人知面不知心的話兒是特為這種人們說的咯。[4] 我還算是儌倖若不留心遠着他必定也受了他的籠絡。

談論篇百章之二十五

哎[1]你的性子也太疲了，若是不能的事情就罷了，既然應承了又不趕緊的辦，只是給人家就擱着，是甚麼意思呢，若像這麽樣兒的行事朋友們還怎麽信你的話呢。 想來[2]你是自己不覺罷了，我實在替你害羞，與其這麽顢預着索性把實在的光景告訴人家，他也好歇了心另外打算哪。

談論篇百章之二十六

這[1]是甚麽話呢，論事情還沒有影兒呢，就略運些兒也不要緊，正經事情的主

談論篇百章之二十四

就罷了，我在老遠的就看見了，有騎着的理麼。是啊[4]，咱們許久沒見了，我進去略坐一坐兒，哎呀，栽了許多的花兒了麼，又養着許多金魚兒山子石兒堆得也好，心思用得很巧，層層都有懷兒，這個書房實在乾淨，怎麼瞧怎麼入眼，正是咱們念書的地方兒．自己沒有甚麼朋友，一個人兒念書很冷清，這有何難呢[6]，你若不厭煩我給你作伴兒來，何如。若是那們着真是我的造化了，我請還恐怕不來呢，若果真來真是我的萬幸略，那兒還有厭煩的理呢。

起初我見他的時候兒待人兒很親熱又很爽快，相貌又體面漢仗兒又魁偉，伶牙利齒的真會說話兒，我看着很羨慕他心裏說怎麼能和他相與，相與幾[1]好，不住口兒的誇獎他。後來交上了一塊兒常混混細細兒考較他所行所[2]為的事情，原來不是個正經人，虛架子弄玄的，而且心裏又陰險，不給人好道

兄台不到家裏坐麼[8]

好離是好啊，但只恨是我[5]

這有何難呢，你若不厭煩我給[6]

若是那們着真[7]

談論篇百章之二十二

我們倆底根兒相好、而且又連了幾層親、如今許多年沒得見面兒了、我打出[1]兵來間、就要找了他去、叙談叙談、不想叫事情絆住、竟沒空兒去、到昨兒順便兒到他家一間、那兒的人說他搬了好久咯、現在小街兒西頭兒、拐灣兒住着呢。我照着告訴的話找了去一瞧、在儘溜頭兒、嚼拉兒裏頭、纔找着了、他的[2]門兒關着呢、我叫了半天、並沒人兒答應、又敲着門兒叫了好一會子、纔出來了一個走不動的老媽兒來了、他說主人沒在家別處兒去了、我說等你們老爺囘來告訴他、說我來瞧來了。這個老媽兒的耳朶又很聾總聽不[3]見、我沒法兒、就在他們隔壁兒小鋪兒裏、借了個筆硯把我瞧他去的話、寫了個字兒留下了。

談論篇百章之二十三

兄[1]台請騎着我失躱避了啊、乏乏的、又下來作甚麼。 甚麼話呢、若沒有看見

得項的地方兒，他總不沾染，這正是合了積善之家必有餘慶的那句話了。

談論篇百章之二十一

咱[1]們這些人裏頭，你還是外人兒麼，要瞧我就一直進來，又何必先通報呢，既到了門口兒怎麼又囘去了呢，想必是我們家裡的人們說我不在家，你惱咯，是這個緣故不是啊，我若不說出緣故來，你怎麼知道呢。這[2]一向咱們那羣孩子們合着影兒開了要錢塲兒了，方纔來起誓發願的，必定叫我去，我不得空兒，你是深知道的，一會兒一會兒的差使，如何能定呢，而且王法又很儼若鬧出一件事來，把臉放在那兒啊。因為[3]這上頭惱，就由他惱罷，我到底沒去告訴家裡的人們，不拘誰來找我，答應不在家，想不到你來了，糊塗奴才們，也照着樣兒答應不在家，打發了去咯，纔進來告訴我，我急忙差人去趕他囘來說，沒趕上，叫我心裏很過意不去，實在我是不知道，你納千萬別計較。

居家過日子是一樸納心兒的勤儉父母跟前又孝順弟兄們跟前又親熱真是沒有一點兒毛病兒况且待朋友們又很護衆不拘誰托他一件事他不應就罷了他若是點了頭必定替你盡力的辦不成不肯歇手因此誰不敬他誰不親近他。是啊他這樣兒的人豈有空過一生的理麼俗語兒說吉人天相天必降福啊。

談論篇百章之二十

那個人哪是咱們舊街坊啊眼看着長大的孩子隔了能有幾天兒如今聽見說很出息了做了官了起初我還半信半疑的來着後來在朋友們跟前打聽果然是真的看起這個來是有志者事竟成和有志不在年高這兩句話真是不假啊。兄台你的話雖然是這麼說也是他老家兒有陰功纔生出這樣兒成人的孩子來呢很樸實又艮善除了學馬步箭的工夫素常在家就是看書荒唐的道兒一步兒也不肯走况且公事上又很小心很勤謹至於有便宜有

的地方兒逛看見道傍邊兒有一個金元寶。他們彼此對讓誰也不肯揀仍

撂下走咯。 遇見一個莊稼漢就告訴他說那兒有個金元寶你去揀去罷。[3]

那個莊稼漢聽了這話趕忙着去到那兒一找並不見金子只見有一條兩頭[5]

兒蛇。 嚇了一大跳連忙使鋤把蛇砍成兩截兒就追趕他們嚷着說我和[6]

你們有甚麼讎啊把一條兩頭兒蛇告訴我說是金元寶差點兒沒要了我的

命。 他們倆不信同去一看仍舊是金子只是砍成兩半兒同去咯。[7]

人拏了一半兒走咯那個莊稼漢還是空着手兒同去咯。 古時候兒的人們[8]

相與的道理是這個樣兒啊。 這話雖是小說兒上的實在可以給如今見利[9][10]

忘義的人們作個榜樣兒。

歇論篇百章之十九

你打聽的不是那位老弟麼。 是啊。 他是個囊中之錐不久就要出頭咯。[1][2][3]

甚麼緣故呢。 他生來得安靜學問淵博行動兒漢仗兒又出眾差使上又勤[4][5]

談論篇百章之十七

弟兄們[1]是一個母親肚子裏生的，小的時候兒在一塊兒喫一塊兒頑兒，不分彼此，何等樣兒親熱來着，後來長大了，漸漸兒的生分的緣故，大約都是聽了妻妾的桃唆，就爭家產，或是聽了傍人離間的話，各自各兒懷着異心的很多。就[2]是天天兒聽了這些讒言，耳濡目染，到心裏都裝滿了，一時間不能忍以致於打架辯嘴，就成了讎咯。也該想一想產業沒了，還可以再置女人死了，也可以再娶，弟兄們若是傷一個就像手腳折了一隻的一個，爲能再得呢。比方[4]偶然鬧出一件禍事來，那還得骨肉相關的弟兄們，拚命巴結着搭救啊，若是傍人，恐怕連累着，躲還躲不迭呢，還肯替你出力麼。看起這個來，再沒有如同弟兄們親的咯人爲甚麼不細細兒的想想這些個呢。

談論篇百章之十八

若[1]說相與朋友應該學古時候兒的管仲，鮑叔。他們倆[2]有一天在荒郊野外

談論篇百章之十六

養兒原為防備老為人子的應該想着父母的勞苦養活的恩就趁着父母在[1]着拏好穿的好喫的孝敬他和顏悅色的叫老家兒喜歡若是喫穿不管饑[2]寒不問的像外人兒似的看待叫兩個老人家傷心生氣到了百年之後任憑你怎麼慟哭中甚麼用啊就算是你出於誠心誰信呢不過因為怕人家笑話假的罷咧就是供甚麼樣兒的珍饈美味誰見靈魂兒來受享了麼也還是活人兒饞搋罷咧死的人有甚麼益處啊還有[8]一種更不好的人說父母上了年紀兒了老輩晦了吵鬧着強要分家的說到這個塲處不由的叫人生氣傷心這種樣兒的人天地不容神鬼都是恨的爲能善終呢你[4]只靜靜兒的看着一眨眼兒的工夫兒他的子孫也就照着他的樣兒學了

行事還正派故此人家都服我願意給我出力啊

就像是他自己的一個樣兒,很着急,必定儘着力兒搭救,眞是一位厚道積福的老人家,故此我若是隔久了,不去看一看心裏頭只是不過意。俗語兒說的,一人有福,托帶滿屋,現在那家業充足,子孫興旺,都是他老人家行爲好的報應啊。

談論篇百章之十五

啊,衆位弟兄們可要小心這位老大人的才情敏捷,有決斷,無論甚麼事情到手,就有條有理兒辦結咯,而且心裏明白認得人,好歹瞞不過他的眼睛去,又最憐愛凡有勤謹體面少年的子弟們,到了挑缺應陞的時候兒眞肯提拔保舉,但是遇着差使上滑的面子上要獻勤兒討好占便宜的這種人可小心着,難免叫他擎住若是叫他摟着了,斷沒有輕放過去的。你們的話雖是這麼說,弟兄們天天兒眼巴巴兒的盼着要仗着我成人,我若是應保舉的不保舉,應約束的不約束,怎麼還能賞功罰罪呢,我是生成的心直口快,想來說話,

當差行走的、只看各自的機會、時運若平常、樣樣兒總不着不論甚麼事、眼看着要成偏會生出岔兒來、有一種彩頭好、走好運的人、眞是沒有不照着他所思所算的爽爽利利兒隨了心的眼聰着、就是優等高陞。你[2]納是這麼說、我心裏却不然、只論巴結不巴結、就是咯若是素餐尸位的、整年家不行走還該當革退呢、再指望陞官能彀麼當差的人、第一要勤謹朋友們裏頭要和氣別各別另樣的別不隨羣兒、有事不擧人、不論甚麼差使一樸納心兒的辦、勇往向前行了去、必定是在高等兒上、有不得的道理麼。

談論篇百章之十四

這[1]姓張的待人很冷淡、我認得一個有了年紀兒的人、却不是這樣兒見了人很親熟、若是坐在一處兒論起學問來、很喜歡講今比古的接連不斷、整天家說也不乏。若[2]是遇見年輕的人兒們了、他和顏悅色的、往好處兒引誘該指撥的地方兒指撥、該教導的地方兒教導、最仁愛又最護衆、見了人家有苦處、

談論篇百章之十二

兄[1]台、恭喜咯、說放韋京揀選上了。是啊、昨兒揀選的把我擬了正了。擬[2]陪的、是誰啊。你[3]不認得、是一個前鋒梭。他[4]有兵麼。沒[5]有兵、寡有圍。我[6]替你納算計熟咯、一定要戴孔雀翎子咯。別[7]過獎咧、我有甚麼奇處兒比我好的[8]多着的呢、一定指望着使得麼、不過是託着祖宗的福蔭、儌倖着也定不得。這[9]是太謙了、你納是甚麼時候兒的人兒們、也都陞了、若論你納行走的朋友、都作了大人咯、在你納後頭年輕的人年久咯、若論起來、和你納一塊兒的差使、出過兵受過傷現在又是十五善射、你納說旗下強過你納的是誰、我知道了、想是怕我來喝喜酒啊。喝[10]酒有甚麼呢、果然若得了、別說是酒合着茶也沒喝、請呀、改日再見到家裡、都替我問好罷。

談論篇百章之十三

你納的意思我請你納。

沒有若有不是的地方兒、請撥正撥正。 你射的步箭、有甚麼說得呢、早晚兒、要仗着太拇指頭戴翎子咯、檫兒又妤又很熟撒得又乾淨、人若都能像你、還說甚麼呢、但只是弓還略頓些兒前手略有一點兒定不住、把這幾處兒毛病兒若改了、不拘到那兒去射一定出衆、有誰能壓得下你去呢。

談論篇百章之十一

兄台新喜啊。[2] 好說大家同喜啊。 兄台請坐。[3] 做甚麼。[4] 給兄台拜年哪。[5]
甚麼話呢。[6] 老兄長啊、是該當磕頭的。[7] 請起請起、陞官哪得子啊、過富貴的
日子啊、請起請上坐、這現成兒的煮餃子、請喫幾個罷。[8] 我在家裡喫了出來
的。[9] 喫得那麼飽麼、年輕的人兒、纔喫了就餓啊、若不喫、想必是粧假罷。[10] 真[11]
的呀、在你納家、我還作客麼、不敢撒謊。[12] 那們就沏茶來。 我不喝。[13] 怎麼。[14]
我還要到別處兒去呢、該去的地方兒多太去晚了、人都犯思量、兄台請喫罷。[15]
別送看帶了味兒去。 那兒有這個理、不出房門兒、使得麼哎、來了窣窣的連[16]

打發那小孩子取去了、我們先叫他去、他肯聽我們的話麼、有要沒緊兒的、躭擱時候兒、後來我說有兄台的話、他纔趕忙着去了、那一部書不是四套麼、他只拿了三套來、我們說他為甚麽漏下了一套、若不趕着取去、等着主人回來必不依你呀、他反倒說、我們告訴得糊塗不明白、抱怨着去了、至今還沒回來呢、若差人迎他去罷、又恐怕走岔了道兒。這種樣兒的滑東西也有麼一定是往那個熱鬧地方兒頑兒去咯、若不嚴嚴兒的管教斷斷使不得、等他回來的時候兒、把他捆上重重兒的打一頓纔好、不然慣了他、就更不堪了。

談論篇百章之十

射步箭、是咱們滿洲人最要緊的事、看着容易、做着難、就是黑下白日的長拉、抱着弓睡的都有、若拉到出類拔萃的、好能出了名的有幾個。難處在那兒呢。身子要正、骼子要平、一身要很自然、沒有毛病兒、還又搭着弓硬、箭出去的有勁兒、再箭兒中綳算得是好呢。兄台、你納看我射箭、比從前出息了

你快補名字罷、別錯過了機會啊。

談論篇百章之八

你[1]別看小說兒這種書若是看書看通鑑可以長學問記得古來的事情以好的爲法以不好的爲戒於身心大有益處啊。至[2]於看小說兒、古兒詞、都是人編的沒影兒的瞎話、就是整千本兒的看了、有甚麼益處呢。有[3]一種人還皮着臉兒念給人家聽呢、從前那一國、誰和誰、打過幾次仗、這個掌刀砍那個使斧架這個又掄鎗扎那個又使棍搪若說是敗了、請了來的、都是雲裏來、霧裏去的神仙剪草爲馬撒豆兒成兵的。明[4]明兒的是謊話那糊塗人們、當成眞事還獃頭獃腦、有滋有味兒的聽呢、有見識的人看見不但笑話、而且懶怠瞧、你往這上頭用心做甚麼。

談論篇百章之九

那[1]個書取了來咯沒有。取[2]去了、還沒拏來呢。使[3]喚誰去的、至今還沒來麽。

談論篇百章之七

你[1]是明白漢字的人哪要學繙譯很容易只是專心別隔斷了挨着次兒的學兩三年的工夫兒自然就有頭緒兒了若是三日打魚兩日曬網的就念到二十年也是枉然。 兄[2]台瞧瞧我的繙譯求你納略攺一攺。 你[3]學得大有長進了句句兒順當字字兒清楚沒有一點兒肬星兒若是考可以操必勝之權這一次考筆帖式遞了名字沒有。 若[4]是考得很好只怕秀才未必准考罷。 這[5]是那兒的話呢像你這懞兒的八旗都許考獨不准你考的理有麼況且義學生、還准考呢、秀才倒不准刚因爲准考你姪兒這個窒兒緫趕着學滿洲書呢、

錯繼子譬如我當了差使回來𣲙下的窒兒歇歇兒那不好麽只是和你們這個那個的爲甚麽呢不過因爲是骨肉叫你們出息成人的意思啊。 我[5]如今也沒法兒了只好盡心的敎導完我的責任就是了聽不聽隨你們罷咧叫我可怎麽懞兒呢。

談論篇百章之六

今兒早起背他們的書一個比一個的生哼啊哼的張着嘴瞪着眼只是站着。看他們這麼着我說且住了聽我的話你們旣然是念滿洲書就該一樸納心兒的學像這麼樣兒的充數兒沽虛名多咱是個了手啊不但你們是虛度日月連我也是白費了勁兒咯這是你們自己咯還是我惱了你們咯呢。已經長成了大漢子的說着也是這個樣兒朶離然聽了並不放在心上太皮臉了罷把我說的苦口良言全當成了耳傍風咯。別說我找你們的
量教我們的是誰啊是師傅麼不是呀是我的一個族兄所有教的都是我們一家兒的子弟再者就是親戚們並沒有外人可怎麼說呢我們族兄又要天天兒上衙門不得閒兒是因爲我們過懶不肯自己用功他萬不得已兒匀着盆兒教我們若不是這麼着兄台要念書也是好事罷咧替你說說又費了我甚麼呢。

談論篇百章之五

老[1]弟、你天天從這兒過、都是往那兒去啊。念書去。不[3]是念滿洲書麽。是[4]。

現[5]在念的、都是甚麼書。沒有新樣兒的書、都是眼面前兒的零碎話和清話指要這兩樣兒。還[7]教你們寫清字楷書不啊。如[8]今天短沒寫字的空兒、等着天長了、不但教寫字、還教學繙譯呢。老[9]弟、我爲這念書的事、真是鑽頭覓縫兒的、那兒沒有找到啊、可惜我們左近沒有念清書的學房、我想着你們念書的這學房、就可以到多儌、我也去念去、請你替我先說說罷。兄[10]台、你打

面。還[3]有一種不念書不修品的、全靠着鑽幹逢迎作他的本事、我不知道他們心裏到底要怎麼樣啊、我實在替他害羞。這[4]一種人不但自己辱身壞名、連老子娘都叫人家咒罵啊。老[5]弟、你白想一想父母的恩情、爲人子的、能彀報得萬一麼、旣不能彀光宗耀祖的罷咧、反倒叫父母受人家的咒罵、沒出息兒到甚麼分兒上了。細[6]想起這個來、人若是不念書不修品、使得麼。

獎、我的清話算甚麼呢、我有個朋友滿洲話說得很好、又清楚、又快、沒有一點兒漢音、很熟練哪、不但這個、而且記得話兒還多、那纔可以算得起是好呢。他比你如何。我怎麼敢比他、我可不是他的對兒啊、差得天地懸隔呢。甚麼緣故呢。他學得日子深、會得多、頗好書、至今還是不住嘴兒的念、不離手兒的拏着看、若要趕他、實在難哪。弟台你這話、只怕有點兒說錯了罷、你忘了、有志者事竟成、這句話了麼、他也是學會得罷咧、並不是生了來、就知道的啊、咱們那點兒、不如他、任憑他是怎麼樣兒的精熟、咱們只要拏定主意、用心去學、雖然到不了他那個地步兒、料想也就差不多兒咯。

談論篇百章之四

人生在世、頭一件要緊、是學念書呢、特為的是明白道理、學得道理明白了、在家呢、孝順父母、做官呢、給國家出力、不論甚麼事、可自然都會成就。人若是學得果然有了本事、無論到那塊兒、不但別人尊重你、就是你自己、也覺着體

談論篇百章之二

聽見說你的清話、如今學得很有點兒規模兒了麽。那兒的話呢、人家說的我雖懂得、我自家要說還早呢、不但我說的不能像別人兒說得成片叚兒、而且一連四五句話就接不上了、還有個怪處兒、是臨說話的時候、無緣無故的怕錯、不敢簡簡决决的說、這麽樣兒、可叫我怎麽說呢、我也灰了心咯、想著就是這麽樣兒學來學去也不過就是這麽個本事兒咯、那兒還能彀有長進呢。這都是你沒熟的緣故、我告訴你、無論他是誰、但凡遇見個會說清話的、你就趕著和他說、再有那清話精通的師傅們、也要往他們那兒去學、或是和清話熟習的朋友們、時常談論、天天兒看書記話、平常說慣了嘴兒、若照着這麽學、至多一兩年、自然而然的、就會順着嘴兒說咯、又愁甚麽不能呢。

談論篇百章之三

老弟、你的清話、是甚麽崆兒學的、聲兒說得好、而且又明白。啊、承兄台的過

談論篇百章之一

[1]我聽見說你如今學滿洲書呢麼、很好、滿洲話是咱們頭一宗兒要緊的事情、就像漢人們、各處兒各處兒的鄉談一個樣兒不會使得麼。[2]可不是麼、我念了十幾年的漢書、至今還摸不着一點兒頭緒呢、若再不念滿洲書不學繙譯兩下裏都躭誤咯、因為這麼着我一則來瞧瞧兄台、二則還有奉求的事情呢。[3]這有甚麼難呢、有話請說若是我做得來的事情、咱們倆只是怪難開口的。我所求的是你納疼愛我就是勞乏些兒可怎麼樣呢、抽空兒我還推辭麼。[4]我所求的是你兄弟若能彀成了人、都是兄台所賜的、我再不敢忘了恩哪、必要重報的。[5]你怎麼這麼說呢、你是外人嗎、只怕你不肯學、旣然要學巴不得教你成人呢、說報恩是甚麼話呢、咱們自己人說得嗎。[6]若是這麼着、我就感激不盡了、只好給兄台磕頭咯、還有甚麼說得呢。

PART VI.

THE HUNDRED LESSONS.

(CHINESE TEXT.)

TZŬ ERH CHI.

COLLOQUIAL SERIES.

PART VII.

THE TONE EXERCISES.

(CHINESE TEXT.)

TZŭ ERH CHI. **Colloquial Series.** PART VII. SOUND TABLE.

A			J								
1 阿	46 窘	88 風	128 染	174 棍	217 米	257 拜	302 孫	340 弔	386 揩		
2 愛	47 窮	89 佛	129 嚷	175 困	218 苗	258 派	303 送	341 挑	387 鼠		
3 安	48 卓	90 否	130 繞	176 工	219 滅	259 半		342 疊	388 嘴		
4 昂	49 綽	91 夫	131 熟	177 孔	220 面	260 盼	SH	343 貼	389 催		
5 傲	50 畫		132 人	178 果	221 民	261 幫	304 殺	344 店	390 奪		
	51 抽	H	133 扔	179 鬪	222 謬	262 包	305 臕	345 天	391 寸		
CH	52 包	92 哈	134 日		223 末	263 飽	306 山	346 定	392 宗		
6 乍	53 取	93 害	135 若	L	224 謀	264 北	307 賞	347 聽	393 葱		
7 茶	54 捐	94 寒	136 很	180 拉	225 木	265 陪	308 少	348 丟			
8 蹇	55 全	95 碎	137 恆	181 來	226	266 本	309 舌	349 多	TZ		
9 柴	56 絕	96 好	138 河	182 懶		267 盆	310 身	350 妥	394 子		
10 嶄	57 缺	97 黑	139 後	183 浪	N	268 迸	311 生	351 豆	395 次		
11 產	58 君	98 很	140 戶	184 老	227 那	269 朋	312 事	352 頭			
12 章	59 羣	99 恆	141 花	185 勒	228 妳	270 必	313 手	353 肚	W		
13 唱	60 卻	100 河		186 累	229 男	271 皮	314 書	354 土	396 瓦		
14 抄	61 主	101 後	K	187 冷	230 饔	272 表	315 刷	355 短	397 外		
15 沙	62 出	102 戶	142 嗑	188 立	231 鬧	273 票	316 拴	356 團	398 完		
16 這	63 抓	103 花	143 卡	189 倆	232 內	274 別	317 雙	357 對	399 往		
17 車	64 敥	104 壞	144 改	190 兩	233 嫩	275 撇	318 水	358 退	400 為		
18 這	65 拽	105 黃	145 開	191 了	234 能	276 扁	319 順	359 敦	401 文		
19 眞	66 專	106 回	146 甘	192 裂	235 你	277 片	320 說	360 吞	402 翁		
20 臣	67 穿	107 混	147 看	193 連	236 娘	278 賓	321	361 冬	403 我		
21 正	68 壯	108 紅	148 剛	194 林	237 鳥	279 兵		362 同	404 武		
22 成	69 牀	109 混	149 炕	195 另	238 捏	280 憑	SS				
23 吉	70 吹	110 火	150 告	196 略	239 念	281 波	322 絲	TS	Y		
24 奇	71 淮		151 刻	197 陋	240 您	282 破		363 雜	405 牙		
25 家	72 春	HS	152 給	198 騾	241 寧	283 不	T	364 擦	406 涯		
26 恰	73 中	111 西	153 刻	199 陋	242 虐	284 剖	323 大	365 在	407 洋		
27 楷	74 充	112 夏	154 根	200 律	243 挪	285 朴	324 他	366 才	408 要		
28 角	75 揣	113 向	155 肯	201 懸	244 糯	286 剖	325 歹	367 慚	409 夜		
29 江	76 中	114 小	156 更	202 略	245 女	287 朴	326 單	368 葬	410 盲		
30 搶	77 充	115 些	157 坑	203 掄	246 虐	288 普	327 炭	369 倉	411 益		
31 交	78 揣	116 先	158 各	204 略	247 奴		328 當	370 早	412 音		
32 巧		117 心	159 可	205 路	248 煖	S	329 湯	371 則	413 迎		
33 街		118 性	160 狗	206 亂	249 嫩	289 撒	330 道	372 策	414 約		
34 且	F	119 學	161 口	207 論	250 濃	290 賽	331 逃	373 賊	415 魚		
35 見	79 嶺	120 修	162 苦	208 龍	251	291 散	332 得	374 怎	416 原		
36 欠	80 恩	121 兄	163 瓜		252	292 桑	333 特	375 參	417 月		
37 知	81 哼	122 須	164 跨	M		293 掃	334 得	376 增	418 雲		
38 尺	82 兒	123 喧	165 怪	209 馬	ngO	294 嗇	335 等	377 層	419 有		
39 斤		124 雪	166 快	210 買	253 詘	295 僧	336 疼	378 作	420 用		
40 親		125 巡	167 官	211 慢	254 偶	296 搜	337 疼	379 錯			
41 井	F	126 學	168 光	212 忙		297 索	338	380 走			
42 輕	83 法		169 況	213 毛	P	298 素	339	381 湊			
43 角	84 反	I	170 規	214 美	255 罷	299 算		382 祖			
44 卻	85 方	127 衣	171 愧	215 門	256 怕	300		383 粗			
45 秋	86 非		172	216 夢		301 碎		384			
	87 分		173					385			

TONE EXERCISES. a — ch‘ên.

20				15				10			5					
臣	眞	這	車	吵	兆	唱	章	産	斬	柴	窘	茶	乍	傲	昂	安	愛	阿
是君臣之臣	是眞假之眞	是這塊兒之這	是車馬之車	是吵嚷之吵	是先兆之兆	是歌唱之唱	是章程之章	是産業生産之産	是斬絞之斬	是柴炭之柴	是寬窘之窘	是茶酒之茶	是乍見乍冷乍熱	是狂傲之傲	是低昂之昂	是平安之安	是愛惜之愛	是阿哥之阿

嗔	眞	○	車	吵	招	娼	章	擾	沾	拆	齋	渣	义	熬	昂	安	哀	阿
臣	○	○	馬	嚷	著	長	○	饒	○	柴	宅	茶	拟	熬	昂	○	挨	○
磣	枕	枕	扯	炒	找	厰	長	産	盞	拟	窘	衤	拃	襖	○	俺	矮	阿
趁	震	震	撤	鈔	兆	唱	賬	○	站	○	債	○	乍	傲	○	岸	愛	○

| 嗔怪 | 眞假 | ○ | 車馬 | 吵嚷 | 招呼 | 娼妓 | 章程 | 擾雜 | 拆毁 | 柴炭 | 齋戒 | 渣滓 | 义手 | 熬菜 | 低昂 | 平安 | 哀求 | 是阿 |

| 君臣 | ○ | ○ | ○ | 長嚷 | 長短 | ○ | ○ | ○ | ○ | ○ | ○ | ○ | ○ | 熬夜 | 昂貴 | 塵埃 | ○ | ○ |

| 阿磣 | 枕頭 | 這塊兒 | ○ | 煎炒 | 著急 | 長饒 | 木厰 | 生長 | ○ | 一盞燈 | 寬窄 | 扭腰 | 一拃 | 割文 | 熬菜 | ○ | 俺們 | 高矮 | 阿甚麽 |

| 趁著 | 地震 | 這塊兒 | 裁撤 | 再者 | 錢鈔 | 先兆 | 歇唱 | 帳目 | 懺悔 | 驛站 | 欠債 | 樹枒 | 乍見 | 在傲 | ○ | 河岸 | 愛惜 | 阿哥 |

PART VII. TONE EXERCISES. chêng — ch'ing.   221

練習燕山平仄編

正	成	吉	奇	家	恰	楷	江	搶	交	巧	街	且	見	欠	知	尺	斤	親	井	輕
			25					30					35						40	
是	是	是	是	是	是	是	是	是	是	是	是	是	是	是	是	是	是	是	是	是
邪	成	吉	奇	佳	恰	楷	大	搶	交	巧	街	況	見	該	知	尺	斤	親	井	輕
正	敗	凶	怪	家	巧	書	江	奪	代	妙	道	且	面	欠	道	寸	兩	戚	泉	重
之	之	之	之	之	之	之	之	之	之	之	之	之	之	之	之	之	之	之	之	之
正	成	吉	奇	家	恰	楷	江	搶	交	巧	街	且	見	欠	知	尺	斤	親	井	輕

正	稱	雞	七	家	招	○	江	腔	交	敲	街	切	奸	千	知	斤	親	○	輕	輕
○	成	吉	奇	夾	○	○	○	牆	嚼	橋	結	茄	○	錢	值	遲	勤	錦	○	啨
整	懲	已	起	甲	卡	○	講	搶	腳	巧	解	且	減	淺	指	尺	寢	近	靜	請
正	秤	記	氣	價	恰	匠	戲	叫	俏	借	見	欠	志	翅	噯					慶

正	稱	雞	七	住	招	○	大	腔	交	敲	街	切	奸	千	知	斤	親	輕
月	呼	犬	八	家	花		江	調	代	打	道	肉	臣	萬	道	兩	戚	重
																紅		眼
																赤		睛
																赤		

| ○ | 成 | 吉 | 奇 | 夾 | ○ | ○ | ○ | 驕 | 嚼 | 橋 | 完 | 茄 | ○ | 錢 | 值 | 遲 | 勤 | ○ | 陰 |
| | 敗 | 凶 | 怪 | 帶 | | | | 壁 | 過 | 梁 | 結 | 子 | | 財 | 班 | 誤 | 儉 | | 啨 |

整	懲	自	赳	盔	卡	楷	講	搶	手	巧	解	況	裁	深	指	尺	錦	井	請
齊	辦	己	初	甲	子	書	究	奪	腳	妙	開	且	滅	淺	頭	寸	繡	泉	安
																	寢	安	慶
																	食	靜	弔

邪	斗	記	氣	價	恰	○	匠	餓	叫	俏	借	況	志	翅	該	尺	翅	遠	狗
正	秤	載	血	錢	巧		人	木	喊	皮	貸	姬	向	膀	面	寸	膀	近	噯
												妾			欠				

角	却	酒	秋 45	窘	窮	桌	綽	畫	抽	句	取	捐 55	全	絕	缺	君	羣	爵	却 60
是	是	是	是	是	是	是	是	是	是	是	是	是	是	是	是	是	是	是	見
角	推	酒	春	窘	貧	桌	寬	畫	抽	句	取	捐	齊	斷	補	君	成	爵	上
色	却	肉	秋	窘	窮	櫈	綽	夜	叚	叚	送	納	全	絕	缺	王	羣	位
之	之	之	之	之	之	之	之	之	之	之	之	之	之	之	之	之	之	之
角	却	酒	秋	窘	窮	桌	綽	畫	抽	句	取	捐	全	絕	缺	君	羣	爵

(Content continues with additional character entries and circle markers)

PART VII. TONE EXERCISES. chio — ên.   223

練習燕山平仄編

80			75				70				65			
恩	額	擉	充	中	春	准	吹	追	牀	壯	穿	專	揣	拽	欻	抓	出	主
是恩典之恩	是額歎之額	是擉撞之擉	是充當之充	是中外之中	是春夏之春	是准駁之准	是吹打之吹	是追趕之追	是牀鋪之牀	是壯健之壯	是穿戴之穿	是專門之專	是揣摩之揣	是拉拽之拽	是欻一聲之欻	是抓住抓破之抓	是出外之出	是賓主之主
恩 ○ 阿額我惡	○ ○ 擉	○ ○ 充虫寵銃	○ ○ 中純腫重	○ ○ 春蠢准駁	○ 吹垂 ○ 墜	○ 追趕打	○ 牀闖創	○ 装船槳壯	○ 穿船喘串	○ 專轉傳	○ 揣揣踹	○ 拽跩拽	○ 欻 ○ ○	○ 抓爪	○ 出廚處處	猪竹主住
恩典太阿		擉撞	充當	中外	春夏		吹打	追趕	牀鋪	裝戡	穿戴	專門	懷揣	拽泥	欻一聲	抓破	出外	猪羊
○ 額歎	○	○	○ 虫蟻	○ 純厚	○	垂手	○	牀鋪	車船	○	○	○	○	○	○	厨房	竹子
○ 爾我	○	○ 寵愛	○ 蠢笨	准駁	○	○	闖入	粗糙	痰喘	轉移	揣摩	鴨跩	○	雞爪子	○	處分	賓主
搵倒 善惡	○	○ 鐵銃	輕重	○	慶墜	○	創始	壯健	串通	經傳	蹬踹	拉拽	○	○	住處	住處	

哼	兒	法	反 85	方	非	分	風	佛	否 90	夫	哈	害	寒	碎 95	好	黑	很
是哼阿之哼	是兒女之兒	是法子之法	是反倒之反	是方圓之方	是是非之非	是分開之分	是風雨之風	是佛老之佛	是然否之否	是夫妻之夫	是哈哈笑之哈	是利害之害	是寒涼之寒	是打碎之碎	是好歹之好	是黑白之黑	是很好之很
哼○○○	○兒耳二	發法髮	翻煩反飯	方房訪放	非肥匪費	分墳粉	風縫	○佛○○	○浮否单	夫扶斧父	哈蝦哈	咳孩海害	頂寒喊漢	碎行○項	蒿毫好好	○黑○黑	痕很恨
哼阿	○	發遣	翻騰	方圓	是非	分開	風雨	○	○	夫妻	哈哈笑	咳聲	齻頂	打碎	蒿草	黑白	○
○	兒女	法子	煩惱	房屋	肥瘦	墳墓	裁縫	佛老	浮沉	扶持	蝦蟆	孩子	寒涼	各行	絲毫	○	傷痕
○	耳朶	頭髮	反倒	訪查	賊匪	脂粉	○	○	然否	斧鉞	哈吧	江海	叫喊	○	好不好	黑豆	好得很
○	二三	佛法	喫飯	放肆	使費	職分	供奉	○	埠口	爻毋	哈什螞	利害	滿漢	好喜	項圈	○	恨怨

練習燕山平仄編

心	先115	小	向	夏	西	紅	火110	混	囘	黃	換105	壞	花	戶	後	河100	恆
是心性之心	是先後之先	是些微之些	是大小之小	是方向之向	是春夏之夏	是東西之西	是紅綠之紅	是水火之火	是混亂之混	是同去同來之同	是青黃之黃	是更換之換	是損壞之壞	是花草之花	是戶口之戶	是前後之後	是江河之河	是恆久之恆

心尋〇信　先開險限　些欹血謝　滑學小笑　香詳想　瞎霞〇夏　西席喜細　剮活火貨　烘紅哄　昏魂渾混　灰囘悔賄　荒黃謊晃　歡環緩換　〇懷〇壞　花滑話話　忽壺虎戶　齁侯吼後　喝河〇賀　哼恆〇橫

哼哈　〇　公侯　忽然　花草　〇　歡喜　荒亂　石灰　昏暗　烘烤　剮口子　東西　瞎子　香臭　消滅　些微　先後　心性

恆久　江河.　茶壺　泥滑　懷想　連環　青黃　同去　鬼魂　紅綠　死活　酒席　雲霞　詳細　學徒　靴鞋　清閒　尋東西

　　牛吼　龍虎榜　話敢人　〇　撒謊　混厚　欺哄　烙丞　水火　喜歡　〇　思想　大小　謝恩　危險　〇

兇橫　賀喜　前後　戶口　說話　損壞　更換　一晃兒　賄賂　混亂　渾厚　煉丞　貨物　粗細　春夏　方向　談笑　謝恩　限期　書信

姓	學	修	兄120	須	喧	雪	巡	學125	衣	染	嚷	繞	熱130	人	扔	日	若135	肉
是姓名之姓	是學問之學	是修理之修	是兄弟之兄	是必須之須	是喧嚷之喧	是雨雪之雪	是巡察之巡	見上	是衣裳之衣	是沾染之染	是嚷鬧之嚷	是圍繞之繞	是冷熱之熱	是人物之人	是扔棄之扔	是日月之日	是若論之若	是骨肉之骨
星行醒姓	○學○○	修○朽袖	兄熊○袖	須徐許續	靴懸選選	熏穴○	靴穴○汎	○	衣一尾易	然染	嚷○讓	饒繞	○饒繞○熱	○人忍任	扔○	○日	○若	揉桑○肉
星宿	○	修理	兄弟	必須	喧嚷	熏蒸	巡察	○	衣裳	○嚷嚷	嚷嚷	○	○	○	扔棄	○	○	揉的一聲
行爲	學問	○狗熊	兄弟	徐圖	懸掛	穴道	巡道	○	一個	然否	瓢子	饒裕	○	人物	○	○	○	剛柔
睡醒	○糟朽	應許	○	擇選	雨雪	○	○	○	尾巴	沾染	嚷鬧	圍繞	○	容忍	○	○	○	○
姓名	○領袖	接續	候選	鑽穴	營汎	容易	○	謙讓	繞住	冷熱	責任	○	日月	若論	骨肉

PART VII. TONE EXERCISES. hsing — k'ên.

練習燕山平仄編

肯 155	根	刻	給	考	告 150	炕	剛	看	甘	改	開 145	卡	嘎		榮	潤 140	瑞	軟	如
是肯不肯之肯	是根本之根	是刻搜之刻	是放給之給	是考察之考	是告訴之告	是火炕之炕	是剛纔之剛	是看見之看	是甘苦之甘	是改變之改	是開閉之開	是卡倫之卡	是嘎嘎笑的聲兒		是榮耀之榮	是潤澤之潤	是祥瑞之瑞	是軟弱之軟	是如若之如
○肯掯	○根哏	○刻○	○給	○高稿考靠	康扛抗炕	剛綆堈杠	看○斫守	甘趕○幹	開慨○	該當改概	卡○倫	嘎嘎嘎嘎		○榮齈○	○潤○	○蕊瑞○	○軟○	如如入入
○根本	○刻搜	○	○圀限	扛擡		剛綏	看守	甘苦	開閉	該當	卡倫	嘎嘎的笑		榮耀	潤澤	蕋瑞	軟弱	如貼
○肯不肯	○放給	○考察	稿案	不抗不卑的	土堈子	刀斫	看見	甘苦	懷慨	改變.	○	打嘎兒		榮耀	花蕋	氄毛	軟弱	強入
一掯子	艮卦	○	依靠	告訴	火炕	擡杠	看見	才幹	追趕	犬概	○	吸雜子		○	潤澤	祥瑞	○	如若
												雞嘎嘎蛋兒.						出入

困 175	棍	愧	規	況	光	寬	官	快	怪	跨 165	瓜	苦	古	口	狗	可 160	各	坑	更
是乏困之困	是棍棒之棍	是慚愧之愧	是規矩之規	是況且之況	是光明之光	是寬窄之寬	是官員之官	是快慢之快	是怪道之怪	是跨馬之跨	是瓜果之瓜	是苦甜之苦	是古今之古	是口舌之口	是豬狗之狗	是可否之可	是各人之各	是抗坎之抗	是更多更少之更
坤 ○ 閫 困	棍 ○ 滾 棍	虧 揆 愧 ○ 僞	規 ○ 詭 逵	誆 狂 ○ 況	光 ○ 廣 逛	寬 ○ 款 慣	官 ○ 管 ○	○ 摳 快	乖 拐 跨 怪	誇 侉 跨 挎	瓜 寡 苦 掛	估 骨 古 固	窟 寠 口 叩	摳 骨 古 固	溝 狗 渴 殼	可 可 渴 客	哥 格 各 個	坑 ○ ○ ○	更 ○ 埂 更
坤道		虧欠	規矩	誆騙	光明	寬窄	官員			誇張	瓜果	料估	窟窿	摳破了	溝渠	可惜了兒	哥哥	坑坎	更改
○	○	揆守	○	狂妄	○	○	○	○	○	○	○	骨頭	○	○	○	可否	影格	○	○
閫閭	翻滾	慚愧	詭詐	況且	廣大	款項	管理	摳瘁瘁	拐騙	侉子	多寡	甜苦	古今	口舌	叩頭	堅固	褲子	懸掛	跨馬	怪道	快慢	習慣	遊逛	況且	富貴	慚愧	棍子棒子	乏因
道埂子	更多	○	幾個	賓客	豬狗	足殼	叩頭	堅固	褲子	懸掛	跨馬	怪道	快慢	習慣	遊逛	況且	富貴	慚愧	棍子棒子	乏因

工	孔	果	闊	拉 180	來	懶	浪	老	勒 185	累	冷	立	倆	雨	了 190	列	連	林	練習燕山平仄編
是工夫之工	是面孔之孔	是結果之果	是寬闊之闊	是拉扯之拉	是來去之來	是懶惰之懶	是波浪之浪	是老幼之老	是勒索之勒	是連累之累	是冷熱之冷	是站立之立	是倆三之倆	是斤兩之兩	是了斷之了	是擺列之列	是接連之連	是樹林之林	
工〇礦	空〇孔空	鍋國果過	闊〇〇共	拉邋蜊蠟	〇來〇賴	鬣婪懶爛	榜狠朗浪	榔勞老潦	勒〇〇樂	累雷累類	〇稜冷愣	璃離禮立	量涼倆〇	〇〇雨諒	〇聊了料	咧咧咧列	連憐臉練	〇林㯉賃	
工夫	空虛	飯鍋	〇	拉扯		鬣鬆	檳榔	打撈	勒索	勒死	〇	玻璃	〇	商量	〇	罷咧	接連	〇	
〇	〇	國家	〇	邋遢	來去	貪婪	狠虎	勞苦	〇	雷電	稜角	分離	〇	涼熱	無聊	瞎咧咧	憐恤	樹林子	
金礦	面孔	結果	〇	蜊蜊蛄		懶惰	光朗	老幼	〇	累次	冷熱	禮貌	倆三	斤雨	了斷	咧嘴	臉面	房櫳	
通共	閉空	過去	寬闊	蠟燭	倚賴	燦爛	波浪	旱澇	歡樂	族類	發愣	站立	〇	原諒	料理	擺列	練習	租賃	

TZǓ ERH CHI. Colloquial Series.

另 195	略	留	駱	陋	律	戀	略	掄	略	路 205	亂	倫	龍	馬 210	買	慢	忙	毛
是另外之另	是謀略之略	是收留之留	是駱駝之駱	是鄙陋之陋	是律例之律	是依戀之戀	是忽略之略	是混掄之掄	是大略之略	是道路之路	是雜亂之亂	是五倫之倫	是龍虎之龍	是馬匹之馬	是買賣之買	是快慢之慢	是急忙之忙	是羽毛之毛
〇零領另	〇略	〇略	遛駵柳六	摟摟褻陋	樓屢律	〇〇戀	〇〇略	掄掄圇論	〇〇略	嚕爐櫓路	窿籠弄	窿龍曨論 輪圇論	〇〇〇〇	媽麻馬罵	〇埋買賣	顢聯滿慢	茫忙莽	貓毛卯貌
	〇	〇	一遛兒	摟起袖子		〇	〇	混掄		嘟嚕		窟窿		簀媽		顢頂	白茫茫	貓狗
零碎	〇	收留	驟馬	樓房	驢馬	〇	〇	人倫		爐灶		車輪	龍虎榜	麻木		蟎理	急忙	羽毛
領袖	〇	楊柳	裸身	酒簍	屢次	〇	〇	渾圇著		船櫓		圇圇	瓦隴	馬鞍		收買	鹵莽	卯刻
另外	謀略	五六	駱駝	鄙陋	律例	依戀	忽略	講論	大略	道路	雜亂	沒論	胡弄	打馬	快賣	〇	快慢	相貌

練習燕山平仄編

內	奶	男	囊	鬧		那	木	謀	末	謬	名	民	面	滅	苗	米	夢	門	美
		230						225					220					215	
是內外之內	是牛奶之奶	是男婦之男	是囊袋之囊	是熱鬧之鬧		是問人那個之那	是草木之木	是圖謀之謀	是始末之末	是謬妄之謬	是姓名之名	是民人之民	是臉面之面	是滅火之滅	是禾苗之苗	是米糧之米	是睡夢之夢	是門扇之門	是美貌之美
◯	◯	◯ 喃 ◯ 耐	攘 囊 攏 纔	撓 鐃 惱 鬧		那 拏 那 那	◯ 模 母 木	◯ 謀 某 ◯	摩 麽 抹 末	◯ ◯ ◯ 謬	◯ ◯ ◯ 命	◯ 民 憫 ◯	◯ 綿 勉 面	咩 ◯ ◯ 滅	喵 苗 藐 廟	咪 迷 米 密	懵 盟 猛 夢	捫 ◯ ◯ 悶	◯ 煤 美 眛
◯ 內	在這兒那	哺哺囌語	呦囔	撓着					搵摩					咩咩的羊叫	喵喵的貓叫	眯瞇眼	懵懂	捫捺	
◯ 內外	拏賊 那個	◯ 男婦 牛奶	囊袋 攮了一刀子	鐃鈸 煩惱			模樣 某人 父母 草木	圖謀 甚麼 塗抹		姓名 憐憫 勉力	民人	綿花		禾苗 藐小	迷惑 米糧 勇猛	結盟 睡夢 機密 廟宇 滅火 臉面 性命	謬妄 始末	門扇 憂悶	煤炭 美貌 愚昧

(Entries reading right-to-left, numbered 235–250)

- 濃 — 是濃淡之濃 ／ 濃弄 ／ 濃淡 ／ 擺弄
- 嫩 — 是老嫩之嫩 ／ 嫩 ／ 老嫩
- 暖 (250) — 是暖和之暖 ／ 暖嫩 ／ 暖和 ／ 老嫩
- 奴 — 是奴僕之奴 ／ 奴努怒 ／ 奴僕 ／ 努力 ／ 喜怒
- 虐 — 見上
- 女 — 是男女之女 ／ 女 ／ 男女
- 耨 (245) — 是耕耨之耨 ／ 挪耨 ／ 懦耨 ／ 耕耨
- 挪 — 是挪移之挪 ／ 挪 ／ 挪移 ／ 懦弱 ／ 拗不過來
- 牛 — 是牛馬之牛 ／ 妞牛鈕拗 ／ 牛馬 ／ 鈕扣 ／ 暴虐
- 虐 — 是暴虐之虐 ／ 虐 ／ 妞兒 ／ 擠壞 ／ 伎口
- 甯 — 是安甯之甯 ／ 甯擠佞 ／ 安甯 ／ 您納 ／ 捻匯 ／ 罪孽 ／ 尿尿
- 您 (240) — 是稱呼人的話你納的字本 ／ 年月 ／ 捻匯 ／ 念誦
- 念 — 是想念之念 ／ 拈年捻念 ／ 拈花
- 揑 — 是揑弄之揑 ／ 揑呆孽 ／ 揑弄 ／ 呆獸 ／ 鳥獸 ／ 尿尿 ／ 藏匿
- 鳥 — 是鳥獸之鳥 ／ 嗅鳥尿 ／ 嗅嗅的貓叫 ／ 爹娘 ／ 擬議 ／ 蘊釀
- 娘 — 是爹娘之娘 ／ 娘擬匪 ／ 泥土 ／ 泥擬 ／ 藏匿
- 你 — 是你我之你 ／ 能泥擬匪 ／ 才能 ／ 老嫩
- 能 (235) — 是才能之能
- 嫩 — 是老嫩之嫩

PART VII. TONE EXERCISES. nên — p'i.   233

練習燕山平仄編

皮	必	朋270	盆	迸	本	陪	北265	跑	包	旁	幫	盼260	半	派	拜	怕	罷255	偶	訛
是皮毛之皮	是務必之必	是朋友之朋	是木盆之盆	是迸跳之迸	是根本之本	是陪伴之陪	是南北之北	是跑脫之跑	是包裹之包	是旁邊之旁	是幫助之幫	是盼望之盼	是整半之半	是分派之派	是拜客之拜	是恐怕之怕	是罷了之罷	是偶然之偶	是訛錯之訛
批皮鄙屁	逼鼻筆必	烹朋棒碰	繃盆○迸	噴盆○噴	奔本奔	披陪配	背○北背	拋袍跑礮	包薄跑抱	幫鄉謗	攀盤盼	班板半	拍牌狐派	掰白百拜	琶扒把	八枚把罷	毆○偶嘔	哦訛○惡	
批評	逼迫	割烹	繃鼓	噴水	奔忙	披衣	背負	拋棄	袍袖	旁邊	幫助	高攀	輪班	拍打	擗開	琵琶	八九	毆打	哦一聲
皮毛	口鼻	朋友	盆礮	○	根本	陪伴	南北	跑脫	保護	厚薄	盤查	○	木牌	○	黑白	扒桿兒	提拔	○	訛錯
鄙俚	筆墨	手捧	○	噴	○	○	○	跑	吹哼	細綁	○	板片	千百	一屁股狐下		把持		偶然	○
屁股	務必	碰破	迸跳	噴香	投奔	配偶	向背	槍礮	懷抱	胖瘦	毀謗	盼望	整半	分派	拜客	恐怕	罷了	嘔氣	善惡

234 TZŬ ERH CHI. Colloquial Series.

散	賽 290	洒灑	普	不	剖 285	不	破	波	憑	兵	貧	賓 280	片	扁	撤	別 275	票	表
是散放之散	是賭賽之賽	是洒掃之洒	是普遍之普	是不是之不	是剖開之剖 不字作詩裏有作上平用的	是培剋之培	是破碎之破	是水波之波	是憑據之憑	是兵丁之兵	是貧窮之貧	是賓主之賓	是片叚之片	是圓扁之扁	是撤開之撤	是分別之別	是文票之票	是表裏之表
三〇傘散	頤頰○賽	撒瞰洒	鋪葡普鋪	培○不補不	培○剖		坡婆筐破	波駁播簸	砰憑○聘	兵○稟病	摒貧品牝	賓○殯	偏便調片	邊扁便	擎○撤	憨別嚮嚮	漂嫖漂票	標○表鰾
三四	○○	撒手	葡萄	○不是	○剖剋		土坡	水波	憑據	兵丁	○貧窮	賓主	○偏正	邊沿	擎開	分別	嫖賭	標文書
○○	○○	一眼瞰著							婆娘				便宜					
傘蓋	洒掃	○	普遍	剖開	補缺		破碎	播米	聘禮	稟報	品級	○	謅拉	圓扁	撤了	嚮嘴	漂布	表裏
散散	賭賽	○	鋪子	不可	○		破碎	聘嫁	聘笑	疾病	殯牡	殯葬	片叚	方便	○	錢拐 票子	嚮拐	鰾膠

PART VII. TONE EXERCISES. piao — shên. 235

練習燕山平仄編

桑	掃	嗇 295	森	僧	索	搜	素	筭 300	碎	孫	送	殺	曬 305	山	賞	少	舌	身 310
是桑梓之桑	是掃地之掃	是吝嗇之嗇	是森嚴之森	是僧道之僧	是勒索之索	是搜察之搜	是平素之素	是算計之算	是零碎之碎	是子孫之孫	是迎送之送	是殺死之殺	是曬乾之曬	是山川之山	是賞賜之賞	是多少之少	是脣舌之舌	是身體之身
桑○嗓喪	騷○掃掃	嗇○嗇	森○森嚴	僧○僧道	搜○餿溲	搜○搜察	蘇○速素	酸○筭	雖○髓碎	孫○榫	松○槓送	殺○傻刣	篩○色曬	山○閃善	商○晌賞上	燒○杓少少	賒○掐射	身神審慎
桑梓	騷擾	嚦嚦的叫狗	森嚴	僧道	搜察	蘇州	酸的鹹的		松樹	子孫		殺死		山川	商量	火燒		身體
						迅速		跟隨							晌午	刀勺	脣舌	神仙
嗓子	掃地			鎖上	老叟		骨髓		損益	毛骨竦然		矇傻		顏色	賞賜	多少	棄捨	審問
喪氣	掃興	吝嗇		追溯	咳嗽	平素	算計	零碎		迎送		擎剪子刣一點		曬乾	雷閃	上下	老少	善惡	謹慎	射箭

生	事	手	書	刷	衰	拴	雙	水	順	說	絲	大	他	歹	太	單	炭
				315					320					325			
是	是	是	是	是	是	是	是	是	是	是	是	是	是	是	是	是	是
生	事	手	詩	刷	衰	拴	成	山	順	說	絲	大	他	好	太	單	柴
長	情	足	書	洗	敗	捆	雙	水	當	話	線	小	人	歹	甚	雙	炭
之	之	之	之	之	之	之	之	之	之	之	之	之	之	之	之	之	之
生	事	手	詩	刷	衰	拴	雙	水	順	說	絲	大	他	歹	太	單	炭

生	失	收	書	刷	衰	拴	雙	○	○	說	絲	答	他	歹	胎	單	貪
繩	十	贖	贖	○	○	誰	○	○	○	○	○	搭	○	○	擔	○	談
省	使	數	數	要	摔	○	爽	水	○	○	死	打	塔	歹	○	膽	坦
膡	事	獸	數	○	率	涮	雙	睡	順	朔	四	大	榻	代	太	蛋	炭

| 生 | 失 | 收 | 詩 | 刷 | 衰 | 拴 | 成 | | ○ | 說 | 絲 | 答 | 他 | 歹 | 孕 | 單 | 貪 |
| 長 | 落 | 拾 | 書 | 洗 | 敗 | 捆 | 雙 | | | 話 | 線 | 應 | 人 | 呆 | 胎 | 雙 | 贜 |

| 繩 | 九 | 生 | 贖 | ○ | ○ | ○ | 誰 | | | ○ | ○ | 搭 | ○ | ○ | ○ | ○ | 談 |
| 子 | 十 | 熟 | 罪 | | | | 人 | | | | | 救 | | | | | 論 |

各		手	數	要	摔	○	爽	山	○	○	死	毆	佛	好	○	膽	平
省	使	足	錢	笑	東		快	水			生	打	塔	歹		子	坦
	喚				西											火	

| 賸 | 事 | 禽 | 數 | ○ | 草 | 涮 | 雙 | 睡 | 順 | 朔 | 四 | 失 | 牀 | 交 | 太 | 雞 | 柴 |
| 下 | 情 | 獸 | 目 | | 率 | 洗 | 生 | 覺 | 當 | 望 | 五 | 小 | 榻 | 代 | 甚 | 蛋 | 炭 |

No.							
	丟	是丟失之丟	丟〇哷〇	丟失	〇	呀哷	〇
	聽	是聽見之聽	聽停梃聽	聽見	停止	樹梃	聽其自然
	定	是定規之定	釘〇頂定	釘子	〇	頂戴	定規
345	天	是天地之天	天田餂掭	天地	莊田	拏舌頭餂	掭筆
	店	是客店之店	掂〇點店	掂量	〇	圈點	客店
	貼	是體貼之貼	貼〇鐵帖	體貼	〇	銅鐵	牙帖
	疊	是重重疊疊之疊	爹疊〇〇	爹娘	重疊	〇	〇
	挑	是挑選之挑	挑條挑跳	挑選	條陳	挑着	跳躍
340	弔	是弔死之弔	貂〇〇弔	貂皮	〇	〇	弔死
	替	是替工之替	梯提體替	樓梯	提拔	體量	替工
	的	是你的我的之的	的敵底地	我的	仇敵	到底	天地
	疼	是疼痛之疼	鼟疼〇撜	鼟鼟的鼓聲兒	疼痛	〇	板撜
	等	是等第等候之等	燈〇等鐙	燈燭	〇	等候	馬鐙
335	得'	是必得之得'	鏑〇得〇	小鑼兒鏑鏑的聲兒	〇	必得'	〇
	特	是特意之特	忑〇〇特	忐忑	〇	〇	特意
	得	是得失之得	叨得〇〇	話叨叨	得失	〇	〇
	逃	是逃跑之逃	叨逃討套	叨恩	逃跑	討要	圈套
	道	是道理之道	刀擣倒道	刀槍	擣線	顛倒	道理
330	湯	是喝湯之湯	湯糖躺燙	喝湯	白糖	躺臥	燙手
	當	是應當之當	當〇攩當	應當	〇	攩住	典當

贊	才	在365	擦	雜	同	冬360	吞	退	對	團	短355	土	妒	頭	豆	安350	多
是參贊之贊	是才幹之才	是在家在外之在	是擦抹之擦	是雜亂之雜	是會同之同	是冬夏之冬	是吞吐之吞	是進退之退	是對面之對	是團圓之團	是長短之短	是塵土之土	是娚妒之妒	是頭臉之頭	是綠豆之豆	是妥當之妥	是多少之多
簪俗攢贊	猜才彩菜	栽〇宰在	擦〇	攢雜咱	通同統痛	冬〇懂動	吞屯〇褪	敦〇眈鈍	推〇骸退	堆〇〇〇	端〇短斷	禿塗土唾	督毒賭妒	偷頭〇透	兜〇斗豆	託駝妥唾	多奪朶惰
簪贇	猜想	擦抹	腌臢	通達	冬夏	吞吞吐吐	敦厚	推諉	堆積	端正	禿子	督撫	偷盜	兜底子	託情	多少
借們	才幹	〇	〇	雜亂	會同	〇	屯田	骸快	〇	團圓	〇	塗抹	毒害	頭臉	〇	駱駝	搶奪
攢錢	雲彩	宰殺	〇	咱的	統帥	懂得	〇	打眈兒	〇	〇	長短	塵土	賭博	〇	升斗	妥當	花朶兒
參贊	菜飯	在家	〇	〇	疼痛	勸靜	褪手	遲鈍	進退	對面	〇	斷絕	唾沫	娚妒	透徹	綠豆	陸沫	懶惰

PART VII. TONE EXERCISES. to — ts'uan.

竄	揩	粗	祖	湊	走	錯	作	層	增	參	怎	賊	策	則	草	早	倉	葬	慚
		385				380						375					370		
是逃竄之竄	是揩住之揩	是粗細之粗	是祖宗之祖	是湊合之湊	是行走之走	是作失之錯	是作爲之作	是層次之層	是增減之增	是參差之參	是怎麽之怎	是賊匪之賊	是計策之策	是則例之則	是草木之草	是早晚之早	是倉庫之倉	是葬埋之葬	是慚愧之慚

馬驥	鑽	粗	租	○	走	○	作昨左	搓矬	噌	參	○	○	○	○	操	○	倉	遭	賊	參
攢○	纂○	細○	足○	○	○	○			層	○	○	○	○	○	槽	○	藏	鑒○	哈○	慚
○竄	○楷	○粗	○祖	湊	奏	錯	作	怎○	怎○	○	怎	賊	策	○	草	早	○	○葬	○嗒	慘
		○醋							贈							造				儳

| 馬驢 | 鑽幹 | 粗質 | 租 | ○ | ○ | ○ | 作房 | 揉搓 | 蹭一聲上了房 | 增減 | 參差 | ○ | ○ | 操練 | 倉庫 | 週遭 | 貪賊 | 參考 |

| 攪湊 | ○ | ○ | 祖宗 | ○ | 行走 | ○ | 挫子 | ○ | ○ | 昨日 | 層次 | ○ | ○ | 賊匪 | ○ | 則例 | 馬槽 | 穿鑒 | 瞞藏 | 晗們 | 慚愧 | ○ | 手足 |

| 纂修 | ○ | ○ | ○ | ○ | 左右 | ○ | 怎麽 | ○ | 怎麽 | ○ | ○ | ○ | 草木 | 來得早 | ○ | ○ | 懷慘 |

| 逃竄 | 揩住 | 喫醋 | ○ | 湊合 | 奏事 | 錯失 | 作爲 | 蹭蹬 | 饞贈 | ○ | ○ | 訐策 | ○ | ○ | 造化 | ○ | 犟埋 | 傖頭 |

練習燕山平仄編

嘴	催 390	尊	寸	宗	葱	子	次 395	瓦	外	完	往	爲 400	文	翁	我	武
是嘴脣之嘴	是催逼之催	是尊重之尊	是尺寸之寸	是大宗之宗	是葱蒜之葱	是子孫之子	是次序之次	是甎瓦之瓦	是內外之外	是完全之完	是來往之往	是行爲之爲	是文武之文	是老翁之翁	是你我之我	是文武之武
堆○嘴罪	催隨○萃	尊○撙	村存忖○寸	宗從○總縱	葱○	貲○子字	齜磁此次	挖娃瓦襪	歪○㕶外	灣完晚萬	汪王往忘	微爲委位	溫文穩問	翁○甕	窩○我臥	屋無武物
一堆	催逼	尊重	村莊	大宗	葱蒜	資格	齜著牙兒笑	刨挖	歪正	水灣兒	汪洋	微翦	溫和	老翁	窩巢	房屋
○	隨他去	○	存亡	○	依從	○	磁器	娃娃	○	完全	王公	行爲	文武	○	○	有無
嘴脣	○	撙節	忖量	總名	○	子孫	彼此	甎瓦	昏早	來往	忘記	委員	安穩	○	你我	文武
犯罪	萃集	○	尺寸	縱容	○	寫字	次序	鞋襪	內外	千萬	爵位	問答	○	水甕	坐臥	萬物

PART VII. TONE EXERCISES. tsui — yung.

練習燕山平仄編

405 牙	涯	羊	要	夜	言 410	盆	音	迎	約	魚 415	原	月	雲	有	用 420
是牙齒之牙	是天涯之涯	是牛羊之羊	是討要之要	是半夜之夜	是言語之言	是損盆之盆	是聲音之音	是迎接之迎	是約會之約	是魚蝦之魚	是原來之原	是年月之月	是雲彩之雲	是有無之有	是使用之用
丫牙雅壓	○	夬羊養樣	腰遙咬要	喧爺野夜	煙言眼沿	揖盆引易	音銀引印	應迎影應	約○○樂	愚魚雨預	寃原遠願	曰喊○月	暈雲允運	憂油有右	庸容永用
丫頭	○	央求	腰㪟	喧住	喫煙	作揖	聲音	應該	約會	愚淘	寃屈	子曰	頭暈	憂愁	平庸
牙齒	天涯	牛羊	遙遠	老爺	言語	盆處	金銀	迎接	○	魚蝦	原來	乾喊	雲彩	香油	容易
文雅	○	饕活	咬一口	野地	眼睛	○	勾引	○	沒影兒	風雨	遠近	○	應允	有無	永遠
壓倒	○	各樣	討要	半夜	河沿兒	用印	易經	報應	音樂	預備	顧意	年月	氣運	左右	使用

END OF PART VII.

THE TONE EXERCISES.

(CHINESE TEXT.)

TZŬ ERH CHI.

COLLOQUIAL SERIES.

PART VIII.

CHAPTER ON THE PARTS OF SPEECH.

(CHINESE TEXT.)

The following Chinese Text has been set up differently from that in any foregoing Part. That of the thirteen divisions which properly constitute the Chapter on the Parts of Speech runs, Chinese fashion, from right to left, ending on page 245. The pages of the Supplement, marked XIV, run from left to right, but the reader must begin with the right hand column of each page. He will be guided sufficiently by the numbers prefixed to each sentence.

TZŬ ERH CHI

—

COLLOQUIAL SERIES.

—

PART VIII.

(CHINESE TEXT.)

PART VIII. CHAPTER ON THE PART OF SPEECH.

那麼順當麼哎³呀你受了這些年的辛苦還不知道憐恤別人麼可惡那個人不但白耽悞工夫還鬧了許多的錯兒可惜了兒他的官都快陞了因為不要緊的事把他革了啊你們外國的機器眞是巧妙得很你那天作的那首詩是王老爺瞧過就讚妙不止一次連呼妙妙⁸奇怪他放着好的不要偏要那個壞的有這個道理麽情願那張老爺的傷快好了就可以來救援我聽見說他好了他好了好極又間他後天可以來後天麼巴不得。

路走他²²是搭輪船從大江去得²³多少天纔到七²⁴天我²⁵估摸輪船從上海到漢口、不是四天就到麼、四²⁶天就到也可以、此次是因為沿江各口、又上貨又下貨、所以不能那麼快。

言語例畧第十二段

雖¹²⁵然下很大的雨他也到過衙門、今²年冬天也不大冷也不大潮、那天那個熱鬧不但小童出來看連小妞兒也看他⁴寫的字不論粗細他想人都可以看得出來不³管你去不去我一定去連⁶他帶我都是受傷我想等你試一回⁷不怕你不喜歡憑⁸你去辦兩個法子都好你⁹快說或東或西是怎麼樣¹⁰、這個事不是竟不喜歡還有實在好處。

言語例畧第十三段

那¹²⁶¹心裡驚訝、嘴裡說出來的話、就是有歎美的、有喜歡的、有憐恤的、有憎惡的、有想不到而驚的、有情願的、各等神氣不同、咳²你學話不彀三個月、說的可以

言語例畧第十一段

費了很大的力沒成效[20]那個地方兒頭裡居民很衆,如今很蕭條,道兒離遠我可以快走,不大工夫就到了。

牆頭兒上露出一個人來,[2]他倚靠着牆那羣人我那時都見過,姓張的不在那裡頭,他們倆交情日子深,我瞧他去他沒在家我留下話日落之前我再來,他[6]們把一根木頭橫在道兒上,絆了我一個觔斗他道兒上遇見了很利害的一個險房子背後有園子沒有山[9]上有個廟山背後洞裡有房子,我們是從東華門外頭過去,[11]你是進園子裡頭去麽我們從裡頭打過個穿兒昨兒個一天都是熱閙們那天論的那個事從分手後還沒聽見甚麽消息那[15]上水的小船兒都是頂水拉着[16]那馬從馬圈裡拉了來,騙上跑了,我昨兒個圍着皇城走了一遭,[18]先是看他往那邊去,後來轉過臉見往我這邊來了,那個人跑過這塊莊稼地從小道兒奔大道跑了,張老爺,他如今往漢口去了,[21]是由水路走是由旱

PART VIII. ON THE PARTS OF SPEECH. X — XI. 251

是這兩個法子,你說那一個好,這一個還可以商量,那一個萬不可行,那兩個人,你找着了沒有,找了姓李的沒在家,姓張的並沒有這麼一個人,風颳得可怕,今兒晚上星宿很亮可喜,那個雪下得過逾深,那茶葉實在是壞的,也不是全壞,還有幾分可用,那位先生教得不好,他唱得很好聽,我身子有些微有點兒乏,那[123]小孩子在那兒呢,左右是在家裡總不過是在家,他[2]辦過這件事是甚麼時候兒甚麼地方兒甚麼緣故甚麼法子辦的,我都知道,他[3]一聽見那件事忽然雲彩鋪滿了這些天裡頭,至今沒好,他[4]剛出門去,瓦面就叫風全脫了,早起天晴了不多,他[5]這些天一霎,他早已有病,如今好了,他[6]這一次來的日子不多,他[7]早已的病不多,立刻就走了,是一時收拾不及那客人們動身晚了,趕不出城來,他[11]每月受五兩銀子的工錢,他[14]差一點兒壞了官,那底下人他差一點兒散了工,我[16]天天兒出去逛一逛,我[17]們到他那塊兒瞧瞧,他總是很喜歡,他[18]和賊對敵,打了個敗仗,他[19]辦那件事

說比初次多到三倍、我也不能應許進去。

$^{122}_1$這個很好、那個不好得很、他^{2}寫得字不大很好、他兄弟寫得十分好、他^{3}十分讚美^{4}你、你納那天請他喫飯他很覺體面京北那件事鬧出來皇上氣極了、你^{6}為一件不要緊的事過於生氣說話太傷雅了、那^{7}人過於糊塗甚麼話都不懂、那^{8}件衣裳可以多喀拏了來昨兒晚上差不多兒得了、料估着這時候准得了、那^{9}房子上月差不多就得了、如今縂全完了、我^{10}好些天縂沒看書通鑑是差不多忘了、那漢書所全忘了今兒遇見的那倆人姓張的差不多我不認得了、那姓李^{11}的所不認得了、頭裡那山上樹木很密、如今差不多沒有了、是百姓太不照應、那^{13}些人都好、最好的是姓李的、那^{14}些人他都不願意要頂不願意要的是姓劉的那^{15}些人他都責罰得利害、偏重的是帶他兒子見我、你^{17}昨兒個不是這麽說的你^{18}昨兒個說的不是這麽着、我說的原是這麽着、這^{19}個不是好法子麽不好、怎麽呢、不是你納的法子麽總不

輛車，我的親戚在左邊，宋都老爺在右邊，勇從左邊擁來了，要搶車把車擠得橫攏下，倆人都甲下來了，我的親戚在上頭，宋都老爺在底下，摔得傷很重哎[19]呀，到這個地步兒勇怎麼不要他們的命，唉，他們脫身，是個徼倖的事，是來了[20]甚麼救星呢，是這麼着勇正把車裡的箱子拉出來的時候兒，他們的那些跟人騎着牲口，趕了來了，勇聽見馬跑的聲兒，不知道是甚麼，都四下裡驚散了。你[121,1]到過那關帝廟是多少回，到過門口兒三回，往裡頭就是一次，頭一次進去，第二次為甚麼不進去，我頭一次進去，是先給了廟裡點兒香錢，第二次呢，是他們不肯要錢麼，他們要是要，我說上回給是因為初次來，總給這一回不給了，既[4]是這麼第二次不教你進去，怎麼第三次和尚怎麼樣呢，他更不愛商量，直此沒說明白，不如再試一試，就[5]是那第三次，又去呢，有人說第二次是彼說斷不能進去，為甚麼原故呢，他說一來是官廟，二來當家的沒在家，三來那一天，你納沒給香資就是了，他[7]既有這個話，你還沒提給他錢麼，我倒提了他

那兒沒有、你問得是那兒、我說得是通州、沒到過通州、到過張[4]家灣、怎麼沒到通州呢、打天津坐船就到了張家灣啊、[5]這麼看起來、你不是京[6]城的人麼、我不是京城的人、那麼你貫處是那塊兒呢、我是江蘇人、[7]還是江蘇[8]那一府呢、本藉是蘇州[9]蘇城東門裡頭的那朱家、你認得不認得怕是東門外[10]罷、內外我不狠記得、是從前作過御史的、原是、我到過他家好些麼、[11]他回了藉不是前年麼、我記不很清楚、他前前後後時常得來往、他在道兒上、受了多少[12]的罪、那是那一次呢、哎、就是前年的事情、我一個親戚同他一塊兒走來着、[13]不是在大名府那個地方兒遇見了賊、不是賊、是鄉勇變了、[14]是叫他們追上了、是遇見了、都不是他風聞得大道兒上有事、他走岔道兒斜着往南去、那麼着[15]那兒不可以躲避呢、不但沒躲避、反倒走到他們跟前兒去了、是坐着車、[16]是騎着性口、是坐車到某處兒前後都是勇、是那進退兩頭兒難、[17]聽見說勇還放槍、沒放槍、那[18]麼是受得甚麼傷呢、傷的是這麼着、我的親戚和朱都老爺坐着一

了、不錯、那就是前十年了、是不是原是也快十年了、初次進京、不是隨王大人一塊兒麼、不是、那是第三次了、你納通共進過幾次京、共總五次、初次是隨着先父、令尊是多喒進京、是那道光二十三年的時候兒、多喒回去的、三四個月的工夫兒、就回去了、二次是怎麼來的、是過了二年、先父打發我有事進京來、我都記得那次你納進京、住得日子也不多、我在京幾天、家裡有個急信來啊、不是令尊病重啊、不是、是舍弟受傷、說是要死、令弟還在罷、不錯、他的傷痕慢慢的好了、我彷彿記得那時候兒、是令尊病着來着、是真的、我在道兒上的時候兒、聽見說病了、到了家幾天、就不在了、是、所以後來你納許久沒進京、自然的、丁憂不能出門的、滿服後就是跟王大人來的那一次、王大人如今還在京麼、現在出差了、過些日子就回來了、聽見說你納慢慢兒的也有出京的意思、不錯、可以快走了、這兒差使的期滿了、就可以回去。他是那兒來的人、他是通州來的、離京是通州遠、是張家灣遠、由齊化門論、到通州近一點兒、你到過

跑了、那人找到他丈人家、求他們給他打算些兒、他們雖然是有錢、囘答說、我們近來的買賣很不好、甚麼都喫虧、萬難相幫、你想他初次叫人寃枉、挨罵挨打、後來是賊搶受傷、並且家裡一無所有、他一身受了這些苦處、還叫他女人家裡見笑、像人受這樣兒苦難、向來還有的麼。

言語例畧第十段

那[119][1]一個人今兒個可以來不可以來、怕今兒不能來、明兒個可以來、他昨兒個爲甚麼不來呢、他昨兒個是來了、來得晚、你[3]來得早、他爲甚麼來得晚、我在衙門裡先散的、他後散的、常是這麼着、他來的是我出門的時候兒沒出門的時候兒、你[4]納先走了、他後來的、你告訴他明兒個散衙門趕着來、恐怕不行、他明兒個來了、我纔可以見他不能先見着、那兒[6]呢、你立刻到衙門裡、不能見麼、一定趕不上、我到衙門裡、他必先走了、他[7]如今住的是那兒住的是我從前住的那個衙衙[8]你說的從前、是甚麼時候兒、是你納初次進京的時候兒、那[9]是早已

拉着你⁶³滿嘴裡的話都是誆哄我我不再問了，咳⁶⁴這是那兒的話，你各自各兒起疑不再問也好啊。

上頭¹¹⁵剛看的那個問答章，原意是作出英話用這活字的榜樣，就是因為那是行的多受的少，現在打算再添幾句補足了那受的格局。父母¹¹⁶都是養兒子，那句話所提是父母行的兒子為父母所養，這一句，是兒子受的。你¹¹⁷打我那字眼兒是分定那打是你行的，我被你打是那打為我所受的，就是那受甚麼的理漢話論的，不止一樣的字眼兒。比方¹¹⁸那人實在可憐，從前在王大人那兒做門上，是被人的冤屈說他私受銀錢，因為這個挨打很利害，就把他辭了²，他回鄉去道兒上又碰見賊，把他擄到山中，不但甚麼都搶乾淨了，還受了傷很重，不是有車從那兒過，有人把他扶起來，他一定要死了，等他回到本村³就知道他那住的地方，新近都是被賊擾亂，他父親的房子也燒了，所有的產業也都毀壞了，他⁴女人原是財主家裡的姑娘，賊鬧的時候兒，是叫兒子拐下

麼
，
殿
與
不
殿
沒
要
緊
，
那
時
候
兒
你
看
見
他
動
身
也
可
以
告
訴
我
，
那
時
候
兒
你
上[35]
樓
，
自
己
可
以
看
見
了
，
那
時
候
兒
你
不
許
我
上
樓
這
時
候
兒
你
許
我
上
樓
麼
，
隨[36]
你[37]
愛
上
樓
愛
找
那
個
人
去
，
都
使
得
找
他
幹
甚
麼
大
概
道
他
半
天
也
看
不
見
，
別
有[38]
氣
，
我
不
是
有
氣
就
是
不
信
你
的
話
，
噯
你
別
這
麼
着
從
前
就
打
量
着
是[39]
誰[40]
是
真
的
，
你
誆
了
是
這
麼
半
天
了
，
就
打
量
着
這
麼
半
天
是
誰
，
與
你
何
妨
總
而
言[41]
之
，
你
想
我
這
會
兒
追
趕
得
上
麼
，
我
頭
裡
叫
你
去
的
時
候
兒
你
就
走
，
還
容
易
趕
得[42][43][44]
上
，
就
是
那
會
兒
走
也
未
必
准
能
按
着
他
的
道
兒
去
，
你
真
矯
情
可
以
不
叫
你
去
罷[45][46]
你
叫
我
去
罷
這
個
人
你
不
認
得
不
能
找
，
我
回
去
了
，
你
如
今
上
來
了
你
先
指
給
我[47][48]
他
往
那
們
去
了
，
指
給
不
指
給
不
要
緊
還
得
等
三
天
，
他
可
以
回
來
，
他
這
三
天
上
那[49][50][51]
兒
去
，
他
上
墳
地
裡
監
工
去
，
你
說
不
認
得
怎
麼
知
道
是
修
墳
地
去
頭
裡
我
不
認
得[52][53]
後
來
我
看
出
來
是
王
立
，
王
立
在
這
兒
打
人
做
甚
麼
我
沒
棍
他
是
打
人
他
還
是
打[54][55][56][57][58][59]
馬
來
着
麼
不
是
打
馬
，
是
打
騾
子
，
他
騎
着
騾
子
我
那
兒
趕
得
上
呢
，
他
不
是
騎
着
是[60][61][62]

打甚麼呢,那[5]個人你認得不認得,我[6]從前沒見過你[7]在這兒坐着看了有多大工夫兒呢[8],不很大的工夫兒[9],恐怕你看錯沒人打甚麼沒[10]錯,到這時候我還看着呢,我[11]還怕是錯了,沒有這個人,那[12]兒沒這個人的時候兒你看是看現在還是看我[13]沒問你的時候兒你看見過沒有呢[14],早我就看見了,你[15]剛纔說在這兒的工夫不大,我[16]那時候兒說的是實話,我[17]出去看一看你看的那個人是有沒有,很好你[18]到那兒就知道有沒有,你[19]等我回來我行不行,你[20]快回來,我還在這兒坐着你[21]沒有甚麼事辦麼事[22]還有,到不了你回來我就准辦結了,到那[23]兒了,果有這個人回來我認錯,等[24]你看明了,至不濟我先有三天的笑話不完怎麼[25]先有三天的笑話呢,我[26]說至不濟,你得等三天纔得問明,我就去看,怎麼[27]會耽誤三天,你[28]立刻去看,還趕不上,那[29]兒你還看着那個人,我怎麼趕不上呢,叫[30]我說他還在那兒,那就是撒謊,你[31]這半天沒有正是看着的話麼當[32]時正看着,未必此時還能趕上,你[33]說他走了,是不是,我[34]若是說他走了,你還能彀我

是爲的、所有時候不同、總不過分三等、是已經的、就是過去的、是未有的、就是將來的、是目下的、就是現在的、這是三個大綱、還有細目得分的。我昨天上衙門、今天看書、明天再歇歇這三句、就是分時候三等的大概、至於那細目[112]來的時候兒、我正在喫飯、到晚上回來、我已經出門去了、你多喒可以過來麼[118]我明兒晌午來好不好不行、你是晌午來、我正要上衙門去、你倒放心罷、敁彼此相見、你那一件事必是我給你先都辦妥了、我是寫信給京城裡叫他們把我那些書、都從船上寄了來、我這半天、也都是寫信來着、到後天我看那個書、已經三個月了、到今天晚上、第八本就看完了、你總得用心罷用心我是用心、我不是不用心買馬的那時候兒、你爲甚麽不找個好的呢、找是找過了總沒找着。[114]你在樓上坐着看甚麽呢、我坐着看那個人、看他在那兒作甚麽呢、我看他是

人的、就有走罷、跑去、是令人走、令人快走的。 他[109]愛看書那句話、裡頭有愛字、看字、都是活字、其中那愛字、旣屬他字所主、就是按英文定例、歸爲直說的式樣、那看字不屬專主、尙算凡論的限制、看書書是個好事、這些看字、是無論看書的是誰、與他看書是專指某人是看書的、兩個說法不同、一見就可以了然。 英文[110]的活字、上頭五個變換畧說明白了、剩有一個是較比難些兒試[2]論當時那姓張的、他那些孩子們、他最疼愛的那個病了、那漢帝最寵的那臣子謀叛、那炸砲炸開的時候兒、那些兵站着的打傷了、躺着的都躱避了、我骨頭那麼疼、是個疼、躺着、站着、不安、國勢大亂、就彷彿牆要躺下了、這些句裡頭那疼愛的寵的、站着、坐着、要下各等字樣、繙做英話都算是歸活字第六個式樣的裡頭細查那的字、着字實用像似活字所議、是作是爲的、專一指的就是那正義、再加那的字、着字、那都是陪出旁義、是爲補足專指其事、或可正在現有、或可正在已有、或可正在將有、各等形勢。 事情[111]是作的能算全是對的、權用也無不可、讓我把兩國隨用那活字、有相對有相反的地方兒勉強做個榜樣。卽[100]如有漢人說馬跑鳥飛虫扒魚游這幾句話、旣是這麼接連着所說的、必是馬類都是跑的、鳥類都是飛的、虫類都是扒的、魚類都是游的、這個意思。或[101]是偶爾聽見那旁人說馬跑那句話、必算他專指有匹馬、正在跑着、還是常說那個馬跑的多。他[102]念書我寫字這兩句所論、可以是現在我們倆正在那兒做這兩件事也可以是向來各人如此分課的意思。這裡頭用活字是作爲的有[103]間的你們倆在那兒都是睡覺麼答的、可是有他睡我醒着他是睡覺我醒着、他睡覺我醒着、我是醒着這些樣子都無不可。光景多那行的受的、可以緩商、先把那英文使用活字、各有分定六個式樣說一說。比[105]方我愛他你肯不肯、那愛字肯字各當直說直間指明准定的意思。他[106]來我必見他、那是包是否准來未定的意思。他[107]可以做先生那句話就是或指他會做先生或指他願意總能夠做先生。叫[108]人用來一個字、那是令

麼多[6]你不要這麼些個還可以轉賣給別人你[7]是多少錢買得是四吊錢一百
斤買的哎[9]買得這麼貴是在那一個鋪子裡買的[10]是平安街泰興煤鋪他這麼
貴你爲甚麼不到別處去呢離這兒左近沒有別的煤鋪那兒[13]的話呢我那一
天上平安街看見好幾個煤鋪子是有還是彼此通氣兒離[15]是
通氣兒還可以還價兒不能這兒要多少那兒也是要多少都是彼此相襯的
意思看煤也不見很好這宗煤要賣四吊錢一百斤實在是豈有此理我彷彿
記得去年這宗煤還貴些兒別[17]的不別的這斤數兒太多我可不能全買懲你
撥出幾成轉賣給別人罷咧[18]你不要全數兒實要多少[19]可以留三四百斤都可
以那[20]煤價呢你可以給了改[21]日子再給罷。

言語例畧第九段

英[99]國無論人物所有議及是爲的是做的是受的這宗字樣都是歸爲那九項
之一漢文並沒有這個限制較難創出個專名子來就是那活字這字樣雖不

那一個不論那一個我都不愛喜，你[13]們這些人進來的時候兒，個個兒都得帶腰牌。你[14]看這兩個那一個都好呢，那一個都好，這兩樣兒玉器你要那一個，兩個都好，論一個那一個都使得。

那磁器他要買那一個呢，通共他都要買，你[3]要買的是那一件兒，我都不要買是你有理，是他有理呢，衆人都說是我有理。他家裡那個病鬧得利害，除了他一個人其餘都死了。那[8]件事是人都可以明白，那[9]件事他爲甚麼不找人打一個主意沒有人能替打算，那兒呢，這宗事情是人都可以打算，大家都說這個人執拗所以他不肯聽別人的主意，他[12]實在可憐人人都不管也不是有幾個人管他不多，却有幾個恨他很利害的啊，有幾個可以數得出來的，你[14]算是幾個。我[15]算着有五個人，我想不止五個人，還多得很呢，有人告訴你怎麼不錯有某人告訴我說，有某家幾個人就很不喜歡他。哎呀[98]你買的這個煤是多少斤共總八百斤，怎麼買的這麼多呢，你說的得買好些個，我說好些個也不要這

告訴上司、不用人告訴他們、他們自己就可以查出來了。[16]

這兩匹馬那一個好、依我說這一匹好、那一匹不好、那一道河的兩岸兒、那一[95][1][2][3]邊兒好、那一邊兒有景致、這一邊兒荒、些個這些牛都是你買的、這三個黃的[4][5][6]是我的、那幾個黑的是他買的、你拏我這些東西作甚麼、那些個你攔下罷。[7][8][9]不是我的呢、這一樣就不是你的、就是了、這一個我可不要那一個[10][11]

國家的百官各人有各人的辦法、賠錢的各自[96][1][2][3]各兒下各自各的注、那兩個主意都不好用、那一天有兩個人給他出主意聽[4][5]誰的都可以救他的命、可惜那兩個主意他都沒肯聽、他問我賃房子是長住[6]是暫住、我說怎麼着都可以、這個單子、你們倆不論誰抄寫都可以、他們倆每[7][8]月三次囘家、每次准一個人囘去、明兒個怕有事、你們倆總得留下一個人不[9]論誰都使得、他那一天喝醉、遇見人就打、你說得那個賊、都是腦袋上纏着紅[10][11]布麼、共總有沒有、我可不知道、我見的是個個纏着紅布的、他們倆、你愛喜[12]

個,說人說物都可以。他⁹⁰在那兒辦的是甚麼事,辦的是甚麼事,他還沒告訴我說。他⁹¹實在要的是這們着。所⁹²有犯法的總得究辦,無論是誰犯了法,就得究辦,無論是誰,該賞,我必得賞那⁹³賊很兒遇誰都殺,凡²有進入內地必取執照,那³話是假的,憑誰說都不可信,憑⁴他保舉是誰,都得陞賞,他⁵叫我辦甚麼,我必得辦甚麼,我⁶不是叫你把那邊所有的書,都拏過來麼,原⁷是還有我沒拏過來的麼,立⁸櫃裡頭的那一本還落下了。他⁹⁴不是你的父親麼,不²是,是我的哥哥,哦,他³的歲數兒多大呢,比我大二十多那⁵一本書是你的,是你借來的,是我本人的,哦⁷是你託那姓張的給你買的麼,不⁸是,是我本人買的,你⁹今兒上東花園兒逛逛罷,不¹⁰行,我今兒有差使,交給我替¹¹你當好不好,費你納的心,必得我自己辦的,你各自個兒辦,和別人辦有甚麼不一樣,不¹⁴但是我本人的責任,若是我自己個兒不辦,必招上司的挑斥,誰¹⁵

你我提起旁人稱爲是他。所稱[82]的不止一個人、爲我們偺們、你們、他們。話裡頭提起會歡來、他字可以說得論死物那他字用不着提起狗來着。可[84]漢[83]以說他會看家、間人那桌子拏過來了麽、不能說拏他過來了。我[85]去拜的那個人沒在家、你[2]去拜的是誰、是[3]從前教我說官話一位先生、他姓[4]甚麽、姓[5]張、是[6]在虎皮衚衕住的那張家的麽、再說[7]是甚麽胡同、我說[8]得是虎皮衚衕、是在東大街南頭兒路西裡、第四條的那個衚衕、那[9]倒不是張先生住得那個衚衕、他住得是城外頭、他[10]如今教得是誰、他[11]教得有倆人、都是我的親戚、教[12]他們甚麽功課呢、教[13]那個大的辦文書、小的看那四書、他們倆那一個[14]見長、我[15]看那小的比大的強、你[16]現在看得是甚麽書、還是你去年送給我的那一本書。說[86]誰字兒就是提人纔用得、說那個這倆字眼兒提人提東西都[17]用得着。叫[87]你來得是誰、叫你來得是甚麽人。你[88]要甚麽來。我要那茶碗來。你在這兒做甚麽我在這兒拾到屋子。你[89]愛喜是那一

字眼兒是輔助的。比方單說好一個字是空說沒有着落好字之外必得添[68]人添物纔爲分項之用。比方這是個好人,那個人好,這兩句那好字是品評[69]人的字眼兒。這個紙白,那個紙紅,這紅白兩個字是分紙項的。粗紙細紙[70][71]這個紙粗,那個紙細,各等句裡頭這粗細兩個字是分等的。

至於用那輔助的字眼兒也得分層次看這一章就可以知道。他[72]明白,你比他明白這些人裡最明白是他,他比他們那些人明白他比人明白[73]他是天底下最明白的人。

這些法子頂做不來的是那個。那是做不來的,那更是做不來的,那再做不來的。[74]比我的錢多。我比不起他的能幹。京城裡頭的房脊頂高的是皇宮。他的錢[75][76]話那一個強姓李的強些兒。他身量高我的身量矮。他們倆說官[77][78][79]

言語例暑第八段

這三個人的學問那一個強,還是姓李的強。[80]

人說話裡頭,稱自己爲我,我向誰說話稱誰爲你,你我偺們兩個之外爲旁[81]人。

不可和他掉換。

那賊匪燒過我老人家的房子這一句裡按着英話的說法,賊匪是頭等,房子是二等,老人家是三等。怎麼見得呢,比方要問放火是誰,是那賊匪,燒的是甚麼,是房子,是誰的房子,是老人家的房子。總之那名目不論甚麼,是行的當為頭等,受的就當為二等,歸為三等。

言語例畧第六段

人[62]分得是男女禽獸分得是公母,凡死物東西,都不分陰陽,山冰木石,都算是死物。那[63]邊兒坐着的一個爺們,一個娘兒們,是夫婦麼不是,是兄妹。我買了七隻小雞子,有兩隻公的,五隻母的。兒[65]馬是公的,騾馬是母的。犍[66]牛話裡頭是公牛,母牛是母牛。

言語例畧第七段

那[67]名目的實字若要分項定等必得加字眼兒,實字像是為主的,分項定等的

言語例畧第五段

英[46]國用名目、是人是物、限定三个式樣、都是隨勢敀換、漢話裏旣是沒有這個分別、權且分出三等、請看以下四段、就是分三等先後的榜樣。那茶碗[47]是誰砸得、是那小孩子砸得。這個字是甚麼人寫得、是姓張的那個人寫得。畜[49]性裏最靈的是甚麼、最靈的是狗。那[50]小小子兒打得是誰、他打得是那妞兒。那[51]樵夫在那兒做甚麼呢、他在那兒砍樹枝子呢。他[52]把那本書丟了、丟得是誰的書、是我的那本書。你[53]那本書不是送給他麼、不是送給他的。是[54]借給的、你跟他要他的那本、補你的罷咧、他那一天和我借給的、就是前天借給他的。你[55]是那一天借給他的。你[56]怎麼這麼借給他呢、他在街上遇見我、拏着這本書、他和我借、我不肯。你[57]不肯他怎麼拏了去得呢、我說不肯、他打手裏頭硬槍了去、說後天還我。他[58]實在可惡、你以後

目用的。有用這眾多多多少好些個都均全大家諸凡等這些字的。到了要說名目的數兒有把數目字加在上頭的有先提出名目後加數目字的。此方聽[33]見眾人說來的人很多。有多少有好些個。都是甚麼人均屬良善。爲[36]甚麼全來了大家有公事求諸位辦理。凡[37]事有個頭緒這些人等自然就回去了。來了[38]多少人那句話也可以當來了許多人。有人[39]來這句話不能定是一個人來是多少人來有兩個人來有三個人以上一個人來那句話也可以說得三個人以[上]常說得是人數較多些兒似乎一看數不清。那[41]家裏那些人們狠不和睦。話[42]裏不提人用不着們字。他[43]來的是賣牛羊這句話必不是賣一隻牛一隻羊的意思。有人說他要賣隻牛賣匹馬賣的一定是一隻牛一匹馬。這[44]間房子是單說一間這房子是間數兒不定。有[45]人來了是幾個人四個人那些人做甚麼來他們是拉了幾匹馬來那幾匹馬是誰要買的不是都要買的買一匹也可以我不大很要買馬。

尊一尊礮也說一位礮一架礮。

尾一尾魚還說一條魚。

位位字的本義是人是物或坐或立各歸其應得之所就是了話裏頭有三位大人一位礮幾位客這宗樣子。

文那文字除了銅錢之外不當陪伴字樣問其原由是周朝鑄錢上頭加字文的時候兒起的一文錢常說是一個大錢或問這東西要幾文錢答的是多少大錢這麼說。

眼眼就是說井用這個眼字作陪伴。

言語例畧第四段

就[32]是剛講的這些陪伴的字看起來每與數目自連着而用的多再要提起名目裏的數兒那有單的有總的不同就是漢話分單數兒總數兒有好些個是有本名目不加數目字眼兒可以當數目字用的有重用名目的字可以當數

是常說的、到了一條河、也說一道河、一條被、還說一林被。

貼　除了一貼膏藥沒別的話、一貼金箔、多說是一張金箔。

頂　這頂字、就是做轎子帽子的陪件。

朶　除了一朶花沒別的用處、那朶還沒開花之先、俗名叫咕朶。

垛　一垛木頭、一垛磚、說得是櫊得齊整。

頭　一頭牛、一頭騾子、一頭驢、隨便說一個騾子、一個牛也使得、惟獨羊是論隻不論頭。

堵　堵是做牆字的陪件、用堵字道字、都是一樣。

堆　堆字和垛字彷彿、但垛是整齊、堆是雜亂、也有說一堆木頭、一堆磚、也說一堆土等類。

頓　一頓飯、一頓打、是這個頓字做陪件、像似因為有些兒足了的意思。

座　一座山、一座墳、一座廟、一座塔、都說得。

檯　檯本是兩個人、或是數人、搭着一樣兒東西、出殯的可以有六十四檯。
嫁粧至少的八檯、富家可以一百多檯。送禮物的檯、都是雙數。

擔¹　擔是一個人拏扁擔挑着東西。
頭兒挑着柴火。比方³僅有一綑柴火、那是用棍子挑着扛在肩髆兒上。他挑着一擔柴火、是他挑扁擔、扁擔兩

刀　刀就是一刀紙這一句話、本是幾十張紙擱平搭在一塊兒、是因用刀力可以裁得開的。

道　一道¹河、一道橋、一道牆、一道口子、一道上諭、都是條字的意思。京城²前門外頭、那是個三道橋。

套　一套書、是幾本書套在一塊兒、可以是一部全書、也可以是一部書分爲幾套。一套²衣裳、是一袍一褂、可以裡邊穿一件外面套一件。

條　一條線、一條繩子、一條帶子、一條鎖、一條狗、一條虹、一條理、一條街、這都

首、那首數兒不是一定必要雙數、做三五首、做幾十首、都好。

匹 馬字的陪伴是專用匹字、到了一匹騾驢、還可以說一頭、若活說一個也可以、駱駝常說是幾個。

疋 疋字專做綢緞綾羅紗布等項的陪伴、必是兩頭兒不缺、纔可以說。

篇 一篇文章、一篇賦、一篇論、都是成章的意思、所以用篇做陪伴。到[2]說這書有多少篇兒、那是論張數兒和成章有點分別。

鋪 除了一鋪炕之外沒有甚麼別的、是林總得說一張牀、那鋪店之鋪是同音不同聲的。

所 一所房子、和一處房子相同、都是總論一個大門之內的。

扇 扇[1]本是趨暑招風的東西、因為門的櫈兒彷彿、故此說扇。那[2]房子門扇不齊、還得做四五扇。

首 首字單是做詩纔用、彷彿限定首尾的意思、詩家做詩、看題隨做詩、首多寡不定、各首句數不同、或有四句、或有八句、最多十二句、十六句、都說一

管　管是長柄的東西中間是空的作為陪伴字即如一管筆一管笛一管簫政說一枝也是一樣

綑　一綑柴火一綑草一綑葱這些說都是因為有束在一塊兒的意思

粒　一粒米一粒九藥都是指那東西的形像而論

領　除了一領蓆子一領葦箔別沒有甚麼用處

面　這面字就是做鑼鼓旗鏡的陪伴字

把　是有把兒手裡可以拏的東西都論幾把。比方一把茶壺兩把刀子一把鏟子一把叉子一把扇子一把鎖頭這類都是。椅子說一把說一張都使得

包　凡是收裏起來的都可以用包字做陪伴的字即如一包糖一包煙土等類就是

本　一本書一本帳都說得一本書還可以說一卷書帳却不能說卷字。

棵 這棵字、就是專做樹的陪伴、沒別的用法。

顆 一顆珠子、一顆首級、都是按那名目形像說的、是圓的東西、都可以分一顆一顆的多。

口 [1]一口鍋、一口鐘、一口刀、一口缸、幾口人、都說得、雖然這口字是這些名目的陪伴、獨論人還有分別、總說男女的人數兒、是論口、單說婦女、也是論口、至於專論衆男人、也說多少名、也說多少個。[2]一口刀、原是兵器、一把刀也可以說、屠戶用的、也是一把刀。 那[3]一口鐘的鐘、是廟裡掛的鐘裡頭沒有鐸、有人撞纔有聲兒。

股 一股道、就是一條道、文話一股路也說得。

塊 一塊洋錢、一塊墨、一塊磚、一塊區、都可以說這塊字的用處、也是最廣的、比方拏一塊銀子、買了一塊氈子。

牀　一牀被、一牀褥子、一牀毡子、都說得。

方　這方字就是做磚石的陪伴。

封　這封字是做書信等字的陪伴、因為這個字本有包藏不露的理、所以說一封書字一封信。

幅　幅幅和張不同與條字近些兒但是寬窄沒甚分別一幅箋紙就是一張箋紙、論布可以說一幅布論綢也有一幅一幅的說、都是兩邊織就的意思。

副　一副對字、一副環子、都是一對的意思。

桿　說一桿槍、一桿秤、一桿叉、都是因那東西的形像總說若是長槍說一條也使得、其餘別的却不能。

根　用這根字陪伴那旗杆棍子杆子燈草木頭頭髮鬍子等名目都是按著形像說的。一根棍子說一條棍子也可以。[1][2]

個　這個字的用處最多、惟獨幾個人、這個理、這個東西是更常說的、別的用

軸　一軸畫兒是一張裱了的條幅因為底下兩頭兒露出木頭軸兒來故此是一枝子兵一枝子勇可以用。總說還有誥封論幾軸也是一樣的意思。

句　這句字就是陪伴話文這兩個字。

卷　一卷册子一卷書還是說一本册子一本書的多。

炷　一炷香是單說一枝香若是好些炷用紙束在一塊兒那為一股五股在一塊兒為一封。

處　處就是地方兒的意思說買了一處房子是一個院牆之內的那些間房子都在裏頭連單間沒院牆的也可以說。

串　一串珠子一串誦珠一串朝珠。誦珠朝珠也說一掛單珠是顆字陪伴。

椿　地下埋的木橛叫椿話裏說有一椿事情是在多少事情裏單要提出這個來說是特立樣子常說還是一件事多。

件　間不等、那樓分間在外頭、說是五七間房子身在裏頭說是五七間屋子
我們倆在一個屋裏住這句話、是那幾間屋子連到一塊兒出入都是由
一個門走或說我們倆在一間屋子住、那是一個單間另有屋門的、這[5]
一溜房子有多少間、是問這橫連着的房子有多少。
這[1]陪伴衣裳的字、是專用件字到了一件事情幾件像伙幾件文書這宗
字樣要換別的字陪伴也可以。比方[2]說一樁事情幾樣像伙幾套文書、
都使得。

隻　那隻字的陪伴、有雞鴨鵝牛羊虎觥箱等字又有鞵靴襪胳臂手脚眼睛
都是原來成雙的要指一半而說、所以纔用這個隻字卽如那個鞵丟了
一隻。

枝　枝是樹上長得一枝枝字、一枝花兒那是好些朵花兒在一塊兒長着、一
枝筆、一枝笛可以說、也沒有一管筆、一管笛說的多、枝子和枝不同用、就

陣 的樣子。
一陣大雨,一陣大風,一陣吵鬧,這個陣字本意原是打仗,是因那個忽然的形勢,故此用做陪伴字,彷彿是來的很急不能等着的神氣。

乘 那乘字本是乘船,乘車,乘馬的乘字。 轎[2]有說一乘的,又說一頂的多。

劑 一劑藥是合好些味藥做湯飲的,若是把好些味藥要配丸藥,那稱為一料藥。

架 一架礮,一架鷹,一架鐘,一架房樑,這裡頭就是兩架房樑,還可以說一對。

間 是[1]四根柱子的中間為一間,故此為房子,屋子這些名目的陪伴,還有得細分的。比方[2]人說我買了房子,那是買了房子在裡頭,或說那個房子好,那是統一個大門裏都算上。或[3]間那個房子裏有多少間,那人回答有三十多間,那都是那個房子裏頭,不分大小,按各間而說。 王公府[4]裏大約北面都有個後樓,上下兩層各分五七

的比方話裏說馬船的大數兒也可說馬匹船隻這麼樣又有本名目剛先提
過接着說的話可以把陪伴字做爲替換之用設若有人買了牛他告訴我說
我昨兒買了牛我問他買了多少隻他囘答買了十幾隻這就是牛字作爲本
名目那隻字就是陪伴的有贘伴的替換本名目就可以不重覆再提
了這替換名目的也是文理有時可以替換總之細察那陪伴字的實用像是
把總類專項分晰辯明的意思卽如皇天之天后土之土是有類無項的名目
那兒有陪伴的字樣至若那些有類可以分項的那宗總名要數出每類多少
項就把那陪伴字當作細目爲方便如今把那些陪伴的字眼兒連各司的名
目一併開列於左爲學話的便用。

盞擎一盞燈來我要看書。[1] 那個燈籠是走道兒屬的。[2] 那盞字也當碗字
用一盞茶一碗茶都可以說。[3]

張 所有桌椅牀凳弓紙機羅這些字用張字做陪伴是因爲像形稍有寬大

泛論。漢話裡用那個其字、像似和英文裡指定的字眼兒、有時相合、也不能常。那[26]可不錯比方其餘的那個其字、原是指定了、早已開除之外所剩的都在裡頭、還有其要在此那一句、是專指最要的地方兒、所論像是那個人其心不可問、這一句裡那其字、不過是當他字講、至於名目裡不用先加指定的字懞、兩國的話裡、都有可去的地方兒、即如人是萬物裡最靈的、金比銀重這兩句裡那人字、金字、銀字、這都是大類的總名、是可以直說的、還有人姓地名等項、也是這麼著。

言語例署第三段

至[27]於漢話裡頭、那名目又有個專屬、是這麼著話裡凡有提起是人是物、可以有上頭加一個同類的名目、是要看形像的用處、做為陪伴的字、即如一個人一位官、一匹馬、一隻船、這四個裡頭、那個字、位字、匹字、隻字、就是陪伴人官馬船這些名目的這陪伴的字、都不但竟是加在上頭、也有可以隨著本名目說

言語例畧第二段

這[21]句叚分的綱目中國也不是總沒有這個道理，但是東家所說的單字分有九項，那是從前還沒有聽見提過。可[22]是先生沒聽見過那單字的分項漢話裡沒有如此指明，就是那英文凡有人物事勢此等字樣所分字項的定制，皆稱爲名目，即如人字書字病字年字這四個字，都是名目，英國不分作文說話裡，凡有遇用那名目多有先加字樣，可以指出所提，是否早已議及，這等字樣漢話裡雖然沒有詳細分別，凡遇其勢也有分其已準未準之法，比方凡說有個人來，有一個人來，這兩句聽了，可以知道所論的人，並不是個早已論及的那傳話的心裡還茫無定向呢，設若傳話的人說，那個人來了，聽了可以知道來的，是早已提過的那個人，傳話的如此分淸了界限，那就是確然指明了。我[23]們這些那字這字原是分別彼此之用。那[24]可自然那個且等後來再說，就是這第二十二句裡，專用那個人的那字，却沒有彼此之分，實因指定不是隨時隨勢可以互相變通的理。變通是全能彀變通的，甚至於有人說不論那個字都可以做半活半死的用。我們英國話文限制死些兒沒有漢字那變換的活動權分其大端有單字有句法那字各歸九項就是論單字的一端至於連字成句連句成段那就是句法。做國向來作文章也有分股分段的式樣東家剛說這句法可以是那麼樣罷。那却不同貴國作文憑那句法是專管那個字句的長短我們成句之理就是無論何句必有綱目兩分方能成句人家所題那人那物那事為綱論綱的是非有無動作承受這都為目看起這個來竟有死字沒有活字難算成句較比人雨竟說這三個字不添活字實屬有頭無尾為能算話竟是有活字沒有死字其理相同不待言矣那人是好下雨那馬快這三句達出來的意思全了所以總成句分其綱目就是這頭一句裡那人字為綱論人的好不好是目第二句下雨雨字是綱論起下雨不下是目第三句馬字為綱論起走得快為目。

的文較比我們中國省事些兒。那是外國的作文其單字各字都歸准類連字成句又有句法明文那些書貴國並無這些指定句法的書成句都是記得書上記載的字㨾句旣作成就可以連句成文至於那單字統分虛實兩大項那是我考察了多少囘至今總沒有透澈這個理。本字[15]裡有正義的統謂是實字其中要看用法還有死活之分虛字較難細辨比方你不要錢麽那一句那麼字本無正義用之竟是因爲指明了是訂間的口氣就是虛字其餘的幾個裡那個不字離有實義漢文裡頭還算是虛字那你字錢字那都爲實字至於那個死的活的不同就是此處你錢這兩個字是死的那要字一個字是活的然而那要字總說是活字在此處固然是活的別處也可以當死的用比方其要在速這一句那要字速字可不是死字麽再問這句裡活字沒有麼就是那在字必算是活字又考這些字裡虛實之分就是那其在這兩字離然本有正義此處仍算是虛字。

看[16]起這個來就是虛字實字這些個名目大有

用處。 那[7]清文頗有幾分相似,漢文離不相同,那漢文寫的還分八筆,稱爲字母,和貴國的筆畫可不同麽。 其[8]用大不相同,那漢文單着的筆畫雖有本音,作成整字,其音與筆畫本音並不相干,比方寫一個十字,那是數目裡一個字,寫的是橫竪兩筆,那橫的原名一字,竪的原名滾字,這兩筆合成十字,一看就知是專管這個字形,於聲音毫無干涉,這是外國人學漢字以爲最難的地方兒。 外[9]國定音的,還有甚麽好法子呢。 是[10]這麽着,外國寫字,那有二十多個筆畫,把那筆畫連成字,也不用很多的工夫,就可以知道那個理,學會之後,遇見甚麽字,都可以定得準他的音,至若漢字,並沒有一個可以準是定音的地方兒,沒念過決不能知道,必得察一察,察過一次,日後再見了,還是不能保其不忘記。 那[11]是不錯的,我們漢人們不怕忘記了,是因爲從小兒先認單字的。 就[12]是了,我們外國旣是沒念過貴國的書,看書的時候兒,未免有那單字的難處,等到把單字連上成文,那作文的難,就比單字更甚萬分。 聽[13]見說外國

言語例畧第一段

看[1]貴國的人學我們的漢話都像是費事得很却是甚麽難處呢。唉[2]那難處不止一樣了有口音的難處有單字的難處更有文法的難處。怎麽[3]呢外國人各國互相學話看着像不用很多的工夫難道我們這漢話和貴國的話全是兩樣的麽。那到[4]不必說天下各國的話沒有全不相同的地方兒是人那念頭發出來隨勢自可分好些神氣有直說有無有間有令有願望有驚訝比方這人死了那人沒死那是直說有無有的話那人死了沒有是問人的話斬那人罷是令人的話把不得那人好了是願望的話可惜了兒那人死了是驚訝的話這是鄙意先生明白不明白。那兒[5]不明白這就可算文話的總例是中外各國人情自然相同之理。可不[6]是麽就是論及單字的那個難處這惟漢文獨異怎麽呢就是除了中國之外是有文各國寫字就有那些筆畫的定數這些筆畫各有本音可以把數筆連在一塊兒不但會整字還有指定聲音的

PART VIII. (Supplement.) XIV. 289

附編

言語例畧第十四段

127.
1. 來。 lai!
2. 嗟。 cha!
3. 拏水來。 na shui lai.
4. 老爺要的是涼水是開水。 lao-yeh yao-ti shih liang shui, shih k'ai shui.
5. 要涼水洗澡要溫水洗 yao liang shui hsi-tsao, yao wên shui hsi

臉。 lien.
6. 臉盆裡有溫水那澡盆是漏的怕不能倒水。 lien-p'ên li yu wên shui; na tsao-p'ên shih lou-ti, p'a pu nêng tao shui.
7. 快叫人收拾罷我那衣裳 k'uai chiao jên shou-shih pa! wo na i-shang

你抽打了沒有。 ni ch'ou-ta-liao mo yu?
8. 衣裳是早已抽打了靴子也刷了。 i-shang shih tsao i ch'ou-ta-liao; hsüeh-tzŭ yeh shua-liao.
9. 怎麼呢那手巾那胰子 tseng-mo ni? na shou-chin, na i-tzŭ

還擱在那裡。 'han ko tsai na li?
10. 那胰子在屉板兒上手巾在架子上掛着。 na i-tzŭ tsai t'i-pan-'rh shang; shou-chin tsai chia-tzŭ shang kua-cho.

128.

1. 老爺的行李來了。
lao-yeh-ti hsing-li lai-liao.

2. 啊狠好,那箱子你數過了沒有,
a! hên hao; na hsiang-tzǔ ni shu-kuo-liao mo yu?

3. 數了,大小通共二
shu-liao; ta hsiao t'ung-kung erh-

十四件。
shih-ssǔ chien.

4. 那裡有那麼些,怕不是都是我的。
na li yu na-mo hsieh? p'a pu shih tou shih wo-ti.

5. 老爺的箱子幾隻記得不記得。
lao-yeh-ti hsiang-tzǔ chi chih, chi-tê pu chi-tê?

6. 有三隻皮箱,一隻木箱,還有鋪蓋,還有零碎包兒兩件,共總七樣兒。
yu san chih p'i hsiang, i chih mu hsiang, 'han yu p'u-kai, 'han yu ling-sui pao-erh liang chien; kung tsung ch'i yang-'rh.

7. 請老爺出去看看,那個是老爺的。
ch'ing lao-yeh ch'u-ch'ü k'an-k'an na-ko shih lao-yeh-ti.

8. 就是了,那車錢呢,還得給多少。
chiu shih la! na ch'ê ch'ien ni, 'han tei kei to-shao?

9. 向來天津來的,那大車都是五塊錢,小車是三塊錢。
hsiang-lai T'ien-ching lai-ti, na ta ch'ê tou shih wu k'uai ch'ien; hsiao ch'ê shih san k'uai ch'ien.

10. 等一會兒,我同那些老爺們算清了,
têng i 'hui-erh, wo t'ung na hsieh lao-yeh-mên suan-ch'ing liao,

給他。
kei t'a.

PART VIII. (Supplement.) XIV.   291

129.

1. 我屋裡的那些傢伙在那兒去買？
wo u li -ti na hsieh chia-huo tsai na 'rh ch'ü mai?

2. 老爺屋裡這些還不彀用的麼。
lao-yeh u li chê hsieh 'han pu kou yung -ti mo?

3. 這

4. 就是那桌子椅子，我可以給老爺在鋪子裡買去。
chiu shih na cho-tzŭ, i tzŭ, wo k'o i kei lao-yeh tsai p'u-tzŭ li mai ch'ü.

5. 還要書架子裝書。
'han yao shu chia -tzŭ chuang shu.

6. 那書架子沒現成的，得叫木匠做；那臉盆架杺，老爺要
na shu chia -tzŭ, tei chiao mu-chiang tso; na lien-p'ên-chia, ch'uang, lao-yeh yao

個不是我的，都是借的。
ko pu shih wo -ti, tou shih chieh -ti.

7. 臉盆架要買；牀有我帶來的。
lien-p'ên-chia yao mai; ch'uang yu wo tai lai -ti.

8. 老爺的牀在那兒。
lao-yeh -ti ch'uang tsai na 'rh?

9. 那牀是鐵的，在那
na ch'uang shih t'ieh -ti, tsai na

不要。
pu yao?

10. 我去找木匠來把他打開。
wo ch'ü chao mu-chiang lai pa t'a ta-k'ai.

11. 還有我的衣裳臟了，得洗。
'han yu wo -ti i-shang tsang liao, tei hsi.

長木箱子裏裝着。
ch'ang mu hsiang -tzŭ li chuang -cho.

12. 我已經告訴洗衣裳的了，可以快來。
wo i-ching kao-su hsi-i-shang -ti liao; k'o i k'uai lai.

130.

1. 老爺點油燈點爛燭。點那個呢？

2. 我帶來的有一盞油燈還有幾包爛。

3. 老爺今兒下鋪毡子不鋪。

4. 今兒快黑了先點爛明兒再買油。

5. 如今天快冷了老爺屋裡地下鋪毡子不鋪。

6. 毡子是要鋪的那燒火的煤炭呢！

7. 那炭是廚子管那煤是老爺們合夥兒買。

8. 後頭那窗戶透風得利害沒有攩住的好法子？此地那窗戶冬天都是拏紙糊上。

9. 此地那窗戶冬天都是拏紙糊上。

10. 啊是這麼着就是明天可以把那後頭的糊上前頭不用糊。

131.

1. 老爺先生來了。 lao-yeh, hsien-shêng lai liao.

2. 請擎茶來啊！先生請坐。 ch'ing na ch'a lai. a! hsien-shêng ch'ing tso.

3. 請坐。 ch'ing tso.

4. 昨天看那話條子,有 tso t'ien k'an na hua t'iao-tzŭ, yu

幾處不懂得。 chi ch'u pu tung-tê.

5. 還有甚麼難處呢,您納說一說。 han yu shen-mo nan ch'u ni? nin-na shuo i shuo.

6. 這一個字我找不着。 chê i ko tzŭ wo chao pu chao.

7. 那是 na shih

8. 就是這個呢。 chiu shih chê ko ni?

9. 那是亂字。 na shih luan tzŭ.

10. 還是歸那個部首? han shih kuei na ko pu-shou?

11. 部 pu-

個俗字字典上沒有的。 ko su tzŭ; tzŭ-tien-shang mo yu-ti.

首本是乙,您納找的是那個部首? shou pên shih Yi; nin na chao-ti shih na ko pu-shou?

12. 我找的是爪部。 wo chao-ti shih Chao pu.

13. 那是錯了,那亂字的意思您納明白不明白? na shih ts'o liao, na luan tzŭ-ti i-ssŭ, nin-na ming-po pu ming-po?

14. 我彷彿記得見過一次,也不定,常說的是連那個字說,先生請告訴我。 wo fang-fu chi-tê chien-kuo i tz'ŭ, yeh pu ting; ch'ang shuo-ti shih lien na ko tzŭ shuo, hsien-shêng ch'ing kao-su wo.

15. 那字眼多了,有雜亂,有反亂,有荒亂,有混亂,有擾亂,有治亂。 na tzŭ-yén to liao lo; yu tsa-luan, yu fan luan, yu huang luan, yu hùn-luan, yu jao-luan, yu chih luan.

唉慢慢的這些字眼兒都是甚麼意思
ai! man-man-ti; chê hsieh tzǔ-yen-'rh tou shih shên-mo i ssǔ?

17. 那亂字本是不整齊的意思東西
na luan tzǔ pên shih pu chêng-ch'i-ti i-ssǔ; tung-hsi

沒布置是雜亂辦事也有雜亂無章之說那賊匪鬧得利害是反亂年歲不收
mei pu chih shih tsa-luan; pan shih yeh yu tsa-luan wu chang chih shuo; na tsei-fei nao tê li-hai, shih fan-luan nien-sui pu shou-

成百姓沒有吃穿各處兒搶奪那就是荒亂家裡沒規矩是混亂世界混亂是
ch'êng, pai-po-hsing mê yu ch'ih ch'uan ko ch'u 'rh ch'iang-to, na chiu shih huang luan; chia-li mei kuei-chü, shih hun luan; shih-chieh hun-luan, shih

說普天下大亂之極那擾亂地方是匪類把某處百姓不是殺就是燒治亂無
shuo p'u tien-hsia ta luan chih chi; na jao-luan ti-fang, shih fei-lei pa mou ch'u 'pai po hsing, pu shih sha, chiu shih shao chih luan wu

常這一句是天下有時太平有時大亂都不能定的意思。 18. 領教就是這些句
ch'ang chê i chü, shih t'ien-hsia yu shih t'ai p'ing yu shih ta luan, tou pu nêng ting-ti i-ssǔ. 18. ling chiao; chiu shih chê hsieh chü

裡頭最常用的是那個字眼兒。 19. 隨常用的怕是雜亂罷;隨便甚麼都可以說
li-t'ou tsui ch'ang yung ti shih na ko tzǔ-yen-'rh? 19. sui-ch'ang yung-ti p'a shih tsa-luan pa; sui pien shen-mo tou k'o-i shuo

雜亂。 tsa--luan.

20. 就是底下見這亂字,我可以記得是雜亂之亂。 chiu shih ti -hsia, chien chê *luan* tzŭ, wo k'o i chi -tê shih tsa--luan chih luan.

TZŬ ERH CHI.

COLLOQUIAL SERIES.

APPENDICES
TO
PARTS III, IV, V, & VI.

Appendix I, contains all characters new to the Student in Part III, or the Forty Exercises; Appendix II, those in Part IV, or the Ten Dialogues; Appendix III, those in Part V, or the Eighteen Sections; and Appendix IV, those in Part VI, or the Hundred Lessons.

The characters in Appendix I, are numbered and arranged exactly as they are in the Vocabulary Columns of Part III. In Appendix II, the characters follow each other in the order of their first appearance in the Ten Dialogues, and the number by the side of each refers the Student to the question or answer in which the character is first found, consequently, to the Note on it, in the Key, which explains its meaning. The same rule is observed in Appendix III, the numbers given indicating the place of each character in the particular Section and sentence to which it belongs.

In the Key to Part VI, it will be seen that the Notes appended to the translation of each Lesson are numbered independently of the paragraphs or other subdivisions of the Text of the Lesson, and the number accompanying each character in Appendix IV will simply guide the Student to the Note explaining it in the Key.

Where an asterisk stands by the side of any character, the Student will observe that there are more forms than one of that character used in the *Tzŭ Erh Chi*, but that the form given in the Appendix is the correct form. In Part III, great pains have been taken to avoid the repetition of any character before met with, except it be used with a new Sound or Tone. In the Appendices to Parts IV, V, and VI, some few characters have been repeated, with or without reason, a second or even a third time; but this need not perplex the Student, who should use these lists, not only as indices of reference, but also, and principally, as tables to test his memory.

Appendix I. CHARACTERS IN THE FORTY EXERCISES.

1.	2.	3.	4.	5.	6.	7.	8.
1. 兩	1. 你	1. 進	1. 前	1. 眞	1. 紙	1. 炕	1. 傢
2. 三	2. 我	2. 城	2. 後	2. 正	2. 張	2. 蓆	2. 伙
3. 第	3. 他	3. 家	3. 叫	3. 抄	3. 筆	3. 床	3. 櫈
4. 四	4. 偺	4. 住	4. 站	4. 寫	4. 管	4. 帳	4. 條
5. 五	5. 們	*5. 著	5. 起	5. 教	5. 墨	5. 鋪	5. 倒
6. 六	6. 倆	6. 街	6. 躺	6. 學	6. 塊	6. 蓋	6. 壺
7. 七	7. 這	7. 上	7. 地	7. 請	7. 把	7. 卓	7. 花
8. 九	8. 在	8. 房	8. 快	8. 賺	8. 本	8. 椅	8. 瓶
9. 幾	9. 那	9. 間	9. 慢	9. 拏	9. 書	9. 蠟	9. 破
10. 千	10. 兒	10. 屋	10. 都	10. 字	10. 念	10. 燈	10. 收
11. 數	11. 的	11. 裏	11. 愛	11. 典	11. 完	11. 盞	11. 拾
12. 百	12. 没	12. 開	12. 坐	12. 話	12. 可	12. 隻	12. 盤
13. 萬	13. 了	13. 鋪	13. 轎	13. 我	13. 以	13. 酒	13. 碟
14. 零	14. 甚	14. 關	14. 樓	14. 看	14. 給	14. 杯	14. 喫
15. 來	15. 麼	15. 臌	15. 下	15. 先	15. 官	15. 茶	15. 點
16. 多	16. 買	16. 出	16. 回	16. 認	16. 會	16. 碗	16. 吹
17. 少	17. 賣	17. 去	17. 到	17. 還	17. 分	17. 盅	17. 滅
18. 有	18. 得	18. 往	18. 驢	18. 肯	18. 聽	18. 廚	18. 使
19. 好	19. 很	19. 外	19. 騾	19. 告	19. 明	19. 煮	19. 燒
20. 些	20. 誰	20. 頭	20. 匹	20. 訴	20. 也	20. 飯	20. 爐
21. 個	21. 要	21. 知	21. 輛	21. 呢	21. 懂	21. 鍋	21. 空
	22. 不	22. 道	22. 步	22. 記	22. 平	22. 錘	22. 滿
	23. 是	23. 做	23. 頂	23. 間	23. 聲	23. 勺	23. 同
	24. 東	24. 過	24. 衙	24. 騎	24. 忘		24. 算
			25. 說	25. 跑	25. 錯		25. 碎

3

Appendix I. CHARACTERS IN THE FORTY EXERCISES.

9.	10.	11.	12.	13.	14.	15.	16.
1. 今	1. 更	1. 怕	1. 儘	1. 銀	1. 煤	1. 京	1. 李
2. 年	2. 夫	2. 裳	2. 摘	2. 銅	2. 炭	2. 遠	2. 箱
3. 時	3. 每	3. 件	3. 戴	3. 鐵	3. 柴	3. 近	3. 包
4. 令	4. 夜	4. 太	4. 擅	4. 錢	4. 麴	4. 南	4. 袋
5. 暖	5. 得	5. 腌	5. 帽	5. 吊	5. 油	5. 北	5. 氈
6. 和	6. 打	6. 臟	6. 砍	6. 票	6. 芝	6. 路	6. 布
7. 昨	7. 罷	7. 换	7. 肩	7. 桿	7. 糖	7. 直	7. 餕
8. 天	8. 早	8. 乾	8. 汗	8. 秤	8. 鹽	8. 繞	8. 駱駝
9. 就	9. 晚	9. 淨	9. 衫	9. 稱	9. 粗	9. 河	9. 牲
10. 定	10. 晌	10. 刷	10. 單	10. 價	10. 細	10. 海	10. 跟
11. 畫	11. 午	11. 洗	11. 夾	11. 值	11. 湯	11. 邊	11. 班
12. 晴	12. 嗒	12. 臉	12. 縣	12. 貴	12. 雞	12. 深	12. 裝
13. 亮	13. 事	13. 盆	13. 褲	13. 賤	13. 奶	13. 淺	13. 帶
14. 鐘	14. 情	14. 縫	14. 裁	14. 便	14. 果	14. 船	14. 馱
15. 半	15. 擱	15. 補	15. 袖	15. 宜	15. 茶	15. 客	15. 追
16. 刻	16. 各	16. 穿	16. 梳	16. 輕	16. 饅	16. 店	16. 趕
17. 氣	17. 樣	17. 鞋	17. 髮	17. 重	17. 喝	17. 掌	17. 喚
18. 候	18. 短	18. 脫	18. 針	18. 借	18. 弄	18. 櫃	18. 無
19. 冷	19. 雲	19. 靴	19. 線	19. 賬	19. 端	19. 計	19. 利
20. 熱	20. 彩	20. 雙	20. 腋	20. 該	20. 撒	20. 受	20. 害
21. 雪	21. 陰	21. 襪	21. 澡	21. 費	21. 熟	21. 累	21. 春
22. 涼	22. 霧	22. 最	22.	22. 當	22. 論	22. 苦	22. 夏
23. 颶	23. 空	23. 溫		23. 於	23. 石	23. 乏	23. 秋
				24. 好		24. 歇	24. 冬
						25. 連	25.

Appendix I. CHARACTERS IN THE FORTY EXERCISES.

17.	18.	19.	20.	21.	22.	23.	24.
1. 腦	1. 眉	1. 君	1. 國	1. 搶	1. 凡	1. 語	1. 兆
2. 辮	2. 鬢	2. 民	2. 章	2. 奪	2. 揣	2. 句	2. 吉
3. 朶	3. 顋	3. 主	3. 程	3. 偷	3. 摩	3. 吵	3. 凶
4. 眼	4. 頰	4. 爵	4. 卡	4. 股	4. 約	4. 喧	4. 祥
5. 睛	5. 巴	5. 位	5. 倫	5. 逃	5. 准	5. 嚷	5. 瑞
6. 嘴	6. 額	6. 參	6. 巡	6. 竄	6. 否	6. 哼	6. 安
7. 脣	7. 脖	7. 贊	7. 察	7. 散	7. 更	7. 阿	7. 寧
8. 鬍	8. 嗓	8. 尊	8. 刻	8. 混	8. 改	8. 哈	8. 順
9. 胳	9. 節	9. 武	9. 搜	9. 懶	9. 爹	9. 嘎	9. 寬
10. 臂	10. 刮	10. 兵	10. 律	10. 惰	10. 當	10. 詑	10. 綽
11. 指	11. 剃	11. 缺	11. 例	11. 棍	11. 專	11. 裹	11. 貧
12. 甲	12. 胸	12. 額	12. 治	12. 扔	12. 失	12. 困	12. 窮
13. 抓	13. 背	13. 捐	13. 理	13. 放	13. 神	13. 極	13. 窘
14. 腰	14. 脊	14. 充	14. 暴	14. 槍	14. 參	14. 夢	14. 恆
15. 腿	15. 梁	15. 謀	15. 虐	15. 恰	15. 差	15. 貌	15. 產
16. 壯	16. 骸	16. 策	16. 亂	16. 巧	16. 忙	16. 美	16. 朋
17. 建	17. 肚	17. 殺	17. 謬	17. 特	17. 向	17. 陋	17. 友
18. 輭	18. 波	18. 退	18. 普	18. 意	18. 規	18. 摔	18. 賞
19. 弱	19. 稜	19. 勒	19. 羣	19. 偶	19. 幹	19. 掉	19. 相
20. 拉	20. 踝	20. 索	20. 耕	20. 然	20. 辦	20. 擱	20. 幫
21. 拽	21. 腳	21. 中	21. 耨	21. 成	21. 法	21. 搭	21. 留
22. 病	22. 體	22. 底	22. 囊	22. 硬	22. 胡	22. 窄	22. 能
23. 疼	23. 斬	23. 全	23. 總	23. 按	23. 鬧	23. 則	23. 丟
24. 奇	24. 賊	24. 姓	24. 謂	24. 思	24. 掄	24. 況	24. 根
25. 怪	25. 級	25. 名	25. 之	25.	25. 催	25. 且	25. 現

Appendix I. CHARACTERS IN THE FORTY EXERCISES.

25.	26.	27.	28.	29.	30.	31.	32.
1. 您	1. 想	1. 某	1. 裱	1. 剛	1. 臺	1. 男	1. 皇
2. 喧	2. 怎	2. 乍	2. 糊	2. 纔	2. 灣	2. 爺	2. 宮
3. 親	3. 却	3. 初	3. 匠	3. 、再	3. 江	3. 娘	3. 朝
4. 旁	4. 睡	4. 和	4. 染	4. 等	4. 湖	4. 幼	4. 廷
5. 祖	5. 覺	5. 別	5. 顏	5. 取	5. 流	5. 輩	5. 建
6. 翁	6. 對	6. 素	6. 紅	6. 送	6. 浪	6. 頑	6. 臨
7. 兄	7. 賽	7. 原	7. 藍	7. 落	7. 闊	7. 耍	7. 強
8. 孫	8. 齒	8. 待	8. 淡	8. 永	8. 浮	8. 蠢	8. 戾
9. 舍	9. 吞	9. 敦	9. 新	9. 湊	9. 橋	9. 笨	9. 禁
10. 弟	10. 疊	10. 厚	10. 舊	10. 挪	10. 井	10. 獸	10. 舞
11. 奴	11. 次	11. 薄	11. 紗	11. 拴	11. 坑	11. 冒	11. 爲
12. 才	12. 增	12. 傲	12. 氈	12. 套	12. 衖	12. 爽	12. 匪
13. 迎	13. 蔥	13. 嫉	13. 必	13. 商	13. 衖	13. 靜	13. 反
14. 接	14. 苗	14. 妬	14. 須	14. 量	14. 巷	14. 舒	14. 犯
15. 葬	15. 嫩	15. 慚	15. 光	15. 殼	15. 野	15. 服	15. 罪
16. 絲	16. 桑	16. 愧	16. 潤	16. 斟	16. 屯	16. 艱	16. 死
17. 團	17. 樹	17. 絕	17. 玻	17. 酌	17. 墳	17. 難	17. 黨
18. 緘	18. 林	18. 交	18. 璃	18. 疑	18. 墓	18. 耐	18. 爭
19. 尺	19. 森	19. 實	19. 料	19. 惑	19. 峯	19. 羞	19. 鬪
20. 貨	20. 綠	20. 憑	20. 擦	20. 喊	20. 嶺	20. 辱	20. 號
21. 昂	21. 草	21. 賓	21. 碰	21. 答	21. 尖	21. 討	21. 靖
22. 替	22. 濕	22. 拜	22. 裂	22. 應		22. 嫌	22. 恩
23. 挑	23. 曬	23. 應	23. 行	23. 從			23. 赦
	24. 晒	24. 陪		24. 末			24. 免
							25. 隨

Appendix I. CHARACTERS IN THE FORTY EXERCISES.

33.	34.	35.	36.	37.	38.	39.	40.
1. 古	1. 倉	1. 揑	1. 歲	1. 常	1. 承	1. 脾	1. 緊
2. 世	2. 庫	2. 洒	2. 紀	2. 屢	2. 差	2. 性	2. 預
3. 孔	3. 宗	3. 灑	3. 壽	3. 公	3. 任	3. 禍	3. 備
4. 聖	4. 考	4. 掃	4. 因	4. 私	4. 署	4. 福	4. 通
5. 儒	5. 如	5. 帚	5. 爲	5. 務	5. 習	5. 命	5. 共
6. 佛	6. 若	6. 砌	6. 緣	6. 閒	6. 部	6. 運	6. 合
7. 廟	7. 雜	7. 磚	7. 故	7. 空	7. 堂	7. 志	7. 除
8. 座	8. 另	8. 狗	8. 耽	8. 悶	8. 司	8. 盆	8. 剩
9. 僧	9. 派	9. 欻	9. 悞	9. 慌	9. 委	9. 活	9. 盈
10. 俗	10. 盼	10. 修	10. 容	10. 樂	10. 員	10. 動	10. 像
11. 尙	11. 望	11. 表	11. 易	11. 煩	11. 吏	11. 聰	11. 似
12. 傳	12. 列	12. 圓	12. 便	12. 急	12. 役	12. 願	12. 橫
13. 經	13. 衆	13. 扁	13. 勁	13. 奉	13. 皁	13. 功	13. 竪
14. 楷	14. 滙	14. 剖	14. 塗	14. 求	14. 隸	14. 虧	14. 傷
15. 率	15. 依	15. 宛	15. 喜	15. 託	15. 供	15. 辜	15. 棚
16. 更	16. 戀	16. 枉	16. 歡	16. 發	16. 稟	16. 負	*16. 著
17. 濃	17. 跨	17. 逆	17. 惜	17. 信	17. 帖	17. 抱	17. 準
18. 貼	18. 捨	18. 跳	18. 欺	18. 雇	18. 存	18. 怨	18. 勢
19. 牆	19. {礙	19. 造	19. 哄	19. 孩	19. 稿	19. 寒	
20. 層	20. 彼	20. 報	20. 誆	20. 撒	20. 陳	20. 悔	
21. 掛	21. 此	21. 彷	21. 騙	21. 謊	21. 案	21. 善	
22. 畫	22. 處	22. 彿	22. 屣	22. 賺	22. 照	22. 惡	
23. 唱	23. 偏	23. 筶		23. 星	23. 式	23. 其	
24. 曲	24. 或			24. 所		24. 餘	
25. 抽				25. 雖		25. 靈	

Appendix II. CHARACTERS IN PART IV. DIALOGUES 1–5.

Dial. 1.		Dial. 2.		Dial. 3.		Dial. 4.		Dial. 5.			
2	敝	1	納	8	哥	103	殿	4	徐	64	孀	1	永	78	躲
2	津	20	哎	13	假	104	館	5	識	64	婦	9	抛	80	酣
2	領	20	呀	18	母	106	沙	6	陳	70	憐	15	查		
4	鄉	20	久	19 {	著	106	窩	7	遇	73	排	20	狂		
9	駕	27	項	21	勿	110	鞭	23	慶	75	殘	21	烟		
12	洋	28	賠	22	恕	114	但	25	讓	75	疾	22	貪		
12	漆	28	墊	23	離	119	折	32	沏	76	景	25	葉		
16	解	31	依	48	敢	123	忠	37	托	77	栽	26	湖		
19	省	32	王	49	院	123	擔	38	恬	77	培	26	藥		
20	廣	32	戚	52	闖	123	竟	38	勞	79	感	32	村		
28	行	34	放	54	曖	123	村	40	糢	79	激	36	微		
28	作	34	撫	54	瑳	123	誠	45	康	79	盡	36	薆		
30	異	37	歡	56	挨	123	決	49	奈	81	提	36	棧		
		38	證	56	伸			52	莫	83	拔	36	藏		
		43	恨	57	與			52	被			44	艇		
		43	勤	57	何			52	竊			49	封		
		43	儉	64	駒			53	惡			52	豐		
		44	唉	65	咳			53	摔			61	虎		
		44	既	65	詳			54	繃			64	撞		
		44	咎	72	伴			55	保			65	哨		
		46	宥	74	加			56	精			66	欽		
		48	由	79	架			57	養			66	劉		
		49	息	88	哟			59	姐			72	驚		
		50	歸	91	昕			59	妹			72	訝		
		53	均	93	只			60	未			74	損		
		54	哪	96	鎭			62	姑			76	寡		
		54	業	96	園			62	嫁			76	敵		
		58	伺	99	猾			63	陣			76	膽		
		59	幕					63	亡			76	虛		

Appendix II. CHARACTERS IN PART IV. DIALOGUES 6–10.

Dial. 6.			Dial. 7.	Dial. 8.		Dial. 9.		Dial. 10.		
1	兊	50	倚	6	孟	3	英	7	蘇	5	洲	50 {	複
1	結	53	推	10	齋	5	皁	9	閣	6	緇		復
9	始			37	戲	9	州	18	漢	7	壁	52	羅
9	終			46	姪	17	擺	36	講	10	整	52	織
9	扣			47	悉	17	渡	38	註	10	贅	54	練
10	資			65	搬	21	浦	40	中	11	習	54	閱
14	涉			72	琉	21	叚	40	秀	16	選	54	歷
16	塲			72	廠	23	楊	41	徴	16	擇	56	拘
21	究			76	婆	23	蔡	41	倖	16	屬	62	清
21	罰			83	翻	23	隔	41	試	19	榜	63	卷
22	遮			88	扭	29	格	42	庚	19	妙	66	刪
22	掩			93	壓	33	蕫	46	榮	20	義	66	談
23	楊			98	哭	35	富	47	縣	20	類	71	彙
23	編			100	郇	35	與	51	緒	21	導	72	啓
24	逌			100	府	55	妨	53	遵	21	周	72	蒙
24	詐					55	駁	54	申	21	密	74	續
27	舉					63	佾			32	題	74	斷
31	靠					63	御			36	絡	75	簷
35	估					69	恐			38	印	75	溜
35	摸					77	鞍			38	篇	76	貽
36	臁					79	籠			38	序	77	登
37	徇					81	嚼			38	譯	77	卑
37	庇					81	扯			39	切	77	邇
38	享					81	慣			40	並	77	互
38	恤					83	夥			40	較	77	及
41	頓					87	吩			44	倍		
49	許					87	咐			47	乎		
50	簡									48	畧		
50	轉									48	僅		

散話九章第二十二字涼，是涼熱的涼，涼是風俗涼薄的涼。以著爲俗字，兩形雖異義實相同。○問答十章第五十節複字單是重複字用，俗多用復，至反復各等字樣，此用復字不能用複。

Appendix III. CHARACTERS IN PART V. SECTIONS 1-12.

Sec. 1.		33	溜		3	弦	35	梘		46	蜂		3	焦	21	陶	27	滑	29	瞭
2	猜	37	伶	5	與	38	逍		46	螯	6	炒	25	藏	27	趄	33	恐
9	禗	37	俐	10	越	38	遙		47	蝎	8	曲	28	圖	27	趑	34	駢
15	餓	41	悢	15	淌	39	種		48	獬	10	滷	32	醉	28	坡	35	防
16	截	48	停	18	壁	40	瓯		48	扮	11	鏡	33	鮮	31	趾	35	唬
19	痊		20	芥	42	機		Sec. 7.	12	腸	35	露	31	穩	37	濺
24	搓	Sec. 3.	30	搖	42	密		4	財	14	餬	36	錦	32	盌	38	屈
24	磨	2	羅	30	鈴	43	捽		7	綁	17	饒	37	戲	33	磐	39	摳
25	痛	3	硯	37	繫	43	結		8	謹	21	形	37	逢	34	側	39	癢
27	板	4	粧	38	紮	43	繩		8	慎	22	餉	37	酬	36	橈	40	籃
28	壽	6	搭	40	忒	45	整		12	鬧	29	蟥	38	渾	37	襟	41	呃
30	差	7	楊	47	透				12	咬	29	蟬	42	含	38	釘	42	摁
33	欖	8	飽	50	凍	Sec. 6.		20	仇	30	宰	46	漆	38	鈕	42	鑼
40	賴	13	顧	50	瘡	4	印		21	仗	32	羅		41	滾	42	檑
45	叨	13	佔		8	俏		23	芽	33	怯	Sec. 10.	41	燙	43	篩
45	耗	14	蛋	Sec. 5.	9	敗		25	圾	40	攪	1	碧	47	佩	43	簸
47	刺	22	纂	3	呆	9	腕		26	鑲	41	變	1	圈		44	罎
50	稍	27	嬌	4	跌	13	核		31	鴉	41	卦	2	翠	Sec. 11.	45	摅
55	臊	27	慣	4	仰	21	熊		35	蚊	45	省	3	鋼	4	痛	45	烙
		31	榴	7	媳	23	胖		37	調			3	駒	6	遭	47	誦
Sec. 2.		35	幹	8	婦	26	煎		37	羹	Sec. 9.	5	鹹	6	遏	48	辣
4	淞	36	岸	8	搢	31	罰		38	艙	3	瘖	6	臭	8	憎	
11	份	37	賜	12	罩	32	蛛		40	擋	4	闢	7	噴	13	楊	Sec. 12.
14	拘	40	玫	12	啞	32	網		41	投	5	劑	10	訓	14	猶	1	邐
15	鎖	40	瑰	14	禮	33	切		44	礅	7	吐	10	酬	18	耿	2	牽
17	仍			23	擋	38	縱				9	紋	11	酸	18	惹	3	攪
26	咳	Sec. 4.	25	遲	39	俊		Sec. 8.	14	絆	12	瀣	20	冠	4	扺
26	嗽	1	妞	28	瞎	40	漸		3	勤	16	閫	19	懸	20	寄	4	椰
28	模	2	擱	33	並	42	螞		3	煳	17	睜	25	努	25	居	5	愁
29	熗	2	騰	34	棵	46	螞				18	侔	26	臘	27	魯		

Appendix III. CHARACTERS IN PART V. SECTIONS 12-18.

5 展	Sec. 13.	28 幅	4 譽	26 篆	12 傘	3 桅	44 罕	32 響								
7 搽	1 哨	31 蠹	4 厲	27 縺	18 埋	3 杆	47 席	34 撥								
9 轉	2 插	32 堵	5 齎	27 綻	20 燻	4 皈	Sec. 17.	34 擷								
16 婆	2 鞘	32 窟	5 擲	29 慈	20 潦	5 牽	1 遞	37 丁								
17 勦	3 莉	32 窿	6 陸	30 熬	21 束	6 謙	4 唸	40 偏								
18 踥	4 謠	33 楔	7 珠	30 伺	22 稼	6 恭	7 擺	45 久								
19 啼	5 毫	33 度	7 寶	31 憋	22 淹	9 緯	9 架	46 棟								
20 瘴	8 嚴	34 飾	8 蜘	33 泉	23 嚥	10 蹉	10 棄	Sec. 18.								
21 藏	9 獨	34 鍍	9 螬	35 餿	25 演	11 蓬	10 樸	1 嘮								
24 平	10 占	35 吐	10 硃	35 踐	27 揲	14 權	10 蛾	3 骰								
24 者	10 鼇	35 瀉	11 醇	37 墅	27 胭	16 顴	11 避	3 髕								
25 篡	11 棋	36 督	13 恬	37 釦	27 抹	19 邪	14 譚	3 肘								
26 怵	11 譜	36 制	13 愧	38 泉	27 粉	20 扇	14 覷	3 腫								
27 覆	14 鳴	38 轆	14 鏝	39 鑲	28 厭	20 欬	14 視	5 鬆								
28 屠	15 睦	38 轤	15 顛	42 仙	29 遐	24 掀	14 稀	6 尾								
29 禿	16 幕	38 台	16 餂	44 黏	30 奸	24 簾	21 爛	6 遛								
30 窨	16 重	40 圖	17 填	44 涎	30 詐	25 險	21 熾	10 齡								
30 磁	17 齋	43 兔	18 墊	45 歆	31 饞	28 陷	22 噴	11 勝								
32 攘	17 戒	43 狐	19 搭	Sec. 15.	39 劍	30 餡	23 拙	12 矇								
34 宿	17 沐	43 悲	20 醬	1 羨	39 贈	31 限	24 呲	15 藝								
35 悄	18 窗	43 物	20 沾	1 慕	39 烈	33 患	25 咕	18 昭								
37 驛	19 符	44 糞	21 靛	2 颱	39 佳	34 綵	25 嚷	18 彰								
38 雀	19 咒	46 櫊	21 缸	3 剝	41 捲	35 閉	26 嘟	27 跡								
39 蟻	20 撇	47 館	22 九	4 檀	43 鱺	36 鈎	26 噥	28 忍								
39 蛀	22 斧	Sec. 14.	22 膏	5 鏃	43 孤	36 環	29 鎖	29 洩								
40 劾	22 劈	1 賄	23 丹	7 漩	44 灌	39 癱	29 匙	30 賒								
40 勞	24 覗	1 賂	24 牆	7 窩		39 瘓	30 欄									
42 椹	25 降	2 軾	24 勻	Sec. 16.		43 翰	32 拍									
43 糟	25 伏	3 磔	24 攤	1 釣		44 希										
43 糕	26 祓			1 竿												

11

Appendix IV. CHARACTERS IN PART VI. LESSONS 1-30.

Les. 1.	7 度	2 箭	6 仁	Les. 17.	13 忘	5 堆	Les. 28.
4 賜	11 譽	4 萃	7 護	2 妻		11 幸	1 奢
Les. 2.	12 責	9 撥	8 救	3 桃	Les. 19.	Les. 24.	1 侈
7 師	Les. 7.	10 拇	9 積	3 唆	1 錐	1 魁	3 溝
7 傳	4 胺	11 翎	13 旺	4 爭	2 淵	1 偉	4 穩
	7 遞	12 壓	Les. 15.	5 間	2 博	2 誇	5 粒
Les. 3.	8 旗	Les. 11.	1 敏	6 懷	3 居	11 勉	6 捆
1 獎	9 獨	2 陞	3 瞞	7 異	5 豈	13 絡	8 折
4 頗	11 姪	4 餃	4 獻	8 讒	7 相		12 隱
			7 束	9 懦		Les. 25.	13 捱
Les. 4.	Les. 8.	Les. 12.	8 賞	10 致	Les. 20.	1 疲	
2 孝	2 鑑	3 擬		11 辯	1 坊	6 率	Les. 29.
5 種	5 影	4 鋒	Les. 16.	12 雛	6 楔	6 索	4 債
6 品	6 瞎	5 校	1 防	13 置	7 唐	7 景	5 嘆
7 鑽	9 扎	6 圍	2 趁	14 娶			
8 逢	10 搪	10 橧	3 饑	15 折	Les. 21.	Les. 26.	Les. 30.
10 咒	13 剪		5 珍	16 搶	3 誓	3 催	3 鬢
10 罵	15 滋	Les. 13.	6 饈	18 送	4 王	6 逼	4 髫
13 耀	18 怠	1 扠	魂		7 較	6 纏	6 紫
		4 瞪	8 享	Les. 18.		8 倘	7 斜
Les. 5.	Les. 9.	5 優	9 饞	1 仲	Les. 22.	9 欄	8 糙
2 覓	1 漏	7 簽	9 糅	2 鮑	3 叙		9 稠
2 縫	2 依	9 攀	10 晦	3 郊	6 拐	Les. 27.	13 噗
5 族	3 嚴	10 勇	14 焉	4 迸	8 嗎	7 舅	13 咻
	5 捆		15 終	5 元	9 敲	8 窩	14 職
Les. 6.	堪	Les. 14.	16 靜	摺	10 媽	10 扎	15 猴
2 瞪	7	3 悦	17 眨	9 蛇		11 鑤	16 歪
4 樸	Les. 10.	4 引		10 嚇	Les. 23.	12 夾	17 韜
5 沽	1 射	4 誘		11 鋤	4 暑	14 趣	

Appendix **IV**. CHARACTERS IN PART VI. LESSONS 31–64.

Les. 31.	Les. 35.	Les. 38.	Les. 42.	Les. 46.	9 慘	6 掏	Les. 59.
6 併	1 響	2 誦	5 侍	3 賭	Les. 51.	7 釘	2 聊
7 幸	2 睜	5 嗜	6 漚	Les. 47.	2 沉	12 哄	3 賴
9 處	4 蓬	6 菩	8 唧	3 赴	3 魷	14 跤	Les. 60.
11 係	4 鬆	8 汗	8 叮	7 藉	4 慰	Les. 55.	3 低
	5 醒	9 漚	8 咕	8 敬	8 嘻	1 佻	5 探
Les. 32.	6 櫃	11 膈	8 咚	9 毒	9 災	2 雕	Les. 62.
1 寫	7 挾	12 踪	11 忍	10 鏡	Les. 52.	塑	
2 霸	8 肶			11 糟	1 曾	Les. 56.	5 頸
3 渾	10 暗	Les. 39.	Les. 43.		2 看	3 畏	6 配
5 潦	11 猛	3 極	3 橛	Les. 48.	3 幾	5 扶	7 競
6 謠			4 跪		4 喪		13 諒
7 升	Les. 36.	Les. 40.	5 哀	4 枕	5 醫	Les. 57.	15 僻
8 槽	3 垣	1 掄		5 腹	6 診	1 臘	16 罵
9 減	4 鍾	4 俐	Les. 44.	6 膨	9 效	2 誇	
	5 烙	5 嗜	3 趴	8 烤		3 即	Les. 63.
Les. 33.	6 愣	5 嚕	9 戒	10 飲	Les. 53.	5 恥	2 譏
1 儋	10 鄂	8 墜		11 臥	1 躁	7 綢	2 誚
2 牽	11 謝	9 轂	Les. 45.	12 停	2 辦	8 裹	3 免
3 顛	12 儀	9 輶	1 刷		5 繃		4 揭
4 裏	14 禱		3 瘦	Les. 49.	7 怒	Les. 58.	5 揉
6 繫	15 祭	Les. 41.	5 掏	1 損	8 冲	3 愚	5 挫
8 鷹	15 奠	2 勸	5 炮	2 延	9 樺	3 蠢	7 恕
9 觀		4 噘	5 燥	7 惦		6 勾	11 磴
	Les. 37.	6 淚	6 袍		Les. 54.	8 坱	
Les. 34.	4 廂	7 汪	7 暈	Les. 50.	2 燎	8 屁	Les. 64.
1 貂	5 諂	8 忠	7 忽	1 闊	3 嘆	股	6 傳
6 緞	6 祟	9 逆	11 妨	2 烘			7 德
7 俸				3 倒			
				6 大			

Appendix IV. CHARACTERS IN PART VI. LESSONS 65—100.

Les. 65.	8 趁	Les. 76.	8 撩	6 蝦	3 涮	Les. 99.	
2 裘游	16 攢	4 喪		5 樓		1 畜豪	
4 筷		5 殯	Les. 85.	Les. 91.	Les. 95.	2 腌	
6 咂	Les. 71.		5 超	2 暢	2 蚊	6 傻	
7 旦	1 莽	Les. 77.	6 迷	3 撐	蚝	7 腴	
9 檀	2 摘	1 挺	7 棄	4 浩	3 蚤	9	
11	4 騷	4 餿	叩	蘆	4 叮		
Les. 66.		6 惡	8 披	葦	6 崩	Les. 100.	
1 囑	Les. 72.		9	5 悠	7 响	1 琵	
	2 刺	Les. 79.	Les. 86.	6 慮	8 陡	2 琶	
Les. 67.	3 休	1 藝	1 堉	7 皆	震	5 絃	
1 渣	4 絮	2 努	3 襟	8 期	11	玷	
7 啐	5 叨		4 盥	10 致		6 洿	
8 沫	8 刷	Les. 80.	5 煞	11 徒	Les. 96.		
	9 蔬	1 悌	7 沿	12	1 霹		
Les. 68.	12 盛	5 獄	9 榙		2 雷		
2 吾	13 設	7 餬		Les. 92.	3 傾		
		8 恃	Les. 87.	3 闞			
Les. 69.	Les. 73.		4 嫂	5 恍	Les. 97.		
1 痼	5 瘖	Les. 81.	5 呶	5 惚	1 飄		
5 啃		1 顧		6 加	2 飆		
	Les. 74.	醜	Les. 88.		3 爐		
Les. 70.	3 棚		5 泡	Les. 93.	4 簾		
1 饞	3 欄	Les. 82.	6 克	4 暑	5 雅		
3 襤褸		1 瑣		5 攀	6 紛		
5 戰	Les. 75.	3 階	Les. 90.	6 眩			
6 料	4 供	4 供	1 曠	喝	Les. 98.		
7 披	6 瑩	Les. 83.	3 桃	Les. 94.	2 吸		
		4 掣	4 柳	1 纏	3 攣		
		5 挽	5 彈	2 稱			

14

Appendix V. CHARACTERS IN PART VII. SYLLABLES 6 – 417

喊 417	萄 288	盟 216	瓢 129	倔 56	泬 6
	瞰 289	睞 217	堈 148	獱 57	册 9
	叟	瞜	杠	茵 58	娼 13
	閃 306	喵 218	尻 151	鴨 66	妓
	孕 326	咩 219	哏 154	踈	歌
	撟 331	喃 229	揹 155	蹬 67	煎 15
	忎 334	躉	埂 156	蹁	鈔
	丕	曬 230	摳 161	痰	砢 20
	鐙 336	欀	礦 176	喘 69	碜
	鏊 337	欀	壂 182	串	㽽 25
	鏑	釰 231	鏊	奘 70	腔 29
	梯 339	嗅 237	熒	閫 71	鈛
	搽 345	屎	稜 187	創	嚼 30
	眈 359	尿	欂 194	墜 72	貸 32
	裉 360	擗 257	遛 197	銃 77	茄 33
	鏧 371	瓢 258	裸 198	椹 80	姬
	蹭 379	胖 262	摟 199	埠 90	奸 34
	剉 381	膀	簍	鋮 91	翅 37
	驟 387	鰾 273	圖 203	蟆 92	噯 39
	忖 391	諞 278	嚕 205	什	槺 45
	齜 395	砰 282	囥 207	蒿 96	軸 50
	盃 396	磅	籠 208	吼 101	渠 53
	刨	簸 283	參 209	烤 109	眷 54
	娃 397	箕	貓 213	汞	吠 55
	甕 408	箞 284	卯	熊 121	嚄 56
	噎 409	籮 284	捫 215	熏 125	撩
	沿 410	葡 288	擞	汛	壓

15

END OF

THE APPENDICES.

北京大学中国语言学研究中心

早期北京话珍稀文献集成

主编 刘云

——西人北京话教科书汇编

分卷主编 翟赟 郭利霞 陈颖

语言自迩集

［英］威妥玛 编著

卷二

北京大学出版社
PEKING UNIVERSITY PRESS

KEY

TO THE

TZŭ ERH CHI.

COLLOQUIAL SERIES.

PART III. THE FORTY EXERCISES, with TRANSLATION AND NOTES.
PART IV. TRANSLATION, with NOTES, of THE TEN DIALOGUES.
PART V. TRANSLATION, with NOTES, of THE EIGHTEEN SECTIONS.
PART VI. TRANSLATION, with NOTES, of THE HUNDRED LESSONS.
PART VII. TRANSLATION, with NOTES, of THE TONE EXERCISES.
PART VIII. CHAPTER on THE PARTS OF SPEECH.

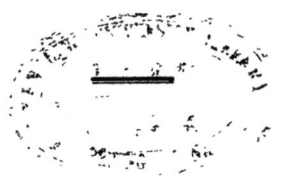

LONDON:
TRÜBNER & Co., 60, PATERNOSTER ROW.
MDCCCLXVII.

OBSERVATIONS ON THE USE OF THE KEY TO PARTS III, IV, V & VI.

Parts I and II speak for themselves. The Student having, with the aid of the Text Tables in these, and the Exercise on page 28, acquired a working familiarity with the Radicals, will proceed to the study of the *San Yu Chang*, or chapters of detached sentences, forty in number. These are to be remembered as the Forty Exercises of Part III.

In the Key to this Part it will be seen that the Chinese Text of the Forty Exercises has been reprinted. By the side of each character in the right hand column stands a syllable representing its pronunciation, which syllable is farther accompanied by a number that is the index of its Tone. The meaning of the characters in this Vocabulary Column will be found in the paragraph headed SINGLE WORDS. The remaining columns of the Exercises exhibit, first, some of the more ordinary combinations of Single Words, and, following them, phrases made up of these ordinary combinations. A translation of these phrases is given on the opposite page in the paragraph headed WORDS COMBINED, and some farther explanation of them in the Notes placed after the fortieth Exercise.

The Student will observe that no character that he has met with among the Colloquial Radicals or in the Vocabulary Column of any Exercise, is repeated in the Vocabulary of a fresh Exercise, unless it appear with a Sound or Tone differing from that previously indicated as belonging to it. When, therefore, in the text of an Exercise new to him, he comes upon characters unexplained, he must assume that they have been met with before, and he must refer either to the Colloquial Radicals, or to the Vocabulary Column of the Exercises he has learned. To shorten his search, the forty Vocabulary Columns have been collected together in Appendix I at the end of the *Tsŭ Erh Chi*.

Part IV, the *Wên-ta Chang*, or pieces of question and answer, contains Ten Dialogues printed, Chinese fashion, from right to left. The text, therefore, begins at page 109, and runs backwards to page 73. In the Key it will be seen that in each page, below the Translation of these Dialogues, are ranged all such Chinese characters as have not occurred in the foregoing Parts of the work, each having, on one side, its pronunciation and tone-index, and, on the other, the number of the question or answer in which it is found. The Notes include an explanation of these new characters, a list of which, in the order of their occurrence, is given in Appendix II.

Part V. consists of eighteen pages, here called for distinction's sake the Eighteen Sections, each containing a number of short idiomatic sentences. These are styled in Chinese, the *Hsu San Yu*, or supplementary phrases, for, although, as stated in the Preface, of older date than the Forty Exercises, they are to be taken as a sort of supplement to these. In the Key, the characters in them new to the Student, are placed, not as in Part IV, but each immediately under the translation of the sentence in which it occurs; the whole of them being arranged for reference in Appendix III.

In the Key to Part VI, the *T'an Lun P'ien*, or Chapters of Conversation, but here entitled the Hundred Lessons, it will be seen that the Notes treat of several characters with which the Student must be already acquainted. Those unknown to him are distinguished by having the Tone Index affixed to the syllable which gives their Sound. In some few cases, for special reasons, the Tone Index is added, although the character be an old acquaintance. Appendix IV. includes all the new characters in this Part.

Observations on the use of Parts VII and VIII will be found prefixed to those Parts.

KEY to the TZŬ ERH CHI. Colloquial Series.

1. 兩 liang³
2. 三 san¹
3. 第 ti⁴
4. 四 ssŭ⁴
5. 五 wu³
6. 六 liu⁴
7. 七 ch'i¹
8. 九 chiu³
9. 幾 chi³
10. 千 ch'ien¹
11. 數 shu⁴
12. 百 pai³
13. 萬 wan⁴
14. 零 ling²
15. 來 lai²
16. 多 to¹
17. 少 shao³
18. 有 yu³
19. 好 'hao³
20. 些 hsieh¹
21. 個 ko⁴

十六九二十三十四五十六十七八。¹

個三五個五七百個人。

百個五十七萬零六百一十七萬零二十。

萬零五百零七十萬。

八九萬八千四百零二一千零

百零三。¹

人有好些個人有多少人來三萬多。⁴

八九個十數個十來個二百多五千多。

肉六斤羊肉幾斤魚。

里有山足高二百里。

第一第二十七，第³ 第一千八百六十五。

一百萬三十五百萬零一千。⁵

七萬零一百九十一千四十六萬一千。

一百十八二百五十四九百九十萬零三千。⁶

第一百萬零⁴ 五萬零八十

有幾個人來有些個⁷

數十個幾十幾個兩個幾個十個多。⁹

長三寸四一身一口五斤牛¹¹

幾個牙長幾萬里足四萬¹³

七斗麥子九斗米一斗黍子。¹²

4

PART III. THE FORTY EXERCISES. *San Yü Chang.*

EXERCISE I.

SINGLE WORDS.

1. *liang*, two; a couple; dual. Also an ounce, sixteen to the *chin*, catty.
2. *san*, three.
3. *ti*, order; series; prefix which makes cardinal numbers ordinal.
4. *ssŭ*, four.
5. *wu*, five.
6. *liu*, six.
7. *ch'i*, seven.
8. *chiu*, nine.
9. *chi*, some; how many?
10. *ch'ien*, a thousand.
11. *shu*[4], number; several; some.
12. *pai*, a hundred.
13. *wan*, myriad, ten thousand.
14. *ling*, fractional; see note on Example 4.
15. *lai*, to come; when used with numbers, to approach.
16. *to*, many; more; with many words indicating number, dimension, &c, to be rendered by the interrogative How?
17. *shao*, few; less.
18. *yu*, to be; to have.
19. *-hao*[3], good; adverbially, very.
20. *hsüeh*, few, some
21. *ko*, used as the Numerative of most nouns, [See Note.]

WORDS COMBINED.

1. Sixteen. Nineteen. Twenty. Thirty-four. Fifty-seven. Sixty-eight.
2. The seventeenth, person or thing. Two or three hundred. Two or three thousand. Two or three thousand. Two or three persons or things Three or five, persons or things. Five or seven hundred persons.
3. Number one; the first; also, figuratively, the best. Number twenty-seven; the twenty-seventh. Number one thousand eight hundred and sixty-five.
4. The one million and three hundredth, person or thing. Five hundred and seventy thousand six hundred and ten. Seven hundred thousand and twenty.
5. A million. Three hundred and fifty thousand. Five million and one. Sixty thousand, five hundred, and seven. One hundred thousand.
6. Seventy thousand, one hundred, and ninety-one. Ten millions; or, figuratively, any number; in any, or, the utmost degree. Four hundred and sixty-one thousand.
7. Fifty thousand and eighty-eight. Ninety-eight thousand, four hundred, and two. One thousand and five. Four thousand and seventy-two. Eight thousand, three hundred, and sixty-seven. Ten thousand and six. One hundred and three.
8. One hundred and eighteen. Two hundred and fifty-four. Nine million, nine hundred, and ninety-three thousand.
9. A number of people are come; or, How many people are come? There are some people. There are a good number of people. How many people are come? Upwards of thirty thousand
10. Several score, *lit.* tens; some score. Some score, or, How many score? Ten and/ more persons or things, or, How many over ten? Two persons or things Some persons or things, or, How many? Ten and more; over ten Eight or nine. Ten and more, ten odd. Near ten persons or things Nine or ten persons or things. Two hundred and more. Five thousand and more
11. Three inches four tenths long. A single individual. Five catties of beef. Six catties of mutton. Some catties of fish; or, How many catties of fish?
12. Seven measures of wheat. Nine measures of rice. One measure of millet.
13. Some teeth. Several myriads of *li* in length; some tens of thousands of miles long; or, How many myriads of miles long? Full forty thousand *li*. There is a mountain, or, there are mountains, full two hundred *li* high.

KEY TO THE TZŬ ERH CHI. Colloquial Series.

1.	你	ni³
2.	我	wo³
3.	他	t'a¹
4.	偺	tsa²
5.	們	mên¹
6.	倆	lia³
7.	這	chê⁴
8.	在	tsai⁴
9.	那	na⁴'
10.	兒	êrh²
11.	的	ti¹
12.	沒	mo⁴ / mu⁴'
13.	了	mei² / liao³
14.	甚	shên²
15.	麼	mo¹
16.	買	mai³
17.	賣	mai⁴
18.	得	tê²
19.	很	hên³
20.	誰	shui²
21.	要	yao⁴
22.	不	pu⁴
23.	是	shih⁴
24.	東	tung¹

¹你的、我的、他的。 ²你們的、我們的、他們的。 ³你們的、我們的、他們的、偺們的。 ⁴我們偺們。 ⁵我們倆。 ⁶偺們倆。 ⁷偺們三個人。 ⁸這個那個。 ⁹這兒那兒。 ¹⁰這麼那麼。 ¹¹甚麼人。 ¹²甚麼東西。 ¹³那個人是誰，那個人是個好人。 ¹⁴買東西賣東西。 ¹⁵他是個買賣人，賣甚麼的，賣好些個東西。 ¹⁶我要好的，有沒有沒有了。 ¹⁷這個很好，那個不好。 ¹⁸有甚麼人來，沒有人來。 ¹⁹他是那兒的人，他不是這兒的。 ²⁰他們來了多少人。 ²¹我不要這個，他們要這個。 ²²這個是我們的，那個是他們的。 ²³你們有這個東西沒有，我們不要這個東西。 ²⁴有多少人在那兒，有十幾個人。 ²⁵他來了沒有他沒有來。 ²⁶這個人很好那個人很好。 ²⁷這個東西是甚麼人的，是我們的，你們有多少這個東西，有不多的。 ²⁸你們那兒有很好的沒有，沒有好的，你沒有很好的，我們不要了。

PART III. THE FORTY EXERCISES. *San Yü Chang.*

EXERCISE II.

SINGLE WORDS.

1. *ni*, thou.
2. *wo*, I.
3. *t'a*, he.
4. *tsa*, properly *tsan*, the first person, not used in the singular, but with 5, generally including the person spoken to; you and I, or you and we, here present, or in this concern.
5. *mên*, plural particle affixed to personal nouns and pronouns.
6. *lia*, familiar abbreviation of *liang*, two, both.
7. *chê*, this.
8. *tsai*, to be; to be at.
9. *na*⁴, that; *na*³, what?
10. *êrh*, a son; like *tzŭ*, added to many nouns without affecting their meaning. It sometimes, when so affixed, converts a verb into a substantive.
11. *ti*, a particle affixed to nouns or pronouns as the sign of the possessive case; used to adverbialise adjectives, especially when these are repeated; otherwise, as a relative pronoun;

also as an indefinite pronoun; also in the place of *tê*, (18,) as an auxiliary verb.
12. *mo*, *mu*, not; *mei*, there is not; *mei*, being a corruption of *mo yu*.
13. *liao*, to end; ended; after verbs, sign of the past, but at the end of a clause very often a mere expletive, and then pronounced *la*, or *lo*.
14. *shên*, extreme, with *mo*, 15, what?
15. *mo*, negative interrogative particle.
16. *mai*, to buy.
17. *mai*, to sell.
18. *tê*, to get; hence, to have, possess, accomplish; a most important auxiliary verb.
19. *'hên*, very.
20. *shui*, who?
21. *yao*, to want, desire; to be about to.
22. *pu*, not.
23. *shih*, to be; yes.
24. *tung*, the east;

WORDS COMBINED.

1. Thine; mine; his.
2. You; we; they; we, the persons present, or concerned in the matter spoken of.
3. Your; our; their; belonging to us here (to our party, country, &c.)
4. We two men.
5. We two.
6. You and I.
7. We three here.
8. This, that.
9. Here; there.
10. As large as this; as small as that.
11. What man?
12. What thing? *Obs.*, thing; *tung-hsi*, east and west; *q d.*, every thing between east and west.
13. Who is that man? or, What kind of man is that? That man is a good man.
14. To buy things; to sell things.
15. He is a trader. What does he sell? He sells a good many things.
16. I want good ones; have you any (or, are there any)? None.
17. This is very good, that is bad; or this is a very good one, &c.
18. Who is it that is come? There is no one come.
19. What place is he from? He is not of this place.
20. How many people is it that are come? A good number.
21. I do not want this one; they want it.
22. This is ours; that is theirs.
23. Have you got this thing? We do not want it.
24. How many people are there there? Ten people and more.
25. Is he come? He is not come.
26. This man is very good; that is a very bad man.
27. Whose is this thing, or, are these things? It is ours; they are ours. How many have you of these? Not many of them.
28. Have you got any very good ones there? None good. Unless you have some very good, we do not want any.

KEY TO THE TZŬ ERH CHI. Colloquial Series.

1.	進	chin⁴
2.	城	ch'êng²
3.	家	chia¹
4.	住	chu⁴
5.	著, 着	cho²
6.	街	chieh¹
7.	上	shang⁴
8.	房	fang²
9.	間	chien¹
10.	屋	u¹, wu¹
11.	裏	li³
12.	開	k'ai¹
13.	鋪	p'u⁴
14.	關	kuan¹
15.	牕	ch'uang¹
16.	出	ch'u¹
17.	去	ch'ü⁴
18.	往	wang³
19.	外	wai⁴
20.	頭	t'ou²
21.	知	chih¹
22.	道	tao⁴
23.	做	tso⁴
24.	過	kuo⁴

住房子。住[2]家。城[3]裏,城外。裏頭,外頭。屋[5]裏。三[6]間房子。十八間屋子[7]。

四[8]個舖子。關[9]門。開[10]牕戶。出[11]去進來。過[12]去。走[13]着。上街[14]。街上[15]走着。

往[16]東往西。東[17]城西城。知道[18]。做甚麼[19]。你在[20]那兒住,我在城裏頭。你們那[21]個人開着[著?]

兒有多少房子,有三十五間房子。開[24]了門,關上牕戶。你知道不知道,上街去了。那[28]個人開着[著?]... 你[22]住的房子大小,我住的是三間小屋子。出[26]去進來[25]。

這[23]個房子比那個房子好多了。

他[27]在家裏做甚麼,沒在家往那兒去了。你知道不知道,上街去了。

七個舖子,他的舖子是甚麼買賣,開在那兒。在[29]城裏頭,東城有三個,西城有四個。

我們這兒沒有那麼大的買賣。那[30]個舖子裏買東西的人很多。外[31]頭來了

五六個人,是甚麼人,我不知道。這[32]個屋子沒有人住,那[33]個舖子是我的。他[34]

沒進來,過去往西去了,他出去做甚麼,上街上買東西去了,街[35]上的人很多。

8

PART III. THE FORTY EXERCISES *San Yü Chang.*

EXERCISE III

SINGLE WORDS

1 *chin*, to enter.
2 *ch'êng*, wall of a city, walled city
3 *chia*, house, home, following *jên*, man, a person, following *tzŭ*, self
4 *chu*, to inhabit
5 *cho*, an important auxiliary verb. When following its verb, and pronounced *cho*, it generally plays the part of our participial inflections. When preceding adjectives, or when pronounced *chao2*, its use is different. See Note at the end of those on Exercise XL
6 *chieh*, street
7 *shang*, up, upon, to go up, to ascend
8 *fang*, house
9 *chien*, properly a space or interval, the Numerative of rooms and houses
10 *u, wu*, room
11 *li*, the inside.
12 *k'ai*, to open
13 *p'ui*, shop
14 *kuan*, to bar or bolt; hence, to be connected with, to concern
15 *ch'uang*, window
16 *ch'u*, to go out, or, go out of
17 *ch'ü*, to go away.
18 *wang*, to go towards, towards; to
19 *wai*, outside
20 *t'ou*, head, front, side, also the Numerative of cattle, mules, asses &c
21 *chih*, to know
22 *tao*, road or way, to speak.
23 *tso*, to do
24 *kuo*, to pass, to pass over, also used as an auxiliary to effect the past tense of verbs

WORDS COMBINED

1 To live in a house
2 To live at home
3 Inside the city walls   Outside the city walls
4 Inside Outside
5 In a room
6 Three houses
7 Eighteen rooms
8 Four shops
9 Shut (*lit* bolt) the door
10 Open the window
11 To go out   To come in.
12 To pass, to go past,
13 Going, or, walking
14 To go up the street
15 Walking in the street
16 To go east and west, eastwards and westwards
17 The eastern and western divisions of the city [in Peking]
18 To know
19 What doing? or, Why?
20 Where do you live? I am in the city
21 How many buildings have you over there? Thirty-five
22. Is the house you live in large or small? I live, in three small rooms
23. This house is a great deal better than that one
24. Open the door, (or, the door is open) Shut the window, (or, the window is shut) *Obs*, shut, the *shang* is an auxiliary completing the action of the verb *kuan*
25 To come into the room
26 There is a great deal of dust outside
27 What is he doing at home? He is not at home Do you know where he is gone? He is gone for a turn (*lit* up the street)
28 That man keeps seven shops Dealing in what? And where are they all?
29. They are inside the city, three in the east division, and four in the west we have no such business here
30 Those shops have a large number of customers
31 There are five or six people come out, who are they? I cannot say
32 No one lives in this room, (or these rooms)
33 That shop is mine
34 He did not come in, he went past, westwards. What is he gone out to do? He is gone up the street to buy something
35 There are a great number of people in the street

KEY TO THE TZŬ ERH CHI. Colloquial Series.

1.	前	ch'ien²
2.	後	'hou⁴
3.	叫	chiao⁴
4.	站	chan⁴
5.	起	ch'i³
6.	躺	t'ang³
7.	地	ti⁴
8.	快	k'uai⁴
9.	慢	man⁴
10.	都	tu¹, tou¹
11.	愛	ai⁴, ⁿgai⁴
12.	坐	tso⁴
13.	轎	chiao⁴
14.	樓	lou²
15.	下	hsia⁴
16.	回	'hui²
17.	到	tao⁴
18.	驢	lü²
19.	騾	lo²
20.	匹	p'i¹
21.	輛	liang⁴
22.	步	pu⁴
23.	頂	ting³
24.	衙	ya²
25.	說	shuo¹

¹躺著坐著起來站著走著步行。²快走慢走。³前頭後頭。⁴回來到了。愛不愛。⁵他在後頭走。⁶叫人叫人來。⁷衙門樓上地下。⁸一輛車一頂轎子三匹馬兩頭騾子⁹四頭驢。他在道兒上躺著叫他起來。¹⁰我在樓上坐著他是地下坐著。我走得快他走得慢我在前頭¹¹他是往那兒去¹²我是坐車來的他是步行兒來的。他那個人回來了沒有他快回來了他是¹³坐轎去是坐車去是坐著一頂小轎子他不愛坐車¹⁴他那個人回來了沒有他們那些人我都不愛。¹⁵他那個人你愛不愛他們那些人我都不愛。¹⁶他買的是馬麼不是買的是騾子驢。¹⁷是買馬這兒一匹都沒有這兒他買了多少頭騾子他買了三頭騾子七頭驢。這兒的騾子那兒的騾子好這兒的騾子沒有那兒的騾子比那兒的慢那兒的騾子驢都快。

10

PART III. THE FORTY EXERCISES. *San Yü Chang.*

EXERCISE IV

SINGLE WORDS.

1. *ch'ien*, before, in time or place.
2. *'hou*, behind, in time or place.
3. *chiao*, to call; to bid.
4. *chan*, to stand up.
5. *ch'i*, to rise.
6. *t'ang*, to recline.
7. *ti*, earth; ground.
8. *k'uai*, fast, soon.
9. *man*, slow.
10. *tu, tou*, all.
11. *ai*, to love; to be wont.
12. *tso*, to sit; to sit on, or in.
13. *chiao*, a sedan-chair.
14. *lou*, an upper story; a building with one or more stories.
15. *hsia*, below; down; to descend.
16. *'hui*, to return.
17. *tao*, to arrive at,
18. *lu*, donkey.
19. *lo*, mule.
20. *p'i*, the Numerative of horses, mules, asses.
21. *liang*, the Numerative of carts, carriages, &c.
22. *pu*, a pace; to pace.
23. *ting*, crown of the head; at the top of; in which sense it often makes the superlative of adjectives; the button of an official cap; the Numerative of official caps, sedans, &c.
24. *ya*, a bureau, public office.
25. *shuo*, to speak. See Exerc. V. *ex.* 10.

WORDS COMBINED.

1. Reclining. Sitting. To rise (from bed, from a seat.) Standing up. Walking. To go on foot.
2. Go fast; make haste and go. Go slow.
3. In front. In rear.
4. To come back. To have arrived.
5. Do you like it, him, them, or not? Not at all.
6. To tell some one to come. Call some one here.
7. A bureau, public office. Up stairs. On the ground; down on the ground.
8. A cart. A sedan-chair. Three horses. Two mules. Four donkeys.
9. He is lying down in the road; tell him to get up.
10. I was, or am, sitting up stairs; he was, or is' sitting down below.
11. He was on foot. I came in a cart; he came on foot.
12. I walk fast; he walks slow; or, I walk faster than he does.
13. I was walking in front; he was behind.
14. Is that man come back or not? He is not back; but he soon will be. Where did he go (is he gone to)? To the *ya-mên*, (office). Did he go in a chair or in a carriage? In a small chair; he does not like being in a carriage.
15. Do you like that man? I do not like any of those men.
16. Has he been buying horses? No; mules and donkeys; if he wanted to buy horses, [he could not, for] there is not a horse to be had here. How many mules or donkeys has he bought? Three mules and seven donkeys.
17. Which are the better, the mules from this place, or those from that? The mules here are not so good as those there. The mules here are slower than what you get there; both the mules and donkeys from that place are fast.

KEY TO THE TZŬ ERH CHI. Colloquial Series.

1.	眞	chên¹
2.	正	chêng⁴
3.	抄	ch'ao¹
4.	寫	hsieh³
5.	教	chiao¹
6.	學	hsiao², hsio²
7.	請	ch'ing³
8.	瞧	ch'iao²
9.	拿	na²
10.	字	tzŭ⁴
11.	典	tien³
12.	話	'hua⁴
13.	找	chao³
14.	看	k'an⁴
15.	先	hsien¹
16.	認	jên⁴
17.	還	'hai², 'han²
18.	肯	k'ên³
19.	告	kao⁴
20.	訴	su⁴
21.	呢	ni¹
22.	記	chi⁴
23.	問	wên⁴
24.	騎	ch'i²
25.	跑	p'ao³

先生¹ 教學² 學生³ 拿字典看字典⁴ 找字認字⁵ 抄寫字⁶ 找先生請⁷ 先生請教。 我問你，請你告訴⁸ 記得不記得。⁹ 口音¹⁰ 正說話眞。 看見你看見過¹¹ 騎著跑著你是步行兒來的是騎馬來的我¹² 你找過先生沒有找過了。 請先生教話。¹³ 請先生請¹⁴ 先¹⁵ 這個字你瞧過沒瞧過瞧過了，你告訴¹⁶ 我問你這個字你認得不認得這個字我¹⁷ 的口音正說話眞。 我請過先生教我他不肯來，請他教你甚麽請他教我們說話。¹⁸ 他說他不肯來。¹⁹ 你²⁰ 告訴我說他那個人的口音沒有甚麽大好，他認得的字比我認得的多。

是騎馬來的，那匹馬跑得快。 沒有你還沒有看見過麽看過了。 生請教。 我問你，請你告訴。 生拿字典看字典。 先生 教學 學生 拿字典看字典 找字認字 抄寫字 找先生請 我說是甚麽字要找瞧字 我說拿字典找字，要找甚麽字要找瞧字 不記得的多。 我說看見過沒看見過呢。 還沒看見過呢。 他說學生多不肯來。 音沒有甚麽大好，他認得的字比我認得的多。

12

PART III. THE FORTY EXERCISES. *San Yü Chang.*

EXERCISE V

SINGLE WORDS.

1. *chên*, true.
2. *chêng*, upright, correct.
3. *ch'ao*, to copy.
4. *hsieh*, to write.
5. *chiao*, to teach.
6. *hsiao, hsio, hsueh, hsuo,* to learn.
7. *ch'ing*, to request.
8. *ch'iao*, to look at, see.
9. *na*, to lay hold of.
10. *tzŭ*, written words.
11. *tien*, a rule, law.
12. *'hua*, oral language.
13. *chao*, to seek.
14. *k'an*, to see.
15. *hsien*, before, in time only.
16. *jên*, to recognise.
17. *'huan*, to return, repay; *'hai, 'han,* yet, still.
18. *k'ên*, to wish, to choose to.
19. *kao*, to announce.
20. *su*, to tell to.
21. *m*, a particle, generally, but not always interrogative.
22. *chi*, to remember.
23. *wên*, to ask, to enquire.
24. *ch'i*, to ride.
25. *p'ao*, to run.

WORDS COMBINED.

1. Teacher.
2. To teach.
3. Pupil.
4. To take hold of the dictionary. To read the dictionary.
5. To look out characters. To recognise characters, to be able to read.
6. To copy. To write.
7. To look out for a teacher. To engage a teacher; also, Please, teacher. Be so good as to inform me.
8. I ask you the question. Be so good as to tell me.
9. Do you remember?
10. Correct pronunciation. Correct or intelligible diction; *lit.*, to speak language true without error.
11. To see; to behold. Have you seen it or not? Have you not seen it yet? I have seen it.
12. Riding. Running or galloping. Did you come on foot or on horseback? I came on horseback. That horse gallops fast.
13. Have you found a teacher? I have.
14. Teacher, please teach me to talk.
15. Teacher, please look out a word in the dictionary. What character do you want looked out? The character *ch'iao*, to see.
16. Have you ever met with (*lit.* seen) this character? I have. Tell me what character it is? I do not remember the character. Are there any other characters that you do not remember? Of course there are. I remember but few compared with the number I forget.
17. Your pronunciation is correct; so is your diction.
18. I will ask you whether you know this character or not? I have never seen this character.
19. I have requested a teacher to come and teach me, [but] he will not come. What is it you requested him to teach? I asked him to teach us the spoken language; [but] he says he objects to come on account of the large number of pupils.
20. Tell me, is that man's pronunciation as good as yours? My pronunciation is not very good; he knows more characters than I.

KEY to the TZŬ ERH CHI. **Colloquial Series.**

1. 紙 chih³
2. 張 chang¹
3. 筆 pi³
4. 管 kuan³
5. 墨 mê⁴, mo⁴
6. 塊 k'uai⁴
7. 把 pa⁴
8. 本 pên³
9. 書 shu¹
10. 念 nien⁴
11. 完 wan²
12. 可 k'o³
13. 以 i³
14. 給 kei³
15. 官 kuan¹
16. 會 'hui⁴
17. 分 fên¹
18. 聽 t'ing¹
19. 明 ming²
20. 也 yeh³
21. 懂 tung³
22. 平 p'ing²
23. 聲 shêng¹
24. 忘 wang⁴
25. 錯 ts'o⁴

一張紙、一本書、兩塊墨、五管筆。¹ 官話、懂得聽見忘了。² 四聲是上平下平上³聲、去聲。不錯、完了、不會明白、可以。⁴ 我看你給我買十管筆兩塊墨。⁵ 我聽見說你學官話學得很好、四聲你會分不會、四聲都可以分得開。那一本書你看完了沒有、十分裏我看過八分明白不⁶明白、有幾分不明白、也有幾個字不認得。你念過多少日子的書、我念過十⁷個月的書、那書上的字都記得麼、不都記得、忘了好些個、也有記錯了的。他那⁸個人懂得官話不懂、我聽見說他不懂、他認得字不認得字、你那兒知道呢。⁹上月我們在一塊兒看書、我叫他抄寫、他可以不可以、沒有甚¹⁰麼不可以的。我問你、他的話、你聽得出來、聽不出來。你¹¹念過的書、千萬不可忘了、不錯、你說得很是。¹²

PART III. THE FORTY EXERCISES. *San Yü Chang.*

EXERCISE VI.

SINGLE WORDS.

1. *chih*, paper.
2. *chang*, properly to open, spread out; hence, when found with paper, *chih*, a sheet; also the Numerative of chairs, tables, &c.
3. *pi*, pencil.
4. *kuan*, tube; also the Numerative of pencils.
5. *mê*, *mo*, ink.
6. *k'uai*, a bit, piece; also the Numerative of Chinese ink, which is in small cakes.
7. *pa*, to hold; often prefixed to what we call the object of a transitive verb; also a noun, the Numerative of various nouns.
8. *pên*, trunk; root above ground; also the Numerative of volumes; under certain circumstances the pronoun *this*.
9. *shu*, a book; writings.
10. *nien*, to think of; to commit to memory; to repeat aloud; to study.
11. *wan*, to end; hence sometimes used to form the perfect of verbs.
12. *k'o*, to be right; to be able.
13. *i*, properly to use; but it has other meanings. See Exerc. XVIII. *ex*. 12.
14. *kei*, properly *chi*, to give; hence, to or for.
15. *kuan*, officer.
16. *'hui*, to meet; come together; be competent to; to know.
17. *fên*, to divide; a portion; specially a tenth.
18. *t'ing*, to hear.
19. *ming*, plain to the sight; clear-seeing.
20. *yeh*, also, even.
21. *tung*, to understand.
22. *p'ing*, even, level; at peace.
23. *shêng*, sound; tone.
24. *wang*, to forget.
25. *ts'o*, to err, wrong. See Radical Test Table III., 10.

WORDS COMBINED.

1. A sheet of paper. A volume. Two bits or cakes of ink. Five pencils.
2. The mandarin dialect; *lit.* official spoken-language.
3. To understand. To hear. To have forgotten.
4. The Four Tones [of the oral language] are the *shang-p'ing*, upper-even; the *hsia-p'ing*, lower-even; the *shang*, ascending; and the *ch'u*, departing.
5. Right! *lit.* no mistake. To have finished or ended, (active or neuter). Not to be able to. Intelligible, intelligent; to understand. To be able; or, It will do well enough.
6. Bring that volume here to, or for, me. Show me that sheet of paper. Buy me ten pencils and two cakes of ink.
7. I hear it said that you are learning mandarin, and getting on very well. Can you distinguish the Four Tones? I can distinguish them all.
8. Have you done reading that book yet? (or, have you finished that book?) I have read four-fifths of it. Do you understand it? There are portions of it that I do not understand; there are also some characters that I do not know.
9. How long have you been reading (studying)? I have been studying ten months. Do you remember all the characters in the book (or books) you have been studying? I do not remember them all. I have forgotten a good number altogether, and there are some that I do not remember accurately.
10. Does *he* understand mandarin?. I have heard people say that he does not. Does he know the written character? That he does; he knows four or five thousand characters. How do you know? We read together last month. If I tell him to copy, will he be able to? There is no reason why he should not.
11. Tell me, do you understand him when he speaks?
12. You must on no account forget the books you read. Certainly not; you are quite right.

KEY TO THE TZŬ ERH CHI. — Colloquial Series.

1. 炕 k'ang⁴
2. 蓆 hsi²
3. 床 ch'uang²
4. 帳 chang⁴
5. 鋪 p'u¹
6. 蓋 kai⁴
7. 桌 cho¹
8. 椅 i³
9. 燭 la⁴
10. 燈 têng¹
11. 盞 chan³
12. 隻 chih¹
13. 酒 chiu³
14. 杯 pei¹
15. 茶 ch'a²
16. 碗 wan³
17. 盅 chung¹
18. 廚 ch'u²
19. 煑 chu³
20. 飯 fan⁴
21. 鍋 kuo¹
22. 鏟 ch'a¹
23. 勺 shao²
24. 壞 'huai⁴

鋪炕一張床。帳子蓆子鋪蓋。一張桌子一張椅子。一盞燈，燭燈。廚房。

一把刀子一把勺子一口飯鍋一個鍋蓋一個茶碗一隻酒杯一個酒盅子。他煑飯壞了。他在炕上鋪蓆子。我要在這張床上躺著你在椅子上坐著。

快把鋪蓋鋪上。那一張床上帳子沒有。他在床上躺著我在椅子上坐著。

這屋裏很黑拏一盞燈來。有人拏了那盞燈去。桌子上的那燭燈誰拏了去

是我給廚子拏過去了。廚房裏沒有火。飯鍋是煑飯用的鍋蓋是飯鍋的蓋兒。

酒杯酒盅子這兩個東西不大很歹。那屋裏

那些桌子椅子都壞了。我叫你買的那茶碗你買了沒買，買過了，買了多少個

買了二十個是在那兒買的，都是在城外頭鋪子裏買的。你們的屋裏有蓆子

沒有，我們的屋裏炕上都有蓆子。

PART III. THE FORTY EXERCISES. *San Yü Chang.*

EXERCISE VII.

SINGLE WORDS.

1. *k'ang*, stove-bed.
2. *hsi*, mat.
3. *ch'uang* bed.
4. *chang*, curtain.
5. *p'u¹*, to spread; the Numerative of stove-beds.
6. *kai*, cover; to cover.
7. *cho*, table.
8. *i*, chair.
9. *la*, wax.
10. *têng*, lamp
11. *chan*, the Numerative of lamps.
12. *chih*, properly the half of a pair; the Numerative of sheep, poultry, shipping, &c.
13. *chiu*, wine.
14. *pei*, cup.
15. *ch'a*, tea.
16. *wan*, bowl
17. *chung*, cup, larger than *pei*.
18. *ch'u*, to cook
19. *chu*, to boil.
20. *fan*, properly cooked rice; also any cooked victuals.
21. *kuo*, a certain cooking-pan.
22. *ch'a*, fork.
23. *shao*, spoon.
24. *'huai*, to spoil; to ruin; hence morally ruined, vicious.

WORDS COMBINED.

1. A stove-bed. A bed.
2. Curtains Mats. Bedding; q d that which is spread and which covers.
3. A table. A chair
4. A lamp. Candlesticks.
5. Kitchen. A knife. A fork. A spoon A cooking-pan, a pan to cook rice. A cooking-pan lid. A tea-cup. Do. A wine-cup. Do. (See below, ex. 16, 17)
6. To boil rice.
7. To have spoiled; he, or it, is spoiled, or destroyed.
8. He spread, or is spreading, a mat on the stove-bed
9. I will (or want to, or, am going to,) lie down on this bed; be quick and make the bed.
10. Are there curtains upon that bed?
11. He is, or was, lying on the bed; I am, or was, sitting on a chair.
12. It is very dark in the room;. bring a lamp here.
13. Some one has taken the lamp away.
14. Who took away the candlestick that was on the table? It was I that took it for the cook (or, to give it to the cook).
15. There is no fire in the kitchen
16. A rice-pan, *fan-kuo*, is a pan for boiling rice; the *kuo-kai* is the cover of the rice-pan; tea-cups, whether *ch'a-wan* or *ch'a-chung*, may both have *kai*, covers.
17. There is no great difference between a *chiu-pei* and a *chiu-chung-tzŭ* (wine cups).
18. The chairs and tables in that room are all spoiled.
19. Have you bought those tea-cups I told you to buy? I have. How many did you buy? Twenty. Where did you buy them? They were bought in a shop outside the city
20. Have you mats in your apartment (or, apartments)? There are mats on all the stove-beds in our apartments.

KEY TO THE TZŬ ERH CHI. Colloquial Series.

1.	傢	chia¹
2.	伙	ʻhuo³
3.	撬	tʻêng⁴
4.	條	tʻiao²
5.	倒	tao⁴
6.	壺	ʻhu²
7.	花	ʻhua²
8.	瓶	pʻing²
9.	破	pʻo⁴
10.	收	shou¹
11.	拾	shih²
12.	盤	pʻan²
13.	碟	tieh²
14.	吃	chʻih¹
15.	點	tien³
16.	吹	chʻui¹
17.	滅	mieh⁴
18.	使	shih³
19.	燒	shao¹
20.	爐	lu²
21.	空	kʻung¹
22.	滿	man³
23.	同	tʻung²
24.	算	suan⁴
25.	碎	sui⁴

傢伙。¹ 一條撬子,²一個撬子也說得。一個爐子。³花瓶,酒瓶,酒壺,茶壺,盤子,碟子,刡水,⁶空壺滿壺空了,壺滿了。使得破壞收拾。⁸家裏用的東西都是傢伙。⁹點燈吹燈燒火滅火。床桌椅撬都是屋裏用的傢伙。¹⁰爐子有大小不同廚房做飯是傢伙炕頭裏吃飯的傢伙有刀子鍘子勺子盤子碟子飯碗酒杯。也是爐子屋裏燒火還是爐子。¹²花瓶也算是傢伙麽花瓶還可以算是傢伙。那¹⁴酒瓶酒壺茶壺茶碗也都是零用的傢伙。那碗裏的水倒在鍋裏。¹⁵倒茶是叫人把茶倒在碗裏。你¹⁷點了燈沒有我點上燈了,是他吹滅了。吹¹⁸燈是滅燈火滅火是滅了爐子的火。那¹⁹倆壺裏頭有水沒有水一個是空的一個是滿的你把那空的倒滿了水。那²⁰花瓶是甚麽人破壞的我不知道是誰快去叫人收拾使得使不得叫人收拾很使得。

PART III. THE FORTY EXERCISES. *San Yü Chang.*

EXERCISE VIII.

SINGLE WORDS.

1, 2. *chia-'huo*, utensils, furniture.
3. *têng*, a stool, a bench.
4. *t'iao*, a branch, twig; the Numerative of stools, and many other dissimilar things that are long and narrow.
5. *tao*, to upset; to pour.
6. *'hu*, a pot, a tea-pot, &c.
7. *'hua*, flowers.
8. *p'ing*, a vase.
9. *p'o*, to crack, break.
10. *shou*, to receive; recover, to put away.
11. *shih*, to pick up; to put in order.
12. *p'an*, plates.
13. *tieh*, plates, saucers, smaller than *p'an*.
14. *ch'ih*, to eat.
15. *tien*, point, particle; to punctuate; to light as a candle.
16. *ch'ui*, to blow.
17. *mieh*, to extinguish.
18. *shih*, to employ.
19. *shao*, to burn, roast.
20. *lu*, a stove.
21. *k'ung* 1, empty.
22. *man*, full.
23. *t'ung*, same; with.
24. *suan*, to reckon.
25. *sui*, in fragments, in tatters.

WORDS COMBINED.

1. Furniture, utensils.
2. A stool or bench; you may also use *t'iao* or *ko* as the Numerative of *têng*.
3. A stove.
4. Flower-vase. Wine-bottle. Wine-kettle. Teapot. Dishes. Plates.
5. Light the lamp. Blow out the lamp. Light the fire. The fire is out.
6. To pour, or upset water.
7. Empty pot, or kettle; full pot. The pot is empty; the pot is full.
8. It may be used (is rightly used, will do. See below *Ex.* 20.). To spoil by breaking. To mend.
9. Every thing that is used in a house is *chia-'huo*, furniture.
10. Beds, tables, chairs, stools, are all *chia-'huo*, room-furniture.
11. The *chia-'huo* for the table are knives, forks, spoons, dishes, plates, bowls, and wine cups.
12. Stoves, *lu-tzŭ*, are of different sizes; some larger, some smaller; the stove on which things are cooked in the kitchen is a *lu-tzŭ*; so is the stove in front of the stove-bed; so also is the stove in which a fire is lit in one's room.
13. May flower-vases also be considered *chia-'huo*? They may be so considered.
14. Wine-bottles, wine-kettles, tea-pots, and tea cups, are also miscellaneous *chia-'huo*.
15. The water in the cup is (or, was) poured into the pan.
16. To say *tao ch'a*, pour tea, is to desire some one to pour tea into the cups.
17. Have you lit the lamp? I lit it; but he blew it out.
18. *ch'ui têng*, *lit.* to blow a lamp, is to extinguish the flame of the lamp; *mieh 'huo*, to extinguish fire, means the extinction of fire [as] in a fire-place.
19. Is there water in those two kettles? One is empty, the other is full. Fill the empty one with water.
20. Who is it that has broken the (or, that) flower-vase? I do not know who it was. Had I not better go at once and desire some one to mend it? Yes; you had much better tell some one to mend it.

1.	今	chin¹
2.	年	nien²
3.	時	shih²
4.	令	ling⁴
5.	暖	nuan³
6.	和	'ho², 'huo²
7.	昨	tso²
8.	天	t'ien¹
9.	就	chiu⁴
10.	定	ting⁴
11.	晝	chou⁴
12.	晴	ch'ing²
13.	亮	liang⁴
14.	鐘	chung¹
15.	半	pan⁴
16.	刻	k'ê⁴
17.	氣	ch'i⁴
18.	候	'hou⁴
19.	冷	lêng³
20.	熱	jê⁴
21.	雪	hsüeh³
22.	涼	liang²
23.	颳	kua¹

前年去年今年明年後年。

[2] 上月本月下月。

[3] 前兒就是前天昨兒今兒今[4] 時令就是一年的四時。[5] 天氣可以分天明兒明天後兒後天都是那麼著。[6] 時候天亮白晝黑下一會兒一點鐘兩刻冷天熱天涼天暖和颳風晴天下雪。[7] 那人他看過二十多[8] 我今兒走下月可以回來。[9] 你今兒八下鐘還半點鐘一點半鐘就是一點鐘兩刻一下鐘就是一點鐘半點鐘做過五六個月的先生。[10] 前年後年可以說前月後月不大很說。[11] 這兒天熱的時候兒下雨，天沒起來。[12] 昨兒黑下颳風天亮的時候兒很冷。[13] 他愛白晝出去騎馬冷的時候兒下雪。[14] 昨兒黑下下雨，今兒晴了天。[15] 今兒是個晴天。[16] 今年天氣暖黑下回家看書。[17] 我們倆到這兒好些年了。[18] 他是去年來的，我是上和得很，沒有去年那麼冷。月到的，他們倆，是去年來過了。

PART III. THE FORTY EXERCISES *San Yu Chang.*

EXERCISE IX.

SINGLE WORDS

1 *chin*, now, the present
2 *nien*, the year.
3 *shih*, time
4 *ling*, to command, commands, also, honorable.
5 *nuan*, also *nan*, warm
6 *'ho, 'huo*, peace, together with
7 *tso*, of yesterday
8 *t'ien*, heaven, a day
9 *chiu*, to follow as a consequence, consequently, then
10 *ting*, to fix
11 *chou*, day time
12 *ch'ing*, clear, fine
13 *liang*, light as day
14 *chung*, bell, clock
15 *pan*, half
16 *k'ê*, to engrave, a quarter of an hour
17 *ch'i*, breath, air
18 *'hou*, to await, hence a section of time
19 *lêng*, cold.
20 *jê*, hot
21 *hsueh*, snow
22 *liang*, cool, cold
23 *kua*, to blow, said to be a vulgar form of *kua*, to rasp or cut, EXERC XVIII 10.

WORDS COMBINED

1 The year before last Last year This year Next year The year after next
2 Last moon, *lit* the moon above This moon Next moon, *lit* the moon below
3 *ch'ien-'rh* is simply *ch'ien-t'ien*, the day before yesterday, and the combinations meaning yesterday, to-day, to-morrow, and the day after to-morrow, all follow the same rule
4 The term *shih-ling*, means simply the four seasons
5 The weather, *lit* air of the sky, may be distinguished as cold, hot, cool, warm, windy, clear, snowy
6 A time Day-break Day-time Night-time A short space of time An hour and two quarters A half-hour An hour and a half is the same as an hour and two quarters Both the following expressions, *i hsia chung* and *i tien chung*, mean an hour
7 That man there has studied upwards of twenty years, and has been a teacher five or six months.
8 I am going to-day, and I may be back next moon
9 You were not up at eight o'clock to-day
10 You may say both *ch'ien nien* for the year before last, and *'hou nien* for the year after next, but one seldom hears *ch'ien yueh* and *'hou yueh*
11 At this place it rains in the hot weather and snows in the cold
12 It blew last night, and at day-break it was very cold
13 It is his habit to go out riding in the day-time, and to go home at night and read
14 It rained last night, but it is fine to-day
15 This is a fine (or, clear) day
16 The weather is very mild this year, not so cold as it was last year
17 You and I have been here a good many years, (or It is many years since you and I came here)
18 He came last year, I arrived last moon, they two were over here last year

KEY TO THE TZŬ ERH CHI. Colloquial Series.

1.	更	ching[1]
2.	夫	fu[1]
3.	每	mei[3]
4.	夜	yeh[4]
5.	得	tei[3]
6.	打	ta[3]
7.	罷	pa[4]
8.	早	tsao[3]
9.	晚	wan[3]
10.	晌	shang[3]
11.	午	wu[3]
12.	喒	tsan[1]
13.	事	shih[4]
14.	情	ch'ing[2]
15.	擱	ko[1]
16.	各	ko[4]
17.	樣	yang[4]
18.	短	tuan[3]
19.	雲	yün[2]
20.	彩	ts'ai[3]
21.	陰	yin[1]
22.	霧	wu[4]
23.	空	k'ung[4]

1 每年，每月，每天，每日，各樣。 2 早起，晌午，晚上，上半天，下半天，夜裏，前半夜，4 陰天，雲彩 5 定更，打更更夫。 6 天長，夜短，多喒，工夫。 8 每年不是年年每月就是月月每天 14 每日還是那麼樣。他 15 是早起起來，晌午街上走，晚上回家看書，到夜裏三更天就躺在炕上罷了。天天都是這麼樣。各自各兒就是自己一個人這個事 17 情得你各自各兒去那房子就是他各自各兒住著。18 前半夜還暖和後半夜冷。三更天就是半夜。19 夜裏那更夫打更一晴了。20 天長做事的工夫多，天短沒有空兒事情得 21 攔著罷。他 22 多喒回來，明兒可以回來。那茶壺擱在那兒了，擱在屋裏桌子 23 上了。天 24 上的雲彩滿了，就是陰天。今 25 兒早起下得霧很大，大山都看不見

22

PART III. THE FORTY EXERCISES. *San Yü Chang.*

EXERCISE X.

SINGLE WORDS.

1. *ching*, properly *kéng*, the night watches.
2. *fu*, a man; specially a husband; commonly, any working man.
3. *mei*, every.
4. *yeh*, night.
5. *tei*, must be; popular contraction of *té yao*; see Exerc. II.
6. *ta*, to strike.
7. *pa*, to end, cause to cease; at the end of a sentence, There's an end of it; but sometimes an expression of doubt, like our Eh?
8. *tsao*, early.
9. *wan*, late.
10. *shang*, noon.
11. *wu*, noon.
12. *tsan*, length of time; popular contraction of *tsao wan*.
13. *shih*, an affair.
14. *ch'ing*, feelings; circumstances.
15. *ko*, to put, to place; to leave unmoved.
16. *ko*, each, every.
17. *yang*, kind; fashion.
18. *tuan*, short.
19. *yun*, cloud.
20. *ts'ai*, colours.
21. *yin*, dark.
22. *wu*, mist.
23. *k'ung* 4, vacancy, leisure.

WORDS COMBINED.

1. Every year. Every moon. Every day (*t'ien*). Every day (*jıh*).
2. Each kind; or, all sorts.
3. Early in the morning. Noon. In the evening, or, at night. The forenoon. The afternoon.
4. By night; during night. Before midnight. After midnight.
5. To set the watch; the watch-setting. To strike [the number of] the watch; to keep watch as a watchman. A watchman.
6. The days are long. The days are short. The nights are long. The nights are short.
7. At what time; when?
8. Work; the time at man's disposal for work; hence his leisure; time taken up by anything.
9. A dull day. Clouds. There is a mist come, or coming on.
10. There must be one, or some.
11. Affairs; an affair.
12. Being put or placed.
13. It is ended; enough about it.
14. Every year, *mei nien*, is the same as year after year, *nien nien*, is it not? Every moon is moon after moon, monthly; so with the phrases *mei t'ien*, *mei jıh*, daily.
15. He rises early; goes for a walk (*lit.* up the street) at noon; comes home in the evening and reads; and in the third watch of the night he goes to bed. He does the same every day.
16. The expression *ko-tzŭ-ko-'rh* means simply one's individual self. In this matter it is essential that you should go yourself. He lives by himself in that house.
17. It rained in the forenoon, but the afternoon was fine.
18. It was warm before midnight, but cold after.
19. The third watch is midnight.
20. As regards the watches which a watchman strikes during the night, the night is divided into five; the beginning of the first of which is the watch-setting.
21. When the days are long, there is more time to do things; when they are short, one has not leisure for them, and they must just wait (be put aside).
22. When will he be back? Possibly to-morrow.
23. Where is the teapot put? On the table in the room.
24. When the sky is overcast, the day is said to be *yin*, dull, obscured.
25. There was a thick mist this morning; the mountains were invisible.

KEY TO THE TZŬ ERH CHI. Colloquial Series.

1. 怕 p'a⁴
2. 裳 shang¹
3. 件 chien⁴
4. 太 t'ai⁴
5. 腌 a¹, ang¹
6. 臢 tsa¹, tsang¹
7. 換 huan⁴
8. 乾 kan¹
9. 淨 ching⁴
10. 刷 shua¹
11. 洗 hsi³
12. 臉 lien³
13. 盆 p'ên²
14. 縫 fêng²
15. 補 pu³
16. 穿 ch'uan¹
17. 鞋 hsieh²
18. 脫 t'o¹
19. 靴 hsüeh¹
20. 雙 shuang¹
21. 襪 wa⁴
22. 最 tsui⁴
23. 溫 wên¹

刷¹洗。腌臢²乾淨。衣裳³靴子鞋襪子。穿上⁴脫下來，換上。縫⁵補。一雙靴⁶。

這盆水腌臢了，換乾淨的拏來我洗臉。那些衣裳腌臢拏刷子刷一刷，這一件衣裳破了叫人來縫⁷補。

子，兩雙鞋，十雙襪子，一條手巾，八件衣裳，一個臉盆。

你⁹快起來穿上衣裳。他¹⁰脫了衣裳躺著。那¹¹一件衣裳他穿了好些日子沒換呢。今¹²兒個天涼你得多穿一件衣裳。他¹³是穿靴子是穿鞋。你¹⁵愛穿的是靴子是鞋。

這¹⁴一條手巾腌臢，擱在盆裏洗一洗。我在家裏坐著穿鞋上衙門去穿靴子。

你¹⁶的那皮靴子擱得日子多得刷洗著靴子來著。你¹⁷洗手是愛使涼水是愛使開水，兩樣兒都不好，涼水太涼，開水太熱最好的是溫和水兒。

你¹⁸快把這個水倒在鍋裏溫一溫。那¹⁹火要滅了，這水溫了半天開不了。

要²⁰洗衣裳使熱水最好，刷洗靴子得使涼水。

24

PART III. THE FORTY EXERCISES. *Sán Yü Chang.*

EXERCISE XI.

SINGLE WORDS.

1. *p'a*, to fear.
2. *shang*, with *i*, Radical 145, clothes.
3. *chien*, properly an item, or unit; the Numerative of clothes, affairs, and other things.
4. *t'ai*, much; very; too much.
5. *a, ang*, (used only with 6,) dirty.
6. *tsa, tsang*, dirty; (often used without 5).
7. *'huan*, to exchange.
8. *kan*, dry.
9. *ching*, clean.
10. *shua*, to brush.
11. *hsi*, to wash.
12. *lien*, face.
13. *p'ên*, basin.
14. *fêng*, to stitch together.
15. *pu*, to patch.
16. *ch'uan*, to bore; to put on clothes.
17. *hsieh*, shoes.
18. *t'o*, to take off or away.
19. *hsueh*, boots.
20. *shuang*, a pair.
21. *wa*, stockings.
22. *tsui*, much; very.
23. *wên*, warm.

WORDS COMBINED.

1. To brush and wash (Chinese boots).
2. Dirty. Clean.
3. Clothes. Boots. Shoes. Stockings.
4. To put on clothes (or any article of clothing). To take off. To change (clothes).
5. To mend by stitching.
6. A pair of boots. Two pair of shoes. Ten pair of stockings. A handkerchief, or napkin. Eight articles of dress. A wash-hand basin.
7. The water in this basin is dirty; change it and bring me some clean water instead to wash my face.
8. Those clothes are dirty; take a brush and brush them. This thing (article of dress) is torn; call some one here to mend it.
9. Get up quick and dress.
10. He is (or, was) lying down undressed; or, has taken off his clothes and is lying down.
11. He has had that thing on for several days without changing it.
12. It is cold to day; you must put on something more.
13. Has he got on boots or shoes? He has got on boots.
14. This handkerchief is dirty; put it in the basin and wash it.
15. Are you in the habit of wearing boots or shoes? When I am not going out, I wear shoes; when I go to the *ya-mên*, I put on boots.
16. Those leather boots of yours have been lying by a long time; they must be washed and brushed.
17. Which do you prefer (or, which are you in the habit of) using when you wash your hands, cold water or boiling water? Both are bad; cold water is too cold; boiling water is too hot; warm water is the best.
18. Be quick and pour this water into the pan, and warm it.
19. The fire is going out; the water has been on some time, and it will not boil.
20. To wash clothes it is best to use hot water. The water used to clean (brush and wash) boots must be cold.

KEY TO THE TZŬ ERH CHI. Colloquial Series.

1.	儘	chin³
2.	摘	chai¹
3.	戴	tai⁴
4.	揮	tan³
5.	帽	mao⁴
6.	砍	k'an³
7.	肩	chien¹
8.	汗	'han⁴
9.	衫	shan¹
10.	單	tan¹
11.	夾	chia²
12.	綿	mien²
13.	褲	k'u⁴
14.	裁	ts'ai²
15.	褂	kua⁴
16.	袖	hsiu¹
17.	梳	shu¹
18.	髮	fa¹
19.	針	chên¹
20.	線	hsien⁴
21.	胰	i²
22.	澡	tsao³

綿衣裳夾衣裳單衣裳。砍肩兒汗衫袴子。帽子戴帽子摘帽子。針¹線二個針一條線。裁縫裁衣裳縫衣裳。撣子撣衣裳。洗澡。頭髮梳頭髮。單衣裳是就有一面兒沒裏兒的。夾衣裳是有裏兒有面兒的。綿衣裳是夾衣裳中間有綿花的。砍肩兒是有前後沒袖子的那一件衣裳汗衫是儘裏頭穿的單衣裳短的就叫馬褂子。這一條褲子是綿的，是夾的。帽子分得是小帽兒官帽兒涼帽暖帽兩樣兒。人在街上得戴帽子進屋裏來可以摘帽子。你會針線不會，我不會就叫一個裁縫來把我那一件汗衫補了。那¹⁴一件砍肩兒裁了還沒縫呢。那¹⁵一件破馬褂子得縫補了。拏¹⁶撣子撣一撣衣裳上的土。那¹⁷一把木梳是誰梳頭髮的。洗¹⁸澡是一身都洗，天天兒洗澡很好。

PART III. THE FORTY EXERCISES. *San Yü Chang.*

EXERCISE XII.

SINGLE WORDS.

1. *chin*, extreme, farthest.
2. *chai*, to uncap.
3. *tai*, to wear on the head.
4. *tan*, to tap, to dust.
5. *mao*, a cap.
6. *k'an*, to cut.
7. *chien*, shoulders.
8. *'han*, sweat.
9. *shan*, a shirt, shift.
10. *tan*, single.
11. *chia*, doubled; having a lining.
12. *mien*, cotton.
13. *k'u*, trowsers.
14. *ts'ai*, to cut (as a tailor).
15. *kua*, an outer coat.
16. *hsiu*, a sleeve.
17. *shu*, a comb; to comb.
18. *fa*, the hair.
19. *chên*, a needle.
20. *hsien*, thread.
21. *i*, soap.
22. *tsao*, to bathe.

WORDS COMBINED.

1. Wadded clothes. Lined clothes. Clothes not lined.
2. Waistcoat. Shirt, or shift. Outer coat. Trowsers.
3. Cap. To have the cap on. To take the cap off.
4. To sew. A needle. A thread.
5. A tailor. To cut out clothes. To stitch, put together, make up clothes.
6. A duster. To dust clothes.
7. To bathe.
8. The hair of the head. To comb the hair.
9. Clothes, *tan*, not lined, are such as have an outside with nothing inside it. Clothes, *chia*, lined, are such as have both a lining and an outside. Wadded clothes are clothes with cotton between the outside and the lining.
10. A *k'an-chien*, *lit.*, shoulder-cutter, is the article of dress which has a back and front and no sleeves; a waistcoat. The *'han-shan* is the garment without lining worn innermost of all. The *kua tzŭ* is the garment worn outermost of all; when short it is called a *ma-kua*, riding-jacket.
11. Is this pair of trowsers wadded, or is it lined?
12. Caps are distinguished as small caps and official caps; and in the category of official caps there are two sorts, the cool (summer) cap, and the warm (winter) cap. In the street (out of doors), one must have a cap on; in a room (or, on going into a room), one may take it off.
13. Do you know how to sew? I do not. Then call a tailor here to mend my shirt.
14. The waistcoat is cut out, but not put together yet.
15. That riding-coat should be mended.
16. Tap the dust off the clothes with a duster.
17. Who is it that combs his hair with that, (or, the,) wooden comb?
18. The expression *hsi-tsao* means to bathe the whole person. It is a good thing to bathe every day.

1. 銀 yin²
2. 銅 t'ung²
3. 鐵 t'ieh³
4. 錢 ch'ien²
5. 吊 tiao⁴
6. 票 p'iao⁴
7. 桿 kan³
8. 秤 ch'êng⁴
9. 稱 ch'êng¹
10. 價 chia⁴
11. 值 chih²
12. 貴 kuei⁴
13. 賤 'chien
14. 便 p'ien²
15. 宜 i²
16. 輕 ch'ing¹
17. 重 chung⁴
18. 借 chieh⁴
19. 賬 chang⁴
20. 該 kai¹
21. 費 fei⁴
22. 當 tang⁴
23. 於 yü²
24. 好 'hao⁴

欠[1]賬借錢該錢。賬[2]目。花[3]費。價值價錢。很賤[4]不貴便宜。銀[5]子銀錢。銅[6]錢鐵錢票子。一兩銀子一吊錢四吊錢的票子。他[7]的輕重拏秤稱一稱。我[8]借錢是我把人家的錢拏來我使我借給人錢是把我的錢拏給人使。他[9]欠人的賬目不少。我[10]借錢是把人家的錢拏他[11]該的賬目不下一千兩銀子。他[12]愛花錢好花錢都花費是把錢使去了,我們家裏天天兒的花費不很多。說[13]得是他過於費錢。那[14]房子價值不貴這一件皮襖子價值很便宜那個花瓶不值錢今年的綿花很賤。他[15]家裏一個大錢都沒有。那[16]當十的大錢裏頭有七分是銅的,有三分是鐵的。票[17]子是一張紙上頭寫著錢數兒買東西同銀子錢一個樣兒。金[18]子比銀子重鐵比銀子輕。買[19]東西要稱分兩的都得使秤。那[20]些秤秤可以稱多少斤兩最大的可以稱三百斤。

PART III. THE FORTY EXERCISES. *San Yü Chang.*

EXERCISE XIII.

SINGLE WORDS.

1. *yin*, silver.
2. *t'ung*, copper.
3. *t'ieh*, iron.
4. *ch'ien*, coin.
5. *tiao*, a five hundred cash note.
6. *p'iao*, a printed note, or written order for money; also a police warrant.
7. *kan*, properly any straight pole or rod of wood; the Numerative of spears, muskets, &c.
8. *ch'êng*, a balance.
9. *ch'êng*, here to weigh; hence, to esteem, to speak of.
10. *chia*, price; value.
11. *chih*, to be worth.
12. *kuei*, dear, valuable; honorable, esteemed.
13. *chien*, cheap; valueless.
14. *p'ien*, a popular pronunciation of *pien* (see Exercise XXXVI.), convenient, advantageous; read *p'ien* only when followed by *i*; it then means cheap.
15. *i*, to be befitting, morally essential.
16. *ch'ing*, light.
17. *chung*, heavy.
18. *chieh*, to lend; to borrow.
19. *chang*, a bill, account.
20. *kai*, to owe anything; morally, to owe duty.
21. *fei*, to expend.
22. *tang*, to represent, stand for.
23. *yü*, in, in the case or matter of; proceeding out of; not colloquially used except in a few phrases.
24. *'hao* 4, to like, be fond of; to be distinguished from *'hao* 3, good.

WORDS COMBINED.

1. To be in debt, *lit* to owe bills. To lend or borrow money. To owe money.
2. Accounts; a bill.
3. To spend; expenses.
4. Price, value. Price, cost.
5. Of very small value. Not dear. Cheap, advantageous.
6. Money; silver money. Not dear. Copper coin. Iron coin. Bank notes.
7. A tael or ounce of silver. A note for 500 Peking cash. A four *tiao* note.
8. This is light. That is heavy. Weigh it in the balance (or with the weighing machine), if you do not know its weight.
9. He owes different people a good deal of money.
10. The expression *wo chieh ch'ien*, means that I am getting money of people for my use; *wo chieh kei jên ch'ien*, means that I am letting another have my money for his use.
11. His debts do not amount to less than 1,000 taels.
12. The expression *'hua fei* means to spend, expenditure. Our daily expenditure is not very large.
13. The expression *t'a ai*, he loves to spend money, or *t'a 'hao*, he is fond of spending money, are equally correct, both mean that he spends too much money
14. That is not a dear house. The price asked, or paid, for this fur riding-jacket is very small. That flower vase is worth nothing. Cotton is very low this year.
15. He has not got a cash to live on.
16. Seven-tenths of those ten-cash pieces are copper and three-tenths iron.
17. A *p'iao* is a paper note on which is written the number of cash it is worth; for buying things it is the same as coin.
18. Gold is heavier than silver; iron is lighter than silver.
19. If one wants to weigh things that one is buying, one must use the balance.
20. What weight are those balances equal to weighing? The largest will bear three hundred catties (three piculs).

KEY TO THE TZŬ ERH CHI. Colloquial Series.

麵

1. 煤 mei²
2. 炭 t'an⁴
3. 柴 ch'ai²
4. 麵 mien⁴
5. 油 yu²
6. 芝 chih¹
7. 糖 t'ang²
8. 鹽 yen²
9. 粗 ts'u¹
10. 細 hsi⁴
11. 湯 t'ang¹
12. 雞 chi¹
13. 奶 nai³
14. 果 kuo³
15. 菜 ts'ai⁴
16. 饅 man²
17. 喝 ho¹
18. 弄 nung⁴
19. 端 tuan¹
20. 撤 ch'ê⁴
21. 熟 shou²
22. 論 lun²
23. 石 tan⁴

1. 柴火煤炭。
2. 米麵饅頭白糖雞子兒牛奶果子
3. 茶端茶撤了。燈油香油。
4. 石米二百斤麵。吃飯喝湯。粗鹽細鹽。
5. 就是燒火。我昨兒買了三百斤炭八十斤柴火四
6. 盆是屋裏用的不能做飯做水。燈油是豆子做的香油是芝蔴做的燈油比香油賤。弄火。
7. 茶是地下長出來的就可以吃得。
8. 天氣冷的時候兒煤炭用得多。
9. 炕爐子是用煤火盆是用炭火
10. 你去給我買一隻小雞子三四個雞子兒還
11. 茶有生的有熟的在火上做的都是熟茶生
12. 要牛奶不要牛奶便宜我可以要幾斤
13. 碗論瓶買果子也不論斤都是論個兒
14. 我愛喝湯愛喝甚麼湯呢肉湯雞湯都好。
15. 你愛吃饅頭愛吃飯兩樣兒都不愛
16. 甚麼是撒了呢你吃完了飯都擎下去那就是撒了。
17. 你快弄飯去飯得了就端了來。

30

PART III. THE FORTY EXERCISES. *San Yü Chang.*

EXERCISE XIV.

SINGLE WORDS.

1. *mei*, coal.
2. *t'an*, charcoal.
3. *ch'ai*, fuel.
4. *mien*, flour.
5. *yu*, oil.
6. *chih*, properly the plant of immortality; used with *ma*, Radical 200, as here, sesame.
7. *t'ang*, sugar.
8. *yen*, salt.
9. *ts'u*, coarse.
10. *hsi*, fine.
11. *t'ang*, broth.
12. *chi*, chicken.
13. *nai*, milk.
14. *kuo*, fruit.
15. *ts'ai*, vegetables; victuals in general.
16. *man*, a dumpling.
17. *'ho*, to drink.
18. *nung*, to make, prepare.
19. *tuan*, upright; to place properly, arrange.
20. *ch'ê*, to remove.
21. *shu*, vulg. *shou*, ripe; cooked.
22. *lun*, to discuss.
23. *tan*, a corrupt form of *shih*, stone, Radical 112; one hundred catties, ordinarily called a picul.

WORDS COMBINED.

1. Firewood. Coal and charcoal.
2. Rice and flour. Bread. White sugar. Fowls' eggs. Cow's milk. Fruit.
3. Lamp oil; sweet oil.
4. Coarse salt. Fine salt.
5. To prepare, cook, food. To put food on the table. To clear away, remove.
6. To eat one's meals. To drink broth.
7. I bought yesterday 300 catties of coal, 50 catties of charcoal, 80 catties of firewood, 4 piculs of rice, and 200 catties of flour.
8. Lamp oil is made from the bean; sweet oil from sesame; lamp-oil costs less than sweet oil.
9. The expression *nung 'huo* means simply *shao 'huo*, to light a fire.
10. When the weather is cold, the consumption of coal and charcoal is larger.
11. In the stove of a stove-bed one uses coal; in a chafing-dish one uses charcoal. A chafing-dish is for use in a room; one cannot cook food or heat water with it.
12. Things to be eaten are either *shêng*, raw, or *shou*, cooked; all that are prepared over fire are *shou*, cooked; the *shêng* are vegetables that may be eaten in their natural state.
13. You go and buy me a small chicken, and three or four eggs. Do you want any milk as well? I should like some catties of milk if it is cheap. In this part of the world we do not buy milk by the catty, but by the cup or bottle. Fruit is not bought by the catty either, but by the piece.
14. Do you prefer bread or rice? Neither, I like broth. What broth? Either meat soup or chicken broth suits me.
15. Go and get the food ready directly, and as soon as it is ready put it on the table.
16. What does *ch'ê liao* mean? The removal of the things when you have done eating.

KEY TO THE TZŬ ERH CHI. Colloquial Series.

1. 京	ching[1]
2. 遠	yüan[3]
3. 近	chin[4]
4. 南	nan[2]
5. 北	pei[3]
6. 路	lu[4]
7. 直	chih[2]
8. 繞	jao[4]
9. 河	'ho[2]
10. 海	'hai[3]
11. 邊	pien[1]
12. 深	shên[1]
13. 淺	ch'ien[3]
14. 船	ch'uan[2]
15. 客	k'ê[4], k'o[4]
16. 店	tien[4]
17. 掌	chang[3]
18. 櫃	kuei[4]
19. 計	chi[4]
20. 受	shou[4]
21. 累	lei[4]
22. 苦	k'u[3]
23. 乏	fa[2]
24. 歇	hsieh[1]
25. 連	lien[2]

進京[1]直走繞著走都可以。筭計[2]道路的遠近直走繞著走遠。南邊[3]北邊。一隻船[4]。坐船[5]過河走海水深水淺。客店掌櫃[6]的辛苦[7]受累乏了歇著。你去年進京在那兒住著在客店裏我聽見說城外頭客店有不很好住的那都看掌櫃的好不好在我說人乏了那兒都好到店裏不過歇著罷了。路愛坐車愛坐船都是看地方兒南邊沒有車走道兒的客人都是坐船走河路都是小船兒走海的船大。河裏[10]的水淺沒有海水深。你前年坐海船不是受了累了麽不錯是颱大風船在山東海邊兒上擱了淺我們那些人辛苦得了不得。船[12]上吃飯是甚麼人管也是船家管。筭計[13]盤費是坐船貴是坐車貴坐車比坐船花的錢多那兒車價比船價貴呢。車價貴都是我們北邊那個車店裏的掌櫃的也要使些個錢。

32

PART III. THE FORTY EXERCISES. *San Yü Chang.*

EXERCISE XV

SINGLE WORDS.

1. *ching*, the capital.
2. *yuan*, far.
3. *chin*, near.
4. *nan*, south.
5. *pei*, north.
6. *lu*, road, way.
7. *chih*, straight.
8. *jao*, winding.
9. *'ho*, river.
10. *'hai*, sea.
11. *pien*, side.
12. *shên*, deep; morally, profound.
13. *ch'ien*, shallow; morally, commonplace, not profound.
14. *ch'uan*, ship.
15. *k'ê, k'o*, stranger.
16. *tien*, shop, inn.
17. *chang*, to superintend.
18. *kuei*, the counter; a till; a safe.
19. *chi*, to reckon; to count.
20. *shou*, to receive; to suffer; hence used in many passive formations.
21. *lei*, to entangle; trouble.
22. *k'u*, bitterness; grief; mental or physical suffering.
23. *fa*, tired.
24. *hsieh*, to rest.
25. *lien*, to join, connect. See Exerc. XVII, ex. 4.

WORDS COMBINED.

1. To go up to, or enter, Peking. To go straight. To go round. Both are practicable; or either will do; or, One may go to Peking either by the straight road or round about.
2. *suan-chi*, to reckon, *tao-lu*, road or journey; *yuan-chin*, distance A straight road is the shortest. A winding road is longer; or, As to distance, the straight road there is the shortest.
3. The south side. The north side.
4. A ship.
5. To be on board ship. To cross a river. To go by sea. The water is deep. The water is shallow.
6. An inn. The inn-keeper; (*lit.* till-director.)
7. Trouble, sorrow. To be in trouble; also, an apologetic expression for giving trouble. To be tired. To be resting.
8. When you went to Peking last year, where did you live? At an inn. I have heard it said that the inns outside the city are some of them not very good to stay at. That is all according as the inn-keeper is a good or a bad one; in my opinion, when one is tired, any inn is good; all you go to it for is to rest yourself.
9. Do you prefer travelling in a cart or by ship? That depends upon the country I am in; there are no carts in the south, and travellers all go by water. The vessels used in river-travelling are small; sea-going vessels are larger.
10. The water in rivers is shallow, not so deep as in the sea.
11. In the voyage you made by sea the year before last, you had a hard time of it, hadn't you? I had. It blew hard, and the ship got ashore on the coast of Shan Tung; all of us who were on board suffered dreadfully.
12. Who looks after the messing on board ship? The people of the ship look after it.
13. Which costs most, travelling by water or travelling in a cart? One spends more travelling in a cart. What? Does the fare of a cart come to more than one's passage on board a vessel? The cart costs more; the reason being that the people we hire our carts of in the north, have also their money to make out of it.

33

KEY TO THE TZŬ ERH CHI. Colloquial Series.

1. 李 li³
2. 箱 hsiang¹
3. 包 pao¹
4. 袋 tai⁴
5. 氈 chan¹
6. 布 pu⁴
7. 餧 wei⁴
8. 駱 lo⁴
9. 駝 t'o²
10. 牲 shêng¹
11. 跟 kên¹
12. 班 pan¹
13. 裝 chuang¹
14. 帶 tai⁴
15. 馱 to⁴
16. 追 chui¹
17. 趕 kan³
18. 喚 huan⁴
19. 無 wu²
20. 利 li⁴
21. 害 hai⁴
22. 春 ch'un¹
23. 夏 hsia⁴
24. 秋 ch'iu¹
25. 冬 tung¹

行李箱子包兒口袋氈子,一定布¹ 餧牲口、駱駝馱子、跟班。² 裝箱子帶³ 東西帶牲口。追趕。⁴ 太利害。春夏秋冬、行李是走道兒的客人帶的東⁵ 西。箱子有皮子做的,有木頭做的,甚麼都可裝得包兒是把東西用甚麼包⁶ 起來,他是拏氈子把那小箱子包起來口袋是裝客碎東西的,我們使的都是⁷ 布口袋。道兒上到店裏得餧牲口。⁸ 駱駝都是口外來的。牲口身上駝著⁹ 東西就叫馱子、驢馱子、騾馱子、馬馱子都說得。你¹⁰ 小心著行李馱子都齊了,我出門去他的¹¹ 跟班的是使喚的人,他叫跟班的把箱子裝在車上,那個人在那兒呢,他出去了,你¹² 跟班的在後頭追趕我追了半天也沒趕上。¹³ 快跑可以趕得上他,他早走了,怕是趕不上罷,無論趕得上趕不上,你快跑著¹⁴ 追他,就是了。

冬¹⁵ 天太冷夏天太熱春沒有冬冷,秋沒有夏熱。

PART III. THE FORTY EXERCISES. *San Yü Chang.*

EXERCISE XVI.

SINGLE WORDS.

1. *li,* properly plums; in the phrase *hsing-li,* baggage, corruptly used for *li,* (see Exercise XX. 13,) to reduce to proper order.
2. *hsiang,* a box, a trunk.
3. *pao,* a bundle; to make into a bundle; to wrap up.
4. *tai,* a bag.
5. *chan,* felt, or similar fabrics.
6. *pu,* cotton fabrics.
7. *wei,* to feed animals.
8. *lo,* the camel with one hump.
9. *t'o,* the camel with two humps; to stow things on the back of a beast.
10. *shêng,* cattle; beasts; (rarely used alone).
11. *kên,* the heel; hence to follow, to accompany.
12. *pan,* properly any set of persons organised to act together; a troop of players; a set of chair-bearers; a guard, &c.
13. *chuang,* to put into; to contain.
14. *tai,* a girdle; to lead, bring.
15. *to,* a beast's load.
16. *chui,* to pursue, fast.
17. *kan,* to pursue, slow or fast.
18. *'huan,* to call aloud.
19. *wu,* not to be, not to have; the opposite of *yu,* to be, to have.
20. *li,* properly sharp-edged; **profit, advantage.**
21. *'hai,* harm; hurt.
22. *ch'un,* spring.
23. *hsia,* summer.
24. *ch'iu,* autumn.
25. *tung,* winter.

WORDS COMBINED.

1. Baggage. Trunk. Bundle. Travelling bag. A blanket, or, piece of felt.
2. A bale of cotton cloth.
3. To feed beasts, domestic or of burden. The camel. The beast that bears a load, whether, horse, mule, ass, or camel.
4. One's retinue; footmen.
5. To put in a box. To carry things with one. To lead, or, to bring, cattle, horses.
6. To pursue.
7. Very dreadful; very dangerous; excessive, but generally of evil in excess.
8. Spring, summer, autumn, winter.
9. The expression *hsing li* comprises whatever a traveller carries with him.
10. Trunks are made some of leather, some of wood, and will hold all sorts of things. A *pao-'rh* is a bundle of things wrapped up in anything. He has wrapped up that small box in a rug. A *k'ou-tai* is a bag to hold odds and ends. The bags we use are made of cloth.
11. On a journey, the beasts have to be fed as soon as one arrives at an inn.
12. Camels all come from beyond the frontier.
13. The beast which bears a load is called a *to-tzŭ.* One may speak of an ass, a mule, or a horse, as a *to-tzŭ.*
14. Take care of the baggage. It will be all right if the baggage is all there.
15. The *kên-pan* are they who take orders (your servants). He called a servant to put his box (or boxes) into the cart (or carts).
16. As I came out his servant came after me, but, though he pursued me for a good while, he did not overtake me.
17. Where is that man? He is gone out. If you run fast enough you will be able to overtake him. He is gone some time, *lit.* early; I fear it will not be possible to overtake him. Whether he is to be overtaken or not, you just run after him as hard as you can.
18. Winter is very cold; summer very hot; spring is not so cold as winter, nor is autumn so hot as summer.

KEY TO THE TZŬ ERH CHI. Colloquial Series.

1.	腦	nao³
2.	辮子	pien⁴
3.	朵	to³
4.	眼	yen³
5.	睛	ching¹
6.	嘴	tsui³
7.	唇	ch'un²
8.	鬍	'hu²
9.	胳	kê¹, ko¹
10.	臂	pei⁴
11.	指	chih³
12.	甲	chia³
13.	抓	chua¹
14.	腰	yao¹
15.	腿	t'ui³
16.	壯	chuang⁴
17.	健	chien⁴
18.	輭	juan³
19.	弱	jo⁴
20.	拉	la¹
21.	拽	chuai⁴
22.	病	ping⁴
23.	疼	t'êng²
24.	奇	ch'i²
25.	怪	kuai⁴

1. 腦袋、辮子、耳朵、眼睛、鼻子、嘴、嘴裏、嘴骨子、鬍子、胳臂、指頭、指甲、腰腿。
2. 壯健、輭
3. 弱。拉著、拽著、拉拽抓破。連著。
4.
5. 有病、很疼奇怪。
6. 人的頭裏頭有腦子就
7. 你這個辮子得梳了。
8. 人老了、耳朵聽不真、眼睛也看不真、那個
9. 人鼻子眼睛長得奇怪。這個人很健壯、那個人輭弱得很。你的身子有病
10. 麼沒有病、我是身子輭弱。
11. 街上那兒躺著的那個人、兩腿都破了。
12. 偺們五六年沒有見你的鬍子都白了、是我的身
13. 子這幾年病得利害。
14. 腰上有病、直
15. 不起來。你這麼慢走、是身子有病麼、不是、是人老了、腰腿都不好。
16. 他的舌
17. 頭有病連嘴骨都破了。嘴裏吃東西、嘴裏說話、都說得。那女人的指甲
18.
19. 長、把他的胳臂抓破了。我的指頭疼。拉車用甚麼牲口呢、用騾子、驢子、馬、
20.
21. 都可以拉得。拽是說人挈手用力的拉、把那門拽住了、他拉拽著我。

PART III. THE FORTY EXERCISES. San Yü Chang.

EXERCISE XVII.

SINGLE WORDS.

1. *nao*, the brains.
2. *pien*, the pigtail; queue worn by Chinese.
3. *to*, a bud; the lobe of the ear.
4. *yen*, the eye. The Numerative of wells.
5. *ching*, the pupil of the eye.
6. *tsui*, the mouth.
7. *ch'un*, the lips.
8. *'hu*, the beard.
9. *kê*, properly the armpit; not used alone.
10. *pei*, the arm in general.
11. *chih*, the finger.
12. *chia*, the nails.
13. *chua*, to catch or claw hold of, as a man with his hand, or a bird with its talons; to clutch.
14. *yao*, the loins; waist.
15. *t'ui*, the thigh; legs.
16. *chuang*, vigorous.
17. *chien*, strong, sound.
18. *juan*, soft.
19. *jo*, weak.
20. *la*, to pull, drag.
21. *chuai*, to haul at.
22. *ping*, illness; disease.
23. *t'êng*, pain, whether from wound or sickness; also, morally, intensity of kindly feeling.
24. *ch'i*, strange.
25. *kuai*, monstrous.

WORDS COMBINED.

1. The head. The queue, or Chinese pigtail. The lobe of the ear. The eye. The nose. The mouth. In the mouth. The lips. The beard. The arm. The finger. The nail. Back and legs.
2. Robust. Weak.
3. Pulling. Hauling at. To haul with great effort. To tear or injure in clutching hold of.
4. Connected, consecutively.
5. To be ill. Very sore. Strange; odd, (in the common sense).
6. A man's *t'ou*, head, has *nao-tzŭ*, brains, inside it, and is accordingly called *nao-tai*, his brain-bag.
7. This tail of yours wants combing.
8. When a man is old, he can neither hear well, *lit*. truly, with his ears, nor see clearly with his eyes.
9. That man has a very odd-looking countenance.
10. This man is very hearty; that man is feeble.
11. Have you anything the matter with you? No; I am weak, but not ill.
12. In these five or six years that you and I have not met, your beard has turned quite white. I have been sadly ailing for some years.
13. That man who is lying on the road has both legs broken.
14. To have something the matter with the back that makes it impossible for one to stand upright.
15. Do you move so slowly because you have something the matter with you? No; it is age which makes me weak both in the back and limbs.
16. He has something the matter with his tongue, and both it and his lips have broken out.
17. It is equally correct to use *tsui li* as the mouth, whether as regards eating or speaking with it.
18. That woman's nails were so long that when she clutched hold of his arm, they tore it.
19. My finger is sore (or, in pain).
20. What beasts are used to draw carts? They may be drawn by mules, donkeys, or horses.
21. The word *chuai* means to pull hard with the hand. Pull the door fast to. He laid hold of me, and would not let me go.

KEY TO THE TZŬ ERH CHI. Colloquial Series.

1. 眉 mei[2]
2. 鬢 pin[4]
3. 顋 sai[1]
4. 頰 {chia[4] / chieh[4]}
5. 巴 pa[1]
6. 頦 k'o[1]
7. 脖 po[2]
8. 嗓 sang[3]
9. 節 chieh[2]
10. 刮 kua[1]
11. 剃 ti[4]
12. 胸 hsiung[1]
13. 背 pei[4]
14. 脊 chi[3]
15. 梁 {liang[2] / niang[2]}
16. 髈 pang[3]
17. 肚 tu[4], tu[3]
18. 波 po[1]
19. 棱 lêng[2]
20. 踝 'huai[2]
21. 脚 chiao[3]
22. 體 ti[3]
23. 斬 chan[3]
24. 賊 tsei[2]
25. 級 chi[2]

1 眉毛、鬢角兒、顋頰下巴頦兒鼻子眼兒脖子嗓子眼兒。2 肩髈兒、脊梁背兒胸前肚子。3 波棱蓋兒踝子骨骨節兒。4 刮臉、剃頭、斬賊首級。5 體面。

6 眉毛是眉棱骨上的毛鬢角兒是腦門子兩邊兒的頭髮。7 顋頰是嘴兩邊兒體面。8 嘴下頭的骨頭是下巴頦兒。9 肩髈兒是胳臂的上頭。10 兩個肩髈後頭的地方兒叫脊梁背兒。11 腦袋下頭叫脖子前頭叫嗓子。12 胸前是脖子以下肚子以上。13 波棱蓋兒是腿中間兒的骨頭節兒脚上頭的骨頭節兒。14 年輕的人沒鬍子的時候兒得拏刀子刮臉。15 剃頭、剃的是那辮子以外的短頭髮不剃頭的那個賊就叫長髮賊。16 拏住賊就斬斬下來的腦袋就叫首級。17 說體面人、是說那個人的行止沒有甚麼不好說那個人長得體面、是說他長得好看。18 他那個房子蓋得體面也說得。

PART III. THE FORTY EXERCISES. *San Yü Chang.*

EXERCISE XVIII.

SINGLE WORDS.

1. *mei*, eyebrows.
2. *pin*, the hair on the temples.
3. *sai*, the jaws.
4. *chia, chieh*, the jaws.
5. *pa*, the name of a place; used corruptly as part of the combination meaning the chin.
6. *k'o*, the lower part of the face.
7. *po*, the neck.
8. *sang*, the throat, within and without.
9. *chieh*, joints, of the bones; of the bamboo tree, &c.
10. *kua*, to scrape with a knife; to scrape the hair off an animal's skin.
11. *t'i*, to shave.
12. *hsiung*, the breast.
13. *pei*, the back.
14. *chi*, the spine.
15. *niang*, the spine; properly read *liang*, a horizontal beam; (the spine of beasts being horizontal.)
16. *pang*, the shoulders.
17. *tu* 4, the belly; *tu* 3, the entrails.
18. *po*, waves.
19. *lêng*, an edge.
20. *'huai*, the ankle.
21. *chiao*, the feet.
22. *t'i*, the body.
23. *chan*, to behead.
24. *tsei*, robbers; rebels; any malefactors.
25. *chi* 4, a step in gradation; here *chi* 2, the heads of criminals.

WORDS COMBINED.

1. The eye-brows. The hair on the temples; *lit.* the temples' horns or corners. The jaws; (read both *sai-chia* and *sai-chieh*.) The chin. The nostrils. The neck. The throat, inside or out. The gullet.
2. The shoulders. The spine. The back between and just below the shoulders. The breast. The belly.
3. The knee-cap. The ankle-bone. The joints.
4. To scrape the face (take the hair off). To shave the head; (the Chinese tonsure). To cut off the head of a malefactor.
5. Respectable; also, and very commonly of persons or things, nice-looking.
6. The eye-brows are the hair above the eyes. The *pin-chiao-'rh* is the hair on either side of the forehead.
7. The *sai-chieh* are the flesh on either side of the mouth.
8. The bone below the mouth is *hsia-pa-k'o-'rh*, the chin.
9. The shoulders are at the top of the arms.
10. The space between, *lit.* behind, the shoulders is called the *chi-niang* and the *chi-niang-pei-'rh*.
11. What is below the head is called the neck; the fore part of it is called the throat.
12. The chest, or breast, is below the throat, and above the belly.
13. The knee, *lit.* knee-cap, is the joint in the middle of the leg. The joint above the foot is called the ankle.
14. When people are too young to have beards, their faces have to be scraped with a razor.
15. In the Chinese tonsure, what is shaved off is the short hair growing outside the pigtail. Outlaws who do not shave the head are called long-haired rebels.
16. When a rebel is laid hands on, he is beheaded, and the head cut off is spoken of as his *shou-chi*.
17. When you say *t'i-mien jên*, you mean that the person's conduct is unexceptionable; when you say that such a person *chang-tê t'i-mien*, you mean that he is goodlooking.
18. You may also say that that house of so-and-so's is *t'i-mien*; (that it is a fine house).

KEY TO THE TZŬ ERH CHI. Collóquial Series.

1. 君 chün¹
2. 民 min²
3. 主 chu³
4. 爵位 {chio² chüeh² ch'io²}
5. 位 wei⁴
6. 參 ts'an¹
7. 贊 tsan⁴
8. 尊 tsun¹
9. 武 wu³
10. 兵 ping¹
11. 缺 ch'üeh¹
12. 額 ngê², ngo²
13. 捐 chüan¹
14. 充 ch'ung¹
15. 謀 mou²
16. 策 ts'ê⁴
17. 殺 sha¹
18. 退 t'ui⁴
19. 勒 lê², lê⁴
20. 索 so³
21. 中 chung¹
22. 底 ti³
23. 全 ch'üan²
24. 姓 hsing⁴
25. 名 ming²

君上下民主子家主兒底下人。¹
爵位參贊尊貴。²
官民文官武官官兵。³
民人姓名百姓。⁴
捐官充當。⁵官人。⁶謀算計策殺退。⁷全是。⁸官民就是官長下民小官民。¹¹

君上是百官萬民的主子家主兒是底下人的主人。¹⁰

爵位尊是說人做的官大說小官不算爵位比方參贊的官爵位的額數有一定的有開了缺的得補沒補的缺得找人充補。¹²

管民的是文官帶兵的是武官。¹³

官兵的額數有一定的有甚麼真本事是人充數兒是假的沒有。¹⁴⁻¹⁵

說民人充兵當那都是他做兵。用銀子錢買官那叫捐官。¹⁶⁻¹⁷

去年賊很多帶兵的大官全是謀算不好不會定計策叫賊全跑了那¹⁸

退到河北裏見人就殺河北的官民會齊了追趕把賊全殺退了。

那賊頭兒¹⁹的姓名知道不知道有一個姓黃名龍是賊中的頭兒。

PART III. THE FORTY EXERCISES. *San Yü Chang.*

EXERCISE XIX.

SINGLE WORDS.

1. *chun*, the sovereign.
2. *min*, the people.
3. *chu*, a master.
4. *chio, chueh*, high rank, whether official or hereditary.
5. *wei*, properly the position of a person, the place where he stands or sits; specially, high position; hence the Numerative of gentlemen, scholars, officials.
6. *ts'an*, to counsel.
7. *tsan*, to assist.
8. *tsun*, honored.
9. *wu*, military.
10. *ping*, soldier.
11. *ch'ueh*, to vacate, vacancy.
12. *ngê*, classically, the forehead; colloquially, a fixed number.
13. *chuan*, to subscribe for a public purpose.
14. *ch'ung*, to stand for, or, in the place of; to act as, play the part of.
15. *mou*, to conceive a design: to plan; to plot.
16. *ts'ê*, plans; means proposed to an end.
17. *sha*, to kill.
18. *t'ui*, to retire; to drive back.
19. *lê*, to bind; to coerce. Obs. *lê* 2 *so, lê* 4 *ling*.
20. *so*, to drag; to extort.
21. *chung*¹, central.
22. *ti*, the bottom; below.
23. *ch'uan*, all; entire.
24. *hsing*, family name.
25. *ming*, name.

WORDS COMBINED.

1. The sovereign. The people below him. The lord or master. The master of the house. His inferiors, the servants.
2. Official position or dignity. The resident minister's assistant or deputy in certain Chinese colonies. Of honorable rank.
3. Officers and people; or, government and people. Civil authorities. Military authorities. Government troops.
4. To remove from office for sickness or misconduct. To fill, succeed to, a vacancy. A given number.
5. To purchase a grade of rank by subscribing to the State's necessities. To serve as.
6. Official understrappers (clerks, &c.)
7. To project, make calculations. Plans, projects. To repulse the enemy with loss.
8. The whole is; or, They all are . . . ; or, it is all because. . . .
9. People, s c. not officials; or Chinese as opposed to Bannermen. Name and surname. The hundred surnames, the people of China; any *plebs*.
10. The *chun-shang*, sovereign, is the lord over all his subjects, official and unofficial; the *chia-chu-'rh*, master of the house, is *chu-jên*, master over his servants.
11. The expression *kuan-min*, government and people, means the authorities and the people below them; the common, *lit* small, people, or lower orders, are also called *po-hsing*, the hundred surnames.
12. When you say that a man's "position" is honorable, you mean that his office is considerable; in speaking of a small official, you do not assume that he has any "position." The *ts'an-tsan*, for instance, is an officer of high position.
13. Officials who have charge of the people are *wên kuan*, civilians; those who command troops are *wu kuan*, military officers.
14. The strength of the army is fixed; when any one is dismissed, his vacancy has to be filled up; people have to be found to supply vacancies that have not been filled up.
15. The expression *ch'ung shu-'rh*, to make up the number, is used of a counterfeit, that does not possess in reality the properties [it claims to have], it may be said either of men or things.
16. If you say that such an one of the people *ch'ung ping* or *tang ping*, you mean, in either case, that he is serving as a soldier.
17. When an office, or, rank, is obtained for money, it is said to be a *chuan-kuan*, an office obtained by subscription.
18. Last year there was a good deal of brigandage, and the measures adopted by the high officers in command of the troops were ill-devised in every instance; they were quite incompetent to plan a campaign; so much so that they let the outlaws all escape. The outlaws retired to the north of the river, where they killed every one they met. The authorities and people north of the river assembled and pursued them, and drove them back with loss.
19. Do you know the name of the brigand (or, rebel) chief? There was a man named Huang Lung who was chief among them.

KEY TO THE TZŬ ERH CHI. Colloquial Series.

1. 國 kuo²
2. 章 chang¹
3. 程 ch'êng²
4. 卡 k'a¹, ch'ia¹
5. 倫 lun²
6. 巡 hsun²
7. 察 ch'a²
8. 刻 k'ei¹
9. 搜 sou¹
10. 律 lu⁴
11. 例 li⁴
12. 治 chih⁴
13. 理 li³
14. 暴 pao⁴
15. 虐 nio⁴
16. 亂 lan⁴, luan⁴
17. 謬 miu⁴, niu⁴
18. 普 p'u³
19. 羣 ch'ün²
20. 耕 kêng¹
21. 耨 nou⁴
22. 囊 nang²
23. 總 tsung³
24. 謂 wei⁴
25. 之 chih¹

章程定章。 卡倫巡察搜拏搜察刻搜。 律例³。 治亂⁴。 治理道理理會。 暴虐大亂太謬。 普天下。 一羣⁸。 耕耨耕田。 囊中¹⁰。 名目¹¹。 西路那邊兒道¹²。

兒上有卡倫是盤察出入人的那卡倫都有一定的章程過客的行李總得搜察。 城門¹³的官兵巡察是有定章也不可太刻搜。 國家¹⁴定的律例是治理百姓的不是出於暴虐中國的道理不教而殺謂之虐。 耕耨¹⁵是小民的本分夏天人人都耕田。 近年¹⁶天下大亂是官長治理得不好是普天下百姓知道的。 那塊兒¹⁷的官太謬不肯聽話百姓告訴他說賊快來了他總不理會全不治理地方也不搜拏賊過了一會兒賊就來了殺燒得利害得很那跑了的一羣百姓囊中都沒有錢苦得了不得。 百姓¹⁸一齊跑著謂之一羣騾馬牛羊好些個在一塊兒也有這個一羣的名目。 天下¹⁹治亂總在於官。

42

PART III. THE FORTY EXERCISES. *San Yü Chang.*

EXERCISE XX.

SINGLE WORDS.

1. *kuo*, a nation, a government.
2. *chang*, a rule, a law.
3. *ch'êng*, a stage in a journey.
4-5. *k'a-lun*, a customs'-barrier; a Manchu word.
6. *hsun*, to go the rounds.
7. *ch'a*, to enquire into.
8. *k'ei*, a popular pronunciation of *k'ê*; see Exerc. IX. 16; only sounded *k'ei* when joined to *sou*.
9. *sou*, to search, as the person, baggage, &c.
10. *lu*, statutes
11. *li*, laws, amendments.
12. *chih*, to regulate; to reform; to restore order.
13. *li*, regulating principle, or force; also, to manage, to regulate.
14. *pao*, passionate, fierce; the opposite of soft, gentle.
15. *nio*, tyrannical.
16. *lan*, *luan*, disorder.
17. *miu*, also read *niu*, perverse, contrary.
18. *p'u*, universal.
19. *ch'un*, a flock, drove.
20. *kêng*, to till.
21. *nou*, to weed.
22. *nang*, a purse, bag.
23. *tsung*, to collect; collectively.
24. *wei*, to speak of; to esteem as; to style or call.
25. *chih*, used in books, as the pronoun of the third person, and the sign of the possessive; also in some instances, comparatively rare, in the spoken language.

WORDS COMBINED.

1. Regulations. To make definite arrangements.
2. An inland customs' barrier. To go one's rounds and make enquiries. To make search for and seize; as robbers, &c. To search, as the person, baggage, &c. To annoy, act vexatiously to.
3. Laws; the penal code.
4. Order and disorder; or, to restore order.
5. To keep order, or, to restore it. Right principle, the principle of anything. To observe, to notice.
6. Brutally tyrannical. Great disorder. Very perverse.
7. The whole empire; or world; *lit*. all under heaven.
8. A whole herd or multitude.
9. To plough and to weed. To till the fields.
10. In a purse or bag.
11. A denomination.
12. In the west country yonder there are *k'a-lun*, customs' stations, on the road, whose business it is to search (or, for the purpose of searching,) every one that is coming in or going out. The *k'a-lun*, have got rules by which the baggage of passengers must in every case be examined.
13. The guards on the city gates have also got fixed rules for their rounds and their investigations; but it is not right that they should be vexatious, (or, over strict).
14. The laws have been passed by the State for the administration of the people; they do not proceed from any tyrannical motive. It is a principle with the Chinese government that to put to death those who have had no instruction, is tyrannical.
15. Agricultural labour is the proper business of the humbler classes; in the summer every one is tilling the ground.
16. That the great disorder [that has prevailed] of late years is due to the maladministration of the authorities, is a fact known to the people of the whole empire.
17. The official there is very self-willed, and would not hear what was said: the people told him that the rebels would be there soon, but he paid no attention; did nothing whatever to restore order in the country; nor did he make any search for rebels. A short time after, the rebels did come, and burned and slaughtered in the most dreadful way. The people fled in numbers, and, not one of the multitude having money in his purse, they suffered sadly.
18. When the people fly all together, they are said to be a *ch'un*, a drove or crowd. The same term *ch'un* may be applied to mules, horses, oxen, or sheep, when collected together in any number.
19. The condition of the empire, its order or disorder, depends altogether upon the government.

KEY TO THE TZŬ ERH CHI. Colloquial Series.

1.	搶	ch'iang³
2.	奪	to²
3.	偷	t'ou¹
4.	股	ku³
5.	逃	t'ao²
6.	竄	ts'uan⁴
7.	散	san⁴
8.	混	'hun⁴
9.	懶	lan³
10.	惰	to⁴
11.	棍	kun⁴
12.	扔	jêng¹
13.	放	fang⁴
14.	槍	ch'iang¹
15.	恰	ch'ia¹
16.	巧	ch'iao³
17.	特	t'ê⁴
18.	意	i⁴
19.	偶	ou³, ngou³
20.	然	jan²
21.	成	ch'êng²
22.	硬	ying⁴
23.	按	an⁴, ngan⁴
24.	思	ssŭ¹

搶奪偷東西。一股賊。¹ 逃竄逃散。² 混跑混說。³ 懶惰。⁴ 一根小棍子一條⁵ 槍一桿槍裝槍放槍。⁶ 扔東西。恰⁷ 巧特意偶然自然按著。⁸ 成人成事。⁹ 背¹⁰

著人拏東西不教人知道是偷把人家的東西硬拏了去就是搶奪不分夜裏白日都說得。那一股賊都逃散了。¹¹ 山東那一股賊竄到河南去了百姓見了賊都四下裏混跑。說話沒有理那算是混說。¹² 人不愛用工夫，謂之懶惰。那¹³ 一天有倆賊一個拏著一條長槍一個拏著一條大棍子混打恰巧有¹⁴ 人拏著一桿槍來了，看見了那個賊混打，趕著裝上槍就打那個賊呢那賊扔下棍子就跑了帶著鳥槍的那個人是特意來的，還是偶然來的，怕是偶然來。那¹⁵ 的也不定。他那個人很懶惰怕不是成人的人不愛念書那兒可以成呢，人¹⁶ 的心裏有力自然可以成事。人不按著道兒走，就是混走。¹⁷

PART III. THE FORTY EXERCISES. *San Yü Chang.*

EXERCISE XXI.

SINGLE WORDS.

1. *ch'iang*, to take by violence.
2. *to*, to snatch away.
3. *t'ou*, to steal.
4. *ku*, classically, but not colloquially, the leg or thigh; also, collectively, of banditti, &c., a gang or band.
5. *t'ao*, to fly as a fugitive.
6. *ts'uan*, to escape as rats, mice.
7. *san*, to disperse.
8. *'hun*, mingled in confusion, like the water of torrents.
9-10. *lan-to*, idle.
11. *kun*, a staff.
12. *jêng*, to cast, to throw.
13. *fang*, to release, let go.
14. *ch'iang*, a spear; a musket.
15. *ch'ia*, to coincide with exactly.
16. *ch'iao*, cunning.
17. *t'ê*, special, particular.
18. *i*, meaning, purpose.
19. *ou*, accidental.
20. *jan*, thus by nature; positively.
21. *ch'êng*, to make, become.
22. *ying*, hard.
23. *an*, *ngan*, properly, to press with the hand; ordinarily, according to.
24. *ssŭ*, to think.

WORDS COMBINED.

1. To steal; take from with violence. To filch things.
2. A body of thieves, brigands, rebels.
3. (Of the above persons,) to make one's way furtively from one place to another. To disperse as fugitives from justice.
4. To run helter-skelter. To talk wild or confusedly.
5. Idle.
6. A small staff. A spear. A musket. To load a musket. To fire it.
7. To fling a thing.
8. In the nick of time; in exact coincidence. On purpose; with express intention. By accident. Of course; naturally; so being of one's own power or authority. According to.
9. To be, or become, a man; hence, to succeed in life. To complete an affair.
10. When a man takes a thing unobserved, without letting any one know, that is *t'ou*, to steal, pilfer. To take away anything from a person by force, is *ch'iang-to*, to rob. The phrase may be used of robbery whether committed by night or by day.
11. That body of robbers have fled and dispersed.
12. The robbers in Shan-Tung have found their way into Ho Nan. When the people saw the robbers coming, they fled pell-mell in every direction.
13. To talk without reference to the right (or to reason), is what is considered *'hun shuo*, talking wild.
14. When a man will not work, he is said to be *lan-to*, idle.
15. The other day two robbers, the one armed with a long spear, the other with a large staff, were assaulting people right and left, when it fortunately happened that some one with a musket came up. Seeing the robbers so engaged, he made haste and loaded and fired. And what did the robbers do? The robber with the staff threw it down and ran away. Did the man with the gun make his appearance designedly, or by accident? Probably by accident, but I am not sure.
16. That man is very idle; I am afraid he will not turn out well. If a man will not study, how is he to succeed in life? If a man has moral energy, he will be sure to accomplish anything he may undertake.
17. Not to keep the path when one is walking, is *'hun tsou*, to walk wild, to run off the line, &c.

KEY to the TZŬ ERH CHI. Colloquial Series.

1.	凡	fan[2]
2.	揣	ch'uai[3]
3.	摩	mo[1]
4.	約	yo[1]
5.	准	chun[3]
6.	否	fou[3]
7.	更	kêng[1]
8.	改	kai[3]
9.	妥	t'o[3]
10.	當	tang[1]
11.	專	chuan[1]
12.	失	shih[1]
13.	神	shên[2]
14.	參	ts'ên[1]
15.	差	tz'ŭ[1]
16.	忙	mang[2]
17.	向	hsiang[4]
18.	規	kuei[1]
19.	幹	kan[4]
20.	辦	pan[4]
21.	法	fa[2]
22.	胡	hu[2]
23.	鬧	nao[4]
24.	掄	lün[1], lun[1]
25.	催	ts'ui[1]

1. 凡事大約。2. 凡論專說。揣摩[3]。3. 揣摩著幹事辦理法子。4. 准否准了、更改妥當。5. 專心失神太忙參差。6. 定向定規。7. 幹事辦事辦理法子。8. 胡鬧混掄催[9]人。10. 凡做事總得有定向。11. 來的人是誰、我揣摩著是姓張的、大約是他[12] 那一件事還沒有辦妥當章程得改也不知道李大人准否、大約沒有甚麼更改了。不可太忙辦事太忙就有參差了。要幹甚麼事先得定規立准了主意就謂之定向。13 念書寫字都得專心也。14 要幹事的時候兒心裏不在、那就叫失神。定[16]安了辦事的法子就叫定規。那[17]個人有一件要事得趕辦他、一點不忙、同人催他快著些兒他不肯聽拏著棍子混掄眞是胡鬧。論[18]事不能指定那就同謂之凡論說那一股賊有幾萬、那就是賊數兒的大凡。以[19]上這幾章是專說大股賊的多。他[20]那個人辦理甚麼事、都辦得不妥當、多有參差不齊。

PART III. THE FORTY EXERCISES. *San Yü Chang.*

EXERCISE XXII.

SINGLE WORDS.

1. *fan*, all whatsoever.
2. *ch'uai*, to feel, or feel for, by thrusting in the hand.
3. *mo*, to feel with the fingers.
4. *yo*, an agreement.
5. *chun*, to authorise; true to a course.
6. *fou*, if not; or, not.
7. *kêng*[1], to change.
8. *kai*, to change.
9. *t'o*, secure, satisfactory.
10. *tang*, to suit, to be fit, or according to rule (or pattern).
11. *chuan*, single, special.
12. *shih*, to lose, miss.
13. *shên*, spirits, divine or human; animal spirits.
14-15. *ts'ên-tsü*, irregular, uneven, *e.g*, like foliage.
16. *mang*, to hasten; busy.
17. *hsiang*, to face towards; towards; direction.
18. *kuei*, rule.
19. *kan*, to concern.
20. *pan*, to administer.
21. *fa*, method, fashion.
22. *'hu*, wildly, blindly.
23. *nao*, to be in a rage; to occur when it should not occur.
24. *lun*, to whirl about, as a mace, &c.; *lun*, to brandish, as the fist.
25. *ts'ui*, to urge.

WORDS COMBINED.

1. All matters whatsoever. Most probably.
2. In general terms. To speak with special reference to.
3. To guess.
4. To authorise or to negative. To have authorised; or, it is authorised. To alter, modify. Secure, satisfactory.
5. With the mind specially devoted to. To be absent in mind. Over hasty. Irregular, incomplete.
6. To determine one's direction. The line to be taken; or, to decide on such a line.
7. To attend to, to interest one's self in, busy oneself about, a matter. To dispose of a matter or matters, despatch business. To be engaged in administering. A way, method.
8. An unreasonable outbreak. To brandish or flourish wildly.
9. To press any one, as for payment of a debt, termination of an affair, &c.
10. In any affair the line to be taken should invariably be determined first.
11. Who is it that is come? I imagine that it is Chang. The probability is that it is he.
12. That matter is not satisfactorily disposed of yet. The regulations require alteration; but I do not know whether His Excellency Li will approve it or not. Most likely no alteration will take place.
13. Reading and writing both require undivided attention; nor must one be in too great a hurry. The consequence of over-haste in the transaction of business, is that mistakes are made; or, that it is not turned out ship-shape.
14. If one wants to engage in any affair, one's line = policy, must be settled beforehand; when one's views are fairly settled, one is said *ting hsiang*, to have laid down a course.
15. When one is engaged in anything, and one's mind is somewhere else, one is said *shih shên*, to be absent.
16. The determination of the way in which anything is to be done, is called *ting kuei*, completion of arrangements, or settlement of course of action.
17. That man had a matter of importance in hand, which it was necessary he should dispose of as soon as possible; but he would not hurry himself at all, and when some one who was acting with him urged him to make a little more speed, he would not listen, but began to strike wildly about him with a big stick; an unreasonable outbreak truly.
18. The treatment of any proposition as general, not particular, is termed *fan lun*. When one says, such a body of banditti is several thousand strong, one is speaking in a general way of their number. (For *nêng*, the fourth word in this example, see Exerc. XXIV. 22).
19. The foregoing exercises (chapters) have most of them been confined to what regards banditti.
20. There is an irregularity and incompleteness in every affair, no matter what, that that man deals with.

47

KEY TO THE TZŬ ERH CHI. Colloquial Series.

1.	諭	yü³
2.	句	chü⁴
3.	吵	ch'ao¹, ch'ao³
4.	喧	hsüan¹
5.	嚷	jang³
6.	哼	ʽêng¹, ʽheng¹
7.	阿	a¹
8.	哈	ʽha¹
9.	嘎	ka¹
10.	訛	ngê², ngo²
11.	衰	shuai¹
12.	困	k'un⁴, k'uên⁴
13.	極	chi²
14.	夢	mêng⁴
15.	貌	mao⁴
16.	美	mei³
17.	陋	lou⁴
18.	摔	shuai¹, shuai³
19.	掉	tiao⁴
20.	擱	ch'o¹, ch'uo¹
21.	揝	tsuan⁴
22.	搋	chai⁴
23.	則	tsê²
24.	況	k'uang⁴
25.	且	ch'ieh³

言語一句話。吵鬧喧嚷哼阿哼的。哈哈的笑嘎嘎的笑冷笑。訛錯氣血衰困極了做夢。貌美貌陋。摔了掉下來掉下去揝了搋住地方兒揝。他的言語你懂得不懂他這麼哼阿哼的我一句話都聽不出來他那一個人我也不愛同他說話一則我一開口他就是哈哈的笑二則他說的話也訛錯的多況且他那個土音我聽著很費事。城門口兒的地方那外頭是甚麼人喧嚷跟班的趕車的他們吵鬧呢。老頭子氣血衰困極了躺在道兒上做著夢說話那些人都嚷嚷的笑他。你看那兩個小人兒一個很貌美一個很貌陋那貌美的笑話那貌陋的生了氣把茶碗摔碎了有人說了他兩句他害怕就說茶碗是掉下去的揝住他的辮子要拉了他去他倒在地下把胳臂揝了。

48

PART III. THE FORTY EXERCISES. *San Yü Chang.*

EXERCISE XXIII.

SINGLE WORDS.

1. *yü*, language; sayings.
2. *chu*, a clause, sentence.
3. *ch'ao*, to wrangle (of two or many).
4. *hsüan*, to make an uproar; (said of many).
5. *jang*, to talk too loud.
6. *ĕng* or *'hĕng*, a stammering sound.
7. *a*[1], an ejaculation; sometimes interrogative.
8. *'ha*, a sound of loud laughter.
9. *ka*, a sound of laughter.
10. *ngĕ, ngo*, wrong, untrue.
11. *shuai*, decayed, worn out.
12. *k'un, k'uên*, surrounded; embarrassed; fatigued.
13. *chi*, extreme, excess.
14. *mêng*, a dream.
15. *mao*, personal appearance.
16. *mei*, handsome; also, (morally,) fine, becoming, goodly.
17. *lou*, mean, vulgar.
18. *shuai*, to throw, dash down.
19. *tiao*, to hang (neuter).
20. *ch'o, ch'uo*, to jar by a fall.
21. *tsuan*, to grasp in the hand.
22. *chai*, narrow.
23. *tsê*, then; in consequence.
24. *k'uang*, besides.
25. *ch'ieh*, also; in the next place.

WORDS COMBINED.

1. Speech, what is said. A sentence of talk.
2. Altercation (*ch'ao* [3] *nao*). Uproar; noise of loud voices; (*ch'ao* [1] *jang*). Stuttering and stammering.
3. To laugh loud. To laugh. Forced smile or laughter.
4. Wrong, in error.
5. Worn out constitution. Extremely tired; as tired as one can be. To dream.
6. Of handsome appearance. Of vulgar appearance.
7. Flung down (*shuai* [1]). To drop down (neuter; said by a spectator who is below.) To drop down (neuter; the spectator being above.) To have jarred, or given a shock to, hand or foot by a fall. To grasp tight.
8. The place is narrow; there is not much space.
9. In the first place; in the second place. Moreover.
10. Do you understand what he says (or, when he talks)? Stammering as he does, I cannot make out one word (*lit.* a single sentence). I don't like talking with the man myself; firstly, because the moment I open my mouth, he bursts out laughing; and, in the next place, a large portion of what he says is incorrect; besides, it gives me a good deal of trouble to understand that dialect of his.
11. There is but little space at the city-gates for the large number of carts and horses that are moving through them in opposite directions.
12. Who is it that is making such a noise outside? The servants and carters are wrangling about something or other.
13. The old man's constitution was broken, and he was as tired as he could be, so much so that he lay down in the road and began to talk in his sleep; on which those people all began to laugh at him.
14. Look at those two little fellows; one of them is very good looking, the other very much the reverse. The good looking one was making fun of the vulgar one, and the latter in a rage smashed a tea-cup. Some one found fault with him for this; he was frightened, and said that the tea-cup had fallen down. They took hold of his pigtail, and were trying to drag him away, when he fell down and hurt his arm by the shock.

1.	兆	chao⁴
2.	古	chi²
3.	凶	hsiung¹
4.	祥	hsiang²
5.	瑞	jui⁴
6.	安	ngan¹
7.	寗	ning²
8.	順	shun⁴
9.	寬	k'uan¹
10.	綽	ch'o⁴
11.	貧	p'in²
12.	窮	ch'iung²
13.	窘	chiung³
14.	恆	hêng²
15.	產	ch'an³
16.	朋	p'êng²
17.	友	yu³
18.	賞	shang³ᵃ
19.	相	hsiang¹
20.	幫	pang¹
21.	留	liu²
22.	能	nêng²
23.	丟	tiu¹
24.	根	kên¹
25.	現	hsien⁴

¹先兆吉兆凶兆祥瑞。²安寗順當。³寬綽貧窮很窘。⁴恆產。⁵好朋友。⁶賞東西賞錢幫人銀錢。⁷留下不能丟了。⁸底根兒現在現今目下。⁹事情不論吉凶都有個先兆兒。¹⁰事情沒來之先看見天上有甚麼可以知道日後有祥瑞凶就謂之吉兆。家裏的錢足用的是寬綽錢太少過日子不順當日後怕過¹²日子有准進的錢那就叫做恆產。¹¹百姓沒有恆產家事就不安寗地方官趕著賞了些米把逃的百姓都留住了。那就謂之吉兆。甚麼是安寗呢。¹³比方去年河南那一塊兒那就是不安寗地方兒鬧得大亂那時候兒我甚麼都丟了找不能安寗了。甚麼是¹⁴有收成民人甚麼都丟了人人兒窘得很。¹⁵一個朋友說俗們這些年的相好你幫我幾個錢肯不肯。¹⁶那¹⁷他說沒有甚麼肯兒真是不能我們底根兒有那些錢現在恆產沒了一個大錢都沒有連我自己也沒喫的。

PART III. THE FORTY EXERCISES. *San Yü Chang.*

EXERCISE XXIV.

SINGLE WORDS.

1. *chao*, a presage, an omen.
2. *chi*, auspicious.
3. *hsiung*, inauspicious.
4. *hsiang*, good fortune; that which bodes good fortune.
5. *jui*, the same as *hsiang*.
6. *ngan*, repose.
7. *ning*, tranquillity.
8. *shun*, obedient; hence, following.
9. *k'uan*, broad; liberal.
10. *ch'o*, of exceeding extent; said of place, fortune, &c. (inseparable in the spoken language from *k'uan*).
11. *p'in*, poor.
12. *ch'iung*, extremity; hence, poverty.
13. *chiung*, straitened, of space or fortune.
14. *'hêng*, constantly enduring.
15. *ch'an*, to produce; productions; property.
16. *p'êng*, friend, properly from circumstances.
17. *yu*, friend, properly from feelings.
18. *shang*, to bestow on.
19. *hsiang*, mutual; also indicating the unreciprocated relation of one person or thing to another.
20. *pang*, to assist.
21. *liu*, to keep, detain.
22. *nêng*, to be able.
23. *tiu*, to lose.
24. *kên*, root of a tree.
25. *hsien*, now; present time.

WORDS COMBINED.

1. A presage. A good omen. An ill omen. Prosperous condition of a person, house, or state.
2. Peace and quietness; (state of freedom from danger) Proceeding as it ought.
3. Comfortable, in easy circumstances. Poor. Having very small means.
4. Property producing regular income; wherewithal to go on with.
5. A good friend.
6. To bestow a thing. To present any one with a present of money. To help any one with a loan, or present, of money.
7. To retain. To be unable. To have lost; it is lost.
8. At the root; originally. Now. At this time. At the present moment.
9. Things that come to pass may be good or evil, but in either case there is a presage of their coming.
10. When, before a thing comes to pass, there is a something in the sky by which it is known that there will be happiness at some future time, that is called an auspicious omen.
11. When there is money enough in a house for its expenses, that is *k'uan ch'o*, comfort; when there is not enough for daily need, that is called *p'in ch'iung*, poverty.
12. When there is a regular income to provide for daily subsistence, there is said to be *'hêng ch'an*, property producing a regular income.
13. The people having no regular income, their households cannot go on comfortably, and it is to be feared that they will be disposed not to be *an-ning*.
14. What is *an-ning*?
15. To give an instance; last year, over in Ho Nan, it rained for several days in succession; there was no autumn harvest; the people lost everything, and every man being in a state of extreme indigence, serious disturbances ensued in the country. That was not *an-ning*, a state of peace. The local authorities lost no time in giving the people some rice, and by this means they prevented those who were about to fly from doing so.
16. I lost everything at the time, and I looked out for a certain friend of mine, and I said to him, "We have known each other these ever so many years, will you help me with a little money?"
17. He said, "It is not that I will not, but really that I cannot. My people had a little money as you know. We have now no income; not a cash. I myself have not bread to put into my mouth."

KEY TO THE TZŬ ERH CHI. Colloquial Series.

1. 您 nin²
2. 喳 cha¹
3. 親 ch'in¹
4. 旁 p'ang²
5. 祖 tsu³
6. 翁 wêng¹
7. 兄 hsiung¹
8. 孫 sun¹
9. 舍 shê⁴
10. 弟 ti⁴
11. 奴 nu²
12. 才 ts'ai²
13. 迎 ying²
14. 接 chieh¹
15. 葬 tsang⁴
16. 絲 ssŭ¹
17. 團 t'uan²
18. 絨 jung²
19. 尺 ch'ih³
20. 貨 huo⁴
21. 昂 'ang²
22. 替 ti⁴
23. 挑 t'iao¹

您¹ 尊重² 旁人³ 祖上、老翁、家兄、舍弟、子、孫、兒子、孫子、奴才、喳得一聲迎⁵ 接⁶ 下葬。一團絲幾尺絨土貨。替我⁸ 挑好的。昂貴¹⁰ 粗細¹¹ 稱人¹² 您我的家祖、就是我父親、喳得一聲、迎⁴ 好阿、令祖好阿、是問您祖您父親的安。向人稱自已的弟兄、可以稱老翁。旁人的父親、可以稱老翁。是有點兒尊重人的意思您好您多喳來的、就使得。一團絲幾尺絨土貨。替我挑好的。令¹⁵ 祖好阿令尊好阿、是問您祖您父親的安。向人¹⁶ 稱自已的弟兄、說的是家兄舍弟稱人家的弟兄、是說令兄令弟。我¹⁷ 兒子的兒女、是我的孫子孫女。奴才¹⁸ 就是使喚的人、有是買的、有不是買的、還是說底下人的多。家¹⁹ 主兒叫底下人喳得一聲、是順著聽話的意思。今²⁰ 兒家祖回來、我去迎接、後兒他們老翁下葬、我得幫幫他們去。那²¹ 絲不是你們這兒的土貨麽、可不是麽那絨還一團是粗的、一團是細的。那²² 絲不是土貨請您替我挑一點兒好的、近來價錢昂貴、一尺不下二錢多銀子。

52

PART III. THE FORTY EXERCISES. *San Yü Chang.*

EXERCISE XXV.

SINGLE WORDS.

1. *nin*, more commonly pronounced *ni-na*, which, again, is short for *ni lao jên-chia*; politely, you my elder; you, Sir, or Madam.
2. *cha* (rather *dja*), a sound taken from the Manchu; Yes, Sir, or Madam.
3. *ch'in*, intimate relationship.
4. *p'ang*, the sides.
5. *tsu*, ancestors.
6. *wêng*, an old man; used of him, not to him.
7. *hsiung*, an elder brother.
8. *sun*, a grandchild.
9. *shê*, a cottage; politely, in certain phrases, my house.
10. *ti*, a younger brother.
11. *nu*, slave,—but also used, disparagingly, of inferiors not slaves.
12. *ts'ai*, talent; but when coupled with *nu*, as below, it does not appear to affect the sense of *nu*.
13. *ying*, to go out to meet an equal or superior; to welcome him.
14. *chieh*, to receive a present, guest, &c.
15. *tsang*, to bury.
16. *ssŭ*, silk, spinning or winding; not yet made into a fabric.
17. *t'uan*, a ball; lump; as of silk, cotton, &c.
18. *jung*2, woollen cloth, velvet, worsted; very coarse silk
19. *ch'ih*, the Chinese foot of ten Chinese inches.
20. *'huo*, goods, merchandise.
21. *ang*, rising, risen.
22. *ti*, to supply the place of; for, instead of.
23. *t'iao*, to carry on the shoulder; to select.

WORDS COMBINED.

1. You, Sir, or Madam.
2. To respect; deserving of respect.
3. A bystander; a third person. One's ancestors. An old gentleman My elder brother My younger brother. Sons and grandsons; posterity A son. A grandson. A slave
4. To *dja*, or to have *dja*-d; to answer. Yes, Sir!
5. To receive, go to meet; as a parent, visitor, &c.
6. To bury.
7. A ball of silk. Some feet of woollen cloth, &c. Native, or local, goods; produce of such a country or district.
8. For me, supplying my place.
9. To choose a good one, or good ones.
10. High price; rising in price.
11. Coarse and fine.
12. The form *nin*, You, Sir, is a somewhat respectful form of addressing a person. To say, *nin 'hao*, Are you well, Sir? or *nin to-tsan*, &c, When did (or will) you come, Sir, is quite correct.
13. My *chia-tsu*, grandfather, is my father's father.
14. The father of a third person may be spoken of as his *lao wêng*, his old man.
15. Is the honored grandfather well? Is the honored worshipful one well? are enquiries after the grandfather or father of the person addressed.
16. When one is speaking to any one of one's own brothers, the form used is *chia hsiung*, the elder brother of my family; *shê ti*, the younger brother of my cottage In speaking any one else of his brothers, the form is the honored elder brother, or the honored younger brother.
17. The sons and daughters of my son, are my *sun-tzŭ, sun-nu*, grandsons and granddaughters.
18. The term *nu ts'ai* means simply servants; some are property (slaves), some are not; but the more common phrase is *ti-hsia jên*, inferiors.
19. When the master calls, and the servant cries out *dja*, his doing so signifies that he hears the call and will obey it.
20. My grandfather returns to-day, and I am going to meet him to offer my respects. Their father will be buried the day after to-morrow, and I shall have to lend a hand at the funeral.
21. One of those balls of silk is coarse, the other is fine
22. Is not silk a product of your country here? To be sure it is; but velvet is not, and I shall be obliged to you to choose me some that is good. The price has gone up of late; it is not less than two mace and more a foot.

KEY to the TZŬ ERH CHI. Colloquial Series.

1.	想	hsiang³
2.	怎	tsên³
3.	却	ch'io⁴ / ch'üeh⁴
4.	睡	shui
5.	覺	chiao⁴ / chio² / chüeh²
6.	對	tui⁴
7.	賽	sai⁴
8.	嗇	sê⁴
9.	吞	t'un¹
10.	疊	tieh²
11.	次	tz'ŭ⁴
12.	增	tsêng¹
13.	葱	ts'ung¹
14.	苗	miao²
15.	嫩	nên¹ / nun¹
16.	桑	sang¹
17.	樹	shu⁴
18.	林	lin²
19.	森	sên¹
20.	綠	lu⁴
21.	草	ts'ao³
22.	溼	shih¹
23.	曬	shai⁴
24.	晒	shai⁴

想[1]著。怎[2]麼。却[3]是。睡[4]覺。相對。倆人賽[5]對賽。嗇[6]刻[7]吞[8]了。向來[9]

怎麽呢。大家都喝酒,你就睡了覺了麽。你想[15]這個錢不是他吞了,却是誰

草木,青草苗兒老嫩,桑樹樹林子綠森森。溼[13]了曬乾。

他們倆人對賽著寫字那個姓李的寫的字比你的好不好,我們向來沒賽過。

怎麽知道他好不好。他[17]那倆兄弟利害得很,都是過於嗇刻,不肯花錢。他們

的銀錢一天比一天增多,那個兄弟還是疊次吞人家的錢,那個[18]葱這兩天

貴不分老嫩,都是二百錢一斤。分[19]牛羊肉的好歹,也有老嫩之說。草[20]木是

花草樹木的總名草本的東西,一出土兒叫苗兒。苗[21]子是四川東南的人分

生的熟的。樹[22]多謂之樹林子那桑樹林子綠森森的。樹[23]林子底下的地溼

得很。要[24]把溼衣裳弄乾了,得鋪在日頭地裏曬一曬,曬乾了就疊起來罷。

PART III. THE FORTY EXERCISES. *San Yü Chang.*

EXERCISE XXVI.

SINGLE WORDS.

1. *hsiang*, to think; to think of.
2. *tsên*, never met with in talk except when followed by *mo*, and then the final *n* is not heard; the dissyllable being pronounced *tsê-mo*. See below.
3. *ch'io, ch'üeh*, properly to reject a present; a strong disjunctive, to be rendered sometimes by our word *but*, sometimes by emphasis only.
4. *shui*, to sleep.
5. *chiao*, properly to perceive, feel, in which sense it is sometimes pronounced *chio* and *chüeh*; when joined with *shui*, to sleep, it does not affect the sense of *shui*.
6. *tui*, opposite to; to agree with; a pair.
7. *sai*, to compete with.
8. *sê*, niggardly.
9. *t'un*, to swallow, bolt down; oftener used figuratively of peculation, avarice, &c.
10. *tieh*, in folds or layers; repeatedly.
11. *tz'ŭ*, the place of any person or thing below the first place in a series.
12. *tsêng*, to add to.
13. *ts'ung*, onions.
14. *miao*, sprouts; the first appearance of any vegetation.
15. *nun*, tender, fresh, as opposed to tough, stale.
16. *sang*, the mulberry tree.
17. *shu*, a tree.
18. *lin*, a wood, forest.
19. *sên*, density as of foliage.
20. *lu*, green.
21. *ts'ao*, grass; plants, not being trees.
22. *shih*, wet; damp.
23. *shai*, a verb describing the action of the sun's rays; not necessarily to scorch.
24. *shai*, a vulgar form of the foregoing character.

WORDS COMBINED.

1. Thinking, to be thinking.
2. How? What?
3. It is nevertheless the fact that . . . .
4. To sleep.
5. Opposite one another; also, agreeing together.
6. Two persons rivalling one another. Competing.
7. Niggardly, miserly.
8. Has swallowed, as food, absorbed, as advantages.
9. Heretofore.
10. There have been many added. Time after time, repeatedly. (Observe *tieh* abbreviated).
11. A catty of onions.
12. Plants and trees, the vegetable kingdom. Grass, herbs. Sprouts of any vegetation Tough and tender. The mulberry tree. A grove or wood. The green (of the foliage) is deep, or dense.
13. To be damp. To dry by the action of the sun.
14. How is this? How is it that you have been in bed, or lying down, when all the rest, or the whole party, are drinking?
15. Just think, if it was not he who absorbed (pocketed) this money, (or the money,) who could it have been?
16. Those two men are writing one against the other. Does that man Li write better than you or not? How should I know how he can write? We have never had a trial together.
17. Those two brothers are dreadful; they are too niggardly; they won't spend anything. Their money increases every day. That younger brother has pocketed other people's money over and over again.
18. Onions have been dear these last two days; stale and fresh alike, they have been all two hundred cash the catty.
19. The words *lao nun*, tender and tough (or, fresh and not fresh,) are used to distinguish the qualities of beef and mutton as well as of other things.
20. The term *ts'ao-mu* is generic of flowers, plants, and trees. Anything which grows as grass, as soon as it comes up, is called *miao-êrh*, sprouts.
21. The Miao Tzŭ are people to the southeast of Ssŭ Ch'uan, they are divided into Wild and Reclaimed.
22. A number of trees is called *shu-lin-tzŭ*, a grove or wood. How deep (or dense) the green of that mulberry grove is!
23. The ground under a grove of trees is very damp.
24. If you want to dry damp clothes, you should spread them out in a sunny place for the sun to shine on them; when the sun has dried them, they may be folded up.

1.	某	mou³
2.	乍	cha⁴
3.	初	ch'u¹
4.	和 別	'hai⁴, 'ho²
5.	別	pieh²
6.	素	su⁴
7.	原	yüan²
8.	待	tai⁴
9.	敦	tun¹
10.	厚	'hou⁴
11.	薄	pao², po²
12.	傲	ngao⁴
13.	嫉	chi⁴
14.	妒	tu⁴
15.	慚	ts'an²
16.	愧	k'uei⁴
17.	絕	chüeh²
18.	交	chiao¹
19.	實	shih²
20.	憑	p'ing²
21.	賓	pin¹
22.	拜	pai⁴
23.	應	ying¹
24.	陪	p'ei²

某人。¹ 乍見。² 起初原是，原來，平素。厚刻薄，傲慢，傲慢，待慚愧嫉妒。某人¹¹是不說出姓名來的人，有某人嫉妒我這個好兒的刻薄原是嘴裏的刻薄話心裏的刻薄卻是敦厚的對面兒。實在。⁶ 憑他。⁷ 可憑。⁸ 賓客相拜。陪着正陪。⁹ 和⁴我和別人待人相待。親熱厚薄敦初乍見某人是平素沒見過的人初次見他，多日沒見的人見了，也可以說乍見，是一見之見。他¹³和我不和別人也不對，他待人沒有不敦厚的，實在沒可慚愧。他們倆起初相好近來絕了交了。他¹⁵不分厚薄待人都是刻薄他這個人不同待人沒有不敦厚大待人有點兒傲慢那一天有賓客來拜他卻不見他說的話呢，您去理應是見我的爵位原來大的沒有一句可憑的我還要拜他去見不見憑他。陪著您去好不好憑他慢待我可以不論。專¹⁶主的是幫同的是陪。

PART III. THE FORTY EXERCISES. *San Yü Chang.*

EXERCISE XXVII.

SINGLE WORDS.

1. *mou*, certain ; as, a certain man.
2. *cha*, suddenly, unexpectedly.
3. *ch'u*, the first ; when first.
4. *'hai*, (properly *'ho*; see Exerc. IX. 6,) together with, in relations with.
5. *pieh*, to distinguish, to separate ; hence another.
6. *su*, of uniform plainness ; hence, uninterruptedly through past time ; heretofore.
7. *yuan*, origin, beginning ; in fact.
8. *tai*, towards ; to await.
9. *tun*, morally sound ; staunch ; generous.
10. *'hou*, thick ; staunch.
11. *pao, po*, thin.
12. *ngao*, proud.
13. *chi*, not used, in speaking, without the following *tu*, with which it is the same in meaning.
14. *tu*, envious, jealous.
15. *ts'an*, to be ashamed.
16. *k'uei*, to be ashamed ; shame.
17. *chüeh*, to cut off, interrupt, as a stream, supplies, intercourse ; to be so cut off.
18. *chiao*, to interchange ; intercourse.
19. *shih*, true ; also solid as opposed to hollow.
20. *p'ing*, to lean upon, depend on.
21. *pin*, guest, stranger, as opposed to *chu*, Exercise XIX. 3, in the sense of host.
22. *pai*, to salute, visit, pay respects to
23. *ying* 1, (not to be confounded with *ying* 4 in Exercise XXIX.) to conform to what is right ; ought
24. *p'ei*, to play second to, as a candidate in reserve; to bear one's guest company.

WORDS COMBINED.

1. A certain person.
2. To meet suddenly; or to come upon for the first time.
3. At the very beginning. In fact ; or, indeed it is. In fact; in the first instance. In all past time; heretofore.
4. With me. With another person. Towards a person , treating, behaving to, a person. Behaviour to each other; or behaviour to another.
5. Very intimate. Thick and thin ; also, intimately and slightly related. Staunch; liberal. Mean; vexatious. Proud, arrogant. To behave to haughtily, discourteously. To be ashamed. Envy, jealousy ; to feel it.
6. True, truly.
7. It depends on him ; as he pleases.
8. That may be relied on.
9. A guest, visitor. To visit one another, behaviour.
10. Acting as second to ; bearing one company. Principal and second ; nominee and reserve nominee.
11. The expression *mou jên*, a certain person, is used when the person's name is not mentioned; [*e.g.*] A certain person begrudges me these advantages, and acts most unhandsomely towards me. The word unhandsome, *k'ê-po*, here means, in a word, that his language is illiberal ; but *k'ê-po*, as a sentiment, is the opposite of *tun-'hou*, staunch, cordial, liberal.
12. *cha chien*, is the sight one gets of another for the first time. When I say I have *cha-chien* a certain person, I mean that I have seen for the first time, a person whom I had never seen before. One may also say it after seeing a person whom one has not seen for a long time.
13. He is not on good terms with me, nor does he agree with any one else ; he makes no difference between friends and acquaintances ; he treats every one with the same illiberality, or, behaves equally ill to all alike This other man is not like him ; he behaves ill to no one; he has certainly nothing to be ashamed of
14. They *were* friends once upon a time, but of late they have discontinued intercourse with one another.
15. *A*. His position is a high one no doubt, and he treats people with some haughtiness. A visitor called on him the other day, but he would not see him. Not a word he says can be relied on either. *B*. I shall go and call on him nevertheless ; he may see me or not as he pleases *A*. You, Sir ? If *you* call, of course he will see you. What do you say to my accompanying you, Sir ? He may be uncivil to me if he pleases ; that will not signify.
16. The chief or principal, the independent authority, is *chêng* ; his auxiliary is *p'ei*, his second (or, acts as second to him).

57

1.	裱	piao³
2.	糊	ʽhu²
3.	匠	chiang⁴
4.	染	jan³
5.	顏	yen²
6.	紅	ʽhung²
7.	藍	lan²
8.	淡	tan⁴
9.	新	hsin¹
10.	舊	chiu⁴
11.	紗	sha¹
12.	氈	tʽan³
13.	必	pi⁴
14.	須	hsü¹
15.	光	kuang¹
16.	潤	jun⁴
17.	玻	po¹
18.	璃	li²
19.	料	liao⁴
20.	擦	tsʽa¹
21.	碰	pʽêng⁴
22.	裂	lieh⁴
23.	行	ʽhang²

裱糊。¹匠人。²一疋紗、一疋布、氈子。³新的光潤、舊的顏色兒太淡染紅的染藍的都行。玻璃料貨、⁵必須、⁶擦一擦。⁷碰著、⁸碰壞了、破了、碰破了、破裂裂了、碎了、破碎。窗戶紙裂了、⁹叫裱糊匠來糊上單張紙糊在那兒是糊雙張兒紙糊在一塊兒是裱。各行的¹⁰手工人叫匠人的多木匠瓦匠鐵匠都說得。布是綿花做的、紗是絲做的。有一塊布、有一塊紗、¹²顏色兒舊了必須染別的顏色原舊的顏色兒是紅的、還可以染藍的要染甚麼顏色、都憑人家的主意。你¹³瞧那一疋紅紗顏色光潤不光潤怎麼是光潤呢、那紗原來是好紗又是新的染得顏色又好看這光潤不止於說紗說別的也行。料貨¹⁴是玻璃東西的總名。我¹⁵拏那個玻璃瓶來、要擦一擦、碰在桌子上、破壞了。有兩隻船¹⁶相碰、這一隻壞了、那一隻破碎了。茶碗¹⁷掉在地下碎了。

PART III. THE FORTY EXERCISES. *San Yü Chang.*

EXERCISE XXVIII.

SINGLE WORDS.

1. *piao*, to paste two sheets of paper together.
2. *'hu*, to paste paper, cloth, &c., against another substance.
3. *chiang*, workman, artificer.
4. *jan*, to dye.
5. *yen*, colours.
6. *'hung*, red.
7. *lan*, blue.
8. *tan*, weak (as of tea); pale (as of colours).
9. *hsin*, new.
10. *chiu*, old.
11. *sha*, crape.
12. *t'an*, a rug, carpet.
13. *pi*, necessarily; must.
14. *hsu*, must.
15. *kuang*, brightness.
16. *jun*, moist.
17-18. *po-li*, (said to be derived from a Sanscrit word,) glass of all kinds.
19. *liao*, properly materials; but, as below, often specially applied to glassware.
20. *ts'a*, to rub with the hand, or a cloth, &c.
21. *p'êng*, to run against, come violently in contact with.
22. *lieh*, to crack of itself, as wood or paper.
23. *'hang*, a vulgar modification of *hsing*, or *'hang*, Radical 144; a trade or calling. (See below, ex. 10.)

WORDS COMBINED.

1. To paste paper against paper or cloth.
2. A workman, or artificer of any kind.
3. A bale of crape. A bale of cotton goods. A carpet, rug.
4. The new are bright; the old, if much faded, may be dyed either red or blue.
5. Glass. Vitreous ware in general.
6. Necessary, necessarily must.
7. To give a thing a rub.
8. Running up against; in collision with. To have injured, or to be injured seriously by a collision. To have broken, or, torn; to be broken or torn. To have broken, or, to be broken by a collision. To crack and break. To have cracked of itself. To be broken into pieces. To break or be broken in pieces; to be in tatters.
9. The paper of the window is cracked; tell a paper-hanger to come and mend it. To paste a single sheet of paper on any place is *'hu*; two sheets pasted together are *piao*. (Observe *ch'uang*, abbreviated. See Exerc. III. 15.)
10. The term *chiang*, is applied to handicrafts men in most trades, you may say *mu-chiang*, a carpenter, *wa-chiang*, a bricklayer, *t'ieh-chiang*, a blacksmith.
11. Shirtings are made of cotton; crape is made of silk.
12. Such a piece of cotton cloth, such a piece of crape, being faded, it must be dyed some other colour; if its old colour were red, it might be dyed blue; what colour it shall be dyed must depend entirely on the opinion of the person interested.
13. Look at that piece of red crape, and tell me if it is not *kuang-jun*. What does *kuang-jun*, mean? That, in the first place, the crape is good crape; then that it is new; and besides that it is dyed a good colour. The expression *kuang-jun*, glossy, is not used only of crape; it is equally applicable to other things.
14. *liao 'huo* is a generic term for all vitreous ware.
15. I was bringing that glass bottle here to give it a rub, when I bumped it against the table, and smashed it.
16. There were two vessels which ran foul of one another; one was injured desperately, and the other was smashed to pieces.
17. A tea-cup fell on the ground and was smashed.

1.	剛	kang¹
2.	纔	ts'ai²
3.	再	tsai⁴
4.	等	têng³
5.	取	ch'ü³
6.	送	sung⁴
7.	落	{la⁴ / lao⁴ / lo⁴}
8.	永	yung³
9.	湊	ts'ou⁴
10.	挪	no²
11.	拴	shuan¹
12.	套	t'ao⁴
13.	商	shang¹
14.	量	{liang¹ / liang²}
15.	彀	kou⁴
16.	斟	chên¹
17.	酌	cho²
18.	疑	i²
19.	惑	'huo⁴
20.	喊	'han³
21.	答	ta¹
22.	應	ying⁴
23.	從	ts'ung²
24.	末	mo⁴

剛纔。等著從來從前。再來再三再四。永遠。末了兒。取東西、送東西。落下了挪開湊到一塊兒。拴牲口套車。量米、不彀。一石。斟酌。剛纔我們在這兒論起這件事來、再三的喊他過來、後永遠不改了。樹酌等了半天他不答應。喊叫答應。剛纔我們在這兒論起這件事來、再三的喊他過來、他都不肯再把錢送了去了。叫你把箱子挪開了、在我說石數兒怎麼挪那麼遠。這米、我量了不彀五石一個單套車就拉了。不止五石不是二套車怕拉不了。我是南邊來的、從來沒坐過車那趕車的到店裏立刻就要錢、我疑惑從來沒這個理、叫他等一等再來。

PART III. THE FORTY EXERCISES. *San Yü Chang.*

EXERCISE XXIX.

SINGLE WORDS.

1. *kang*, properly, hard, which meaning in certain combinations it retains; with the following character it has an intensive force.
2. *ts'ai*, just now; but a moment ago.
3. *tsai*, again, the second time; then.
4. *têng*, a class or grade; to wait.
5. *ch'u*, to fetch, bring; take for oneself.
6. *sung*, to carry to, or present; to accompany.
7. *la, lao, lo*, down; to descend; *la*, to leave behind
8. *yung*, eternal. [one, leave out.
9. *ts'ou*, to add to a body or number; to assemble, of men or things; active or neuter; see note on *ex* 17; (corruptly written with Radical 15).
10. *no*, to move, actively, from one place to another.
11. *shuan*, to tie up, animals, things; not men.
12. *t'ao*, generally a closely-fitting case or envelope; a noose; a loop; a head-stall; the leader's reins in a cart.
13. *shang*, a trader; to consult.
14. *liang*, to calculate.
15. *kou*, enough.
16. *chên*, properly to pour out wine. In colloquial language it has not this sense, but is joined with
17. *cho*, the combination signifying to deliberate, whether with another or oneself.
18. *i*, doubts; to doubt.
19. *'huo*, to doubt; not used alone in the spoken language.
20. *'han*, to cry aloud; to halloo.
21. *ta*, to reply.
22. *ying*^{4}, echo; to echo; to respond to.
23. *ts'ung*, proceeding from; forth from.
24. *mo*, the end; *lit.* the tip of anything that runs to a point.

WORDS COMBINED.

1. A moment ago.
2. Waiting. Heretofore. Formerly.
3. Come again. Thrice and four times.
4. For evermore.
5. At the end; at last.
6. To take or fetch a thing. To carry a thing to; to present a thing.
7. *la hsia liao*, to have omitted a thing; to be dropped out of a number of persons or things. To move a thing away from. To assemble things or persons together.
8. To tie up the beasts. To get a cart ready; to harness the mules or horses, or put them to.
9. To measure rice.
10. Not enough.
11. One stone, or picul.
12. To deliberate, alone or with another. To consult with or together. To doubt.
13. To call to. To answer; also, to assent, promise.
14. We were talking of this affair here just now, and we called to him again and again to come over and consult with us, but after waiting ever so long he made no answer. I suspect he did not hear.
15. We were, (or have been,) deliberating half the day before we made our arrangements definitively, and they will now never more be changed.
16. He was requested again and again to come over to us, but he did not; and, after all, I had to go to him before he would.
17. Ten of us agreed in the first instance to put some money into a business. Some time after, two withdrew, and others took out their capital; and when I saw this, I did not choose to put any more money in either.
18. Because I told you to move the box away, why should you have moved it so far?
19. *A.* According to my estimate this rice does not amount to five piculs, and a one-horse cart will do to draw it. *B.* In my opinion there is not so little as five piculs, and I don't think that less than two beasts will draw it.
20. I am from the south, I have never travelled by cart before; and the moment we got to the inn, the carter asked for his money. I suspected that this was not the rule, so I told him to wait awhile and come again.

1.	臺	tʻai²
2.	灣	wan¹
3.	江	chiang¹
4.	湖	ʻhu²
5.	流	liu²
6.	浪	lang⁴
7.	闊	kʻuo⁴
8.	浮	fou², fu²
9.	橋	chʻiao²
10.	井	ching³
11.	坑	kʻêng¹
12.	衚	ʻhu²
13.	衕	tʻung²
14.	巷	hsiang⁴
15.	野	yeh³
16.	屯	tʻun²
17.	墳	fên²
18.	墓	mu⁴
19.	峯	fêng¹
20.	嶺	ling³
21.	尖	chien¹

臺灣。江河湖海長江流水順流波浪寬闊。浮橋。一眼井一個坑一條衚衕。大街小巷野地屯裏墳墓。山峯山嶺兒峯嶺。尖兒。臺灣是中國東南海裏的地方兒南北兩頭兒山嶺兒也多也大那峯嶺也很好看。江河湖海是天下大水的總名兒。俺們這兒的小河兒很窄有浮橋就可以過去那江面有地方兒寬闊和湖相同一路都是順流到了江西那兒的山水也可以。那長江之流打西到東湖北來的船到江西去同山峯是高而尖的山嶺也高就是沒有那尖的。尖兒那個字眼兒是個個不廢刀尖筆尖都說得。京城裏沒有河水喝的都是井水。京城裏的買賣大半在大街上開鋪子衚衕小巷都是住家兒的多。城外頭沒甚麼住家兒的就叫野地連有墳墓的也罷。民人湊到一塊住的北邊那就叫屯。

PART III. THE FORTY EXERCISES. *San Yü Chang.*

EXERCISE XXX.

SINGLE WORDS.

1. *t'ai,* a terrace.
2. *wan,* curving; a bay or indentation in the sea-shore.
3. *chiang,* a river; see *'ho,* Exercise XV. 9.
4. *'hu,* a lake, any large sheet of water.
5. *liu,* to flow.
6. *lang,* waves, larger than *po;* see Exerc. XVIII. 18.
7. *k'uo,* spacious.
8. *fou, fu,* floating, moveable.
9. *ch'iao,* a bridge.
10. *ching,* a well.
11. *k'êng,* a pit, natural or artificial.
12-13. *h'u-t'ung,* a small street; an alley.
14. *hsiang,* a small street, an alley.
15. *yeh,* properly uninhabited ground, but often country as opposed to town; hence, wild, savage.
16. *t'un,* a village; the country as opposed to the town.
17. *fên,* a grave, tomb.
18. *mu,* a grave, a tomb; rarely used without the preceding word *fên.*
19. *fêng,* the peak of a hill.
20. *ling,* a height not peaked.
21. *chien,* a projecting point, of a knife, a hill, &c.

WORDS COMBINED.

1. T'ai-wan, Formosa, the island and its principal city.
2. Rivers and streams, lakes and seas. The Long River, (the Yang-tzŭ Chiang.) Water flowing. Following the stream; hence, moving, proceeding freely, smoothly. Waves. Wide, of large space.
3. A flying or floating bridge.
4. A well. A pit. A street or lane.
5. A large street. A small street or lane. Uncultivated ground, or desert; the country. In the country; out of town. A tomb, or cemetery.
6. The peak, or peaks of a hill. Mountains not peaked. Hills or mountains collectively.
7. A point; (pronounced *chierh.*)
8. T'ai-wan (Formosa) is a place in the sea southeast of China, the northern and southern extremities of which are very mountainous, the heights being of considerable elevation; the mountain scenery is at the same time very picturesque.
9. The phrase *chiang, 'ho, 'hu, 'hai,* rivers, streams, lakes, and seas, designates in general terms the greater waters of the empire.
10. Our small rivers here are so narrow that they can be crossed by moveable bridges. The Great River is as broad as a lake in some places.
11. The course of the Great River is from west to east. Vessels from Hu Pei to Chiang Hsi go with the stream all the way. The scenery when you get to Chiang Hsi is rather fine.
12. The mountain peaks in a *shan-fêng* are no two alike. A *shan-fêng* is lofty and pointed. A *shan-ling* is also a height, but not of peaked form.
13. The term *chien-'rh* may be equally applied to the point of a knife, a pencil, or the like.
14. There is no river water in the capital; what is drunk is all well-water.
15. Trade in the capital is for the most part conducted in shops on the great streets; the houses in the lanes and small streets are, principally, dwelling houses.
16. The country outside the city-walls where there are no habitations, is called *yeh ti;* even when there are graves on it, it is so regarded.
17. Any place [in the country] where people come together so as to form a community, is called in the north a *t'un.*

KEY TO THE TZŬ ERH CHI. Colloquial Series.

1. 男 nan²
2. 爺 yeh²
3. 娘 niang²
4. 幼 yu⁴
5. 輩 pei⁴
6. 頑 wan²
7. 耍 shua³
8. 蠢 ch'un³
9. 笨 pên⁴
10. 獃 tai¹
11. 冒 mao⁴
12. 爽 shuang³
13. 靜 ching⁴
14. 舒 shu¹
15. 服 fu²
16. 艱 chien¹
17. 難 nan²
18. 耐 nai⁴
19. 羞 hsiu¹
20. 辱 ju², ju⁴
21. 討 t'ao³
22. 嫌 hsien²

¹男女男人女人爺們娘兒們老爺老爺²老幼老少長輩晚輩獃子蠢笨冒失。爽⁵快拉縧。安靜熱鬧。舒⁷服欠安。艱⁸難耐著。羞⁹辱討人嫌。男¹⁰女就是爺們娘兒們賊把男女老少都殺了。是不分年高年輕的都不舒服。和祖父一輩兒的是長輩和兒孫一輩兒裏的事情。蠢笨是粗而無能的別名就是獃子是外面不明白的樣子某人獃得很實在蠢笨都可以說得。頑¹³耍¹⁴是小人兒們弄甚麼頑意兒要刀就是武本事的是晚輩了。是不該說的話說了不該做的事做了就是冒失。說¹⁶話做事不會拉縧就是爽快。人¹⁷心安靜是說人心裏平定他是個安靜人不愛熱鬧。心¹⁸裏沒累是舒服身上欠安也謂之不舒服。日¹⁹子不好過是艱難總得耐著。自²⁰已不體面討人嫌受了人的不好話謂之羞辱他吞了錢受大家羞辱。

PART III. THE FORTY EXERCISES. *San Yü Chang.*

EXERCISE XXXI.

SINGLE WORDS.

1. *nan*, male.
2. *yeh*, properly a father, but forming part of certain appellations of honour, and other words.
3. *niang*, properly a mother; but, in certain combinations, any woman.
4. *yu*, of tender years.
5. *pei*, a generation.
6. *wan*, childish, trifling; to trifle, to play.
7. *shua*, to flourish as a weapon in fencing.
8. *ch'un*, loutish, in form, or mind, or both.
9. *pên*, of things, unwieldy; of man, stupid.
10. *tai*, silly; idiotic.
11. *mao*, out of place; a word descriptive of obtrusiveness, of doing that which one ought to let alone.
12. *shuang*, of weather, bright, cheery; of man, lively, free from care.
13. *ching*, at rest, as opposed to unquiet.
14. *shu*, properly open, unrolled.
15. *fu*, complying, obedient; (it has many meanings beside.)
16. *chien*, very difficult.
17. *nan*, difficult.
18. *nai*, to endure, put up with; to endure, or last.
19. *hsiu*, shame; to blush.
20. *ju*, to insult.
21. *t'ao*, to exact, demand.
22. *hsien*, to dislike.

WORDS COMBINED.

1. Man and woman. One's husband. One's wife. The men. The women. Sir, or, a gentleman.
2. *lao yu*, old and young. *lao shao*, old and young. Observe *shao* 4, not as in Exerc. I. 17, *shao* 3. One's elders. One's juniors.
3. To play, trifle. A toy; or, playing with a toy. To play with the sword, or other weapon of the kind.
4. An idiot. Stupid. To blunder, in act or speech.
5. Frank, prompt, brisk. To dilly-dally.
6. Still, quiet. Noisy; bustling.
7. Comfortable; well in health. To be indisposed.
8. Difficult. Bearing patiently.
9. To abuse, revile deservedly. To provoke people's dislike.
10. The words *nan nu* simply mean men and women. The rebels slew all without distinction of age or sex.
11. Were you to say, His whole family, *lao* and *yu*, are sick alike, you would mean that both those who are of a respectable age, and those who are not, are all indisposed without distinction.
12. The generation which is the contemporary of your father and your grandfather, is the *chang pei*, the senior generation; that which is the contemporary of your son and your grandson is the *wan-pei*, the junior (later) generation.
13. *wan-shua* is the playing of little children with anything; *shua-tao* is to play (fence, &c.) with the sword; it is a martial accomplishment.
14. The expression *ch'un-pên* describes a person who is coarse or vulgar, and without ability; *tai-tzŭ* means that a man, to judge from his appearance, is not intelligent. You may either say, Such a person is very *tai*, or that he is indeed *ch'un-pên*.
15. To say what one ought not to say, to do what one ought not to do, is *mao-shih*, to blunder, to commit oneself.
16. *shuang k'uai* is the reverse of hesitation in speech or dilatoriness in action.
17. A man's mind is said to be *an-ching*, when it is steady or sober. He is a quiet, or sober-minded person; he does not like noise (bustle, gaiety, &c.)
18. When the mind is free from care, a man is *shu-fu*; when he is indisposed, it is equally correct to say of his body that it is not *shu-fu*.
19. It is a hard case when one is troubled to get one's daily bread; there is nothing for it but patience.
20. One is said to be *hsiu-ju*, (deservedly abused, denounced in strong language, put to shame,) when having provoked people to dislike one for disreputable conduct, one is reviled by them. Every one tells him what a scoundrel he is for the way he gets hold of money.

KEY TO THE TZŬ ERH CHI. Colloquial Series.

1. 皇	ʻhuang²
2. 宮	kung¹
3. 朝	chʻao²
4. 廷	tʻing²
5. 建	chien⁴
6. 臨	lin²
7. 強	chʻiang²
8. 良	liang²
9. 禁	chin⁴
10. 舞	wu³
11. 爲	wei²
12. 匪	fei³
13. 反	fan³
14. 犯	fan⁴
15. 罪	tsui⁴
16. 死	ssŭ³
17. 黨	tang³
18. 爭	chêng¹
19. 鬪	tou⁴
20. 號	ʻhao⁴
21. 靖	ching⁴
22. 恩	ngên¹
23. 赦	shê⁴
24. 免	mien³
25. 隨	sui²

皇上朝廷。建立²皇宮³。臨民臨死⁴。鼓舞⁵。良民強暴。禁止⁷禁地。反了⁸爲匪、賊匪死黨爭鬪⁹。號令地方不靖犯罪¹⁰。恩典赦罪寬免難免¹¹。皇上¹²朝廷、都說得是主子家。朝廷隨地酌情建立地方官爲臨民的官。臨¹⁴地方官賞給銀錢。有事情民人出了力。地方官賞禁止民人不准出入。這地方¹⁷頭裏都筭禁地、向例禁止民人不准出入。皇宮¹⁶裏頭都筭禁地、向例禁止民人不准出入。走、是快要走的時候臨死是就要死。那是鼓舞的意思。皇宮¹⁶裏頭大爲不靖、每有強暴兩下裏爭鬪難爲良民那官不管末了兒良民也反了、近來的官很好把從前的事情都反過來、把那賊匪全都平了。賊匪湊¹⁸的多、爲黨爲股。和賊頭兒最親近的是死黨。號令¹⁹是帶兵的官出的口號法令、兵不聽號令、就是犯了大罪。赦罪²⁰、是人犯了罪皇上隨事酌情寬免了、那都是皇上的恩典受恩赦罪之後、再有爲匪的那寶在難免死罪。

PART III. THE FORTY EXERCISES. *San Yü Chang.*

EXERCISE XXXII.

SINGLE WORDS.

1. *'huang*, august, imperial.
2. *kung*, an imperial palace.
3. *ch'ao*, properly to see the emperor, as at court; any dynasty of China.
4. *t'ing*, properly a hall of assembly; specially the emperor's court.
5. *chien*, to set up, establish.
6. *lin*, to descend, to approach to.
7. *ch'iang*, energetic; often over-energetic, violent.
8. *liang*, virtuous, good.
9. *chin*, to prohibit.
10. *wu*, to gesticulate, make postures like a dancer.
11. *wei* ², to do, to be.
12. *fei*, wrong-doing; wrong-doer.
13. *fan*, to turn upside down; hence, to rebel.
14. *fan*, to stumble against; to offend; to incur a penalty.
15. *tsui*, properly punishment; also, offences, great or small.
16. *ssŭ*, to die.
17. *tang*, a gang, a band; in a bad sense, a political party.
18. *chêng*, to emulate; to wrangle, or fight with.
19. *tou*, to fight with or without arms.
20. *'hao*, a signal; visible, as a flag; audible, as a bugle-call.
21. *ching*, quiet, as a country free from disorder.
22. *wên*, goodness to an inferior.
23. *shê*, pardon, amnesty; as of the act of a government.
24. *mien*, to avoid; to cause to avoid, dispense with.
25. *sui*, following after; according to.

WORDS COMBINED.

1. His Majesty. The court.
2. To establish.
3. The Imperial Palace.
4. Near, in immediate relations with the people. To be about to go. To be about to die.
5. To encourage zeal.
6. Virtuous people, or, good subjects. The lawlessly violent.
7. To prohibit. Forbidden ground.
8. Upset; to turn rebel. To play the robber; to become one. Brigands, rebels, outlaws of any kind. The sworn rebels, or robbers, of the gang. To fight, squabble.
9. Words of command.
10. A country, or region, not quiet; in a state of disorder. To commit an offence.
11. Grace or bounty. To grant amnesty. Gracious remission. To escape with difficulty; hardly avoidable.
12. The meaning of both '*Huang-Shang* and *Ch'ao Ting*, (or the person meant by both expressions,) is the Sovereign.
13. The sovereign is guided by place and circumstances in his establishment of local authorities to be in near relations with the people.
14. *lin-tsou* means that the time is near when one will be going; *lin-ssŭ* means that one is about to die presently.
15. When the people have exerted themselves in any matter, and the local authorities make them a present of money, they do so for the purpose of stimulating their zeal.
16. The interior of the emperor's palace is all considered sacred ground; the common people have always been forbidden to pass through it.
17. This place used to be in very bad order. There were constantly cases of ruffians falling out with one another, and molesting honest people. The authorities took no notice of this, and so at last the honest people also became rebels. Of late, the authorities have been very good; they have completely reversed the old order of things, and have entirely suppressed the rebellion (or, put down the outlaws, bad characters, &c.)
18. When outlaws collect together in any number, they form a *tang* or a *ku*, a gang, body, &c. Those who are nearest attached to, (most in the confidence of,) the chiefs, are the *ssŭ-tang*.
19. The *'hao-ling* are the words of command spoken to soldiers by the officers commanding them, their orders, (written or spoken); disobedience of orders by a soldier is a very serious offence.
20. An amnesty is a remission by the Emperor in consideration of particular circumstances, of the punishment incurred by offenders. It is altogether an act of grace on the part of His Majesty. If a man, after having had his offence thus graciously pardoned, returns to vicious courses, he will hardly escape capital punishment.

1.	古	ku³
2.	世	shih⁴
3.	孔	k'ung³
4.	聖	shêng⁴
5.	儒	ju²
6.	佛	fo²
7.	廟	miao⁴
8.	座	tso⁴
9.	僧	sêng¹
10.	俗	su²
11.	尙	shang⁴
12.	傳	ch'uan²
13.	經	ching¹
14.	楷	{ch'iai³ / k'ai³}
15.	率	shuai⁴
16.	更	kêng⁴
17.	濃	nung²
18.	貼	t'ieh¹
19.	牆	ch'iang²
20.	層	ts'êng²
21.	掛	kua⁴
22.	畫	'hua⁴
23.	唱	ch'ang⁴
24.	曲	ch'ü³
25.	抽	ch'ou¹

古¹來往古後世。孔²子聖人聖教儒教佛爺佛教老子道教。幾³座廟僧家道士念經。俗家俗說俗話。和尙。告⁶示。楷⁷書行書草字草率墨濃。裱⁸幾層貼在牆上掛著。畫⁹兒。抽空¹⁰兒唱曲。早已過¹¹的時候兒，是往古。古¹²來有個聖人姓孔他的教後世謂之聖教爲中國最尊的同時還有老子的教謂之道教佛教是西方僧家傳來的尊佛爺出家的是僧家俗說叫和尙尊老子出家的是道士聖教又名儒教儒教裏的人叫俗家三教的總名就是僧道儒。京¹³城的廟多有幾座是和尙廟有幾座是道士廟在那兒念經的聲兒是和人唱曲兒一個樣。牆¹⁴上貼的告示，寫的得用楷書用行書那就算草率那草字更使不得寫楷書比寫行書墨得濃。我¹⁵屋裏牆上掛的那一張古字今兒拏新紙裱上一層。老¹⁶弟畫得這麼好怎麼不裱上掛在屋裏呢。

PART III. THE FORTY EXERCISES. *San Yü Chang.*

EXERCISE XXXIII.

SINGLE WORDS.

1. *ku*, ancient.
2. *shih*, an age, generation.
3. *k'ung*, properly, a hole; the surname of Confucius.
4. *shêng*, virtuous as heaven; sainted; canonised.
5. *ju*, generally a scholar; specially, a Confucianist, as opposed to the Taoist and Buddhist.
6. *fo*, Buddha.
7. *miao*, a temple.
8. *tso*, properly a seat or throne; also the Numerative of cities, temples, &c.
9. *sêng*, a Buddhist priest.
10. *su*, properly common, in vulgar use; but, under certain conditions, Confucian.
11. *shang*, properly eminent; but most commonly a conjunction, when even; here it is a sound linked to *'ho*; see *ex.* 5.
12. *ch'uan*, to communicate by tradition, or propagate by preaching.
13. *ching*, a canonical book; also a sign of the past tense.
14. *ch'iai*, *k'ai*, properly the stalk of grain'; applied to a clerkly kind of Chinese writing somewhat corresponding to our round text
15. *shuai*, to follow one's nature; properly in a good sense, but here careless.
16. *kêng* 4, before adjectives, more; (*keng* 1, to change.)
17. *nung*, thick, of fluids.
18. *t'ieh*, to stick, or be sticking to, as a bill on a wall.
19. *ch'iang*, a wall.
20. *ts'êng*, layers or sections of various things, from front to rear, side to side, or top to bottom.
21. *kua*, to hang up; to be hung up.
22. *'hua*, to draw or paint.
23. *ch'ang*, to sing.
24. *ch'u*, one kind of songs.
25. *ch'ou*, to draw out one of many, as a stick from a faggot.

WORDS COMBINED.

1. In ancient times. In times long gone by. After ages; posterity.
2. Confucius. The virtuous, the sainted man; viz. Confucius. The sainted doctrine or philosophy, viz that of Confucius. The doctrine of lettered men; Confucianism. Buddha. Buddhism. Lao Tzŭ. The doctrine of reason; Taoism.
3. A number of temples. A Buddhist priest. A Tao priest, (*lit.* scholar.) To recite the books of Buddha, or of Tao.
4. Of the ordinary persuasion; *sc.* not Buddhist or Taoist, but Confucian. It is common to say. The vulgar tongue.
5. A *'ho-shang*, Buddhist priest.
6. A proclamation.
7. Round hand, clerkly writing. Running hand. A running hand (*lit.* grass characters) much abbreviated. Careless. The ink is thick, glutinous [as for the Chinese pen it should be].
8. To paste [sheets of paper together] several folds thick. To stick up against a wall. Hanging, suspended.
9. A painting, or drawing.
10. To find time; *lit.* to pull out a portion of leisure. To sing ballads.
11. *wang-ku*, past antiquity is time long gone by.
12. In ancient times there was a sainted man of the family (*lit.* surname) of K'ung. His doctrine was entitled by subsequent generations the *shêng chiao*, the doctrine of the sainted man. It is that most honored in China. There was also contemporaneous with this the doctrine of Lao Tzŭ, which is called the doctrine of *tao*, reason or right. The doctrine of Buddha was propagated (or preached) by the *sêng-chia*, priests, of the west. Those who leave their home for the honor of Buddha are *sêng-chia*. In common parlance they are called *'ho-shang*. Those who leave their homes for the honor of Lao Tzŭ are *tao-shih*, priests of Tao. The *shêng chiao* (doctrine of Confucius) is also called *ju chiao*, doctrine of the men of letters. Persons belonging to the *ju chiao* are called *su-chia*, members of the ordinary persuasion. The three sects, or persuasions, are spoken of collectively as the *sêng, tao, ju*, Buddhism, Taoism, and Confucianism.
13. There are several temples in the Capital. There are some that are temples of Buddhist priests, some, temples of Taoist priests The recital of the books in these, sounds as if people were singing songs.
14. The proclamations that are posted on the walls must be written in round hand. It would be considered slovenly were running hand to be employed. The *ts'ao-tzŭ* hand is even less admissible. To write round-hand, thicker ink is required than for writing running-hand.
15. I pasted a fresh piece of paper to-day under (or, at the back of) that slip (or scroll) of old writing that hangs on the wall of my room.
16. How is it, Sir, when you paint so well, that you do not mount your paintings and hang them up in your room?

KEY to the TZŬ ERH CHI. Colloquial Series.

1.	倉	ts'ang¹
2.	庫	k'u⁴
3.	宗	tsung¹
4.	考	k'ao³
5.	如	ju²
6.	若	jo⁴
7.	雜	tsa²
8.	另	ling⁴
9.	派	p'ai⁴
10.	盼	p'an⁴
11.	望	wang⁴
12.	列	lieh⁴
13.	衆	chung⁴
14.	涯	{ya² / yai²}
15.	依	i¹
16.	戀	{lien⁴ / luan⁴}
17.	跨	k'ua¹
18.	捨	shê³
19.	礙﹛碍﹜	ngai⁴
20.	彼	pi³
21.	此	tz'ŭ³
22.	處	ch'u⁴
23.	偏	p'ien¹
24.	或	huo⁴

倉¹庫米倉銀庫。國²計民生大宗兒。如³若。考察⁴。雜亂⁵。另派⁶。別人⁷彼此衆人。盼望⁸。列位⁹散了。此處¹⁰。海角¹¹天涯。依戀¹²。跨著¹³。倉庫¹⁴是米倉銀庫的總名。米石¹⁵銀兩是國計的大宗兒米銀不足實在礙於國計民生。派來的那一位爵位大些兒百姓盼望他來好考察衆人甚麼是這¹⁶一件事辦得雜亂無章聽見說要另派別人不是要派衆人甚麼是已經派過了又說重辦。列¹⁷位是你們這些位是尊稱衆人的字眼兒衙門裏列位都散了是衆官都回去了。海¹⁸角天涯是說彼此相離的過遠的話頭兒。出¹⁹門往遠處去臨走的時候兒難免依戀那依戀是捨不得的意思或親戚或朋友或本家都說得。人²⁰跨馬是偏在馬一旁坐著車外頭跨著是一條腿空著坐在車外邊兒。

PART III. THE FORTY EXERCISES. *San Yü Chang.*

EXERCISE XXXIV

SINGLE WORDS.

1. *ts'ang*, a granary.
2. *k'u*, a store-room, money-vault, &c.
3. *tsung*, a sort; also used as a collective pluralising the noun that precedes it.
4. *k'ao*, to compare, to examine competitively.
5. *ju*, if, as.
6. *jo*, if.
7. *tsa*, miscellaneous, not uniform.
8. *ling*, additional.
9. *p'ai*, to distribute, to send on a mission.
10. *p'an*, to look for anxiously.
11. *wang*, to expect; to look towards; towards.
12. *lieh*, separated in due order.
13. *chung*, a number of persons; all; every one.
14. *ya, yai*, the horizon.
15. *i*, to lean against; closely following; hence, according.
16. *lien, lüan*, to be warmly attached to a person or place.
17. *k'ua*, to bestride, to be seated with one leg hanging.
18. *shê*, to let go, not to detain.
19. *ngai*, to obstruct, interfere with. (The second character is an abbreviation of the first.)
20. *pi*, that.
21. *tz'ŭ*, this.
22. *ch'u*, a place.
23. *p'ien*, to lean towards; hence partial; specially; particularly.
24. *'huo*, expressive of uncertainty; if; perhaps; either, or.

WORDS COMBINED.

1. The granaries and treasuries of the empire. A rice-granary. A treasury; money-vault.
2. The finances. The people's life or welfare. The generality; the kind of which there is most; the larger proportion.
3. If; supposing that.
4. To enquire into conduct, or circumstances.
5. Confusion; muddle.
6. To send, or detach, some functionary in addition to, or instead of, the one sent.
7. Another person. We two, you two, the two, in relation of reciprocity. People; men; all hands.
8. To hope for, to expect anxiously.
9. All the gentlemen are gone.
10. This place.
11. The end, *lit.* corner, of the sea, and heaven's boundary line; the horizon.
12. To be fondly attached to.
13. Seated so that the legs hang, either or both.
14. The term *ts'ang k'u* is generic of granaries and treasuries.
15. Rice and money form the bulk, or largest proportion, of the state's revenue. An insufficient supply of rice or money is of serious consequence to the finances of the state and the existence of the people.
16. A. A great mess has been made of this affair. It is said that some one else is to be sent [to manage it] B. Not *is to be* sent; he has been sent already, and it is stated, too, that the officer sent is of somewhat high rank. The people are on the look out for him, hoping that he will look well into the conduct of every body. A. What is meant by *chung jên*, every one? B. In this place it means the small mandarins who are subordinate to the higher. The high officer [who is coming] will look into the conduct of affairs by the inferior officers, and if it has been made a mess of, the latter will hardly escape severe punishment.
17. The expression *lieh wei* either means, you gentlemen present, or is a respectful form of speaking of a number of persons. When you say the *lieh wei* in the *yamên* have *san*, dispersed, you mean that the officials there have all gone home.
18. The expression ocean's limit, heaven's bound, is one used in speaking of one's absent friend, meaning that he is very far off.
19. When one is about to leave home for some distant spot, one can hardly help *i-luan*. The words *i-luan* signify unwillingness to separate from; it may be of separation from one's relatives, one's friend, or one's home.
20. A man riding *k'ua* sits on one side only of the horse; to be *k'ua-cho* outside a cart, is to have one leg seated, and one in the air.

1.	揌	nieh¹
2.	灑	sa³
3.	洒	sa³
4.	掃	sao³
5.	帚	chou³
6.	砌	ch'i⁴
7.	磋	'hang¹
8.	狗	kou³
9.	欻	ch'ua¹
10.	修	hsiu¹
11.	裘	piao¹
12.	圓	yüan²
13.	扁	pien³
14.	剖	p'ou³
15.	寃	yüan¹
16.	枉	wang³
17.	逩	p'êng⁴
18.	跳	t'iao⁴
19.	造	tsao⁴
20.	報	pao⁴
21.	彷	fang³
22.	彿	fu²
23.	管	t'iao²

揌¹著揌做。揌²造揌報，彷彿水灑³了。掃⁴地一把條帚，砌⁵牆，打磋。一條⁶那狗⁷欻一聲迸跳過去。修⁸理。時辰⁹鐘表。圓¹⁰的，扁的，剖¹¹開分剖。寃¹²枉。他手¹³裏揌著管筆，彷彿要寫甚麼。那¹⁴瓦盆兒是盆兒揌做的。那¹⁵他帶著貨物¹⁶揌報是行李叫卡倫察出，全收入官。擎條帚來把地掃乾淨了。洒¹⁷字和灑字是一個字水在地下散開了，是水灑了。賊揌造告示做爲官出的。那¹⁸一條狗害怕，欻一聲跳過牆去見了他的主人滿地跳迸。我這個時辰表有點兒毛病，得找個鐘表匠修理。若論圓扁的不同，那西瓜就是圓的，那一本書就是扁的，那個鐘表了¹⁹。要砌牆先得打磋。那²⁰個人打牆上迸下來。又²³圓又扁的。我²⁴沒犯法，人告我是賊，那不是我的寃枉麼，有人替我說明白了，那就是他給我分剖了。剖²⁵開是用刀子破開，單說西瓜不說別的。

PART III. THE FORTY EXERCISES. *San Yü Chang.*

EXERCISE XXXV.

SINGLE WORDS.

1. *nieh*, to hold between the fingers, as a flower; to work up as clay.
2, 3. *sa* to sprinkle water; the second character being an abbreviation of the first.
4. *sao*, to sweep.
5. *chou*, a broom.
6. *ch'i*, to raise in courses or layers as a wall.
7. *hang*, to beat the ground for building, before bricks or stones are laid. This character according to some Chinese should be written with *ta*, great, above *li*, strength.
8. *kou*, a dog.
9. *ch'ua*, to produce the sound made when a dog jumps up suddenly.
10. *hsiu*, to keep, or to put, in order.
11. *piao*, properly the outside; hence, to shew; hence, a watch.
12. *yüan*, round as opposed to square.
13. *pien*, flat and thin.
14. *p'ou*, to cut open, as a melon.
15. *yuan*, to be aggrieved.
16. *wang*, properly, not straight; hence, injustice.
17. *pêng*, to jump off the ground.
18. *t'iao*, the same as 17.
19. *tsao*, to make.
20. *pao*, to announce, give notice of; to recompense.
21. *fang*, to resemble.
22. *fu*, only used with 21.
23. *t'iao*, used interchangeably with the *t'iao* in example 18, as the Numerative of brooms.

WORDS COMBINED.

1. Holding in the fingers. To make with the hands.
2. To forge, fabricate. To forge a statement; to make a false return. Resembling; as if; for instance.
3. There has been water sprinkled.
4. To sweep the ground. A broom.
5. To raise a wall. To beat the ground, before laying foundations.
6. A dog.
7. Gave a jump, whisk! To jump, leap about. To leap over, to have leaped over.
8. To put in order; to repair.
9. Watches. Clocks and watches.
10. Circular. Flat and thin.
11. To cut open, specially of a water-melon. To shew the truth on behalf of a man calumniated; to be the advocate of a man aggrieved.
12. To accuse wrongfully.
13. He has hold of a pencil in his fingers, as if he wanted to write something.
14. Earthenware bowls are made by the hand of the potter.
15. The rebels forged a proclamation, which was to pass as one issued by the authorities.
16. He returned the merchandise he had with him as baggage; which being detected at the customs' station, the whole was confiscated.
17. The characters *sa* and *sa* are one and the same; *sa* means to sprinkle water about the ground.
18. Bring a broom and sweep the ground (or floor).
19. Before a wall is run up, the ground [on which it is to stand] has to be beaten (pounded with a rammer).
20. The dog was frightened, and whisk! he was over the wall; then, seeing his master, he began to jump all about the place.
21. The man jumped down off the wall.
22. There is something the matter with this watch of mine; I must get hold of a watchmaker and have it repaired.
23. As regards the difference between *yüan*, round, and *pien*, flat, a water-melon is round, a book is flat; a cash is both the one and the other.
24. If I have not broken the law and I am accused of being an ill-doer, that is an injustice to me, is it not? Then, whoever explains the matter for me is said to *fên p'ou*, lay the truth bare.
25. The expression *p'ou k'ai* means to cut open with a knife; it is used only of the water-melon; of nothing else.

KEY TO THE TZŬ ERH CHI. Colloquial Series.

1.	歲	sui⁴
2.	紀	chi⁴
3.	壽	shou⁴
4.	因	yin¹
5.	為	wei⁴
6.	緣	yüan²
7.	故	ku⁴
8.	耽	tan¹
9.	惧	wu⁴
10.	容	jung²
11.	易	i, yi
12.	便	pien⁴
13.	勁	chin⁴
14.	塗	t'u², tu⁴
15.	喜	hsi³
16.	歡	huan¹
17.	惜	chʻi¹
18.	欺	chʻi¹
19.	哄	hung³
20.	誆	kʻuang¹
21.	騙	pʻien⁴
22.	屜	tʻi⁴

歲數兒年紀高壽。¹ 因為緣故。² 耽惧耽擱。³ 容易費事。⁴ 方便宜。交情⁶ 您高壽我今年四十五。¹³ 我是年輕⁷ 的他是有年紀的他多大歲數兒他有六十多歲了。歲。那一件事耽惧了，是因為甚麼緣故那緣故太多不容易說。這個辦法⁸容易那個費事得很。可惜那個人過於糊塗說不明白耽擱了我半天的工夫實在是不方便。屯⁷ 裏有好些個不便宜我喜歡在京裏住。我們倆彼此¹⁸很對勁可惜他那個兄弟很會欺哄人去年還誆騙了我幾兩銀子誆騙這兩個字我懂得他欺哄人是怎麼著呢。比方那一天他知道某人和他父親有交情他揑造一個字兒算是他父親要借皮袚子後來他給賣了。把抽屜¹⁹ 是使勁兒拉出來，抽屜是桌子裏櫃子裏拉得出來的屜子。把抽屜關上。

74

PART III. THE FORTY EXERCISES. *San Yü Chang.*

EXERCISE XXXVI.

SINGLE WORDS.

1. *sui*, the year, but used more limitedly than *nien*.
2. *chi*, anciently a period of twelve years; hence any period of years; or, to reckon one.
3. *shou*, old age.
4. *yin*, a cause; because of.
5. *wei*, because of.
6. *yuan*, origin; clue; cause.
7. *ku*, ancient; a cause of.
8. *tan*, to loiter, delay.
9. *wu*, to leave undone; to fail in doing.
10. *jung*, alone, the countenance; but, with 11, easy.
11. *i* or *yi*, properly to change; easy.
12. *pien*, convenience; (see *ex. 7.*)
13. *chin*, muscular strength; inclination.
14. *t'u* 2, properly mud; but in *'hu-tu*, stupid, *tu* 4.
15. *hsi*, joy; to be pleased.
16. *'huan*, to rejoice, shew pleasure.
17. *hsi*, to pity; to feel for; to like; to spare; to save, economically
18. *ch'i*, to deceive.
19. *'hung*, to beguile.
20. *k'uang*, to attempt to gain one's end, by lies, false promises, &c.
21. *p'ien*, to defraud one of.
22. *t'i*, a tray or drawer.

WORDS COMBINED.

1. The number of years [any one, old or young, is aged.] One's age. Your age; (politely, and not except to a middle-aged person).
2. Because of. The reason why.
3. To mar; to occasion failure. To delay.
4. Easy. Giving trouble; difficult.
5. Convenient. Suited to one's purpose, or the occasion.
6. Interchange of friendly sentiments; friendly relations. To suit one's liking.
7. To exert one's strength; make an effort.
8. Stupid.
9. To be pleased. To be fond of. What a pity!
10. To cheat; also, to tell lies to. To cheat.
11. A drawer.
12. I am young; he is old, or, of a certain age. How old is he? He is more than sixty years of age.
13. May I ask your age, Sir? I am forty-five years this year.
14. What is the reason why that affair has not succeeded? There are a great number of reasons; 'too many to make it easy to tell them.
15. This is an easy method; that is a very difficult one.
16. What a pity it is that that man is so exceedingly stupid that he cannot make himself intelligible. He has taken up ever so much of my time. It is really most inconvenient (or, a great bore really).
17. There are many things that make it inconvenient to live in the country; I prefer the capital
18. *B*. He and I suit each other very well. Unfortunately his brother is a great cheat. He got some taels out of me last year. *A*. The two words *k'uang-p'ien*, getting money out of you, I understand; but what do you mean when you say that he *ch'i-'hung*, takes in, people ? *B*. I will give you an instance: the other day, knowing that a certain man was a friend of his father's, he forged a letter the purport of which was that his father wanted to borrow a fur-jacket, and when he got it he sold it.
19. The word *ch'ou* means to pull out with some force; *ch'ou-t'i* is a drawer that can be pulled out of a table, or out of a press.
20. Push the drawer in.

1.	常	ch'ang²
2.	屢	lü³
3.	公	kung¹
4.	私	ssǔ¹
5.	務	wu⁴
6.	閒	hsien²
7.	空	k'ung⁴
8.	悶	mên⁴
9.	慌	'huang¹
10.	樂	lê⁴, lo
11.	煩	fan²
12.	急	chi²
13.	奉	fêng⁴
14.	求	ch'iu²
15.	託	t'o¹
16.	發	fa¹
17.	信	hsin⁴
18.	雇	ku⁴
19.	孩	'hai²
20.	撒	sa¹
21.	謊	'huang³
22.	賺	chuan⁴
23.	星	hsing¹
24.	所	so³
25.	雖	sui¹

平¹常屢次。公私公道。²事務家務。閒空兒。³煩悶悶得慌。⁴奉求奉託⁵ 您⁶打發送信。屯裏。雇人。⁷孩子⁸。撒謊賺錢。所以⁹雖然。那流星也¹⁰

是常有的我屢次的看見過。說某事是平常多有是說他常見的意思。公¹¹事原是官事大衆的事也謂之公事就是家務都可以分得公私事情不分公私總得按著公道辦。他¹²在家裏閒坐悶得慌我心裏有些煩悶。您¹³的公事雖然煩雜心裏還樂我有一件要事實在累得慌奉求您替我打筭。昨兒¹⁴我那相好的因爲小孩子病心裏煩悶急要發信到屯裏閒一問託我替他雇一個人送信我雇了一個人打發他去了,到後半天他回來說沒有找著,我知道他¹⁵是撒謊所以不肯給錢。小¹⁶價錢買來的大價錢賣,那就是賺錢那貨是一兩銀子一斤買的還是一兩銀子賣的所以不能賺錢。

PART III. THE FORTY EXERCISES. *San Yü Chang.*

EXERCISE XXXVII.

SINGLE WORDS.

1. *ch'ang*, constant, continual.
2. *lu*, frequent.
3. *kung*, public, just, disinterested.
4. *ssŭ*, private; illicit; interested.
5. *wu*, business; the verb *must*.
6. *hsien*, empty; without occupation; leisure.
7. *k'ung*⁴, leisure.
8. *mên*, sad, in low spirits.
9. *'huang*, intensive of adjectives describing certain disagreeable sensations.
10. *lê, lo*, joy in the heart, gladness in the countenance.
11. *fan*, to put, or be put, to trouble.
12. *chi*, quick, in movement, temper; rushing of water.
13. *fêng*, properly to raise the hands as when presenting anything; to receive; as orders, an appointment, &c.
14. *ch'iu*, to request; to seek.
15. *t'o*, to commission, request one to act as an agent.
16. *fa*, to issue forth; to cause to issue.
17. *hsin*, good faith; to believe; a letter.
18. *ku*, to hire as a servant, horse, conveyance; not said of a house, furniture, &c.
19. *'hai*, a child.
20. *sa*, to scatter from the hand; as seed, &c.
21. *'huang*, falsehood.
22. *chuan*, to gain (as money).
23. *hsing*, a star.
24. *so*, properly a place; a relative pronoun.
25. *sui*, although.

WORDS COMBINED.

1. Constantly; commonly; also, not excellent or remarkable. Several times.
2. Public and private; disinterested and selfish; openly and clandestinely. Justice; just.
3. Business. House business; affair at home.
4. Leisure.
5. Harassed in mind from much care. Very dull for want of occupation.
6. To request. To request one to execute a commission. May I request you, Sir, to . . . .
7. To send a person. To send a letter.
8. In the country; the country [as opposed to the city or town].
9. To hire a man.
10. A child.
11. To tell a falsehood. To make money.
12. Therefore; wherefore; for that reason. Although.
13. Meteors are of common enough occurrence. I have often seen them.
14. To say that such or such a thing is *p'ing-ch'ang*, common, *to yu*, that it is frequent, means that it is a common object.
15. The phrase *kung shih*, public matters, means official matters, business in which a community is interested may also be called *kung shih*; and, similarly, the affairs of a family may be distinguished as *kung*, public, or common to all its members, and *ssŭ*, private, or regarding individuals. Whether public or private, all affairs ought to be conducted with fairness.
16. He is very dull at home with nothing to do. I am somewhat troubled in mind.
17. Although your public business gives you a good deal of trouble, Sir, you are happy in mind. There is a question of much importance to me which really embarrasses me greatly. I should be much obliged to you, Sir, to turn it over in your mind for me.
18. Yesterday a friend of mine, who was in great distress about a child of his in the country that is ill, wanted to send a note to enquire how he was, and asked me to hire some one to take it. I did hire a man and sent him off, but he came back in the afternoon, and said that he had not been able to find the place. I knew he was not telling the truth, and so I would not give him anything.
19. To buy cheap and sell dear is *chuan ch'ien*, to make money. Such or such goods cost a tael a catty, and are sold a tael a catty. There is consequently nothing made on the transaction.

KEY TO THE TZŬ ERH CHI. Colloquial Series.

1. 承 ch'êng²
2. 差 ch'ai¹
3. 任 jên⁴
4. 署 shu⁴
5. 習 hsi²
6. 部 pu⁴
7. 堂 t'ang²
8. 司 ssŭ¹
9. 委 wei³
10. 員 yüan²
11. 吏 li⁴
12. 役 yi⁴
13. 皁 tsao⁴
14. 隸 li⁴
15. 供 kung⁴
16. 稟 ping³
17. 帖 t'ieh¹
18. 存 ts'un²
19. 稿 kao³
20. 陳 ch'ên²
21. 案 an⁴
22. 照 chao⁴
23. 式 shih⁴

差使¹。實任署理署任、本任、幫辦學習。六部³堂官。平行⁴、司官委員。書吏、書手、書班、供事皁隸、衙役。稟帖⁵、稟報知會、存稿、稿底子、陳案、文書、來文、去文、照會、家信。式樣承辦。官事⁸不論大小都叫差使。本任的官、或是公出、或是撤任、有官替他辦事、那就是署任和實任不同、所出的缺不大上司派委員署理。六部¹⁰的上司、都稱堂官、堂官之下、就是司官新到衙門候補的司官爲學習行走。文書¹¹所論的是公事家信論的是私事、從下往上告報事件、當用稟帖、行文的式樣不同、中外各國有事情得知會、平行的官來往用照會。京城¹²的衙門辦稿底子、不是司官辦、就是書班辦、這宗官人也叫書吏書手、供事、是有頂子的書班、還是相同的差使。文書¹³發了、把存稿存著、那叫陳案。衙門¹⁴裏使喚的承辦零碎差使的人、總名叫衙役皁隸。

PART III. THE FORTY EXERCISES. San Yü Chang.

EXERCISE XXXVIII.

SINGLE WORDS.

1. *ch'êng*, to receive on commission, be entrusted with.
2. *ch'ai*, to send, whether as an envoy, or, on ordinary occasions, as an official messenger.
3. *jên*, to hold an office, the office so held.
4. *shu*, an official bureau; before certain words, it indicates provisional tenure of office.
5. *hsi*, to practise when learning.
6. *pu*, any great category.
7. *t'ang*, a large hall; in certain departments of state, collective of the chiefs of any establishment.
8. *ssü*, to manage, direct; to manage one of the departments in a great office; the department so managed.
9. *wei*, to depute, as a higher officer a lower.
10. *yuan*, any officer of the civil or military service.
11. *li*, properly to exercise authority over others, is used with reference to the civil service in various ways; also, to mean clerks.
12. *yi*, properly, any employé, but, specially, such people as constables, &c.
13. *tsao*, properly, black.
14. *li*, properly, one under the authority of another.
15. *kung*, properly, to supply for use.
16. *ping*, to represent to a superior.
17. *t'ieh*, a slip of silk or paper with writing upon it.
18. *ts'un*, to preserve; to retain.
19. *kao*, the rough draft of a document.
20. *ch'ên*, to spread out, hence, to state, here and very commonly, stale, used.
21. *an*, in legal or official language, a case or question; also, the correspondence regarding a case.
22. *chao*, properly, to reflect light; hence, according to.
23. *shih*, a fashion; the fashion.

WORDS COMBINED.

1. The official mission of any employé from the highest to the lowest.
2. An appointment on the regular establishment of the empire, as opposed to a special mission; an effective as opposed to an acting appointment. To administer provisionally. A provisional as opposed to an effective appointment. One's own appointment, or this appointment, *sc.* that which the speaker holds. To assist in the administration of business, or settlement of an affair. To study, practise, a language, an art, &c.
3. The Six Boards, or chief departments of the central government. The chiefs of any such board, or other principal department.
4. To be of equal rank with, on equal terms with. (Officially speaking,) one's superior. The officers managing sections of any great department, as distinguished from the *t'ang kuan*. Officers deputed by a superior officer.
5. *shu-li*, *shu-shou*, *shu-pan*, clerks or copyists; *kung-shih*, clerks or copyists [but of higher degree]. Lictors. Constables; runners.
6. A written representation presented to a superior. To represent, orally or in writing, to one's superior. To communicate to an equal. To keep a draft; the draft so kept. The rough draft. Correspondence in a case that is put by. The official as distinct from the literary style of writing; an official document. The official document received in correspondence. The official document sent. The term used in the treaties for the form of despatch to be used between native and foreign authorities of equal rank. A home or family letter.
7. Form, or pattern to be followed. To undertake to manage, to be invested with the management of.
8. The business of any one in official employ is all called *ch'ai-shih*, whatever the degree of its importance.
9. If the proper officer of a post is absent on duty, or removed from it [on duty or in disgrace], and an officer is administering business for him, the appointment of the latter is in that case a *shu jên*, an acting appointment, as distinct from a *shih jên*, a post filled by its proper incumbent. When the appointment vacated is of no great importance, the superior of the jurisdiction will depute any officer to fill it.
10. The superior officers of the Six Boards are called the *t'ang kuan*, the chiefs, those under them are the *ssü-kuan*, sub-chiefs, or chiefs of departments. An expectant *ssü-kuan*, newly come to any *yamên*, serves a noviciate.
11. The matter treated of in *wên-shu*, despatches, is public business; that of *chia-hsin*, home letters, is private business. The form of document an inferior should use when he has a representation to make to a superior, is a *ping-t'ieh*. The forms of official letters differ. When communication is necessary on any subject between China and a foreign government, the officers corresponding, if of equal rank, use the form *chao-'hui*, communication.
12. The drafts of public documents in the *yamêns* in the capital, when not prepared by sub-chiefs of departments, are prepared by the *shu-pan*, clerks. This class of employés are also called *shu-li*, *shu-shou*. The *kung-shih* are clerks with an official button; their duties, are, however, of the same kind.
13. When a despatch has been sent off, and the draft placed in the archives, it is said to be *ch'ên-ngan*, a case or a correspondence of the past, no longer in hand.
14. The generic denomination of the understrappers employed in any *yamên* to execute miscellaneous duties; *ya-yi* and *tsao-li*, runners and lictors.

79

1.	脾	pʻi²
2.	性	hsing⁴
3.	禍	ʻhuo⁴
4.	福	fu²
5.	命	ming⁴
6.	運	yün⁴
7.	志	chih⁴
8.	益	yi², yi⁴
9.	活	ʻhuo²
10.	動	tung⁴
11.	聰	tsʻung¹
12.	願	yüan⁴
13.	功	kung¹
14.	虧	kʻuei¹
15.	辜	ku¹
16.	負	fu⁴
17.	抱	pao⁴
18.	怨	yüan⁴
19.	寒	ʻhan²
20.	悔	ʻhui³
21.	善	shan⁴
22.	惡	ngê⁴, ngo⁴
23.	其	chʻi²
24.	餘	yü²
25.	靈	ling²

脾氣志氣性情性急好性兒。[1]

禍福命運運氣天命。[2]

各處處好處益處。[3]

聰明活動死樣。[4] 用功力量。[5] 願意情願情願意。[6] 喫虧。[7] 辜負。[8] 抱怨。[9] 後悔、善惡。[10] 其餘。[11]

他脾氣好不好他性急得很也不是不好性兒。你性[13]情愛抱怨日後難免後悔。他[12]那一件事情成了是他的命運好在我說不關運氣都是他有志氣肯用功的好歹也是天按着善惡的功過命定了的禍福。人[16]處各有不等說是運氣的好歹也是天命所定。活的壽數長短都是天命所定。那姓李[17]的好處騙他的銀錢令他很喫了虧、如今姓李的後了悔願意相幫他倒情願意喫虧不用姓李的力量。在那些人裏分其善惡內有三個是善其餘全是[18]惡人。聰[19]明是心裏有靈動是蠢笨的對面活動是死樣的對面。

善人惡人處處都有他們的好處苦[15]處各有不等說是運氣的好歹也是天按着善惡的功過命定了的禍福。

PART III. THE FORTY EXERCISES. *San Yü Chang.*

EXERCISE XXXIX.

SINGLE WORDS.

1. *p'i*, a part of the stomach that produces digestion.
2. *hsing*, nature, natural dispositions.
3. *'huo*, adversity, calamity.
4. *fu*, prosperity.
5. *ming*, decree; of fate, or of a superior.
6. *yun*, to convey; to bring to pass.
7. *chih*, resolution.
8. *yi*, addition; advantage; colloquially, far oftener *yi²* than *yi⁴*.
9. *'huo*, alive, living.
10. *tung*, to move; to be moved.
11. *ts'ung*, quick to apprehend what one hears.
12. *yuan*, to wish, be willing.
13. *kung*, exertion in a good cause.
14. *k'uei*, to be deficient.
15. *ku*, properly fault, specially ingratitude; to be ungrateful for.
16. *fu*, to turn the back on, bear on the back.
17. *pao*, to hold in the arms, or bosom; hence to cherish.
18. *yuan*, resentment.
19. *'han*, cold.
20. *'hui*, to repent, of good or evil.
21. *shan*, virtuous.
22. *ngê, ngo*, vicious.
23. *ch'i*, used in particular locutions as the definite article; *the* person or thing.
24. *yu*, surplus, remainder.
25. *ling*, spiritual, intelligent.

WORDS COMBINED.

1. Temper. Resolution; determination in a good sense. Disposition. Quickness of temper; or, the temper is quick. Good-nature.
2. Weal and woe. Revolutions of destiny. Fortune; luck; *lit.*, influence of revolving destiny. Heaven's decree; destiny.
3. Each or every place. All places; every place. Good quality or merit; kindness shown. Advantage (*yi² ch'u⁴*).
4. Quickness of ear and eye; intelligence. Capable of movement; lively, as intelligence; conditional. Deathlike; inanimate.
5. To make effort, to be industrious. Power, capacity; resources.
6. *yuan-i*, to wish, to be willing; *ch'ing-yuan* and *ch'ing-yuan-i* have the same meaning.
7. To suffer loss.
8. To be ungrateful for or to.
9. To feel resentment. To repent, or, to regret. The feeling produced by ingratitude.
10. Virtuous and vicious.
11. The remainder.
12. What sort of a temper has he? He is very quick, but not ill-natured.
13. Your disposition is resentful; you will be pretty sure to repent it hereafter.
14. That success of his is due to his luck. I do not attribute it to his luck; I think it was all due to his own merits, his determination and his industry.
15. There are good men and bad everywhere, and good and evil befal both without any regularity. One may say that it is all chance that makes the difference, but the truth is that heaven decrees happiness in one case and unhappiness in another, according as men deserve the one for their virtue or the other for their wickedness.
16. The length of time a man has to live is settled by heaven's decree.
17. The reason why he is so hurt at Li, is that Li has been ungrateful to him for his kindness; has cheated him of money and put him to serious loss. Li is sorry for it now and wants to help him, but he prefers bearing his loss and not being assisted by Li.
18. As to the proportion of good to bad in that set of people, there are three of them virtuous, and all the rest are vicious.
19. The expression *ts'ung-ming*, means intelligence, liveliness of mind; it is the opposite of *ch'un-pen*, stupid. The expression *'huo-tung*, alive, lively, is the opposite of *ssŭ-yang*, deathlike.

1.	緊	chin³
2.	預	yü⁴
3.	備	pei⁴
4.	通	t'ung¹
5.	共	kung⁴
6.	合	ho²
7.	除	ch'u²
8.	剩	shêng⁴
9.	盈	ying²
10.	像	hsiang⁴
11.	似	ssŭ⁴, shih⁴
12.	橫	hêng²
13.	豎	shu⁴
14.	傷	shang¹
15.	棚	p'êng²
16.	著 着	chao²
17.	準	chun³
18.	勢	shih⁴

¹要緊,緊急。 ²預備。 ³通共。 ⁴合式。 ⁵合算,除了,下剩,盈餘。 ⁶像似不像。 ⁷平擱橫豎。 ⁸傷心着急。 ⁹馬棚。 ¹⁰你天天兒來不來,都不要緊,有緊急的事去叫你去。 ¹¹你預備的那車輛都很合式。 ¹²可惜他蓋的那房子不像房子的式樣,實在像馬棚兒似的,住著很不合式。 ¹³那房子通共多少間,通共有百餘間。除了人住的下餘還有四五十間。我合算起來,有一萬兩銀子的賬,除了還人之外,下剩還有一二千兩銀子的盈餘。 ¹⁴我月月兒進的錢,總不夠沒有盈餘反倒剩下些個賬目,不能還過這個日子,實在傷我的心,彷彿天天兒着急,沒有法子。 ¹⁵有個人放槍把他那小孩子打傷了很重。 ¹⁶在地下平擱的東西,說橫說豎,那都是隨勢兒,豎的門上下的木頭是橫的。 ¹⁷門旁邊兒的木頭是豎的,門上下的木頭是橫的。 ¹⁸在面前直著的為豎,在旁面的人就以為是橫的活動話,如若情的。

PART III. THE FORTY EXERCISES. *San Yü Chang.*

EXERCISE XL.

SINGLE WORDS.

1. *chin*, tight; pressing.
2. *yu*, beforehand.
3. *pei*, to prepare; ready.
4. *t'ung*, passing from one point to another without hindrance; to understand.
5. *kung*, collectively; together with.
6. *'ho*, united; agreeing with.
7. *ch'u*, to take away, subtract from.
8. *shêng*, to remain, as the balance of a sum.
9. *ying*, excess; overplus.
10. *'hsiang*, properly a figure resembling; to resemble, seem like.
11. *ssŭ, shih,* (differently pronounced under different circumstances,) resembling.
12. *'hêng*, horizontal as opposed to perpendicular.
13. *shu*, perpendicular as opposed to horizontal.
14. *shang*, to wound, injure; of man's person or feelings; of many things beside, animate and inanimate.
15. *p'êng*, a mat-shed, or pent-house.
16. *chao*, so pronounced with *chi*. See *ex.* 8; also, the last of the Notes on the Forty Exercises.
17. *chun*, to adjust, equalise, hence a rule.
18. *shih*, properly power, authority; hence, power to change; hence, circumstances.

WORDS COMBINED.

1. Important. Pressing.
2. To be ready; to make ready.
3. All taken together; the total; in sum.
4. Agreeing with the right form or pattern; as it should be
5. To add together, reckon the sum of. To deduct. To remain after deduction. The remainder, or balance. A surplus, over and above a proper or fixed quantity.
6. To be like; it appears; (see below *ex.* 12.) Not to resemble.
7. To lay straight; of a thing that can be laid flat, or with reference to something else lying crosswise. Horizontal and perpendicular.
8. To be sore of heart; melancholy; perplexed. Hard-pressed, troubled for want of time; also, over-eager, shewing excitement.
9. Stables; a shed for horses.
10. Whether you come every day or not is of no consequence; if there be anything of pressing importance, you shall be sent for.
11. You have turned out those carts very properly.
12. It is a pity that he has built that house so little like what a house ought to be; it looks just like a stable; it is quite unfit to live in.
13. How many apartments are there in that house altogether? There are altogether above a hundred; some forty or fifty over and above what people are living in.
14. I put the total of what is due to me at ten thousand taels, and, after paying my own debts, I shall have a credit of one or two thousand taels.
15. My monthly income is insufficient. I have nothing left from it; on the contrary, I have some debts I cannot pay. I am sadly perplexed to know how to live. Indeed it seems as if I was to be put to it every day. I don't know what to do.
16. A man let a gun off and hurt his little child very badly.
17. The doorposts of a door are perpendicular; the [beams of] wood above and below the door are horizontal.
18. The direction of things laid flat will be said to be perpendicular or horizontal conditionally; if the direction of a thing lying end on to one person be held to be perpendicular, it will be regarded as horizontal by any one whose face is turned at right angles to that of the first person.

KEY TO THE TZŬ ERH CHI. Colloquial Series.

Observations on the Text and Notes of the Forty Exercises.

EXERC. II. *ex.* 18, *yu shên-mo jên lai*, otherwise emphasised, may also mean, Is there any one come? or, Are any people come?
IV. 3, 叫 is more commonly written 呌.
XIII. 7, *kan*, is also written 扞
XIV. *ex.* 5, *ex.* 16, for 撒 read 撤.
XV. *ex.* 13, for 貫 read 貴.
XVI. 5, *ch'un*, is properly written 罎.
XVII. in Note on 18, for *k'ê pei* read *kê pei*.

XVIII. 1. for 踭 read 脖; in *ex.* 11 and *ex.* 12, for 脖 read 脖.
XXI. *ex.* 10 for 槍奪 read 搶奪.
XXII. in Note on 8, for *currupt* read *corrupt*.
XXV. in Note on 12, for *chea* read *chia*.
XXVI. 10, *tieh*, also written as in *ex.* 10. 22, *shih*, is also written 溼.
XXVI. Single Words 12; for 7, read 5. See *Obs.* above, on XIII. 14.
XXVII. *chuan*[4] may also be written 賺.

The subjoined information regarding Chinese Weights and Measures has been condensed from the Canton Chrestomathy, the highly valuable work compiled by the late Dr. Bridgman. The characters for the words referred to are placed at the foot of the page.

LENGTH. As in England we commence with *barley-corns*, so in China have the natives started with a certain number of kernels of grain, whether disposed lengthwise or crosswise, is disputed. One grain is held to make a *fên*, ten *fên* a *ts'un*, the Chinese inch; ten *ts'un* a *ch'ih*, the Chinese cubit, covid or foot, and ten *ch'ih*, a *chang*. "The *ch'ih*," says the Chrestomathy, "fixed by the Mathematical Board at Peking, is 13.125 English inches; that used by tradesmen in Canton varies from 14.625 inches to 14.81, and that employed by the engineers of public works is 12.7 inches; while that by which distances is usually measured is 12.1 nearly. The *li*, or mile, is 1897½ English feet; and 192½ *li* used to be reckoned for a degree of latitude or longitude. But the European mathematicians at the capital, deviating from their predecessors, divided the degree into 250 *li*, reducing it to 1826 English feet, or the tenth part of a French league; and this, at present, is the established measure. Accordingly, the *li* is a little *more* than one-third of an English mile.

"The *fên* may be taken as equivalent to a line in rough calculations; it is (calling the *ch'ih* 14.625 inches) exactly 1.015625 of the twelfth of an inch. The *ts'un* in Canton, is equal to 1.21875 of an inch, or one inch and one-fifth. The *chang* is frequently used by carpenters and other artisans in measuring their work, its length of course depends on that of the *ch'ih* employed, but it is usually about 14.35 feet."

N.B. The *chang* of the Tariff of 1858 is 141 English inches, the *ch'ih*, 14.1 English inches.

LAND MEASURE. Five *ch'ih*, Chinese feet, make one *pu*, pace, 240 *pu*, one *mou* or *mu*, = about one-sixth of an English acre, and 100 *mou* one *ch'ing*.

WEIGHT. It must be borne in mind that, except copper cash, the Chinese have no current *coin*, and that, except where foreign coin is employed, all payments in silver are calculated with reference to weight. The maximum money-weight is the *liang*, say ounce, commonly known as the *tael*, the subordinate divisions of which are the *ch'ien*, or mace, *fên*, candarin, *li*, cash, the three last named denominations respectively equalling the one-tenth, one-hundredth, and one-thousandth of the *liang*. The cash of the copper currency which should properly be worth a tael a thousand, are spoken of as *t'ung ch'ien* or *ch'ien*, the latter term being moreover generic of money like our word cash.

In what we should call Avoirdupoise, the weights to be remembered, in addition to the above, are the *chin*, catty or Chinese pound of 16 *liang*, or ounces, the ounce being subdivided as in money weight. The *chin* is equal to about 1⅓ ℔ English, and one hundred *chin* make the *tan* or *shih*, known by us as the picul = 133⅓ ℔ English. The terms *tan* and *shih* are used interchangeably at Peking, or rather, the latter is seldom used with its proper sound.

分 *fên*	步 *pu*	兩 *liang*	斤 *chin*
寸 *ts'un*	畝 *mou* or *mu*	錢 *ch'ien*	擔 *tan*
尺 *ch'ih*	頃 *ch'ing*	分 *fên*	石 *shih*
丈 *chang*		釐 *li*	
里 *li*		銅 *t'ung*	

NOTES ON THE FORTY EXERCISES.

EXERCISE I.

THE NUMERATIVES. Chinese nouns substantive have commonly associated with them certain other nouns substantive, here styled Numeratives, between the meaning of which and their own there is an affinity. This may be generic, specific, formal, qualitative, and is sometimes so vaguely defined that nouns, being names of things in categories widely different, may have the same Numerative. The latter, in virtue of this affinity, acts as the unit of the class, body, or other plurality, that may be indicated by the noun on which it is dependent; and it should be borne in mind that a large number of Numeratives are never used independently of those nouns to which they are related. We have, in English, nouns that do somewhat the same duty. We say so many *head* of oxen; so many *stand* of arms; a crew of so many *hands*; a fleet of so many *sail*. These are all plurals or collectives; but if we were speaking of oxen, we might also say that there was not a *head* left; or, if of arms, that every *stand* was destroyed. The Chinese Numerative will be found to play both the parts here illustrated; but it also plays a part of its own. Where it comes between a number, one or more, and its substantive, it cannot be translated. For *i ko jên*, one man, *san ko jên*, three men, the Cantonese, in the broken English which is the *lingua franca* of the open ports of China, would say, "one piece man" "three piece man." We have nothing analogous to this in our language.

Familiarly, the Numerative, where the noun is singular, stands sometimes before it without the number one; as *yu ko jên lai*, for *yu i ko jên lai*, "there is a person come or coming." Some Numeratives are occasionally placed after the noun with which they are joined, and whenever they are, that noun must be construed as in the plural number, or as a generic term.

A full list of the Numeratives will be given in the chapter on PARTS OF SPEECH.

Ex. 2. *Obs.* three, five, seven; the Chinese do also use four or five, six or seven.

Ex. 4. *Obs.* 1. and three hundredth; *ling*, fractional, indicates an interruption of the series; it is used in any place but the last in a series of numbers in which we should insert zero; also with *yu*, to be, as *odd*, after myriads, thousands, hundreds, or, if the number spoken of be more than thirty, after tens. Thus *i pai yu ling*, one hundred and odd. *Obs.* 2. and ten; the *i*, one, before *shih* could not be omitted. In reckoning myriads it is equally correct to use *i* or to omit it. You may say *shih wan, shih pa wan*, or *i shih wan, i shih pa wan*.

Ex. 10. *Obs.* score; the Chinese have no word for a score, but it is un-English to say some tens. Note that ten odd are supposed not to amount to fifteen.

Ex. 11. *Obs.* four-tenths; the word *fên* (Exerc. VI. 17), part, emphatically, tenth part, is understood after *ssŭ*.

Ex. 13. *Obs.* full; see Radical 157.

EXERCISE II.

Ex. 2. *Obs.* persons present; the expression *tsa-mên* is believed to be peculiar to northern mandarin. It is seldom made to include an absent person unless he be a party equally concerned with the speakers in whatever is the subject of conversation. On the other hand, *wo-mên* may include an absent person, or it may not. In northern mandarin it would generally not include him.

Ex. 9. *Obs.* here, there; the *êrh* here stands for place. Note that these combinations, in accordance with the rule of pronunciation before given, are pronounced *chê-'rh, na-'rh*.

Ex. 10. *Obs.* The *mo* is sometimes written *mên*, 5; but this is then pronounced *mo*.

Ex. 15. *Obs.* what does he sell; the *ti* here stands for *tung-hsi*, things; *q. d.* he sells what ones?

Ex. 16. *Obs.* none; the *liao*, here pronounced *la*, or *lo*, rounds the sentence so far as sound is concerned, but adds nothing to the sense.

KEY TO THE TZŬ ERH CHI. **Colloquial Series.**

Ex. 18. *Obs.* that is come; *lit.* there is what man come? &c.
Ex. 19. *Obs.* he from; it is simplest here to construe *ti* as the sign of the possessive; *q. d.* he is what place's man.
Ex. 20. *Obs.* are come; *lit.* they have come how many persons?
Ex. 22. *Obs.* ours; not including you.
Ex. 28. *Obs.* got any; or, at your place are there any; *yu* meaning as often to be as to have; so again the last clause, unless there be some very good &c.

EXERCISE III.

Ex. 18. *Obs.* to know; *chih-tao*, to know to say, as in French, Italian, &c. The word *tao* is much used as the verb *to speak* in novels, and in certain special phrases of congratulation, condolence, and apology, it is so employed in ordinary parlance. With *nan* difficult (Exerc. XXXI. 17), it makes an interrogation somewhat resembling our You don't mean to say, &c.
Ex. 23. *Obs.* better; *lit.* this house compared with that house good, or goodness, more.
Ex. 27. *Obs.* for a turn; *shang* has not here any sense of ascending; the phrase has the indefiniteness of He is gone out, when the speaker does not specify where the person spoken of is gone to.
Ex. 28. *Obs.* 1. keeps; *k'ai-cho*, is in the act of keeping. *Obs.* 2. where are they; *lit.* where opened.
Ex. 29. *Obs.* we have; *wo-mên*, the person addressed being an outsider. We here have not here, in our quarter, that-magnitude—'s trade.
Ex. 30. *Obs.* customers; the buy-thing—'s persons.
Ex. 35. *Obs.* persons; *lit.* the in-the-street—'s persons [are] very many.

EXERCISE IV.

Ex. 8. *Obs.* two mules; some Chinese maintain that *p'i*, not *t'ou*, is the correct Numerative of mules.
Ex. 11. *Obs.* he came; *lit.* he in his act of moving was a foot moving. In our idiom the value of *ti* is lost; it stands for the manner in which; *q. d.* my [manner of coming] was seated-in-a-cart-to-come—'s [manner].
Ex. 12. *Obs.* faster; *lit.* I in my movement attain to quickness, &c.
Ex. 14. *Obs.* 1. that man; the *t'a*, he, preceding, the demonstrative *na-ko* for emphasis' sake. Some Chinese dispute the propriety of prefixing the *t'a* to *na-ho* unless the question refer to the man's character, moral qualities, &c. The common people of Peking certainly use it as it is here; and with *wo* and *ni*, *chê-ko* is similarly used. *Obs.* 2. soon will; in *k'uai 'hui lai liao*, the *liao* need not be translated.
Ex. 16. *Obs.* three mules; *lit.* the bought ones are three mules, &c.

EXERCISE V.

Ex. 1. *Obs.* teacher; *lit.* elder born. Compare senior, signor, sir.
Ex. 2. *Obs.* to teach: this may be pronounced *chiao hsio* or *chiao hsüeh*. The latter word is as often as not *hsiao*. The pronunciation *hsüo* is merely given because some Chinese use it instead of *hsio*. The last is nearest the original pronunciation, to wit *hio*.
Ex. 3. *Obs.* pupil; this may be read *hsio-shêng*, or *hsüeh-shêng*; never *hsiao-shêng*.
Ex. 4. *Obs.* dictionary; *lit.* the authoritative law of characters.
Ex: 8. *Obs.* tell me; *kao-su*, often read *kao-sung*.
Ex. 13. *Obs.* have found; *kuo* here sign of the past.

PART VI. THE FORTY EXERCISES. Notes.

Ex. 15. *Obs.* look out; *lit.* [I] pray [you], teacher, holding the dictionary, look out words. The verb *na*, when used as here, is one of those by which the Chinese form what we should call the instrumental case. This is a very common use of *na*, but it will be found also as the index of the object. Followed by *lai*, to come, it means to bring; by *ch'ü*, to go, it means to take away. The object brought or taken away may precede the whole combination *na-lai* or *na-ch'ü*, as in Exerc. VI. *ex.* 6; if it do not, it will be between the verb *na* and the verb *ch'ü* or *lai*, but not after either.

Ex. 16. *Obs.* of course there are; *lit.* How should there not be, eh? The remembered ones are few, &c.

Ex. 18. *Obs.* know this; here a particular character, but the phrase *jên-tê tzŭ*, to recognise characters, when no character is so specified, means to know how to read.

Ex. 19. *Obs.* will not; *pu k'ên*, not to choose to, or, to refuse.

Ex. 20. *Obs.* tell me; *lit.* you telling to me say, &c. Observe *ta*, very; but you could not use it after *mei* without the *shên-mo*. You might say *pu ta 'hao*, if you were depreciating some other person's character or abilities.

EXERCISE VI.

Ex. 6. *Obs.* bring here; *lit.* do you take hold of that one volume book; holding [it] come; give [it] to me.

Ex. 8. *Obs.* four-fifths; *lit.* eight parts, namely of ten.

Ex. 9. *Obs.* how long; *lit.* you have recited, committed to memory, how many days' characters?

Ex. 10. *Obs.* 1. that he does; *lit.* characters, *'hai, 'han*, on the other hand he knows; he *jên-kuo*, has made an acquaintance with four or five thousand characters. *Obs.* 2. read together; *tsai i k'uai 'rh*, *lit.* in one or the same place, but used of moving or acting together. *Obs.* 3. not be able to; *lit.* I have seen there is nothing that is not *k'o-i* available. The *ti* at the end of the last clause represents the word incident or circumstances; or some such word must be understood after it; *q. d.* there is not any unavailility's [reason]. It will construe as a relative pronoun, *q. d.* there is nothing that is not *k'o-i*, available; but were the Chinese word for cause or reason expressed, which it might be, *ti* would not be dispensed with. *Obs.* 4. available; *k'o-i, lit.* can rightly use, or be used, sometimes, simply, to be able; sometimes, to be tolerable. Compare *shih-tê*, Exerc. VIII. 20.

Ex. 11. *Obs.* understand; *ch'u* has nothing to do with movement; it completes the meaning of *t'ing*, to hear, *q. d.* hearing do you understand?

Ex. 12. *Obs.* 1. no account; *lit.* a thousand times, ten thousand times must you not forget. *Obs.* 2. quite right; *lit.* you speaking attain to the very right.

EXERCISE VII.

Ex. 2. *Obs. p'u¹*, to spread, not *p'u⁴*, a shop.

Ex. 9. *Obs.* be quick; *lit.* quickly taking hold of the bedding spread [it]. It would be as correct to say *na p'u-kai*; especially if the bedding was not already on the bed.

Ex. 14. *Obs.* who took; *lit.* on the table there being that lamp, who taking hold of [it] went away? It was I that for the cook took hold of [it, and] passing over, went away. The *kuo*, to pass, is here used because the candlestick is removed from one place to another.

Ex. 16. *Obs.* both; *tou* is rendered both, only because the articles referred to are but two in number.

Ex. 17. *Obs.* no great; you might say here, *pu 'hên fên*; but you could not say *pu ta fên*, though you may say, of a phrase rarely used, *pu ta shuo*.

KEY TO THE TZŬ ERH CHI. Colloquial Series.

Ex. 18. *Obs.* the chairs; *hsieh,* properly few, is constantly used, as here, to mark the plural, without reference to number or quality.

EXERCISE VIII.

Ex. 5. *Obs.* fire is out; to put out the fire, would be *pa 'huo mieh la:* were one speaking of the event as past, this might also mean that some one had put out the fire, or had let it out; for the phrase in the text you might oftener use *mieh liao 'huo.*

Ex. 12. *Obs.* different sizes; *lit.* greatness and smallness not the same. A large proportion of English substantives signifying quantity or quality are rendered, as in this case, by a combination of opposites.

Ex. 13. *Obs.* also; the words *'han,* still, and *yeh,* also, in this example as in the preceding, might each take the other's place.

Ex. 14. *Obs.* 1. where you have the pronoun *na* preceding the subject at the beginning of a sentence as here, it is resumptive. The subject of the sentence must have been earlier alluded to. Do not translate *na.* *Obs.* 2. miscellaneous; *ling,* fragmentary, fractional; *sui,* broken, in fragments.

Ex. 15. *Obs.* the water; here *na* is demonstrative, and may be rendered by that or the.

Ex. 17. *Obs.* 1. lit it; the *shang* after *tien* completes the action of the latter. It is so combined with several verbs, where the action is that of placing on, applying to, &c. *Obs.* 2. but he; *lit.* it is the fact that he blew it out.

Ex. 19. *Obs.* one is empty; *ti* represents the noun *'hu.*

Ex. 20. *Obs.* 1. better go; *lit.* quickly to go to tell a person to mend [it], can [this means] be employed, [or] can it not be employed? *Obs.* 2. much better; although, when analysed, *shih-tê* and *k'o-i,* would seem identical expressions, there is this difference between them; the former always affirms positive fitness or utility; the latter, sometimes, no more than a tolerable degree of either.

EXERCISE IX.

Ex. 3. *Obs.* all follow the same rule; *lit.* all are thus.

Ex. 4. *Obs.* seasons; *shih-ling, lit.* time-command, time-law. Four spirits are believed to *ling,* rule, each one a season.

Ex. 5. *Obs.* warm, *nan-'ho, nuan-'ho,* or *nuan-'huo,* warm and peaceful; windy, *lit.* there blows wind; snowy, *lit.* there falls snow.

Ex. 6. *Obs.* 1. following expressions; literally, *i hsia chung* proceeds to be, then is, *i tien chung*: the word *chiu,* to pass on to, hence, then, in that case, is here hardly to be translated. It emphasises any proposition it introduces, *q. d.* when one says so-and-so, then one means such and such a thing. *Obs.* 2. an hour; the words *i hsia,* one down, mean one blow or stroke in general; *i tien,* one point, viz. on the dial.

Ex. 9. *Obs.* not up; *ch'i-lai* is often joined to other verbs as an auxiliary, but, when not so joined, means, as here, to rise from a sitting or recumbent posture.

Ex. 14. *Obs.* fine; *lit.* the sky is clear: the *liao* after *ch'ing* shews that the sky has cleared, or, is become clear, having been previously overcast. Notice the difference in construction between this and the following sentence.

Ex. 16. *Obs.* very mild; *lit.* the warmth of this year's weather *tê 'hên,* attains to excess.

Ex. 18. *Obs.* over here; the *kuo* in the last clause shews that the persons did come over from another place but are not here now.

EXERCISE X.

Ex. 8. *Obs.* the *fu* in *kung-fu* cannot be explained.

PART VI. THE FORTY EXERCISES. Notes.

Ex. 14. *Obs.* 1. is it not; the Chinese constantly affirm by an interrogation of this sort. *Obs.* 2. every moon &c.; *chiu* might be rendered by a pause after the word moon, or by the words *in fact* after *is*: coming as it does here in the second clause, however, it might be rendered, *similarly, consequently*. *Obs.* 3. so with; *lit.* [the phrases specified] also are in that fashion.

Ex. 15. *Obs.* 1. goes to bed; *lit.* lies down on the stove-bed, the ordinary bedstead of northern Chinese. Some say simply *shang k'ang*, ascend the stove-bed. Be careful not to use *shang ch'uang*, for that is to take to one's bed in mortal sickness.

Ex. 16. *Obs.* living alone; the expression may mean that the person spoken of is senior or master in the house; or that no out-siders live there.

Ex. 20. *Obs.* as regards; *lit.* [with reference to the question of night watches], in the night the watchman strikes the watches (*lit.* changes); a whole night's divisions are five watches; [the beginning of] the foremost (*lit.* head first) watch, is [the time known as] the *ting-ching*, the setting of the watch.

Ex. 21. *Obs.* must just wait; *lit.* must be left unmoved, and that is all about it. The *pa* at the end is not essential.

Ex. 24. *Obs.* overcast; *lit.* when the clouds in the sky have filled [the sky], *chiu*, in such cases, there is a dull day.

Ex. 25. *Obs.* invisible; *k'an-pu-chien*, behold not see; *q. d. k'an-pu-tê-chien*. This insertion of *pu* between two cognate verbs is a very common construction where the action they together imply is impossible. Its possibility on the other hand is expressed by the insertion of *tê*; visible would be *k'an-tê-chien*. See below Exerc. XI. 19.

EXERCISE XI.

Ex. 2. *Obs.* dirty; pronounced both *ang-tsang* and *a-tsa*.

Ex. 7. *Obs.* change it; *lit.* exchange it for *ti*, some, clean.

Ex. 9. *Obs.* dress; put on your clothes; the *shang* here, as in '*huan shang*, (see *ex.* 4,) meaning on the person.

Ex. 12. *Obs.* more; you must additionally put on clothes.

Ex. 13. *Obs.* 1. has he got; this might be equally well, Had he got &c.; the answer of course being, He had got &c. *Obs.* 2. The *lai-cho* implies that he was *in the act* of wearing boots at the time spoken of; as we should say, puts the verb in the imperfect tense.

Ex. 16. *Obs.* must be brushed; this is our idiom, but it should be remembered that there is really no passive verb in Chinese; *lit.* some person *tei*, ought to wash and brush them.

Ex. 17. *Obs.* 1. boiling water; *k'ai shui*, opening, bubbling water. *Obs.* 2. the best; *ti* representing [the water] which is best. *Obs.* 3. *wên 'huo*, the warmth of water, or steam, or breath.

Ex. 19. *Obs.* 1. going out; *yao* is about to. *Obs.* 2. the water; *chê shui*, this water, is the object of *wên*, here a verb, the subject of which is a person understood. *Obs.* 3. will not boil; on *pu* so placed see Exerc. X. 25; *k'ai-tê-liao*, boil-achieve-completed, would mean that the water can be made to boil; *q. d.* got to boil; *k'ai-pu-liao*, cannot be made to boil, is most likely, as before observed, a corruption of *k'ai-pu-tê-liao*, which is not in use. This construction *pu-liao*, = *pu-tê*, indicating, that is, that the action of the verb which precedes cannot take effect, is very common.

EXERCISE XII.

Ex. 2. *Obs.* waist-coat; *lit.* cut-shoulders; a short-waisted garment without sleeves, worn over some of the long Chinese dresses, and under others.

KEY TO THE TZŬ ERH CHI. Colloquial Series.

Ex. 4. *Obs.* a needle; observe that the nouns needle and thread, combined, make the verb to sew. In the next example, the verbs to cut out and stitch make the noun tailor.

Ex. 9. *Obs.* 1. cotton; *mien 'hua*, cotton flowers. *Obs.* 2. between; *chung*, middle, *chien*, intervening space; *lit.* cotton, = wadded, clothes are those having, or which have, cotton in the space between [the lining and outside of] lined clothes. The *ti* at the close represents *i-shang*, clothes.

Ex. 10. *Obs.* 1. the article of dress; *lit.* is the hav-ing, *yu-ti*, back and front, &c., that garment. *Obs.* 2. riding-jacket; *tuan-ti*, the short one, that which is short.

Ex. 12. *Obs.* 1. distinguished; *lit.* caps divided attain-to being small caps, and official caps. *Obs.* 2. may take it off; in China it is respectful to keep the cap on.

Ex. 14. *Obs.* is cut out; *lit.* that waist-coat [the tailor] has cut out, &c.

Ex. 15. *Obs.* should be mended; *lit.* that torn riding-coat [some one] ought to mend.

Ex. 16.* *Obs.* 1. duster; a small stick with some rags at the end of it. *Obs.* 2. tap off; *lit.* holding, = with, a duster tap-a-tap, give a tap to, the on the clothes—'s dust.

Ex. 17. *Obs.* that combs; *lit.* that wooden comb is whose comb, is who-to-comb-head-hair—'s [comb]? *ti* standing for *mu-shu*.

Ex. 18. *Obs.* whole person; *yi*, one = indivisible.

EXERCISE XIII.

Ex. 8. *Obs.* weigh it; instead of *ch'êng i ch'êng*, it is equally correct, and more popular to say *yao i yao*; (see Exerc. II. 21.)

Ex. 9. *Obs.* 1. good deal of money; *lit.* the bills owed by him to people [are] not few. *Obs.* 2. the word *chang* is not authorised by the native dictionaries. It means, says a teacher, an entry or memorandum of expenditure; *mu*, the eye, combined with *chang* has something of the force of our word *heads* in a discourse; sections or other subdivisions.

Ex. 10. *Obs.* the expression; *lit.* [the words] *wo chieh ch'ien* are, = mean [that] I holding people's money bring it [to me for] my use; *chieh hei jên ch'ien* means [that I] holding my money take it [to people for] people's use.

Ex. 13. *Obs.* to spend money; *lit.* [what the two phrases] he loves to spend money, he is fond of spending money, both in speaking arrive at, is [this, that] he exceeds *yü*, in-the-matter-of, spending money.

Ex. 15. *Obs.* not a cash; *lit.* he in his house one large cash [even] has he not got. This might mean equally that his *family* were all in as great distress; but were it an object to isolate the individual, *shou-li*, in his hand, might be used instead of *chia-li*.

Ex. 16. *Obs.* 1. ten cash; large cash *tang*, representing ten. *Obs.* 2. cash-pieces; the *ti* is simplest construed as *ones*; *q. d.* there are seven-tenths being-copper ones, there are three-tenths being-iron ones. Were it meant that each cash contained seven-tenths copper to three-tenths iron, the text might be variously modified; you might omit *li-t'ou*, and then proceed *tou shih ch'i fên t'ung, san fên t'ieh ti*, all are seven-tenths, &c.; or, *mei i ko shih yu ch'i fên t'ung*, every one is seven-tenths, &c.

Ex. 17. *Obs.* a paper note; *lit.* a *p'iao tzŭ* is a slip of paper; [on its] surface [man] writes a number of cash; [in] buying things [it is] with money of one and the same fashion. Instead of *i ko yang-'rh*, you may read *shih i ko yang ti*.

EXERCISE XIV.

Ex. 11. *Obs.* 1. stove-bed; *lit.* [as regards, or, in the case of] stoves of stove-beds it is the fact that [one] uses coal, &c. Observe that if *ti* were added to each of these clauses, the translation would be

PART VI. THE FORTY EXERCISES. Notes.

thus:—The stove is that, the thing, in which one uses coal; the chafing-dish that in which one uses charcoal, &c. *Obs.* 2. cannot; *nêng*, see Exerc. XXIV. 22.

Ex. 12. *Obs.* natural state; *lit.* the *shêng ts'ai* are [these; such as] growing out of the ground, [man] thereon, or immediately, can eat. The *k'o-i* is very often supported by the *tê* as here, but the latter might be exchanged for *liao*.

Ex. 13. *Obs.* 1. milk; not by the catty, *lit.* you do not consider or reckon the catties' number. *Obs.* 2. fruit; *lit.* [man] buying fruit also not reckons the catties; *tou*, in-all-cases, it is the fact [that he] reckons individual ones. This is true at Peking except in the case of dates and grapes.

Ex. 14. *Obs.* prefer; *ai* is so rendered here because, by the answer, the question seems to refer to the present moment. The question itself might equally mean, Which are you in the habit of eating?

Ex. 15. *Obs.* food ready; *tê*, having achieved that which is in preparation. The expression *tê liao* is used of several other operations completed.

Ex. 16. *Obs.* removal; *lit.* you having eaten the food, [persons] everything holding down go. The *hsia*, down, as elsewhere *shang*, up, refers to the table, and not as we might suppose to an upper or lower story.

EXERCISE XV.

Ex. 8. *Obs.* 1. inns outside; *lit.* I have heard it said [that among the] walls-without inns there are-not-very good-to-inhabit ones. *Obs.* 2. according as, *lit.* that all regards the till-director's goodness or badness. *Obs.* 3. in my opinion; *lit.* it is my saying [that when] man is tired, *na-'rh*, what places [he will], all are good; [the object of] going to an inn is not more than to rest, and there an end!

Ex. 9. *Obs.* 1. by water; *lit.* sit in vessels. *Obs.* 2. *shui-lu*, *'hai-lu*, *'ho-lu*, are all correct expressions for travelling by water, sea, river.

Ex. 10. *Obs.* so deep; *lit.* the water in rivers [is] shallow; [it] has not sea-water's depth.

Ex. 11. *Obs.* 1. hard time; *lit.* you *shou*, were the recipient of, suffered, trouble. *Obs.* 2. got ashore; *lit.* [the wind] put the ship on a shoal place. *Obs.* 3. dreadfully; *lit.* we, those persons, = I and the others there, suffered trouble, *lit.* bitterness, infinitely; the adjective *hsin k'u* being verbalised by *tê*.

Ex. 12. *Obs.* the people; *lit.* also is it the fact that the people of the ship look after it; *q. d.* they look after the meals as well as after other things.

Ex. 13. *Obs.* 1. travelling expenses, *p'an-fei*; *p'an* properly is a circular dish, bowl, plate; see Exerc. VIII; combined with a certain word it means in lettered language to travel for pleasure, to tour; thence it passes into the present phrase. *Obs.* 2. one spends more; *'hua ti*, though more commonly so pronounced, should properly be written *'hua tê*, the construction being literally, Sitting on a cart compared with sitting in a ship [one] *'hua tê*, succeeds in expending, comes to expend, more money. *Obs.* 3. the cart costs more; *lit.* the cart's cost [is relatively] dear. *Obs.* 4. the reason being; *lit.* wholly is it that, (all because,) the till-directors in the cart-establishments of our northern region, &c. *Obs.* 5. have their money to make; *lit.* also, = as well as other people, require to make a few cash. The word *shih*, properly to use, when placed as here, means to use another's money; of course, unfairly.

EXERCISE XVI.

Ex. 10. *Obs.* hold all sorts of things; *lit.* anything all = everything whatsoever, *k'o*, by rights, properly, hold can [they]. *Obs.* 2. bundle; *lit.* a *pao-'rh* is [what is effected as follows; a person] taking things, *yung*, using, = with, anything wraps [them] up. Treat *pa tung-hsi* as if it were the object of the verb *pao-ch'i-lai*. *Obs.* 3. in a rug; the verb *na* before *chan-tzŭ* like *yung* in the preceding sentence, puts the noun following it in what we term the instrumental case.

KEY TO THE TZŬ ERH CHI. Colloquial Series.

Ex. 12. *Obs.* frontier; *k'ou*, literally mouths; the openings, passes, or gates in the Great Wall, from beyond which are brought the camels.

Ex. 14. *Obs.* all there; *lit.* if the baggage be all *ch'i*, complete, in that case it is well.

Ex. 15. *Obs.* 1. a servant; in southern mandarin an individual servant is spoken of as *kên-pan*; in Peking as *kên-pan-ti*, oftener *'kên-pan-'rh-ti*. *Obs.* 2. take orders; *lit.* are those whom [one] sends and calls: but the verb *shih-'huan* is also used subjectively as to serve, attend, &c.

Ex. 16. *Obs.* a good while; *lit.* half a day.

Ex. 17. *Obs.* 1. fast enough; *lit.* running quickly, you will be able pursuing-to achieve-coming-up-with him. *Obs.* 2. hard as you can; quick running pursue [him] then it will be right or well.

EXERCISE XVII.

Ex. 1. *Obs.* the lips; some Chinese prefer to omit the *tzŭ*.

Ex. 4. *Obs. lien* EXERC. XV. 25.

Ex. 9. *Obs.* 1. *lit.* that man's nose and eyes, = his face, growing has attained to singularity. *Obs.* 2. *chang*, to grow, must generally be construed *is*; much as we say, is turning out, or, has turned out.

Ex. 11. *Obs.* weak; *lit.* I am [in this condition that my] body is weak.

Ex. 12. *Obs.* sadly ailing; *lit.* it is the fact that of my body these some years the sickness has attained to *li-'hai*, sharp hurt. Compare our acute pain, acute disease, &c.

Ex. 13. *Obs.* literally, of the on the road there lying man the two legs both are broken.

Ex. 14. *Obs.* impossible; *lit.* in the back, or loins, to have an ailment [such that] straight [one can]-not rise up. See above Exerc. X. *ex.* 25, XI. *ex.* 19.

Ex. 15. *Obs.* matter; *lit.* you move thus slowly; is it that in your body there is an ailment?

Ex. 18. *Obs.* so long; *lit.* that woman's nails being long, holding his arm in clutching tore it. The object of the verb *chua-p'o*, in clutching to tear, is *k'ê-pei* the arm. The verb *pa* is in our idiom superfluous.

Ex. 20. *Obs.* drawn by; *lit.* [whether one] use mule, ass, horse, all can draw [carts]. Notice the two auxiliary verbs for can.

Ex. 21 *Obs.* 1. pull hard; *lit.* [the character] *chuai* is [one that] means that a person with-the-hand-using-force-wise draws. Notice the *ti* adverbialising the whole clause from *jên to li*. *Obs.* 2. fast to; *lit.* laying hand on that door, *chua*, pull it, [until it be] *chu-liao*, fixed in a position. *Obs.* 3. would not let me go; *la* is to pull, but not so violently as *chuai*. One Chinese lays down that *la* is to drag after one, and *chuai* to pull in towards one; but the distinction is not carefully observed.

EXERCISE XVIII.

Ex. 5. *Obs.* respectable; *t'i-mien*; *lit.* form and face. The word *t'i*, commonly body, hence the right body or proper form; the totality from which nothing must be taken; *shih t'i* (see Exerc. XXII. 12,) is to lose, or come short of, what is right, in conduct or administration; so *tiu lien* (see Exerc. XXV. 23,) to lose face, to have done what makes one blush, is to have damaged one's repute. The phrase *t'i-mien* signifies that there is no short coming in conduct, no blemish on reputation.

Ex. 6. *Obs.* forehead; *lit.* the brain's door or gateway.

Ex. 10. *Obs. pei-'rh* is pronounced almost *pêrh*.

Ex. 12. *Obs.* below, above; one of the senses of *i* is to follow; hence with words indicating place it means in the direction of; thus *i-tung* to the east of, *i-wai*, outside of. See below *ex.* 15, outside the pigtail.

Ex. 13. *Obs.* 1. knee-cap; *kai-êrh* is pronounced *karh*. *Obs.* 2. the leg; the thigh is *ta t'ui*.

Ex. 15. *Obs.* outlaws; *tsei* is any person violating the law, especially if he overtly opposes authority. From a Chinese point of view we are *tsei* during war with China.

PART III. THE FORTY EXERCISES. Notes.

Ex. 17. *Obs.* 1. conduct; *lit.* a man's *hsing*, moving, and *chih*, standing still. *Obs.* 2. unexceptionable; *lit.* there is not anything not good. *Obs.* 3. is good-looking; see *chang-tê* above Exerc. XVII. ex. 10.

Ex. 18. *Obs.* so-and-so's house; observe *t'a*, another person, a third person.

EXERCISE XIX.

Ex. 10. *Obs.* 1. all subjects; *lit.* over the hundred officials and the myriad non-officials. The Manchus more particularly speak of the Emperor as their *chu-tzŭ*, master; a Chinese consulted objects to *chia-chu-'rh*, for head of the family, except when applied to the Emperor. *Obs.* 2. the hundred surnames; hundred used as an indefinite plural, but the surnames of all China do not amount to six hundred.

Ex. 12. *Obs.* the *ts'an-tsan*; the dependencies of China beyond the borders of Kan Su and Ssŭ Ch'uan are some of them administered by high officers styled *pan-shih ta ch'ên*, to whom the *ts'an-tsan* is second; the title is also given to the civilian who aids a high commissioner of war.

Ex. 14. *Obs.* strength; *lit.* [as to] the government troops' quota-number, there is *yi*, one uniform, fixed one; the *ti* standing for *shu*, number.

Ex. 15. *Obs.* 1. properties; *pên-shih* does not mean, as might be supposed from its formation, inborn qualities that ought to be possessed, but acquired ones. *Obs.* 2. men or things; *lit.* be it man, be it thing, *tou*, in every case, [men] may say it.

Ex. 16. *Obs.* *tang-ping* is more common than *ch'ung ping*.

Ex. 18. *Obs.* 1. last year; *lit.* last year robbers [were] very many; the high officers leading troops all were planning and calculating not well; were not competent to decide estimates and stratagems; [thus] caused, = enabled, the robbers all to run away. *Obs.* 2. retired; *lit.* those robbers retiring came to *li*, the place, north of the river; [whenever they] saw a person then they slew. *Obs.* 3. with loss; *lit.* laying hand upon the robbers utterly slaughtering drove them back.

Ex. 19. *Obs.* man named; *lit.* there was one surnamed 'Huang and named Lung. Observe that in Chinese the surname always precedes the name.

EXERCISE XX.

Ex. 5. *Obs.* principle; *tao*, road, morally, the right road; *li*, the principle implanted in man, if he conform to which he will keep the right road; *tao-li* is hence right principle; next, any principle conformity to which produces the normal estate of men or things, the rationale or logical condition of anything. It is against *tao-li* in the first sense to steal; but to steal is the *tao-li* of a thief; he would not be a thief did he not steal: a Chinese would say *mei chê-ko tao-li*, it is not logical, there is no sense in such a proposition as that a man should be a thief and yet not steal. Lastly, the term *tao-li* is used as the principles collectively, the philosophic system, of any teacher. Confucianism is the *tao-li* of Confucius.

Ex. 10. *Obs.* denomination; *lit.* name-eye; the latter word being apparently employed on account of the distinguishing property of the organ; compare *chang-mu*, accounts, Exerc. XIII. ex. 9.

Ex. 14. *Obs.* 1. administration; *ting-ti* should be properly *ting-tê*; *q. d.* [the purpose of] the state in passing laws, is [the to] well-govern the people—'s [purpose]. *Obs.* 2. proceed from; *lit.* it is not [this, namely a purpose that] comes *yü*, out of, *pao*, passionate violence, *nio*, tyrannical disposition.

Ex. 16. *Obs.* 1. authorities; *kuan-chang*, the latter word in its sense of great. *Obs.* 2. maladministration; *chih-li-ti*, as in 14, properly *chih-li-tê*; the authorities in governing, or the government of the authorities, attained to badness. *Obs.* 3. fact known; *ti* representing fact, circumstance, or any like noun. *Obs.* 4. Notice the construction of the whole sentence: [the fact that of] late years the empire's great disorder is [the result of] the authorities' maladministration, is a by-the-entire-empire's-people-known one.

KEY TO THE TZŬ ERH CHI. **Colloquial Series.**

Ex. 17. *Obs.* 1. there; *lit.* in that piece, = that quarter. *Obs.* 2. search; search with a view to apprehend. *Obs.* 3. did come; *lit.* there passed an interval, the rebels *chiu*, then, came. *Obs.* 4. all depends; *lit.* altogether *tsai*, is in, rests with, the officials. *Obs.* 5. dreadful way; *li-'hai* may of course be rendered by any adjective signifying excess of damage; *lit.* the rebels did come [and], slaying and burning, accomplished injury that attained-to excess.

EXERCISE XXI.

Ex. 8. *Obs.* by accident; *jan*, thus by nature, makes several adverbs: by accident thus, = accidentally; of itself thus, = naturally, for certain.

Ex. 10. *Obs.* unobserved; *pei*, the back, is here used as a verb signifying to do acts behind another; the addition of *cho* makes it construe as a participle.

Ex. 12. *Obs.* 1. every direction; *hsia-li*, in the sense of place or direction; properly, the four points of the compass. The Chinese say similarly the four faces, four seas, &c.

Ex. 13. *Obs.* is said to be; *lit.* [men] *wei chih*, style him, or, esteem him, lazy.

Ex. 15. *Obs.* 1. large staff; notice the difference of the Numerative, according as the staff is large or small. *Obs.* 2. so engaged; *lit.* wildly striking. In Chinese such repetitions are more common than with us. *Obs.* 3. made haste; *lit.* pursuing, viz. his purpose; he was not in chase of the thief. *Obs.* 4. loaded; as elsewhere, the *shang* does not indicate the direction of the movement, but the completion of the act. *Obs.* 5. fired; *lit.* hastening loaded; *chiu*, then fired. The verb *ta* does not here mean that he struck, but that he fired intending to strike, the thief. *Obs.* 6. probably; *lit.* I fear, but constantly used to express uncertainty.

Ex. 16. *Obs.* 1. turn out; *lit.* he is not a making-man one. *Obs.* 2. energy; *lit.* vigour of mind, specially used of laudable ambition.

EXERCISE XXII.

Ex. 1. *Obs.* most probably; *yo*, originally to bind; hence league, contract, agreement; *ta yo* general agreement, viz. of the grounds on which the estimate is based.

Ex. 6. *Obs.* the line; *kuei* is *lit.* a pair of compasses; hence a rule laid down; *ting*, may be here the active verb to determine, or its past participle.

Ex. 7. *Obs.* 1. administering; *pan*, is to despatch, *li*, to attend to; *pan-li*, to attend to with a view to the despatch of. *Obs.* 2. method; also means, resources, *moyens*; the common expression for a condition in which there is no alternative, no help, is *mei fa-tzŭ*.

Ex. 8. *Obs.* outbreak; *'hu* is used with various verbs to denote a wild random manner of acting or speaking. The dictionaries do not justify this meaning. The character is very possibly a currupt one.

Ex. 10. *Obs.* invariably; *lit.* whenever [man] does things, in every case, *tei*, must he have, or, must there be, a determined direction; = a direction determined.

Ex. 11. *Obs.* 1. imagine, *ch'uai-mo*; see Single Words 2 and 3. *Obs.* 2. Chang; *lit.* the surnamed Chang one.

Ex. 12. *Obs.* alteration; *lit.* the regulations [one] must alter; *yeh*, still does [one] not know [if] Li, the great man, sanctions or the reverse. The *kai*, to alter, would as often as not be repeated; *kai-kai.* *Obs.* 2. take place; the *liao* at the close of the sentence is simply expletive.

Ex. 13. *Obs.* 1. nor must one; *lit.* also it is not right too much to hurry. *Obs.* 2. consequences; *lit.* [if one] dispatches business too hastily, *chiu*, then is there *ts'ên tz'ŭ*, unevenness.

Ex. 14. *Obs.* 1. fairly settled; *lit.* [when one] has *li*, planted, *chûn*, with true aim, one's *chu-i*, guiding or dominant idea. *Obs.* 2. one is said; then [men] style it, (the having so done,) *ting hsiang*, the having

PART III. THE FORTY EXERCISES. Notes.

determined one's direction. *Obs.* 3. the character *chun* is identical in meaning with the 17th character given in the Single Words of Exerc. XL; the form of the latter is much more common when *chun* is used as in this example.

Ex. 15. *Obs.* somewhere else; *lit.* [when the thought] in the mind is not present, that then [men] call *shih shên*.

Ex. 16. *Obs.* way in which; *lit.* the having settled securely the method of disposing of any matter, [men] *chiu*, proceed to, call *ting kuei*. Observe that *chiu* is fully represented, in the free English translation in the text, by a comma after the word *done*; that is after the clause which is, in the English, the subject of the verb *is called*, but, in Chinese, one of the objects of the transitive verb *chiao*; the other object being *ting-kuei*.

Ex. 17. *Obs.* 1. acting with him; *t'ung jên*, = *t'ung shih ti jên*. *Obs.* 2. not listen; *lit.* he would not hear; taking a staff he wildly whirled it; *'hun lun* is here a verb having for its object the staff, but without an object it is adverbially used to mean wantonly, at random.

Ex. 18. *Obs.* 1. as general; *lit.* [when one] speaking of matters does not, *lit.* cannot, point to [details so as to give] certainty, that [men] proceed to term *fan lun*, generalisation. *Obs.* 2. general way; the *ta* in *ta-fan*, means comprehensively, on the whole; so in *ta-chia*, the whole party, and other combinations.

Ex. 19. *Obs.* foregoing; *i shang*, up-wards; see Exerc. XVIII. *ex.* 12.

Ex. 20. *Obs.* irregularity; *lit.* whatsoever business that man administers, *tou*, all administering he attains to no *t'o-tang*, security or completeness; *to*, in excess, or for the more part, is there *ts'ên-tz'ŭ*, jaggedness, and *pu-ch'i*, unevenness.

EXERCISE XXIII.

Ex. 5. *Obs.* constitution; *lit.* breath and blood.

Ex. 9. *Obs.* 1. first place; *tsê* is an illative particle; it may indicate that what follows is a logical consequence of what goes before, as in *jan tsê*, (see Exerc. XXI. 21,) such being the case, then—&c.; but, in this example, it has much the force of *chiu*; firstly, then so-and-so; secondly, then so-and-so; implying sequence rather than con-sequence. *Obs.* 2 moreover; *lit.* additionally also.

Ex. 10. *Obs.* make out; *t'ing-tê-ch'u* does not mean to hear but to understand; the *ch'u* out, or, to go out, is an auxiliary joined to several verbs implying, like *ex* in Latin and Greek compounds, completion. *Obs.* 2. the moment; *q. d.* at one and the same time that I open my mouth. *Obs.* 3. trouble; *lit.* besides too, those local sounds of his, I listening to much expend exertion.

En. 11. *Obs.* opposite directions; the coming and going carts and horses are numerous.

Ex. 12. *Obs.* 1. old fellow; *lit.* old head. *Obs.* 2. constitution; *lit.* breath and blood. *Obs.* 3. tired; *lit.* his body's fatigue being extreme.

Ex. 14. *Obs.* 1. rage; *ch'i*, air, breath, in Chinese physiology often untranslateable; best taken as matter; here *nu-ch'i*, wrath-matter; the vulgar boy begot or generated wrath-matter. *Obs.* 2. smashed; taking a tea-cup dashed it down into fragments; *pa* marking the object. *Obs.* 3. found fault; *shuo*, to speak, followed by a personal noun or pronoun, means to blame; but when the same nouns or pronouns are so circumstanced as to be in what we call the dative case, *shuo* means to speak to. *Obs.* 4. frightened; *'hai* to hurt, merely intensifies the expression of fear in *p'a*; compare our *sore* afraid; so in *'hai lêng*, said of a sick person who feels chilly.

EXERCISE XXIV.

Ex. 2. *Obs.* proceeding; literally *shŭn*, obedient to, *tang*, what is proper.

Ex. 8. *Obs.* present; *lit.* under the eye.

KEY TO THE TZŬ ERH CHI. Colloquial Series.

Ex. 9. *Obs.* observe the construction of the sentence, which will equally well construe, Things, [we will] not discuss their good or ill luck, in every case have a presage; or, As to things, we will not discuss their good luck or ill luck; in all cases is there a presage.

Ex. 10. *Obs.* 1. when before; *lit.* things-not-come—'s before; the word *chih* here like *ti*, forming a number of words preceding it into a predicate of the word following it. See Exerc. XX. 25. *Obs.* 2. that is called; *lit.* that [men] then call it.

Ex. 11. *Obs.* when there is; the second *ti*, stands for the noun condition; *q. d.* [the condition described in the words preceding *ti*, namely] house-within—'s-money-equalling-expenditure—'s [condition], is *k'uan-cho*.

Ex. 12. *Obs.* regular income; *lit.* certainly incoming; on *chun*, see Exerc. XXII. *ex.* 14.

Ex. 15. *Obs.* 1. raihed; *lit.* there descended rain for a succession of dark [days]. *Obs.* 2. harvest; *shou* to ingather; *ch'êng*, [the grain] full grown. *Obs.* 3. prevented; *lit.* taking the-about-to-be-fly—ing people, all kept fast; *pa* governing the object of the verb *liu chu*. *Obs.* 4. *tou* in this position should never be translated; it merely pluralises the noun it immediately follows. *Obs.* 5. the *chu* merely completes the action of *liu*; it does not imply compulsory detention.

Ex. 17. *Obs.* 1. as you know; this clause is introduced to bring out the force of the *na*; *lit.* in the beginning we had *that* little money [you know of]. *Obs.* 2. bread; *lit.* even, or, also, I myself have not-a-to-eat *ti*, anything.

EXERCISE XXV.

Ex. 12. *Obs.* 1. addressing; *nin*, or *ni-na*, is an abbreviation of *ni lao jên chia*. *Obs.* 2. *lit.* [when one] accosts any one as *nin*, it is [that one] has a somewhat to respect the person—'s intention. *Obs.* 3. somewhat; *tien*, a particle of such an intention.

Ex. 14. *Obs.* 1. third person; *lit.* side person; though the term is one of respect, you do not use it when speaking to the son of the person spoken of. *Obs.* 2. *ch'êng*, here, to speak of; translated in example 12 by *addressing*, because its object is there in the second person.

Ex. 15. *Obs.* Notice the interrogative, *a*.

Ex. 18. *Obs.* but; still is [it the fact that] men saying *ti-hsia-jên*—'s [fashion is the] more frequent.

Ex. 19. *Obs.* 1. signifies; *lit.* [when] the master calls and the servant makes the sound *dja*, [the meaning of this] is an obediently-hearing command—'s meaning; not the man's meaning, but that of his cry. *Obs.* 2. cries out; *tê* verbalising *cha*, or as it is pronounced *dja*; the servant by *dja* achieves a sound, *dja*—s a sound.

Ex. 20. *Obs.* 1. respects; *lit.* I go to welcome and receive, receive with welcome. *Obs.* 2. buried; *lit.* the day after to-morrow their father [they] bury; I must to help them go. *Obs.* 3. to bury; *hsia-tsang*, are two verbs compounded; not a verb and its object. *Obs.* 4. here, as in many places, the object *lao wêng* preceding the verb, may be made in our idiom the subject of a passive verb. *Obs.* 5. though *wêng* is properly an old man, it is applied to any one's father without reference to his age.

Ex. 21. *Obs.* one of those; *lit.* of those two balls silk, one is a coarse one, one is a fine one; the *ti* in each clause representing *t'uan*, a ball.

Ex. 22. *Obs.* 1. silk; *na*, indicating silk in general; not translateable in English; compare the French *la soie*. *Obs.* 2. country here; *lit.* of your this place's native merchandise. *Obs.* 3. to be sure; *lit.* can it not be; *k'o* morally right or possible. *Obs.* 4. but velvet; *lit.* velvet, on the other hand, (*'huan* pronounced *'hai*,) is not, &c. *Obs.* 5. some; *ti* standing for *jung*; *q. d.* for me choose a little good velvet.

PART III. THE FORTY EXERCISES. Notes.

EXERCISE XXVI.

Ex. 14. *Obs.* 1. in bed; *shui-chiao* does not necessarily imply sleep; *shui-chao* does; for *chao* see Exerc. XL. 16. *Obs.* 2. have been; the *liao* shews that some time has elapsed; *q. d.* in bed all this time, while the others, &c. Were the phrase *shui chiao liao*, it would mean, how is it that you are gone to bed &c.; *shui chao liao* that you are asleep, or went to sleep; the *liao* in the latter not marking the time.

Ex. 15. *Obs.* 1. just think; so translated to bring out the force of *ch'io*, or *ch'üeh*; *lit.* think, this money, were it not he who stole it, *ch'io*, on the other part, who was it?

Ex. 17. *Obs.* 1. dreadful; see *li-'hai* Exerc. XVI. *ex.* 7. *Obs.* 2. too niggardly; *lit.* both are exceeding in parsimony.

Ex. 19. *Obs.* 1. qualities; *lit.* when distinguishing beef and mutton's good and ill. *Obs.* 2. as well as; *lit.* also is there *lao nên*—'s expression. *Obs.* 3. *chih*, as before in Exerc. XXIV. *ex.* 10.

Ex. 20. *Obs.* 1. generic; *lit.* all including name. *Obs.* 2. grows as; *lit.* grass-stem—'s things. *Obs.* 3. comes up; *lit.* once it issues from the ground.

Ex. 21. *Obs.* wild; *lit.* unripe and ripe, reclaimed and unreclaimed.

Ex. 24. *Obs.* 1. to dry; *nung*, here, and often elsewhere, pronounced *nou*, verbalises the adjective *kan*, dry. *Obs.* 2. sunny place; *lit.* you must spread them on a sun place. *Obs.* 3. folded; *lit.* [when the sun] has warmed them dry, then fold them up. *Obs.* 4. fold them up; *ch'i-lai* the auxiliary verb of *tieh*, not necessarily implying movement upwards.

EXERCISE XXVII.

Ex. 4. *Obs.* behaviour; *tai*, towards; *hsiang*, though properly implying reciprocity in relations, is here, and very frequently in other combinations, onesided; the *ad* in *admoneo* rather than the *con* in *communis*.

Ex. 6. *Obs.* true; *tsai*, to be; true it is.

Ex. 11. *Obs.* 1. advantages; *'hao-êrh* for *'hao-ch'u*, good places, points. *Obs.* 2. unhandsomely; *k'e-po* is, literally, cutting thin, paring down; here used, as the following clause explains, as a verb of injurious speaking; *q. d.* censures, disparages me infinitely. Notice the *'hên* preceding the verb which is followed by *liao-pu-tê*, a double intensive common enough; also the *wo-ti*, so pronounced, but properly *wo-tê*. *Obs.* 3. but as a sentiment; *lit. k'ê-po* in the mind, *ch'io*, on the other part, is generosity's opposite. Notice the disjunctive *ch'io* between the subject, and the verb.

Ex. 12. *Obs.* 1. the sight; *lit. cha chien* is the beginning, the first moment, of *chien*, a seeing. *Obs.* 2. when I say; *lit.* [the phrase I have] *cha chien* a certain person is [this; there is] a person whom heretofore [I] have not seen; [I] for the first time see him; of a man that for a long time [one] has not seen also can [one] say *cha chien*. *Obs.* 3. first time; Chinese teachers differ much as to the correct application of *cha chien*; it is not strictly confined to the first sight of the object; the *cha* points to suddenness, unpreparedness, in meeting with persons or things; but if they be not met with for the first time, a certain interval must have elapsed since they were last seen.

Ex. 13. *Obs.* 1. this other; notice *t'a* before *chê-ko*; *celui-ci*; the latter person not being necessarily present. *Obs.* 2. ashamed of; *lit.* truly is there not [such a state of things that he] is *k'o*, by rights, ashamed.

Ex. 14. *Obs.* 1. of late; notice the *lai* similarly implying progress of time in *chin-lai*, of late, *'hou-lai*, hereafter, *ku-lai*, anciently, *hsiang-lai*, and *ts'ung-lai*, heretofore; but not so in *ch'ien-lai*, which is to advance, to come to the front. *Obs.* 2. discontinued; *lit.* they have severed intercourse; the second *liao*, or *la*, is merely expletive.

KEY TO THE TZŬ ERH CHI. Colloquial Series.

Ex. 15. *Obs.* 1. no doubt; *yüan-lai*, to come down from the source, may be rendered in various ways; in the first place, as in Exerc. XXVIII. *ex.* 13; or, as here, in fact, the fact is, &c.: it is a strong affirmative which here authorises this disjunctive in the second clause; *q. d.* he *has* rank, it is true, but &c. *Obs.* 2. either; *lit.* in his talk, also is there not a sentence [on which men] can by rights depend. *Obs.* 3. nevertheless; *'huan, 'hai*; notice *pai t'a ch'ü*; it would be equally correct to say *ch'ü pai t'a. Obs.* 4. as he pleases; *lit.* it depends on him, *q. d.* I leave it to him. *Obs.* 5. you, Sir; *lit.* what language, what manner of language; a common form of deprecation; the Sir being taken in English, for symmetry's sake, from the *nin* which begins the clause following. *Obs.* 6. of course; *lit.* if you go, Sir, in accordance with reason there will be a reception (or an interview.) *Obs.* 7. uncivil; *lit.* [I] leave it *to* him to be uncivil to, uncivilly treat, me; [I] cannot speak of it, or take it into consideration.

Ex. 16. *Obs.* independent; *chuan*, sole, undivided; *lit.* the undivided master, = independent authority; one is *chêng*, properly the upright, as contrasted with the deflected; the true, or *bonâ-fide* one.

EXERCISE XXVIII.

Ex. 4. *Obs.* 1. the new; *sc.* rugs. *Obs.* 2. dyed; *lit.* if the colour of the old ones be greatly faded, a dyed red [colour], a dyed blue [colour] will both do.

Ex. 8. *Obs.* to crack and break; where the fissure is produced, not by violence, but, as in paper, wood, or rocks, under the action of heat, &c. You do not use *lieh* of cracks in crockery; these are *wên*, streaks, Radical 67; which word will be joined to a different verb according to the cause of the damage, fire, water, or collision.

Ex. 9. *Obs.* 1. paper-hanger; *lit.* a pasting artisan. *Obs.* 2. mend it; *lit.* to paste it up; *shang* indicating completion of the act, not upward movement.

Ex. 10. *Obs.* 1. trades; *'hang*, is not a character recognised by the dictionaries; from the original meanings of the character without the dot, namely to move, the way or course of movement, the order of proceeding, it comes to mean class, calling, &c. *Obs.* 2. *lit.* of the several trades' handicrafts-men, the called *chiang-jên* ones [are the more] numerous.

Ex. 11. *Obs.* shirtings; the word *pu* includes of course many fabrics besides those of our manufacture.

Ex. 12. *Obs.* 1. faded; *lit.* the colour has oldened. *Obs.* 2. some other; *lit.* [men] must dye other kind of colour; *ti* representing *yang* kind or sort. *Obs.* 3. old colour; *lit.* original old. *Obs.* 4. interested; *lit.* all depending on [the] person's, or, on one's, idea.

Ex. 13. *Obs.* 1. first place; *yuan-lai*; see above Exerc. XXVII. *ex.* 14. 15. *Obs.* 2. besides . . . . dyed; *lit.* the colour [men] dying it achieved, = the colour it is dyed, also is good to see. *Obs.* 3. not used only; *lit.* does not halt in the speaking of crape; to speak of some other [things] also it suits; *yü*, in the case of; see Exerc. XIII. 23.

Ex. 15. *Obs.* bump against; *p'êng* implies that the movement that occasions the shock is either lateral, or from below.

Ex. 16. *Obs.* desperately; *'huai* here implies ruin past recovery.

EXERCISE XXIX.

Ex. 7. *Obs.* assemble; *lit.* to bring together to one piece.

Ex. 11. *Obs.* one stone; see Exerc. XIV.

Ex. 14. *Obs.* 1. talking over; *lun-ch'i*, the latter being auxiliary of the former verb, not in the sense of raising but beginning; so also *lai*, which is not to be construed in the sense of to come. *Obs.* 2. this affair; notice the object of the verb between its two auxiliaries *ch'i* and *lai*; a common construction. *Obs.* 3. ever so long; *lit.* we waited half a day, he did not reply; [I] doubt, &c.

PART III. THE FORTY EXERCISES. Notes.

Ex. 15. *Obs.* never more; to eternity will not, or, can not, be changed. The Chinese who added *liao* maintains that the force of the phrase = that of *kai-pu-liao*.

Ex. 16. *Obs.* 1. again; the *ti* adverbial, standing for fashion; *q. d.* three times, four times, fashion. *Obs.* 2. had to go; *lit.* in the end, '*hai*, still, was it my going to his side or place; the *ti* representing a word for the cause or circumstance which made him come.

Ex. 17. *Obs.* 1. agreed; *ting tê*; most Pekinese would say and write *ti*. *Obs.* 2. first instance; *lit.* from before, *q.d.* starting from an earlier date. In citing dates some way back, the words used in Chinese will generally translate *from*, where we should use *at*. *Obs.* 3. to put money; *ts'ou* properly written with Radical 159, means to converge as spokes to the nave of a wheel; to contribute money to do trade. *Obs.* 4. withdrew; *lit.* there dropped out two men. *Obs.* 5. and others; *lit.* yet more there were laying-hand-on capital took [it] back ones. *Obs.* 6. did not choose; *pu k'ên* translates very well as decline or refuse, where there is evidence that a proposal has been made.

Ex. 18. *Obs.* because; *lit.* [I, or, man] tell you to move apart the box; [this being so], why move [it] thus far?

Ex. 19. *Obs.* 1. one-horse cart; *lit.* single halter cart. *Obs.* 2. so little as; *lit.* in my opinion the piculs' number is not simply five piculs; [if the cart brought] be not a two halter cart, [I] fear [the single beast] will not be able to draw [it]. Notice *liao*, as *to be able* in both clauses; *la liao* and *la pu liao*.

Ex. 20. *Obs.* 1. the moment; *lit.* the carter having arrived in, = at, the inn, *chiu*, immediately thereon, wanted, or demanded money; *chiu*, proceeded to, ask for. *Obs.* 2. the; *na*, that carter belonging to the cart just spoken of. *Obs.* 3. not the rule; *lit.* suspected that theretofore there was not this *li*, a principle or rule that should obtain because it was just. The carter would plead that to pay at once was *li*, justice; the traveller suspects that this never had been the principle in accordance with which action ought to be taken.

EXERCISE XXX.

Ex. 8. *Obs.* 1. very mountainous; *lit.* the heights both numerous and large. *Obs.* 2. elevation; were they not lofty as well as extensive, they would be *ch'ang*, long, but not *ta*, great.

Ex. 11. *Obs.* rather fine; *lit.* those mountains and waters will do; see *k'o-i* above in Exerc. VI. 10; VIII. 20.

Ex. 12. *Obs.* also a height; the construction is somewhat elliptical, *q. d.* a *shan ling* is also high [like a *shan fêng*; but when it is a *shan ling*,] *chiu*, then there is not that point-ed form.

Ex. 13. *Obs.* 1. term; *lit.* characters' eye, *q. d.* characters seen together; it is not applied to single characters; compare *ming-mu*, in note on Exerc. XX. *ex.* 11. *Obs.* 2. the like; understand *chê tsung yang-tzŭ ti*, this kind of ones, after *pi chien*; because there are many things to the point of which the term might apply; and were these two kinds not specified, the indefinite *shên-mo*, here meaning *quot* or *quæcumque*, would still stand.

Ex. 16. *Obs.* 1. where; *lit.* outside the walls a-not-having-any-houses-to-live-in-'s [place, men] *chiu*, consequently call a *yeh ti*. *Obs.* 2. regarded; *lit.* even let there be a cemetery's [place, that place men] also reckon to be [a *yeh ti*].

EXERCISE XXXI.

Ex. 1. *Obs.* the women; *niang-êrh-mên*, pronounced *niarmên*. It is also used as *a* woman.

Ex. 5. *Obs.* 1. frank; *shuang* is properly the freshness of day-break. *Obs.* 2. dilly-dally; *lit.* to draw out silk.

KEY TO THE TZŬ ERH CHI. Colloquial Series.

Ex. 11. *Obs.* respectable age; *lit.* years high, *q. d.* piled up, as opposed to the lesser burden of years which is *ch'ing*, light.

Ex. 12. *Obs.* 1. contemporary; *lit.* the with [a man's] father and grandfather one and the same generation's ones are the senior generation, &c. *Obs.* 2. grandfather; see Exerc. XXV. *ex.* 10, where *tsu-fu* combined make one word; they are here separate.

Ex. 13. *Obs.* 1. anything; *lit* any plaything; the *ěrh* making the concrete noun when added to *wan-i*, trifling intention, purpose of play. *Obs.* 2. accomplishment; see above, Exerc. XIX. *ex.* 15, on *pên-shih*. *Obs.* 3. fence; *lit.* whirling the sword to play.

Ex. 16. *Obs.* reverse of; *lit.* in speaking and acting not to know to draw silk, [that] consequently is *shuang-k'uai*, briskness; *'hui*, to know, = as in French or Italian, to be able to do.

Ex. 18. *Obs.* equally correct; *lit.* also [do men] term it *pu shu-fu*.

Ex. 20. *Obs.* disreputable; see Exerc. XVIII. *ex.* 5. *lit.* [when,] from one's own disrepute inviting men's disgust, [one] has been the subject of bad language; [men] call it, (that is, the application of such language for such a cause), *hsiu-ju*, putting to shame.

EXERCISE XXXII.

Ex. 5. *Obs.* to encourage; the combination is of classical origin; *ku* and *wu* were originally both parts of a sacrificial bell; latterly, *ku*, a drum, or to drum; *wu*, to dance, or make postures, to music; hence to set people dancing, to stimulate to action.

Ex. 12. *Obs.* the sovereign; *chu-tzŭ-chia*, the master, a phrase in vogue more among the Manchus than the Chinese. See Exerc. XIX., note 10.

Ex. 13. *Obs.* is guided; *lit.* following, acting according to, place, considering circumstances, establishes officers [for the government] of the locality. The phrase does not include judicial or fiscal authorities, nor, in the capital, the departments of the central government, unless these be executive.

Ex. 16. *Obs.* always forbidden; *lit.* heretofore, the law has by prohibitions stopped the people; has not authorised them to go out and come in.

Ex. 17. *Obs.* 1. used to be; *lit.* in the beginning greatly was unquiet. *Obs.* 2. falling out; *lit.* constantly were there violent [persons] on the two sides fighting.

Ex. 19. *Obs.* 1. words of command; *lit.* the *'hao-ling* are the *k'ou-'hao*, oral signals, and *fa-ling*, law-commands, issued by the officers, &c. *Obs.* 2. serious offence; *lit.* a soldier disobeying commands is [in this case, that he] has consequently run against, incurred, great punishment.

Ex. 20. *Obs.* graciously; notice the construction; receive-grace-remit-punishment—'s after, again-being-a-doing-evil-one, that [man] in truth with difficulty avoids death punishment.

EXERCISE XXXIII.

Ex. 3. *Obs.* Buddhist priest; *lit.* a *sêng* person; *sêng* represents the first syllable of a Sanscrit word the meaning of which is Buddhist, or follower of Buddha.

Ex. 5. *Obs.* *'ho-shang* is also a foreign word, the sound, not the meaning of which is represented by the two characters employed.

Ex. 12. *Obs.* 1. most honored; *ti* representing *chiao*; it is the China-most-honors-one. *Obs.* 2. also called; other name. *Obs.* 3. collectively; *lit.* the three doctrines' all-including term is *sêng-tao-ju*; notice *chiu* after the subject *tsung-ming*; it emphasises, but is untranslateable in English.

Ex. 13. *Obs.* 1. sounds as if; *lit.* the in that place reciting book—'s sound is with men singing songs, one, or the same, fashion. *Obs.* 2. *nien*, to recite, see above Exerc. VI.

PART III. THE FORTY EXERCISES. Notes.

Ex. 14. *Obs.* even less; *lit.* that grass character more [men] use not can, = still less to be used. *Obs.* 2. thicker ink; *lit.* [one] writing *ch'iai shu*, as compared with [one] writing *hsing shu*, ink requires thick.

Ex. 15. *Obs.* under; *lit.* on, but it must have been under, or at the back of, the other which is covered with writing.

Ex. 16. *Obs.* 1. Sir; *lit.* old younger brother, *q. d. signor giovane*. *Obs.* 2. to mount; see *piao*, Exerc. XXVIII.

EXERCISE XXXIV.

Ex. 8. *Obs.* gentlemen; see *wei* Exerc. XIX.

Ex. 16. *Obs.* 1. great mess; *lit.* confusion and no rule; *tsa-luan* would stand alone, *wu chang* could not. *Obs.* 2. subordinate; *lit.* the here mentioned ones are [the superior's] hand beneath—'s small officials.

Ex. 18. *Obs.* 1. absent friend; *lit.* ocean's corner, sky's bound, is a '*hua-t'ou-'rh*, phrase, meaning that that [person] and this, = the speaker and his friend, are mutually separated exceedingly far. *Obs.* 2. expression; *lit.* an end of talk; compare the French *bout*.

Ex. 19. *Obs.* 1. hardly help; *lit.* it is hard to avoid. *Obs.* 2. unwillingness; *lit.* not able to let go, or part with. *Obs.* 3. signify; *lit.* [the meaning of] those [words], *i-lüan*, is [a man's] inability-to-part-with's meaning.

Ex. 20. *Obs.* one side; *lit.* a man, if he *k'ua* a horse, is specially on a horse's one side seated, or, sitting.

EXERCISE XXXV.

Ex. 15. *Obs.* 1. proclamation; a noun formed of two verbs *kao*, Exerc. V. 19, and *shih*, Radical 113. *Obs.* 2. to pass as; *tso-wei*^{2}, both verbs, and both here meaning to play a part, to act as. *Obs.* 3. issued; *ch'u*, to issue, here an active verb, of which *kuan*, officer, or, the government, is the subject; *lit.* to act as an-authorities-issue one, = one that is issued by the authorities.

Ex. 16. *Obs.* 1. being detected; *chiao*, *lit.* to cause; *q. d.* [some agent or incident] caused [the police of] the *k'a-lun* to find out [the truth]; = the truth was discovered by the *k'a-lun*. *Obs.* 2. was confiscated; construction as before, that of the active verb; *q. d.* [they, the people of the *k'a-lun*] the whole *shou*, put away, *ju*, that it might revert to government. *Obs.* 3. There is not in Chinese any verb properly passive, but the passive construction is effected, as in the two clauses here cited, by a verb like *shou*, to receive, or *pei*, to suffer; or by statement of the action that caused what was received or suffered; the action being indicated by an active verb the subject of which, whether agent or incident, is understood.

Ex. 17. *Obs.* sprinkle; *lit.* disperse and separate.

Ex. 20. *Obs.* all about; *lit.* the full, or whole, place.

Ex. 21. *Obs.* off; *ta*, literally, to strike; corruptly used for one of many words, it is not known which, signifying *from* a place.

Ex. 22. *Obs.* 1. something the matter; *mao-ping*, literally, an ailment small or trivial as a hair. *Obs.* 2. get hold of, but often to be rendered find; see Exerc. V. *ex.* 13.

Ex. 23. *Obs.* as regards; *lit.* if [one would] consider *yüan* and *pien's* un-sameness.

Ex. 24. *Obs.* 1. then whoever; observe that *chiu*, then, does not occur till the second clause; *lit.* let it be that a person for me speaks plainly, or explains, that then is [this, that] he for me *fēn p'ou*.

KEY TO THE TZŬ ERH CHI. Colloquial Series.

EXERCISE XXXVI.

Ex. 5. *Obs.* suited; be careful not to confound this *pien⁴-i²* suitable, with *p'ien²-i²* cheap; see Exerc. XIII. *ex.* 5.

Ex. 6. *Obs.* one's liking; *lit.* to correspond to one's nerve or muscle.

Ex. 9. *Obs.* pity; *q. d.* [the person or case referred to, men] *h'o*, ought to, by rights do, pity; = the person or case is justly deserving of pity.

Ex. 12. *Obs.* how old; see *to* above, Exerc. I. 16.

Ex. 16. *Obs.* exceedingly; *lit.* exceeds in the matter of stupidity; on *yü* see Exerc. XIII. 23.

Ex. 18. *Obs.* 1. great cheat; *lit.* is very competent, well knows how, to cheat people. *Obs.* 2. an instance; *lit.* for instance, that day. *Obs.* 3. the purport; more literally, a writing [which the reader would] reckon to be, = to mean, that his father wanted, &c. *Obs.* 4. and when; *lit.* subsequently he sold it for [him]; the *hei* being almost in his stead. The Chinese say similarly that a thing has been lost *for* a person; see *t'i*, for, Exerc. XXV.

Ex. 20. *Obs.* push in; or shut to; *shang* as above Exerc. III. *ex.* 24.

EXERCISE XXXVII.

Ex. 7. *Obs.* may I request; *lit.* I commit or entrust to you, Sir.

Ex. 13. *Obs.* 1. meteors; observe *na*, that, = *the* meteor. *Obs.* 2. common enough; *lit.* also is a constantly being thing; *yeh*, also; *q. d.* although not so common as other celestial phenomena, still it is by no means uncommon; *ti* representing any such noun as phenomenon.

Ex. 14. *Obs.* 1. means; the construction will be apparent if the reader ask the question to which the whole example is an answer; viz. What is a man's meaning when he says that such a thing is common or frequent? Construe the answer thus; [the meaning of a man who] says that a thing is common &c., is the meaning [of a man] who says that it, [the meteor, he] constantly sees. *Obs.* 2. the *t'a* = it, the object, not man the subject.

Ex. 15. *Obs.* 1. community; *ta chung*, the multitude in its greatest extent. *Obs.* 2. distinguished; *lit.* thus is it that family affairs all can [men] divide into *kung* and *ssŭ*.

Ex. 16. *Obs.* nothing to do; *hsien-chu*, is similarly to be living without an occupation.

Ex. 17. *Obs.* 1. trouble; *lit.* although your public business is *fan-tsa*, troublesome and irregular. *Obs.* 2. embarrasses; *lit.* I have an important matter; true it is that it embarrasses intensely. *Obs.* 3. obliged; *lit.* I prefer a prayer to you, Sir, in my behalf to cast a calculation.

Ex. 18. *Obs.* 1. a friend; observe *na*, as in *na i t'ien*, see Exerc. XXI. *ex.* 15. *Obs.* 2. in the afternoon; *tao*, when the time came to be afternoon. *Obs.* 3. find the place; see note on *chao* at the end of Exerc. XL.

Ex. 19. *Obs.* 1. to buy; *ti* representing the word goods, or any like word; *lit.* [when men] at a great price sell [they] at a small price bought *ti*, goods, articles, = the goods bought by them, *na chiu*, that then, = such a transaction, is making money. *Obs.* 2. such goods; *na*, as in *ex.* 18, indefinite; *ti*, again as above; *lit.* those goods, any goods you please, are for one tael a catty [a dealer] bought ones; yet are they for one tael [the dealer] sold ones; *so-i*, wherefore, [the dealer was] not able to make money.

EXERCISE XXXVIII.

Ex. 9. *Obs.* 1. absent on duty; *lit.* on public [service] gone forth. *Obs.* 2. as distinct from; *lit.* that then is [an] acting post ['s] with a real post ['s] unsameness. *Obs.* 3. will depute; *lit.* [when] the post from which [the incumbent] goes out is not great, the superior *mei*, on every occasion, = usually, deputes, &c.

PART III. THE FORTY EXERCISES. Notes.

Ex. 10. *Obs.* 1. noviciate; *lit.* is, or acts as [one who] to learn by practice moves [therein]. *Obs.* 2. expectant; *lit.* waiting to fill; *'hou* being here the verb *to wait.*

Ex. 11. *Obs.* 1. China; *lit.* the within and the without; or the central [state and the states] without. *Obs.* 2. document; *lit.* [when a man] from his inferior position to a superior represents matters, he ought to use [the paper styled] *ping-t'ieh. Obs.* 3. corresponding; *lit.* going and coming.

Ex. 12. *Obs.* employés; *lit.* officers' people, government persons, but not applied to officers. *Obs.* 2. however; *lit.* still, [though wearing the insignia mentioned, their duties] are the same duties.

Ex. 13. *Obs.* 1. understrappers; *lit.* the persons serving and undertaking the execution of miscellaneous official duties in a *yamên. Obs.* 2. lictors; the *tsao-li* are, in law, the lictors charged with the infliction of corporal punishments, but, in practice, there is no distinction between them and the *ya-yi*.

EXERCISE XXXIX.

Ex. 5. *Obs.* power; *lit.* strength-measure, used morally and materially; also as means, resources, whether financial or intellectual.

Ex. 13. *Obs.* pretty sure; [you will find it] *lit.* hard to avoid.

Ex. 14. *Obs.* 1. not attribute; in my saying, = opinion, it is not connected with luck; see *kuan* Exerc. III. 14, to concern. *Obs.* 2. all due; *lit.* wholly is it that he has resolution-and-willingness-to-use-exertion—'s good points or advantage.

Ex. 15. *Obs.* 1. regularity; *lit.* good places and bitter places, = advantages and disadvantages, *ho*, severally, have non-assortment. *Obs.* 2. may say; *lit.* [one] says it is chance's good or evil, = different qualities of chance; yet is it that heaven according to virtuous and vicious [men's] merits and demerits, by decree decides woe and weal's un-sameness.

Ex. 16. *Obs.* length of time; *lit.* length of the measure of the longevity of man's living. Note long and short, = length, as in *ex.* 15 good and evil, = quality.

Ex. 17. *Obs.* 1 hurt at Li; *lit.* the surname Li one has made him thus chill-hearted. [Why?] It is that Li, &c. *Obs.* 2. kindness; note *'hao-ch'u*, as in *ex.* 15, objectively. *Obs.* 3. serious loss; *ling*, caused him, greatly to eat, = suffer, loss. *Obs.* 4. sorry for it; *lit.* now Li has *'hou'hao*, given after effect to, *'hui* repentance; the words *'hou-'hui*, combined, are a very common equivalent of the verb *repent*, and might stand here without the *liao. Obs.* 5. prefers; *lit.* he however willingly desires to eat loss [and] not to use Li's resources.

Ex. 18. *Obs.* deathlike; *ssŭ-yang* is used of persons only; when opposed as here to *'huo-tung*, the two terms may well be rendered animate and inanimate.

EXERCISE XL.

Ex. 10. *Obs.* sent for; if there be a pressing matter, [some one shall] going to call you go. Note the *ch'ü*, to go, repeated.

Ex. 11. *Obs.* turned out; *lit.* by you prepared those carts all greatly conform to [the proper] fashion; *ti* properly *tê*.

Ex. 12. *Obs.* 1. just looks; *lit.* truly it resembles; observe the object resembled between *hsiang* and *shih*, the two words which combine to produce our verb *resemble*; the latter had better be construed as a noun; *q. d.* truly like a horse-shed's likeness. *Obs.* 2. *hsiang-shih*; the latter character is always pronounced *shih* when with its present adjunct, or when it is followed by *ti*; but when with *hsiang*, mutual, (XXIV. 19,) it makes *hsiang-ssŭ*, resembling each other, it is always pronounced *ssŭ*; and so in various combinations in which it is the first word or syllable. *Obs.* 3. to live in; *lit.* [for a person] inhabiting very improper.

Ex. 13. *Obs.* over and above; *lit.* having excluded the persons inhabiting ones, below-remaining, still are there forty or fifty apartments.

Ex. 14. *Obs.* after paying; read '*huan* not '*han*, or '*hai*.

Ex. 15. *Obs.* perplexed; *lit.* [how] to get through, = subsist myself through, this, = the, day, truly wounds my heart.

Ex. 16. *Obs.* very badly; *chung* heavy, grave.

Ex. 17. *Obs.* 1. conditionally; *lit.* of a thing laid flat on the ground the saying '*hêng* and the saying *shu* are an according-to-the-case-and-considering-the-circumstances '*huo-tung* '*hua*, moveable expressions. *Obs* 2. end on; if that before [one's] face, *chih*, in a right line, confronting, be *shu*, [whoever] *tsai*, may be, a side facing man, then will regard it as '*hêng*. *Obs.* 3. held to be; *wei*, to make of, as before in *tso-wei*; see Exerc. XXXV. *ex.* 15. *Obs.* 4. regarded; the same verb *wei* preceded by *i*, to use, here acting as the sign of the objective case of a noun, the object of *wei*, understood; *q. d.* of the direction specified, the side-facing man makes horizontal, = he regards it as horizontal. Treat *i-wei* as the verb to regard, remembering that the object may either precede the combination or come between its two parts. It is equally correct to say *chê-ko i-wei shih* '*hêng*, and *i chê-ko wei* '*hêng*.

NOTE that *cho*², or *chao*², is written in the two different forms given in EXERC. III. 5, but that the second is that more commonly employed except when *cho* signifies to command. It is especially used in this latter sense in Imperial Decrees, to express the WE WILL of the Emperor. When preceding adjectives or adverbs, it is read both *cho* and *chao*; we have, for instance, *cho-shih*, of that which is real and true, *bonâ-fide*; *cho-lo*, of the settlement of a doubt, claim, enquiry, &c., but *chao-chi*, anxious, duly eager, or over eager, and, from the latter, impatient. After verbs, when nothing intervenes, it is most commonly, almost universally, *cho*; as in *tsou-cho*, going, *p'ao-cho*, running; but if the auxiliary *tê*, or *pu* representing *pu tê*, come between it and the verb, it is invariably *chao*, as in *chao-tê-chao*, has found or can find, *chao pu chao*, cannot find. In either case, whether *chao* or *cho*, after a verb its meaning is almost identical with that of *tê*, which, again, as has been before observed, is often corruptly supplanted by *ti*. The probability is that the *ti* used now to produce what we call the inflection of the possessive case, was originally *tê*, and it is reducible to an equivalent of *tê* in almost every construction in which we find it, except perhaps those which we should term adverbial; those, that is, where *ti* may be rendered by our terminations *like*, as in *sailorlike*, or *wise* in *cross-wise*. Even in these *tê* would do their duty, but as the parallel constructions in classical written Chinese are formed by *jan*, thus, and there is between the primitive meaning of *jan* and that of *ti*, a certain affinity, it may be safer to infer that, in these, *ti* figures in its earlier and uncorrupted sense. This was brightness, manifestness, like the white part of a target; hence, that which is evident. The word *jan*, originally the flashing of fire, came to mean *thus* by apparently a similar process.

END OF KEY TO PART III.

PART IV. THE TEN DIALOGUES. Wên-Ta Chang. I.

DIALOGUE I.

1. What part of the country are you from, Sir?
2. I am a T'ien-ching (T'ien-tsin) man. May I ask your country?
3. I am a Chih Li man too.
4. Ha! We are fellow-provincials then.
5. Who is that gentleman?
6. He is a foreigner.
7. Do you know what brings him here?
8. I do not. You had better ask him yourself.
9. May I ask what brings you to our country, Sir?
10. I am in business.
11. What have you brought with you, Sir?
12. Small things in the Japanese lacquer-ware way.
13. Oh! You are from Japan, Sir?
14. Yes. I am a Japanese.
15. Indeed! I had been told that no one could get into Japan or out of it.
16. That difficulty did exist once; but of late the restrictions have been relaxed, and intercourse is an easier matter than it used to be.

2. 敝 pi⁴	2. 領 ling³	9. 駕 chia⁴	12 漆 ch'i¹, ch'ih⁴
2. 津 chin¹, ching¹	4. 鄉 hsiang¹	12. 洋 yang²	16. 解 chieh³

1. *Obs.* what part; *kuei*, honorable, for the possessive pronoun of the second person.
2. *Obs.* 1. I am; *pi*⁴, vile, in ill condition, for the possessive of the first pronoun; my humble place is T'ien-chin¹, or T'ien-ching¹. *Obs.* 2. may I ask; *lit.* I have not *ling*³, received your instruction; you have not said whence you come.
4. *Obs* fellow-provincials; *hsiang*¹, properly village; both the speakers are men of the province of Chih Li.
8. *Obs.* yourself; *tzŭ-chi* does not agree with *t'a*.
9. *Obs.* Sir; *tsun chia*⁴, literally honored chariot.
12. *Obs.* 1. Japanese; *yang*², literally the eastern sea; the sea. *Obs.* 2. lacquer-ware; *ch'i*¹, the gum with which lacquer-ware is covered.
15. *Obs.* no one, *nan*, difficult is as often as not used for impossible.
16. *Obs.* 1. did exist; *t'ou-li*, formerly, *ch'io*, [however easy now, it was] nevertheless difficult. *Obs.* 2. relaxed; *chieh*³, to loosen, *chin*, the prohibitions; hence the state of things is 'hao hsieh-'rh, somewhat better.

KEY TO THE TZŬ ERH CHI. Colloquial Series.

17. Have any of our merchants gone over there yet?
18. There are some Chinese there.
19. From what province of China do the majority of them go?
20. The greater part are from the provinces of Kuang Tung and Fu Chien.
21. Do they do a large business?
22. Not very large I shŏuld imagine.
23. Why not? Have n't they money?
24. Well, I should say not much.
25. Why do they go to Japan, then, if they have n't money?
26. Most of them have accompanied Europeans.
27. What do Europeans carry them with them for?
28. It is to take charge of their hongs and to act as brokers for them.
29. Do they get on well with the Japanese?
30. Neither has much confidence in the other I imagine.

19. 省 *shêng*³   20. 廣 *kuang*³   28. 行 *'hang*²   28. 作 *tso*⁴   30 異 *i*⁴

19. *Obs.* province; *shêng*³, of which there are eighteen in China.
20. *Obs.* Kuang Tung; *kuang*³, broad.
23. *Obs.* money; *pên ch'ien*, one's own money, capital.
26. *Obs.* Europeans; *t'ai hsi kuo*, nations of the west; *t'ai* acting as a sort of collective.
28. *Obs.* 1. hongs; *'hang*², a vulgar form of *'hang* the 144th Radical. *Obs.* 2. act as; *tso*⁴-*wei*, both verbs signify to do; *tso* is but another form of *tso*, Exerc. III, 23. *Obs.* 3. brokers; *ching*, in the sense of to pass through, *shou*, the hand
30. *Obs.* confidence; *i*⁴ *hsin*, estranged minds, hearts not well affected.

DIALOGUE II.

1. Is not the horse you are riding, Sir, a horse of our country here?
2. It was bought in your country.
3. Who bought it for you?
4. The people in the horse-yard chose it for me.
5. How much did they ask you for him?
6. They asked 30 taels.
7. Did you give it?
8. I did not. I thought they asked too much.
9. And how much did you give?
10. I closed with them for 22 taels.
11. The horse was mine once.
12. Was he really? Why did you sell him?
13. I sold him because I wanted money.
14. It was not on account of any defect, was it?
15. Not at all. He had no defect whatever.

1. 納 *na*⁴

1. *Obs.* Sir; *ni na*⁴; see *nin* Exerc. XXV, 1.
9. *Obs.* And how much; *q. d.*, [though you did not give what they asked], *tao*, yet, how much &c

PART IV. - THE TEN DIALOGUES. Wên-Ta Chang. II.

16. What did you pay for him in the first instance?
17. A good deal. I had money then.
18. Ah! You had something in the public service had you not?
19. I was in a public office until my father died. I gave up my employment then, and returned home to look after my family.
20. Dear me! Was your father long ill?
21. Oh yes! Pretty near ten years.
22. And during his illness who took charge of his family?
23. He was able to attend to his affairs in-doors, though he could not go out.
24. Should you have remained in office had you not lost your father?
25. I might have remained or I might not, I am not sure.
26. How not sure?
27. I would have staid in the place if there had been more to be made out of it.
28. Did your salary in it not cover your expenses?
29. Well it did. Still a little addition was required to make one comfortable.
30. Don't think it odd if I say that you were wrong to give up your place.
31. Why, what do you think I ought to have done?
32. Is not His Excellency Wang your connection by marriage?
33. More; he is my blood relation.
34. Better still. Was not he made governor of a province the other day?
35. He was; Governor of Ho Nan. But what do you imply by your question, Sir?
36. My idea is that were you still in public employ, His Excellency Wang would beyond doubt be willing to give you a lift.

20.	哎 *ai*1	27.	項 *hsiang*4	31.	依 *i*1	34.	放 *fang*4
20.	呀 *ya*1	28.	賠 *p'ei*2	32.	王 *wang*2	34	撫 *fu*3
20.	久 *chiu*3	28.	墊 *tien*4	32.	戚 *ch'i*4		

16. *Obs.* first instance; *kên-'rh-li*, literally at the root.
19. *Obs.* 1. father died; *hsien fu*, my late father, *ch'u* departed from, *shih*, the world. *Obs.* 2. gave up; *ko hsia*, laid down, the appointment. *Obs.* 3. look after; *hao-li*, the first word signifying, here, the calculation, the second the administration, required in *chia wu*, household business.
20. *Obs.* 1. dear me! *ai1-ya1*. *Obs.* 2. your father; *ling tsun*; both words signifying honorable. *Obs.* 3. long; *jih-tzŭ chiu3*, days long enduring.
22. *Obs.* 1 his illness; *t'a na*, like *ni na*; a respectful form. *Obs.* 2. took charge; *chao-ying*, looked to every thing, and met every requirement.
24. *Obs.* remained in office; *tang*, here to bear.
27. *Obs.* more to be made; *hsiang*4, properly the neck; items, subdivisions; *tê hsiang*, the items, sums, obtained; specially used of the profits of an office.
28. *Obs.* cover expenses; *p'ei*2, to make up a deficiency; *tien*4, to fill up a hollow space.
29. *Obs.* well; [though I could have wished more], *tao*, yet, I had not to *p'ei-tien*.
30. *Obs.* 1. don't; *pieh*, short for *pu yao*. *Obs.* 2. think it odd; *kuai*, to be angry with. *Obs.* 3. were wrong; in laying down your office you were *pu-tang*, not right.
31. *Obs.* you think; *i*1, to follow; to lean against; according to; *lit.* in that case according to your idea, [you would have] *chiao*, caused me to do what?
32. *Obs.* 1. his excellency; *Wang*2 *ta-jên*; the two last words make an honorable appellative proper to a large number of officials whom we should not style excellency. *Obs.* 2. connection; *ch'in-ch'i*1, related by marriage.
34. *Obs.* made governor; *fang*4, to let go; in the higher grades to appoint; *hsun-fu*3, the former character signifying to go rounds as a watch, the latter, to soothe, conciliate.
35. *Obs.* imply by your question; *lit.* what is your lofty view, the view of your superior intelligence?

KEY TO THE TZŬ ERH CHI. Colloquial Series.

37. You are wrong. He never liked me.
38. That's all imagination. What evidence have you that he did not?
39. The last time he left home, I asked him to take me with him.
40. And what answer did he make?
41. He said. If there were not another man in the world, I would n't have you.
42. Dear me! Was there any reason for such sternness?
43. He can't bear me because I was idle and extravagant when I was young.
44. Oh! Be easy about that. Bygones are bygones. His Excellency surely doesn't bear you ill will now.
45. You don't know. He said more than what I have told you.
46. But not that he would never forgive you?
47. He said that no matter what luck he might have, he would never shew me any favor.
48. What a pity, that with such an opportunity as this you shouldn't be able to avail yourself of it.
49. There is no help for it. It's no one's fault but mine that I did not make better use of my time long ago.
50. Did your father's property all come to you, or was it divided?
51. Not all to me; my two brothers elder and younger have each a share.
52. Has your elder brother a larger share than the rest?
53. No. It is equally divided amongst the three of us.
54. What sort of property was it? Money?
55. There was some ready money, and some house property; and business as well.
56. How came the house to you when you were not the eldest son?
57. While my father was alive, my eldest brother always looked after the shop.
58. Oh? And you live in the house to take care of your mother.

37. 歡 'huan 1	43. 儉 chien 3	46. 宥 yu 4	53. 均 chun 1
38 證 chêng 4	44. 唉 ai 1	48. 由 yu 2	54. 哪 na 4
43. 恨 'hên 4	44. 既 chi 4	49. 息 hsi 2	54. 業 yeh 4
43. 勤 ch'in 2	44. 咎 chiu 1	50. 歸 kuei 1	58. 侍 tz'ŭ 4

37. *Obs.* never liked; he heretofore has not *hsi-'huan* 1, rejoiced in me.
38. *Obs* evidence; *lit.* what is a *tui-chêng* 4; the latter word, *chêng*, signifying witness, that *tui*, accords with, what you advance.
39. *Obs.* 1. last time; *shang tz'ŭ*, the time or turn last above the present. *Obs.* 2. left home; *lit* went outside; said of any one going to some distance to trade, on duty, &c.
43. *Obs.* 1. can't bear; *'hên* 4, to hate, be wrath with. *Obs.* 2 idle; was not *ch'in* 2, diligent, and *chien*, 3 economical
44. *Obs.* 1 Oh! *ai* 1, an interjection. *Obs.* 2. bygones; *chi* 4, of time that is past; since; *chi wang*, as to what is past, or, since the thing is past, *pu chiu* 1, there is no fault [imputed].
46. *Obs* forgive; *yu* 4, to forgive; *k'uan-yu*, to have the liberality to forgive.
47. *Obs.* luck; *lit* no matter what share of promotion, wealth, &c, he might reach.
48. *Obs.* opportunity; *yu* 2, from, proceeding from, *shih-yu-êrh*, that from which any thing proceeds, its occasion.
49. *Obs.* better use; *hsi* 2, properly, rest; the profit, interest, accruing on money put out; *ch'u-hsi*, to make profit, or, the profit made.
50. *Obs.* all come, *chuan*, exclusively, *kuei* 1, to revert to.
53. *Obs.* equally; *chun* 1, in even shares.
54. *Obs.* 1. was it; *na* 1, an interrogative particle. *Obs.* 2. property; *ch'an yeh* 4, may mean land, house, or business.
56. *Obs.* the house; *lit.* the dwelling house below your person.
57. *Obs.* alive; *tsai*, existing.
58. *Obs.* 1. take care of; *tz'ŭ* 4 -*'hou*, to wait on; both words meaning to wait, to wait for. *Obs.* 2. your mother; *hsuan-t'ang*, the latter word, properly a hall, being elliptically used for *hsuan-t'ang*, a poetical term for mother.

PART IV. THE TEN DIALOGUES. Wên-Ta Chang II & III.

59. Exactly; my younger brother being also away from home. He has got a private secretary's place somewhere or other.

59. 幕 *mu*⁴

59. `Obs.` private secretary; *mu*⁴, properly a curtain or screen, behind which the secretary would sit, his employer being in court. The allusion is classical.

DIALOGUE III.

1. Come here somebody.
2. Here, Sir. What did you want, Sir?
3. Who are you?
4. My name is Lai-fu.
5. What is your surname?
6. My surname is Chang.
7. What do you do here?
8. I came to do my elder brother's work?
9. Who is your elder brother?
10. My brother's name is Lai-shun.
11. What, the Lai-shun who looks after the library?
12. Yes the same.
13. How came he to go away without asking leave?
14. He thought he oughtn't to trouble you about leave, Sir, when you were unwell.
15. Why couldn't he wait till I was well again?
16. He was wanted at home on very particular business.
17. What particular business?
18. His mother was very ill.
19. If so, why should you and he have changed places?
20. He went because his father desired it, and I came for fear your work might not be done, Sir.
21. Well, be all that as it may, servants should never leave the house without asking leave.
22. Don't be hard on my brother, Sir, pray; he will be back soon.

8. 哥 *ko*¹   18. 母 *mu*³   21. 勿 *wu*⁴
13. 假 *chia*⁴   19. 著 *chê*   22. 恕 *shu*⁴

4. *Obs.* my name; *hsiao tı*, the little one); servants so style themselves to their masters; in a court, prisoners and witnesses do the same; differently used in Part VI, Lesson LXXXVII.
8. *Obs* elder brother; *ho*¹-*ko*¹, borrowed from the Manchu language; notice *t*ı first as the preposition instead of, and then as the verb to replace, or do instead of
13. *Obs* ask leave; *chia*⁴, to rest, take a holiday; not to be confounded with *chia*³, false; *kao chia*, to give notice of leave.
14. *Obs.* he oughtn't; *pu pien*, it was not expedient that he should.
18 *Obs* his mother; *mu*³ being also the mother of the speaker, she is spoken of as the mother of the family; compare Dial II, 58
19. *Obs.* if so, since it is *chê-mo-cho*, thus; the *cho*² at the end of this combination is sometimes written as *cho*, Exerc. III, 5; sometimes as *chê*, the classical relative; see Part V, Section XII, 24.
21. *Obs.* be all that, *wu*⁴, a negative imperative particle; lit of other matters, before [I speak of this most essential matter], do not speak.
22 *Obs* don't be hard; *k'uan-shu*⁴; *shu*, properly, to forbear doing to others what one does not wish done to oneself; hence, to shew mercy.

KEY TO THE TZŬ ERH CHI. Colloquial Series.

23. Is your house far from this?
24. I should not call it very far.
25. What do you mean by not very far?
26. It's not more than four *li* at the most. It's in the Eastern Division too.
27. Well you can go home. I sha'n't want you.
28. Must my brother come back directly?
29. It will do if he is here by to-night.
30. Oh! Here is Lai-shun himself!
31. Ha! Tell him to come here. You can go.
32. You have no farther orders for me, Sir?
33. None whatever. You go. Here, Lai-shun!
34. I have made a sad mistake, Sir, but I hope you will forgive me.
35. It was a mistake indeed. Why did you go out without saying a word to me?
36. You were not well, Sir, and they were pressing me for the money.
37. Who were *they*, and what was *the* money?
38. The shop, Sir, where I bought the table for you the other day, wanted to be paid for it.
39. Isn't that shop in the Western Division?
40. No Sir; outside the walls.
41. Outside the walls! Near which gate?
42. I don't know much about the town outside the walls, Sir.
43. But you know whether the shop was north or south of this, don't you?
44. Oh! I remember. It's outside the An-ting Gate.
45. There's something I don't quite understand in all this.
46. What is it you don't understand, Sir?
47. You have got to speak the truth, mind.
48. I shouldn't venture to tell you a lie, Sir.
49. Halloa! Who is it that's making such a noise in the court?
50. Shall I go out and see, Sir?
51. No, you needn't go. Shut the window.
52. Dear me! What can the matter be? There's some one coming rushing into the house.
53. Why you are a waggoner are you not? What do you mean by rushing in in this way?
54. O Sir! My humble service to you. I want you to stand my friend, Sir.
55. What do you mean?
56. O Sir! Justice, if you please. I've been thrashed and I've lost my money.

23. 離 li^2 49. 院 $yuan^4$ 54. 噯 ai^1 56. 挨 ai^2, $ngai^2$
48. 敢 kan^3 52. 闖 $ch'uang^3$ 54. 磕 $k'o^1$ 56. 伸 $shen^1$

23. *Obs.* far from; li^2, to separate; hence, from; is your house from this far or near?
28. *Obs.* directly; li-$k'ê$, the moment now present; *q. d.* now standing before us.
48. *Obs.* venture; kan^3, to dare.
49. *Obs.* court; $yuan^4$, an enclosure surrounded by walls; the open spaces between the buildings in a Chinese house are so called.
52. *Obs.* rushing in; $ch'uang^3$, to burst a way into; said of man or beast.
54. *Obs.* 1. oh Sir; ai^1, a mere exclamation. *Obs.* 2. humble service; $k'o^1$, to knock, $t'ou$, the head, perform a kotow.
    Obs. 3. stand my friend, *lit.* I pray you, Sir, to $tso chu$, to play the master, to manage my business for me.
56. *Obs.* 1. have been thrashed, $ngai^2$, originally to beat; more commonly, side by side with; in northern mandarin, to suffer, be the recipient of; hence, when with other verbs, what we should call a sign of the passive. *Obs.* 2. justice; *lit.* I pray you, Sir, $shen^1$, stretch out so as to straighten, $yuan$, my wrong.

PART IV. THE TEN DIALOGUES. Wên-Ta Chang III.

57. And what have I to do with your thrashing or your losses?
58. If you have nothing to do with it, Sir, your servant has, at any rate.
59. My servant! What, Lai-shun here, perhaps?
60. Ha! Yes indeed! That is the man. I didn't notice him before.
61. What has he had to do with you?
62. He hasn't paid me my fare.
63. Your fare from the Northern Division?
64. Northern Division? No. We belong to an inn at Foal's Bridge.
65. Dear! Dear! This really requires explanation. Take care what you say.
66. You may take my leg off, Sir, if I say a word that's not true.
67. What time did you start from Foal's Bridge this morning?
68. The team was put to at cock-crow.
69. Had you one beast or two?
70. A pair. We were to go quick.
71. Had you no passenger but Lai-shun here?
72. There was a companion of his as well.
73. And which of the two was it that proposed to go so fast?
74. Lai-shun hired the cart, and when he came to hire it, he said that if I made haste he would pay me something extra.
75. What did you and he agree should be the fare?
76. It was settled that I was to have five tiao.
77. Including the extra charge for speed.
78. Yes; the extra fare included. I never take in anybody.
79. Oh! The fare is fair enough. Was it about this you came to blows?
80. We didn't come to blows at all.
81. What! Didn't you say just now that you had had a thrashing?
82. Yes, but it was not Lai-shun that thrashed me.
83. Who then?
84. A number of people; I don't know any one of them.
85. What, a lot of people headed by Lai-shun?
86. No, no. Lai-shun did not bring any one.
87. They were thieves then?

    57. 與 yu³   64. 駒 chü¹   65. 詳 hsiang²   74. 加 chia¹
    57. 何 'ho²   65. 咳 'hai¹   72. 伴 pan⁴   79. 架 chia⁴

57. *Obs* to do with; *yu*⁴, with; your loss of money &c. has with me, *'ho² kan*, what connection, or concern?
64. *Obs*. Foal's Bridge; *chü*¹, horse, ass, or mule, not full grown. *Ma-chü Ch'iao* is a village a few miles east of Peking.
65. *Obs* 1. dear! dear! *'hai*¹, an interjection. *Obs* 2. explanation; *lit.* this *shang*, still, requires *hsiang*²*-hsi*, explicitness and minuteness.
72. *Obs*. companion; *pan*⁴, partner, associate.
74. *Obs*. extra; *chia*¹, to add to; *lit* he said if I made haste he could add some cash.
78. *Obs*. take in; *ngo*, in Exerc. XXIII, 10, as erroneous; here, as inducing error, deceiving.
79. *Obs*. came to blows; *chia*⁴, properly a frame; to ward off blows; with *ta*, to fight, with arms or without.

KEY TO THE TZŬ ERH CHI. Colloquial Series.

88. No not thieves either. Oh dear it's a long story to tell.
89. Well, but you have got to tell it, whether it be long or short.
90. Oh Sir, please pay me the fare that's due to me, and I'll go about my business.
91. Not so fast. I want to understand all this.
92. It's not worth taking up your time, Sir.
93. Don't you trouble yourself about that. All you've got to do is to answer my questions.
94. Well, Sir, what do you want me to tell you?
95. Is Chang Lai-shun here a Foal's Bridge man?
96. His father is a market-gardener outside the town there.
97. Oh! Then of course Lai-shun is an old acquaintance of yours?
98. I used to see him when he was quite a little fellow playing about the streets.
99. Was he honest as a boy, or the reverse?
100. Sir, I had rather not tell tales of anybody.
101. But I don't want you to tell tales. You can tell me any good you know of him, can't you?
102. Sir! Please pay me my fare and let me go about my business.
103. Well, tell me; where did the people come from who fell upon you?
104. They belonged to a tea-house on the road.
105. How far from the city?
106. Not far. Just outside the Sha-wo gate.
107. And Lai-shun had some tea there?
108. No, no tea; some spirits and something to eat besides.
109. Did you breakfast with him?
110. No. I was away getting my whip mended.
111. Well, and when it was mended you came back to the house?
112. Yes, I came back; and when I got back I found that they were off.
113. Off! Having done you out of your money?
114. Yes, and not only me, but the tea-house as well.'

88.	哟 yo¹	96.	鎮 chên⁴	103.	毆 ou¹	106.	窩 wo¹
91.	晰 hsi¹	96.	園 yuan²	104.	館 kuan³	110.	鞭 pien¹
93.	只 chih³	99.	滑 'hua²	106.	沙 sha¹	114.	但 tan⁴

88. *Obs.* oh dear; *ai yo*¹, an interjection.
91. *Obs* to understand; *hsi*¹, bright, clear; I must *fên-hsi*, distinguish one part from another *ming-pai*, clearly.
93. *Obs.* all you have to do; *chih*³, only; I only require that, when I ask you something, you say that something
96. *Obs.* 1. town; *chên*⁴, properly to control, amongst many other meanings it has that of a town, less in importance than a district city; *chên-tien* is a place of trade larger than a village. *Obs.* 2 gardener; *yuan*², a garden; his father keeps, lit. opens, a *ts'ai-yuan*, vegetable garden, as distinct from *'hua yuan*, a flower garden, *kuo-mu yuan*, an orchard.
99. *Obs.* reverse; *'hua*², slippery; *tsei-'hua*, thief-like slippery, dishonest.
100. *Obs.* tell tales; to tell people's *tuan ch'u*, short places, demerits; *ch'ang-ch'u* is a man's special merit.
103. *Obs.* fell upon; *ng ou*¹, to beat, with or without a weapon.
104. *Obs.* tea-house; *kuan*³, a term to be differently translated according to circumstances; a school, an hotel, the temporary residence of an official travelling on duty, &c.
106. *Obs.* gate; *sha*¹ *wo*¹, popularly pronounced *sha-'huo*; literally dust, or sand, nest, *wo* is the nest or lair of bird or beast.
110. *Obs.* whip; *pien*¹; mended *shuan*, as before, to tie on to, or round.
112. *Obs.* 1. when; *kan*, as before, to overtake, come up to. *Obs.* 2. they were off, they had, before the time so described, run away.
114. *Obs.* not only; *tan*⁴, only; not only the waggon fare, *lien*, also, &c.

PART IV. THE TEN DIALOGUES. Wên-Ta Chang III & IV.

115. Oh! That was it! And the tea-shop wanted you to pay your passengers' bill?
116. That *was* it; and when I wouldn't pay they set upon me.
117. Well, so far as the beating you got at the tea-house goes, I don't see that I can do anything for you. Eh?
118. Oh! The beating doesn't signify, but please, Sir, pay me my fare, and let me go about my business.
119. There is no difficulty about the fare. I shall stop it out of Lai-shùn's wages for you.
120. Could you give it me at once, Sir, if you please, and let me go home?
121. Don't disturb yourself about the fare; but have you nothing to say to him about what took place at the tea-shop.
122. No, no; nothing whatever. Please pay me my fare, Sir, and let me go home.
123. Well you are a right good fellow to put up with your neighbour's wrong-doing in this way; but when you get back to your village, you may tell Lai-shùn's father, that neither of his sons has any honesty in him, and that I will have nothing whatever to do with such servants.

   119. 折 *chê*²   123. 擔 *tan*¹   123. 村 *ts'un*¹   123. 決 *chueh*²
   123. 忠 *chung*¹   123. 竟 *ching*⁴   123. 誠 *ch'êng*²

115. *Obs.* wanted you; *wang*, Exerc. XXXIV, 11, to look towards; often used as the prepositions *to*, or *of*, in such phrases as, speaking *to* me, requiring *of* me.
119. *Obs.* stop it, *chê*², properly to snap off, here, as elsewhere, to deduct from one account in favor of another.
123. *Obs.* 1. right good, *chung*¹; honest, loyal, *'hou*, thick; morally, sound, liberal, the opposite of mean. *Obs.* 2. put up with; *tan*¹; to bear on the shoulder, but read *tan*⁴ when used materially; *tan-tai* to behave towards men as one bearing their *pu-shih*, faults, on one's own shoulder. *Obs.* 3. but when; *ching*⁴, a strong disjunctive. *Obs.* 4. village; *ts'un*¹. *Obs.* 5 honesty; *ch'êng*², true of heart, *shih*, of word. *Obs.* 6. nothing whatever; *chueh*², literally to cut; positively, decidedly.

DIALOGUE IV.

1. Lung-t'ien!
2. Sir!
3. Who is that in the court?
4. His name is Hsu.
5. Oh! A man you know, is it?
6. Yes Sir; an old acquaintance.
7. Where did you meet?

   4. 徐 *hsü*²   5 識 *shih*²   6. 陳 *ch'ên*²   7 遇 *yü*⁴

1. *Obs* Lung-t'ien; the name of the person addressed, not the surname, this, in familiar intercourse, especially with a junior, is omitted. Were the surname expressed, it would precede the name as above in Dial. III, 95
4. *Obs.* Hsu²; a surname. There are in all China but some 540 single syllabled surnames, with perhaps 30 of two syllables.
5. *Obs* know; *shih*², to know, recognise.
6. *Obs.* old acquaintance; *ch'ên*², old, of things long in use, also, stale.
7. *Obs.* meet; *yu*⁴, to meet by accident.

KEY TO THE TZŬ ERH CHI. Colloquial Series.

8. We met at Shanghai.
9. When was that?
10. Many years ago.
11. Were you intimate?
12. Pretty well, Sir. We are distantly connected.
13. Ho! You're distantly connected? Do you know what he wants here?
14. No, Sir, but I can ask him. Shall I?
15. Do. I have no objection.
16. He says he is come to see Your Excellency.
17. Come to see me! What about?
18. His father has sent him to pay his respects he says.
19. His father! What is his father?
20. He was in business once. At present he has no occupation.
21. I don't remember the man at all. What line of business was he in?
22. Surely you remember the large draper's shop in the Western Division, Sir?
23. Oh! Hsu Fu-ch'ing! I do remember him. It's *his* son is it?
24. His son, Sir.
25. Ask him to step in.
26. His Excellency begs you will walk in.
27. I hope Your Excellency is well.
28. Take a seat! Take a seat!
29. When Your Excellency is seated.
30. Take a seat! Take a seat! Here! Somebody!
31. Dja!
32. Some tea! Your name is Hsü, Sir?
33. Hsü, at your service, Sir.
34. The son of Hsü Fu-ch'ing?
35. Hsü Fu-ch'ing is my father.
36. I used to know him years ago. I hope he is well?
37. Very well, thank you Sir. He sent me to enquire after Your Excellency's health.
38. It was very good of him to think of me, I am sure, and very good of you to take so much trouble.

23. 慶 ch'ing⁴   32. 沏 ch'i¹   38. 惦 tien⁴
25. 讓 jang⁴   37. 托 t'o¹   38. 勞 lao²

18. *Obs.* respects; sent to *ch'ing*, for *ch'ing-wên*, to beg to be allowed to enquire after your *an*, health, comfort
21. *Obs.* the man; *q.d.* this man is one *so*, whom I do not remember; the addition of the *so* is held to emphasise the affirmation.
23. *Obs.* Hsü Fu-ch'ing; *ch'ing*⁴, prosperity, congratulations upon prosperity; here, part of a man's name.
25. *Obs.* ask him; *jang*⁴, properly to concede to, hence, to offer to, invite to benefit by; very commonly used of invitations to eat, drink, smoke, &c
32. *Obs.* some tea; *ch'i¹*, to pour boiling water on tea.
33. *Obs.* your service; *chien*, cheap, lowly, like *pi* Dial. I, 2, for the pronoun of the first person.
37. *Obs.* thank you; *t'o¹*, the same as *t'o¹*, Exerc. XXXVII, 15; to be beholden to *fu*, the prosperity of the person addressed; his goodness, which Heaven rewards by making him prosper, has a beneficial influence on the speaker
38. *Obs.* 1. good of him; *chiao*, to cause, as elsewhere puts the verb in the passive; *tien*⁴, to be anxious about persons or things; not recognised by the dictionaries. *Obs.* 2. I am sure; *cho-shih*, in very truth. *Obs.* 3. take trouble; *lao*², trouble, to trouble; *lao cha*, to trouble the chariot, politely for to trouble you.

PART IV. THE TEN DIALOGUES. Wên-Ta Chang IV.

39. Oh! Sir, it was no more than my simple duty.
40. Your father used to suffer from his eyes if I remember rightly. Do they still give him trouble?
41. His eyesight is pretty good thank you, Sir, considering his age.
42. Age! Why he is much the same age as I am I fancy?
43. He is sixty-nine, Sir.
44. Then I beat him by two years, for I am seventy-one.
45. I should be well satisfied if he looked as young as Your Excellency.
46. Well, I don't understand why he should not. He has not gone through what I have.
47. As a public man Your Excellency has had great cares no doubt; but my poor father has had his anxieties.
48. Well but they are over now. I hear he has retired from business.
49. Yes, Sir, he *has* retired, but that was because he could not help himself.
50. Oh indeed! He was unfortunate in business?
51. Not exactly, Sir.
52. No? Then was he robbed?
53. Far worse, Sir. He was cheated out of almost all the money he had made.
54. Dear me! I'm sorry to hear that. How was it? Did some one who owed him money make off with it?
55. No, Sir, a friend he went security for —
56. Absconded! How abominable! And the loss has told on your father's health, has it?
57. Naturally Sir. He has a large family and nothing to give them.

40 模 mo¹	52. 莫 mo⁴	53. 惡 wu⁴	55. 保 pao³
45. 康 k'ang¹	52. 被 pei⁴	53. 掙 chêng⁴	56. 精 ching¹
49. 奈 nai⁴	52. 竊 ch'ieh⁴	54. 繃 pêng¹	57. 養 yang³

40 *Obs.* if I remember; *mo*¹, a word not used separately from *'hu*; the combination implying dimness of sight or sense.

42. *Obs.* much the same; *ch'a*¹, properly, 'diverging; not to be confounded with the same character read *ch'ai*¹, Exerc XXXVIII, 2, or *tz'ǔ*¹, XXII, 15; *ch'a-pu-to*, differing not much, nearly the same as.

45. *Obs.* 1. as young; *k'ang*¹, free from ailment, *k'ang-chien*, stout and hearty. *Obs.* 2. well satisfied; literally, when I behold your excellency so stout and hearty, [I say if] my father *nêng-kou*, could be thus, that [would be a thing that, though] one asked for it, one could not obtain it; too good a thing to be got.

49. *Obs.* not help; *nai*⁴, properly, a certain fruit, but, as used in this phrase, untranslateable; *wu nai 'ho*, and *wu k'o nai 'ho*, both mean that the case is without any remedy, there is no help for it.

52. *Obs.* 1. no?; *mo*⁴, generally, negative imperative; *mo pu*, if it were not; was it not then that he was robbed? *Obs* 2. robbed; *pei*⁴, to cover; hence to suffer; hence sign of the passive; *ch'ieh*⁴, to steal, pilfer.

53 *Obs.* 1. worse; *wu*⁴, to hate; *k'o wu*, deserving hate, detestable, abominable. *Obs.* 2. made; *chêng*⁴, to make an effort, as when trying to extricate oneself from bonds; *chêng ch'ien*, to make money by exertion.

54. *Obs.* make off with; did the *ch'ien chu*, debtor, *pêng*¹, flick it, the money, away? *pêng*, which is not a recognised character, is used of the action of a bow-string, or of a piece of wood so set as to propel anything, upon the missile propelled.

55. *Obs.* security; *pao*³, to secure, ensure, in any sense.

56. *Obs.* health; *ching*¹, properly, minute, subtle; *ching*, the spirit within one as distinguished from *shên*, its external manifestation; *ching shên*, animal spirits, health.

57. *Obs.* nothing to give; *lit.* he has not *li-hang*, resources wherewith to *yang-'huo*, to keep them alive; *yang*³, to feed, rear, man or beast.

KEY TO THE TZŬ ERH CHI. **Colloquial Series.**

58. How many are there of you?
59. Four sons and three daughters.
60. But not all at home?
61. All at home, Sir.
62. I thought your father's daughters were all married? [campaign in the west.
63. Two of them were married to officers of the army, but their husbands were killed in that last
64. And their widows are come home again?
65. Yes, Sir; one with her two children and the other with six.
66. That is a large family to keep indeed. And there is another lady unmarried?
67. She is quite a young thing, and always ailing.
68. Ah! What does she suffer from?
69. My mother died while she was a baby at the breast, and she never throve afterwards.
70. This is very sad, really. But you and your brothers are doing something for the family I suppose.
71. I should be very glad to do anything, but I can get nothing to do.
72. Are you the eldest son?
73. The eldest but one, Sir.
74. And what is your eldest brother about?
75. He is a cripple and quite unfit for anything.
76. Well this is a terrible case. And your younger brothers?
77. They were quite children when my father failed, and as he couldn't pay for their schooling, they have been very imperfectly educated.

59. 姐 *chieh*³	62. 嫁 *chia*⁴	64. 婦 *fu*⁴	75. 疾 *chi*²
59. 妹 *mei*⁴	63. 陣 *chên*⁴	70. 憐 *lien*²	76. 景 *ching*³
60. 未 *wei*⁴	63. 亡 *wang*²	73. 排 *p'ai*²	77. 栽 *tsai*¹
62. 姑 *ku*¹	64. 孀 *shuang*¹	75. 殘 *ts'an*²	77. 培 *p'ei*²

59 *Obs* daughters; *chieh*³, elder sisters of the speaker; *mei*⁴, his younger sisters.
60. *Obs.* but not; *wei*⁴, not; not yet, *wei pi*, it does not necessarily follow.
61 *Obs* all; *ko ko 'rh*; every individual
62. *Obs*. 1. daughters; *ku*¹-*niang*, a spinster Obs 2 married, *chia*⁴, of the woman married, to leave home.
63. *Obs*. 1 married; those they were given to were military officers. *Obs*. 2. killed, *chên*⁴, a rank; the ranks of a force, *wang*², to die, *chên-wang*, died in battle; were killed the last time that in the west, *lit*. on the western road, [beyond the frontier], there was a *ch'u ping*, going forth to war.
64. *Obs* widows; *shuang*¹, widowed, *fu*⁴, a wife, *fu-jên* is used of any woman.
67 *Obs.* always ailing; *ai*, to love, here and often, in the sense of *to be used to*.
69. *Obs*. 1. while; *ts'ung* proceeding from; hence, at the time when. *Obs* 2. at the breast; *ch'ueh nai*, she wanted, was deficient in milk. *Obs*. 3. throve; *tsu ch'uang*, sufficiently vigorous.
70. *Obs* very sad; *lien*², to compassionate, *k'o lien*, that rightly may be, deserves to be, pitied; but it is used simply as *to pity*
71. *Obs* but, *lit*. I, *ch'ueh*, for all that may be argued to the contrary, am very willing, *k'o hsi*, lamentably, there is no *tao-lu*, road
72. *Obs*. eldest son, *chang fang*, literally, the chamber first in order, the sons, while children, are all in one apartment; as each one marries, he has a room to himself, the eldest will be first married.
73. *Obs* eldest but one; *p'ai*², to arrange in order; *p'ai êrh*, I stand second among the sons, a daughter might say it of her place among her sisters. [*chi*², ailments in general.
75. *Obs*. cripple, *ts'an-chi*, dreadfully ailing in the legs and feet, *ts'an*², to destroy, seriously injure; hence cruel.
76. *Obs*. 1. terrible case, *huang-ching*³, circumstances; the latter word, alone, being more strictly applicable to scenery, features of a landscape Obs 2. *k'o*, is properly; may properly be said to be *hao-pu-ti*³, infinite, *sc* in its badness.
77. *Obs*. 1. pay for schooling; *tsai-p'ei*, properly of trees; *tsai*¹, to plant, *p'ei*², to pile earth round the roots; could not take care of them [so as to enable them] to read. Obs. 2. imperfectly; *lit*. their learning, [though they have some,] *'hai*, or *'han*, for all that, cannot either be considered deep.

PART IV. THE TEN DIALOGUES. Wên-Ta Chang IV & V.

78. Well, I suppose the long and the short of it is that you want me to find you a place, eh?
79. Oh, Your Excellency, I should be inexpressibly grateful if you would take so much interest in me.
80. And that was the real object of your visit to-day; wasn't it?
81. I shouldn't have presumed to mention the subject, Sir, if you had not alluded to it.
82. Well, I'll see what I can do for you. Be so good as to call again about ten days hence.
83. I am greatly indebted to you for the preference you are shewing me, Sir. I will wait on Your Excellency again in a few days.
84. Good bye then for the present.
85. Good bye to Your Excellency.

79. 感 kan³   79. 激 chi¹   79. 盡 chin⁴   81. 提 t'i²   83. 拔 pa²

79. *Obs.* 1. interest; *t'êng ai*, to tenderly love. *Obs.* 2. grateful; *kan-chi*; the character *kan*³ meaning to move the heart, or to have the heart moved; *chi*¹, the out-bursting of the heart so moved. *Obs.* 3. inexpressibly; *chin*⁴, to exhaust; words will hardly exhaust.
81. *Obs.* 1. allude to; *t'i*², properly to pick up.
83. *Obs.* preference; *t'i-pa*²; the first word as in 81; the second means, to draw one out of a bundle; *t'i-pa*, to help on any one in preference to others.

DIALOGUE V.

1. Lung-t'ien, when Hsü Yung calls again you tell him I've left town.
2. Poor fellow! He'll be sadly disappointed. What has he done to offend Your Excellency?
3. Offend! His whole story was a tissue of falsehoods from beginning to end.
4. Why isn't he the son of Hsü Fu-ch'ing?
5. Oh yes, he's Hsu Fu-ch'ing's son.
6. And didn't his father fail as he said?
7. He did fail; but not as he said.
8. How did he fail then?
9. It was his own extravagance and folly that broke him; nothing else.
10. Still he has an immense family to support.
11. Nothing of the sort. In the first place, Hsü Fu-ch'ing himself has been dead some years.
12. Dead some years! And who maintains all those sons and daughters of his?
13. His daughters all died before him, and he never had any son but this impostor.
14. Sir, I think Your Excellency must be misinformed.
15. Not in the least. I've been making very careful enquiries. Didn't you say that you were connected
16. I did.   [with these people by marriage?
17. But you have seen nothing of them for four or five years?
18. Oh, more than that; nine or ten years.
19. Just so. Now, when old Hsu kept the draper's shop, what was his character?

1. 永 yung³   9. 拋 p'ao¹   15. 查 ch'a²

1. *Obs.* Hsu Yung; *yung*³, eternal, here the name of the man surnamed Hsü.
2. *Obs.* 1 disappointment; *shih wang*, to lose hope. *Obs.* 2. offend; *tê tsui*, to get blame of you; before *ni-na* 'you, understand *yu*, Exerc XIII, 23, in the sense of *from* or *of*.
3. *Obs.* beginning to end, *t'ung shên*, entire body.
9. *Obs.* extravagance; *p'ao*¹, to let go suddenly of what is held in the hand; *p'ao-fei*, to spend without restraint.
15. *Obs.* careful enquiries, *k'ao-ch'a*², the latter character being identical, in the colloquial language, with *ch'a*, Exerc. XX, 7.

KEY TO THE TZŬ ERH CHI. Colloquial Series.

20. They used to say he was a very proud man. I never heard anything else against him.
21. Wasn't he very much given to smoking?
22. He did smoke certainly; and he was pretty fond of his glass too.
23. Exactly. Now, when you met his son at Shanghai, what was he doing there?
24. He said he had been commissioned to buy produce for exportation.
25. What produce? Tea or silk?
26. Tea, and silk, and medicines.
27. And where were they to have been carried?
28. I forget whether he said north or south.
29. And did he say nothing about purchasing imports?
30. Nothing that I remember.
31. Nothing about opium?
32. Yes, yes! Now you mention it, I recollect that he had some little difficulty about his opium.
33. Why, wasn't there as much as he wanted in the market?
34. Oh yes! The price of the drug was rising every day, but there was plenty of it for sale.
35. What, publicly?
36. Not exactly. It was stowed away snugly in the receiving ships, or in foreign warehouses.
37. And had it to be smoked on foreign premises?
38. No. The divan Hsu Yung used to frequent was in the back of a small house up a narrow street.
39. Ho! He used to frequent a divan did he? Like father like son.
40. Well he didn't smoke so much after all.
41. Only purchased it for others, eh? And what was the difficulty he got into about it?
42. The prohibitions against the trade were still in force, and after he had purchased what he wanted, he couldn't get it away for a long time.
43. And how did he succeed at last?
44. He shipped it in a cargo boat freighted with firewood, and smuggled it out of port.

20	狂 k'uang²	25	葉 yeh⁴	26	材 ts'ai²	36	棧 chan⁴
21	烟 yen¹	26	湖 hu²	32	微 wei¹	36	藏 ts'ang²
22	貪 t'an¹	26	藥 yao⁴	36	躉 tun³	44	艇 t'ing³

20. *Obs.* proud; *k'uang²*, of unbridled temper, or passions, *k'uang-ao*, ungovernably proud; contemptuous.
21. *Obs.* smoking; *yen¹*, smoke of any kind; *ch'ih yen*, to eat smoke, to smoke; nowadays more particularly used of opium-smoking.
22. *Obs* fond of his glass; *t'an¹*, to covet, desire immoderately.
24. *Obs* produce, *t'u 'huo*, merchandise of the place or country.
25. *Obs.* tea; *yeh⁴*, a leaf; *ch'a yeh*, tea-leaves; tea in the market.
26. *Obs.* silk; *'Hu² ssū*, properly silk of 'Hu-chou Fu, in the province of Chê Chiang (Chê Keang), but used generically of the finer silk. *Obs* 2 medicines, *yao⁴*, drug, *ts'ai²*, materials; the latter word used particularly of timber.
27. *Obs.* carried; *yun*, to convey, Exerc. XXXIX, 6
31. *Obs* 1. nothing about, *lit.* did he not mention that he was *pan*, managing, engaged in an operation of, (that is, as it is very commonly used,) buying. *Obs.* 2. opium; *yang yao*, foreign drug, drug from the seas.
32. *Obs.* some little, *wei¹*, minute; *hsieh wei i tien*, a very common diminutive.
35. *Obs.* publicly; *kung-jan*; the latter word as in Exerc. XXI, 20.
36. *Obs* 1. receiving ships; *tun³ ch'uan*; the first character meaning to buy wholesale. *Obs* 2 warehouses; *chan⁴-fung*. *Obs* 3 stored; *ts'ang²*, to conceal, put out of sight.
44. *Obs.* 1. cargo-boat, *t'ing³*, not an open boat, but still a smaller vessel than a sea-going junk. *Obs.* 2. smuggled it out, *t'ou*, to steal; *t'ou-cho*, stealthily, went out of port.

PART IV. THE TEN DIALOGUES. Wên-Ta Chang V.

45. I thought firewood all came to Shanghai? Where could it be going to *from* the port?
46. To some place in the neighbourhood I suppose. The junk, you may be sure, had more opium than
47. And so he got into a scrape? [firewood on board.
48. Yes. His junk was dropping down the tide, when a revenue cruiser pounced upon her.
49. And put the cargo under seal?
50. No; but the tide-waiters threatened to search her if Hsü Yung didn't behave liberally.
51. How much did they ask?
52. They named no sum. They only said he must make them a handsome present.
53. And what did he offer?
54. Well, like a fool, he offered a hundred taels.
55. That was pretty liberal. Didn't the Custom House people think so?
56. They thought it much too liberal for a boat loaded with fuel; and they said that unless he paid down three hundred taels, they would seize the whole cargo.
57. And did he pay three hundred taels?
58. He hadn't got it to pay.
59. Then how did he manage?
60. He gave them an order on a foreign house in Shanghai.
61. I wonder they took it. He was in great luck to get away at all.
62. But he didn't get away immediately, that was the best of it.
63. What, did the Customs' people repent of their bargain after they had got the order for the money?
64. No; but while all this negociation had been going on, the Customs' boat and the junk had been dropping down the tide side by side, and ran foul of two other boats, that were lying at anchor.
65. What two other cruisers?
66. No, not cruisers; two boats belonging to the Imperial Commissioner Liu; one for himself and the
67. Capital! Was it very late at night? [other for his suite.
68. Not very late. About nine o'clock.
69. Still the Commissioner and his people were all asleep I suppose?
70. The Commissioner, I should think, was at his rooms in the city; but his people were laughing, and singing, and keeping it up on board.
71. But his people had no concern with a Customs' question.

| 49. 封 *fêng*¹ | 61. 虎 *'hu*³ | 65 唷 *shao*⁴ | 66. 劉 *liu*² |
| 52. 豐 *fêng*¹ | 64. 撞 *chuang*⁴ | 66. 欽 *ch'in*¹ | |

48. *Obs.* formed; *ch'ou lêng-tzŭ*, an expression indicating unlooked for occurrences; on a sudden *chua-chu*, clapped the paw, or claw, upon, and held or stopped the boat. The word *lêng*, cold, may refer to the shock of any occurrence unlooked for, but *ch'ou*, to draw, is scarcely explicable.
49. *Obs.* under seal; *fêng*¹, properly to stop up an orifice; here to close by pasting certain official papers over a door, hatch, &c.
52. *Obs.* handsome; *fêng*¹, abounding, plenteous; *ts'ung fêng*, in an abounding manner, in the most abounding manner
60. *Obs* 1. an order; *lit.* he wrote *ko tzŭ-erh*, a [paper of] characters; applicable to any note, memorandum, &c. *Obs* 2 on a house; *kên*, commonly, following; in the presence of; here, of or from, of the foreign house *ch'u ch'ien*, to take the money.
61. *Obs.* get away; *'hu*³, the tiger; that he got out of the tiger's mouth was his *p'ien-i*, advantage.
64. *Obs.* 1. ran foul; *chuang*⁴, to run up against; collision of persons or things. *Obs.* 2. at anchor; *wan*, Exerc. XXX, 2; there, a bay; but here, and often, to be at anchor.
65. *Obs.* cruisers; *shao*⁴, properly to whistle, or make the like sound; hence to make it as a signal, *hsun shao ch'uan*, circulating signal-making vessels.
66. *Obs.* 1. not cruisers; *kuan*, here short for *'hai-kuan*, maritime customs establishment. *Obs.* 2 commissioners, *ch'in*¹, imperial, *ch'ai*, envoy; *Liu*², a surname.

KEY TO THE TZŬ ERH CHI. Colloquial Series.

72. True; but when his boat ran bump up against them, it frightened them; and then, when they had recovered from their alarm, they came down on him for compensation.
73. Compensation for what?
74. For the fright, and damage done to the Imperial Commissioner's boats, and any thing else you please.
75. I wonder Hsu Yung didn't shew fight.
76. They were too many for him, and besides he had a guilty conscience.
77. As well he might have. But how did it all end?
78. The Customs' boat had hauled off, but his experience in her case had taught him not to be too liberal this time; so he offered the Commissioner's people ten taels only.
79. And they were satisfied.
80. Oh yes. They would have taken anything. They were much too far gone to overhaul his junk.

72. 驚 *ching*1		76. 寡 *kua*3		76. 虛 *hsu*1	
72. 訝 *ya*4		76. 敵 *ti*2		78. 躲 *to*3	
74. 損 *sun*3		76. 膽 *tan*3		80. 酣 *'han*1	

72. *Obs.* frightened; *ching*1 *ya*4, both words indicating surprise, but the former also terror.
74. *Obs.* damage; *sun*3, to injure; *sun-'huai*, to injure seriously.
76. *Obs.* 1. too many; *kua*3, the few, could not *ti*2, stand before, as equal to, *chung*, the many. *Obs* 2. guilty conscience; *tan*3, the liver, was *hsu*1, the opposite of *shih*, true, sound, solid. With the Chinese the liver is the seat of courage. Compare our term *white-livered*.
78. *Obs.* 1. had hauled off; *tsao*, early, some time before; *to*3, withdraw; *to-k'ai*, to get out of the way. *Obs.* 2. experience; he *ching kuo*, having passed through that [other affair], *chang*, had added a piece of *chien-shih*, seeing and knowing.
80. *Obs.* 1. oh, yes; *li* how should they not consent. *Obs.* 2. too far gone; they had all drunk to a state of *pan 'han*1, half intoxication.

DIALOGUE VI.

1. Well to return to his fabrications. Did he tell you whom he was buying for?
2. I forget.
3. He didn't tell you it was for his father?
4. I don't remember really.
5. It *was* for his father however, and his father's bankruptcy was due to this very transaction.
6. It was a bad speculation?
7. In one sense, yes. The opium was shipped for T'ien-ching.
8. What and seized there?
9. It never arrived. The junk it was on board of was taken by pirates off the Shan Tung coast.

1. 岔 *ch'a*4	1. 結 *chieh*2	9. 始 *shih*3	9. 終 *chung*1	9. 扣 *k'ou*4

1. *Obs.* to return; *lit.* that digression let us consider ended; *ch'a*4, a forked road, *p'ang-ch'a*, branching off from one side. *chieh*2, to tie a knot; to close an affair or a conversation.
5. *Obs.* was due; *yuan-yu*, the cause from which the bankruptcy proceeded.
9. *Obs.* 1. never; *shih*3, beginning, *chung*1, end; *shih chung*, from first to last. *Obs.* 2. taken by pirates, *lit.* was by sea robbers *k'ou*4*-chu*, kept fast; *k'ou* is properly to strike, as one knocking at a door.

PART IV. THE TEN DIALOGUES. Wên-Ta Chang VI.

10. And old Hsü lost all the money he had invested in it?
11. Yes, and not only that, but his button to boot.
12. But I didn't know that he had any rank.
13. He had purchased a grade the year before.
14. Purchased a grade! But how could the piracy affect his rank? It is not alleged that he was in relations with the pirates, surely?
15. The piracy did not affect it, but the smuggling did.
16. What? Did the smuggling come to the knowledge of the authorities?
17. Do you suppose large sums are ever extorted without the knowledge of the authorities?
18. Three hundred taels was not so very large a sum.
19. Quite large enough to be divided, and the cruiser's people kept more than their share, and fought about what they kept.
20. And then one told on the rest?
21. Precisely; and, once the authorities got wind of it, the whole operation was traced to its source, and old Hsü had to pay the heaviest fine that could be inflicted, and was stripped of his rank.
22. Well, one can't wonder at Hsü Yung's desire to keep his father's disgrace quiet.
23. Certainly not. He wasn't obliged to publish such a thing. But that is no reason why he should come here with a long invention about his father being the victim of misplaced confidence.

10. 貲 tzŭ 1   21. 究 chiu 1   22. 掩 yen 3
14. 涉 shê 4   21. 罰 fa 2   23. 揚 yang 2
16. 塲 ch'ang 3   22. 遮 chê 1   23. 編 pien 1

10. *Obs.* invested; *tzŭ* 1, properly, goods; here money; *tzu-pên*, capital.
11. *Obs.* button; *ting-tai*, literally, that which is borne on the crown of the head; but it means, generally, the insignia of office.
12. *Obs.* rank; *kung-ming*, elliptically for the credit one has gained, the name one is leaving; commonly used for official rank, whether obtained by merit or purchase.
14. *Obs* 1 but; *jan erh*, pronounced *jaⁿ 'rh*; the case being *jan*, thus, *érh*, yet —. *Obs.* 2. could affect; *shê* 4, properly to ford; *kan-shê*, to be affected by prejudicially; *q d.*, the thing *kan* strikes me; I am *shê*, implicated in it; as a man fording a stream is wet by the water. *Obs.* 3 not alleged; *nan-tao*, see Exerc. III, 22. *Obs.* 4 in relations; *t'ung*, to penetrate; here, to be in communication with, league with.
15. *Obs.* smuggling; *tsou-ssŭ*, the *ssŭ* is applied to any act unauthorised by law; a Chinese here understands *'huo*, goods, after it, and treats *tsou* as an active verb.
16 *Obs.* authorities; *ch'ang* 3, an arena; *kuan-ch'ang chung*; in the official arena, amongst the authorities.
19. *Obs.* divided; with their *t'ung-shih*, fellows in the business, *chun fên*, in equal parts shared; *t'ung-shih* is as often applied to associates in a lawful undertaking, those one acts with.
21. *Obs.* 1. traced; *chiu* 1, to investigate; they carefully investigated [in such wise that there was] a water-descending-stone-appearing, a discovery of the truth. *Obs.* 2. heaviest; *ts'ung chung*; see *ts'ung fêng*, Dial. V, 52. *Obs.* 3. fine; *fa* 2, properly, to punish, but, colloquially, to fine. *Obs.* 4 stripped, *kê*, Rad. 177, lit to skin.
22. *Obs.* 1. father's disgrace; *tiu lien*, to lose, throw away, face. *Obs.* 2. to keep quiet; *chê* 1, to screen wholly; *yen* 3 to half-screen; *chê-yen* may be used literally, but is oftener figurative.
23. *Obs.* 1. publish; *chang-yang* 2, the first word meaning to spread wide, the second to raise high. *Obs.* 2. invention; *pien* 1, to weave; *pien-tsao*, to fabricate a story.

KEY TO THE TZŬ ERH CHI. **Colloquial Series.**

24. That was too bad I admit.
25. I half mistrusted him at the time, and I resolved to ask Li Yung-ch'êng about him. I knew that he used to be very intimate with his father.
26. And his account of him was not satisfactory, I suppose?
27. Not at all. He knows Hsü Yung very well. He was weak enough to get him a place once without examining him.
28. As what?
29. As an office copyist, but he didn't keep the place a month.
30. Why not? Was he ill-conducted or incompetent?
31. Both. He could not write round hand at all, so he was of no use as a copyist; and they never could believe a word that he said.
32. I wonder how he contrives to dress as well as he does, with nothing to live on.
33. The coat he had on the other day was no great things I am sure.
34. Great things or not, it was a coat that must have cost something; and so must that mule he was on.
35. I thought he came in a cart.
36. No; he rode here; on a stout mule in very good case.
37. And yet, with all you know of his dishonesty and extravagance, you seem inclined to take his part.
38. I can't help pitying people that have known better days, when I see them in extremity.
39. Pity him as much as you will, but don't ask me to get him employment, for I wo'n't do it.
40. He'll be on the streets before long, poor fellow.
41. Well when he comes to want a meal I'll give it him, but recommend him for any place I will not.

24. 逾 *yü* 4	31 靠 *k'ao* 4	36. 膘 *piao* 1	38 享 *hsiang* 3
24 詐 *cha* 4	35. 估 *ku* 1	37. 徇 *hsün* 2	38 恤 *hsü* 1
27. 舉 *chü* 3	35. 摸 *mo* 1	37. 庇 *p'i* 1	41. 頓 *tun* 4

24. *Obs.* too bad; *yü* 4, to overpass, exceed; *cha* 4, falsehood; *kuo-yü*, to exceed in, *hsü-cha*, what is empty and false.
25. *Obs.* 1. intimate; *shou*, ripe. *Obs.* 2 resolved; *ta-cho*. *Obs.* 3 to ask; *ta-t'ing*, to enquire.
26. *Obs.* 1. I suppose; *ta kai*, in all probability. *Obs.* 2 account; *shuo*, not here to blame, but to talk of.
27. *Obs.* get him a place; *chü* 4, classically to raise; *pao-chü*, to recommend, guarantee the goodness of, a person. That man formerly besought him *k'ei'chao*, for him to seek, something, he being in heart *juan*, soft, consented; not having examined him, *chiu*, yet proceeded, to recommend him.
29. *Obs.* office copyist; *t'ieh hsieh*, literally, to write memoranda that are *t'ieh*, appended, to the document; see Exerc. XXXVIII, 17, for another form of the same character.
30. *Obs.* ill-conducted; *hsing-chih*, moving and being stationary, = conduct under all conditions, not good
31. *Obs.* 1. not write round hand at all; *ht.* as to *ch'tai shu*, round hand, *so*, it was what, he could not write; the *so*, as before observed, is sometimes regarded by a Chinese however, as intensive or emphasising, not as relative pronoun. *Obs.* 2. believe; *k'ao* 4, to lean against, rely upon; *k'ao-pu-chu*, not be relied on.
32. *Obs.* wonder; *lit.* that man is strange; being without money, how is it that what he wears is so respectable?
33. *Obs.* no great things; also not anything
35. *Obs* I thought; *ku* 1 *-mo* 1, from *ku*, to estimate as number or value, *mo*, to feel with the fingers.
36. *Obs* good case, *piao-chuang*, sleek and stout; *piao* not used except of beasts.
37. *Obs* take his part; *hsün* 2 *-p'i* 1; from *hsün*, to follow his lead, acquiesce in the line he takes, and *p'i* to give shelter to; *hsün-p'i* is only used where the party upheld is undeserving support.
38. *Obs.* 1. better days; having formerly *hsiang* 3, enjoyed, *fu* happiness. *Obs.* 2. pitying; *lien*, to pity, as in Dialogue IV, 17; *hsü* 1, means the same as *lien*.
40. *Obs.* 1. poor fellow; *k'o-hsi-hao-'rh-ti*, one deserving of pity. *Obs.* 2. before long; *yen-k'an-cho*, while the eye is beholding. *Obs.* 3. on the streets; he will, or is about to, want rice.
41. *Obs.* 1. a meal; *tun* 4, originally to bow the head a time or turn; hence, one time of eating. *Obs.* 2. recommend; *pao*, to guarantee; see above *pao-chü*.

PART IV. THE TEN DIALOGUES. Wên-Ta Chang V.I & VII.

42. He was to be here the day after to-morrow.
43. Then tell him what I told you.
44. That you will have nothing to say to him Sir?
45. No; that I am gone out of town.
46. And if he asks when he may call again?
47. You can't say. You don't know how long I shall be away.
48. But he'll be calling every day to find out.
49. Let him call as often as he likes, he is not to be admitted.
50. Wouldn't it be better to tell him plainly that he mustn't count on Your Excellency's support?
51. No, no! That will involve explanations into which I am still less inclined to enter with him.
52. If I don't mistake I hear his voice in the yard.
53. Then you may just put him off in the best way you can; for see him I wo'n't.
54. I was only joking. It's the block-cutter come for his money.
55. Let him come at the end of the month.
56. The man has been here twice already, Sir.
57. So he has, and I promised to pay him; so he must be paid.
58. I'll pay him Sir. Don't trouble yourself.

49 許 *hsu*³   50. 簡 *chien*³   50. 轉 *chuan*³   50. 倚 *i*³   53. 推 *t'ui*¹

42. *Obs* was to be here; according to what was that day agreed to, you *yo*, engaged, him to come the day after to-morrow.
43. *Obs.* what I told you; *ch'i-hsien*, at the beginning
49. *Obs.* he is not to be; *hsu*³, to permit; I do not permit you to make him come in.
50. *Obs* 1 better; *pu ju*, nothing so good as, interrogatively, would it not be best? *Obs.* 2. plainly; *chien-chih*, from *chien*³, concise, summary, and *chih*, straight   *Obs* 3 mustn't count; *lit.* if you are *ta suan*, speculating on any thing, do you *chuan*³, turning round, commission some one else; *chuan*, as here, constantly used as a disjunctive; *q.d.* so far from commissioning you, *chuan*, on the contrary, commission some one else.   *Obs.* 4. Your Excellency's support; it is of no use ¹ ³-*k'ao*, to lean against Your Excellency; *i* and *k'ao* are nearly identical in meaning.
51. *Obs* 1. no, no, note the force of *ch'io*.   *Obs.* 2. explanations; *lit.* it will be necessary to tell him minutely and plainly so *i jun ti 'hua*, words stating the so *i jan*, wherefore thus, the reason why.
52. *Obs* if I don't mistake; *êng*², here, an interrogative word; ha? what? See Exerc. XXIII, 6.
53. *Obs.* I put him off; *t'ui*¹ *tz'ŭ*, to push or put forward excuses; the latter word meaning originally language; *kao tz'ŭ*, to make one's excuses, is to take leave; as a verb *tz'ŭ*, means to decline, also to dismiss from one's employ.   *Obs.* 2. see him I won't; *chueh chi*, it is my fixed design, positively my plan.   [a type-cutter.
54. *Obs.* block-cutter; *k'o*¹, to engrave, not to be confounded with the same character read *k'o*⁴, Exerc IX, 16; *k'o tzŭ chiang*,
57. *Obs* promised; *ying-hsu*, both words in the sense of responding favorably to what is proposed, promising to perform
58. *Obs.* I'll pay him; *lit.* I for you, Sir, will *k'ai-fa*, distributingly issue; *k'ai-fa* in strictness applying to the settlement of a number of accounts.

DIALOGUE VII.

1. Was it you who were knocking at the door?
2. It was I.
3. Where are you from?
4. I am from outside the city.
5. Who are you looking for?
6. A person named Mêng.

6. 孟 *mêng*⁴

1. *Obs.* knocking; *lit.* calling, *sc.* some one to come out.
6. *Obs.* Mêng⁴, a family name; the surname of the philosopher known to us as Mencius.

KEY TO THE TZŬ ERH CHI. Colloquial Series.

7. Well, that's my name.
8. Oh! You are Mr. Mêng?
9. Yes. I am Mêng. What do you want of me?
10. I was sent from the Kuang Wên Chai.
11. Is not the Kuang Wên Chai a bookseller's?
12. Yes, a bookseller's.
13. What book is it you were told to bring?
14. I have not brought any book.
15. What? Isn't that a book you have in your hand?
16. No. It's a book-cover, not a book.
17. If you had no books to bring, why bring an empty book-cover?
18. The book-cover is not empty.
19. If it isn't, what has it got inside?
20. A few drawings.
21. Drawings! You've come to the wrong house I suspect.
22. No, it's all right; 1 was to bring them here.
23. How so? I've bought no drawings.
24. No; I know that it was not you who bought them.
25. Well then, why bring them to me?
26. Some one bought them for your house.
27. What could any one have meant by buying drawings for me?
28. Oh, Sir, you needn't ask what his motive was.
29. Well but who was it that bought them for me?
30. Do you know Mr. Chang who lives in the T'ang-tzŭ 'Hu-t'ung?
31. I do know him; and it was he was it?
32. No it was not he.
33. Not he! Then why mention him?
34. I have a reason for mentioning him.
35. If you have why don't you state it?
36. You're in a great hurry, Sir. You will understand more about it presently.
37. Come, I won't stand this. You're quizzing me.

10. 齋 chai¹   37. 戲 hsi⁴

10. *Obs.* Kuang Wên Chai; *chai*¹, properly, a swallow's nest; a pavilion in which to repose; elegantly used of certain shops. See below Part VI, Lesson LXXX, 2.
16. *Obs.* book-cover; *t'ao*, see Exerc. XXIX, 12; here the cover of pasteboard and cloth, in which Chinese volumes are wrapped.
30. *Obs.* T'ang-tzŭ 'Hu-t'ung; see above Exerc. XXX, 12; *t'ang*², properly a hall; *t'ang-tzŭ* may also mean a bathing establishment, but is, specially, the name of the chapel in which the emperor sacrifices to his ancestors.
36. *Obs.* presently; '*hui-lai*, in a turn of time; not, when you return.
37. *Obs.* quizzing; *hsi*⁴, to play, dramatically or otherwise; this is *shua-hsi*, joking language; I *pu fu*, will not submit to it.

PART IV. THE TEN DIALOGUES. Wên-Ta Chang VII.

38. Quizzing! I shouldn't think of such a thing.
39. But why not speak, if you have got anything serious to say?
40. It's a long story to tell.
41. Well if you can't tell it me, I'll go in. Be off with you.
42. Stop, stop! Don't be in such a hurry. I've got something more to say.
43. Be quick about it then; I've no time to waste.
44. You say you know Mr. Chang, Sir?
45. Yes. I told you so before.
46. Do you know his nephew, Sir?
47. Not much. I've seen him once.
48. Well, it is he that ordered these drawings to be sent to you.
49. He ordered them? When did he return?
50. Return? Has he been absent?
51. Wasn't he away with some officer?
52. I don't know. How many years ago was it?
53. I recollect his going to Chiang Hsi the year before last.
54. Indeed! I've seen him in Peking ever since last year.
55. Never mind. What did he send me the drawings for?
56. It was not for you that he bought them.
57. Then what have you brought them here for? I am not going to buy them I can assure you.
58. Buy them! No. He has paid for them.
59. Well, I do not understand one word of all these contradictions.
60. But you will if you let me say a few words more.
61. Quick then; don't keep me here all day.
62. Isn't your son employed in the Board of Revenue?
63. You do nothing but ask questions. My son *is* under the Board of Revenue.
64. He doesn't live with you, does he?
65. He has a separate establishment at present.
66. May I ask where his house is?
67. He lives at the west end of Chiao Min Hsiang on the north side of the way.
68. Lives in Chiao Min Hsiang?

46. 姪 *chih* 2   47. 悉 *hsi* 2   65. 搬 *pan* 1

39. *Obs* serious; *chêng-ching*, literally, upright and straight; often used as we vulgarly use the word regular; here, the opposite of *shua-hsi*, fun.
46. *Obs* nephew; *chih* 2, the son of a brother, not of a sister
47. *Obs*. not much, *hsi* 2, properly, exhaustive; hence, to explore exhaustively; hence, to know; *shu-hsi*, to know well, persons [or things
61. *Obs*. all day, *chin-tzŭ*, completely, utterly.
62. *Obs*. 1. your son; see *shao*, Exerc. XXXI, Ex. 2; his junior worship. *Obs*. 2. Board of Revenue; 'Hu Pu, *lit*. the Department of the Population, = of the Census.
64. *Obs*. does not live with you, *tan chu*, to live alone, apart from parents, or brothers.
65. *Obs*. separate establishment; *pan* 1, to remove from one place to another; not used of small things; specially used of a change of residence; he at this time has in singleness removed [his establishment] out, *sc*. of his father's house.

KEY TO THE TZŬ ERH CHI. Colloquial Series.

69. To be sure he does. What makes you doubt it?
70. I thought he lived in the Chinese town.
71. What all that way from the Board's Office? That would never do. What made you think he lived in the Chinese town?
72. I met his cart yesterday at sunset in the Liu Li Ch'ang.
73. How could that be? He was here with me last night.
74. The cart was his, but he wasn't in it.
75. How did you know then that the cart was his?
76. An old woman in the cart said that it was Mr. Mêng's cart.
77. An old woman with a child in her arms?
78. Exactly; a child some seven or eight years old.
79. Dear me! It must have been my grandson. Where could he have been going so late?
80. Don't be alarmed, Sir. They had met with a little accident.
81. What was it pray? Had the mule taken fright?
82. No the fact is that the roads were in a sad state.
83. Oh! And the cart had been upset?
84. No; not that either; it and another cart had run against each other.
85. Well, and were they still discussing the collision at that hour?
86. It wasn't that any discussion they might have had wasn't over.
87. Then the little boy was hurt?
88. Not severely; he jumped out of the cart, and in jumping out he sprained himself.
89. Confound that other cart! Do you know whose it was?
90. It belonged to Mr. Chang's nephew.
91. Mr. Chang's nephew! And the drawings that he has sent—?
92. Are for your grandson, Sir.
93. But why should he buy drawings of all things in the world to pacify the child?
94. He had bought the drawings; he didn't buy them on purpose for the child.
95. And he had them with him in his hand I suppose?
96. Yes he had; he had just bought them at our shop.
97. And did the child ask him for them?

72. 琉 *liu*²   76. 婆 *p'o*²   88. 扭 *niu*³
72. 厰 *ch'ang*³   83. 翻 *fan*¹   93. 壓 *ya*¹

72. *Obs.* 1. sunset; *jih-t'ou lao*. *Obs.* 2. Liu-li Ch'ang; literally, Glass Ware Manufactory, the name of a street in the Chinese city; *liu*², glass-ware; *li* as in *po-li*, *ch'ang*³, properly a large booth
76. *Obs.* old woman; *p'o*², any married woman.
79. *Obs.* so late; *na tsao wan*, = such a time of day.
83. *Obs.* upset; *fan*¹; originally, flight or other movement backwards and forwards.
84. *Obs.* run against each other; the cart had with a *tui-t'ou-'rh ch'ê*, an opposing cart, made collision
85. *Obs.* still discussing; *lit.* the collision having taken place, had they *lao*, in so long a time, not *shuo-k'ai*, talked it out, thoroughly explained it.
88. *Obs.* sprained; *niu*³, to twist; here twisted, or sprained, the leg.
93. *Obs.* to pacify; *ya*¹, properly to press down, to suppress; *ching*, fright.

PART IV. THE TEN DIALOGUES. Wên-Ta Chang VII & VIII.

98. No; your grandson cried, and he said. "Don't cry and I'll send you something to play with."
99. Oh! And these drawings are for him to play with; but why didn't you take them to his house instead of bringing them here?
100. Mr. Chang's nephew came to our shop this morning to find out where your son lived, Sir; we said we couldn't say, but that we knew your house; and then he told us to bring the drawings here. He'll call himself in a day or two.

98 哭 *k'u*1   100. 郎 *lang*2   100 府 *fu*3

98. *Obs.* cried; *k'u*1, to cry as a human being.
100. *Obs* 1. your son, *lang*2, properly a male, a man; *ling lang*, your son's, *chu-ch'u*, abiding place. *Obs.* 2 Sir; this word is introduced here to give the force of *ling*, honored. *Obs.* 3. here; *fu*3, properly a treasury, a palace; politely, *fu-shang*, your residence, the *shang* also indicating the superiority of the person addressed. *Obs.* 4. himself; *ch'in-tzŭ*, his own self.

DIALOGUE VIII.

1. Your servant, Sir.
2. Thank you. Who are you?
3. I have been sent by the Ying-shun Hong to shew you the way to Peking, Sir. When do you propose going, Sir?
4. I want to be off to-morrow.
5. Do you intend to go by land or by water, Sir?
6. Which is the best way?
7. I should say by land. The river will be so high with the heavy rains we have had these last few days, that it will be hard work tracking the boat up stream; and if you were to come in for a northerly wind, I don't think you could fetch T'ung Chou in five or six days.
8. Dear me! It won't do to go by water then. How about going by land?
9. If you were off to-morrow morning, Sir, and pushed on, you ought to be at Peking by the following evening. If you took your time you would be well able to reach it on the third day.
10. Do you know the land road well? [and more.
11. Know it well? I should think I did. I've been travelling it back and forward for these ten years
12. Then can you tell me enough about it to enable me to dispense with a guide, supposing I don't take one?
13. Yes; there is no difficulty about that. Do you know the floating bridge to the east as you leave this
14. Yes, I know the bridge. [city, Sir?
15. When you are on the other side of it, Sir, you will be in a street where there is a good deal going on. You must enquire there for another bridge; and when you are across the second bridge, you will be in a road going north-west which is the high-road to Peking.
16. I have heard that one has to cross a river somewhere. Is there one?

3. 英 *ying*1   5. 旱 *'han*4   9. 州 *chou*1

3. *Obs.* Ying-shun 'Hong; *ying*1, properly bursting into flower; hence gallant, heroic, *shun*, obedient, that flows without check; *ying-shun* might translate as the Prosperous; the hong, mercantile firm, whose sign is Prosperity.
5. *Obs.* by land; *'han*4, dry.
9. *Obs.* 1. were off; *tung-shên*, to move the person, specially, to start on a journey. *Obs.* 2. T'ung Chou; *chou*1, one of the minor jurisdictions into which a *fu*, prefecture, is ordinarily divided; see *hsien*, Dial IX 47.
13. *Obs.* floating bridge, *fou ch'iao*, or *fu*2 *ch'iao*.
15. *Obs.* good deal going on; *jê-nao chieh-'rh*, a bustling street.

KEY TO THE TZŬ ERH CHI. Colloquial Series.

17. That's the ferry. There *is* a ferry.
18. There is a ferry! And how do the carts and horses manage?
19. There is no trouble with them; they can be ferried over.
20. Well, and after the ferry what then?
21. When you leave the ferry station, you keep along the high-road for thirty odd li from T'ien-ching, when you come to a market town called P'u-k'ou. That is the first stage.
22. What? The first stage is Ho-si-wu, is it not?
23. No, Sir; Ho-si-wu is a long way on. It's the end of the first day's journey. When you have passed through P'u-k'ou, you come next to Yang-ts'un, and after that to Nan Ts'ai-ts'un, and you may then reach Ho-si-wu towards night-fall. These places are all something over thirty li from each other.
24. And how much of the road to Peking are you supposed to have done when you get to Ho-si-wu?
25. It's about half way. You spend the night there, and you may be in Peking next day.
26. And where does one pass the night?
27. Some of your countrymen stop at the inns, Sir, some in the temples.
28. Which are the best; the inns or the temples?
29. I think the inns more convenient myself. At the temples, strangers are taken in only now and then; and it is not certain, in the first place, whether there is accommodation to be had in them or not. Then, if there is a large number of carters, the priests do not like it. And besides, if anything is missing there is no one to make responsible.
30. Ha! Then the inn-keeper has to look to it, if things are lost at an inn, has he?
31. Yes, Sir. That's the way of it. And there is another consideration. The inns have everything you want to eat or drink at hand. In the temples there is not even a kitchen.
32. No kitchen! Then where do the people cook?
33. The people in the temples cook nothing but *maigre*; they may not cook meat.
34. Humph! One will be best off in an inn then. Which is the best inn in Ho-si-wu?
35. There is the Fu Hsing and the Shun Lai both of them large inns. One stands at the south end of the street, and the other at the north.

17.	擺 *pai*³	21.	段 *tuan*⁴	23.	隔 *ko*²	35.	富 *fu*⁴
17.	渡 *tu*⁴	23.	楊 *yang*²	29.	格 *ko*²	35.	興 *hsing*¹
21.	浦 *p'u*³	23.	蔡 *ts'ai*⁴	33.	葷 *'hun*¹		

17 *Obs.* ferry; *pai-tu*, from *pai*³, to shake, as the ferryman must the boat, and *tu*⁴, to cross water

21. *Obs* 1. ferry-station; *k'ou*, mouth, on the sea-coast, a port; here specially of the hollow in the banks where they are touched by the ferry-boat going and returning. *Obs.* 2. P'u-k'ou; *p'u*³, a bend in the bank of a river *Obs.* 3 stage, *tuan*⁴, properly a piece, a section.

23. *Obs.* 1. Yang Ts'un; lit the village of the family of Yang². *Obs.* 2. Nan Ts'ai Tsun, the southern village of the family of Ts'ai⁴. *Obs.* 3. from each other; *hsiang kê*², or *ko*², mutually separated

24. *Obs* much of the road; *lit.* speaking according to, with reference to, the length of the road

25. *Obs.* about half way; *lit* it may be reckoned to be *chung-chien*, in the middle.

29. *Obs.* now and then; *kê*², or *ko*², from various other meanings comes to signify a bound or rule; *ko-wai*, beyond rule, in the temples *liu k'o*, the keeping strangers, is an extraordinary thing, a thing not usual.

33. *Obs* 1. *maigre*; *su*, see Exerc. XXVII, but here used of food which is not meat; *'hun*¹, properly that which has a relish, but simply meat or fish when opposed to *su*, *maigre*.

35. *Obs.* 1. Fu-hsing; *fu*⁴, rich, *fu-hsing*, wealth and prosperity, say, the sign of the Well-to-do. *Obs.* 2 Shun-lai; the inn to which guests come *shun*, in an uninterrupted stream; say, the Ever-going.

PART IV. THE TEN DIALOGUES. Wên-Ta Chang VIII.

36. And which will it suit me best to go to?
37. It must be for you to decide, Sir, whether it suits you best to stop at a south end inn, or an inn at the north end. The fare and accommodation are pretty much the same at both.
38. What does it signify whether I stop at the inns north or the inns south? Are the two a great way apart?
39. No great way apart. Ho-si-wu is not large place like our city here. It is only a market-town; one long street with some shops on either side of it.
40. Very well; then what difference is there between the north end and the south?
41. There is no difference; but the gentlemen I have shewn the road to, have in most instances put up at the inn nearest at hand after they had got into the town.
42. You mean, put up at the south end, if they were coming from T'ien-ching, and at the north, coming from Peking, don't you?
43. Exactly so, Sir.
44. All right. Now, when I get to my inn, what had I best tell them to get ready for me?
45. I dont't suppose you have tried our Chinese fare, have you, Sir?
46. No, I have not.
47. Well, if you have not, Sir, you had best have something that will carry got ready at T'ien-ching, and take it with you.
48. Take it with me! But if I don't feed at the inns, they won't like it, will they?
49. It doesn't signify. The inn-people will charge you for your accommodation.
50. Is there any fixed sum that one pays for one's lodging?
51. *We* pay much the same under any circumstances, but the man-in-charge will probably make a foreign traveller pay a little more than we do.
52. Is the man-in-charge the proprietor of the inn?
53. There is no rule. In some cases the proprietor takes charge himself; sometimes he engages a man-in-charge to look after the business for him.
54. I understand. And how much is it likely that I shall be asked to pay for my lodging?
55. I can hardly tell; but you speak Chinese, Sir, and so you can have a talk with them about that before you take your rooms. If their charge is too high, there's no harm in objecting to it, and offering something less.
56. Yes, that will do very well. Now, to get to Peking next day, which way am I to go?
57. After leaving Ho-si-wu in the morning, you still keep north-west, and, at twenty odd *li* on, you come to An-p'ing, and at some twenty *li* more, to Ma-t'ou; and then, twenty *li* from Ma-t'ou, you come to the old walled town of Chang-Chia Wan.
58. Isn't there a small stream somewhere before you reach Chang-Chia Wan.

55 妨 *fang*¹   古. 駁 *po*²

37. *Obs.* fare; *ch'ih-shih*
39. *Obs.* some shops; *p'u-tzŭ*, shops, *shên-mo-ti*, and anything you like.
41. *Obs.* nearest at hand; *i chin chieh*, once they entered the street.
47. *Obs.* with you, *pu ju*, there is nothing so good as that *ts'ung*, at, T'ien-ching, [the place *from* which you are moving,] you should *tso*, having prepared, a little good-to-carry victuals, *tai-cho*, carry them with you.
55 *Obs.* 1. no harm; *pu fang*¹, no hurt, no objection. *Obs.* 2. objecting; *po*², properly, to turn sharp round; to contradict.

KEY TO THE TZŬ ERH CHI. Colloquial Series.

59. No, Sir. The town is on the river, part north of it, and part south. You will go in at the south gate, up the main street, across the river, and out by the north gate. Outside the north gate there is a forked road; the road north takes you to T'ung Chou; the other, which is nearly west, takes you to Peking.
60. How far is it from that to Peking?
61. That depends on the gate you go in by, Sir. If you stop at an inn in the Chinese city, you will go in by the Sha-wo Gate, and that is some fifty *li* from Chang-Chia Wan. If you are going into the city by the East Wicket, you must keep north two or three *li*; no great distance farther.
62. Which gate should one go in by to get to the Foreign Legations?
63. They are all inside the 'Ha-ta Gate in the neighbourhood of the Imperial Canal Bridge. I should say the best way would be by the East Wicket.
64. Very good; I understand perfectly. There is another question I want to ask. If I am to go so fast, what am I to do with my baggage?
65. How much baggage have you, Sir?
66. Those things lying outside the door.
67. What? Are all those large cases yours too, Sir?
68. To be sure they are.
69. If you intend to be in Peking in two days, I am afraid you must leave some of the baggage behind, Sir. You would have to pay a good deal for the hire of so many large carts, and, not only that, it would be impossible for you to go any pace.
70. Well, then what do you recommend me to do?
71. I think, Sir, you might hire a small cart to carry your bedding and all that sort of thing with you, and ship the rest of the baggage for T'ung Chou.
72. In that case do I ride in the cart with the baggage I take with me?
73. Better hire another small cart to ride in, Sir. Don't you think so?
74. Will they be carts with one beast or two?
75. If you want to get on, Sir, you must have two beasts; indeed you might as well have three; for there will be a good deal of water on the roads after the rain, and they will be heavy.
76. Ah! But if the roads are so heavy I don't much fancy riding in a cart. Can I hire a horse here?
77. Yes, Sir, or a mule; but I am afraid our saddles will not do for you.
78. I've got English sadlery, and all that sort of thing, with me.
79. I don't think that will do, all the same. The saddle might be put on one of our horses, but I don't think he would stand the *lung-t'ou*.

63. 岱 *tai*⁴   63. 御 *yu*⁴   69. 恐 *k'ung*³   77. 鞍 *an*¹   79. 籠 *lung*¹

59   Obs. 1. on the river, *ch'i-cho*, bestriding the river face. Obs 2 forked road, two *ku*, literally limbs, of a diverging road
     Obs. 3 nearly west; *p'ien*¹, swerving from a right line, leaning off the perpendicular, *lit* going west swerving slightly
63. Obs. 1. 'Ha-ta Gate, properly 'Hai Tai; the name given the gate by the late dynasty, *tai*⁴, classically a hill.
     Obs. 2. Imperial Canal Bridge; *yu*⁴, properly, to drive a chariot; prefixed to certain words, imperial.
69   Obs. afraid, *k'ung*³, the same in meaning as *p'a* with which it is joined
71. Obs. all that sort; *têng hsiang*, such items; *têng*, a class, here, and often, pluralising the word which follows it
77. Obs. 1. afraid; *chih p'a*, I only fear. Obs. 2 saddles; *an*¹.
79   Obs. 1. he put on, *lit* our horses *'han*, after all, can *pei*, take on the back. Obs. 2 *lung-t'ou*; *lung*², properly, a basket such as poultry are carried in.

PART IV. THE TEN DIALOGUES. Wên-Ta Chang VIII & IX.

80. What is the *lung-t'ou?*
81. The bit and the reins. What I am afraid of is, that, as the horse is not used to carrying the like, you might have trouble with him, Sir. I should say you would do better to buy a foreign horse.
82. But how am I to buy a foreign horse here at T'ien-ching?
83. There's a horse in our hong that one of the partners wants to sell. He is a very good horse; quiet and fast; and he has been to Peking and back three or four times.
84. Good. I'll go to the hong and have a talk about it. And now, when these boxes go up to T'ung Chou, whom can I hire to go with them to Peking?
85. Would it do to hire me, Sir?
86. It would do very well, but I doubt whether the house will let you go. I don't think they could spare you for so many days.
87. They can spare me, Sir. What did they send me here to-day for but to take your orders?

   81. 嚼 *chiao*².   81. 慣 *kuan*⁴.   87. 吩 *fên*¹.
   81. 扯 *ch'ê*³.   83. 夥 *'huo*³.   87. 附 *fu*⁴.

81. *Obs* 1. bit; *chiao*², properly to bite, whether of man or beast. *Obs* 2. reins; *ch'ê*³, to draw; *ch'ê-shou*, the bridle used by a rider. *Obs* 3 not used; *kuan*⁴, accustomed to.
83. *Obs*. 1. partners; *'huo*³, originally, a number of persons or things; thence, the same with, associated with; *'huo-chi*, one who is associated with one in a place &c; partner, associate. *Obs* 2. quiet; *lao-shih*, honest; hence, simple; when applied to animals, inoffensive.
86. *Obs* let you go, *jung*², the same character as that read *yung* in Exerc. XXXVI, but here meaning to allow, to tolerate; I fear [the people] in your hong *li-pu-k'ai*, unable to separate from you, to part with you, will not let you go.
87. *Obs* orders, *fên*¹ -*fu*⁴, to give orders to; the combination is not well explained by the dictionaries; by some teachers the two words are said to mean no more than they would without the Radical *k'ou*, namely, to allot to different persons their several functions.

DIALOGUE IX.

1. *(Servant.)* There's a teacher who wishes to see you, Sir.
2. *(Master.)* Ask him to walk in.
3. The teacher, Sir.
4. *(Master to the Teacher.)* Take a seat, Sir.
5. *(Teacher.)* Thank you, Sir. Pray be seated.
6. May I ask your name, Sir?
7. My name is Su.
8. And your business with me is—?
9. I heard that you wanted to engage a teacher, Sir. A friend of mine mentioned it yesterday.
10. Ah! It must have been Chang *hsien-shêng* who was speaking of it.
11. It was Chang *hsien-shêng*.
12. Did he tell you that I was looking out for a teacher for myself, or for some one else, Sir?

    7. 蘇 *su*¹   9. 閣 *ko*²

7. *Obs*. Su; *su*¹, properly, reviving; here a surname.
9. *Obs*. sir; *ko*², properly an upper story; *ko-hsia*, in ancient times, applied only to certain ministers; now, as used in the text, Sir.

KEY TO THE TZŬ ERH CHI. Colloquial Series.

13. He did not specify whether it was for yourself or not, Sir. Is it not for yourself?
14. It is not. I do not want a teacher myself; but a friend of mine has commissioned me to engage one for him.
15. Is your friend a countryman of your own, Sir?
16. He is. He has not been in China long.
17. Then he does not understand Chinese I suppose?
18. He does not speak a word of Chinese, nor does he know a character.
19. How am I to read with him then?
20. You will have to teach him to talk first, Sir. When he begins to speak, we shall see what can be done in the written language.
21. But how am I to begin if he doesn't know a character.?
22. Oh! Sir, a teacher of your experience who has had so many pupils among your own countrymen will not find it impossible to teach him, surely?
23. Teaching as we are taught is another affair. We become able to speak Chinese without learning it, and we acquire the written language by learning books off by heart when we are very young. But I don't think it likely that your friend will put himself to the trouble of keeping to the same order of proceeding as our Chinese boys, Sir.
24. That of course not. Still we may hit upon something. How old were you when you began to read, Sir?
25. I began at seven.
26. Did you begin with the Three Character Classic, and the Poem in a Thousand Characters, Sir?
27. Yes; they were my first studies.
28. The Chinese all begin with those little books. What is the real advantage of their so doing?
29. The Three Character Classic is in sentences of three characters each, and this makes it easy for little children to commit it to memory. The Poem in a Thousand Characters has no character twice repeated, and, therefore, when they have learned this, they know a thousand characters.
30. And what do they learn after these?
31. As a rule, the Four Books, and, after these, the Five Canons.
32. How many years did it take you, Sir, to learn them all; from the time you began the Four Books until you knew the Five Canons?
33. Some six or seven years from the beginning of the course to the end of it.
34. Ha! Then, by the time you had learned the Five Canons, you were fourteen Sir?
35. Yes; in my fourteenth year.
36. And how old were you, Sir, when you began to have them explained to you?
37. I was twelve years of age.

18. 漢 'han 4   36. 講 chiang 3

13. *Obs.* specify; he did not tell me *hsiang-hsi*, explicitly.
18. *Obs* Chinese; 'han 4, the name of the dynasty in which the Christian era commenced; now applied generally to all men and things Chinese.
19. *Obs.* read with; *chiao kei*; the *kei* being untranslatable in English. Grammatically, we should say that it puts *t'a* in the dative case
22. *Obs.* 1. experience; *lao-shou*, an old hand. *Obs.* 2 pupils; *mên-shêng*, the word *shêng* being construed as man; those who come to the *mên*, gate or door, of the *hsien-shêng*, teacher.
23. *Obs.* without learning; *êrh*, and yet, we do not learn, and yet we are able.
31. *Obs.* five canons; *ching*, Exerc. XXXIII, 13; here specially of the five great classical books of China
36 *Obs.* explained, *chiang*³, properly to tell; specially to explain the meaning of a character or a text; *k'ai chiang*, to begin explaining.

PART IV. THE TEN DIALOGUES. Wên-Ta Chang IX.

38. Did you study the commentary, or did you have the text explained to you orally by your teacher?
39. At first, by my teacher; but, after listening to his explanations a year or so, I began to read the commentary myself. Then I worked at prose composition some two years or more, and then I
40. At sixteen! That was early. You must be a first-rate man, Sir. [graduated.
41. Nothing of the kind indeed. It was all luck. I had to stand several examinations for my licentiate's degree, and I didn't get it for seven or eight years after.
42. May I ask your age, Sir?
43. I am thirty, Sir.
44. And what has been your occupation, Sir, in the six years since you took your licentiate's degree?
45. I have been doing nothing to speak of. I took pupils at home for the first two years, and for some time after that I acted as private secretary to a friend.
46. What office did your friend hold, Sir?
47. He was magistrate of a district in Shan Tung. He died last year, and I came home again.
48. Your having acted as a private secretary is an additional recommendation, Sir.
49. How an additional recommendation?
50. In this respect. My friend who wishes to engage you, will want to study official correspondence when he has learned the spoken language.
51. It's a pity that one can't see one's way to beginning the spoken language. [it over with me?
52. I have a plan, but I am too busy to-day to explain it. Could you come and see me to-morrow, and talk
53. By all means. I'll wait on you to-morrow as you desire, Sir. At what o'clock?
54. Shall we say between three and four?
55. Very good, Sir; then I take my leave.
56. Good day, Sir.
57. Good day.

38	註 chu⁴	41.	徼 chiao³	42	庚 kêng¹	51	緒 hsu⁴
40	中 chung⁴	41	倖 hsing⁴	46.	榮 jung²	53.	遵 tsun¹
40	秀 hsiu⁴	41.	試 shih⁴	47.	縣 hsien⁴	54	申 shên¹

38 *Obs* commentary; *chu*⁴, properly, to make a note of; thence, to annotate.
39 *Obs* 1 prose composition; *wên-chang*, literally, forms of literature, literature which conforms to the rules of composition; poetry is not included in the term *Obs* 2 graduated; *chin hsio*, to enter *hsio*, the colleges, or literary establishments, of which the graduates who have taken the first degree are members.
40. *Obs*: 1. early; what, at sixteen, *chung*⁴ (not to be confounded with the same character read *chung*¹), you obtained the degree of *hsiu-ts'ai*, fine talent, your B A *Obs*. 2 *chung*⁴, properly to hit a mark, *hsiu*⁴, fair, elegant. *Obs* 3 first-rate man; your *t'ien fên*, share of ability assigned you by heaven, is *kao*, of high degree
41 *Obs* 1. all luck; *chiao*³, amongst many meanings, has that of a bye-way; *hsing*⁴, properly, fortunate; *chiao-hsing*, generally, of success beyond merit *Obs* 2 licentiate; *hsiang shih*⁴, literally, village trial, see Dial I, 4, an allusion to ancient competitive examination in one's native district; but, now, technically signifying the examination for the second degree held in the capital of the province.
42. *Obs* your age; *kêng*¹, one of the characters used in the Chinese time-cycle; colloquially, as here, the years of one's age.
46. *Obs* what office; *jung*², properly, of vegetation, flourishing; used, as here, complimentarily, *jung jên*, your post.
47. *Obs* district; *hsien*⁴, one of the minor jurisdictions into which a prefecture is divided, somewhat less important than a *chou*, the magistrate governing it is called a *chih-hsien*, as in the *chou*, a *chih-chou*.
50 *Obs*. correspondence; *wên-shu*, generic of all official documents.
51 *Obs*. see one's way; *hsu*⁴, a skein of silk; *t'ou-hsu*, the clue to unravel a skein.
53 *Obs* as you desire; *tsun*¹, to obey; I will just obey your commands.
54. *Obs* three and four; *shên*¹, the ninth of the twelve two-hour periods into which the twenty-four hours are divided; it extends from 3 to 5 P M; *shên ch'u*, the first part of the period *shên*.
55. *Obs*. take leave, *shih*, to lose, deprive oneself of [the pleasure of] *p'ei*, bearing you company.

KEY TO THE TZŬ ERH CHI. Colloquial Series.

DIALOGUE X.

1. The teacher Su, who came yesterday is here, Sir.
2. Shew him in. Ha! You've come as you said you would, Sir.
3. It was agreed yesterday, I believe, that we should meet again to-day.
4. It was, Sir; it was. Have you hit upon any means of beginning with my friend who wants to learn the language of you?
5. Our people have a sort of phrase-book for studying Manchu with. Have you any elementary works of this kind in England?
6. We have, but when the phrases are in English only, the students have no means of putting them into Chinese; and, on the other hand, if they are in Chinese without English, it is impossible they should understand them.
7. Of course, without a dictionary. They must have a dictionary in the two languages and look the words out.
8. True; they *must* look the words out; but they must learn the Radicals first, must they not?
9. In our country, we never make a special study of the Radicals.
10. No, because when you learn to read you learn to know the characters without analysing them, and so you have no occasion to bore yourselves with distinguishing the Radicals to which they belong, or with the number of strokes of the pen in them.
11. You are right, Sir. Still, when we meet with a character we don't know, we have to look it out by its Radical, even without a special study of the Radicals. This is not very difficult, however. There are only some two hundred of them altogether; and it requires no great effort to become familiar with them.
12. No great effort. Now, I referred yesterday to a method of my own for learning the language. I have divided the Radicals into three sections; the first containing all such characters as *jên*, man, *k'ou*, mouth, *niu*, oxen, *ma*, horses; 136 in number, and all in constant use colloquially. The second section contains 30 characters such as *yüeh*, to speak, *ch'üan*, the dog, *chiu*, a mortar, *yi*, a city, which are found in writing but not in conversation. The remaining 48 characters act simply as Radical Indices of other characters; they are not found in books, nor are they used in the spoken language. These form the third section. Do you understand the principle of this [distribution, Sir?
13. Oh! yes.

5. 洲 *chou*1		7. 璧 *pi*4		10. 贅 *chui*4	
6. 繙 *fan*1		10. 整 *chêng*3		11. 習 *hsi*2	

5. *Obs*. 1. Manchu; *chou*1, properly a river-shoal; also an island; not used colloquially; here merely as a sound to represent the second syllable of the word Manchu, the name of the original territory of the present dynasty. *Obs*. 2. elementary; *ju shou*, to introduce the hand.
6. *Obs* putting into; *fan*1, to translate; see *fan-yi* below in 38.
7. *Obs*. in two languages; *pi*4, properly, a round piece of jade worn for ornament on the person; it is now called by other names; *'ho-pi* is a *pi* in two parts which may be *'ho*, put together, so that the back cannot be distinguished from the front. The expression is applied to the form in which Chinese and other texts are printed side by side.
8. *Obs*. radicals; *pu shou*, literally, heads of categories; the characters we call radicals, 214 in number, under which as *shou*, heads, the characters of which they are the indices are ranged.
10. *Obs*. 1. analysing; *chêng*3, formed, completed; *chêng tzŭ*, characters in their integrity. *Obs*. 2. bore; *lei*2, much the same in meaning with the same character read *lei*4, Exerc. XV, 21; embarrassing, restricting; *chui*4, properly, to trouble with excess of talk; *lei-chui*, whether of words or things, is boring, troublesome.
11. *Obs*. familiar; *hsi*2, to practise; *shou-hsi*, or *shu-hsi*, thoroughly versed in, well acquainted with.

PART IV. THE TEN DIALOGUES. Wên-Ta Chang X.

14. Well then, my three sections being definitively settled, an exercise was composed for the use of the student, consisting of phrases formed out of the Radical characters that are available in conversation. While studying these, he will acquire a certain number of colloquial phrases, and he is at the same time acquainting himself with the Radical characters employed. What's your opinion of this method, Sir? Will it do, think you?
15. It will do very well, Sir; you attain two ends by the one means. But what is your plan, will you tell me, for teaching the Radicals in the second and third sections?
16. I was just going to speak of them. The second and third sections contain in all 78 Radicals; which, as these were unavailable colloquially, could not of course be made into colloquial phrases; and I was obliged, therefore, to choose some of the characters most in colloquial use that are ranged under these Radicals. Of these a separate exercise was composed, which, like the other, has the advantage of teaching the student to talk at the same time that he is learning the Radical. Do I make myself clear to you, Sir?
17. Not quite, Sir, though I do understand to a certain extent. I should like to look at these two exercises* if you could lay your hand on them.
18. These are they. Will you have the goodness to look at them?
19. I see. The first set of phrases is made out of those Radicals only which belong to the first section. In the second there are some Radicals belonging to the first Section, and the characters not Radicals, are characters that you have selected [in the General Table] to illustrate the Radicals of the second and third Sections.
20. That's too great praise; however, besides these two exercises which the student will have to study, there is another in which the Radicals are classed according to their meanings. By occasional reference to this, when he is nearly perfect in the other two, he will be able to refresh his memory.

16	選 $hsüan^3$	16.	屬 shu^3	19.	妙 $miao^4$	20.	類 lei^4
16.	擇 $tsê^2$			19.	榜 $pang^3$	20.	義 i^4

14. *Obs.* phrases; *tzŭ yên*, characters which, when placed together, the eye takes in as forming one phrase; taking the *pu-shou*, radicals, that in talk may be used, *tso-ch'êng*, to form a *chang*, chapter or section, of phrases
15. *Obs.* two ends; *chu*, see above Dialogue IX, 41; here, to make a move; by one move or enterprise, *liang tê*, two things are attained
16. *Obs* 1. just going; *chêng tsai*, exactly at the being about to speak. *Obs* 2. of course not; note the interrogative clause; a very common form of affirmation. *Obs* 3. obliged; *chih 'hao*, the only course that was, or seemed to me, good. *Obs.* 4 to choose; *hsüan³-tsê²*, both words meaning to choose, and both used separately. *Obs* 5. ranged under; *shu³*, belonging to, under the authority of, *lit* I was obliged to choose some of the characters that are ranged under the Radical. of such as are commonly used in talk, I additionally made a section &c. *Obs* 6 clear to you; *lit* I do not know whether you, the teacher, understand the *li-i*, established purpose, of this.
17. *Obs.* not quite; although I do *ming-pai*, understand, yet, for all that, my intelligence is not quite *liao jan*, in a state of completeness; *liao jan* is not used except in connection with the act of the understanding.
19. *Obs.* 1. examples; *pang³*, amongst other meanings, the list *posted up* to shew the order in which successful graduates stand; *pang-yang*, a kind or fashion, q d. posted up for example's sake; an example. *Obs* 2. very good; *miao⁴*, excellent as shewing ability.
20 *Obs.* 1 too great praise; *lit.* what language is this? *Obs* 2 classed according to meanings; *i⁴*, originally right principle, justice, public spirit; as here, the true spirit or signification; *lei⁴*, class, species; the radicals in the table referred to are *an i*, according to their meanings, *fên lei*, class-divided, classified. *Obs.* 3. occasional; *sui shih*, from time to time. *Obs* 4. refresh memory; *t'i pu*, to lift up and supply what is wanting. *Obs* 5. nearly perfect; *k'uai shou*, soon ripe.

---
* The first of these Exercises is that in the Colloquial Radicals, Part II, page 28, the second has been suppressed.

KEY TO THE TZŬ ERH CHI. Colloquial Series.

21. Really, Sir, your system provides for every contingency. And how long do you suppose it will take an English student with all these approaches to the question at his command, to get the Radicals well into his head?
22. That must depend on the memory of the individual. A sharp fellow will have them off by heart in a fortnight, and even for a stupid man it would not be an impossibility in a month.
23. Very few would know them all in a fortnight, I suspect. And what do they go on to, pray, when they are well up in the Radicals?
24. When they are up in the Radicals there are forty sheets of detached sentences for them, which I have made with the help of my teacher.
25. I have heard of them. They are of words classed according to subjects, are they not?
26. To a certain extent they are, but it has not been possible to adhere in all cases to this principle of classification.
27. Not quite possible? Why so?
28. It was my original intention to have the words belonging to any category of subjects, such as the numbers, the pronouns, articles of furniture, man's actions, &c., so classed that each category should have a sheet to itself; but, on trial, I found this to be impracticable.
29. How impracticable?
30. It was impossible to construct phrases on the subjects of the categories, so long as no words were employed but those proper to any particular category. It was absolutely necessary, therefore, to add to the stock of words some that were not within the limits of the category.
31. Can you let me have a look at those sheets of phrases, Sir?
32. Certainly. I have them here. This the first sheet. You will observe, if you please, that the words in the first column are the subjects [of the phrases formed in the adjoining columns]. It contains all the numbers.
33. Not all surely. Where are the characters for one, two, eight, and ten?
34. Those are Radicals. The student will have learned the Radicals, and there is consequently no occasion to re-introduce them among the words treated of as subjects.
35. I see. Yes; including the Radicals, the numbers are all there.
36. They are all there. Well then, following the numbers, you see the words *chi, shu, ling, lai,* and the like. These are words to which the numbers had to be linked in order to make short clauses, and this accomplished, the short clauses were connected, as you will see if you look, so as to form longer sentences. Do you understand this, Sir?

   21. 導 *tao*⁴ 21. 周 *chou*¹ 21 密 *mi*⁴ 32 題 *t'i*² 36 絡 *lo*⁴

21 *Obs.* 1 system; *sc.* [system of] instruction; *tao*⁴, to guide; *chiao-tao,* to instruct; often, to admonish. *Obs* 2 every contingency; *chou*¹, surrounding, all round, *mi*⁴, close, so that nothing can pass. *Obs* 3 approaches; *mên-lu,* doors and ways, by which they may *k'ai shou,* commence

22 *Obs* memory; *chi-hsing,* natural power of remembering.

24 *Obs* detached sentences; *san*³, meaning the same as the same character read *san*⁴, Exerc XXI, 7, *san 'hua,* scattered talk or phrases

28 *Obs* man's actions; *tung-tso,* movements and doings.

32 *Obs* 1 column, *'hang,* the 144th Radical, here used as a column of characters *Obs* 2 subjects; *t'i*², originally, the forehead, that which is put forward; a theme, proposition, *t'i-mu,* a subject

36 *Obs* 1. all there; *k'o tzŭ-jan-ti,* a strong affirmative, translation of which may be varied at pleasure, lit [what you say] *k'o,* by rights, *tzŭ-jan-ti* is absolutely, or, naturally the fact. *Obs.* 2 following, *lo*⁴, amongst other things a net; *lien-lo,* linked like the cordage of a net.

PART IV. THE TEN DIALOGUES. Wên-Ta Chang X.

37. Perfectly. But there is one thing I don't see; if the student cannot read Chinese, how is he to know the sound or the meaning of the characters?
38. When we print our book, one page will be in Chinese and the other in English. The words to be illustrated in any exercise will have each one its sound opposite it, and their meaning will be explained by English translations of the several sections of the exercise, each following the other in the order of the sections.
39. When you write down Chinese sounds with English characters, do you employ our method of spelling, Sir?
40. Our method differs in some regards from yours, Sir. It is more elaborate. Chinese spelling is simply a sound above for the initial, and another below for the final, and the union of the two does not produce [the sound to be represented] with any great exactness. We have an alphabet of twenty odd characters for the representation of sound, which we do not regard as words. When written separately, our characters have properly no meaning; they are simply available for the determination of sounds, and when four or five of them are combined to give the sound of a Chinese character, though the syllable they make does not, in every case, exactly correspond to that sound, it is a nearer approximation to it than can be effected by the *fan-ch'ieh* method of China. Do you happen to know the actual number of sounds in the Peking dialect, Sir?
41. I do not. It's a calculation we have never any occasion for, so we have never made it.
42. It would be of no use to a Chinese certainly. I *have* reckoned up the sounds, and they amount in all to something over four hundred and ten.
43. That includes the tones as well as the syllabic sounds, does it?
44. No; not the tones; only the sounds; the tonic distinctions would nearly treble the number.
45. I should not have supposed there was so large a number, had you not counted them, Sir.
46. The number is correct, Sir. If you will look at this sheet of characters you will see that the sounds are all in it.
47. There seem to be some repetitions.

38. 印 yin^4	38 譯 yi^4	40. 較 $chiao^4$
38. 篇 $p'ien^1$	39. 切 $ch'ieh^4$	44. 倍 pei^4
38. 序 hsu^4	40. 並 $ping^4$	47. 乎 $'hu^1$

38. *Obs.* 1. print; yin^4, a seal, to seal; hence, to print; *shua*, to brush the sheets against the block of characters; *ch'u-lai* completes the action of the verbs *shua* and *yin*, which must be taken separately, not treated as a dissyllable. *Obs* 2. one page; $p'ien^1$, a page; *lit* half the page Chinese &c ; the Chinese regarding as a page the two sides of a sheet which they bend back till its edges meet. *Obs.* 3. order; hsu^4, series, order; $tz'ŭ-hsu$, proper order. Construe, *ch'i yu*, the remaining, *chieh-fa*, explanations, all according to the proper order of the *fên tuan*, several sections, are, translated clearly.
39. *Obs.* spelling; *fan-ch'ieh*; the latter word more commonly read $ch'ieh^1$, here $ch'ieh^4$; properly, to cut; here, possibly, to decide, but this is not certain. The rude process styled *fan-ch'ieh* consists in placing together two characters one of which shall guide the reader to the initial, and the other to the terminal, sound; thus *mei* and *ping* will give *ming*.
40 *Obs.* 1. alphabet; *yin-mu*, sound-mothers, twenty odd. *Obs* 2 regard as words; $ping^4$, together; *ping mei*, have not at all, *shih i*, real meanings *Obs.* 3. nearer; $chiao^4$, to compare; *chiao chin*, comparatively near.
44. *Obs.* treble; pei^4, a multiple; *san pei*, three-fold
47. *Obs.* 1. seem to be; $'hu^1$, classically, the preposition *in* or *at*; here, scarcely more than an expletive; on *ssŭ*, see Exerc. XL, Ex. 12 *Obs* 2. repetitions; $ch'ung^2$, repeated, not to be confounded with the same character read $chung^4$, meaning heavy, Exerc. XIII, 17.

KEY TO THE TZŬ ERH CHI. **Colloquial Series.**

48. That was unavoidable. It sometimes happens that there are two or three sounds to but one character. The character *lio*, for instance, is read with more sounds than one.
49. That's true. In the combination *mou-lio*, strategical ability, it is read *lio*; in *ta-lueh*, a summary, or general outline, it is read *lueh*.
50. Just so, and therefore in this sound-table it was impossible to avoid repetitions.
51. I observe that all the words set down in the sound-table are words in common use.
52. They are; all words constantly used in conversation; and, in the exercises in colloquial phraseology, they have been inserted among the characters treated of in the different exercises.
53. What is it that makes you so particular about this sound-table, Sir?
54. Well this: the sounds in the Chinese and English languages differ in many particulars, and my reason for interweaving the sounds proper to the Peking dialect in the phrases made for students was that, while studying these, they might practise themselves in the sounds, and that there might be no sound that they should not have met with.
55. You said, Sir, I think, that there were forty exercises in all?
56. Forty exercises.
57. And that the Radicals were to be learned first, and the exercises after?
58. That is not an absolute rule. A student may be learning the Radicals and reading the forty exercises at one and the same time.
59. And when he has got up the forty exercises is there any progressive work for him to read?
60. There are two works; one is ready, and the other is in course of preparation.
61. What is the name of the one that is ready?
62. Have you ever seen the Ch'ing Wên Chih Yao, (Guide to the Essential in Manchu), Sir?
63. I think I have. It is a book of a few chapters containing phrases in Manchu and Chinese in parallel columns, is it not?

48.	畧 *lio*4, *lueh*4	52.	羅 *lo*2	54.	閱 *yueh*4	62.	清 *ch'ing*1
48	僅 *chin*3	52.	織 *chih*1	54.	歷 *li*4	63	卷 *chuan*4
50.	複 or 復 *fu*4	54	練 *lien*4	58.	拘 *chü*1		

48 *Obs.* 1. unavoidable; that *k'o*, it may be said, is not to be avoided. *Obs.* 2. more than one; *chih*3, only; is not only in possession of one *mên-fu*, way of being read.

50 *Obs.* repetitions; *fu*4, properly, one coat over another; *ch'ung-fu*, repeated. Note that *fu* is correctly written with the 145th Radical, but commonly with the 60th. [good and evil.

52 *Obs.* inserted, *lo*2, a net, *chih*1, to weave; *lo-chih*, to interweave, to work into; used only figuratively, and both of

53. *Obs.* 1 so particular; *chuang-chu*, in the consideration or treatment of a subject, to enquire; to be particular in one's researches, or in one's attention to anything, also, as an adjective, curious, particular; that to which much attention has been paid *Obs* 2 what makes you; *'ho so ch'u i*, = *so ch'u i tsai 'ho*, what, or wherein, is the principle which you get hold of in being so particular

54 *Obs* 1 my reason......was; my interweaving the sounds in the exercises [was] *wei tê*, in order to obtain, that *shih*, there should be,......what follows *Obs.* 2. practise themselves; *lien*4, originally, to boil meat until it was done; hence, among other meanings, to practise. *Obs.* 3. met with; *yueh*4, to see, to pass in review; *li*4, to pass through in succession, as years, events, places.

58. *Obs.* 1. absolute; *chü*1, to lay hold of, hold on to tenaciously; *pu chü*, it is of consequence. *Obs* 2 same time; *i mien*, one and the same face or front.

59. *Obs.* progressive, *chin yü*, advancing and adding to.

62. *Obs.* Manchu; *ch'ing*1, pure; the style by which the Manchu dynasty is distinguished, just as that preceding it was by the style *ming*, bright, glorious; *ch'ing wên*, Manchu literature; *chih*, to point out, *yao*, the requisite.

63 *Obs.* 1 I think; *fang-fu*, to seem like; see Exerc. XXXV, 21; also Exerc. in the Radicals, III, 21. *Obs.* 2. chapters; *chuan*4, books or sections of a work.

PART IV. THE TEN DIALOGUES. Wên-Ta Chang X.

64. That's the book.
65. It's an old work, that. There is a good deal of the Chinese of it that doesn't run as it should.
66. You're right, Sir; there is; and for that reason I got a teacher to remodel it some time ago, and, after a good deal of deliberation, it has been corrected throughout so as to accord with the forms of the language as it is now spoken. It is now called the T'an-Lun P'ien, the Book of Conversation.
67. That is very satisfactory. You mentioned just now another work that was in course of preparation. Is that also taken from an extant Chinese work?
68. No. It is a work I have been engaged on with my teacher at intervals for several months past.
69. Does it resemble the T'an-Lun P'ien, or the exercises in phraseology?
70. Neither. The work is not merely to enable the English student to learn Chinese, but one which will also be useful to Chinese if they want to learn English.
71. Is it in the style of a vocabulary or dictionary?
72. No, not that either. I doubt whether there is any work of the kind in China unless it be the Manchu Accidence, and even in that the points of resemblance require to be carefully particularised.
73. From what you say of your work, Sir. I take it to be a grammar explaining the spirit and construction of our language.
74. It is something in that way. However, the first thing is to get out all these works; when they are off my hands, I may have some others to form a supplement to them. My grand object is that the student may be enabled to advance progressively; and, with these books, if he be not enterrupted, he will not fail to become an abler scholar every month.
75. That of course he will. The water dripping off a roof will go through a stone in time.

66. 刪 shan¹	72. 啟 ch'i³	74. 斷 tuan⁴
66. 談 t'an²	72. 蒙 mêng²	75. 簷 yen²
71. 彙 hui⁴	74. 續 hsü⁴	75. 溜 liu⁴

66. *Obs.* 1. some time ago; *tsao*, early; *i*, past, already. *Obs.* 2. remodel; *shan*¹, to cut out; *ts'ung-hsin*, anew; *shan-kai*, to cut out and alter. *Obs.* 3. conversation; *t'an*², to chat together; *t'an-lun*, to discourse together.
67. *Obs.* extant; is it *pên-cho*, at root, a *ch'êng shu*, a book existing.
71. *Obs.* vocabulary; *'hui*⁴, properly a collection; *tzŭ-'hui*, a dictionary the explanations in which are something less copious than in a *tzŭ-tien*.
72. *Obs.* 1 unless; *ch'u*, to exclude. *Obs.* 2. Accidence; *ch'i*³, to open, to commence; *mêng*², concealed, covered up; *ch'i mêng*, the letting light into darkness, said of elementary studies. The *Ch'ing Wên Ch'i Mêng* is the title of the Manchu Primer or Accidence.
73. *Obs.* 1. I take it; *hsiang-lai*, I am thinking. *Obs.* 2. spirit; *shên-ch'i*, the spirit, or character shewn by a man in his actions, also, the spirit of language or writings. *Obs.* 3. construction; *ts'êng-tz'ŭ*, order of stratification or succession.
74. *Obs.* 1. supplement; *hsü*⁴, originally, to add a piece of thread, sc. to one too short, or broken. *Obs.* 2. not interrupted; *chien*⁴, to make a vacancy, not to be confounded with the same character read *chien*¹, Exerc. XXX, 9; *tuan*⁴, to cut with a knife. *Obs.* 3. *tzŭ-jan*, as a matter of course. *Obs.* 4. abler; *ch'iang*, Exerc. XXXII, 7; here, strong; *chien ch'iang*, will be seen to be stronger; the comparative being formed by the *pi* in the clause preceding. Note that *chien* is used with various adjectives where gradual increase, or diminution, of the property they describe is implied.
75. *Obs.* 1. of course; *pi jan*, certainly thus it must be. *Obs.* 2. dripping; *yên*², the eaves of a house; *liu*⁴, of water running smoothly and rapidly.

KEY TO THE TZŬ ERH CHI. **Colloquial Series.**

76. Just so; and, for that reason, I am sure you will not laugh at these simple things I have been shewing you, Sir.
77. Laugh indeed! [The Book of Odes says] "To rise high you must begin low; to go far you must start from what is near;" and the English and Chinese must both begin in their depth if they want to learn about each others' countries.

   76. 貽 i²   77. 卑 pei¹   77. 互 'hu⁴
   77. 登 têng¹   77. 邇 êrh³   77. 及 chi²

76. *Obs.* 1. simple things; *ch'ien*, shallow, *chin*, within easy reach. *Obs.* 2. not laugh; i², to leave behind one; *ta-fang*, an expression complimentary to the intelligence of the person addressed; I am not afraid of giving a laugh to so superior a person as you.
77. *Obs.* 1. to rise; *têng*¹, to ascend, not common in ordinary conversation. *Obs.* 2. low; *pei*¹, low, lowly. *Obs.* 3. near; *êrh*³, not colloquial. *Obs.* 4. learn about each other; *'hu*⁴, mutually; mutually receive instruction. *Obs.* 5. must both; *tou wu fei*, both cannot but adopt this *li*, principle. *Obs.* 6. begin in their depth; *yu ch'ien*, from shoal [water], *chi*², to, *shên*, deep.

END OF KEY TO PART IV.

PART V. THE EIGHTEEN SECTIONS. *Hsü San Yü.* I.

SECTION I.

1. He struck me; [that is with a sword or similar weapon; not with a spear, a stick, the hand &c].
2. I imagine that it is thus, or in this way.

    猜 *ts'ai*³

    Obs. imagine; *ts'ai*³, to guess.

3. This is right.
4. You want to kill yourself.
5. This is of no use.
6. That does not suit; or, will not agree with some other question already attended to.
7. Who says so?
8. You must speak out.

    Obs. speak out; *p'o*, breaking, as it were, the outer casing in which the matter lies hid.

9. To put on, or have on, a short *ao*³, lined or wadded under-coat.

    襖 *ao*³

10. Bring him here.

    Obs. bring; if the speaker meant, He has been brought, another *liao* would follow *lai*.

11. Go and do it directly.
12. Call the children here.
13. When will you be able to do it?

    Obs. ts'ai, just after; then; *lit.* you at what time then will be able to do it?

14. I am giving you trouble; (a form of apology).
15. I am hungry.

    餓 *ngo*⁴

    Obs. hungry; *ngo*⁴.

16. Are your things all ready?

    截 *chieh*²

    Obs. ready; *chieh*², to cut off; hence, to bring to an end; *ch'i-chieh*, to bring into a state of completeness or order; to be in such a state.

17. Have you got them all ready?
18. Go with me.

    Obs. kên, as *with.*

19. Is your father well again?

    痊 *ch'üan*²

    Obs. 1. your; *tsun,* honored. *Obs.* 2. *ch'üan*², to be recovered, *yu,* to get the better of.

20. Come here and play.
21. What is this made of?
22. If you are thinking of going, just go; or, All you have got to do is to go.

    Obs. just go; *ching,* is to pass through; often signifying past time; here corruptly used as *simply*; *lit.* simply attend to going.

23. You can't catch me up
24. Don't keep on worrying him.

    搓 *ts'o*¹   磨 *mo*²

    Obs. 2. keep on; *ts'o*¹, to rub between the hands; *mo*², to grind; used of continuous annoyance.

25. My finger is in pain.

    痛 *t'ung*⁴

    Obs. pain; *t'ung*⁴, sore, suffering; morally used as an intensive of feelings; oftenest of anger, hate, &c.

26. Get up and let me pass.

    *Obs. jang*⁴, to yield, concede, hence also to invite, specially of eating and drinking.

27. I have not a farthing.

    板 *pan*³

    Obs. 1. farthing; *pan*³, properly a board, which is a flat thing, hence used of cash which are also flat things. *Obs* 2 *kuan-pan,* government money, in contradistinction to base coin.

KEY TO THE TZǓ ERH CHI. Colloquial Series.

28. What do you want? or What are you looking for?

尋 *hsin*² or *hsun*²

Obs. want, *hsin*²; looking for, *hsun*²; like our verb *seek*, the word has two meanings.

29. Don't be too long about it.
30. Nearly the same; differing but a fraction.

差 *ch'a*¹

*Obs. ch'a*¹, to deviate from the right line.

31. A little too short; or, a little shorter, viz. than some other.
32. Do not dawdle.

Obs. dawdle; *to*³, to withdraw from, *lan*³, idle; *q. d.* separating oneself from one's work to idle.

33. Do not disturb, or, bother me.

擾 *chiao*³

Obs. disturb; *chiao*³, to stir up, throw into disorder.

34. Go and help him.
35. He has gone to Su-chou.
36. His father lives at Hsiang-shan; [the district in which Macao lies].
37. Why do you act in this way?
38. Where have you been?

Obs. been; *q.d.* you having been, *tsai*, in what place, are now come?

39. What wind has blown you here to-day?
40. Don't be importunate.

賴 *lai*⁴

Obs. importunate; *sa*¹, to cast as a net; *lai*⁴, to lean against, *q. d.* besiegingly to rely on, to pin down, fasten on, some man now wants to oblige one

41. Come another day.
42. All but this one have been taken away.

*Obs. ch'u*², to exclude; *lit.* excluding this one, all have [men] taken away.

43. This one ought to be put here.

Obs literally, this one is the [men]-ought-to-put-here one.

44. This is the proper place for this one.
45. The cat has got a mouse in her mouth.

叼 *tiao*¹ 耗 *'hao*⁴

Obs. got; *tiao*¹, to hold in the mouth *'hao*⁴, rat or mouse.

46. You may go home to-day.
47. [The person spoken of] has pricked his finger with a knife.

刺 *tz'ŭ*⁴ or *la*²

*Obs. tz'ŭ*⁴, to wound with the point of; also read *la*². *p'o*, to break.

48. On that side of the tree, or trees.
49. Tell the coolie to bring some water.

Obs. coolie, *ta-tsa-'rh-ti*, the one who does the dirty, miscellaneous, work.

50. To carry a note to so-and-so.

稍 *shao*¹

Obs. carry; *shao*¹, properly, the tip of a branch, &c.; hence, (rather circuitously,) to take a note for another, *q. d.* in excess of one's own business.

51. The right thing is to give your whole mind to it.

Obs. mind; *lit.* heart and breast.

52. What day of the moon is to-day?
53. Near night time.

Obs. night; *lit.* soon the lamps, or lanterns, will have been handled.

54. Are you a stranger, pray?

Obs. stranger; *lit.* are you made a stranger; said when a man is standing on ceremony.

55. Are you not ashamed?

臊 *sao*⁴

Obs. ashamed; *sao*⁴, *lit.* fat; but here, the face; *'hai* intensive, as in *'hai-p'a*.

SECTION II.

1. Without a sense of shame.
2. That's my view too.
3. Don't play in the sun.

Obs. sun; *lao ye'rh*, a popular name for the sun.

4. He has got a bran-new over-coat.

湛 *chan*⁴

Obs. bran-new; *chan*⁴, the brightness of fresh dew.

5. Near dark.
6. Will my teacher let me go?

Obs. 1. let; *hsü*³, to permit. *Obs.* 2. *mo*, expressive of doubt.

7. I like this the best of them all.

Obs. like best; *ting*, the crown or top; *hsi-'huan*, to rejoice in.

8. You mind your own business.

PART V. THE EIGHTEEN SECTIONS. *Hsu San Yu.* II.

9. I suspect it is not.

   Obs. suspect; *ku*¹, to estimate, *mo*¹, as in *ch'uai-mo*, Exerc. XXII, 11.

10. I don't believe that.
11. Is this lot mine?

    份 *fên*⁴

    Obs. lot; *fên*⁴, a portion, allotment.

12. What is there to laugh at?
13. Isn't it properly settled?
14. All are equally good.

    拘 *chü*¹

    Obs. equally; *chü*¹, to lay fast hold of; *lit.* not laying fast hold of any, = no matter which, all are good.

15. Lock that door.

    鎖 *so*³

    Obs. lock; *so*³, verb and noun.

16. Take up that child and carry it in.

    Obs. take up; *pao*⁴, to hold in the bosom; *lit.* laying hand on that child, put it in the bosom, and entering go.

17. He is as bad as ever.

    仍 *jên*² or *jêng*²

    Obs. as ever; *jên*², or *jêng*², still as before; *jêng-chiu*, still in the old way.

18. I have never seen him; or, I have never seen him before.
19. Nor are there many left; or, There are but a few left.

    Obs. nor, — but; *lit.* also not many.

20. He was here just now.
21. To judge from appearances he, or it, will do well enough.

    Obs. enough; *lit.* [one may] indeed say there's an end of it.

22. Put it a little way off.
23. To have done all over again from the beginning.

    Obs. all over; *cheh*, properly to receive is corruptly used for *tzŭ*, Radical 132, in its sense of from; *lit* to have done from the head or beginning,...... additionally or afresh.

24. It has long been so.
25. He has a feverish cold.

    Obs. feverish; the transposition of *shang*, to wound, and *'han*, cold, is not to be explained.

26. He coughs a good deal.

    咳 *k'ê*² 嗽 *sou*⁴

    Obs coughs; *k'ê*²-*sou*⁴; both words mean to cough; the latter is used with other words besides *k'ê*, or *k'o*.

27. Do you wish me to help you or not?
28. My eyes are dim.

    糢 *mo*¹

    Obs. dim; *mo*¹ not used without *'hu*, rice-paste; confused, jumbled.

29. The sun dazzles the eyes.

    熀 *'huang*³

    Obs. dazzles; *'huang*³, the action of any strong light on the eyes.

30. Whose business do you do (or, are you doing)?
31. Don't bother me just now.
32. Properly you ought not to be doing this, acting thus.
33. Come with me for a stroll.

    溜 *liu*¹

    Obs. stroll; *liu*¹, the flowing of water; *ta* is not to be explained by any of its known meanings.

34. I am afraid of what will be said about it.
35. The horse is frisking about.

    Obs. frisking; *sa-'huan*, flinging about in joy; of course without a rider.

36. How do you rate him? or, What sort of a man is he?

    Obs 1. rate; superior, middle or lower.
    Obs. 2. class; calling, station.

37. He is a very clever child.

    伶 *ling*² 俐 *li*⁴

    Obs clever; *ling*²-*li*⁴; the combination is colloquial; see Sec. XI, 23.

38. It is as hot as it can be to-day.

    Obs. as it can; *ting*, the crown, top; see above *ex.* 7.

39. It is of no great use.
40. Wait here till I return.
41. He comes at odd times.

    愰 *'huang*⁴

    Obs. odd; *'huang*⁴, classically, of uncertainty of mind.

42. When does he sail?

    Obs. sail; *lit.* open; *k'ai*, in the sense of moving apart, as in *no-k'ai*. The *tsan* used here is the same as that in Exerc. X, 12.

KEY TO THE TZŬ ERH CHI. Colloquial Series.

43. Don't be so careless.
    Obs. careless; *mao*⁴, properly to protrude, so as to disturb a series, disorder a set; q. d. by such action to cause *shih*, for *shih tang*, breach of propriety.
44. How many days do you require?
    Obs. require, your *yao*, requirement, *tei*, must require &c., to accomplish the matter in hand
45. How long will you be away?
    Obs. long; within the present day; *lit* how many half days, *'hao pan t'ien*, a good while, but always within the present day's limit.
46. Let him talk.
    Obs. let; *kuan* for *pu kuan*, don't mind.

47. How many days must you be away?
48. Is it not settled yet?

停 *t'ing*²

Obs. settled; *t'ing*², to stop, cause to cease; *tang*¹, as it ought to be

49. Act in all things, (or, exactly) as I desire you.
50. Won't that one do better than the other?
    Obs. 1 do; *lit* to take that one is it not better? *Obs.* 2 *ch'iang*, properly of brute force, is often used, as here, in the sense of good, superior; as we say the *stronger* man, with reference to mental or moral power.

SECTION III.

1. I take medicine every day.
   Obs. medicine; *yao*⁴, drugs.
2. To lend a hand every now and then.

羅 *lo*²

Obs. lend a hand; *chang lo*², *lit* to spread a fowler's net, q. d. to take any and sundry things into one's net for some one else

3. Have you seen my ink-slab?

硯 *yen*⁴

Obs. ink-slab; *yen*⁴-*t'ai*, the latter character being identical with *t'ai*, Exerc XXX, 1.

4. His difficulty in getting along is *bonâ fide*.

粧 *chuang*⁴

Obs. 1. getting along; understand *jih-tzŭ* after *kuo*
Obs. 2. *bonâ fide*; not *chia chuang*¹, *lit.* false paint, or decoration, such as Chinese females put on.

5. His doing it was perfectly intentional.
   Obs. 1. perfectly; *chin*⁴, exhaustively. *Obs.* 2. intentional; *ku*, properly, cause. Cf. the French *motivé*.
6. What do two added to five make?

搭 *ta*¹

Obs. add to; *ta*¹, to add to a number; hence, to take a passage in a ship.

7. He is very careful to keep himself respectable and to hold his own.

揚 *yang*²

Obs. hold his own; *yang*² *ch'i*, to hold up his spirit, not to be overridden.

8. He gives, or, has given his horse a full feed.

飽 *pao*³

Obs. full feed; *pao*³, to eat to fulness.

9. He has got every thing ready to feed his horse.
   Obs. 1 got ready; *an p'ai*², *lit* to put down and to distribute *Obs.* 2 to feed; the *'hao* indicates completion of the act described by *wei*.
10. Whose is otherwise; or, It is the same as every one's, is it not?
11. This can't go on long.
12. That child cares for nothing but play.
    Obs. cares for; *t'an*¹, to covet.
13. All he has an eye to is to get some advantage for himself (his own interest).

顧 *ku*⁴   佔 *chan*⁴

Obs. 1. an eye to; *ku*⁴, *lit* to look over the shoulder.
Obs. 2. to get; *chan*⁴, to encroach upon.

14. Take out these eggs one by one.

蛋 *tan*⁴

Obs. eggs; *tan*⁴.

15. He pays attention to nothing whatever.
16. Don't be officious; *lit.* out of three nostrils, (one more than is natural) there comes more air than out of two.
17. Have you built your new house?
18. I shall go a month hence.
19. He has property worth more than ten thousand taels.
    Obs. *tang*¹, here meaning true, *bonâ fide*.

PART V. THE EIGHTEEN SECTIONS. *Hsü San Yü.* III & IV.

20. I had a pretty piece of work to understand it.
    Obs. pretty piece of work; ironically, It was very easy.
21. What do you do all day?
    Obs. chia is a corruption.
22. Women wear the *tsuan.*

纂 *tsuan*³

Obs. wear; *lit.* comb, their top knots; *tsuan*³, including various methods of gathering up the back hair.

23. Men wear a queue.
    Obs. wear; *ta,* make, or prepare, *pien,* the queue.
24. I have no help for it.
    Obs. help, *lit* I have nothing that by rights, or that can be, *nai*⁴ *'ho*²; the latter character meaning how? what? The former, in its present position, has no assignable signification.
25. I am not master in the matter.
26. I don't venture to give an opinion.
    Obs. venture; *kan*³.
27. He is used to delicacy, or luxury.

嬌 *chiao*¹   慣 *kuan*⁴

*Obs. chiao*¹ *-yang*³, delicately to rear; *kuan*⁴, to be used to.

28. He has been here several times.
29. I should consider your coming in that time (the time named) expeditious.
30. He is an honest fellow enough.
31. Are you fond of pomegranate?

榴 *liu*²

Obs. pomegranate; *shih-liu*².

32. What dialect is that?
    Obs dialect; *lit.* the sounds of what *hsiang,* village, country, quarter, district, province.
33. He is gone on board ship.
34. There is nothing clearer, more intelligible, than this.
35. What had we best attend to?

幹 *kan*⁴

Obs. attend to; *kan*⁴, to dispatch business.

36. Is he gone ashore?

岸 ⁿᵍ*an*⁴

Obs. ashore; has he ascended ⁿᵍ*an*⁴, the beach or shore?

37. The sun is set.

陽 *yang*²

Obs. 1. the sun; *t'ai yang*², the great male principle of nature, light or heat. *Obs.* 2. has set; *lit.* is level with the west.

38. The sun will soon be up.
39. Come very early to-morrow.
40. A fresh smelling rose.

玫 *mei*²   瑰 *kuei*⁴

Obs. 1. fresh; *ch'ing,* pure. *Obs.* 2. rose; the *mei*² - *kuei*⁴, a red and very sweet rose.

41. When shall you go?
    Obs. when; *wan* here only means after-time, *q. d.* how much later.
42. All you have to do is to arrest him.
    Obs. all; *chih* only; you only attend to arresting, then will it be well.

SECTION IV.

1. Whose little girl are you?

妞 *niu*¹

Obs. 1. whose; *chia* for person. *Obs.* 2. girl; *niu*¹, a Corean surname; not a classical character in this sense.

2. Don't keep on fiddling with the things.

捫 *fan*¹   騰 *t'êng*²

Obs. fiddling; *'hun,* wildly, disorderly; *fan*¹ *-t'êng*², upsettingly lift.

3. I forgot, or have forgotten, to wind my clock up.

弦 *hsien*², properly, *hsüan*²

Obs. wind up; *shang,* to make to ascend the *hsien*², thread or spring, of my clock.

4. As light and little bulky as paper.
5. Who let you do it?

興 *hsing*¹

Obs. let; *hsing*¹, properly, to raise, or to rise; here, to authorize; *lai-cho* puts it in the imperfect tense.

6. Handle it, or, Do it, with a little more care.
7. What put it into your head? or, What made you think of it?
8. It is not so at all.
9. This is very useful.
10. The more the better.

越 *yüeh*⁴

Obs. the more; *yüeh*⁴, to overpass.

11. I can't lift it.

Obs. lift; *t'i*¹-*liu*²; the latter character not to be construed by its proper meaning; *lit.* I lifting do not stir it.

12. Can you swim?

Obs. swim; *lit.* do you know how to *fu*⁴, float on, water?

13. Can you swim?

Obs. swim; *lit.* do you know, are you up to, water?

14. What did you say? or, What were you saying? [namely, on the occasion referred to].
15. [The rain, or the water from a watering-pot,] has come in and has made the whole room so damp.

潲 *shao*⁴

Obs. 1. come in; *shao*⁴, of the action of rain blown by the wind, or water thrown by any one holding a watering-pot. *Obs.* 2. so damp; *ching*, properly minute, here, used intensively; as we use fine, nice, &c. *Obs.* 3. *ti* for *tê*.

16. Whose turn will it be to go next?

Obs. turn; *lit.* next turn ought who to go?

17. Who wants to go next time?
18. His shop is next door to ours.

壁 *pi*³, properly, *pi*⁴

Obs. 1. next door; *chieh*²-*pi*⁴, or *ko*²-*pi*⁴; the first word meaning to divide, the second, a partition wall. *Obs.* 2. *pi* in *ko-pi-erh* becomes *pi*³.

19. Go and put it back in its old place.
20. He flounced in; or, burst in without any one asking him.

莽 *mang*³

Obs. 1. flounced in; *mang*³, properly, tangled, like brushwood, &c.; *chuang*⁴, to run up against. *Obs.* 2. without asking; *ko-ko-'rh*, of, or by, himself, no one inviting him.

21. That does not follow surely? or, That is not so certain, is it?
22. You are certain to be benefited by it.
23. What is absolutely necessary to make it all right?

24. He does not mind so well what is said to him [as some other person alluded to].
25. It cannot but be false (of words or things).
26. There are none but what are false (of words or things).
27. This is your business and no one's else.

Obs. else; *tso*, properly, left; originally, *tso-yu*, left and right; *q. d.* left and right [I thought of people], but it was the business of you alone.

28. Dear me! What is this?

Obs. dear me; *ai*¹, an interjection.

29. Too communicative.
30. The men with the bells are thread-sellers.

搖 *yao*² 鈴 *ling*²

Obs. bells; *yao*², to shake, *ling*², a small bell; here, specially of one of those small plates of brass with knotted cords attached to it, and which the pedlar strikes against it by turning his wrist.

31. The ladies' packman; *lit.* one who shakes the *po-lang* drum; see Exerc. XVIII, 18, and XXX, 6. (The drum is struck by two knots attached one to each end of it).
32. Pour half [out, or, in].
33. Half packed (said either of the receptacle half full, or of the things that the receptacle is to hold).
34. This oil won't light.
35. Whose turn is it to read?
36. Won't you retrench a little?
37. Tied tight.

繫 *hsi*⁴ or *chi*⁴

Obs. tied; properly *hsi*⁴, but colloquially *chi*⁴, to tie.

38. Tied up tight.

紮 *tsa*¹

Obs. tied up; *tsa*¹, of cord tied round and round, as round the tip of a queue, the mouth of a bag, &c.

39. I'm too weak to walk so far.
40. This tea is too weak; *lit.* too pale.

忒 *t'ê*⁴

Obs. too; *t'ê*⁴, classically to exceed; apparently identical with *t'ê*, special, particular. See Exerc. XXI, 17.

41. As hard as stone.
42. Who would meddle with him?

Obs. meddle; *lit.* move the hand, *sc.* to strike him, he being weakly, &c.

PART V. THE EIGHTEEN SECTIONS. *Hsü San Yi.* IV & V.

43. Don't be too rough in your romps.
44. Who owns this property?
45. A running knot is the easiest untied.

   Obs. 1. running; *'huo*, living; *k'ou*⁴, *lit* to deduct, here, a knot. *Obs.* 2. untied; *chieh*, to loosen, solve.

46. What does that signify to you?

   Obs. signify; *q. d.* as to its interfering with you, what connection is there between you and it; mind your own business.

47. This meat is not boiled enough.

   透 *t'ou*⁴

   Obs. enough; *t'ou*⁴, to penetrate thoroughly.

48. This meat is not roasted enough.
49. Don't come here again.
50. I've got chilblains on my feet.

   凍 *tung*⁴ 瘡 *ch'uang*¹

   Obs. chilblains; *lit.* I have grown *tung*⁴ *ch'uang*¹, frost ulcers.

SECTION V.

1. It's hot; let it cool a little.
2. You just do it carelessly [and you'll catch it].

   Obs. you just; literally, *ni*, you, *k'o*, by rights, = had as well, *pieh*, (corrupt for *pu yao*,) not choose, *hsiao hsin*, carefully, *tso*, to act or do.

3. Go on! What are you standing staring at?

   呆 *tai*¹

   Obs. staring at; *tai*¹ the 'same as *tai* in Exerc. XXXI, 10.

4. He fell down on his back with his legs out.

   跌 *tieh*¹ or *tsai*¹   仰 *yang*³

   Obs. 1. fell down; *tieh*¹, also, in this sense, colloquially read *tsai*¹, of men to fall. *Obs.* 2. back; *yang*³, to look upwards. *Obs.* 3. legs out; with the feet like the character *pa*, eight.

5. Put it back in it's old place.
6. Pull back the cart a little way.
7. My wife is his younger sister.

   媳 *hsi*²   婦 *fu*⁴

   Obs. 1. wife; *hsi*²-*fu*⁴; each character meaning wife. *Obs.* 2. sister; *mei*⁴, a sister younger than oneself. Where a number of sisters are so, the eldest is called the *ta mei-mei*, the second *êrh mei-mei*, and so on.

8. Prop up this window now.

   撑 *chih*¹

   Obs. prop; *chih*¹, to keep from falling by putting a stick under; here, applied to the outer leaf which is hung horizontally from the frame of the Chinese window.

9. My foot is asleep.

   Obs. asleep; *ma-mu*, properly, hemp and wood, is applied to the numbness, stiffness of the limbs of old men.

10. There are some of every kind and sort.
11. He does not pay attention to what he is about.
12. He was born deaf and dumb.

   聾 *lung*²   啞 *ya*³

   Obs. deaf; *lung*², dumb, *ya*³.

13. I can't, and how much less can you.
14. There are seven days to a [foreign] week.

   禮 *li*³

   Obs. week; *li*³, moral and ritual observances; *pai*, see Exerc XXVII, 22; here, to pay homage to, to worship; in seven days there is one worship with ceremonies. The Chinese have no week.

15. There must be a little of every sort.
16. I want it made to take to pieces.

   Obs. to pieces; *huo*, alive, moveable, *pien*, convenient; then it will do.

17. He has been here a considerable time.

   Obs. time; less than a day.

18. That one can't be sure of.
19. Get up and move away a little; don't come up against me again.
20. This is the deepest well.
21. Take care, or you'll be down.
22. He has no other ability.

   Obs. ability; *nai*, see Exerc. XXXI, 18; here, corruptly used, apparently for *wei*², Exerc. XXXII, 11.

23. Get up; clear the road.

   攩 *tang*³

   Obs. clear; *lit.* do not *tang*³, bar, the road.

24. He has no other ability.
25. What makes you so late?

   遲 *ch'ih*²

   Obs. late; *ch'ih*².

KEY TO THE TZŬ ERH CHI. **Colloquial Series.**

26. Attend to that and to that alone.
    Obs. alone; *chung*⁴, properly, after all, notwithstanding; *q. d.* whatever betide, attend, &c.
27. It ought to be done in this interval.
    Obs. interval; *chên*⁴, properly a rank of soldiers; used also somewhat in the present sense of a certain duration, with rain, wind, &c.
28. Don't listen to his fibs.
    瞎 *hsia*¹
    Obs. fibs; *hsia*¹, properly, blind.
29. He tells every thing no matter what.
30. Don't take up so much room.
    Obs. take up; *chan*⁴, to encroach on, absorb, so wide a place.
31. Try with all your might.
    Obs. might; *hang*⁴ = ˊli-hang, Exerc. XXIX.
32. That is just what I think.
33. It is not here at all.
    並 *ping*⁴
    Obs. at all; *ping*⁴, properly, collected together; *q. d.* all conditions granted, it is not, or, there is none, here.
34. Pluck up this shrub, or, small tree.
    棵 *k'o*¹
    Obs. 1. pluck, *pa*². *Obs.* 2. shrub; *k'o*¹, Numerative of trees.
35. Don't shake the table.
    㨪 ˊ*huang*⁴
    Obs. shake, yao-ˊ*huang*⁴, to move vibratingly, active or neuter.
36. You lean to, are biassed in favor of, that side.
37. Incline to my side; let your opinion be in my favor.

38. He is a hearty happy fellow.
    逍 *hsiao*¹   遙 *yao*²
    Obs. 1. hearty; *hsiao*¹, not used without *yao*², which properly means far distant; the combination of the two characters signifying unconstrained as a bird *Obs.* 2. happy; ˊ*huai-lo* applies rather to the mind, *hsiao-yao*, to the body.
39. How many acres do you farm?
    種 *chung*⁴   畝 *mu*³ or *mou*³
    Obs. 1. farm; *chung*⁴, to plant. *Obs.* 2. acres; *mu*³.
40. Don't mention that subject on any account.
    Obs. mention; *t'i*², to talk of.
41. To be blind of one eye.
42. He managed that matter with all secrecy.
    機 *chi*¹   密 *mi*⁴
    Obs. secrecy; *chi*¹, besides other meanings, the spring of any mechanism; *mi*⁴, close, secret.
43. Help me to twist that cord tight (or, to belay that rope).
    捽 *ning*³   結 *chieh*¹   繩 *shêng*²
    Obs. 1. twist; *ning*³, here, to twist by the leverage of a piece of wood inserted. *Obs.* 2 tight; *chieh*¹-*shih*, solid, secure; the word *chieh*, by itself, signifying to bind together, but not so used colloquially. *Obs.* 3. cord; *shêng*², cords large or small.
44. Help me to tighten this cord round [whatever it may be encircling].
    Obs. round; see Exerc. XV, 8.
45. There are thousands and tens of thousands of persons.
    整 *chêng*³
    *Obs. chêng*³, to constitute; to be entire or complete.

SECTION VI.

1. Somewhat deaf.
   Obs. deaf; *pei*, properly the back; *q. d.* turned back.
2. Lest it should fade.
   Obs. 1. lest; *p'a*, to fear. *Obs.* 2. to fade; *lao*, see Exerc XXIX, 7, but here in the sense of to descend or decline.
3. Where was this book printed?
   Obs. printed; *li* brushed.

4. There are no copies of this book for sale here now.
   印 *yin*⁴
   Obs. 1. copies, *yin*⁴, a seal or stamp; to seal, take an impression. *Obs.* 2. here; the book was printed elsewhere, as the *lai* shows. *Obs.* 3 now, the *pu* and *liao* shew that copies used to come, but now do not; had none ever come, *mei* would stand for *pu*, and *ti* for *lao*.

PART V. THE EIGHTEEN SECTIONS. *Hsü San Yü.* V & VI.

5. This book is not printed now.
   Obs It is not necessarily out of print.
6. Never to have had any other intention (or, idea).
7. Open it out on the grass.
8. This present of yours is very nice.

俏 *ch'iao*⁴

Obs 1 nice; *ch'iao*⁴*-p'i*, properly, of persons; well-favoured. *Obs.* 2. present; *lit.* this that you have sent as a present.

9. His whole family is utterly ruined.

敗 *pai*⁴

Obs. ruined; *pai*⁴, defeat.

10. Will this suit your fancy?
11. This is the son he is fondest of.
    Obs. fondest; *t'êng*², see Exerc. XVII, 23.
12. He has sprained his ankle.

腕 *wan*⁴

Obs 1 sprained, *niu*³, to twist. *Obs.* 2. ankle; *t'ui wan*⁴*-tzŭ*, the *wan-tzŭ* of the leg; *wan-tzŭ*, unqualified, is the wrist

13. Don't throw away even the kernels.

核 *'hê*² or *'hu*²

Obs kernel; *'hê*² or *'hu*².

14. Just as you please.
15. The fruit is just formed upon that tree.
    Obs. formed, see *chêh* above If it be said of a young tree, it may mean that the tree has just come to be able to bear.
16. The fruit is forming on this tree for the first time.
17. This really differs tremendously; or, this makes a tremendous difference.
    Obs difference, see the character *ch'ai*, Exerc. XXXVIII, 2, but here pronounced *ch'a*¹, to diverge from or differ; *ti* for *tê*.
18. Can I, then, manage it?
    Obs 1. then; *'hai*, for all there is against the supposition. *Obs.* 2. manage; *lai* being auxiliary.
19. I can stand it no more.
20. I can bear it no longer.
21. Have you ever seen a bear?

熊 *hsiung*²

Obs. bear; *hsiung*²

22. I had rather not go.
    Obs. rather; *ning*; see Exerc. XXIV, 7; but with *k'o*, as here, to prefer, *q d.* I shall be more at ease under the conditions specified.

23. He is the fattest of men.

胖 *p'ang*⁴

Obs fat, *p'ang*⁴, fleshly, corpulent.

24. Don't go so fast.
25. I am become his partner.
    Obs 1. become; *lit* am added to; see *ta* above, Sec. III, 6. *Obs* 2 his; *kên*, in the sense of in the presence of, by the side of. *Obs.* 3. partner; *'huo*³*-chi*, one who calculates, plans, with his mate.
26. Just fry a little of it, and boil the rest.

煎 *chien*¹

Obs. fry; *chien*¹.

27. Who has got money to pay the amount?
    Obs pay; *fang*, to loosen; compare *solvere*; the phrase would only be used where there was a good deal of money to pay.
28. Set it on the floor of the upper story.
29. At what wages a month?
30. You don't mean to say you would give so much?
    Obs. 1. don't mean; see note on *tao*, Exerc. III, *ex.* 18, so much; *to-shao*, here, not interrogative.
31. He was fined a tael (ounce of silver).

罰 *fa*²

Obs. fined; *fa*², to punish; he received punishment, was punished.

32. Sweep away that spider's web.

蛛 *chu*¹   網 *wang*³

Obs. 1. spider; *chu*¹ *chu*¹. *Obs.* 2. web; *wang*³, properly, a net.

33. Cut it up small.

切 *ch'ieh*¹

Obs. cut; *ch'ieh*¹, to cut with a knife.

34. That we can never do.
    Obs can never; *lit* that is *ti*, something that, we to all eternity can not do. Note the verb *lai* auxiliary of power.
35. Away quick, or you will be late; *or*, you will miss it.
    Obs. miss; see *wu*, Exerc XXXVI, 9; *lit.* you look [that you do not] miss, or, cause to miss.
36. He is always losing knives.
37. They are like as two brothers.
    Obs brothers; *ho*¹; *lit.* they much resemble brothers two Note that *ko-ko* is elder brother, being properly the second syllable of the Manchu word *agê* or *ako*, elder brother, reduplicated

KEY TO THE TZŬ ERH CHI. Colloquial Series.

38. He lets his children run wild.

    縱 *tsung*⁴

    Obs. 1. lets; *tsung*⁴, to loosen, let go; hence also, pronounced *tsung*³, supposing that *Obs.* 2. run wild; see *sa*, Exerc. XXXVII, 20, and *yeh*, Exerc. XXX, 15.

39. This is, or is turning out, a fine child.

    俊 *chün*⁴

    Obs. 1. fine; *chun*⁴, superior in mental and bodily qualifications; applicable only to young persons of either sex, but not much before ten or twelve years of age; classically, the cleverest man in a thousand.

40. There has been, or is, a gradual improvement, [in health or conduct].

    漸 *chien*⁴

    Obs. 1. gradual, *chien*⁴, properly beginning from the spring or source. *Obs.* 2. improvement; *lit.* ʽ*hao*, good, *shang*, moving onwards; *lai* auxiliary of *shang*.

41. Improving more and more every time.
42. Getting worse and worse every time.

    濟 *chi*⁴

    Obs. 1. worse; *pu chi*⁴, properly, not even, not regular as it should be *Obs.* 2 the word ʽ*hai* is scarcely translateable in our idiom; we should reproduce it by an emphasis; *q. d.* worse *and* worse.

43. Who is to blame for that?

    Obs. to blame; *ting*, the crown of the head, here to bear on it; *pu shih*, not right, *q. d.* that is on what person's head borne fault?

44. Better than it was at the beginning.
45. The older the better.
46. I have been stung by a wasp.

    螞 *ma*³   蜂 *fêng*¹   螫 *ché*¹

    Obs. 1. wasp; *ma*³-*fêng*¹. *Obs.* 2. stung; *ché*¹; of bees, wasps, scorpions, not of centipedes, serpents, &c., which bite.

47. A scorpion has stung my hand.

    蝎 *hsieh*¹

    Obs. scorpion; *hsieh*¹.

48. Dressed like a man who performs feats in a circus.

    獬 *hsieh*⁴   扮 *pan*⁴

    Obs. 1. dress; *ta* gives activity to *pan*⁴, to dress. *Obs.* 2. circus; *hsieh*⁴, a fabulous animal of the unicorn kind, supposed to be very fleet; mountebanks in a circus are said to be *pʻao-hsieh-ma-ti*, unicorn runners or riders.

SECTION VII.

1. Dressed nicely or properly.

    Obs. 1. properly; the *chêng* meaning that nothing is broken or torn; *chʻi*, that the whole is complete.

2. The house wants a thorough repair; or, must be rebuilt.

    Obs. repair; see *hsiu*, Exerc. XXXV, 10.

3. Is this any business of yours?
4. What is he worth?

    財 *tsʻai*²

    Obs. worth; *lit* how largely, to what extent, is he a master of *tsʻai*², wealth.

5. I have not seen him this long time.

    Obs. long time; *chʻêng*, see Exerc. XX, 3.

6. This is not right; do it all over again.

    Obs. over; *chʻi tʻou*, *lit.* raising the head; beginning; from the beginning.

7. It is too loose. Tie it tighter.

    綁 *pang*³

    Obs. tie; *pang*³.

8. You must be more careful; *or*, all the more careful.

    謹 *chin*³   慎 *shên*⁴

    Obs. careful; *chin*³, properly of solemn attentiveness, as in a temple; *shên*⁴, also attentive.

9. It has struck four.
10. Go and look for some one who can make good [supply what is wanting].
11. All he thinks of is making money.

    Obs. making; *fa*, to put forth, as a tree its leaves.

12. To set on the dog to worry the pig.

    閧 ʽ*hung*⁴   咬 *yao*³

    Obs. 1. set on; ʽ*hung*⁴, used also of exciting men to fight. *Obs.* 2. to worry; *yao*³, to bite, as man, beast, or reptile; not as birds.

PART V. THE EIGHTEEN SECTIONS. *Hsu San Yu.* VI & VII.

13. He won't admit at all that it was he who did it.
    Obs at all; *lit* his mouth is hard.
14. Holding this end uppermost.
    Obs 1. This would be said of a bag, bottle, vase, cup, or other round thing open at one or both ends.
    Obs 2. uppermost, *ch'ao*, see Exerc XXXII, 3; here meaning *towards*.
15. He is the older traveller; has seen more.
    Obs. traveller; *lit* he is more [than I, or some one,] an old river-and-lake [man], *i e*, speaking as a northern Chinese, He has seen more of the southern provinces than I.
16. I used to sleep in the morning.
    Obs sleep; *lit* sleeping used early to sleep; see Exerc. XXVI, Single Words, 4, 5.
17. The doctor is not giving him any medicine.
    Obs The case being past help.
18. Has he revived again?
19. He has always been so.
20. Those two men are at feud.

仇 *ch'ou* 2

Obs. feud, *ch'ou* 2, hate, enmity.

21. Those two states are at war.

仗 *chang* 4

Obs. war; *chang* 4, properly and very commonly, to lean against, depend on, also, to fight as armies.

22. He lives in our village.
    Obs. village; *ts'un* 1.
23. The trees you planted are all budding.

芽 *ya* 2

Obs budding, are all putting forth *ya* 2, buds.

24. The water is up to one's chin.
25. The mud is up to one's instep.

坭 *ni* 2

Obs. mud; *ni* 2.

26. The setting is of pure gold.

鑲 *hsiang* 1

Obs. 1. setting; *hsiang* 1, a border, to border; *ch'êng*, to be made; *q. d* the border-making is all of gold.

27. A man's load and this fraction over.
    Obs. load, *t'iao*, Exerc. XXV, 23, here, to carry on the shoulder.
28. There are several rats in the room.
29. To delay too long.
30. Are there any figs here?
    Obs. figs; *lit.* the fruit without blossom.

31. Where does opium come from?

鴉 *ya* 1

Obs opium; *ya* 1 -*p'ien yen* 1, *ya-p'ien* smoke; the first two characters, pronounced in Cantonese *o-pin*, being an attempt to reproduce the word opium

32. Hang this up.
33. Make a loop and hang it up.
34. That is an old fashioned cap.
35. What a lot of musquitoes!

蚊 *wên* 2

Obs. musquitoes; *wên* 2, any gnat.

36. Can you cure this disorder?
37. There is one of those spoons missing.

調 *t'iao* 2   羹 *kêng* 1

Obs. spoons; *t'iao* 2, to stir up. *kêng* 1, broth; the *t'iao-kêng* may be of metal or earthenware. See *shao*, Exerc. VII, 23.

38. Down in the hold.

艙 *ts'ang* 1

Obs. hold, *ts'ang* 1, the interior of the ship between decks.

39. That would not be as much as I gave for it.
    Obs. gave, *pên* for *pên ch'ien*, the money originally given.
40. Who was taken in in this?

檔 *tang* 4

Obs taken in; *shang*, went into, the *tang*, *tang* 4, properly, a framework; here, a trap.

41. What was said was beside the question; (did not hit it).

投 *t'ou* 2

Obs hit it; *lit* the talk did not *t'ou* 2, when thrown [hit], *chi*, the spring, *t'ou* is used figuratively of tendering, making to be seen, allegiance, enmity, and much more.

42. He took us in.
    Obs. took in; *tsuan*, Exerc. XXIII, 21; here, to humbug.
43. He made a good thing by the sale of this.
    Obs good thing; *chuan* 4, to make profit.
44. [The child] will be well enough once it is in some one else's house.

檻 *k'an* 3

Obs. 1. some one else; *lit.* when it shall have passed the *k'an* 3, threshold, it will be well; *fig.* = as soon as it shall have been adopted into some other family. *Obs* 2. the *ko* is not here the Numerative of *k'an*, but of *'hui*, a time, or turn, understood; *q d* once it gets a passage across the threshold, it will recover.

KEY TO THE TZŬ ERH CHI. Colloquial Series.

SECTION VIII.

1. Somewhat stupid to-day.
2. Turn round [the box] before you pack it.

   Obs. before; *lit.* and then.

3. Take a little pains to keep it stirring, so as not to let it burn.

   勤 *ch'in*² 烔 *'hu*² 焦 *chiao*¹

   Obs. 1. pains; *ch'in*², diligent. *Obs* 2. stirring; see *chiao*, Sec I, 33 *Obs.* 3. burn; *'hu*², burning black; *chiao*¹, burning yellow.

4. Not more than just enough for us to use.

   Obs. just enough; *chin*³, only.

5. Don't mind about making anything on it; sell it and have done with it.
6. Have not these beans been roasted?

   炒 *ch'ao*³

   Obs. roasted; *ch'ao*³.

7. I will help you to manage it with all my might.
8. For some time the road went on turning and winding.

   曲 *ch'u*¹

   Obs. 1. road; *lit* [the traveller] went. *Obs.* 2. turning and winding; *ch'u*¹, crooked; *wan*¹, curved like the sea-shore; a bay.

9. Take good care of this beast.

   Obs. 1. take care; *chao*, Exerc. XXXVIII, 22; *ying*, Exerc XXIX, 22; *chao-ying*, to reflect back the light, to respond to a call; *q. d.* to answer claims on one's attention *Obs.* 2. beast; *shêng*¹-*k'ou*, horses, cattle, sheep, &c.; not cats or dogs.^.

10. Wanting to eat a salted chicken.

    滷 *lu*³

    Obs. 1. salted; *lu*³, brine, pickle. *Obs.* 2 chicken; the *shêng-k'ou* being specially so applied in this combination.

11. To look at one's face in the glass.

    鏡 *ching*⁴

    Obs. look at; *lit.* laying hold of, = with, *ching*⁴, the mirror, reflect the face.

12. Having no heart to attend to business.

    腸 *ch'ang*²

    Obs. heart, *lit.* heart and *ch'ang*², bowels.

13. To pay great attention to one's writing.

14. What does he depend on for his subsistence?

    餬 *'hu*¹

    Obs. 1. depend on; *chang*; see above Sec. VII, 21.
    Obs. 2 subsistence; *'hu*¹ *k'ou*, to put in the mouth, *lit.* soil the mouth.

15. Translate these words.

    Obs. translate; *fan*, properly, to translate one's own tongue into another; *yi*, properly, to translate a foreign language; combined, the two words mean merely to translate. .

16. That is all vain talking.

    Obs. vain; *pai*, white, blank.

17. That is quite superfluous.

    饒 *jao*²

    Obs superfluous; *pai*, vainly, *jao*², to superadd; superabundant.

18. Unreasonable, and outrageous.

    Obs To come forth, be produced, in [the region] outside of [man's] feelings [and heaven's] right principle The phrase is not necessarily applied to questions of great importance

19. He is but a middle-aged man.
20. The interest of his debt comes to more than the principal.

    Obs interest; *lit.* the profit money; see *li*, Exerc. XVI, 20.

21. Tell me the particulars of the case.

    形 *hsing*²

    Obs particulars; *hsing*², the outer form; *ch'ing*, rather of motives or inner causes; *hsing*, of the visible external circumstances.

22. To-morrow will be pay-day.

    餉 *hsiang*³

    Obs pay; *kuan*, probably in its original sense of bar or bolt, closing, limiting, *hsiang*³, soldiers' pay; *q d* the limiting of pay, giving as much as is due and no more; hence, the receipt of pay.

23. Better than nothing at all.

    Obs better; *lit* stronger. See Sec. II, 50.

24. Somewhat better so than empty-handed.
25. He is very wealthy now.
26. Living is very dear at this place.

    Obs living; *'huo-shih*, the first character the same as in *chia-'huo*, apparently synonymous with *'huo*, fire

PART V. THE EIGHTEEN SECTIONS. Hsü San Yü. VIII & IX.

27. I don't belong to this part of the country.
    Obs. country; *lit.* I am an outer village man; from another province, department, or district.
28. I will send some one for it.
    Obs. 1. will; *chiu*, I proceed to, am sending. *Obs.* 2. for it; to come and take.
29. Kill that cockroach.

    蜣 *ch'iang*¹ 螂 *lang*²

    *Obs. ch'iang*¹*-lang*², in the north, a certain kind of beetle.
30. They are going to kill an ox.

    宰 *tsai*³

    Obs. 1. to kill; *tsai*³, to kill with a knife any beast or bird good for eating; it would not generally be used of game. *Obs.* 2. ox; *niu* is either male or female.
31. We want to put in for a little at Chusan.
    Obs. put in; *wan*, see above, *ex.* 8; here, to anchor one's vessel; to anchor an anchoring, at Chou Shan, junk island.
32. I have eaten too much pine-apple.

    蘿 *lo*²

    Obs. 1. pine-apple; *po-lo*², a combination apparently intended to give the sound of the foreign word. *Obs.* 2 too much; *p'a*, to fear; *q.d.* eaten enough to make a man afraid; compare our use of *fearfully*.
33. Don't be nervous.

    怯 *ch'ieh*⁴

    Obs. nervous; *lit.* don't put forth *ch'ieh*⁴, timidity; not so strong a word as *p'a*.
34. A very unreasonable man.
    Obs. a man not *t'ung*, understanding throughly, feeling or principle.

35. He is not either versed in composition.
    Obs. composition; *wên-li*, the principle by conforming to which a man writes good *wên*, literary composition.
36. He was only joking.
37. Why do you mind him; or, Why mind, concern yourself about, *him?*
38. This does not do very well.
39. Is there any powder in that fowling-piece?
    Obs. powder; *yao*, see Sec. III, 1, properly drugs, &c.; here short for *'huo-yao*, fire chemicals, *sc.* gunpowder.
40. To eat of the two mixed together.

    攙 *ch'an*¹

    Obs. mixed; *ch'an*¹, to mingle, *'ho-cho*, combiningly.
41. He has gone round.

    變 *pien*⁴ 卦 *kua*⁴

    Obs. round; *pien*⁴, to change, transform; *kua*⁴, certain symbolical groups of lines, of classical origin, but here spoken of with reference to divination; *q.d.* the good *kua* originally selected has been changed. *fig.* for some one's change of purpose after passing his word. See the Tone Exercises 153, *hên*³.
42. He does not speak the truth.
    Obs. truth; *lit.* his words do not answer, are not suited to, his mouth; *q.d.* are not what words should be coming out of the mouth.
43. He is a well-mannered man.
    Obs. well-mannered; *ssŭ*, classically, that, the; *wên*, here, in the sense of politeness; the combination *ssŭ-wên* is classical.
44. Keep this to be used along with the rest.
45. She is a thrifty woman.

    省 *shêng*³

    Obs. thrifty; *shêng*³, to save; the word has many other meanings.

SECTION IX.

1. What would this phrase be in Pekinese?
2. Have you anything for me to do, Sir?
    Obs. Sir; the speaker is a Chinese teacher, and as such addresses his employer as *tung chia*; the east being anciently the place of the head of the house, as the west was that of his visitors.
3. He has ague.

    瘧 *yao*⁴

    Obs. ague; *yao*⁴, aguish fever.

4. This chicken can't beat that.

    鬭 *tou*⁴

    Obs. beat; *tou*⁴, to fight; *kuo*, to pass over, become superior to; *lcannot* in fighting become superior to the other.
5. This is a dose of medicine.

    劑 *chi*⁴

    Obs. dose; *chi*⁴

6. That is in breach of the law.
7. Don't spit out the kernels. [Eat them].

吐 *t'u*³

Obs. spit out; *t'u*³.

8. He is a man of no manners.

Obs. manners; *li*, here, in the sense of politeness, *mao*, appearance, externals.

9. This is pure silver.

紋 *wên*²

Obs. 1. pure; *lit* ten parts complete. *Obs.* 2 silver; *wên*², literally streaks; specially, the marks on the metal by which its quality may be known.

10. Sickly visaged.

Obs. sickly; *lit.* burned yellow.

11. Insatiably avaricious.
12. [In a bad sense,] the farther he goes, the farther he wants to go.
13. A liar.

Obs. the two first words would suffice; what the *tiao p'i*, to push back the skin, may mean is not so clear.

14. To be speaking one fair, and to trip one up.

絆 *pan*⁴

Obs. trip up; below the feet, with the feet of the man who is speaking fair, to use a *pan*⁴, the action of a wrestler's feet.

15. To have got a clue, or base, *lit.* a side, in the matter in hand.
16. Don't swear, or say unlucky words in the forenoon.

溷 *'hun*⁴

Obs. swear; *'hun*⁴ *shuo*, the first word being identical with *'hun*, Exerc. XXI, 8.

17. A blind man whose eyes will not shut; *fig.* for one who cannot read, or, for one who cannot see a thing under his nose.

睜 *chêng*¹

Obs. not shut; *chêng*¹, to stare, keep the eyes open wide.

18. Every word he says is a lie, and he takes people in by it.

侉 *'hu*⁴ or *wu*⁴

Obs. takes in; *'hu*⁴, properly read *wu*, to deceive; *lung*, or *nung*, completes the action as elsewhere; both alone and in combination it is more frequently used of bad actions than good.

19. He is given to wearing a high cap; *fig.* for a praise loving, conceited man.
20. Swaggering along the road.

Obs. swaggering; *pai* has various meanings; here, like *yao*, to shake or wave with the hand.

21. This child is a dreadful fidget.

陶 *t'ao*²

Obs. fidget; *t'ao*², properly, joy; *q.d.* has great spirits; but fidgettiness is included.

22. Ready enough to eat, but not to work; a good-for-nothing.

Obs. good-for-nothing; *lit.* he is not, cannot be reckoned, a thing.

23. To commit robbery in broad daylight.

Obs. daylight; *lit* there being *tai*, over head, the sun, [yet even] then to play the robber.

24. Too meddlesome; a dog catching rats.

Obs meddlesome; in excess attending to idle matters, matters that do not concern one.

25. To speak out without reserve.

藏 *ts'ang*²

Obs. reserve; *ts'ang*², to conceal, *ssŭ*, what is private.

26. He does not spare you when he speaks to you.

Obs. spare; *jao*, above as superabundant; here, lenient, leaving a man room.

27. Very open-handed.

Obs. not necessarily in a good sense; the *ta* indicating not liberality, but extravagance.

28. What is your object in taking so much trouble?

圖 *t'u*²

Obs. object; *t'u*², a plan or map; hence, to lay out plans, to scheme after; of good or evil.

29. Turning it over and over in one's mind in great difficulty [as to the decision to be given].
30. A very improper thing to happen.

Obs. happen; *nao ti* for *nao tê*; *lit.* it has occurred not [the right] mode or fashion.

31. He can do anything once he has seen it done.
32. Drink or no drink, always three parts drunk.

醉 *tsui*⁴

Obs. drunk; *tsui*⁴.

33. He is very eccentric.

鮮 *hsien*¹

Obs. eccentric; *lit.* he only attends to *hsin-hsien*¹, new fresh fashions; here, out-of-the-way practices.

PART V. THE EIGHTEEN SECTIONS. *Hsü San Yü.* IX & X.

34. Bowing and scraping.
   Obs. bowing; *ti*¹, low, to make low; *lit* dipping three and descending four.
35. [Of a woman], to exhibit oneself to the world.

露 *lu*⁴ or *lou*⁴

   Obs. exhibit; *p'ao*¹, to cast, throw; *lu*⁴, or *lou*⁴, properly the dew; as a verb, to become manifest, allow to be seen A Chinese woman should be rarely seen; one shewing herself unnecessarily is said to throw her head [at the public], to disclose her countenance.

36. Most people will add flowers to embroidery; will court the great or wealthy.

錦 *chin*³

   Obs. embroidery; *chin*³.

37. [It is not that I am fond of] the amusement; it was only because the occasion presented itself that I indulged in it to oblige my friends.

戲 *hsi*⁴   逢 *fêng*²   酬 *ch'ou*²

   Obs. 1. the amusement; *ch'ang*², properly an arena, the place where various things may be done, hence, the doing of those things, the occasion of their being done; *hsi*⁴, properly to perform a play; *tso hsi*, to do anything that amuses. *Obs.* 2. presented itself; *fêng*², to meet, to encounter. *Obs.* 3. oblige; *ying*⁴-*ch'ou*², the latter word properly to return a favor, but not so here; the combination meaning to shew kindness to. *Obs* 4. Construe thus. Meeting an occasion to indulge in the amusement, I oblige my friends and that is all about it. The speaker is a musician, or possesses some other accomplishment.

38. The rain has come down so that my clothes are quite wet.

濯 *cho*²

   Obs. come down; *cho*², of rain falling heavily; *q. d.* the rain has beaten wet the clothes.

39. A very becoming proceeding, is it not?
   Obs. becoming; not ironical, but strongly affirmative; *lit* [is the act in question] a face-making one or the reverse?
40. Very mysterious in his dealings; [with a view to mislead people].
41. The sight of the money (or other gain) put it into his head.
42. Very reticent in his communications.

含 *'han*²

   Obs. reticent; *'han*², to hold in the mouth, *'hu*, in the sense of mystery, confused; *'han-'hu* is want of distinctness or completeness in speech or action.

43. Murderous, or, bloodthirsty.
   Obs murderous; *lit* life destroying; applied to those who are wont to shed blood, whether of man or beast.
44. Snow white cheeks.
   Obs. cheeks; *lit.* the egg of the face.
45. Fresh red lips.
46. Jet black hair.

漆 *ch'ü*⁴ or *ch'i*¹

   Obs. jet; *ch'u*⁴, properly *ch'i*¹, the gum of which lacquer is made.

SECTION X.

1. Ear-rings of greenish blue.

碧 *pi*⁴   圈 *ch'üan*¹

   Obs. 1 greenish; *pi*⁴, a certain stone; both green and blue are found. *Obs.* 2. ear-rings; *ch'uan*¹, a circle, or ring.

2. A long robe of pale blue.

翠 *ts'ui*⁴

   Obs. pale blue; *ts'ui*⁴-*lan*⁴; the latter character being generic of deep blue; the former meaning the feathers of the kingfisher.

3. A bright yellow gold bracelet.

鐲 *cho*²

   Obs. 1. bright; *chiao*, properly, scorched; see above; here, an intensive of yellow. *Obs.* 2. bracelet; *cho*².

4. He had on an article that was not exactly either blue or green.
5. They have put in too much salt; it is bitter salt.

齁 *'hou*¹   鹹 *hsien*²

   Obs. 1. put in; *fang*⁴, see above; here, to put down. *Obs.* 2. bitter salt; *'hou*¹, properly to snore; but here intensive of *hsien*², salt in flavour.

6. Strong smelling; stinking.

臭 *ch'ou*⁴

   Obs. stinking, *ch'ou*⁴.

7. Smelling gratefully.

噴 *p'ên*⁴

   Obs. gratefully; *p'ên*⁴, to puff out as from the mouth, *hsiang*, fragrance.

8. Insipid for want of salt.
   Obs. insipid; *ching,* see above; properly, subtle; *tan,* see above; thin, as colours; weak, as tea.
9. Dreadfully bitter.
10. Very sweet.
    訓 *hsün*4   甜 *t'ien*2
    Obs. the first word *hsün*4, properly, instructions; here, corruptly used as intensive of *t'ien*2, sweet.
11. Very sour.
    酸 *suan*1
    Obs. sour; *suan*1.
12. Very rough to the tongue.
    澁 *sê*4
    Obs. very, *huai,* devilish; rough, *sê*4, that sets the teeth on edge.
13. A very boisterous day.
14. It is past noon.
    Obs. past; *ts'o* in the sense of varying from what is exactly right.
15. Rambling talk.
    Obs. rambling; *lit.* to talk *la,* pulling east, and *ch'ê,* hauling west.
16. [The same as the foregoing example].
17. It is cooler sitting in the shade.
18. To be talking absolute nonsense.
    Obs. nonsense; *'hu shuo,* random speaking, *pa tao,* in eight directions talking; *q. d.* all round the compass.
19. There is a certain question which keeps me in great anxiety.
    懸 *hsüan*2
    Obs. anxiety; *hsüan*2, to suspend; suspense.
20. Line of action difficult, turn which way you will.
    Obs. action; *tso jên,* to do, or act, of a man's proceedings; *wei jên,* to be, of his character.
21. It will not work either way.
    Obs. work; *ti* for *tê* in the sense of to succeed.
22. [The same as the foregoing example].
23. [So secret in his doings] that neither man nor devil can tell anything about them.
24. Where two people are of one mind [anything becomes possible to them]; clay may be turned into gold.

25. To join heart and hand in the despatch of any business.
    努 *nu*3
    Obs. heart and hand; *lit.* with united hearts, *nu*3 *li,* exerting strength.
26. The weather is cold in the three winter months.
    臘 *la*4
    Obs. three months; the tenth, the eleventh in which there is the *tung chih,* winter solstice, and the twelfth, *la*4 *yueh,* the month in which, anciently, game was *la,* offered in sacrifice. The name remains, but not the practice.
27. I slipped and overbalanced myself; [but did not fall].
    滑 *'hua*2 趔 *lieh*4 趄 *ch'ieh*4
    Obs. 1. slipped; *'hua*2, slippery. *Obs.* 2. overbalanced, *lieh*4 *ch'ieh*4; the latter character means sloping, deviating from the perpendicular; *lieh* is not met with separately.
28. A very high sloping bank.
    坡 *p'o*1
    Obs. bank; *p'o*1 is of itself a sloping bank.
29. It is easy enough to go down hill; the difficulty is to go up.
30. Every tooth in his head is loose; *lit.* moving.
31. It will be all right if one's two feet are planted firmly; [of a man on a roof, or other height].
    跐 *tz'ŭ*3   穩 *wên*3
    Obs. planted firmly; *tz'ŭ*3, to put the foot upon; *wên*3, firm, stable; morally or physically.
32. Staggering about, unable to hold oneself up.
    盪 *tang*4
    Obs staggering; *'huang,* see above; the flickering of light; *li*2, separate; off; apart; *tang*4, tossing about like a ship.
33. To squat on the hams.
    蹳 *p'an*2
    Obs. to squat; *p'an*2, to sit crosslegged; a Manchu practice acquired when the Manchus were dwellers in tents.
34. To be lying on one side.
    側 *chai*1
    Obs. side; *chai*1, classically the side; colloquially, leaning to a side   One is said to lie either *yang-cho,* supine, *'ho-cho,* on the face, or *chai-cho.* See next example.

PART V. THE EIGHTEEN SECTIONS. *Hsü San Yü.* X & XI.

35. Lurching backward and forward; unable to hold oneself up.

    Obs lurching, *q d* though moving the body forward, yet *yang*, throwing the face up; though moving the body backward, yet *'ho*, doubling it up

36. To burst open the door with an iron poker.

    撬 *ch'iao*⁴

    Obs. 1. poker; *t'ung t'iao*, *lit* penetrating rod
    Obs. 2 burst open, *ch'iao*⁴, to prize open.

37. That cap has no throat-lash.

    襻 *p'an*⁴

    Obs. throat-lash; *p'an*⁴ is any catch, regularly made of cord or like substance, that secures one part of the dress to another. See next example.

38. Take a needle and put on the button loop.

    釘 *ting*¹, 鈕 *niu*³

    Obs 1 put on; *ting*¹, properly, a nail; to nail.
    Obs. 2 button; *niu*³, the clothes-button made of cloth, metal, &c.

39. The horse is startled.

    Obs startled, *ching*¹.

40. Iced water makes one shudder.

    Obs. shudder; *'huang*¹, a thrilling sensation that occasions some pain to the heart; *q.d.* ice-cold water ices to shuddering.

41. Boiling tea will scald fearfully.

    滾 *kun*³ 燙 *t'ang*⁴

    Obs 1 boiling, *kun*³ *Obs.* 2. scald; *t'ang*⁴, the action of fire or hot water; *kuai*, as before, monstrous, devilish

42. The expression *ma-shang* (on a horse), means the same as *li-k'o*, immediately.
43. A man of no experience.
44. My eye was just taken off it and it was gone.

    Obs. off it; the eye diverged and not looking, &c.

45. [I wanted to say another word to him, but] my legs did not move as fast as my thoughts did; I could not catch him up at all.

    Obs as fast; *lit* my mind was eager, my legs were slow

46. The poorer one is, the worse luck one meets with.
47. I have a great regard, or respect for, him.

    佩 *p'ei*⁴

    Obs regard; *p'ei*⁴, to carry on the person; *fu*, above as clothes, here, a verb signifying to feel submission to, be attached to, have confidence in.

48. The only way if you don't want people to know that you are doing a thing, is not to do it.

    Obs. 1. only way; *lit.* if you do not want people to know, *ch'u-fu*, except, *chi*, self, *mo*⁴, not, *wei*², doing, [there is no way of preventing them].
    Obs 2 *ch'u*, as before, to cut out; *fei*, not; *q d.* exclude [the one means, and there is] not [any other].

SECTION XI.

1. Too loquacious.
2. Without the sense to tell one thing from another.

    Obs. to tell; *lit* not distinguishing green, red, black, and white; black, *tsao*; see Exerc. XXXIII, 13.

3. The weather is so cold that there is no warmth in the fire.
4. To speak very frankly and straightforwardly.

    痛 *t'ung*⁴

    Obs. very; *t'ung*⁴, painful; here, an intensive.

5. He is a fine straightforward character.

    Obs. fine; *kuang-ming*, as opposed to darkness, secrecy; *chêng*, upright; *ta*, nothing small about him.

6. To malign people at random.

    遭 *tsao*¹ 遢 *t'a*¹

    Obs. malign; *tsao*¹-*t'a*¹, to injure, to spoil, men or things. Cf. the French *abimer*.

7. A place in which there is neither a village ahead of [the traveller], nor an inn behind him.

    Obs. inn; *tien* for *k'ê-tien*; see Exerc. XV, *ex.* 6.

8. A dreadful headache.

    惛 *'hun*¹

    Obs. dreadful; *lit* the head *'hun*¹, confused, the brain sad, very hard to bear.

9. You have a somewhat confused idea of right and wrong. You have not got much sense.
10. I beg you not to say a word about it on any account.

   Obs any account, *'hao-tai*, whatever betide, q. d. come weal, come woe

11. You can make no impression on him, do what you will.

   Obs. impression; *lit* he is indeed a piece of meat that *kun's tao*, gets a knife boiling, a piece of meat so sinewy that the knife flies off it; said of an ill-doer that cares neither for words nor blows

12. I shall not tell any one on any account.

   Obs. any account, *'hêng shu*, as above *'hao tai*, *tso yu*; which way you will.

13. Capricious.

   杨 *yang*²

   Obs. capricious; *lit* of the nature of water, like the blossom of the *yang*², a kind of willow; q. d. like gossamer.

14. Undecided; irresolute.

   犹 *yu*²

   Obs. 1. In the mind *yu*²-*yu*⁴, irresolute, not *chueh*², decided *Obs.* 2. the *yu-yu* is a kind of monkey, said to climb when it should come down, and vice-versâ. *Obs* 3 *chueh*, properly to cut.

15. Each party in fear of the other.
16. Very averse to anxiety.

   Obs averse; *nai*, to bear, but *pu nai* does not here mean impatient.

17. Don't violate the different rules of politeness.

   Obs. rules; *chueh*², joints of the bamboo; hence limits, rules; *kuo*, to pass; here, in the sense of succeeding, q d. the rules that follow one another.

18. Talk in a way you know will be agreeable; out-spokenness provokes people.

   耿 *kêng*³   惹 *jé*³ or *jo*³

   Obs. 1. agreeable; *s'un*, in accord with, *ch'ing*, people's feelings *Obs* 2 outspokenness; *kêng*³, much the same as *chih*, straight, used, morally, of plain-speaking *Obs* 3 provokes, *jo*³, to draw down, as evil things; *hsien*, dislike.

19. Properly dressed.

   冠 *kuan*¹

   Obs properly, *lit* the clothes and *kuan*¹, the cap, *ch'i*, all complete, and *ch'u*, in due order The praise is less of the clothes than of the way they are put on

20. Staying or sojourning in this place for a while.

   寄 *chi*⁴   居 *chü*¹

   Obs. staying; *chi*⁴ *chu*¹, the first word signifying to deposit temporarily, the second, to reside.

21. In easy circumstances.

   Obs. easy, *lit* the hand at ease; it does not mean open-handed.

22. Somewhat reconciled [to something that had not been acceptable].

   Obs. reconciled; *lit* the heart moveable.

23. Eloquent; ready of speech.

   伶 *ling*²   俐 *li*⁴

   Obs. ready; *ling*²-*li*⁴, of any kind of cleverness; *ling*, classically, is an actor or musician; *li* is not used without *ling*

24. A man of kindly and loyal feelings.

   Obs. kindly; *ch'ing*, properly the feelings or the passions, good and evil; here, specially the feelings of a friend; *i*, properly, the principle which makes man just or public-spirited; here, of truth and zeal in friendship.

25. He is wide awake.

   Obs. awake, *lit.* the eye of his mind, his intelligence, does him good service.

26. Feelings in perfect accord.

   Obs. accord; see *t'ou* above, Sec. VII, 41.

27. He is a rough-looking fellow.

   鲁 *lu*³

   Obs. rough-looking; *ts'u-lu*³; the latter word meaning rough, stupid-looking, but not colloquially used separate from the word *ts'u*.

28. The fact is that he is a bad article.
29. Let it cool before you eat it.

   晾 *liang*⁴

   Obs. 1. cool; *liang*⁴, properly, to put in the sun to air; to air; hence, to cool. *Obs* 2. before; *lit.* cool it a cool; then eat.

30. He is in fact a bad article.
31. There is a fire in the great street leading to the front gate [of Peking].
32. Things said [by third parties] without personal communication between the two principals concerned.
33. He is afraid that, were the two parties to meet, the truth would come to light.

   恐 *k'ung*³

   Obs 1 afraid, *k'ung*³ *Obs* 2 to meet; *tui-ch'uh*, the two parties meeting would put forth, show, *kuang*, light.

PART V. THE EIGHTEEN SECTIONS. *Hsü San Yü.* XI & XII.

34. He is always cheating one way or another.

骿 *pêng¹.*

Obs cheating; if he be not *pêng¹*, cheating people [by lies, without contrivances,] then is he *p'ien*, cheating them [by contrivance or intrigue].

35. To be startled; one's heart made to jump.

防 *fang²* 唬 *hsia⁴*

Obs startled; *fang²*, properly to ward off; *lêng*, cold, here, a shock; *lêng-pu-fang-ti*, in the manner of one who receives a shock he cannot ward off; *hsia⁴*, to be frightened, 1 *t'iao*, a jump.

36. A deserted lonely spot.

Obs. lonely; *lit.* cold and clean.

37. Splashed all over by the water.

濺 *chien⁴*

Obs. splash; *chien⁴*, the rebound upwards of water thrown on the ground.

38. One's heart full of the wrong done one, yet unable to speak of it.

屈 *ch'ü¹*

Obs 1. heart; *lit* belly full of *wei-c'hü¹*, wrong; for *wei*, see Exerc XXXVIII, 9; but, here, in the sense of real, positive; *ch'ü*, is crooked; hence, bent by oppression. *Obs.* 2. unable, for shame

39. To scratch what is itching.

撾 *k'uai³* 癢 *yang³*

Obs. scratch; *k'uai³*; itching; *yang³*, any tingling of the skin, as from a gnat-bite or from graver cause.

40. To take a basket on one's arm.

籃 *lan²*

Obs basket; *lan²*; *k'uai*, here, to pass the hand through the loop or handle.

41. To belch after eating too much.

呃 *ko²*

Obs belch; *pao³*, having eaten to repletion; *ko²*, a mere sound tacked on to *pao*; the *ko* of repletion

42. Gonging and drumming.

摚 *shai¹* 鑼 *lo²* 擂 *lei²*

Obs. gonging; *shai¹*, to strike, specially, the *lo²*, gong; *lei²*, to beat, specially, the drum.

43. Pass the rice through a sieve.

篩 *shai¹* 簁 *shai¹*

Obs sieve; *shai¹*, holding the sieve *shai¹-shai¹*, sift the rice; these characters, both sounded *shai*, are merely different forms of the same word.

44. The wine is cold; warm it.

醋 *shai¹*

Obs warm; *shai¹*, to warm, specially wine, which the Chinese always drink warm.

45. To knead dough and bake cakes for eating.

撗 *ch'uai¹* 烙 *lao⁴*

Obs. 1. knead; *ch'uai¹*, to work flour or meal with the hands. *Obs.* 2. bake; *lao⁴*, to heat on a flat plate of iron.

46. To do business briskly.

Obs briskly; *ma-li*; the first word commonly used of numbness, here, an intensive of the second, in the sense of alacrity; *q d.* deadly lively.

47. Don't interrupt people when you have no business to.

謠 *ch'a¹*

Obs. do not at random *ch'a¹*, thrust in, *yen*, your word.

48. He has no experience of the troubles of life.

辣 *la⁴*

Obs troubles; *lit.* he has not received, been the subject of, the sour, the sweet, the bitter, and *la⁴*, the pungent or acrid.

SECTION XII.

1. This cook is very dirty in his cooking.

邋 *la²*

Obs dirty, *la²-t'a*; according to the native dictionary, hastening, like one hastening; hence, probably, careless, but colloquially used as here.

2. The dog's ears hang down; or, hanging down like dog's ears.

耷 *ta¹*

Obs. hang; *ta¹*, to hang down; *la*, to drag; used of any thing pendulous, cord, curtain, &c.

KEY TO THE TZŬ ERH CHI. **Colloquial Series.**

3. Always clambering and climbing; up some wall or another; he never can be still.

爬 *pa*¹ 撓 *nao*²

Obs. 1. clambering; *pa*¹, of the action of the feet in climbing; *nao*², of the action of the hands.
Obs. 2. some wall; *pi*, like *ch'iang*, a wall.

4. The old lady chews betel-nut and keeps her thoughts to herself.

梹 *ping*¹ 榔 *lang*²

Obs. 1. old lady; *t'ai-t'ai*, term of respect by which you speak to a man of his mother, or, to a third person, of a man's wife; but also commonly used to any old woman; as we used to say Dame *Obs.* 2 betel-nut; *ping*¹-*lang*². *Obs.* 3 thoughts; *mên*¹, (not *mên*⁴, melancholy XXXVII, 8,) covered up, as for instance wine or anything of which it is feared the odour might escape The phrase is used of any one who loves to keep his own counsel.

5. A fixed air of melancholy.

愁 *ch'ou*² 展 *chan*³

Obs. melancholy; *ch'ou*², sad; eyebrows that will not *chan*³, open.

6. Flinging away large sums and haggling about little expenses.

7. Dawdling, drivelling; fiddle-faddle.

搎 *so*¹

Obs. dawdling, *mo*, as above, feeling for with the fingers; *so*¹, not used alone, but when doubled, *so-so*, meaning to draw slowly towards one

8. [The disposition of a bully; of one who] takes advantage of inoffensive people, but is in dread of those who are not.

9. To lose one's bearings.

轉 *chuan*⁴

Obs. bearings; *chuan*⁴, to turn; *lit* to have changed, [without knowing it, one's] direction.

10. Wagging the head [to give emphasis to some proposition that is false].

Obs wagging; *yao* and *huang* combine to form a common expression for shaking, jogging.

11. Don't provoke him just now while he is so angry.

Obs. so angry; *t'ou* does not here mean the beginning.

12. This affair is somewhat at a stand-still.

Obs stand-still; *lit.* there is something of a *nao-t'ou*, scratching the head; as men do when they have nothing else for it.

13. Every thing is difficult at first.
14. What on earth is he to give himself such airs?

Obs airs; *lit* putting on a fashion, *lit* a mould, though affecting a style, he is not a thing, not deserving of being considered at all.

15. Not seeing too much of other people's doings; *lit.* one eye open, the other shut.
16. Given up to tittle-tattle.

婆 *p'o*²

Obs given up; *lit* only [caring to] drag [from one place to another] *lao-p'o*², old wives', babble, *lit.* tongues.

17. To give any money for.

剮 *'huo*¹

Obs. any money; *'huo*¹, to cut off as a limb from the body; hence, absolutely regardless of consequences.

18. Wrists and ankles both sprained.

踒 *wo*¹

Obs sprained; *wo*¹, to wrench, by no great effort, either wrist or ankle; not used of other sprains.

19. Tittering and roaring with laughter.

唏 *hsi*¹

Obs tittering; *hsi*¹-*hsi*¹, merely describes the sound of faint laughter.

20. A *pieh-tsui-tzŭ* is a man without teeth.

癟 *pieh*³

Obs the first word, *pieh*³, means one whose lips have fallen in because he has no teeth.

21. Keeping down one's indignation, unable to let it off in any direction.

癟 *pieh*¹

Obs 1. keeping down; *pieh*¹, used only as here.
Obs 2 direction; *lit* with no place to *shêng* *ch'i*, generate the anger-matter; *ch'i* standing for *nu-ch'i*.

22. To give a man one's money and get no good by it; or, to get harm by it.

Obs give; *t'ieh*, properly to stick on, as a placard; figuratively used in various combinations; *lit.* giving, helping a man with, one's money, and buying punishment, receiving evil, thereby.

23. Keeping himself out of people's sight, lest he should be seen.

Obs keeping out of sight; *chê*¹ to screen; *yen*³, to cover partially.

24. A pedant; one who never speaks without using classical phraseology.

乎 *'hu*¹ 者 *chê*³

Obs. pedant; *lit* the mouth full of *chih*, *'hu*¹, *chê*³, *yeh*; four particles of which the first and fourth are explained in the Forty Exercises; the second is, properly, *in*, or *at*; the third, the classical relative.

PART V. THE EIGHTEEN SECTIONS. *Hsü San Yü.* XII.

25. To comprehend nothing of anything.

    竅 *ch'iao*⁴

    Obs. nothing; *ch'iao*⁴, a small hole; by not a single hole does he penetrate.

26. I am only a simple fellow.

    体 *pên*⁴

    Obs. 1. simple; *pên*⁴, also, and more commonly written under the 118th Radical, stupid. *Obs.* 2. fellow; *'han*⁴, the style of the dynasty which governed China from about two centuries before Christ to about two centuries after, and since commonly used, in China, as Chinese; *e g* Chinese man, Chinese language, &c. The term '*Han tzŭ*, is used as we use fellow; a good fellow, a big fellow, &c.

27. Capricious; of uncertain temper.

    覆 *fu*⁴

    Obs. capricious; *fan-fu*⁴, backward and forward.

28. A *t'u-'hu* is a pork butcher.

    屠 *t'u*²

    Obs. butcher; *t'u*², properly, to kill; here specially, pigs; also used of wholesale massacre.

29. The point of this pencil is blunted.

    禿 *tu*¹

    Obs. blunted; *tu*¹, of men's hair, bald; said of a Chinese pencil, or writing-brush, when, from much use, the point has opened out.

30. Porcelain from an old manufactory; old China.

    窰 *yao*²　磁 *t'zŭ*²

    Obs manufactory; *yao*², a kiln, or similar building; porcelain, *t'zŭ*² *ch'i*, china utensils.

31. A man without hair on his head is a *t'u-tzŭ*.
32. [To make a sign of intelligence by] protruding the lips; to wink the eyes, [for the same purpose].

    擠 *chi*³

    Obs protruding; *nu*, above and commonly, to exert oneself; *chi*³, to wink; properly, to shoulder as one man another in a crowd.

33. Softly, softly; not a word!

    Obs. softly; *lit.* stealthily; but here used simply as a caution not to speak so loud as to let people know of something.

34. Not to have slept the whole night long.

    宿 *su*² or *hsiu*³

    Obs. 1. whole night; read *su*², a constellation; also, to rest oneself by night; read *hsiu*³, as here, a night's duration. *Obs.* 2. the *chiao* at the end of the phrase might be omitted.

35. Hush! Don't speak!

    悄 *ch'iao*⁴

    Obs. hush; *ch'iao*⁴, still, quiet.

36. Very handsome; [of the person].
37. He was riding a large she-ass.

    騲 *ts'ao*³

    Obs. she-ass; *ts'ao*³, the female of the ass.

38. A bird lit, or, was lighting, on the very top of the tree.

    雀 *ch'iao*³

    Obs. bird; *ch'iao*³, birds generally.

39. The root of the tree has been eaten through and through by the ants.

    蟻 *i*³　蛀 *chu*⁴

    Obs. 1. ants, *ma*²-*i*³. *Obs.* 2. eaten through; *chu*⁴, specially of the action of any insect on wood, paper, &c.

40. Pains thrown away.

    效 *hsiao*⁴　勞 *lao*²

    Obs. 1. thrown away; *pai*, white, blank; hence, vain, useless; often *pai-pai*. *Obs.* 2. pains; *hsiao*⁴, to exert, *lao*², labour, pains.

41. To be full of apologies; to ask pardon with all one's might.

    Obs apologies; *kao*, to announce; here, almost to *beg* the person addressed; *jao*, to give space to, not to press hard upon.

42. On the stern of the vessel was seated a man steering.

    柁 *to*⁴

    Obs. 1. stern; *shao*, the tip. *Obs.* 2. steering; *to*⁴, a vessel's rudder, or helm; *to-kung*, the helmsman; *kung*, properly, labour; here, for labourer.

43. The whole party concerned were in a great rage one with the other.

    糟 *tsao*¹　糕 *kao*¹

    Obs. 1. concerned; *'huo-'rh*, a comrade, partner; *ta-chia*, the whole of the parties associated. *Obs* 2. great rage; *nao*, were angry to the making of a *tsao*¹ *kao*¹, the first word used of any thing so rotten as to have lost its consistency, the second signifying a cake of a certain kind.

161

KEY TO THE TZŬ ERH CHI. **Colloquial Series.**

SECTION XIII.

1. To whistle.
   Obs. whistle; *shao*⁴, a whistle of bamboo; but *ch'ui shao-tzŭ* may be said of simple whistling with the lips.
2. To put a sword into its sheath.
   插 *ch'a*¹   鞘 *ch'iao*⁴
   Obs. 1. to put; *ch'a*¹, to stick; the *ch'ui* being but auxiliary. *Obs.* 2. sheath, *ch'iao*⁴; were the thing put into it not a sword but a knife, *tao* would be *tao-tzŭ*.
3. When the skin is irritated, take a bath.
   刺 *tz'ŭ*⁴
   Obs. 1 irritated; *tz'ŭ*⁴, thorns; as if there were thorns so as to make one *nao*, scratch. *Obs.* 2 a bath; *lit.* wash a bathe.
4. To fabricate rumours; to tell lies.
   謠 *yao*²
   Obs. rumours; *yao*², falsehood in circulation.
5. Perfectly correct; minutely exact.
   毫 *'hao*²
   Obs. minutely; *lit.* not a thread of silk, or *'hao*², a hair, in error.
6. The single bite of a criminal will go three tenths of an inch into bone.
   Obs. bite; *yao*, of any bite; the expression applies to the false admission of a criminal who incriminates the innocent when called on to name his accomplices.
7. Glib, eloquent.
8. Every man has his own way of doing a thing.
   Obs. own way; *lit.* every man's *ch'iao-miao*, cunning and cleverness.
9. Orders positive or peremptory, and explicit.
   嚴 *yen*²
   Obs. positive; *yen*², severe.
10. To have stood first for the highest degree; (hence, figuratively, to have achieved a great success; as in trade, in politics, &c.)
    獨 *tu*²   占 *chan*⁴   鰲 *ao*²
    Obs. stood first; *tu*², singly, standing alone; *chan*⁴, for *chan*, Exerc. IV, 4, to stand up; *ao*², a sea monster, on whose head is painted a representation of the divinity, he is the patron of candidates for literary honors.

11. There are treatises to teach chess, and treatises to teach drawing. [There is a rule for everything].
    棋 *ch'i*²   譜 *p'u*³
    Obs. 1. chess; *ch'i*², a chessman; *hsia-ch'i*, to put down chessmen. *Obs.* 2. treatises; *p'u*³, primarily, a register, for instance, of a family; a book of rules and diagrams.
12. Be cautious! Pay attention to every step you take.
    Obs. every step; this phrase is only used figuratively; were caution intended to a person walking, *hsiao hsin* would be substituted for *lu hsin*.
13. There is no telling the male from the female.
    Obs. 1 male, *kung*; for its other senses, see Exerc. XXXVII, 3 *Obs.* 2. female; *mu*³, properly mother.
14. The hen lays eggs; the cock crows.
    鳴 *ming*²
    Obs. crows; *ming*², the sound made by any bird; also applied to other sounds; the *ta* makes a verb of it.
15. The two brothers are not on good terms.
    睦 *mu*⁴
    Obs. good terms; *'ho*, peace; *mu*⁴, friendly.
16. To beg subscriptions for the repair [of Buddhist temples].
    募 *mu*⁴   重 *ch'ung*²
    Obs. 1. to beg; *mu*⁴, to hire, to enrol; *'hua*, expenditure, here, the persons contributing the funds needed. *Obs.* 2. repair; *ch'ung*² over again, afresh; not to be confounded with the same character pronounced *chung*⁴, heavy; *hsiu*, to build, to repair.
17. Fasting, abstinence, and purification.
    齋 *chai*¹   戒 *chieh*⁴   沐 *mu*⁴
    Obs. 1 fasting; *chai*¹, to abstain from meat, and to keep the heart devout; *chieh*⁴, to beware of; here specially, of lust and drink. *Obs.* 2 purification, *mu*⁴, to wash the hands and face; *yu*, to bathe the person.
18. Bean-curd boiled in fair water; [said of dishes that are insipid; also of a novel, or of poetry, that is flat].
    腐 *fu*³
    Obs. bean-curd; *tou-fu*³, the latter word properly meaning matter from a sore.

PART V. THE EIGHTEEN SECTIONS. *Hsü San Yü.* XIII.

19. Making up spells, and reciting incantations; so very ridiculous!

符 *fu*² 咒 *chou*⁴

Obs 1 spells; *lit* drawing, sketching, *fu*², properly slips of bamboo, used for conveying orders *Obs.* 2 incantations; *chou*⁴, prayers in gibberish recited to bring rain, &c.

20. To skim off the scum of any liquid.

撇 *p'ieh*¹

Obs 1 scum; *fu t'ou,* the floating surface *Obs* 2. *p'ieh*¹, properly to cast from one, here to skim.

21. Not to keep either the dregs.

Obs dregs; *chin,* close, pressing; that which is close to the bottom, also, not to want, not to choose to keep

22. To split up wood into fuel with an axe.

斧 *fu*³ 劈 *p'i*¹

Obs axe; *fu*³; to split, *p'i*¹; *ch'ai-'huo,* fuel. See Exerc. XIV, 3

23. To have filled out in the face.

Obs filled out, *fa,* to have put forth flesh, as one who has *fu,* happiness, = no sorrow.

24. Something one has seen with one's own eyes.

親 *tu*³

Obs seen; with *mu,* the eye, *tu*³, beholding, with *yên,* the eye, *chien,* seeing

25. I can keep him in better order than any one.

降 *hsiang*² 伏 *fu*²

Obs keep in order; *lit* I am best able to make him *hsiang*²-*fu*²; the first word meaning obedient, the second, to prostrate oneself

26. To wrap clothes up in a wrapper.

袱 *fu*²

Obs wrapper; *pao-fu*².

27. Engaged in nothing but what is disreputable.

Obs. disreputable, things done by a person who does not *yao,* seek to have, face.

28. There are four rolls with drawings (or paintings) on them, hanging on the wall.

幅 *fu*⁴

Obs. rolls; *fu*⁴, long and rather narrow slips of silk or paper, with either writing or designs upon them.

29. There is no one I respect less.

Obs. respect; *pin-fu;* the word *pin* meaning guest; see Exerc XXVII, 21; but, here, to respect; *fu* as in *p'ei-fu.*

30. The present sovereign.

Obs sovereign; *lit* old Buddha; a phrase used by the lower orders.

31. Old books have bookworms in them.

蠹 *tu*⁴

Obs bookworms, *tu*⁴, an insect somewhat like a fish in appearance, which destroys books.

32. Stop up this hole.

堵 *tu*³ 窟 *k'u*¹ 窿 *lung*²

Obs 1. stop; *tu*³, to close a passage, *chu,* fast. *Obs* 2 hole; *k'u*¹-*lung*²; the two words are colloquially inseparable

33. Considering all aspects moral and material.

揆 *k'uei*² 度 *to*⁴

Obs all aspects; *k'uei*², to estimate, *ch'ing* the circumstances; *to*⁴, to ponder, *li,* the principles; *to* not to be confounded with the same character read *tu*⁴, to reckon, measure.

34. These head-ornaments are gilt.

飾 *shih*¹ 鍍 *tu*⁴

Obs 1 ornaments; *shou,* head, *shih*¹, to adorn; *shou-shih* of women's head-gear in general. *Obs.* 2. gilt; *tu*⁴, to gild.

35. Vomiting and purging.

吐 *t'u*⁴ 瀉 *hsieh*⁴

Obs vomiting; *t'u*⁴, properly to spit; purging, *hsieh*⁴.

36. The provincial governors-general are *chih*⁴-*t'ai*².

督 *tu*¹ 制 *chih*⁴

Obs. 1. provincial; *shêng,* above as the verb to economise, here, a province *Obs.* 2. governor-general; *tsung-tu*¹, the latter word meaning to direct, administer *Obs* 3. the term *chih-t'ai,* may be rendered His Excellency the chief authority; *chih*⁴ meaning to control, restrain; *t'ai,* which is identical with *t'ai,* Exerc XXX, 1, meaning worshipful presence. Note that *chih-t'ai* is only used of the *tsung-tu.*

37. A solitary horseman; (also, figuratively,) single-handed.

38. There is a windlass over the well to draw water.

轆 *lu*⁴ 轤 *lu*² 台 *t'ai*²

Obs. windlass; *lu*⁴-*lu*², the wooden apparatus for lowering the bucket, which stands on the *ching-t'ai*², the level surrounding the well's mouth. See the full form of *t'ai,* Exerc. XXX, 1.

39. The whole house to himself (or to themselves). [No other resident on the premises].
40. A case of murder for gain's sake.

圖 *t'u*²

Obs. gain; *t'u*², plotting after *ts'ai*, gain, *'hai*, mortally injuring, *ming*, life.

41. Have you sealed?

Obs. sealed; *t'u-shu*, the mark made by the *t'u*, seal, on a document; *ta* makes a verb of it.

42. A portrait stuck upon, or, sticking to, the wall.

Obs. portrait; *hsing-lo-t'u*, the *t'u*, of one who *hsing-lo*, is enjoying joy, that is, who is alive; the portrait executed after death being known by another term..

43. When the hare dies the fox grieves; it is natural to feel for one's kind.

兎 *t'u*⁴   狐 *'hu*²

悲 *pei*¹   物 *'wu*⁴

Obs. 1. hare *t'u*⁴, the hare dies; *'hu*², the fox, *pei*¹, is mournful. Obs. 2. natural; *wu*⁴, created beings, *shang*, are wounded in the heart for, *ch'i*, their, *lei*⁴, kind, species.

44. Silver is but dirt; reputation is worth any money.

糞 *fên*⁴

Obs 1. dirt; *fên*⁴, dung, with *t'u*, as here, dirt. Obs 2 reputation; *lit* the face is worth a thousand pieces of gold, or money..

45. Irritation at the insult grew into violent rage.

Obs grew into, *pien*, changing, *ch'êng*, became, was made into

46. He hired a boat with a long paddle.

櫓 *lu*³

Obs. 1. hired; *hu* identical with *ku* in Exerc. XXXVII, 18 Obs. 2. paddle; *lu*³, a long oar worked over the stern, or over the quarter.

47. Get two bowls of vermicelli with sauce from the eating-house, and put them on the table.

館 *kuan*³

Obs. 1. get; *lit.* having gone to the *kuan*³, tea-house or eating-house. Obs. 2 vermicelli; *mien*, flour, here specially vermicelli, with *lu*, thick broth or gravy, poured over it. Obs. 3. put on; *tuan*, see Exerc. XIV, 19

SECTION XIV.

1. On no account take presents.

賄 *'hui*⁴   賂 *lu*⁴

Obs. presents; *'hui*⁴-*lu*⁴; both words signifying bribes; the first sometimes used without the second.

2. Rolling all about the place.

軲 *ku*¹

Obs. rolling; *ku*¹-*lu*, properly the wheel of a cart; said of round things; also, says one, of things lying in no regular order.

3. Very hard worked.

碌 *lu*⁴

Obs. worked; *lao*², labour, trouble; *lu*⁴, properly, the unevenness of stony ground.

4. A large number of musk-deer, and one-horned deer, and wild deer.

麇 *chang*¹   麃 *p'ao*²

Obs. musk-deer, *chang*¹; the *p'ao*², Dr. Williams thinks, may be the *nylghau*; the *yeh-lu*, any and every kind of deer.

5. A thumb-ring of deer-horn.

觭 *chi*¹   搬 *pan*¹

Obs. 1. horn; *chi*¹-*chiao*, the horn of any horn-bearing animal Obs. 2 thumb-ring; *pan*¹, properly, to draw in to one, with the hand, or with an instrument; *pan-chi-'rh*, the-drawing-of-finger-thing, is the ring worn on the right thumb by archers.

6. May you have a prosperous journey! or, Have you had a prosperous journey?

陸 *lu*⁴

Obs journey; *shui*, by water, *lu*⁴, by dry land, may you have, have you had, peace, comfort.

7. Pearls, jewels, and articles of precious stone.

珠 *chu*¹   寶 *pao*³

Obs 1. pearls, *chu*¹; jewels, *pao*³; precious stone, *yu*, commonly but not necessarily, what we call jade; agate or other similar material might be included. Obs 2 articles; *ch'i*, utensils

PART V. THE EIGHTEEN SECTIONS. *Hsü San Yü.* XIII & XIV.

8. There is a spider's web on the eaves of the roof.

蜘 *chih*¹

Obs. 1. eaves; *yên*, the edge of the roof. *Obs.* 2. spider; *chih*¹-*chu*, above written *chu-chu*; the form *chih-chu* is correct.

9. To rest awhile.

暫 *chan*⁴

Obs. awhile; *chan*⁴, temporary; the addition of *ch'ieh*, as in some other combinations, adverbialises the word it follows.

10. [One takes the colour of one's company;] by vermilion, one is red; by ink, one is black.

硃 *chu*¹

Obs. vermilion; *chu*¹, cinnabar.

11. Very fond of dumplings.

餑 *po*¹

Obs. dumplings; boiled *po*¹-*po*¹, a term including several varieties of pastry.

12. Where is your residence, Sir?

Obs. 1. Sir; *ni-na*⁴; see Exerc. XXV, 1.
Obs. 2. residence; *fu*³, a noble's palace; the *shang* is also used respectfully, as to the superior of the speaker.

13. This child is very shy.

恦 *mien*³ 愝 *t'ien*³

Obs. shy; *mien*³-*t'ien*³; these words, not used separately, both mean embarrassed in manner.

14. The characters on the reverse of the copper cash are Manchu.

鏝 *man*⁴

Obs. reverse; *man*⁴, or *man-'rh*, properly, the Manchu words on the one face of the cash, as distinguished from the *tzŭ*, Chinese characters, on the other face.

15. To make a great jumble of one's business.

顛 *tien*¹

Obs. jumble; *tien*¹, like *tao*, to upset; managing business turn-over-three-upset-four-wise.

16. To touch with one's tongue.

餂 *t'ien*³

Obs. touch; *t'ien*³; it has no other meaning.

17. Fill up this hole with earth.

填 *t'ien*²

Obs. fill up; *t'ien*², to fill up, *p'ing*, level.

18. Put something under the leg of the table to keep it steady.

墊 *tien*⁴

Obs. steady; *tien*⁴, to put one thing under another to make the latter level, or, *wên*³, steady.

19. Feel it in your hand, and see what it weighs.

掂 *tien*¹

Obs. feel; *tien*¹, to weigh in the hand.

20. Dip it in pickle and eat it.

醬 *chiang*⁴ 沾 *chan*⁴

Obs. 1. pickle; *chiang*⁴, originally dry pickle; *ch'ing*, properly, pure; here, liquid. *Obs.* 2. *chan*⁴, to dip into any fluid. *Obs.* 3. *na*, to be rendered by the instrumental preposition; *lit.* holding liquid pickle, dipping eat.

21. Cloth cannot be drawn out white from an indigo vat. [Thou canst not touch pitch, &c].

靛 *tien*⁴ 缸 *kang*¹

Obs. indigo, *tien*⁴; vat, *kang*¹.

22. Pills, powders, plasters, and pills, are all medical articles.

丸 *wan*² 膏 *kao*¹ 丹 *tan*¹

Obs. pills; *wan*²; powders; *san*³, purgatives; not to be confounded with the same character read *san*⁴, to disperse; *kao*¹, properly, lard, unguent; pills, *tan*¹; in what differing from *wan*², does not appear. The *tan* are said by some to be mythic, *q.d.* fairy medicines; *tan-wan* is used as generic of pills.

23. With a porter's pole in the hand.

擔 *tan*⁴

Obs. pole; *tan*⁴, properly to carry on the shoulder; hence, that with which the load is carried. The pole is *pien*, flat.

24. Share and share alike.

均 *chün*¹ 匀 *yün*² 攤 *t'an*¹

Obs. share; *chün*¹ and *yün*², or *chün*¹-*yün*², mean, in even parts; *t'an*¹, properly to contribute to, but, here, merging its sense in that of *san*, which is to receive what is distributed.

25. Fold up the clothes without rumpling them.

Obs. 1. fold up; *tieh*, see Exerc. XXVI, 10.
Obs. 2. rumpling; *shu*, see Exerc. XXXI, 14, *chan*, properly to open; *shu-chan*, free of wrinkles, or frowns; *lit.* these clothes fold free of wrinkles.

165

26. The four kinds of Chinese text.

　　篆 *chuan*⁴

　　Obs. chên, the tune, fairly formed; *ts'ao*, the running hand, resembling grass, or herbs; *li*, a style introduced shortly before the Christian era, *chuan*⁴, ordinarily known as the Seal Character.

27. Stitching and patching are a matter of duty.

　　縺 *lien*² 　　綻 *chan*⁴

　　Obs 1. stitching; *fêng*, to close a seam; *lien*², means the same, but is not found apart from *fêng*. *Obs* 2 patching; *chan*⁴, a rent. *Obs*. 3. duty; *pên fên*, one's proper share or lot.

28. To have the run of the house.

　　Obs. run; *lit*. to penetrate houses, to enter rooms; one who is intimate enough with the family to do this.

29. Of kind heart and looks.

　　慈 *tz'ŭ*²

　　Obs. kind; *tz'ŭ*², kind as a mother to her offspring; *lit*. heart tender, looks soft.

30. Attended him in his sickness and gave him his medicine.

　　熬 *ao*² 　　伺 *tz'ŭ*⁴

　　Obs. 1 medicine; *lit* frying the broth, = heating the hot drinks; *ao*², scorching the medicines. *Obs*. 2. attends; *tz'ŭ*⁴-*'hou*, to wait upon.

31. A very fine fellow may be ruined by a row about a single cash.

　　憋 *pieh*¹

　　Obs 1. cash; *wên*, the numeral of copper cash. *Obs* 2. row; *pieh*¹, in this phrase, evil circumstances which *tao*, upset. *Obs* 3 fine fellow; *ying*, a hero or genius; *hsiung*, properly the male of birds, hence, masculine, *ying-hsiung*, a hero; for *'han*, see above Sec. XII, *ex* 26.

32. An incessant succession of people.

　　Obs. incessant; stream flowing never *hsi*², resting; of people employed, people in a thoroughfare.

33. The place is full of springs; or, All the water there is spring water.

　　泉 *ch'üan*²

　　Obs. 1. spring; *ch'üan*², a spring or source. *Obs*. 2. full of; *k'o*, scarcely translateable; *q d* the properly being, that which rightly is, that place, — is all spring water.

34. A disposition to look only to the front without looking to the rear; impetuous; precipitate.

　　Obs. to look; *ku*, see above; according to Chinese ideas, a soldier should guard eight points.

35. A farewell-dinner is given him to-morrow.

　　餞 *chien*⁴

　　Obs. farewell-dinner; *chien*⁴, to present food to one about *hsing*, to journey.

36. Don't worry him, or, Don't spoil that in that way.

　　踐 *chien*⁴

　　Obs. 1. that way; *'hun*, as above. *Obs*. 2. worry; *tso chien*⁴, the latter word, properly, to trample on.

37. Buttons with flowers in relief.

　　鏨 *tsan*⁴ 　　釦 *k'ou*⁴

　　Obs. 1. relief; *tsan*⁴, properly to chisel, but so as to throw out the design, not to engrave it. *Obs*. 2. buttons; *niu-k'ou*⁴, the latter word meaning the same as the former; sometimes used apart from it.

38. On the road to the grave there is no distinction of age. (Young people and old die alike).

　　泉 *ch'üan*²

　　Obs. grave; *lit* on the road to *'huang ch'üan*², the yellow spring, = a hollow in the yellow clay deep as springs lie.

39. Messing apart though living in the same building. A divided family.

　　爨 *ts'uan*⁴

　　Obs. messing; *ts'uan*⁴, to light a fire to cook by.

40. Skipping and jumping; or, galloping.

　　Obs. skipping; *lit ts'uan*⁴, making way, properly burrowing like a mouse; said of children running, horses galloping.

41. One should have some one to recommend one.

　　Obs. 1. should have; one *yao*, must have, — then will it be well. *Obs*. 2 recommend; *chu*, to lift up, *chien*⁴, to recommend.

42. Better off than the gods.

　　仙 *hsien*¹

　　Obs. the gods; *shên*², spirits in general; *hsien*¹, fairies.

43. There are both dry fruits and fresh.
44. Running at the mouth.

　　黏 *nien*² 　　涎 *hsien*²

　　Obs. running; *nien*², to make to stick as paste does; *hsien*², the saliva of a sick man.

PART V. THE EIGHTEEN SECTIONS. *Hsü San Yü.* XIV & XV.

45. He is quite a reformed character.

    歛 *lien*⁴

    Obs. reformed; *shou-lien*⁴; the first word in the sense of to put by out of sight; the second, to ingather, of a man who has put away his vices.

46. One small chance of escape remains.

    Obs. chance; *lit.* there is only remaining a path the size of one thread.

47. Bring a needle and thread and stitch the book.

    Obs. stitch; *ting*, properly, to nail; there is no other expression for binding a Chinese book; any volume you look at will show why *ting* = to bind.

SECTION XV.

1. I admire him greatly.

    美 *hsien*⁴   慕 *mu*⁴

    Obs. admire; *hsien*⁴*-mu*⁴, the first word meaning to admire as superior to oneself, the second, to feel devotion to as superior to oneself.

2. A *hua hsüan* wind, whirl-wind, is a *yang-chio*, rams-horn, wind.

    颴 *hsüan*⁴

    Obs. whirl-wind; *hsuan*⁴, of the spiral movement of wind.

3. To skin, or flay, with a knife.

    剝 *pao*¹

    Obs. flay, *pao*¹, to flay an animal.

4. If the shoes are small they must be stretched on the trees.

    楦 *hsüan*⁴

    Obs. trees; *hsuan*⁴, properly a stop-gap; anything put in to fill up a space.

5. The legs of the table are of wood turned.

    鏇 *hsüan*⁴

    Obs. turned; *hsüan*⁴, properly a pulley; to turn as a lathe.

6. No strength left in one's body [from sickness or fatigue].

    Obs. no strength; *lit.* the whole person *suan*, sour, and soft.

7. There is a whirl-pool in the bed of the river.

    漩 *hsüan*⁴   窩 *wo*¹

    Obs. whirl-pool; *hsuan*⁴*-wo*¹, the first word meaning the whirling action of water, the second, a nest, as of birds, beasts, reptiles.

8. An officer waiting in the capital for an appointment.

    Obs. appointment, *hsuan*⁴, to select; awaiting selection, in one's turn, by the Board of Civil Office; not otherwise used in this tone; see below Sec. XII, 2.

9. *Very* clear in his accounts; [a niggard].

    Obs. 1. accounts; the reckoning-board cast clear. *Obs.* 2 very, the *cho* following *ch'ing* is intensive.

10. The button he wears on his cap is coral.

    珊 *shan*¹   瑚 '*hu*³

    Obs. coral; *shan*⁴*-'hu*³.

11. They have broken up, or, are dismissed.

    Obs. they; *pan*, see Exerc. XVI, 12; a company, troop, any set of persons.

12. How much are these umbrellas apiece?

    傘 *san*³

    Obs. umbrella; *san*³, used with or without *yü*, rain.

13. Intolerable injury.

    Obs. intolerable; *shou-pu-tê*, not able to take, be the subject of, the *yuan-ch'u*, wrongful oppression.

14. A family reunited.

    Obs. reunited, *t'uan*, like a ball, *yuan*, round; *t'uan-yuan*, said of persons who have come together again after being dispersed.

15. Purchased rank is a mere delusion.

    Obs. delusion; *lit.* to purchase office with money is simply to fall into a trap.

16. In fact the proper way is this.

17. Visible from the other side of the wall of the court.

    Obs. visible; *lit.* the wall of the *yuan*⁴, court, separating, thus does one see [it or them].

18. Don't be wrath with a man in that way without a cause.

    埋 *mai*² or *man*²

    Obs. cause; *mai*², to bury, here read *man*², and meaning, by mistake, without grounds.

19. You and I are equally willing in this matter.

20. Grimy and scorched; very dirty indeed.

    燻 *hsun*¹   燎 *liao*³

    Obs. grimy, *hsun*¹, sooty, stained by smoke; scorched; *liao*³, properly to burn; here, of the colour produced by the action of heat.

21. In official cap and sash.

束 *shu*⁴

Obs. cap; *lit.* on the crown, *kuan*, a cap, *shu*⁴, girt with, *tai*, a sash.

22. The crops have been swamped by a flood.

稼 *chia*⁴ 淹 *yen*¹

Obs. 1. crops; *chia*⁴, ripe grain; *chuang*, (see above,) hamlet, farm-house; *chuang-chia*, grain-crops in general. *Obs.* 2. swamped; by much water *yen*¹, drowned; *yen* used of persons or things.

23. Unable to swallow, [whether from illness or repletion].

嚥 *yen*⁴

Obs. to swallow; *yen*⁴, to gulp down.

24. Where are the Tuan ink-slabs produced?

Obs. Tuan¹, for Tuan-hsi, a place in Kuang Tung, famous for its *yen*, ink-stones.

25. Shall we have a trial of strength, passage of arms, together?

演 *yen*³

Obs. trial; *shih*⁴, to try anything; *yen*³, to make trial of weapons; the *tsa-mên* shews that the trial is to be between the speaker and the person addressed; it may be with arms or without.

26. You screen me a little.

Obs. screen; *lit.* do you for me *ché*¹-*yen*³, somewhat; *ché*, is to screen wholly, *yên*, to half screen; *ché yen* may be used literally, but is oftener figurative.

27. Rouged and smeared with white.

搽 *ch'a*² 胭 *yen*¹
抹 *mo*³ 粉 *fên*³

Obs. 1. rouged; *ch'a*², to smear, *yen*¹, ordinarily *yen-chih*, rouge. *Obs.* 2. smeared; *mo*³, to rub on with the flat of the hand or the finger, *fên*³, white pigment.

28. To excite people's disgust greatly.

厭 *yen*⁴

Obs. disgust; *yen*⁴.

29. To forget oneself in what one says.

遜 *hsün*⁴

Obs. forget; *lit.* to utter words that are not *hsün*⁴; *hsun*, properly, to follow another from a due sense of one's own subordinate position; *pu hsun*, is to forget this.

30. Extremely treacherous, or disloyal.

奸 *chien*¹ 詐 *cha*⁴

Obs. treacherous; *chien*¹, evil hearted; *cha*⁴, false.

31. What the eye does not see, the mouth does not desire; nor is the heart troubled by what the ear has not heard.

饞 *ch'an*²

Obs. desire; *ch'an*², gluttonous appetite.

32. He has lost caste, or character, greatly.
33. You had the opportunity of doing yourself credit, but you wouldn't.
34. Dreamy, vapouring, language.
35. Don't ever be such a fool as to believe people.

Obs. ever; *tsai*, not another time, but any time.

36. Seeing is believing.
37. He has no sympathy at all [with his relatives, fellow-men, &c].
38. To found [an empire, a family, &c.

Obs. to found; *chien*⁴, to commence, *kung*, an effort, hence the credit it brings; *li*, to establish, *yeh*, that which is achieved and the merit of the achievement; an estate.

39. One gives the precious sword to the dashing warrior; rouge and pearl-powder to a pretty woman, [Don't cast pearls before swine].

劍 *chien*⁴ 贈 *tsêng*⁴
烈 *lieh*⁴ 佳 *chia*¹

Obs. 1. sword; *chien*⁴, a two edged sword. *Obs.* 2. gives; *tsêng*⁴, to present to. *Obs.* 3 to; *yü*³, also, and more commonly, with. *Obs.* 4. dashing; *lieh*⁴, properly blazing. *Obs.* 5. pretty; *chia*¹, good, fair, of persons and things; but used only in certain rather classical phrases.

40. To be serving oneself, under pretence that one is serving the public.

Obs. serving; *chi*⁴, to assist, to benefit, *ssŭ*, one's private ends.

41. To roll up a roll of bedding.

捲 *chüan*³

Obs. roll up; *chüan*³, to roll up.

42. Quite ready to take his place.

PART V. THE EIGHTEEN SECTIONS. *Hsü San Yü.* XV & XVI.

43. Bachelors, widows, orphans, and people without heirs.

鰥 *kuan*¹ 孤 *ku*¹

Obs. bachelor; *kuan*¹; widow; *kua*³, properly few, here lone; orphans, *ku*¹, properly, fatherless, but used of one without either parent; *tu*², properly, single, but used of men in years who have no son.

44. Try and pour the wine into his mouth, and see if he will drink or not.

灌 *kuan*⁴

Obs. try and pour; *kuan*⁴, properly of water flowing in a given channel; used, as here, of the attempt to force a man to drink at a drinking-bout.

SECTION XVI.

1. With a fishing-rod in the hand fishing.

釣 *tiao*⁴ 竿 *kan*¹

Obs. fishing-rod; *tiao*⁴; a hook, to hook; *kên*, a root; here, Numerative *tiao-yu-kan*¹, a hook fish rod.

2. To touch, regenerate, his heart, by kindness.

Obs. to touch; *kan*, to affect, to influence, generally for good; *'hua*, properly, to create, to change, regenerate.

3. The three masts on board the vessel are very lofty.

桅 *wei*² 杆 *kan*¹

Obs. masts; *chih*, a stem, Numerative of *wei*², a mast; *wei* might stand without *kan*¹, as any lofty pole.

4. Shoes down at heel; slip-shod.

趿 *sa*¹ or *t'a*¹

Obs. slip-shod; *sa*¹, or *t'a*¹, the back of the shoe doubled under the heel; *la*, dragging.

5. In great anxiety about an absent relative.

牽 *ch'ien*¹

Obs. anxiety; *ch'ien*¹, classically, to drag, as, for instance, an ox; the absent person drags *chang*, the bowels, *kua*, is hung upon, *tu*, the belly.

6. You must be a little more modest and humble, both in word and deed.

謙 *ch'ien*¹ 恭 *kung*¹

Obs. modest; *ch'ien*¹, humble; *kung*¹, reverential.

7. Pretending not to see.

Obs. pretending; *chia*, false; *chuang*, to assume a false appearance.

8. Not to have paid yet what is owing to people.

Obs. yet; *'hai*, still; *'huan*, to render back.

9. A number of the crew were tracking the grain-junk.

縴 *ch'ien*⁴

Obs. 1. crew; *shang-t'ou*, on board. *Obs* 2. tracking; *ch'ien*⁴, the tow-rope by which the crew *la*, drew the vessel.

10. With one leg stretched out and the other doubled up.

踡 *ch'üan*²

Obs. stretched out; *shên*¹, to stretch straight; doubled up; *ch'uan*², to double up arm or leg.

11. He lends a helping hand.

搒 *p'êng*²

Obs. lends; *lit* he for a person hoists *p'êng*², the sail, and drags the tow-rope.

12. To strike a person with the doubled fist.

Obs. fist; *tsuan*, (see above,) doubling, *chüan*, the fist; *t'ou*, merely an auxiliary noun.

13. With nothing but two empty fists to live upon.

Obs. nothing; *chang*, above, as to fight; here, to depend on.

14. The military power is in his hand.

權 *ch'üan*²

Obs. power; *ch'uan*², properly a balance; hence authority, responsibility.

15. He is both a boxer and a wrestler.
16. High cheek-bones.

顴 *ch'üan*²

Obs. cheek-bones; *ch'uan*².

17. He is very versatile or ingenious.

Obs. versatile, *ch'uan*, here, what suits the occasion; *pien*, to change; ready with means to meet all emergencies.

18. Universal massacre; not so much as a dog or a fowl left alive.

KEY TO THE TZŬ ERH CHI. Colloquial Series.

19. Recommend him to give up his vicious courses, and return to virtue.

    邪 *hsieh*²

    Obs. 1. to recommend; *ch'üan*, to exhort. *Obs* 2. give up; *lit* to change; *hsieh*², properly, deflected, sloping; hence, morally, depravity. *Obs* 3 return; *hue*¹, to return to *chêng*, upright, rectitude.

20. Don't put a name on the fan.

    扇 *shan*⁴   款 *k'uan*³

    Obs. 1. fan; *shan*⁴. *Obs.* 2. a name; *k'uan*³, a form, a section; when used, as here, with *lao*, to put down, *sc.* the name and surname either of the person presenting a fan, or of the recipient; or of both.

21. Not to have violated any specific law.

    Obs. specific; *t'iao*, in the sense of column or section; *k'uan*, a clause or section of the law.

22. Keep a good watch over it; don't let it be lost.

23. I have a certain grudge against him.

    Obs. grudge; *tsêng*, like *hsien*, to dislike.

24. Lift up the curtain and go in with you.

    掀 *hsien*¹   簾 *lien*²

    Obs. 1 lift up; *hsien*¹, to raise, as a hanging screen, a sheet of paper lying flat. *Obs.* 2. curtain; *lien*², any hanging screen; here, of split bamboo or silk.

25. He is a very dangerous man.

    險 *hsien*³

    Obs. dangerous; *hsien*³, properly of precipitous places, &c.; *he wei jên*, plays the man, his character is, very dangerous.

26. That is a very dangerous affair.
27. Crying aloud, both weeping and crying out.

    Obs. crying; both *k'u*¹, sobbing, and *'han*, crying out; *chiao 'huan*, to cry in grief or pain.

28. Heaven and earth collapsing.

    陷 *hsien*⁴

    Obs collapsing; *lit.* the sky *t'a*, falling down in ruins, the earth *hsien*⁴, falling in; figuratively of any great crisis in public or private affairs.

29. A person of official family.

    宦 *'huan*⁴

    Obs. official; the word *'huan*⁴, is a somewhat classical equivalent of *kuan*, an official.

30. *Man-t'ou*, bread, is [a preparation of flour] with nothing inside it.

    餡 *hsien*⁴

    Obs. inside; *hsien*⁴, the meat or stuffing inside a dumpling; *man-t'ou* is used of any kind of wheaten bread.

31. How many days will it take to make?

    限 *hsien*⁴

    Obs. take; *hsien*⁴, to limit; how many days do you prescribe it *tso 'hao liao*, to be finished.

32. In great suspense.

    Obs. suspense; *hsüan*², to hang suspended.

33. A tried friend; one who has shared great trouble with one.

    患 *'huan*⁴

    Obs. trouble; *'huan*⁴, misfortune; calamity.

34. [A wedding] very gay with lanterns hanging, and silks festooned.

    綵 *ts'ai*³

    Obs silks; *ts'ai*³, any coloured silk; *chieh ts'i*, bound up silks.

35. [No company frequents them]. The door is closed, and they are wretched and lonely.

    閉 *pi*⁴

    Obs. 1 closed; *pi*⁴, means the same as *kuan*, and *'hu* the same as *mên*. *Obs.* 2. wretched; see *lêng ch'ing* above.

36. Things hooked on and linked together.

    鉤 *kou*¹   環 *'huan*²

    Obs 1. hooked; *kou*¹, an iron hook; *ta*, to hook together, as with two fingers. *Obs.* 2. linked; *'huan*², a ring.

37. I don't care to change the article once you have taken it out of my shop.
38. Friends so long as there is meat and drink going; a loving couple while there is rice and fuel to cook it with.

    Obs. couple; *ch'i*, the wife as distinct from the concubine.

39. He is paralytic.

    癱 *t'an*²   瘓 *'huan*⁴

    Obs. paralytic; *t'an*², properly, *t'an*¹, paralysis; *'huan*⁴, a word of the same meaning, never separated from *t'an*.

PART V. THE EIGHTEEN SECTIONS. *Hsü San Yü.* XVI & XVII.

40. Don't be too hard on him, or, on it.

    Obs. too hard; *'han*², to hold in the mouth; *pao-'han*, to keep silence; *q. d.* bundle up the matter in your mouth.

41. Not to speak out.
42. To do anything with alacrity.

    Obs. alacrity; *t'ung*, painful; here, an intensive.

43. He commenced his career as a Han Lin.

    翰 *'han*²

    Obs. 1. Han Lin; *'han*², a pencil; *'han lin*, the forest of pencils, the Academy, or great literary establishment, of China. *Obs.* 2. career; *ch'u shên*, put forth his person as an official.

44. To feed on rare food and look on rare things.

    希 *'hsi*¹   罕 *'han*³

    Obs. rare; *'hsi*¹, and *'han*³, both mean rare, few; said of a traveller.

45. I don't think those things of yours curious.
46. A small man.

    Obs. man; for Han see above Sec. XII, *ex.* 26; also, Sec. VII, *ex.* 21, for *chang*, which here means style, fashion.

47. Very nice dinners, either in the Manchu or the Chinese style.

    席 *hsi*²

    Obs. 1. dinners; *chiu hsi*²; the latter word, properly, the mat on which people used to sit; now only used as here. *Obs.* 2. nice; *chiang chiu*, curious, particular, *recherché*.

SECTION XVII.

1. If you delay any longer, you won't be in time.

   遲 *ch'ih*²

   Obs. delay; *ch'ih*², late; *lit.* if *tsai*, again, farther, there be delay &c.

2. I have not seen him for a long time.
3. Hand me that water-pipe.

   Obs. 1. hand; *ti*⁴, to send, convey; specially, despatches; *ti-hei*, to hand to. *Obs.* 2 water-pipe; *lit.* water-smoke-bag; *yen-tai* is the ordinary tobacco pipe.

4. To cough up water as one is swallowing it.

   嗆 *ch'iang*¹

   Obs. cough up; *ch'iang*¹, to eject anything that has gone down the wind-pipe.

5. I can't make out this matter at all.
6. To dress entirely for effect.

   Obs for effect; *nao*, as usual, indicating that the contrary of what ought to be is being done; *p'ai*, arrange things in their proper order; *p'ai-tzŭ*, a person over fastidious, or particular;

7. He is all for show.

   擺 *pai*³   架 *chia*⁴

   Obs. show; *lit.* to the death, extremely, does he *pai*³, distribute, set out his wares upon, *chia*⁴, the frame on which goods are exposed for sale; *pai-chia-tzŭ* may be used substantively for a person who tries to make a display in any way.

8. With but one person to do it, it cannot be done.

9. The merit of past service utterly lost.

   棄 *ch'i*⁴

   Obs. lost; *ch'i*⁴, to fling away, abandon.

10. The moth has put the light out.

    撲 *p'u*¹   蛾 *o*²

    Obs. moth; *p'u*¹-*têng-o*², literally, the knocking-lamp-moth has *p'u-mieh*, by its blow extinguished, the lamp.

11. I keep out of his way; or, I have kept the matter from him.

    避 *pi*⁴   諱 *'hui*⁴

    Obs. kept out, from; *pi*⁴, to avoid; *'hui*⁴, to conceal from another one's deed or thought.

12. Let him stay at home and reflect on his error.

    Obs. stay at home, *lit.* close his door; a common command of the Emperor to recreant ministers.

13. To hold him cheap, look down on him, *lit.* to behold and not raise him, *sc.* to the level of one's view.
14. To despise him.

    藐 *miao*³   視 *shih*⁴

    Obs. despise; *miao*³, minute, petty; *shih*⁴, to regard, behold; *miao-shih*, regarding as small.

15. A very able woman.
16. [This affair must be proceeded with]. The hand must positively not be taken off it.

    Obs. taken off; *tiu*, properly to lose; *tiu-k'ai-shou*, to let out of one's hand; only used figuratively.

KEY TO THE TZǓ ERH CHI. **Colloquial Series.**

17. This affair is not to be accomplished.
    Obs. not to be; the *pu liao* means cannot be; see Note on Exerc XI, *ex* 19.
18. To drink as much wine as one can carry.
19. It cannot turn out well.
20. I did not hear very plainly what was said.
    Obs plainly, *ch'ing-c'hu*, clear, distinct; as speech, calculations, &c
21. Beat him to the consistency of a man's brain.

    稀 *hsi*¹   爛 *lan*⁴

    Obs. consistency, *lit* till he was *lan*⁴, broken, as the brain, which is *hsi*¹, watery, *'hu*, pasty.
22. He has chopped up, or minced, the meat so fine, and it smells so good.

    燉 *'tun*⁴   噴 *p'ên*⁴

    Obs. 1. minced; *tun*⁴; so fine, *hsi-lan*; note the *ko* preceding, *lit* laying hand on the meat, he has chopped a fineness *Obs.* 2 smells; *p'ên*⁴, properly, to puff from the lips; the meat, while being cooked, or, when served, *p'ên hsiang*, puffs forth fragrance.
23. A boggler who cannot say what he has got to say.

    拙 *chuo*¹

    Obs boggler, *chuo*¹ *tsui pên*⁴ *sai ti*, one with awkward lips and clumsy cheeks; used, not of the lips or cheeks, but, figuratively, of a man's lack of power to express himself; *chuo-pên* is awkward, clumsy, in large things and small
24. Uttering nothing but the most perfect nonsense; (or, the foulest abuse).

    呎 *ch'in*⁴

    Obs It is scarcely possible to give a literal equivalent of this phrase, which is abusive of a man for being unreasonable or abusive; the fifth word *ch'in*⁴, means to vomit like a cat or dog.
25. What are you saying to yourself?

    咕 *ku*¹   嚷 *nang*¹

    Obs saying; *ku*¹-*nang*¹, to move the lips without uttering sound.
26. What are you muttering?

    嘟 *tu*¹   噥 *nang*¹

    Obs muttering; *tu*¹-*nang*¹, to utter sounds the purport of which cannot be made out.
27. If you dare to argue, I'll beat you.
    Obs. argue; *ch'iang*, of using strength; said to a child, or an inferior, who will have the last word
28. Life in great danger.

29. The key of that lock is lost.

    鎖 *so*³   鑰 *yao*⁴, *yo*⁴   匙 *shih*², *ch'ih*²

    Obs 1. lock; *so*³, the Chinese padlock. *Obs* 2 key; *yao*⁴-*shih*², properly, *yo*⁴-*ch'ih*², the key of the padlock, *ch'ih*, means properly a spoon
30. A piece of stone of coarse grain; that will not take a polish.

    糲 *la*¹

    Obs. coarse grain; *ts'u*, coarse, *la*¹, rice with the husk on; the expression *ts'u-ts'u-la-la-ti*, applies also to wood, rough skin, &c.
31. He is a great help; a chief aid.
32. One palm of the hand will not make a sound unless the other be struck against it. [Had one party in the quarrel given way, there could have been no collision].

    拍 *p'ai*¹   響 *hsiang*³

    Obs palm; *pa-chang*, one alone *p'ai*¹, struck as one hand against another, *pu hsiang*³, will not sound.
33. A single thread of silk will not make a skein, nor a lone tree a forest. [There are things a man cannot do single-handed].
34. To separate, make a space in, with the hand.

    撥 *pa*¹ or *po*¹   擺 *la*¹

    Obs. separate; as a crowd, or as grass in which one is looking for something, *pa*¹, properly *po*¹, to set apart; *la*¹, never used without *pa*, means the same.
35. All labour in vain.
36. To found a house without means, without support.
37. He is a humble individual; a man without rank.

    丁 *ting*¹

    Obs. individual; *tang*¹, originally a nail or pin, but not so used; here, the unit in a family
38. Come and try which is the stronger.
39. Which is the stronger and which is the weaker?
40. To have been to every part of the world.

    徧 *p'ien*⁴

    Obs world, whatever is beneath the whole sky, all to have *tsou p'ien*⁴, gone round; *p'ien*, everywhere, to visit every spot.
41. The conversation had nothing in it to irritate him, but he colored up.
    Obs colored up; *fan*¹, to turn over, change, *hen*, the countenance

172

PART V. THE EIGHTEEN SECTIONS. *Hsü San Yü.* XVII & XVIII.

42. The couple do not agree.
    Obs. couple; *k'ou*, as before, a member of a family; the two, specially husband and wife.
43. [Not twins], but as like as if they were.
    Obs. 1. but; *tao*, as before, yet; notwithstanding the fact is otherwise, *hsiang*, they seem. *Obs.* 2. twins; a pair of twin born ones; *shuang* in this sense is accented *shuang*⁴. See Exerc. XI, 20.
44. To have spent a life in vain; [to have done no good in one's generation].
45. [It will do for the present;] but how will it be in the long run?

久 *chiu*³

Obs. long run; *chiu*³, long in duration.

46. Take them as they come to your hand; don't be picking and choosing.

揀 *chien*³

Obs. picking and choosing; *t'iao*, see above, Exerc. XXV, 23; *chien*³, to select.

47. To be near sighted, and not to see plainly.
    Obs. sighted; *shih*, to behold.
48. I have but few acquaintances.
    Obs. few; *lit.* as to the persons I know, *yu hsien*, there is a limit; were *jên* the subject of *yu*, — were the phrase, that is, *jên yu hsien*, it would mean that the person was deficient, morally or intellectually.

SECTION XVIII.

1. He provokes people with his incessant fault-finding.

嘮 *lao*²

Obs. fault-finding; with *tsui sui*, mouth, that is talk, in broken fragments, *lao*² *tao*¹, criticising [people's acts].

2. He is very suspicious.
   Obs. very; *chung*, heavy; we talk of *grave* suspicion.
3. The elbow is swollen.

骹 *ko*¹   髆 *po*²
肘 *chou*³   腫 *chung*³

Obs. elbow; *ko*¹-*po*², the arm, *chou*³, the elbow, *chung*³, to swell from a blow, disease, &c.

4. The seller wanting so much, the buyer offering so much.
5. Very immaterial, or insignificant, [person or thing].

鬆 *sung*¹

Obs. immaterial; *hsi sung*¹; the *hsi*, properly, rare, is intensive of *sung*, scattered like dishevelled hair, the etymological opposite of *yao-chin*, important; *p'ing-ch'ang*, common, of every-day occurrence.

6. To have read it all through from begining to end.

尾 *wei*³ or *i*³   遍 *p'ien*⁴

Obs. 1. all through; *p'ien*⁴, nearly the same as *p'ien* in Sec. XVII, 40; to pervade, visit every part. *Obs.* 2. end; *wei*³, properly, an animals's tail; but, when so used, read *i* and coupled with *pa*, Exerc. XVIII, 5; *i-pa*.

7. Not to concern any one else.
8. He never turned to any account.
   Obs. account; never became, was, *ts'ai*² *liao*, materials, with which anything could be constructed.
9. To invite misfortune by one's own impetuosity or violence.
   Obs. violence; *ch'uang*³, to burst into, calamity, to invite evil.
10. Just at an age when the beauties of mind or person begin to shew themselves.

齡 *ling*²

Obs. age; *miao*, as above, excellent, beautiful; *ling*², years of life.

11. Not equal to the duties of his post.

勝 *shêng*¹ or *shêng*⁴

Obs. equal; *shêng*¹, to sustain, be equal to sustaining; also read *shêng*⁴, to overcome; *jên*, see Exerc. XXXVIII, 3.

12. To start before dawn.

矇 *mêng*¹

Obs. before dawn; *mêng*¹, to see indistinctly; *to start* when *liang*, the light, is but *mêng-mêng*; were the verb *to rise*, you would say *ch'i-lai*.

13. When you have learned it throughly, say it off by heart.
    Obs. by heart; when you have *nien*, recited it, so that you are *shou*, ripe, then *pei shu*, turn your back on the book, [and repeat it].
14. One man cannot do the work of two.
    Obs. work; *yi*, see Exerc XXXVIII, 12; cannot *tang*, serve as, two *yi*, official servants.

KEY TO THE TZŬ ERH CHI. **Colloquial Series.**

15. He is a craftsman.

    艺 *i*⁴

    Obs. craftsman; *i*⁴, skill; hence, art, specially, mechanical art.

16. He is a man of no antecedents; an adventurer.

    Obs. antecedents; *lai yu*, an origin from which some thing or person has come forth.

17. An old fellow, and a young fellow.

    Obs. young fellow; *'huo*³, commonly a partner, associate.

18. It is manifestly the justice of heaven.

    昭 *chao*¹   彰 *chang*¹

    Obs. manifestly; *chao*¹, bright light, *chang*¹, manifestation of light; the justice of Heaven shewing itself in retribution for good or for evil.

19. Who will venture to bear the blame?

    Obs. to bear; *tan*¹ to carry on the shoulder; see *tan*⁴, Sec XIV, 23.

20. To lose in trade.

    Obs. to lose; *p'ei*, properly, to make good; hence, to have to make good; *p'ei pên*, to have to make good capital.

21. Every one trusts him.
22. Growing up a fine lad; most fortunate!

    Obs. 1. growing up; see *chang* above; fine lad, or, more rarely, girl; *lit* with eyebrows, *ch'ing*, well-defined, and eyes *hsiu*, here, intelligent. *Obs.* 2. the graces spoken of are those of the mind rather than the person. *Obs.* 3. most fortunate; he has been born with much *fu-ch'i*, prosperity, blessings given him by heaven.

23. Very graceful, or comely.

    Obs. graceful; *hsiu* is here the opposite of *ts'u*, coarse, clumsy.

24. Equally able as a military man and a civilian.
25. A petty nature; [one that busies itself about people's minor shortcomings].
26. Covetous of small things, unable to see anything without wanting it.

    Obs. unable to see, *lit.* the skin of the eye shallow.

27. To be unable to make out whose the handwriting is.

    跡 *chi*⁴

    Obs. handwriting; *pi chi*⁴, *lit.* the pencil's footsteps.

28. To bear in silence.

    忍 *jên*³

    Obs. to bear; *jên*³, to bear patiently, *ch'i*, one's own anger, *t'un*, to bolt down, *shêng*, one's words.

29. He has told on himself in the matter.

    洩 *hsieh*⁴

    Obs. told on; *hsieh*⁴, to leak, to let leak, *ti*, the bottom or sediment of any fluid; he has let out a secret that tells against him.

30. Prices low and no credit given.

    賒 *shê*¹

    Obs. credit; *shê*¹, to buy or sell on credit; here, the latter; selling cheap, [I] give not credit.

31. Paying attention to whatever [such a person] says, and following whatever he suggests.

    Obs. suggests; *lit.* [he] *yên*, speaks, I hear and obey; [he] *chi*, plans, I follow; the *ti* making the whole into an adverb; *q. d.* follow-my-leader-like.

END OF KEY TO PART V.

Circumstances leaving rendered it necessary to print the foregoing and following Parts at different presses, the order of the pages has been unavoidably disturbed. The first page of Part VI is therefore page 1 of a fresh series which will be found to continue unbroken through the remainder of the Key.

KEY TO PART VI. THE HUNDRED LESSONS. T'an Lun P'ien.

PART. VI. THE HUNDRED LESSONS. **T'an Lun P'ien.** I–II.

LESSON I.

1. *Senior.* So I hear you are studying Manchu, eh? That's right. Manchu is with us Manchus, the first and foremost of essentials. It is to us, in short, what the language spoken in his own part of the country is to a Chinese; so it would never do to be without a knowledge of Manchu; would it?

2. *Junior.* To be sure not, and I have an additional reason for wishing to acquire it. I've been studying Chinese for the last ten years, but I am still as far as ever from seeing my way in it. I've now begun Manchu, but if I can't master enough of it to pass for a translatorship, I shall have broken down at both ends of the line. So I am come to-day, Sir, in the first place, to pay my respects to you, and, in the next, to ask a favour of you. I find it not so easy to open the subject, however.

3. *Senior.* What's your difficulty? Pray say what you have got to say. If it's anything that I can do for you, do you suppose that, with the relations existing between us, I shall try to back out?

4. *Junior.* What I have to ask, then, is this; that you will so far take an interest in me as to put yourself to a little trouble on my account. I will tell you how. Find time, if you can, to compose a few phrases for me to study, and if I manage to succeed at all, I shall regard it entirely as your work. Sir, I shall never forget your kindness. I shall not fail to be most grateful.

5. *Senior.* What are you talking about? You are one of us, are you not? My only fear would have been that you were not anxious to learn; but, since you are willing, I wish you all success. Talk of handsome return indeed! People as intimate as you and I are should never use such language to one another.

6. *Junior.* Well, Sir, if that's the way of it, I am sure I feel extremely obliged. I have only to make you my best bow, and I shall say no more.

1. 怪難 *kuai nan,* monstrously difficult. 2. 能彀 *nêng-kou;* power sufficing.
3. 兄台 *hsiung-t'ai;* my elder brother's worship; you, Sir. 4. 賜 *tz'ŭ*4; to confer on an inferior.
5. 巴不得 *pa-pu-tê,* may it be that; *pa* is probably used for *pa,* EXER. XVII. 5; *q. d.,* not to be laid hands on, too good to get, or, to be caught.

LESSON II.

1. *Senior.* Well, I hear that you have made such way in Manchu that you are beginning to speak it quite correctly.

2. *Junior.* Nonsense! I understand it, certainly, when I hear it spoken, but it will be some time yet before I can speak it myself. It is not only that I can't go right through with a piece of conversation of any length like other people, but I can't even string half a dozen sentences together. Then there is another odd thing, I do. Whenever I am going to begin, without being the least able to say why, I become so alarmed about mistakes, that I dare not go on without hesitating. Now, so long as this continues to be the case, how am I to make a speaker? Indeed, so far from considering myself one, I quite despair of ever learning to speak. I say to myself that, if, with all my studying, I have not got farther than this, I shall certainly never be a proficient.

3. *Senior.* This is all mere want of practice. Listen to me. Whenever you meet a man, no matter who, that can talk Manchu, at him at once, and talk away with him. You must go and take lessons of competent professors of the language as well, you know; and if you have any friends who are good Manchu scholars, you should be for ever talking with them. Read some Manchu every day, commit phrases to memory, and talk incessantly, until the habit of speaking comes quite naturally to your mouth. If you follow this rule, in a year or two at the farthest, you will speak it without an effort; so now don't despair any more.

KEY TO THE TZŬ ERH CHI. **Colloquial Series.**

1. 規模 *kuei-mo*; compasses-mould; a mould or form on which anything should be fashioned; only figuratively used.
2. 接不上 *chieh-pu-shang*; do not become connected; *chieh* specially of connection between what is above and what is below, *shang* an auxiliary verb, to a certain extent in affinity with *chieh*.
3. 簡簡決決 *chien-chien-chueh-chueh-ti*; summarily and decidedly.
4. 可叫 *k'o chiao*; [the causes specified above] properly make me how speaking? that is, not speaking, unable to speak.
5. 灰 *hui*¹; ashes; here verbally used; my heart is made ashes, it despairs. 6. 但凡 *tan-fan*; whether singly or universally, all whatsoever. 7. 師傅 *shih*¹-*fu*⁴; any master of a craft; *shih*, among other meanings, means a model, hence a teacher; *fu*, originally to aid by counsels. 8. 要 *yao*; here imperative.
9. 愁 *ch'ou*²; to grieve; [after what I have said,] *yu*, still, do you lament what inability?

LESSON III.

1. *Senior.* Why, when did you find time to learn all the Manchu you know, Sir? Your pronunciation is good, and you speak quite intelligibly.
2. *Junior.* Oh Sir, you are too complimentary. My Manchu does not amount to a great deal. There's a friend of mine who really does talk well. He is thoroughly at home in the language; intelligible, fluent, and speaks without a particle of Chinese accent. Then, besides this, he has such a stock of words and phrases. Now, that is what one may call proficiency, if you please.
3. *Senior.* Which is the better scholar, he or you?
4. *Junior.* Me! I should never venture to compare myself with him. I am as far from being his match as the heavens are from the earth.
5. *Senior.* What is the reason of that?
6. *Junior.* Oh! he has been much longer at it, and knows a great deal more. Then, he is very studious; he has been committing to memory, steadily, ever since he began, without stopping; the book is never out of his hand. I should have trouble enough to come up with him.
7. *Senior.* Nay, my young friend, I think you are making a slight mistake. Don't you remember what the proverb says: "Be resolved, and the thing is done." What he knows he knows only because he has learnt it. It has not come to him by intuition. And are we in any way otherwise constituted? Not at all! Well then, no matter how exact or practised a speaker he may be, all we have to do is to make up our minds, and apply ourselves to the language; and if we don't quite reach the point he has attained, we shall not be very far behind him, I suspect.

1. 獎 *chiang*³, to praise; I, *ch'êng*, am the recipient of, my worthy elder brother's too great praise.
2. 清楚 *ch'ing-ch'u*, distinct, clear, applied also to transaction of business, settlement of accounts, &c.
3. 懸隔 *hsuan-ko*; separated by space, the division caused by space; *hsuan* is properly to hang; *g. d.* the vacuum in which the heavens are hung. 4. 頗 *p'o*¹, a strong intensive, only used with certain adjectives.
5. 竟 *ching*, after all, in any contingency, to him who has *chih*, resolution, an affair [he commences will be] *ching*, happen what may, completed.

LESSON IV.

1. The chief thing that every man who comes into this world has to do is to study, and the great object of his reading is the understanding of the rights of things *(tao-li)*. Such an understanding once arrived at, a man will do his duty by his parents, while he is at home; he must do his best for the state, when he enters the public service; and he will be certain to succeed in whatever he undertakes. 2. Once you have really acquired the knowledge you ought to have, you are respected wherever you go. I don't mean only by other people; you have yourself a sense of your own title to be respected. 3. There is a class of persons who do not read, and who take no pains to be well-conducted, relying exclusively on their attainments, as they regard them, in the arts of intrigue and adulation. For my part, I can't comprehend what their minds can be like, but I know I feel sorely ashamed for them. 4. Such men not only bring discredit and disrepute on themselves, but they make people execrate the parents that could have had such children. 5. Now, my young friend, just reflect a moment, and tell me whether the obligation a man is under to his parents for their goodness to him, can ever be repaid in the very smallest degree? Well then, the least a child can do is to behave himself. If he cannot make his family illustrious, and bring glory to his line by great achievements, that can't be helped; but, on the other hand, what can be more utterly good-for-nothing than so to conduct oneself as to bring down curses on one's father and mother? 6. A careful consideration of the subject, then, satisfies us, does it not, that no man can with propriety neglect the study of books and the regulation of his moral conduct?

PART VI. THE HUNDRED LESSONS. T'an Lun P'ien. II–V.

1. 特 爲 的 *t'ê mei ti;* the special wherefore; *wei*⁴, because of; *ti*, as a relative, representing the word cause understood.
2. 孝 *hsiao*⁴, pious to parents; *hsiao-shun*, filially obedient; here construed verbally.
3. 成 就 *ch'êng-chiu;* to accomplish satisfactorily, make a good job of; *chiu* here differing little from *tê*.
4. 覺 *chio*, to perceive, be sensible of.   5. 種 *chung*³, (to be distinguished from *chung*⁴, to plant,) a kind or sort.
6. 品 *p'in*³, properly a kind or class; hence select; *p'in-hsing*, each man's peculiar nature; *hsiu-p'in*, to study, take care of one's moral nature.
7. 鑽 *tsuan*¹, to pierce as with a *tsuan*⁴, a centre-bit; to make way through a small aperture; *tsuan-kan* is elliptical for a longer phrase, *tsuan ying mou kan*, to study the accomplishment of business by intrigue; *mou-kan* may be used of a good object as well.
8. 逢 *fêng*², to meet; *ying*, to go to meet, to welcome; *fêng-ying*, to play up obsequiously to what you know to be a superior's wish, to endeavour to ingratiate oneself with a superior.
9. 害 羞 *'hai hsiu*, sorely ashamed; *'hai* as in *'hai p'a, 'hai sao*, &c.   10. 咒 *chou*⁴, to curse; 罵 *ma*⁴, to revile.
11. 白 *pai*, white, blank, in vain; *q. d.* whether there be such a case or not, just think, &c.
12. 萬 一 *wan i*, here, one part in ten thousand; also used elsewhere as ten thousand chances to one.
13. 耀 *yao*⁴, *yo*⁴, brightness, glory; here to glorify; *tsung*, for *tsu tsung*, ancestral plurality, one's ancestors; illustrate one's house, make glorious one's ancestors.
14. 出 息 *ch'u-hsi*, to make profit, interest; to cause one's parents to be reviled by people is to be unprofitable up to what *fên*, in what degree!

LESSON V.

1. *Senior.* I observe you pass this way every day, Sir. What place is it that you go to?
2. *Junior.* I go to my studies.
3. *Senior.* To read Manchu, isn't it?
4. *Junior.* It is.
5. *Senior.* What are you reading in Manchu?
6. *Junior.* Oh! no new books; nothing but the two old things; detached sentences on common subjects, and the Ch'ing 'Hua Chih Yao (guide to the Essential in Manchu.)
7. *Senior.* Are they teaching you to write Manchu round-hand yet?
8. *Junior.* The days are too short at present to leave any time for writing; but presently, when they begin to lengthen, we shall be taught to write and to translate too.
9. *Senior.* Well, Sir, I have been wanting to study Manchu myself, and I have looked, I assure you, in every hole and corner for a school; I have tried every imaginable means of procuring instruction; left no place unexamined; but, in our neighbourhood, I am sorry to say, there is no school for Manchu. I was thinking that the one you go to would do for me well enough, and that, one of these days, I might commence my attendance. Will you be so good as to say a word for me to the master beforehand?
10. *Junior.* Ah! I see you think that it is a regular professor that teaches us; but that is not the case. Our instructor is one of the elders of our clan, and he has scarcely any pupils but our own near cousins; any others that may attend are relations by marriage. There is not an outsider among them. But the fact is, that our elder is too busy to give regular lessons; for, besides teaching us, he has to go to the *ya-mên* every day. It is only because we are so idle that we don't work by ourselves, that he feels obliged to find time to play the tutor. Under these circumstances I fear I cannot help you, Sir. Were the case otherwise, your desire to study Manchu is a thing commendable in itself, and as for the trouble of speaking in your behalf, I should not have thought it any trouble at all.

1. 眼 面 前 兒 *yen mien ch'ien*, before the face and eyes; things of constant occurrence.
2. 覓 縫 *mi*⁴, to seek for; *fêng*⁴, a seam, a crevice to be distinguished from *fêng*², to stitch, EXERC. XI, 14; *tsuan t'ou*, boring with the head, *mi fêng*, searching for a crevice; trying every approach to a question.
3. 左 近 *tso-chin*, neighbouring.
4. 打 量 *ta-liang*, to reckon, *sc.* the merits or chances of anything; not used of numbers or amounts.
5. 族 *tsu*², properly class, species; colloquially, clan or tribe of men; *tsu hsiung*, an elder brother of the tribe.
6. 子 弟 *tzŭ-ti*, sons and younger brothers, *sc.* of the clan; the speaker's near cousins.
7. 再 者 *tsai-chê*, here, those who [may come] in addition, *sc.* to the blood relations aforesaid; but, in argument, *tsai-chê* constantly means in the second place, or furthermore.
8. 萬 不 得 已 *wan pu tê i*, feels obliged; *i* is properly to stop; ten thousand times can he not stop; he cannot in any way [help himself.
9. 勻 著 *yun-cho*, properly, dividing into even shares; here simply apportioning a part of *k'ung 'rh*, his leisure.
10. 費 *fei*, as in *fei shi*, DIAL. VI, 58.

KEY TO THE TZŬ ERH CHI. Colloquial Series.

LESSON VI.

1. This morning, when I went to hear those lads their lessons, I found one less prepared than another. There they stood, humming and hawing, gaping and staring, and nothing else could they do. 2. I saw how the land lay, so I said to them, "There! Stop and listen to me! It's your business, now that you are studying Manchu, to give your whole mind to your work. But when will it be accomplished if you go on in this fashion, making believe that you are students, and endeavouring to get credit that you are not entitled to? It is not only that you are wasting day after day, and month after month, but I am expending my energies to no purpose either. You are the sufferers, but the harm done you is your own doing, not mine, remember. 3. Really, it shows a want of all shame," I said, "that grown up lads like you should pay so little attention to what is said to them. You treat the lecturing that I give you for your good just as if it was so much wind in your ears. 4. I don't go out of my way to find fault with you. Don't say that. There are plenty of arguments against such a hypothesis. With the little leisure that is left me, don't you think that, when I come home from my business, I should be glad enough to repose myself, for instance? Why don't I? Why, instead of sitting down to rest, do I set to work to find one fault after another with you? Simply because, being my flesh and blood, I want you to turn to some account. I want to make men of you." 5. I am really quite at my wit's end. I can only throw my whole soul into the advice I give them, and so acquit myself of my responsibility. They may listen to me or not, as they please. I've done all that I can do.

1. 生 *shêng*, raw; here, unprepared with a lesson.
2. 瞪 *têng*[4], to open the eyes wide.
3. 且住 *ch'ieh chu*, there! stop, *ch'ieh* for *chan-ch'ieh*, temporarily, for the time being.
4. 撲 *p'u*[1], colloquially of the forward movement one would make with one's arm to catch a bird, insect, &c.; *i*, undividedly, *p'u*, making such a forward movement, *na hsin*, tender your mind.
5. 沽 *ku*[1], properly, to buy wine, *ku hsu ming*, to buy an empty name, false credit.
6. 了手 *liao shou*, to bring one's work, *lit.* hand, to an end.
7. 度 *tu*[4], to pass; *hsu-tu*, to pass to no purpose.
8. 皮臉 *p'i lien*, a skin face, a face with too thick a skin to blush.
9. 當成 *tang ch'êng*, you *tang*, let it represent, make it *ch'êng*, to be, wind by the side of the ear.
10. 錯縫 *ts'o fêng*, fault-crevices, holes in one's coat.
11. 譬 *p'i*[4], to compare with, *p'i-ju*, for instance, used in argument, as we say, do you suppose, &c.
12. 責 *tsê*[2], originally, amongst other meanings, a fault, to punish for a fault, hence responsibility, I desire *wan*, to complete, what my *tsê-jên*, responsibility, requires; then will it be right.

LESSON VII.

1. *Senior.* As to becoming a translator of Manchu, you are a Chinese scholar, and you can have no difficulty in learning to translate. All you need is an exclusive devotion of your mind to the one subject. Don't let anything interfere with your studies, and let these be progressive; and in two or three years, as a matter of course, you will be well on your way. If you go to work like the fisherman, who fishes for three days, and then is two days drying his nets, you may read for twenty years, but it will come to nothing.
2. *Junior.* Will you do me the favour to look over these translations, Sir, and make a few corrections?
3. *Senior (examining them).* Oh, come; you really have made very great progress. Every sentence runs as it should; every word is clear. I have not a fault to find. If you go up for your examination, success is in your own hands. Have you returned yourself as a candidate at these examinations that are coming off now?
4. *Junior.* I should be glad enough to stand, but I am afraid that, being a *hsiu-ts'ai*, I am not qualified.
5. *Senior.* What? When any Bannerman can go up, do you mean to say that a man of your attainments would not be allowed to? Nonsense! Why, even the *i-hsio shêng* may stand, and if so, how should a *hsiu-ts'ai* not be qualified? But the *hsiu-ts'ai* are entitled to stand, I can assure you, and it is for this reason that my son is now working as hard as he can at Manchu, for the little time that remains before he has to go up. Don't you throw away the opportunity. Add your name to the list at once.

PART VI. THE HUNDRED LESSONS. T'an Lun P'ien. VI–IX.

1. 隔斷 *ko-tuan*, to interrupt; *ko*, by interposition, *tuan*, to cut.   2. 挨 *ai*, in the sense of side by side, *ai-cho tz'ŭ-'rh*, in
3. 枉然 *wang-jan*, in vain; for *wang*, as crooked, unjust, see EXERC. XXXV, 16, here, useless.   [proper order, seriatim.
4. 疙 *ko*¹, a pimple, *hsing*¹, a star; *ko-hsing*, any spot on paper, wood, porcelain, &c.; hence figuratively, defect, blemish.
5. 操 *ts'ao*, to grasp in the hand; you will be able to grasp *ch'üan*, the balance, power, of *pi shêng*, certain success.
6. 筆帖式 *pi-t'ieh-shih*, three words used to produce the Manchu word *bitgheshi*, a lettered man, a clerk.
7. 遞 *ti*⁴, to tender, to hand up; have you returned your name?   8. 旗 *ch'i*², a flag, banner, *pa ch'i*, the Eight Banner
    Corps, of mixed civil and military organisation, in which the Manchus are enrolled. There are also eight Mongol Banner
    Corps, and eight of Chinese descended from those who sided with the Manchus when they invaded China.
9. 獨 *tu*, only; the *li*, justice of exceptionally not permitting you to be examined, can there be?
10. 義學 *i-hsio*; a *hsio*, school, whether Chinese or Manchu, founded by one or more persons of *i*, public spirit, where boys are
    taught to read gratis. The *i-hsio shêng* of the Banner Corps are distinguished from the *kuan-hsio shêng*, candidates from the
11. 姪 *chih*², nephew; here, the son of the speaker who addresses the other person as his brother.   [government establishments.
12. 補名字 *pu ming-tzŭ*, add your name, lit. supplementarily, as you have not yet returned it.
13. 機會 *chi 'hui*, opportunity; *chi*, as elsewhere, the motive spring; *'hui*, a conjuncture, the right moment.

LESSON VIII.

1. Never read novels. If you read anything, read the Mirror of History. That will extend the range of your scholarship for you, and if you keep the events of the past in your memory, making the good your pattern and taking warning by the bad, you will find yourself all the better for it, body and mind. 2. As to novels and old tales, fictions without a shadow of truth that different people have composed, it will do you no good if you read a thousand volumes of them. 3. There are people who have got no sense of decency, who will go on reading to their audience how that, once upon a time, in such and such a state, so-and-so fought ever so many fights with so-and-so; how that this one made a cut with his sword, which the other one parried with his axe; how that this one made a thrust with his spear, which the other one stopped with a staff. If either of the parties is supposed to be defeated, the auxiliaries he invokes are spirits and fairies, who come on clouds and go in mist; grass that, when cut, makes horses, or beans that he scatters, on which they become fighting men. 4. All this is evidently false, yet the stupid people it is told to, receive it as gospel. There they stand like idiots, taking it in with a positive gusto. Men of sense not only ridicule works of the sort, but have a certain distaste for them. So don't you bestow any pains on such trash. Put your novel away, pray!

1. 小說 *hsiao shuo*, tales, romances.   2. 鑑 *chien*⁴, a mirror; the *t'ung-chien*, universal mirror, is a famous historical work.
3. 至於 *chih yu*, to come to; very common where a new proposition is introduced.
4. 詞 *tz'ŭ*, talk expressions; *ku-êrh tz'ŭ*, talk about the men of old, *êrh* for *jên*, man.   5. 影 *ying*³, shadow.
6. 瞎 *hsia*¹, properly, blind, *hsia 'hua*, falsehood. 7. 整 *chêng*, becoming, made up to.   8. 斧 *fu*³, an axe, carpenter's or other.
9. 扎 *cha*¹, to thrust at with the point of a stick or weapon.   10. 搪 *t'ang*², to fend off a blow.
11. 敗 *pai*, originally, damaged, destroyed; here, and commonly, defeated.
12. 神 *shên*², spirits in general; 仙 *hsien*¹, fairies; *shên-hsien*, a collection of such beings.
13. 剪 *chien*³, scissors, to cut with scissars; to cut with a knife, &c.   14. 撒 *sa*³, to scatter; see *sa*¹, EXERC. XXXVII. 20.
15. 滋 *tzŭ*¹, a pleasant flavour; 味 *wei*⁴, any flavour, *tzŭ-wei*, a pleasant flavour, a relish.
16. 見識 *chien-shih*, experience; the sense derived from it.   17. 笑話 *hsiao-'hua*, to laugh at.
18. 怠 *tai*⁴, slow, taking no interest in; *lan-tai*, lazy; not eager *ch'iao*, to read such books.

LESSON IX.

1. *Senior.* Has that book come yet?
2. *Junior.* It has been sent for, but it is not come yet.
3. *Senior.* Not come yet! Who was sent for it?
4. *Junior.* The young lad, Sir. When we first told him to go, he wouldn't stir for us, but kept loitering here ever so long, as if it didn't matter whether he went or not. At last I told him it was you who had desired that the book should be brought, and then he started off post-haste. But when he came back he brought only three *t'ao*, and as you know, Sir, the book is in four. So we asked him: "What made you leave a *t'ao*? You had better make all the haste you can, and get it," we said, "or when your master comes in, he

KEY TO THE TZŬ ERH CHI. Colloquial Series.

won't be best pleased with you." However, he would not plead guilty; on the contrary, he tried to put us in the wrong. We had bungled the directions we gave him, he said; and so he went off in a huff, and he is not back yet. Some one might be sent to meet him, but then he would be most likely returning by one road, while the messenger was going another.

Senior. Was there ever such a slippery article in this world? Of course, he is off to some place where there is something going on, to amuse himself. The right thing, beyond all doubt, is to correct him severely; so, as soon as he returns, I shall tie him up and give him a very sound thrashing. Otherwise, this kind of thing will grow into a habit, and he will become a greater good-for-nothing than he is now.

1. 漏 *lou*⁴, to leak, as anything holding fluid; to leak out as the fluid itself; frequently used, as here, of things left out, omissions in writing, business, &c.
2. 依 *i*¹, to lean against, hence, to incline to, assent to; *pu i*, not to assent to, to be dissatisfied with.
3. 嚴 *yen*², severe; *kuan-chiao*, to keep in order and teach; here, much as we often use the word correction.
4. 斷斷 *tuan-tuan*, decidedly, positively; beyond doubt.   5. 捆 *k'un*³, to bind with cords, things or persons.
6. 頓 *tun*, in the sense of turn or time.
7. 堪 *k'an*¹, to have strength to bear, to be equal to duty, responsibility, &c; *pu k'an*, here, unequal to doing what he ought; elsewhere it may mean that more is laid on a person than he can bear.

LESSON X.

1. *Senior.* Foot-archery is, with us Manchus, a most important consideration. Easy as it seems, it is so much the reverse in practice that, notwithstanding the number of archers who shoot from morning till night, ay, take their very bows to bed with them, there are but a small number who come to shoot so well as to distinguish themselves above their competitors.
2. *Junior.* What is the difficulty?
3. *Senior.* The body must be kept quite upright; the shoulders of the same height; the attitude of the whole person perfectly unconstrained. Then the bow should be so stiff, withal, that, when the arrow leaves it, it goes with force; and then, if every arrrow hits the mark, the shooting may be pronounced good.
4. *Junior.* Well, look at my shooting, Sir, and see if I have improved. If there is anything to find fault with, please correct me.
5. *Senior.* No there is nothing to be said against your shooting as a foot-archer. Trust to your thumb, and sooner or later you will wear the peacock's feather. Your style is good, you show training, and you shoot clean. If everyone shot like you, there would be no fault to find with anyone. The only thing to remark is that your bow is not quite stiff enough, and that the bow-hand is slightly unsteady. Reform in these few particulars, and, no matter where you go to shoot, you are certain to shoot better than the majority. No one will be able to keep you under him.

1. 射 *shih*², in books *shê*⁴, to shoot arrows.   2. 箭 *chien*⁴, an arrow; *pu-chien*, foot archery.
3. 長拉 *ch'ang-la*, continually to draw the bow.
4. 萃 *ts'ui*⁴, reeds or grass growing in tufts; *pa ts'ui*, to draw out one stem or blade from such a tuft, thereby giving it pre-eminence; if there be any whose *la*, shooting, come to be so good as to *ch'u lei*, excel their class, [and, as such,] to be extracted from the bunch. See below, *ch'u chung*.
5. 出名 *ch'u ming*, to put forth a name, become famous, of those who have done so, there are how many?
6. 自然 *tzŭ jan*, as of itself, unconstrained.   7. 毛病 *mao-ping*, evil or fault even so large as a hair.
8. 搭著 *ta-cho*, additionally; it may be used with *yu* preceding it, as here, or without *yu*.
9. 撥 *po*², in books *po*¹, properly to move apart with the hand; *po chêng*, to set right, not used of moving material things.
10. 拇 *mu*³, a finger, not used alone; *chang-cho*, relying on, *ta mu-chih-t'ou*, the great finger; great in the sense of first in the series, the forefinger being *erh mu-chih-t'ou*. The middle finger is *chung-chih*; the next, *ssŭ mu-chih-t'ou*, but also, politely, *wu-ming chih*, the finger without a name. The little finger is *hsiao mu-chih-t'ou*.
11. 翎 *ling*², feathers; here, a feather from the tail of the pheasant or the peacock; the latter being much more honorable than the former; *tai-ling*, to wear such a feather in the cap.
12. 壓 *ya*¹, to press down, as anything laid on another presses that which is below it. Observe *ni* the object of *ya* between its auxiliaries *hsia* and *ch'u*.

PART VI. THE HUNDRED LESSONS. T'an Lun P'ien. IX-XII.

LESSON XI.

1. *Junior (entering).* A happy new year to you, Sir!
2. *Senior.* You are very good. A happy new year to both of us.
3. *Junior.* Please take your seat, Sir.
4. *Senior.* What for?
5. *Junior.* That I may make my new-year salaam to you.
6. *Senior* No, no! I won't hear of such a thing.
7. *Junior.* Indeed, Sir, I must make you a kotow. It's my bounden duty.
8. *Senior.* Get up, get up, I beg of you. There; may you have promotion! May you have posterity! May you pass your life in wealth and honour! Now please get up off your knees, and sit down on the upper seat. Let me give you a few of these dumplings I have here.
9. *Junior.* Not any, thank you; I ate some at home, before I came out.
10. *Senior.* Well, but you did not eat so much that you can't eat any more, surely? At your time of life, a man has no sooner done eating than he is hungry again. Do eat some, or I shall certainly think that your abstemiousness is all pretence.
11. *Junior.* I am in earnest, I assure you, Sir. You don't suppose, do you, that in your house I should do otherwise than make myself at home? I should never think of telling you an untruth, depend on it.
12 *Senior.* Here, then, make some tea for this gentleman.
13. *Junior.* No tea for me, thank you, Sir.
14. *Senior.* But why not?
15. *Junior.* I must be off elsewhere. I have a number of places to go to, and if I don't pay my visits in good time, it will set people wondering. Now, don't get up from table, Sir. Let me find my way out by myself. You'll spoil your dinner, if you come away from it.
16. *Senior.* What, not see you out? A likely story! Dear me, to think that you have had the trouble of coming for nothing; not even a cup of tea! Well, good bye, till we meet again. Make my compliments to all your people, will you?

1. 新喜 *hsin hsi,* new [year's] congratulations.   2. 陞 *shêng*[1], properly, to rise; *shêng-kuan,* to obtain promotion.
3. 富貴 *fu-kuei,* rich and honorable.   4. 餃 *chiao*[3], flour dumplings with or without meat inside.
5. 糚假 *chuang-chia,* pretending, specially pretending to have no appetite; *chia-chuang* is used of any other kind of pretence.
6. 犯思量 *fan ssŭ-liang;* I shall *fan,* offend, run foul of people's *ssŭ-liang,* speculations as to the cause of my not coming to see them Construe, people will all be [by me] *fan ssŭ-liang.*
7. 別送 *pieh-sung,* do not accompany me, *sc.* to the door.
8. 看 *k'an,* lest, look to it that you do not carry away the *wei,* relish of your dinner.
9. 空空 *k'ung-k'ung-'rh-ti,* emptily, specially where a visitor has had nothing to eat, or nothing presented to him.
10. 改日 *kai jih,* another day, *tsai chien,* we shall see each other again.

LESSON XII.

1. *Junior.* I congratulate you, Sir. They say you have been selected for a *chang-ching*-ship.
2. *Senior.* Yes; at the selection yesterday, they decided on proposing me as the effective nominee.
3. *Junior.* On whom did they decide as nominee in waiting?
4. *Senior.* A man you don't know; a subaltern of the Vanguard.
5. *Junior.* Has he seen any service?
6. *Senior.* Only with the Hunting Camp. He has never served a campaign.
7. *Junior.* Well, I feel satisfied that you will be wearing the peacock's feather presently.
8. *Senior.* Don't flatter me, pray. I have no particular merits of my own, and there are too many better men than I in the field to admit of my counting on the appointment as a certainty. I may have the luck to lay hold of it, but, if I do, it will be by the virtue of those who have gone before me and have found favour with heaven; and I can't be sure about getting it at all.
9. *Junior.* You underrate yourself, Sir. Why, think of the number of years you have been in the service! You're a man of good standing; all your friends of the same date, if you come to that, are now *ta-jên,* and those who entered the army later than you did, have all been promoted. Then, as to your services, you have been in the wars, you have been wounded, and you are now one of the Picked Archers. Who is there, therefore, in your Banner Corps that is a better man than you are? I know what you are thinking of. You are afraid, I suppose, that I am come to get a glass of wine out of you in honour of the occasion.
10. *Senior.* Wine, indeed! I can only tell you that, if the news is true, it's not to say wine, but anything you like I shall be happy to offer you.

KEY TO THE TZŬ ERH CHI. Colloquial Series.

1. 章京 *chang-ching*; the words are supposed to give nearly the sound of a certain official designation in Manchu.
2. 選 *hsüan*³, to choose; see above SECTION XV. 8; *chien-hsuan*, colloquially used only of choosing officers, not, (as in SEC. XV,) in their turn, but by merit; *shang* is an auxiliary verb, but indicating at the same time the *superior* merit of the person chosen. 3. 擬 *ni*³, commonly to suggest, here, of submitting a name to the throne.
4. 前鋒校 *ch'ien-fêng*¹ *hsiao*⁴; the *hsiao* are military officers in Manchu corps, of the sixth grade; *fêng*, the point of a weapon; the *Ch'ien Fêng*, is one of the grand divisions of the Manchu army, the point in advance, or vanguard.
5. 有兵 *yu ping*, to have seen military service.
6. 圍 *wei*², to surround; hence applied to hunting as carried on with a corps of beaters; *hua*, only, has he done *wei*, hunting camp service. 7. 孔雀 *k'ung ch'io*, the peacock. 8. 指望 *chih-wang*, to point to and look towards; to hope.
9. 蔭 *yin*⁴, the shade cast by trees, plants, &c., *fu yin*, the overshadowing of prosperity [due to the virtues] of *tsu-tsung*, one's ancestors. 10. 撈 *lao*¹, to take up out of water, with the hand or otherwise.
11. 善射 *shan-shê*, those who have fifteen merits in their shooting; not the fifteen best shots.
12. 旗下 *ch'i-hsia*, serving under the chiefs of your *ch'i*, Banner Corps, who is *ch'iang*, more able, than you.
13. 喜酒 *hsi-chiu*, congratulation wine. 14. 果然 *kuo-jan*, in very deed.
15. 要 *yao*, for *jo*, if, which in Pekinese is often so pronounced.

LESSON XIII.

1. *Senior*. Success in the public service all depends on the opportunities of the individual. If you have no more than ordinary luck, nothing will go well with you. Your object, whatever it be, may seem on the point of attainment, and some *contretemps* will present itself expressly to foil you. There are people who hold such hands, who have such a run of luck, that there really is nothing that does not turn out as they desire and expect. They have their own way without let or hindrance, and, in the twinkling of an eye, there they are in the highest places they can fill.

2. *Junior*. Well, Sir, I am of an entirely different opinion. I think it is all a question of exertion or no exertion. If an *employé* idles the year away, showing no sign of life, and spending his pay without doing any duty for it, how can he possibly expect to be promoted? Why, he ought to be dismissed from the service. The foremost duties of an *employé* are diligence and attentiveness. He must also keep on good terms with his friends; not taking a line of his own, nor refusing to do as others do; never bringing in his comrades for a share of trouble that belongs only to him; and when any duty, no matter what, devolves upon him, it behoves him to give his whole mind to the discharge of it, and to push gallantly to the front. Let a man take this line, and he is certain to rise. How can he fail of success?

1. 扠 *ch'a*⁴, stumps or lesser boughs branching out from the stem of a tree; figuratively for an occurrence out of the plain course one would pursue.
2. 彩頭 *ts'ai-t'ou*, colour-end; the right colour side of the dice; you might say that the *ts'ai-t'ou* is bad; but this is rare.
3. 爽利 *shuang-shuang-li-li-ti*, quickly and without hindrance; *shuang*, as in EXERC. XXXI, free as the morning air, untrammelled, as a sky without clouds, *li*, sharp, quick.
4. 瞅 *ch'ou*⁴, to see, look at. 5. 優 *yu*¹, excellent; *yu-têng*, highest degree of *kao shêng*, rising to high place.
6. 巴結 *pa chieh*, in a good sense, as here, to exert one's-self, in a bad sense, to intrigue for patronage. The expression is purely colloquial, and *pa* evidently stands for some other character.
7. 餐 *ts'an*¹, what is eaten; to eat; *su*, properly white, here used like *pai*, vainly; *su ts'an*, vainly eating, doing no work for one's wages; *shih-wei*, a corpse personage, a dead person; but rarely used except in this combination, the upper and lower parts of which are sometimes transposed.
8. 革退 *kê-t'ui*, to strip off [office and compel] to retire.
9. 攀 *p'an*¹, to drag towards one with the hand; here, of pulling in others to do one's own work. 10. 勇 *yung*³, brave.

LESSON XIV.

1. This Chang is anything but cordial to his acquaintance; not like an old gentleman that I know, who is quite another style of old man; very friendly with everybody; delights in a long literary conversation; will sit talking history a whole day, and never tire. 2. He is very amiable, too, with any young people he happens to meet; tries to win them to the right road; reproves what there is to reprove, and gives them good

PART VI. THE HUNDRED LESSONS. T'an Lun P'ien. XII–XV.

advice when it is needed. 3. Then he is so kindhearted and charitable; as eager to help any one he finds in distress as if he were the party concerned; sure to leave nothing undone that may relieve the sufferer. He really is an old man who has to thank his virtues for all the blessings he enjoys, and I feel this so strongly that I am quite dissatisfied with myself when I let any great length of time pass without paying him a visit. 4. He brings luck on all belonging to him. As the proverb says: "The man who is blest himself, brings blessings on his whole house." And there is the old man with an ample fortune, and sons and grandsons in plenty; all the reward of his own well-doing.

1. 冷淡 *lêng-tan*, cold and thin, or tasteless, not cordial. 2. 親熱 *ch'in-jo*, the opposite of *lêng-tan*.
3. 悦 *yueh*⁴, to rejoice; *'ho-yen*, with friendly colour, and *yueh-shê*, gladsome tint.
4. 引 *yin*³, to lead, guide, *yu*⁴, to tempt, draw on, in a good or bad sense, here *yin-yu*, to draw on to *'hao ch'u*, good ways.
5. 指撥 *chih-po*, to point to and set right, see above, *po* in *po-chêng*, LESSON X.
6. 仁 *jên*¹, benevolence, humanity, disinterestedness, Christian charity, *jên-ai*, kind-hearted.
7. 護 *'hu*⁴, to assist, *'hu-chung*, charitable, philanthropic.
8. 救 *chiu*⁴, to save, *ta-chiu*, to come to the rescue of, *q d.* adding one's own hand or person.
9. 積 *chi*¹, to accumulate, his *fu*, blessings, accumulate, thanks to his *tao*, way of life, the characteristic of which is *'hou*, that is, *chung-'hou*, sincerity and unselfishness.
10. 不過意 *pu kuo i*, not to be able to get over the thought. Observe the emphasis given by *chih shih*, it is simply the fact [that, &c.
11. 托帶 *t'o-tai*, not used except in this proverb; the whole house *t'o*, being beholden to his *fu*, blessings, (which prove the greatness of his virtues,) *tai*, are drawn, follow him, and share these blessings.
12. 充足 *ch'ung tsu*, amply sufficing; *ch'ung* in the sense of filling to the full.
13. 旺 *wang*⁴, brilliancy, great success; *hsing-wang*, flourishing, either as here, or of commerce, harvests, &c.
14. 報應 *pao-ying*, heaven's reward of good or retribution of evil.

LESSON XV.

1. *Junior.* You must mind what you are about, gentlemen, before his Excellency here. He is very quick and decided, and whatever comes to his hand is certain to be turned out shipshape. Then he is very clear-sighted. He knows what people are worth. He is not to be humbugged as to any man's real qualities. With all this he is very kindhearted, and when the young fellows belonging to those about him are diligent and respectable, he will never fail to bring them forward, and support their claims to appointments or promotion at the fitting season. But if he comes across fellows who shirk duty, eye-servants who try to make their game by a show of diligence, they may as well look out. They can't escape him, and once they fall into his hands they will not get away very easily.

2. *Senior.* You young gentlemen may say what you please on the subject; what else can I do? When you are watching me, day after day, with all your eyes, in the hope that I shall make a career for you, how would your respective merits be done justice to, if I did not recommend those who deserve to be recommended, and pull up these who deserve to be pulled up? As to coming down on delinquents, it is my nature to say out what I feel. Still, my conduct and my language are pretty much what they ought to be, I suspect; and this is the reason why people obey me, and are ready to exert themselves when I require it.

1. 敏 *min*³, quick intelligence; *chieh*, quick in movement, active; his *ts'ai-ch'ing*, abilities are, in character, those of a man clear-seeing and prompt.
2. 有條有理 *yu t'iao yu li*, a figure taken from thread duly sorted, not in confusion, *li* representing the word *order*.
3. 瞞 *man*², to hoodwink.
4. 獻 *hien*⁴, to make offer to a superior of a present, or of a suggestion, here, to make a show of tendering diligence.
5. 占 *chan*¹, so pronounced, to take without right; *chan p'ien-i*, to gain advantage unduly.
6. 巴巴兒 *pa-pa 'rh*, of the eye fixed on a mark, not to be explained etymologically, unless *pa*¹ is taken as corrupt for the same character written with the 177th Radical, *pa*³, a target.
7. 束 *shu*⁴, to tie up as a bundle of sticks; *yo*, also properly to bind; *yo-shu*, to control, enforce discipline upon.
8. 賞 *shang*³, to confer on an inferior; hence to reward; *kung*, exertion, hence well-doing, merit.
9. 正派 *chêng p'ai*, right course, correctness; *p'ai*, in the sense of divergent courses of water poured out.

KEY TO THE TZŬ ERH CHI. Colloquial Series.

LESSON XVI.

1. Children are reared to be the prop of age, and a son should remember all the trouble he has given his parents; how kind it was of them to bring him up as they did; and this should make him show his sense of filial duty now, while they are alive, by finding them good food to eat and good clothes to put on, and by rejoicing the heart of the old folks with his amiability and cheerfulness. 2. If a son neglects to feed and clothe his parents, if he does not trouble himself about what they may suffer from want or from weather, and so, by treating them as if they did not belong to him, pains and vexes the old people, while they are yet with him, he may weep and wail as he will a hundred years later, but what good will that do? Supposing his grief to be sincere, no one will believe in it. It will be put down as a sham, got up because he is afraid of people's contempt. And as for sacrifices, you may set any dainties you please before the dead, but who ever knew the spirits enjoy these dishes? They are all gobbled up by the living; the dead don't gain anything by them. 3. There are some children who are worse than neglectful; children who will tell you that their parents are so old that there is no making them understand anything they ought to do; and who go on clamour, clamour, in the house, until at last they insist on having a separate establishment. Language such as this makes one distressed and angry in spite of one's self. Such persons revolt the powers of nature, and the spirits abhor them. How is it possible, one asks, that they should die in their beds? 4. Just observe these undutiful people, and, in the twinkling of an eye, you will see their children and their children's children as undutiful as they have been.

1. 防 *fang*2, to guard against; *fang-pei*, to make preparation against possible evil.
2. 趁 *ch'ên*4, properly to avail one's self of an opportunity.   3. 饑 *chi*1, to hunger, starve.
4. 看待 *k'an-tai*, is explained by the clause preceding it, without which *tang-tai* or *tai*, alone. would be used, *k'an-tai* is not used except, as here, of indifference to relatives, it must be construed as if *k'an* were detached from *tai*, and linked with the words preceding it.
5. 供 *kung*, here to set out for sacrifice.   6. 珍 *chên*1, jewels, 饈 *hsiu*1, dainty fare, *chên-hsiu*, dainty fare; *mei-wei*, goodly [taste.
7. 魂 *hun*2, the spirit of life which leaves man when he dies, not his *ch'i*, the breath, *'hun-ling*, this same spirit belonging to men dead or dreaming, in abeyance when a man is half-drowned, in ordinary men, not immortal.
8. 享 *hsiang*3, to enjoy, as happiness, *shou-hsiang*, the same.
9. 饢 *nang*3, to eat, 搡 *sang*1?, properly to push back with the hand, *nang-sang*, filling the mouth with food like a glutton.
10. 晦 *'hui*4, of the sight darkened, *lao pei 'hui*, the old turn the back on what is right and go in darkness, are drivelling, doting.
11. 塲 處 *ch'ang ch'u*, arena-place, this length.   13. 不由的 *pu yu ti*, without one's permission, whether one will or no.
14. 不容 *pu jung*, not to tolerate, Heaven and Earth, the powers of nature, cannot bear them.
14 焉 *yen*1, a classical interrogative, how can they, &c.
15 終 *chung*1, the end, here, to die, *shan chung*, comfortably to die, *shan*, as in the phrase *shan fa*, good, commendable, methods, not virtuous, righteous, &c.
16 靜 *ching*4, still, tranquil, *ching-ching-ti*, silently.
17. 眨 *chan*3, also colloquially read *cha*3, and in books, *pien*3, to wink the eye.   18. 學 *hsiao*, to imitate.

LESSON XVII.

1. Touching quarrels in families: brothers are borne in the one mother's womb, and while they are little they eat together, play together, and each one will love the other as much as himself. Up to a certain time they will be as affectionate as possible. And if, later in life, they become less intimate, it is in most cases because they are egged on by their wives to fight about property, or because they listen to persons not connected with them, who tell them things calculated to produce estrangement; the result of which cause is, in very many instances, a state of selfish indifference on the part of each to the interest of the other. 2. And so, when their senses have become so affected by daily calumnies that they can think of nothing else, some fine day they lose all patience, and then come blows and altercations, and in fine, there is a feud between them. 3. But they should remember that if they lose goods or property, they can buy more; that if the wife were to die, they could marry again; but that injury done to a brother is like injury done to a hand or foot; if you snap it off, it cannot be reproduced. 4. They should remember also that there is no ally like a brother. Who else, if you are in any serious difficulty, will feel to you like the brother who is bone of your bone, and flesh of your flesh? will risk his life in his efforts to help you? Will any outsider make such an effort? Not a bit of it. He will sheer off for fear of being compromised; he won't be able to get out of the way fast enough 5. All this proves that there is no friend so near one as a brother. Why can't people bear these facts somewhat more particularly in mind?

PART VI. THE HUNDRED LESSONS. **T'an Lun P'ien.** XVI–XVIII.

1. 何 等 'ho têng, what degree, a form of the superlative; in the highest degree.
2. 妻 ch'ɩ¹, the wife, who is espoused, 姜 ch'ɩeh, the concubine, who is purchased; a man cannot legally have two ch'ɩ.
3. 挑 t'ɩau², to set trouble going privily; not to be confounded with t'ɩau¹, to carry on the shoulder; 唆 so¹, to make mischief, t'ɩao-so, to incite to contention.
4. 爭 chêng¹, to quarrel, to quarrel about.
5. 間 chɩen¹, to divide, not to be confounded with chɩen¹, EXERC. III, 9; language that li-chien, separates.
6. 懷 'huaɩ², the breast, to carry in the breast or heart.   7. 異 ɩ⁴, strange, here estranged.
8. 讒 ts'an², to criticise ill-naturedly, to backbite.
9. 濡 ju², thoroughly saturated, as a thing steeped in water; the ear saturated, mu jan, the eye dyed.
10. 致 chɩh⁴, to cause; ɩ, using [the means above described,] chɩh, they cause, what follows, yu, classically governing the object of chɩh.
11. 辯 pan⁴, (properly, and often, pɩen⁴,) to distinguish in discussion; pronounced pan only in this phrase, pan-tsui, altercation.
12. 讎 ch'ou², hate, feud.   13. 置 chɩh⁴, to make, provide; hence, as here, to buy.
14. 娶 ch'ü³, to take a woman to wife.
15. 折 chê³, to snap off, also read shê².   16. 捨 shê³, to fling away; shê ming, to fling away life.
17. 連累 lɩen-leɩ, entanglement, complication.
18. 迭 tɩeh², here in the sense of achieving satisfactorily, to-pu-tɩeh, cannot succeed in escaping.

LESSON XVIII.

1. As to friendship, men should imitate Kuan Chung and Pao Shu of the olden time. 2. These two were walking together one day out in the country, when they saw an ingot of gold lying by the road side. 3. Each wanted the other to take it, but as neither would pick it up to keep for himself, they left it and walked on 4. until they fell in with a labouring man. "There's an ingot of gold over there," said they to him. "you go and take it up now." 5. Away went the labourer as hard as he could, to look for the gold, but no gold could he see, and all he did see was a snake with two heads. 6. This startled him considerably. Without further loss of time he cut the snake in two with his hoe, and then gave chase to his two informants. "Here, I say!" shouted he, when he had caught them up, "What bad blood is there between you and me, that you should have told me a two-headed snake was an ingot of gold? You have pretty near cost me my life, let me tell you." 7. Not believing what he said, they went back to the spot to take a look, and there they found the lump of gold lying where they had first seen it, but cut in two pieces. 8. Kuan Chung took one half, and Pao Shu the other, and off they went, while the labourer had to go his way empty-handed. 9. Such was friendship as it subsisted between friends of the olden time. This story comes out of a story-book, it is true; still the conduct of these two men, as here related, undoubtedly reads a lesson to the profit-at-any-price folks of our own day.

1. 仲 chung⁴, properly, the second son in a family; here, a name.   [father.
2. 鮑 pao¹, 叔 shu², the first character always a surname, the second, here a name, means the younger brother of one's
3. 郊 chɩao¹, originally the land at a radius of 10 li round a capital city; 'huang-chiao, the country as opposed to ground that is built over, yeh-waɩ, nearly the same.
4. 逛 kuang⁴, to stroll, walk for pleasure.
5. 元 yuan², properly, original; here, in the sense of great; pao, a jewel, here, in the sense of something precious; chin yuan-pao, means simply a large lump of gold fashioned into the shape in which the government silver is usually cast.
6. 揀 chɩen, to pick up.   7. 擱 lɩao⁴, properly, to throw down; here, to leave on the ground.
8. 莊稼漢 chuang-chɩa'Han, Chinese who has to do with grain crops; an agricultural labourer.
9. 蛇 shê², a serpent.
10. 嚇 hɩa⁴, in books read 'ho⁴, to frighten; [the sight] frightened him a great start.   11. 鋤 ch'u², a hoe.
12. 兩截 lɩang chɩeh, two fragments; observe the construction; pa before the object shê, snake; k'an, struck, [so that the snake] ch'êng, became two chɩeh, fragments, the verb chɩeh, meaning to cut off.
13. 忘 wang², here so intoned, but identical with wang⁴, to forget, the phrase chɩen li wang ɩ, to forget justice at the sight of gain, is classical.

KEY TO THE TZŬ ERH CHI. Colloquial Series.

LESSON XIX.

1. You mean that young friend of ours, don't you?
2. I do.
3. Ah! he's a regular awl in a bag. He is certain to make his way before long.
4. How is this?
5. He is naturally very steady; highly educated, uncommonly well conducted, and well looking; and so diligent in the discharge of his public duties. When he has none to discharge, and he is living quietly with his family, he gives himself up entirely to the management of household affairs, and to the care of home expenditure. He is dutiful to his parents, and affectionate to his brothers; he really has not a single fault. Then, again, he is such a friend to have if you want his assistance. If a man apply to him he will help if he can, or he will tell him plainly if he can't, be the applicant who he may. If he does not promise his aid, that's all about it; if he gives you to understand that you shall have it, he will not fail to do all he can for you, and, till the question is settled, he won't take his hand off it. Every one, consequently, respects him, and entertains an affection for him.
6. No doubt; and such a man as this will never go through life empty-handed. "Heaven," says the proverb, "stands by the good man," and Heaven will not fail to bless him.

1. 錐 *chui*1, an awl.
2. 淵 *yuan*1, a deep place with water in it; an abyss; only used in certain set phrases; 博 *po*2, of learning, extensive; his *hsio-yên*, learning, is deep and wide.
3. 居 *chu*1, to dwell in, inhabit, *chu-chia*, to live at home, not elsewhere on business or pleasure.
4. 點 頭 *tien t'ou*, to nod the head in token of assent, if he do not *ying*, promise, enough; if he assent, then, &c.
5. 豈 *ch'i*3, how? *ch'i yu*, how can there be, is a common form of negation; how can there be *li*, a rational just possibility, that he should go *k'ung*, without advantage, through life.
6. 相 *hsiang*4, (not *hsiang*1,) to aid, stand by; hence, anciently, a minister or counsellor.
7. 降 *chiang*4, (not *hsiang*2,) to descend, or, as here, to cause to descend. Observe *chi jên*, the fortunate, or prosperous, man, identical with the good man.

LESSON XX.

1. *Senior.* That young fellow is our old neighbour, you know; the lad we have seen grow up here. He has not been away from us so very long, and now one hears that he is doing very well; that he has got an appointment. I only half believed the report when I first heard it, until on inquiring of friends, I find it really is the case. It shows the truth of the proverb, "If a man but resolve, the thing he wants to do is done;" and of the other proverb, "No man is too young to make a resolution"
2. *Junior.* That is all very well, Sir; still, his father's virtues must have had claims known to Heaven to enable him to beget a son of such promise; a young man so plain and honest; so well-conducted; spending any spare time his archery drill may leave him at home, and there always at his studies; never moving in the direction of a dissolute life. Then he is so careful in the discharge of his public duties; so diligent; and as to looking out for himself, or turning a penny underhand, he is perfectly spotless. It's quite a case in which one may observe that, "The house where virtue accumulates from generation to generation will not fail to have more than an ordinary share of happiness."

1. 坊 *fang*1, properly, in past times, a region or quarter of a city; *chieh-fang*, neighbours, a neighbour.
2. 能 有 *nêng yu*, can it be how many days, *q. d* it is but a few days, *ko liao*, that he has been separated from us.
3. 來 著 *lai-cho* implies the continuance of the action of the verbs *hsin* and *i*, until the time indicated by *'hou-lai*, by-and-bye.
4. 陰 功 *yin kung*, secret desert, merit known to heaven only.
5. 繼 *tsai*, [his father's claims being known to heaven,] *tsai*, then, or thereon, was he enabled; his claims must have been known before he could, &c.
6. 樸 *p'u*2, properly, wood as yet untouched by tools, paint, &c.; *q. d.* in primitive simplicity; *p'u-shih*, plain and true, guileless.
7. 唐 *t'ang*2, a Chinese surname, taken as its style by a celebrated dynasty; here, most likely, corruptly used for some other character; *'huang-t'ang*, wild, dissolute in conduct.
8. 沾 染 *chan-jan*, dipped and dyed; only used morally as here.
9. 合 了 *'ho liao*, that agrees with; [the case] is indeed one that agrees with that *chü 'hua*, saying.

PART VI. THE HUNDRED LESSONS. T'an Lun P'ien. XIX–XXII.

LESSON XXI.

Host. 1. But you're not a stranger here, surely. If you wanted to see me, you should have walked straight in. What occasion was there for you to have yourself announced at all? And once you had got to the door, why turn back without coming in? The fact is, that you were put out, I suppose, because my people said I was not at home; eh? Well, you won't see why they should have said so, unless I explain; so listen. 2. For some time past our young fellows have had a gambling-club going, and they had just been here vowing and protesting that I must attend too. Now, in the first place, as you very well know, I haven't time to play; I never can tell from one moment to another but I may be wanted on duty; and, in the next place, even if I had the time, the laws against gaming are extremely severe, and if anything were to go wrong, I should lose my character. 3. So I resolved, *coute que coute*, not to go to the club, let them take it as they pleased, and I told the servants to deny me to all visitors, without distinction of persons. Well, *you* call, and the stupid beggars make the same answer to you as to A or B, and send you about your business before they come in to say a word to me. I did send after you post-haste, but, to my great annoyance, my messenger came back and reported that he had not been able to catch you up. Now, don't, pray, think that I am to blame in this matter. I do assure you that you were denied without my knowledge.

1. 通報 *t'ung-pao*, announced; *t'ung*, passing through; *sc.* from the door to the rooms within. [coming; heretofore.
2. 一向 *i hsiang*, for some time past; *i*, unity unbroken, continuity; *hsiang* as in *hsiang-lai*, of time towards this point
3. 誓 *shih⁴*, an oath; *c'hi shih*, make oath, *fa yuan*, utter a vow; the words *c'hi shih* are used without *fa yuan*, but the latter seldom, if ever, without the former.
4. 王 *wang⁴*, a king or prince, the title in ancient times of the ruler, *wang-fa*, the laws of the state.
5. 儻 *t'ang*, if, but if.   6. 到底 *tao-ti*, literally, to the bottom; used in various ways; here, happen what might.
7. 較 *chiao⁴*, properly, to compare two sides; *chi chiao*, to reckon and compare; to think over a wrong.

LESSON XXII.

1. He and I were friends a long time back, and then we became connected by various intermarriages; and, as we had not met for years, when I came home from the wars, I wanted to hunt him up and have a chat with him. However, one thing or another prevented my going to see him, and I never could find time until yesterday, when, as I was passing that way, I took the opportunity of calling at the house he used to live in. When I got there, I asked for my friend, but they said he had long removed elsewhere, and was now residing round a corner at the west end of a certain small street. 2. I went in search of the house, according to their directions, and, up a blind alley, at the farthest end of the street, I found it; but the door was fast, and no one made answer, though I called and called for half an hour. At last, when I had been knocking and shouting ever so long, there appeared an old woman who could not put one foot before the other, and she said that her master was not at home; he was gone somewhere or other. Then, said I, when he comes home, tell him I called, will you? 3. But, in addition to her other infirmities, the old woman was so deaf that she could hear nothing, and I was obliged to borrow a pen and ink of a small shop next door and write a note, which I left, to tell my friend that I had been to see him.

1. 底根 *ti-kên*, in the root, at the beginning.   2. 打 *ta*, as often elsewhere, from.
3. 叙 *hsu⁴*, written sometimes with the 29th, sometimes with the 66th Radical; properly, to state in order; not used alone colloquially, *hsu-t'an*, to converse, to chat.
4. 順便 *shun pien*, following convenience; the opportunity presenting itself.
5. 搬 *pan*, see SECT. XIV, 5; here, for *pan chia*, to shift one's home.
6. 拐 *kuai³*, to gull, deceive; but probably, in the combination before us, confounded with the same character written with the 75th Radical, meaning a crutch; *kuai-wan*, crutch-like bending, round a corner.
7. 儘溜頭兒 *chin-liu-t'ou-'rh*, the farthest end, *liu*, properly, to fall as water after running down a rock, a roof, &c.; *q.d.* the extreme point before the fall commences.
8. 旮 *ka¹*, has no meaning alone; *ka-la-'rh*, in Manchu, means the opening of a seam in wood; in Peking, it is used of a *cul-de-sac* round a corner.
9. 敲 *ch'iao¹*, to strike.   10. 媽 *ma¹*, properly, an old woman; children call their mothers *ma* or *ma-ma*.
11. 字兒 *tzŭ-êrh*, a short letter or note.

KEY TO THE TZŬ ERH CHI: Colloquial Series.

LESSON XXIII.

1. *Junior.* Keep on your horse, Sir, pray! I ought to have got out of your sight. Now, why should you go through the form of dismounting when you are so tired?
2. *Senior.* Not dismount, indeed! If I had not seen you, well and good; but when I did see you ever so far off, you wouldn't have had me keep on my horse, would you?
3. *Junior.* Well, Sir, won't you step in and sit down?
4. *Senior.* Oh! yes; I'll step in and sit down a moment; it's so long since we met. But, dear me! what a show of flowers you have, and what a stock of gold fish! And your rockery, so ingeniously conceived; every tier of it has a character of it's own! And what a tidy library! Every thing in it looks so nice. It's quite the place for reading men like us.
5. *Junior.* It's nice enough, no doubt; the misfortune is that I have no friend to study with, and studying all alone is tame work.
6. *Senior.* Well, there needn't be much difficulty on that score. I'll be your fellow-student; provided that I don't bore you. What say you?
7. *Junior.* Bore, indeed! It will be a real blessing if you will. I never asked you to come, because I feared you would refuse; but if you really are coming I shall be the most fortunate of men.

1. 躲避 *to-pi*, to get out of the way; I *shih*, failed, to *to-pi*.
2. 老遠 *lao yüan*, very far off; *lao* intensive of *yüan*; has no reference to time.
3. 許久 *hsu chiu*, very long time; *hsu*, purely intensive.
4. 暑 *hao*⁴, diminutive of time, as here, or of quantity. See Sound Table, *lio, lieh, lio*.
5. 堆 *tui*¹, a pile; to pile up; *shan-tzŭ shih-êrh*, stones making a hill; *tui-tê*, piled up, very nicely.
6. 心思 *hsin-ssŭ*, hearts' thoughts, one's fancy, has been employed *hên ch'iao*, very ingeniously.
7. 入眼 *ju yen*, to enter the eye; said of a sight that causes pleasure.
8. 冷清 *lêng-ch'ing*, cold and clear; no warmth in the thing; dull work.
9. 厭煩 *yen-fan*, disgust and trouble; to regard as a bore; the object being *wo*, me, understood.
10. 造化 *tsao-'hua*, properly, to create; often, as here, the good fortune bestowed on one by Heaven when one was created.
11. 幸 *hsing*⁴, good fortune; *wan hsing*, immense felicity.

LESSON XXIV.

1. When first I met that man, I thought his manner very frank and hearty. Then he looked so like a gentleman, that, with his fine handsome person and his powers of conversation, he took my fancy greatly. I used to ask myself how I should best cultivate his acquaintance, and never ceased singing his praises.
2. But, by-and-bye, as we grew better acquainted, and we came to be constantly thrown together, I had occasion to observe his conduct more carefully, and then began to see that he was not at all what he ought to be. There was display enough in him, but no solid qualities. A dark and dangerous man withal; always setting people wrong, and, however fair he might be to your face, doing you serious damage behind the scenes. Let a man drop into his net, and he is laid on his back at once. He has been the ruin of I can't say how many people; more than you could count on your fingers. 3. His acquaintance, consequently, never speak of him without remarking that he is a man to be afraid of. There is not one of them that he has not made smart. 4. He is just one of those men, in fact, to whom the proverb applies exactly: "The heart is concealed by the coat of the stomach; you may see a man's face, but you don't see his mind." 5. I have had wonderful luck in escaping him. He would have had me in his grip for certain like other men, if I hadn't taken great care to give him a wide berth.

1. 魁 *k'uei*², properly, the head; eminent; a hero; 偉 *wei*³, great, remarkable; *k'uei-wei*, of large stature; *'han-chang*, as to stature, a fine person.
2. 誇 *k'ua*¹, to boast; *k'ua-chiang*, to praise.   3. 交上 *chiao shang*, as intercourse began, or proceeded.
4. 混混 *'hun-'hun*, properly, the mingling of water.   5. 考較 *k'ao-chiao*, examine and compare; to observe.
6. 正經 *chêng-ching*; of persons, rightly going, well-conducted; of things, right and proper.
7. 弄空 *nou k'ung*; the first character commonly read *nung*; working out hollowness; without, an empty frame; in his heart,
8. 陰險 *yin-hsien*, dark and dangerous; treacherous.   [an impostor,

PART VI. THE HUNDRED LESSONS. T'an Lun P'ien. XXII—XXVI.

9. 好道 *'hao tao;* not letting men go the right way; observe *pu kei,* and various analogous constructions, mean, in Chinese, [to prevent.
10. 圈套 *ch'uan t'ao,* a ring, circular enclosure, and a trap; figure from hunting.
11. 肋 *chin*[1], properly, the same as the 69th Radical, a catty; here read *kên*[1]; why *kên-tou* should mean a somerset, or fall, is not explained; it is so used whether of man or beast.
12. 坑害 *k'êng 'hai,* injured by falling into a pit; not used except figuratively.
13. 絡 *lo*[4], netted cords; a small net; *lung,* a cage; *lung-lo,* only used, as here, figuratively.

LESSON XXV.

1. No, really, you take things too easy. If you can't do what you are asked to do, there's an end of it. But when you have undertaken a thing, what do you mean by keeping people waiting, instead of making all the haste in your power? What confidence will your friends ever place in your promises, if this is the way you get through your business? 2. And you don't seem to think you are to blame either? Well, *I* feel ashamed then, I can assure you. It would have been far better, instead of dawdling along in this way, to have told the man the truth plump, and plain, in the first instance. His mind would have been set at ease, so far as you were concerned, and he might have turned his attention to some other means of attaining his end.

1. 疲 *p'i*[2], properly, wearied, exhausted; here, callous, not paying due attention to.
2. 應承 *ying-ch'êng,* to promise, to undertake a commission.
3. 信 *hsin,* earlier used as a letter, news; here, in its proper sense of to believe.
4. 與其 *yu ch'i,* as compared with ...... the proposition following *ch'i.*
5. 顢頇 *man*[1]*-'han*[1]; dawdling, not exerting one's-self as one should. Neither character in this dissyllable is found apart from the other.
6. 索 *so*[3], properly, a cord; in combination with various words, to draw, to exhort, &c; here, apparently, used corruptly for *-shuai**, to the sense of which it does not either adhere; *so hsiang,* with all one's might, with one's whole attention.
7. 景 *ching*[3], properly the light of the sun; scenery; *kuang-ching,* circumstances.

LESSON XXVI.

1. What is all this about? The affair has not even assumed shape yet, and if it had, a little delay would make no difference. Besides, the party principally interested is in no hurry whatever about it, so why on earth should you take the initiative in pressing one so violently on the subject? 2. The grand essential is that a question should be carefully considered again and again, and that one should give out nothing until one's mind is made up as to the proper solution of it. It does not do to begin talking in the headlong random fashion you would have me talk. 3. But, however, I am so constituted that in any thing I undertake, I must be left unfettered. If people try to make me act prematurely, by getting my head into chancery, it's my nature to decline all action whatever. If our friend has confidence in me, let him bide my time. If he has not, let him apply to some one else to do his business. Who would prevent him?

1. 有影 *yu ying,* to have a shadow, which a thing cannot have till it has form or shape.
2. 尙且 *shang ch'ieh,* a strong affirmative; *q.d.* the *chêng ching,* rightful principal in the affair, even he is in no hurry.
3. 催 *ts'ui*[1], to urge on, 逼 *pi*[1], to press, to constrain; that you should *hsien,* moving before he does, urgently press, is what reasonableness?
4. 糊裏麻裏的 *'hu-li-ma-li-ti,* in a wild, irregular fashion.
5. 攣 *ch'an*[2], to tie a cord about persons or things.
6. 得實 *tê shih,* to get or become solid, as the fruit after the blossom has fallen.
7. 斷不 *tuan pu,* a strong dissent; on no account, under no circumstances.
8. 倘 *t'ang*[3], if, but if; not used colloquially without *jo,* and then, as a general rule, disjunctively. This character is used interchangeably with *t'ang,* in LESSON XXI, note 5.
9. 攔 *lan*[2], properly, to stop with the hand; to hinder.

---

* 率 *shuai*[4], in the classical passage to which *shuai hsing* properly belongs, is rendered by some commentators to lead, by others, to follow.

KEY TO THE TZǓ ERH CHI. **Colloquial Series.**

LESSON XXVII.

1. Ah! you don't know yet that there are other men as able as you are. This fondness for feats of strength is all along of your youth; the hey-day is in the blood; but when you have met with a few reverses, naturally, you won't be so full of heart. 2. I'll tell you my own case. I was once very fond of martial exercises, and I used to practise them every day. But after a time I gave them up, and for this reason. My elder brother was equally fond of these gymnastics. His weapon was the lance, and he was so handy with it that not one in a score could get within his guard. 3. One day, however, at my uncle's, he fell in with a lame man who had come in from the country and who was a swordsman, and they proposed, one to the other, that they should have a trial of skill; each man to use the weapon he was accustomed to. 4. Well, my brother made nothing of an antagonist like this. He took his lance in his hand and made a thrust straight at the lame man's heart. But the lame man, without hurrying himself the least in the world, deliberately parried the thrust with his sword; the head of the lance was snapped straight across and the piece broke off. My brother made all haste to draw the lance in, but, before he could recover it, the lame man's blade was upon his neck, and as he tried to dodge, he was caught by his foe under the throat and jerked to a considerable distance. 5. This gave him a great distaste for the thing, and I left off learning too. But this shows, doesn't it, that I am right in maintaining that there is no dearth of powerful men in the empire?

1. 旺 *wang*, properly bright; colloquially, of anything that is succeeding, or, at its best; here, of the *hsieh-ch'i*, blood and breath, the constitution, which is *wang*, in its prime. See above, LESSON XIV, note 13.
2. 打把勢 *ta pa-shih*, to do feats of strength or of arms; a good authority explains *pa* to be the hand or arm; *pa-shih*, the condition, or circumstances, in which the arm is placed while performing martial exercises (?).
3. 演習 *yen-hsi*, to practise in order to proficiency.
4. 手歇 *hsieh shou*, to rest the hand, to give up some practice or habit.
5. 勳勁 *tung ching*, to move the muscles.
6. 跟前 *kên ch'ien*, here, of getting *at* the person of the opponent.
7. 舅 *chiu*⁴, one's maternal uncle.   8. 瘸 *ch'üeh*², lame, whether a person or an animal.
9. 那兒有他 *na-'rh yu t'a*, in his mind where had he him? he held him cheap.
10. 扎 *cha*¹, to thrust with any pointed weapon.
11. 犨 *ch'a*², a character not recognised by the dictionaries; a crack or split. Observe the idiom, *ch'i*, even; *ko*, individual; *ch'a*, crack, *ch'i-ko-ch'a-rh-ti*, in the manner of cracks evenly separating.
12. 夾 *chia*¹, not to be confounded with *chia*², EXERC. XII, 11; to keep fast hold of, as between the fingers, under the arm, in the leaves of a book, &c.
13. 撂出 *liao ch'u*, to jerk away; *liao*, properly to put down, or let fall.   14. 趣 *ch'ü*⁴, pleasing savour, taste.

LESSON XXVIII.

1. No, really, you are too extravagant; I can't help taking you to task for your wastefulness. If a man wants to live, he must accustom himself to economy in everything. Instead of throwing the rice you don't eat into the kennel, wouldn't it be better to give it to your servants? I wonder the very thought of such waste doesn't make you uneasy. 2. The fact is that all you trouble yourself about, my friend, is *eating* the rice. You ignore altogether the trouble people have had growing it, and tracking it up the canal, before it arrives here; such trouble that even to get a single grain is no easy matter. 3. Besides, men like you and myself can't go on like your millionaires, who have plenty of money at their command, who eat this and fancy that. If you habituate yourself to your present way of living, eating for ever and without limit to the variety of your dishes, you'll not only have no luck, but you'll beggar yourself to boot. 4. Old men tell us, "Waste not, want not;" and be your luck as good as you please, if you don't become a better manager, look to it that you don't starve in the long run. It will be too late to repent when that day comes.

1. 奢 *shê*¹, extravagance; 侈 *ch'ih*³, extravagance, also pretentiousness; *shê-ch'ih*, wastefulness.
2. 省儉 *shêng-chien*, or *chien-shêng*, economy.   3. 溝 *kou*¹, a ditch, a sewer; *kou yen*, the kennel.
4. 穩 *wên*³, stable, not to be shaken; *an-wên*, of a person's sobriety of demeanour; or, as here, of the mind's contentment.
5. 粒 *li*⁴, a grain of rice.
6. 捆 *k'un*³, or *k'uên*³, properly, to tie up persons or things; here, q.d. put a stopper on the mouth to prevent eating.

PART VI. THE HUNDRED LESSONS. T'an Lun P'ien. XXVII–XXX.

7. 盡頭 *chin t'ou*, extreme end, farthest limit.
8. 折 *ch'ê*², in LESSON XVII; read also *shê;* here, as there, to snap off; *ch'ê fu*, to do a damage to the happiness which Heaven meant one to enjoy.
9. 惜衣 *hsi i*, to be fond of one's clothes; hence, to save or spare them.
10. 福田 *fu t'ien*, the field of your blessings, the region of your luck; a Buddhic expression.
11. 會過 *'hui kuo*, to know how to get through *jih-tzŭ*, one's days, understood; to take proper care of one's money.
12. 隄 *ti*¹, an embankment; *ti-fang cho*, be on your guard.
13. 挨 *ai*², to suffer; the *shang* auxiliary, and marking progress of time; you will come to suffer hunger.

LESSON XXIX.

1. *Neighbour.* What is the use of stowing your money away so safe and never spending any? A hundred years, if a man live so long, are past in the twinkling of an eye. How few days, I say to myself, will this vagrant dream-stuff body of mine have any enjoyment? In the space of a flash of light, we become fit for nothing. We had best make use of our time, then, and occupy ourselves a little with the table and the toilet before we grow old. When our bones and sinews are become stiff, dress don't become us, we have no great relish for what we eat, and we have to do our children's bidding. What pleasure is there in life under such circumstances? No; all that is incumbent on a man is to avoid excess; and then, when we know what we have got to spend, it is quite proper that we should enjoy ourselves to a certain extent.

2. *Host.* Are you speaking with any knowledge of my affairs, pray? or is it all mere speculation? Were I indeed the man of money you make me out, with enough and to spare, it would be quite right that I should enjoy myself like other people. But how if I have not the money and estate that other people have? Would you have me run in debt for dress, or eat myself out of house and home? Supposing that I did what you recommend, what would become of me when all my gear was gone, and I was left bemoaning my lot in such misery that death would be a blessing? And if, which is most likely, I did not die, but was to drag on existence with just enough breath left to live, how should I support myself? If I turned to you, would you listen to my application?

1. 浮生 *fou shêng*, life as if on waves, *ju mêng*, like to a dream.
2. 聽著 *ch'ou-cho*, regarding our children's chins, watching what they say, we pass our days.
3. 所得 *so tê*; the *fen*, portion, that we have got.
4. 債 *chai*⁴, debt; hence, *chai-chu*, debt-proprietor, a creditor.
5. 嘆 *t'an*⁴, to sigh; *k'ou ch'i*, a breath of the mouth; to heave a sigh and then to die, that would be well; [but] ten thousand to one not dying, still having breath I should live; rightly, possibly, how should I live?

LESSON XXX.

1. *Senior.* Who has been here to-day?
2. *Junior.* Two visitors came just after you left the house, Sir; they came to congratulate you, they said, on your promotion.
3. *Senior.* Who went out to speak to them?
4. *Junior.* I was standing at the door at the time. I told them you were out, and I said: "Gentlemen, will you walk in and sit down;" but they declined and went away again.
5. *Senior.* What were they like?
6. *Junior.* One was a stout man, Sir, a little taller than you. He had a square face, with a beard up to his temples, prominent eyes, and a dark ruddy complexion. The other was quite a figure of fun; shockingly dirty; but one eye, and he squinted with that. His face was densely pitted with pockmarks, too; he had a curly beard that covered his whole chin, and he talked as if his tongue was too short. He said something to me, and I was within an ace of bursting out laughing.
7. *Senior.* The stout man I know, but who can the other be?
8. *Junior.* I asked them their names, and they each left a card. Wait, and I will bring you the cards to look at, Sir.
9. *Senior.* Dear me! That monkey, eh? Where is he from, I wonder? You fellows must not look down on *him* though. His form may be as crooked as you please, but he is very able with his pen, and he has all his wits about him. He has long had a reputation, that man. You can name him to no one that has not heard of him.

KEY TO THE TZŬ ERH CHI. Colloquial Series.

1. 道喜 *tao hsi*, to offer congratulations.
2. 來著 *lai cho*, auxiliary of *chan-cho;* so, below, after *wên*, to ask.
3. 鬢 *pin*⁴, the temples; *lien pin*, connected with the temples.   4. 鬍 *'hu*², the beard.
5. 纍子 *pao-tzŭ*, applied to the eyes only, and not used without the word for eyes; *pao*, in the sense not of fierceness, as above, but of conspicuousness.
6. 紫 *tzŭ*³, purple; here, the deep colour of dark sugar.
7. 斜 *hsieh*², slanting, diverging from the right line, whether perpendicular or horizontal.
8. 糨 *chiang*⁴, flour paste.   9. 稠 *ch'ou*², standing thick together.   [boiled rice.
10. 麻子 *ma-tzŭ*, a man pitted with small pox, the marks of which were *chian-ch'ou*, close together like the grains of over-
11. 捲毛 *chüan mao*, curly-haired.
12. 咬著舌兒 *yao-cho she-'rh*, literally, biting his tongue, unable to speak out, clipping sounds, especially the sound *êrh*.
13. 噗哧 *p'u*¹ *ch'ih*¹, of short abrupt sounds, the bursting of paper, the falling of a thing in the mud.
14. 職 *chih*², properly, office, department; *chih-ming*, properly, one's official title, but used now of one's card, whether it bear one's title or not.
15. 猴 *'hou*², a monkey.
16. 歪 *wai*¹, deflected, crooked; the opposite of *chêng*, upright; *wai-wai-niu-niu*, turning and twisting.
17. 韜 *tao*¹, properly, the case for a bow; to put the bow in its case; it would then be concealed; *liao*, in the sense of to ponder, to devise; *t'ao liao*, concealed devices; specially stratagems in war.

LESSON XXXI.

1. *Senior.* What! are you not off yet?
2. *Junior.* Oh! I shall be off by and bye. My travelling baggage and other traps are all packed right enough; what I am a little short of is money to pay my travelling expenses. I believe to-day in the truth of the saying, that it's easier to go up a hill after a tiger, than it is to begin speaking about a thing one wants. I have been begging with the greatest effrontery in every direction, but to no purpose. I couldn't get any one to lend me the money. So in my extremity, Sir, I'm come to look for you, to beg you to oblige me with a slight loan, either of money or of some article to pawn. As soon as I return I shall do myself the honour of repaying you both principal and interest.
3. *Senior.* It is lucky you came to me when you did. If you had been a little later you would not have been in time. I happen to have in hand a few ounces that have just been brought in from the country. You take the half of them for your use. When you have drunk your tea, I'll weigh them out to you. By the way, tell me, are you not leaving home now for the first time?
4. *Junior.* I am.
5. *Senior.* Well, then, a word in your ear. The right line to take when you are going to a distance from home, is this. Let your first care be to keep on good terms with the friends you live amongst. Show kindness to all the common *employés* who serve under you, without distinguishing between those who are in more immediate contact with you and the rest. If you get on ground where you may turn a penny, never forget that reputation is the grand essential, and hold your hand. Ill-gotten gain will seriously compromise a good name.
6. *Junior.* I fully appreciate the value of your advice, Sir, and to the end of my days I shall never forget it.

1. 起身 *ch'i shên*, to be in movement for a journey.
2. 整理 *chêng-li*, to put in proper order; for *to-tzŭ*, see EXERC. XVI.   [your waist.
3. 盤纏 *p'an ch'an*, travelling expenses; *p'an*, see *p'an-fei*, EXERC. XV, ex. 13; *ch'an*, to tie, q.d. tied in your girdle, about
4. 擒 *ch'in*, to lay hands on, make prisoners of, evil doers, wild beasts.
5. 當頭 *tang t'ou*, a something that will stand for money at the *tang p'u*, pawn shop.
6. 併 *ping*⁴, collected together; *pên li*, principal and interest, *i ping*, entirely and together, will I *fêng 'huan*, tender back.
7. 幸 *hsing*⁴, fortunate, auspicious; *k'uei*, to be deficient, has not here any translateable meaning, *hsing-k'uei*, luckily.
8. 遠門 *yuan mên*, as if it were *li mên yuan*, far from your own door.
9. 處 *ch'u*³, to dwell in or amongst, not to be confounded with *ch'u*⁴, a place.
10. 手長 *shou ch'ang*, the hand long, too far reaching; let not this be.
11. 係 *hsi*⁴, properly, to connect as by threads; very commonly in books, the verb *to be*, the participle *being*; but not so here; *kuan-hsi*, to have relation to, affect, concern, but always of evil consequences.

PART VI. THE HUNDRED LESSONS. T'an Lun P'ien. XXX – XXXIII.

LESSON XXXII.

1. *Senior.* When did you come in from the country, Sir?
2. *Junior.* I've been here some days.
3. *Senior.* I never heard a word about your return, Sir, or I should have called on you long ago.
4. *Junior.* It was not likely you should hear, Sir; we live so far from one another; and besides you have your official duties to attend to.
5. *Senior.* Will you allow me to ask whereabouts it is that you are stationed?
6. *Junior.* It's a place in the jurisdiction of Pa Chou.
7. *Senior.* By the Liu-li River, is it?
8. *Junior.* No; by the 'Hun River.
9. *Senior.* And how have the crops turned out there this year?
10. *Junior.* Very well indeed. The harvest has been perfect.
11. *Senior.* How odd! Wasn't there a talk of floods there first, and then of drought?
12. *Junior.* All mere report; no truth in it. Take black pulse alone; it is down to ten cash, or so, a *shêng*. It has not been so low this many years.
13. *Senior.* You don't say so!
14. *Junior.* But I do say so.
15. *Senior.* Well, in that case, the next time you send there, please buy a few piculs of pulse for me; and when you have made out the account, if you'll tell me, I'll pay you whatever it cost you.
16. *Junior.* Aye; you are right. I see you have a number of horses standing in your stables, which, of course, you must have pulse to feed; and it will be much better to have it brought in from down yonder at half-price, than to be paying for it at the rates they are charging here.

1. 窎 *tiao*^{4}, properly, the nest of a large bird; deep; not used alone colloquially; *tiao-yüan*, far off.
2. 霸 *pa*^{4}, properly, to domineer; here, the name of a district in the province of Chih Li.
3. 浑 *'hun*^{2}, properly, confused like pure and turbid water mingling; here, the name of a river.
4. 收成 *shou ch'êng*, in-gathered in a state of completeness, used only of crops whether of fruit or grain.
5. 潦 *lao*^{4}, to flood with rain.
6. 谣 *yao*^{2}, properly, to sing as one works; *yao-yen*, gossip, idle report.
7. 升 *shêng*,^{1} a measure; the tenth of the *tou*.
8. 槽 *ts'ao*^{2}, a trough, whether for water or forage; *ts'ao-shang*, in the stable, speaking of any cattle; *ma ts'ao*, a horse stable; but you cannot put the name of any other beast before *ts'ao*.
9. 减 *chien*^{3}, to diminish.

LESSON XXXIII.

1. *Senior.* If you buy a horse at all, buy a good one, and then it will be a pleasure to see it in the stable; but why waste forage on the keep of a such a screw as this?
2. *Junior.* You don't know his points, Sir, but I do; for when they brought the horse home yesterday, I took him outside the walls and tried him, and I found that he would do well enough to ride; his amble was even; his gallop was fast; at the archery-practice he didn't swerve a hair's breadth; off the course or within it; he has a good mouth, and he is sure-footed.
3. *Senior.* From what you say on the subject it's quite clear to me that you don't know a horse when you see one. A good horse must have his legs sound, must be equal to hard work; he should know the drill of the hunting-field, and he should be well-shaped and handy. That's the sort of horse that one of your fine young fellows will mount, with their quivers on their backs, and away they fly like the hawk; a sight worth looking at. But what manner of horse is this beast of yours? He's old in the teeth, with his lower jaw drooping, and so gone in the legs that they are always coming down with him. Besides, with a figure as unwieldly as yours, he is not at all a suitable horse for you.
4. *Junior.* Well, but what am I to do? The horse is bought and paid for, and so there is nothing for it but to see to his keep, such as he is. I have no business of much importance to take me out, nor any that sends me a great way from home. There's one point in his favor, he has no vice; so he'll answer my purpose. It's better to be on him than on foot, at any rate.

KEY TO THE TZŬ ERH CHI. Colloquial Series.

1. 傖 *ts'an*⁴, a word disparaging appearance; *ts'an-t'ou*, speaking of men, a blockhead; here, simply poor-looking, good-for-nothing.
2. 牽 *ch'ien*¹, to drag, or lead along, animals.
3. 顛 *tien*¹, here, to amble like a horse or mule; *tien tê wên*, his amble is secure, even.
4. 裹 *kuo*³, properly, to wrap round with cord or cloth; in the Chinese riding-school, the horse gallops along a trench; if he swerve outwards, he is said to *chang*, if inwards, to *kuo*.
5. 英雄 *ying hsiung*, a hero; a fine fellow.   6. 繫 *chi*⁴, to bind on; also pronounced, but more rarely, *hsi*.
7. 撒袋 *sa-tai*, a quiver.   8. 鷹 *ying*¹, a falcon.   9. 觀 *kuan*¹, to look at, attend to.
10. 搭拉 *ta-la*, hanging down; both characters used corruptly.
11. 前失 *ch'ien shih*, to miss the footing forward, this horse *k'ên*, is in the habit of, tripping.
12. 笨 *pên*, of the body, clumsy.   13. 相宜 *hsiang-i*, suited.
14. 將就 *chiang-chiu*, here means, by an effort to make a thing suit; *chiang*, being corruptly used for another word that means to move from one place to another.
15. 老實 *lao-shih*, honest; of horses and like animals, quiet, harmless.   16. 究竟 *chiu-ching*, seeking to the end; after all.

LESSON XXXIV.

1. *Senior.* Where did you buy that cloak of sable? In a shop?
2. *Junior.* No. I bought it at one of the fairs.
3. *Senior.* How much did you give for it?
4. *Junior.* Guess.
5. *Senior.* It's worth at least three hundred ounces.
6. *Junior.* I began with an offer of two hundred, and went up, and when I got to two hundred and fifty, the man let me have it.
7, *Senior.* What could have made it so cheap? I remember some time ago, the common price of such a cloak as this was as much as five hundred ounces. Why, just look at it; how deep the colour is, and the fur so thick and smooth. Then the hair along the edges is quite even; the lining is a piece of thick satin, the figure on that is of a new pattern, and, to add to all this, the cloak itself is of the latest fashion. As to fitting you, it couldn't have fitted you better if it had been made for you.
8. *Junior.* If I don't forget, Sir, you used to have one.
9. *Senior.* Mine! That's worth nothing. You can *call* it a cloak by courtesy, but that's all one can say for it. The hair is coming out, and the colour is faded. I can't wear it with the fur outside.
10. *Junior.* Well, well, if that's the case, you must get yourself a good one next pay-day.
11. *Senior.* Oh! I'm too much a man of the past to be nice about dress. All I require is something to keep me warm. You are one of the younger fellows just commencing a career. It's quite right for you to put on good clothes, and turn out smart on a levée day; but if I were to dress in that way, we won't say how I should look; I should be so uncomfortable as well. Besides, we who have got military duty to do, have no occasion for fine clothes. We just put on anything; it may be old, or it may want mending, but we are quite satisfied with it all the same.

1. 貂 *tiao*¹, the marten or sable.
2. 廟上 *miao shang*, in the temple; one of two temples in Peking where fairs are held on certain days every month.
3. 至不濟 *chih pu chi*, most not complete; farthest from completeness; at the very least.
4. 毛道兒 *mao tao êrh*, the fur; *tao*, not translateable by any of the meanings ordinarily assigned it.
5. 風毛 *fêng mao*, the fur edge that projects beyond the silk or satin lining on which the fur is laid.
6. 緞 *tuan*⁴, satin.   7. 俸 *fêng*⁴, official salary; see *kuan*, SECTION VIII, 22.
8. 巴結 *pa-chieh*, here, to make an effort to get on in one's career.
9. 朝會 *ch'ao 'hui*, a levée at court.   10. 倒 *tao*, notwithstanding; all the same.

LESSON XXXV.

1. I've a friend who is a man of great nerve. He was lying one summer's night with the window propped open, and in the midst of his slumbers he became sensible that something was making a noise. He opened his eyes to see what it was, and there, in the bright moonlight, was an elfin thing hopping along, with a face the colour of yellow paper, blood running out of its eyes, its whole body white as snow, and its hair all in

PART VI. THE HUNDRED LESSONS. T'an Lun P'ien. XXXI–XXXVI.

confusion. 2. Such an apparition presenting itself to my friend as he was startled out of his sleep, made him shudder with horror. "Dear me!" said he, "it's a ghost; let us watch him quietly and see what line he takes." 3. Well, for a time the ghost went hopping about; but, before very long, he began to open the doors of a standing-press. Out of this he took a large quantity of clothes, clapped them under his arm, hopped out of the window, and away he went. 4. Come, thought my friend to himself, if this were a *bonâ-fide* ghost, he would not be taking clothes, I should think; and he was discussing this phenomenon with himself when the gallows-bird came in again. My friend jumped up at once and gave the creature a blow with a sword, on which it fell to the ground with a loud *ai-ya*. 5. The servants were called, and the lamp being lit, it turned out that the ghost, a good joke really, was a thief, who, intending to rob the house, had disguised himself as a ghost in order to frighten any one he might come across.

1. 響 *hsiang* 3, sound of any kind, it may be used alone, or, as here, in composition. 2. 睜 *chêng* 1, to open the eyes.
3. 渾身 *'hun shên*, the entire person, see *'hun*, LESSON XXXII, 3, of streams mingling in confusion, undistinguishable; *q. d.* all parts of the person without distinction.
4. 蓬 *p'êng* 2, a kind of flag; in disorder like the foliage of such plants; should, probably, be written with the same Radical as the following character; 鬆 *sung* 1, dishevelled hair; tumbled; confused.
5. 醒 *hsing* 3, to wake, *ching hsing*, to be startled out of one's sleep. 6. 立櫃 *li kuei*, a standing press.
7. 挾 *chia* 1, to put under the arm; read *hsia* 2, to put pressure on a superior.
8. 肐 *chih* 4, the upper part of the arm, not used alone, nor without the characters here immediately preceding and following.
9. 窩 *wo* 1, a nest or den of bird or beast; *ko-chih wo*, the arm-pit.
10. 暗 *an* 4, secret; *an-hsiang*, thought to himself.
11. 猛 *mêng* 3, fierce, courageous; *mêng-jan*, moving rapidly, *q. d.* without fear.
12. 腰刀 *yao-tao*, a sword, not a dagger. 13. 一照 *i chao*, the moment [the light] shone on him.
14. 故意 *ku i*, with intent, designedly.

LESSON XXXVI.

1. Well, gentlemen, as ghosts have been your subject of conversation, I'll tell you a curious thing now. Your stories are all out of story-books; mine is an adventure of my own. 2. Some years ago, I and some friends had been outside the city for a walk, and we were on our way home again when we came to a large cemetery that was by the road-side. It was in a very tumble-down condition; walls and buildings in a state of utter dilapidation; but, inside the enclosure, there was a fine thick growth of trees of every kind. 3. "So," said we, "this is a nice cool place; let us go in and rest awhile;" and we put out the fruit and other eatables we had brought with us, and sat ourselves down in front of the tomb, and began to eat and drink. While we were so engaged, all of a sudden the wine we had in our cups blazed up of itself, with a purring sound, like a thing on fire. 4. Every one was afraid at the sight, and we were all for getting out of the way, when an uncle of mine shook his hand and stopped us before we had time to move. "Stand up, and don't be frightened," said he; "there used to be a saying, 'Leave a thank-offering for the spirit on the boundary of his jurisdiction;' and the spirit of this spot has now alighted here." So saying, he filled a cup with wine and poured a libation, praying to the spirit at the same time; and the flame of the wine that had been in a blaze went out immediately. 5. This was a thing I saw myself. Curious, wasn't it?

1. 經過 *ching kuo*, to have passed through.
2. 墳院 *fên yuan*, grave enclosure; cemetery. Observe the Numerative *tso*.
3. 垣 *yuan* 2, properly, a large wall; *ch'iang-yuan*, a wall, not necessarily large.
4. 鍾 *chung* 1, a cup; the same as *chung*, EXERC. VII, 17; this is larger than that, and probably distinguished as being made [of metal.
5. 焴 *'hu* 1, the sound of fire as it catches anything.
6. 愣 *lêng* 4, stupefied; not recognised by the dictionaries. 7. 叔叔 *shu-shu*, my father's younger brother.
8. 擺手 *pai shou*, to wave the hand. 9. 站住 *chan-chu*, literally, stand and stop; don't go.
10. 鄂 *ao* 4, here, a sound to express that of the first syllable in *ao-po*, or *o-bo*, a Mongolian word for boundary line. The spirit disturbed was the god Terminus.
11. 謝 *hsieh* 4, to thank. 12. 儀 *i* 2, has many meanings; here, a ceremony; *hsieh-i*, a thank-offering.
13. 斟了 *chên liao*, see EXERC. XXIX, ex. 12; *chên*, here, to pour out.
14. 禱 *tao* 3, properly, to pray for happiness.
15. 祭 *chi* 4, properly, to make an offering of meat; 奠 *tien* 4, to pour a libation; *chi-tien*, to offer a meat and drink offering; or either without the other.

KEY TO THE TZŬ ERH CHI. Colloquial Series.

LESSON XXXVII.

1. *Junior.* What sort of house is that opposite yours?
2. *Senior.* Why do you inquire?
3. *Junior.* A friend of mine wants to buy it.
4. *Senior.* The house is uninhabitable; it's haunted. An elder brother of mine did live there once on a time, and a fine spacious house it is; seven rooms in front, and five rows of buildings from front to rear, all distributed as they ought to be in a dwelling-house, and in good order. But after his death, when the place came into my nephew's hands, according to his account, the side buildings got out of repair, and though he had them rebuilt, all of a sudden ghosts and hobgoblins commenced their antics there. They were not so bad at first, but, as time went on, sounds came to be heard in broad daylight; these were followed by apparitions; and the women in the family were so scared by their constant encounters with these horrors, that some of them actually died of fright. The wise women called in only wasted their arts on the spirits: the other exorcists were of no use either, and so there was nothing for it but to let the house go for anything it would fetch.
5. *Junior.* Well, you know, Sir, this is all because the owner was not in luck's way. When a man has luck with him, these evil spirits, if there be any by, keep out of sight, and have no power to hurt. On the other hand, he is a very timorous subject, that friend of mine. I shall tell him the truth as I have heard it, and then I shall have done my duty. It will be for him to buy the house or not, as he sees fit.

1. 所 *so*, originally, a place; here, a collective Numerative of *fang-tzŭ*; all the buildings in the house being included in the [question.
2. 地勢 *ti shih*, the circumstances of the ground, its dimension, condition, &c.
3. 門面 *mên mien*, not the face of the gate, but the gate-face, the face in which the gate stands.
4. 廂 *hsiang*¹, the lesser buildings that commonly flank the central building at right angles to it, not used colloquially without *fang*.
5. 欻 *ts'ao*², colloquially, in disrepair; *ts'ao-lan*, all in ruins.
6. 祟 *sui*⁴, properly, evil done spontaneously by spirits; *tso-ch'i sui lai*, [the spirits] began their pranks.
7. 動不動 *tung-pu-tung*, on every occasion, used only in speaking of unpleasant occurrences.
8. 撞磕 *chuang k'o*, to run up against.
9. 跳神 *t'iao-shên*, the act of female exorcists; they stand on a table and affect by *t'iao*, posture-making, moving the limbs, to attract the spirits to themselves.
10. 送祟 *sung sui*, to see the *sui*, the evil influence, to the door; also the act of exorcists, male or female.

LESSON XXXVIII.

1. *Junior.* That string of beads of yours, Sir, that I said I would take away, I have never taken.
2. *Senior.* Why haven't you?
3. *Junior.* I have been here several times, but you were not at home, and I couldn't think of taking your things without saying a word to you; and that was impossible, as you were not to be found. So I came to-day for the express purpose of seeing you and telling you what I was going to do, after which I could take the beads with a clear conscience. I'll buy anything you fancy in return for your liberality, and if it's something that is not to be got in the shops, I shall do my best to hit upon a means of procuring it for you somewhere or other. What do you say?
4. *Senior.* If you had just carried off the beads whether I was at home or not, it would have been better, I can tell you.
5. *Junior.* How do you mean?
6. *Senior.* They're lost.
7. *Junior.* Oh, what a pity! There are *p'u-t'i* beads enough in the world, but it's seldom one sees any like those. From being carried about daily, they had become saturated with the sweat of the hand, and it had made them quite bright and smooth. You ought to have put them away in the press when you hadn't them in your hand.
8. *Senior.* Ah! They were doomed to be lost. I was going into the garden one day last month, and they were hanging against the wainscoting of the stove-bed, and I forgot to put them by. When I came in I went to look for them, and where were they? Not a sign of them to be seen. I don't know who stole them.

PART VI. THE HUNDRED LESSONS. T'aŭ Lun P'ien. XXXVII-XL.

1. 盤 *p'an*, not as above; snakes *p'an*, coil themselves; *p'an* is here a coil or set of beads.
2. 誦 *su*⁴, properly, *sung*⁴; pronounced *su*, it means to recite as the Buddhists do their books; *su-chu*, properly, the Buddhist chaplet. The character given in the Chinese text of this note is the correct one.
3. 遭 遭 *tsao tsao*, every time; *lit.* every rencontre.
4. 好 *'hao*; having told you, I could then without wrong take them away. 5. 嗐 *'hai*, an exclamation.
6. 菩 *p'u*², merely gives the sound of the first syllable of *p'u-t'i*, a Thibetan word.
7. 卻 *ch'ueh* or *ch'io*; observe its relation to *sui*, although, and its place after the subject of the verb it immediately precedes.
8. 汗 *'han*⁴, sweat of man or beast.
9. 漚 *ou*⁴, to saturate; 透 *t'ou*, to penetrate thoroughly. 10. 光 滑 *kuang 'hua*, bright; glossy.
11. 桶 *ch'uch*, properly, *ch'a*¹, the planking at the end of the stove bed, when but one end of this rests against a wall; not used except as in the combination *p'ai-ch'a*.
12. 踪 *tsung*¹, man's foot-print, *tsung-ying*, foot-print and shadow. 13. 叫 *chiao*; by whom they were stolen.

LESSON XXXIX.

1. *Junior.* Perhaps you've heard, Sir, have you, of the new arrival in the suburb? An astrologer that they say is as sharp as if he had come back from the other world. He makes out one's past history as truly and tells it as correctly as if some one had told it him. People of our acquaintance are going to him in such numbers, the whole day long, that his booth is quite crowded. If he is so first-rate, why shouldn't you and I go too, and make him tell us our fortunes?

2. *Senior.* I heard of him some time ago. Friends of mine have been going to him for some days past, and I went there myself the day before yesterday, and had my nativity calculated by him. He made out my father and mother's age, the number of my brothers, my wife's family name, and the date of my admission into the service, without a mistake in the minutest particular; but, thought I to myself, although he was quite right about all that *has* happened, it's not quite so certain that things that *have not* will turn out as he predicts.

3 *Junior.* Well, that may be all true enough; still, what is there that you and I wouldn't spend the few hundred cash he asks upon? So, come along. It is better for us to be out walking than sitting at home here with our hands before us. It's only to cheer one up a bit, and there is nothing improper in going there either.

1. 新 近 *hsin-chin*, near in time, lately. 2. 轉 世 *chuan shih*, returned to the world.
3. 極 *chi*², properly, the ridge of a roof, extremest, most.
4. 堆 對 *chun tui*, see note on EXERC. XXII, ex. 14, exactly corresponding.
5. 八 字 *pa tzŭ*, the eight characters, taken from the Chinese cyclic system of sixty combinations of the ten stem, and twelve branch, characters, the first combination marks the year, the second the month, the third the day, the fourth the hour, in which the person was born, and on the eight his fortune is calculated.
6. 屬 *shu*, to belong to, here, to belong to a certain year.
7. 毫 *'hao*, a small hair, *ssŭ 'hao*, anything small as a thread of silk, or a single hair; the minutest degree.
8. 只 當 *chih tang*; observe *tang*⁴, not *tang*¹; it only represents, amounts to.
9 解 悶 *chieh mên*, to relax, dissipate, sadness.
10. 不 可 *pu k'o*, impropriety. Observe the force of *yu*, at the beginning of the clause, followed as it is by the negative, *q. d.* when all is said, *yu*, on the other part, what impropriety is there.

LESSON XL.

1. I'll give you something to laugh at. I was sitting here all alone just now, when I saw that a bird had lit on the window-frame. The sun cast his shadow against the window as he hopped about. 2. So I stole over very softly to the place where he was, and made a grab at him through the window paper, tearing a large hole in it; but I made a good shot, and got him safe in my hand, when I saw directly that he was a sparrow. 3. I was in the act of passing him from one hand to the other, when P-r-r-rh! away he flew. I made haste and shut the door, but, just as I had got hold of him a second time he freed himself again, and I was chasing him all round the room, when the boys, hearing that a bird had been caught, came in a body, and we all chased and chevied, until one little fellow popped his cap over him and secured him. 4. Well, then I interceded for the bird. "Why," I said, "some people even buy birds to give them liberty. What can you do with this one? Let him go, can't you?" But he would not hear of it, and he held out with such stubbornness that I was obliged to let him have the bird. This made him quite happy, and away he went, hopping and skipping, as pleased as could be.

KEY TO THE TZŬ ERH CHI. Colloquial Series.

1. 捻 *nieh*¹, also read *nien*⁴, to nip in the fingers; *nieh-shou-nieh-chiao-'rh-ti*, used of moving mincingly, softly, so that one may not be heard.
2. 抓住 *chua chu*, the first verb indicating the motion of the hand, the dash made at the object; the second, its success; *ch'ia 'hao*, by good fortune, the issue being just what I desired, I made the dash and got hold of the bird.
3. 家雀 *chia ch'iao*, a house-sparrow.
4. 倒 *tao*³, to fall down as a man, a wall, &c.; here, to pass from one hand to another; used in this sense of transferring a shop, business in trade; not to be confounded with *tao*⁴, to pour, EXERC. VIII, 5.
5. 嗜嚨 *p'u*¹ *-lu*¹, of no meaning but to express the sound of a bird's wings in motion, or the like.
6. 扣住 *k'ou-chu*, the first word signifying to cover over either with the hand, a cap, a cup, or the like. See *k'ou*, in a different sense, SECTION IV, 45.
7. 放生 *fang shêng*, to let go alive; in conformity with the doctrine of Buddhism, which teaches to spare life.
8. 墜 *chui*⁴, to be kept hanging by a weight.
9. 轂 *ku*¹, an axle tree, 轆 *lu*, see SECTION XIII, 38; *ku-lu*, properly, the wheel of a cart; but *chui-ku-lu* is a circular stone weight hung to awnings or curtains to keep them from shifting in the wind.
10. 跳 *t'iao*, to jump; 鑽 *tsuan*, properly, to bore; here, indicating the action of the head as the child skips away.

LESSON XLI.

1. *Junior.* Was there ever such a brat, Sir, as that boy there! Other people have given him all sorts of advice, only for his good, and to keep him from learning what is bad for him. For all men are alike in that regard; they find it just as hard to acquire what is right and proper, as it is easy to pick up what is vicious. 2. As for this boy, I have blown him up till my mouth is quite sore with talking, but he pays no attention to what I say. On the reverse, it makes him sullen, and he pouts and looks black. I could stand it no longer, and just now I lost my temper, and gave him a very severe thrashing. 3. He coloured up, and says he, "Why can't they do something else besides picking holes in my coat?" and he went off with his eyes full of tears. Blockhead that he is; he's born to do no good. 4. The proverb says, "Good medicine is bitter to the taste, and honest advice grates on the ear." If he didn't belong to me, I should be glad enough, I'm sure, to speak in a way that would be pleasanter to him to listen to. Why should I be doing what is certain to disgust him, if it wasn't for this reason?

1. 壞孩子 *'huai 'hai tzŭ*, not *spoiled* in our sense of the term, but so bad that he will do no good.
2. 勸 *ch'uan*⁴, to advise, to admonish.
3. 無精打彩 *wu ching ta ts'ai*; see *ts'ai-t'ou* LESSON XIII, 2; *q. d.* he has no spirit to play, though gambling be a pleasant thing, yet has he no soul for it. This is one explanation; another is, that *ta ts'ai* means any enjoyment. It is not used in either way except with *wu ching*, the latter character being the *ching* in *ching-shên*, animal spirits.
4. 噘 *chueh*¹, to protrude the lips; to pout.　　5. 撂臉 *liao lien*, literally, to let down the face.
6. 淚 *lei*⁴, to weep.　　7. 汪 *wang*¹, properly, wide and deep; of a wide expanse of water.
8. 忠 *chung*¹, faithful, loyal, as a minister to his sovereign, as a friend to a friend.
9. 逆 *ni*⁴, the opposite of *shun*, obedient, compliant, rebellious, opposed to.
10. 哄著 *'hung-cho; lit.* would that humbugging him I might make him glad.

LESSON XLII.

1. Just see what a miserable creature that is; he is not a man at all; he is a beast; the very counterpart of his father; the more one sees of him, the more he disgusts one. 2. Wherever he goes, he gets into the same scrape; his eyes are so closed up, that he can't see, and he runs against everything; and when he talks he stammers and stutters, like a real lout as he is. 3. As for doing anything that he ought to do, he's of no use whatever. He's ready enough for any tom-foolery. If you allow him no leisure, and keep him constantly attending upon you, he does a little better; but, otherwise, he is all play without ceasing; and such a fidget as he is, up with one thing and down with another, like a monkey; trouble, trouble, never quiet for an instant. 4. When I am angry, I feel as if nothing short of his life would satisfy me; then I cool down, and I say to myself, No; even if he didn't belong to the family, I could never seriously set about killing him; and then he does belong to the family, and, whatever his shortcomings, he is of more use in the house than no one at all. A poker may not be the length it ought to be, but it's better than one's hand to stir the fire with. And when I'm in this vein, I am so far from wishing him any harm, that if any money comes in, or if I've anything nice to eat or drink, I give him a little for love's sake.

PART VI. THE HUNDRED LESSONS. T'an Lun P'ien. XL–XLIV.

1. 賤貨 *chien 'huo*, commodity of small value; *ching*, [though he seems to be a man,] yet he is not at all a man.
2. 活脫 *'huo-t'o*, while living to put off the skin; he has grown up so that he resembles his father as if his father, without dying, had thrown off his skin.
3. 擠顧 *chi-ku*, to gaze with the eyelids closed together.
4. 磕磕巴巴 *k'o-k'o pa-pa*, stammering.   5. 漚人 *ou jên*, a booby that people dislike and ridicule.
6. 侍 *shih*³, amongst other meanings, to attend upon; *fu-shih* is used of the personal attendance of the wife on the husband, or of the other women of the harem upon husband and wife; or of the children upon both parents; in helping them to dress and undress, &c.
7. 鬧事精 *nao-shih ching*; the *ching* is here elliptically used for 精靈 *ching-ling*, or 妖精 *yao-ching*, impish, devilish; *q. d.* clever as an imp, in *nao shih*, making trouble; how, is explained in the words that follow.
8. 唧叮咕咚 *chi*¹ *ting*¹ *ku*¹ *tung*¹; the combination does not admit of analysis; no character in it is intended to do more than express a sound; the whole means a jumble of sounds.
9. 當真 *tang chên*; observe *tang*⁴, in the sense of to stand for, to represent.
10. 打殺 *ta sha* differs somewhat from *sha*, alone, which would imply that death was inflicted by a lethal weapon.
11. 忍 *jên*³, the pain felt by the heart; to bear to do, bear to see; *huai*, devilishly, that is, exceedingly not can I bear.
12. 家生子 *chia shêng tzŭ*, one born in the house, not bought, though he may be the son of a slave.
13. 火棍 *'huo kuên*, a poker, whether of wood or metal, though short, is *ch'iang*, better, than *shou pa*, stirring with the hand. See *po*, LESSON X, 9.
14. 偏疼 *p'ien t'êng*, specially tender, to shew special kindness to.

LESSON XLIII.

1. Yesterday, while I was out, those rascally servants of mine began to wrangle and make a row as if the house belonged to them, and by the time I came home there was a fine uproar. Pack of monkeys! I gave a cough and walked in, and they all became dumb together, and then they sneaked out one by one, looking at each other as guilty and frightened as possible.   2. This morning, just as I was out of bed, in came the villains and dropped down on their knees as stiff as posts, and began, "Oh! we deserve to die," and so on; and they kept on praying and kotowing, and begging pardon so dolefully, that my wrath began to cool a little, and I said to them, "Do you feel as if you *wanted* the stick, that you can't be quiet? If you oblige me to give you a thrashing, what good will it do you, pray? Now, if this happens again, look out for your skins; for I'll thrash you very soundly, I promise you. You won't mind unless I do."   3. And when I had done, they took themselves off, all *dja*-ing as they went.

1. 賊眉鼠眼 *tsei mei shu yen*, eyebrows of wrongdoers, eyes of mice; the *ti* adverbialising the phrase.
2. 使眼色兒 *shih yen-shai 'rh*, using colour of the eyes, with an expression of the eyes, to wit, such as is described in the foregoing clause; *q. d.* thief and mice-like glancing at each other, took themselves off one by one.
3. 橛 *chueh*², a short wooden post; straight-post-like.
4. 跪 *kuei*⁴, to kneel down.   5. 哀 *ai*¹, painful feeling; *ai ch'iu*, to implore.
6. 好好兒的 *'hao-'hao-'rh-ti*, of things, satisfactorily, arranged as they ought to be; of persons, quiet, orderly; your disorderliness [is it because] your flesh *yang*, itches, *s.c.* for the stick.
7. 再要 *tsai yao*, if on another occasion you are so minded, are set on like doings.

LESSON XLIV.

1. *Senior.* Just look at him, Sir; there he is, drunk again to-day; dead drunk, so that he can't keep his legs. I asked him if he had given the orders I desired, and he stared straight at me, heeling and lurching to and fro, without answering a word. Why couldn't he answer? He is neither deaf nor dumb. I'll give the scoundrel a very severe correction this minute; if I don't, I vow I wish something may happen to me.
2. *Junior.* Come, come, Sir, I dare say he forgot to go; and, then, as he knew he was to blame, he became frightened, and this was the reason why he did not answer you. As I happen to be by to-day, forgive him this once in consideration of that circumstance; and warn him from this time forth to make up his mind to beware of drink. You know what the proverb says, "The stocking is a sure find under the boot, and the

KEY TO THE TZŬ ERH CHI. Colloquial Series.

slave has as little chance of giving his master the slip." You can always get at him. If he reforms, so much the better. If he does not, and if he gets drunk in this way any more, thrash him as much as you please; and if I chance to be a witness, I shall not say a word for him.

3. *Senior.* Ah! you don't know, Sir, what a hopeless thing he is, and always has been; and as for drink, he'll give his life for it; it's dearer to him than his father's blood. I may let him off to-day, but I'll answer for it he won't reform. He'll not abstain for more than a couple of days, at the longest, and then he'll be drinking again as hard as ever.

1. 成泥 *ch'êng ni*, has become as mud, lies unable to rise; used only of persons lying senseless from drink, or who have been beaten till they were insensible.
2. 前仰 *ch'ien yang*, the body coming forward and the head *yang*, looking up; 後合 *'hou 'ho*, the body going backward and the head, *'ho*, meeting, doubling forward.
3. 叭 *pa*¹, not used alone; *ya-pa*, a dumb person.
4. 痛快 *t'ung k'uai*, not quite as in SECTION XI, 4, but as indicating a combination of promptitude and completeness; it may be applied to the despatch of any business.
5. 責罰 *tsê-fa*, to punish, but specially of corporal punishment.
6. 起誓 *ch'i-shih*, to make oath; observe the idiom; *q. d.* if I don't beat him [may I incur the penalty of breaking] the oath I swear to beat him.
7. 既然 *chi-jan*, since it is so that I am present.
8. 面上 *mien shang*, having regard for my face, not to put me to shame.   9. 戒 *chieh*⁴, to beware of.
10. 成器 *ch'êng ch'i*, to make an utensil, to be of some use or other.

LESSON XLV.

1. *Junior.* Why, what's the matter, Sir? Your face is as pale as if you had whitened it; and, since I saw you a short time ago, you have quite fallen away.

2. *Senior.* Yes, but you don't know what has happened since then. Sir, these last few days they have been cleaning the drains, and the stench was very bad; and besides this the weather has been so variable, cool one moment, and hot the next, that a man couldn't say how he was to take care of himself. As for me, the day before yesterday, it had been very cool up to breakfast time, but soon after it became so hot that no one could stand it. A violent perspiration broke out all over me, and I took off my long dress to cool myself, and drank a cup of cold tea, on which I was seized with a violent pain in the head, my nose began to run, a hoarseness came on in my throat, and I felt as sick and dizzy as if I was in the clouds.

3. *Junior.* You're not the only person in the same condition. I am out of sorts myself, and not moving about more than I can help. However, yesterday, I had the luck to throw up all there was in my stomach. If I had not, I should not have been able to hold myself up to-day even as well as I am doing.

4. *Senior.* I'll give you a rule to follow; a simple one. When you are hungry, eat sparingly. If you will do this, a little cold won't do you any harm.

1. 刷 *shua*⁴, not different in meaning from *shua*¹, to brush.
2. 冷孤丁 *lêng-ku-ting*, as inexplicable as *lêng-pu-fang*, SECTION XI, 35; something the same in meaning, except that the latter would rather be used where there had been cause of alarm.
3. 瘦 *shou*⁴, thin.   4. 搯 *t'ao*¹, to cleanse out a well, or a ditch; *t'ao kou*, to clean the drains.
5. 炮 *p'ao*⁴, properly, the action of fire upon meat; 燥 *tsao*⁴, dried by fire-heat; *p'ao-tsao-ti*, as if I had been roasted, my whole person *t'ou-'han*, throughout perspired.
6. 袍 *p'ao*², properly, the long dress open in front below, worn by officials under the *kua-tzŭ*; in hot weather the latter is dispensed with. The common people erroneously apply *p'ao-tzŭ* to other long robes.
7. 暈 *yun*⁴, dizzy.   8. 忽 *'hu*¹, properly, to forget; hence not to attend to; *'hu-'hu*, wool-gathering.
9. 吐 *t'u*⁴, to spit out; *ch'uan t'u*, to throw up everything.
10. 扎掙 *cha-chêng*, to hold one's-self up by an effort; *q. d. cha*, planted in the ground, *chêng*, struggling. Observe the construction; [having done what I did I am able to-day to hold myself up by an effort;] had it not been thus, *yeh chiu*, then, even though I made the effort, I could not succeed.
11. 妨 *fang*¹, to injure, interfere with; though you *chao-lang*, encounter cold, even so it will not hurt you.

PART VI. THE HUNDRED LESSONS. T'an Lun P'ien. XLIV–XLVII.

LESSON XLVI.

1. *Senior.* Dear, dear! what does this mean, Sir? It was only the other day that we met, and here you are with your beard grown grey, and your whole appearance that of an old man? Now, don't be angry with me for speaking out; but I do hear that you play, and that you have a number of gambling debts unpaid. This is no joke, if it's true; you had best give up the habit.
2. *Junior.* This is all the merest gossip; not a shadow of truth in it. Enquire carefully if you don't believe me, and then you'll see.
3. *Senior.* No, no; why should I enquire of any one else? No man is ignorant of his own doings. I could not but think there must be some truth in the charge when I found all our friends making it. Now, gambling is an evil without bounds; a bottomless pit to any victim that falls into it. If he does not get foul of the law, he plays away till he hasn't a cash left, and he is cleaned out of house and land before he gives over. I won't say that a hundred is a very large number, but I have seen or heard of more than a hundred cases of the kind. You and I are very intimate; and what would our friendship be worth if I knew of such a thing as this, and did not try to dissuade you from it? One word for all, don't gamble. That's all I have to say. You needn't insist on my "enquiring."

1. 陷進 *hsien-chin*, to fall into; if it be that you fall into [gambling], *na*³, in what [place] is there a bottom? *chiu-shih*, we may proceed hence to say that, &c.
2. 精光 *ching-kuang*, clean and bright. Observe the construction; *ti* representing the noun, of which *ching-kuang* is the attributive; *q. d.* in every case is it that the family estate is *nung*, worked-to, a clean bright [condition]; then,= before that, [the player] will let go his hold.
3. 賭 *tu*³, to play, gamble.

LESSON XLVII.

1. You drink very hard, I observe; you're never away from the wine; you're too fond of it, really. And when you drink, you will get so drunk; you never think you have had enough till you can't stand on your legs. This is not as it ought to be. Wouldn't it be better if you were to drink a little less than you do? 2. If one is dining out, or at a wedding, a little excess doesn't matter much; but what good can come of it, if, with special reason or without special reason, you have always the cup to your lips? You simply excite the disgust of your wife and children, and you get blown up by your elders, when they see you in this state. The least penalty you will pay will be the ruin of some business or other of importance; and you may do far worse; you may bring very serious calamity upon yourself. On the other hand, as for any man making wine the means of acquiring any particular accomplishment or developing any faculty, so as to be able to do what is right and proper in such wise as to make people respect one, *that*, I should say, is a thing that very rarely comes to pass. 3. In a word, wine is a poison as injurious to the mind as it is harmful to the body, and a man should on no account give way to indulgence in it. Look in the glass if you don't believe me, and you'll see how thoroughly the wine has stained your nose and face. What makes it worse in you, too, is that you are a man of a certain class, and to drink night and day as you do is an act of suicide, so far as your career is concerned.

1. 每逢 *mei fêng*, every time you meet with; every time it happens.
2. 算了 *suan liao*; the latter is, here, the verb to finish; you *then*, when you can't stand, consider you have finished; not [before.
3. 赴 *fu*⁴, to repair to; *hsi*, see SECTION XVI, 47; *fu hsi*, to go to a great dinner.
4. 喜事 *hsi shih*, a joyful affair, a wedding.
5. 不是 *pu-shih*, a fault; here, the blame for it; *tê pu-shih*, to be found fault with.
6. 輕著 *ch'ing-cho*; observe the antithesis of *ch'ing* and *chung*, and our corresponding idiom; also that *cho* is here equal to *ti*, or to the classical relative *chê* so often used to isolate the thesis.
7. 霑 *chieh*⁴, to be beholden to.   8. 敬 *ching*⁴, reverence, reverential; *ching-chung*, to respect.
9. 毒 *tu*², poison; *tu-yao*, a poisonous drug.   10. 鏡 *chung*⁴, a mirror.
11. 糟 *tsao*¹, properly, the dregs left after distilling spirit; hence, a soft broken condition such as that of grain so used; hence, thoroughly saturated as grain must be so to break; *tsao t'ou*, thoroughly saturated, the spirit within shewing itself in the face.

KEY TO THE TZŬ ERH CHI. **Colloquial Series.**

LESSON XLVIII.

1. I have had a great deal to do the last few days, and, after sitting up for two nights in succession, my whole frame was so exhausted that I had no spring left in me. 2. So, last night, I thought I would be in bed early, but it was'nt to be. There was a rendezvous of the family at my house, and how was I to go to bed and leave them to take care of themselves? Well, though it was a great effort, I did contrive to stay up and keep them company; but, oh! it was sore work for the eyes. My eyelids drooped, and I was quite stupid. However, there was no help for it till my guests departed. The moment they did, I clapped my head on a pillow, and lay down, all dressed as I was, and slept till about two o'clock, when I woke rather chilly. What had made me so I can't say. My stomach was puffed out and uncomfortable; I was burning from head to foot as if I had been over a fire; and, to add to all this, I had a pain in the ears which was so severe that it inflamed the whole jowl. I had no appetite left, and I was equally uncomfortable lying down or sitting up. 3. I thought the best thing I could do would be to abstain from eating altogether, and to take a purgative. This I did, and when it had carried away every thing inside me, good, bad, and indifferent, my stomach began to feel a little more at ease than it had been.

1. 熬夜 *ao-yeh*, to burn the night; to sit up all night working by lamp-light.
2. 普裏普兒 *p'u li p'u 'rh*, all, the whole tribe, said of persons or things.
3. 會齊 *'hui ch'i*, all met together; observe here, *'hui ch'i-êrh*, as if it were *'hui ko ch'i-êrh*, meeting made a full number.
4. 枕 *chên*³, a pillow for the head.   5. 腹 *fu*², the bowels.
6. 膨 *p'êng*², puffed out; used only of the stomach; *p'êng-mên*, puffed out and uncomfortable.
7. 發燒 *fa shao*, burning hot; *fa jo*, to be feverish.   8. 烤 *k'ao*³, to roast.
9. 搭上 *ta shang*, to add to; observe the construction; also add to this [there was that which] hurt the inside, *lit.* bottom, of the ear, the pain was such that also the whole cheek swelled.
10. 飲 *yin*³, to drink, not so used colloquially alone.   11. 臥 *wo*⁴, to recline, lie down; not used colloquially alone.
12. 停 *t'ing*², to stop, or cause to stop; I thought that the case was one for *t'ing-chu*, stopping eating.
13. 服 *fu*, not differing in sound or tone from the same character in SECT. X, 47, but, here, to swallow a dose; *i chi ta yao*, a dose of purging medicine.
14. 鬆快 *sung k'uai*, the opposite of *p'êng-mên*, the comfort derived from getting rid of the latter; *sung-k'uai*, may also be applied to the mind.

LESSON XLIX.

1. He had not much strength to begin with, and he never took proper care of himself. He was too fond of wine and women, and now his constitution is paying the penalty. 2. His present illness has been a long affair, but yesterday, when we went to see him, he managed to bring himself into the drawing-room to speak to us: "Really, gentlemen," he said, "you do me too much honour, putting yourselves to the trouble of coming to call on me so often this hot weather, and I am sure I can't thank you enough for the different things you are so good as to send me; there is always something coming from you. Of course I attribute the interest you take in me to our relationship. If you had no connection with me, I could not reasonably expect you to take such an interest in me. I don't say much, but I shan't forget your attention, and when I am well again I shall make you the fullest acknowledgments." 3. He went on in this strain, but it was evident at the same time what an effort it was to him to hold himself up. 4. We merely observed, "You are too sensible a man, Sir, to make it needful for us to say more to you than that you must take good care of yourself, and you will soon be well. We'll come and see you again when we have time." When we had said this we came home.

1. 損 *sun*³, to injure; his *ch'i-hsüeh*, breath and blood, his constitution, *k'uei-sun*, is deficient and injured, fails him.
2. 延 *yen*², properly, to go to a distance, or to go on for a long time; *yen chan*, as of a long cord wrapped round.
3. 勞動 *lao tung*, I with fatigue stir you, I give you the trouble of moving.
4. 不敢當 *pu kan tang*, I do not venture to bear, be the recipient of so much kindness; I am not worthy.
5. 感情 *kan ch'ing*; my *kan*, feeling in my heart, your *ch'ing*, kindly disposition, my gratitude for it, is *pu chin*, inexhaustible.
6. 相干 *hsiang kan*, to be concerned with; if you were *p'ang*, bystanding persons with no concern in me.
7. 惦 *tien*⁴, to think kindly of; *tien-chi*, to remember one with kindness. The character *tien* is not in the dictionaries.
8. 可露 *k'o lou*; the *k'o* has a certain disjunctive power, in answer to the *sui-jan* in the preceding clause; although such words were in his mouth, his person, to say the truth, *lou ch'u*, allowed to escape the appearance of one who could not hold himself up. Observe *lai liao* at the close, auxiliary of *lou ch'u*, the object intervening between the verb and its auxiliary.

PART VI. THE HUNDRED LESSONS. T'an Lun P'ien. XLVIII-LI.

LESSON L.

1. Last summer he did contrive to walk, but he has grown much worse in the last few days; so much so, indeed, that he has taken to his bed altogether. His people have no idea what to do for him; they are all confusion and racket; and the old folks are in such affliction that they have quite fallen away. 2. I went to see him the other day, and found him lying on the stove-bed, gasping for breath, and so thin that he was no longer the same man. I went up to him very gently and I said, "Are you any better than you were?" 3. He opened his eyes wide, and when he saw it was I, he grasped my hand in his own very tight, and he said, "Ah! Sir, no doubt I deserve my fate; I don't suppose that, after sinking so low, I can possibly recover. Of course I know it's my lot. Since I first fell ill I've been treated by every physician there is here, and I have taken every description of medicine, and again and again, just as I was beginning to improve, I have had a relapse. It's my destiny. I've done myself no injustice. But what moves me is the thought of my father and mother, who are now well on in years, and of brothers who are still children; and then all my nearest relations are up here too, and I must tear myself from every one belonging to me." 4. Before he had done speaking, his eyes were streaming with tears. It was a most distressing scene. Had one been iron and stone, one must have been quite upset at hearing him talk in this way.

1. 闔 ‘ho², properly, a folding door; to close it; hence, all within it; hence, of persons, all; ‘ho chia-tzŭ, the whole family.
2. 烘 ‘hung¹, properly, the flickering or flaring of flames; ‘hung-‘hung-tı, of restless, anxious, movement.
3. 倒 tao¹, not tao³, LESSON XL, 4, nor tao⁴, EXERC. VIII, 5; tao¹, especially of the breath when it is short; to gasp.
4. 大料 ta liao, most likely, ta, on the whole, liao, I imagine. See EXERC. XXVIII, 19.
5. 自從 tzŭ-ts‘ung, both words meaning from in time; ever since. 6. 大 tai⁴, only so read in tai fu, physician.
7. 重落 ch‘ung-lo, of sickness only; to go down a second time, to relapse.
8. 委曲 wei-ch‘u, injustice, oppression; wei means truly; ch‘ü, as before, to bend; really no injustice; q. d. had I not taken all the pains I have to get well, I should have been unjust to myself.
9. 慘 ts‘an³, to be moved in the heart; tê ‘huang, as in EXERC. XXXVII, ex. 5.

LESSON LI.

1. If a man is not to be killed, it must be because it is his destiny to be saved. That night I was with our friend, he was very bad. He lost all consciousness, and didn't come to his senses again for a long time; and though I tried to quiet his parents, by begging them not to be alarmed, and assuring them that there was no danger, in my own mind, I must confess, I thought the case desperate. 2. However, the sick man and his parents had better luck than one gave them credit for. The day after I was there, a fresh physician was called in, and, from the time he began to treat him, the patient improved visibly from day to day. 3. I paid him a visit the day before yesterday, and though he is not quite himself yet, he has got back his colour, and he has picked up a little flesh. He was leaning against his pillow, eating. "Well," I said to him, "are you all right again? I congratulate you most sincerely on your escape. Your attack was a pretty severe one. You were at death's door, I can tell you." 4. He chuckled as I spoke, and, said he, "It's no merit of mine; it's heaven's love for you and the rest of my friends. As to danger, there is none now; it's a bonâ-fide recovery, I take it."

1. 救星 chiu hsing, a redeeming star, a spirit that will save one.
2. 沉 ch‘ên², to sink in water; hence, in some phrases, weighty; ch‘ên-chung, heavy, of things; grave, of affairs.
3. 甦 su¹, to revive, from death or from a swoon; su-hsing, reviving, to wake up, to come to life again.
4. 慰 wei⁴, sense of comfort in the mind; to cause it; to console; an-wei, to comfort, console.
5. 還元 ‘huan yuan, to restore the original ch‘i, breath, animation.
6. 氣色 ch‘i sê, the colour due to his reanimation. Observe the k‘o for k‘o wei, may be said to.
7. 脫皮 t‘o p‘i, you put off one layer of skin, sc. before you could get through your difficulty; you had a very narrow escape.
8. 嘻 hsi¹, to smile; in conversation, always doubled as here.
9. 災 tsai¹, any misfortune inflicted by heaven.
10. 大好 ta ‘hao, as opposed to ‘hao i tien, a slight improvement. Observe again the k‘o modifying the affirmation.

KEY TO THE TZŬ ERH CHI. **Colloquial Series.**

LESSON LII.

1. It's all very well your recommending me to take physic; but I have an idea of my own on the subject. If it was really necessary that I should take physic, I am not too stingy to buy some; one isn't such a fool as to love money better than life. But the reason why I object to medicine is, that the year before last I took the wrong dose, and very nearly killed myself. It makes my heart beat to think of it even now. 2. And then, as to the doctors of the present day, there may be some good ones among them, but not more than one per cent. All the rest care for is to get in the money as hard as they can. What does it signify to them whether a patient lives or dies? 3. Call one in, if you don't believe me, and try him. He may understand medicine or he may not; but if he doesn't, he won't flinch from undertaking the case. He comes bustling into the house, and, as he calls it, feels your pulse; that is to say, he puts his finger somewhere or other for a moment; then he dashes off a prescription, pockets his fee, and away he goes. If the case turns out well, then, it's all the skill of the doctor; if it does not, he says it was your destiny; it doesn't concern him the least in the world. 4. In the present instance I know very well what I'm about. Instead of swallowing every variety of medicine, all to do me no good, I shall keep quiet and take care of myself. I shall get well enough.

1. 曾 *ts'êng*², properly, past in time; here, it in no way affects the sense of *'ho*.
2. 看 *k'an*¹, to take care of; to be distinguished from *k'an*⁴, to see, EXERC. V, 14.
3. 幾 *chi*¹, nearly; to be distinguished from *chi*³, EXERC. I, 9; *chi-chi-'hu*, nearly; the *'hu* being here merely an adverbial termination. Observe the idiom, ours would require *yu*, not *mê yu*, before *sang liao ming*.
4. 喪 *sang*⁴, properly, to die; here, to cause to die; *sang ming*, to do mortal injury to one's own life; not used of injury to another's.
5. 醫 *i*¹, to treat as a medical man; *i-shêng*, a physician. [another's.
6. 診 *chên*¹, properly, to regard, here, specially to feel the pulse, 脈 *mo*⁴, properly, any artery; here, specially [the pulse.
7. 藥方 *yao fang*, a prescription; *fang* being used in the sense of *fang-fa*, a way or means.
8. 馬錢 *ma ch'ien*, horse money, the doctor's fee. *Similar to char money*.
9. 效 *hsiao*⁴, to succeed, result favorably; *pu chien hsiao*, to be sensible of no favorable result. Observe the *yü ch'i*, as compared with [the first proposition], *pu ju*, there is nothing so good as [the second proposition].
10. 倒好 *tao 'hao*; this reinforces the *pu ju*; the second proposition, whatever the merits of the first, *tao*, notwithstanding, is better.

LESSON LIII.

1. *Senior.* What does it signify to you if other people find fault with him? And then when I try to mollify you, why get more and more angry? Oh! you are too hot, really. Wait till they're gone, and then speak if you like. Why must you argue the whole case this very minute? 2. *Junior.* Come, Sir, I cannot stand this sort of language from you. We are both in the same boat. You yourself have a certain interest in this question; you don't mean to maintain, do you, that it doesn't concern you at all? Well, when they discuss him, it brings you and me more or less under review, and it is your place to stop them; but, instead of this, you take the same side as they do. This I don't understand, and I certainly do feel somewhat dissatisfied. 3 *Senior.* No, no. I did nothing of the sort. All I meant was, that if a man has anything to say, he should be gentle and quiet about it; but to fly into such a passion as you did, to be actually bursting with rage, is surely not the way to settle the matter, is it? All these people who are sitting here, are come here solely on your account; and what must you do but boil up in such style that one might suppose you wanted to turn everybody out of doors. They were so scandalized that they were all thinking of going away, and the reason that they did not go was that they didn't want to cause you the mortification you would have felt if they had gone; but if you keep on raving and storming in this way you'll make it as unpleasant for them to stay as to go; and then the next thing will be that you'll be cut by all your acquaintance.

1. 躁 *tsao*⁴, properly written with this, the 157th Radical, of the heart, easily moved; *chi-tsao*, impetuous.
2. 辨 *pien*⁴, to distinguish in the mind; *fên-pien*, to argue a point, not necessarily with vehemence.
3. 罣 *kua*⁴, properly, to hook on to, *ai*, generally, to impede; *kua-ngai*, to affect, more or less prejudicially.
4. 稍上 *shao shang*; see SECTION I, 50, *q. d.* the matter with its extreme end touches us, it more or less regards us.
5. 繃 *pêng*¹, properly, to tie up; *pêng-pêng-ti*, tied tight, as, for instance, a drum-head.
6. 在坐 *tsai tso*, in this presence sitting, or, engaged in sitting. 7. 怒 *nu*⁴, rage, furious anger.
8. 冲 *ch'ung*¹, of water bursting embankments; your only concern is rage boiling over.
9. 攆 *nien*³, to drive out, observe the construction; [instead of being calm,] *tao*, on the contrary you are *hsiang-shih ti*, one seeming, to want to drive away [every one, no matter] whom.
10. 山嚷 *shan jang*, clamour as within a mountain; *kuai chiao*, devilishly crying out.

PART VI. THE HUNDRED LESSONS. T'an Lun P'ien. LII-LV.

LESSON LIV.

1. *Senior.* Well, now, from what I have seen of you in this affair, I should say that however well you may talk, you haven't the sense that, to look at you, one would suppose you had. If he chose to leave you alone, so much the better for you. Why should you go and provoke him? I advised you not to do it, but, instead of listening to me, you tore away as if you were possessed; and now here you are again having got the worst of it.

2. *Junior.* Oh! you don't half know him, the villain. Every one says he's a terrible fellow. He never shows mercy to any one that comes in his way. So long as he is not interfered with, it's all right; but if you cross him ever so little, he sets to work, might and main, to make his own side win, and he never stays his hand till he has carried the day.

3. *Senior.* Exactly so; but then, why not let a sleeping tiger lie? What is the fun of going out of your way to look for trouble? Remember what the proverb says, "Take a staff in your hand when you walk, and you won't tumble down; take counsel in action, and you'll make no false moves." Well, you had best lean on me now. Your own experience, unaided, won't carry you very far; I'm many years ahead of you on any given subject; and if the course you preferred had been the right course, so far from offering opposition, which would have been unjustifiable on my part, I should have felt it my duty to remind you that it *was* the right course; aye, and to urge you to follow it, had you been of another way of thinking.

1. 就是 *chiu shih;* observe that *chiu* is connected with *shih,* and not with the *chih* which precedes it.
2. 燎 *liao³,* originally, a torch; hence to illumine, *liao-liang,* of intellectual brightness.
3. 嗔 *ch'ên¹,* also written with other Radicals; to be angry with; to shew anger by speech or looks; *hsing ch'ên,* to provoke by anger or censure.
4. 你可 *ni k'o,* that you must provoke him, that you should think it right to provoke him. The Chinese, however, here assign *k'o* something of the power of the disjunctives, *ch'io, tao,* &c.
5. 指使 *chih-shih,* to give direction to and make to act, here, impelled by, *shên kuei,* demons.
6. 拗 *niu⁴,* also read *nung³.* to twist as a cord, a wire, &c.
7. 釘 *ting¹,* a nail, *p'êng liao ting-tzŭ,* to run foul of a nail; kick against the pricks.
8. 該死 *kai ssŭ,* construe thus, that one deserving death, tell me [if you can] what is he? There is no end to [his viciousness], he is a notoriously terrible man.
9. 留分 *liu fên,* literally, to leave a portion, *sc.* of consideration for; *fên* being *ch'ing fên,* the apportionment of the feelings, of which more would be shewn to one man, and less to another.
10. 疊著 *tieh-cho,* reiterating, redoubling, *ching-'rh,* muscle, muscular effort.
11. 佔住 *chan-chu,* to stand fast, here, to effect a position; that is if *chan* be written with the 117th Radical; if written without it, it means to usurp; but, so written, it is not found with *chu.*
12. 哄 *'hung¹,* to rouse to motion by a cry, not *'hung³,* to deceive.
13. 趣兒 *ch'u-'rh,* pleasure from seeing or hearing.
14. 咬 *chiao¹,* by itself, vulgarly, to struggle hard together like wrestlers, both with hand and foot; if you have *kuai kun-'rh,* a staff such as old men lean on, you will not *tieh chiao,* get a fall.
15. 失著 *shih chao;* to err in your move, a figure taken from chess or draughts; *chao* is to move a piece in the one, or to put one down in the other.
16. 光 *kuang,* often vulgarly used as here, for only, alone; is it only your *chien-shih,* experience.
17. 提撥 *t'i-po,* to bring to the recollection, to remind of.
18. 豈有 *ch'i yu,* how should there be *tao,* on the contrary, *ch'ing-li,* justice, in stopping you.

LESSON LV.

1. (*Elder brother to younger.*) Why can't you behave yourself in society? People won't set you down as having nothing in you because you sit still, as a decent, orderly person should. If you never say a word, no one will accuse you of not having the use of your tongue. And what pleasure can there be in going on as you do whenever you find yourself in society; irritating this person or the other person by talking as if you wanted to raise a laugh against him. You don't perceive how ill it looks, but it makes all the rest of the company uncomfortable, and one of these days you will fall in with some one who is not to be trifled with, and when you come to grief, you'll understand the risk you run by this sort of conduct.

2. (*Friend, addressing the younger brother.*) What your brother says is very true, Sir. Quizzing leads to warm words, and, in the long run, to no good. You should mind what he says, for no one not connected

KEY TO THE TZŬ ERH CHI. **Colloquial Series.**

with you would take the same interest in you; and, though you are so tall for your years, you are still young; you really must make a serious effort to break yourself of this habit.

  3. (*Continuing to the elder brother.*) You and I have been young, you know, and, in youth, one is all for play. I should recommend you, without loss of time, to get him some man of good repute as a tutor, and let him read with him. He'll add by degrees to his stock of information, and as soon as he knows more of the world, he'll mend of himself. Don't distress yourself with the notion that he'll go to the bad.

1. 穩重 *wên-chung*, of gravity, decorum, opposed to 輕佻 *ch'ing t'iao*¹, levity, want of manners.
2. 雕 *tiao*¹, to carve wood.   3. 塑 *su*⁴, to model the human figure out of clay.
4. 廢物 *fei wu*, a thing to throw aside; who would say you were a thing to throw aside, a worthless article, carved of wood, or fashioned of mud.
5. 關切 *kuan-ch'ieh*, affectionately interested in; *kuan*, to connect, *ch'ieh*, to cut deep into.

LESSON LVI.

  1. *Friend.* What odd behaviour to be sure! He stammers so when he is with anyone that it's impossible either to make out what he wants when he speaks to you, or to get an intelligible answer out of him; and he's in such a state of trepidation all the time, that he never knows when he ought to come forward, or when to go back. He always seems asleep; a perfect apology for a man, really. How can any one be such a booby as he is, at his time of life. You and his other friends ought to take him to task a little. It might do him good perhaps.

  2. *Host.* Ah! you haven't been long enough acquainted with him to know him thoroughly. He has many an absurd trick besides those you have been enumerating. You may be sitting with him talking, and just as you have got upon one subject, some other comes into his head, and he'll make a remark about that; or he'll be staring at you with his eyes fixed, and his mouth open, and, all of a sudden, he'll blurt out some piece of incoherent nonsense, and make people split their sides with laughing. He came to pay me a visit the day before yesterday, and when he got up to go away, instead of walking straight on, he turned himself half round and moved backwards. I called out to him, "Take care of the doorsill, Sir!" but before the words were out of my mouth he had caught his foot against it, and over he tumbled on his back. I ran to help him in such a hurry that I was very near getting a fall myself. As to taking him to task, I have spoken to him often enough before now, but I found he was the kind of good-for-nothing that advice won't improve; so I don't see the use of wasting my breath on him any longer.

1. 動作 *tung-tso*, behaviour, whether as regards speech or action.
2. 結巴 *chieh-pa*, to stammer; as if, says one Chinese, *hsia-pa*, the chin, were *chieh*, tied to something.
3. 畏 *wei*⁴, to fear; *wei-shou-wei-wei-tı*, fearing the head, fearing the tail; extremely nervous.
4. 指教 *chih chiao*, to point out a man's errors for his edification; to pull him up.
5. 扶住 *fu*²*-chu*, properly, to support by holding under the arm, *fu-chu* may be used with persons or things.

LESSON LVII.

  1. Did you observe, Sir, how ill natured he was all the time about my old clothes?   2. I don't want to boast of my superiority, but, really, for his years *he* knows nothing. As for this question of dress, neither he nor any of them understands it at all. New clothes are intended to be worn on extraordinary occasions. What does it matter if my home suit here, the clothes that I put on every day, be a little the worse for wear? If a man is an ignoramus he has something to be ashamed of; but what can it signify how he dresses? Take myself. I am not a dressy man I admit, but I am a great deal better off than people that are.   3. How so? Why, because I contrive to keep out of debt without applying to any man for help, and therefore I have nothing to feel shame about. As for our young friends there, I've something less than contempt for them. All they are good for is to dress themselves out in fine new clothes, and to swagger jauntily about; as if *that* made them respectable. They learn nothing that makes a man useful. And what is there wonderful in being swathed in silk and satin from head to foot, as they are?   4. Your thoroughly low fellows, who have not eyes to distinguish a lout from a gentleman, may mistake them for gentlemen, and make up to them accordingly; but I regard them simply as so many clothes-horses.

PART VI. THE HUNDRED LESSONS. T'an Lun P'ien. LV–LIX.

1. 膪 ts'ao², the same as ts'ao, LESSON XXXVII, 5; ts'ao-chiu, worn out.
2. 誇 k'ua¹, to praise another, to boast of one's self.
3. 即 chi², a word as common in the written language as chiu in the spoken, and used much as chiu is; chi-ju is more elegant than chiu pi-fang, well, for instance.
4. 求告 ch'iu kao, praying and appealing to.   5. 恥 ch'ih⁴, to be ashamed of.
6. 眼角 yen chiao, the corner of the eye; not even in the corner of my eye do I hold them.
7. 綢 ch'ou², silk, tuan, satin.
8. 裹 kuo³, to wrap about as a cord or bandage; swathed in silks and satins, tao ti, down to the bottom, sc. the feet.

LESSON LVIII.

1. *Senior.* You have no right to be taking him in in this way. When people ask you for an opinion in the most respectful manner, if you know the thing, good; if you don't know it, you should say you don't; but it makes you look as if you wanted to do them a mischief when you set them wrong by telling them what isn't the case. If the man were some scoundrel that one ought to have no love for, I shouldn't pull you up; but I can see that he's a very simple fellow. A single glance shows one that he is too slow to do any great harm. Supposing it was any one else that was humbugging him, it would be our place to remonstrate; and that you, instead of taking his part, should be using him so ill, is really more than I can put up with.

2. *Junior.* You don't understand him, Sir. He'd get round you soon enough, if you had anything to say to him. He's just that sort of being that *seems* to have no sense, while, in reality, he's extremely mischievous. You couldn't form an idea of his viciousness without some experience of it. He's full of shifts, and he'll circumvent any body. His way is to make sure of the line you are going to take. He'll lead you on till he has wormed your views out of you, and then he'll stand off and watch his opportunity. The moment he sees an opening, no matter how small, he'll follow it up and he'll checkmate you then and there. Now, with the risk I run in the case he was speaking of, do you think, Sir, it would have done for me to put him in full possession of my intentions? Admit that you have been censuring me unjustly.

1. 慢性子 man hsing-tzŭ, a slow-natured fellow; no great quickness either for good or for evil.
2. 過不去 kuo pu ch'u, not to be able to pass, said of places through which there is no way; here, of the feelings, unable to pass by, put up with, the objectionable matter in question.
3. 愚 yü¹, stupid, inwardly, 蠢 ch'un, loutish, outwardly, both are used separately; yü-ch'un may be used of either stupidity within, or loutishness without.
4. 險惡 hsien-ngo, treacherous and evil; vicious, malevolent.   5. 據 chu, properly, to lay hold of; p'ing-chü, proof.
6. 勾 kou¹, to hook; kou-yin, to lead on.   7. 破綻 p'o chan, a rent and opening seam; a hole in one's coat.
8. 兜屁股將 tou¹-p'i⁴-ku³-chiang, to checkmate; tou¹, to raise as a napkin having something in it that one does not wish spilt, also, to take in the rear, p'i-ku, the buttocks, chiang, in the sense of a general, q. d. a general who takes his adversary in the rear; the king in Chinese chess is called chiang.
9. 徹 ch'ê, properly written with the 85th Radical, to clear as water of its sediment; 底子 ch'ê ti-tzŭ, cleared to the bottom.

LESSON LIX.

1. What has befallen our friend So-and-so? There he has been for the last few days with a face full of woe, looking as if he cared for nothing and had nobody to care for him. What is it all about?
2. I can't tell you. He used to be always out of doors; never at home, except on a wet day. If it wasn't snowing or raining, he was sure to be off in some direction or other. They never could get him to sit in the house with his hands before him. For some time past, however, he hasn't shown at all, so yesterday I paid him a visit.
3. Yes? And didn't you find him changed?
4. He's grown very thin, and he seems worn; in fact he looks as if he got no rest, night or day. His appearance disquieted me a good deal, and I was just going to ask him a question, when, as luck would have it, a relation of his came in, and I said no more.
5. Dear me! From what you say, I should infer that it's the difficulty he finds himself in about that business, you know, that is disturbing him so. Still, a man that has lived through hard trials, as the proverb says, is not to be frightened by the lesser ills of life; and seeing that What's-his-name has always come very well out of any serious difficulty he may have had on his hands in times past, I don't see why he should attach so much importance to a trifle like this. It's not worth so much distress of mind, surely.

KEY TO THE TZŬ ERH CHI. Colloquial Series.

1. 愁容 *ch'ou-jung*, sorrowful appearance, *man mien*, all over his face; *jung*, the same character as *yung*, EXERC. XXXVI, 10, but with a different meaning.
2. 聊 *liao²*, properly, to lean against, depend upon.
3. 賴 *lai⁴*, much the same as *liao*, and more in use; *wu-liao-wu-lai-ti*, in a listless apathetic manner.
4. 然而 *jan-erh*, read *jan-'rh*, nevertheless; *jan*, thus, this being so, *erh*, yet, notwithstanding.
5. 值得 *chih-tê*, is it indeed worth that *yu-ch'ou*, sadness and dissatisfaction.

LESSON LX.

1. You can have seen nothing of life to be in such a state of nervousness as this. If you have anything to say to him, why keep it on your mind, when, by going to him and telling him plainly what you think, you could bring the thing to a conclusion? He is only a man like yourself; he's not a beast; and, of course, he must act like a reasonable being. Why should he not? - What you have to do is, first, to state how all this came about, and then to go over the whole ground step by step, arguing each point separately. Do you suppose that he will take your life in some way or other? that he'll murder you? or devour you? which? 2. Besides, when every one else interested is perfectly at his ease, is it manly in you to be in this state of chronic alarm, and taking all these precautions? 3. Follow my advice, and keep your mind easy like the rest of them. If he doesn't intend to let you have your way in the matter, if he's going to try a fall with you, he'll give you no law; and don't suppose that the state of terror you are in at this moment will bring you through without scathe; for it will do nothing of the kind. I have observed that, so far, no one has hinted that he does intend hostility, and my own idea is that the thing has long passed out of his recollection. If you think otherwise, set to work quietly, and try and get some information. But I believe he has forgotten it, and I'll engage that you have no trouble at all.

1. 動靜 *tung ching*, literally, to stir what is still; *mei tung ching*, not to move, to give no sign of concern; *lai pu lai ti*, whether anything is happening or not.
2. 味兒 *wei erh*, read *wê-'rh*, the odour, by which the true quality is known of *'han-tzŭ*, a Chinese; that is, a man.
3. 低 *ti¹*, low; *kao ti*, the height of anything, but, here, the keeping up or falling down; if, [like a wrestler,] he is about to see with you who is to be *kao* and who *ti*, to try a fall.
4. 而今 *erh-chin*; up to the present time. So says a Pekinese, but, to judge from another dialect, *erh* has simply the sense of *ju*, EXERC. XXXIV, 5, *q. d.* as at this time.
5. 探 *t'an⁴*, properly, to reach to one's self from a distance; to spy out; *t'an-tzŭ*, a spy; *t'an-t'ing*, to look out for information.
6. 管保 *kuan-pao*, to warrant; the first character adds nothing to the force of the second.

LESSON LXI.

1. *Senior.* You two used to be such friends, and now he never crosses your threshold; what's the reason?
2. *Junior.* I don't profess to understand him. I suppose some of our people here must have offended him. If not, I can only account for it in one other way, and that is that he took offence at something I said myself. It was only a few words, and nothing that, considering the terms we had been on, need have put him out so that he couldn't forget it; but it did, and he gave up coming to see me Not that that would have mattered so much, but what I don't understand is, why he should never be saying anything but evil of me behind my back; making me out so bad and so dangerous; never meeting any of my acquaintances without introducing my name and disparaging me. A short time ago, I was marrying my son, and feeling that it would be a shame not to ask an old friend like that to the wedding, I did write him an invitation, and he didn't send so much as a dog to acknowledge it. I may as well make no more acquaintances, really. Every one I have met has treated me with just the same want of regard.
3. *Senior.* Didn't I tell you you couldn't trust him, either for word or for deed? And you wouldn't even go into such a question. Indeed, you were far from satisfied with me for saying what I did.
4. *Junior.* True enough. As the proverb says, "You may know a man's face, but you can't tell what his heart's like" I couldn't see into his so as to know all that was in it of good or evil. All one can do is to be more careful in future.
5. *Senior.* That's the right thing undoubtedly. It won't do to call every man you meet your very good friend, indiscriminately.

PART VI. THE HUNDRED LESSONS. T‘an Lun P‘ien. LIX – LXII.

1. 好好端端 *‘hao-‘hao-tuan-tuan*, well and rightly; we indeed were in the habit of going on [with one another well and rightly.] See *hsing-tsou*, again below.
2. 上 *shang*, on or in; it was because of [what was] on, or in, a half sentence of talk.
3. 不犯 *pu fan*, here, to regard, concern; not worth remembering.
4. 當作 *tang-tso*, to treat as, to make of; treating me as *‘hua pa ‘rh*, a handle of discourse; *tsao-t‘a*, to injure me, this is what *hsin-i*, intention?
5. 臉上 *lien shang*, must be construed as a noun, the subject of *hsia-pu-lai*, to be unable to lower, to let pass away, *sc.* not the face, but the regard it would shew to a friend.
6. 往後 *wang-‘hou*, in after time, hereafter; *chieh-chiao*, to knit intercourse, make acquaintance.
7. 透徹 *t‘ou-ch‘ê*, thoroughly, to the bottom. 8. 一概 *i-kai*, the whole collectively, of men or things.

LESSON LXII.

1. *Senior.* He began it. Who was finding fault with *him*, I should like to know? It was *he* who forced me to speak by what he said. You are the last man I should think of trying to deceive, and I tell you that since New-year's day he has never once been to the office; and now to-day he comes in, after having been drinking somewhere or other, and the moment he sees me he calls out, "Hallo! how is it I find you here?" In other words, instead of being grateful to me for working double tides, and doing his duty for him a whole month, he attacked me as if I had been neglecting my own duty. I certainly felt very angry. However, I didn't think necessary to argue the point with him to-day. We'll see about it to-morrow.

2. *Junior.* I wouldn't join issue with him on the subject, Sir. Why should you be contentious? That's the very thing that he is. All you have got to do is to go on just as if you had heard nothing and seen nothing, and there will be an end of it. You are not obliged to take notice of him, are you?

3. *Senior.* Yes; but I can tell you, Sir, that forbearance to a bully like this, who is as insolent as he is cowardly, merely makes him more cock-awhoop. If he had said "I was only in joke; what I said slipped out unintentionally; I apologise for the rudeness of my remark," one might have forgiven him; but it wasn't so at all; he was flushed with anger when he spoke to me. Now, who is going to be afraid of him? I am sure I'm not.

4. *Junior.* Don't let him put you in a rage, Sir; I'll get in a rage for you. The drunken villain! I'll take him to some quiet corner, out of the way, and I'll shake my finger in his face, and call him all sorts of names.

1. 瞞 *man*², to blind, deceive.
2. 自從 *tzŭ-ts‘ung*, from, a certain time; the combination has no greater force than either of its parts separately.
3. 走了 *tsou-liao*, on what *ch‘ai shih*, official duty, has he gone? You could not, however, say *tsou-liao ch‘ai-shih*, for having been on duty.
4. 脫空 *t‘o k‘ung*, withdraw [the person in order to enjoy] leisure; construe, if it were as he says, I, [though I] without allowing myself leisure, for a whole month have been bearing his office for him, [instead of having done well,] on the reverse am in the wrong, am I?
5. 頸 *kêng*³, the back of the neck, written properly with the 181st Radical; *po-kêng-tzŭ*, the back of the neck, which, say the Chinese, stiffens as one's choler rises.
6. 配 *p‘ei*⁴, the mate of, to match with; *i pan*, of the same sort; *i p‘ei*, a match with.
7. 競 *ching*⁴, to strive or to wrangle; not used colloquially alone, or otherwise than as here, in *chêng-ching*.
8. 要嘴皮子 *shua tsui p‘i-tzŭ*, literally, to fence with the lips, to bandy words with, in fun or in earnest.
9. 只當 *chih tang*, only to represent, to bear one's self just as if.
10. 跟前 *kên-ch‘ien*, in the presence of, when you stand before this sort of *tung-hsi*, who insults the soft and fears the hard,
11. 長價 *chang chia*, to increase in price or value of; said of things, or, as here, of self-esteem. [&c.
12. 冒失 *mao-shih*, by my abruptness, or inconsiderateness, I erred, a common form of apology.
13. 諒 *liang*⁴, originally, faith, confidence; hence, to assume as fact; in *yuan-liang*, it signifies forgiveness, this combination being an elliptical form of 原情諒事 *yuan ch‘ing liang shih*, bethinking you of the matter, *sc.* my fault, forgive that matter.
14. 不成 *pu ch‘êng*, a common form of ending a sentence interrogatively, especially when *nan ‘tao* has preceded it See
15. 僻 *p‘i*¹, unfrequented by man, out of the way and quiet. [EXERC. VIII.
16. 罵 *ma*⁴, to revile, *chih-cho*, pointing with the finger at his face.
17. 出出氣 *ch‘u ch‘u ch‘i*, to vent rage; here, for another.

35

KEY TO THE TZŬ ERH CHI. **Colloquial Series.**

LESSON LXIII.

1. You false-hearted villain, you! To be showing these airs to *me!* Am I not fit company for *you*, I should like to know? What do you take yourself for, pray, that, right or wrong, you must always be laughing in your sleeve at me? If I were disposed to talk, we have been long enough in daily contact to enable me to do so; but I don't, because, if I were to go back on the past, the next thing you would accuse me of would be of trying to show you up. 2. I know as much about you in your home as you know about me in mine; it is not so very long ago that you used to catch it from everybody; and now, forsooth, you miserable wretch! you affect superiority over me. What do you mean by it? If you had said, "I had no business to say what I did," one might have forgiven you; but no, not a bit of it; nothing will make you give in; you are determined not to admit you were in the wrong. 3. What it is that you consider entitles you to conduct yourself with such impertinence to me, I cannot understand. We're too fairly matched, remember, for either to be afraid of the other. If you want to try a fall, I'm ready. If I hang fire, I'm no true man.

1. 壞了 *huai-liao*, here, attributive of *ch'ang-tzŭ*, literally, the bowels, figuratively, for the inner man; ruined, corrupted, heart.
2. 譏誚 *chi¹-ch'iao⁴*, to criticise covertly, the first character used alone; the second not without the first. The combination may be used of criticism either to a man's face or behind his back, the critic not speaking plainly, but employing *ch'iao 'hua*, cunning talk, clever innuendoes.
3. 免 *mien³*, to avoid, *wei mien*, inevitably. *yu*, in the next place, you would say.
4. 揭 *chieh¹*, to open, disclose, *chieh tuan*, to shew up the short comings of.
5. 揉 *jou²*, to rub between the hands, used, by itself, of things; of persons, as here, with 搓 *ts'o*, a verb of the same meaning, used only with the first, *jou-ts'o*, to bully. Observe the construction; [since] you have ceased *shou*, to be subject to, people's bullying, then how many days is it?
6. 作足 *tso, tsu*, to play the part of a self-sufficient man. Observe the place occupied by the auxiliary verbs *ch'i* and *lai*.
7. 恕 *shu⁴*, to pardon.
8. 死扭 *ssŭ-niu*, literally, determined to twist something held in the hand. You were in the wrong, yet you, *p'ien*, specially, were ready to die rather than not twist; determined to have your way.
9. 一口 *i k'ou*, holding one language unchanged; *yao tîng*, biting fast, not yielding.
10. 舉動 *chu tung*, rising and moving; conduct, behaviour.
11. 磴 *têng⁴*, properly, stairs, steps, of stone; *ta i ko têng*, is used of a halting advance, as if the person were mounting steps, not walking on a smooth level.

LESSON LXIV.

1. He's no good, that fellow; how came you to take a fancy to him? He may be a man in form, but he's a beast by nature. Keep clear of him, whatever you do. 2. Mind what I'm saying to you. He's a mischief-making scoundrel; a dark and dangerous man. According to him there's always a storm brewing somewhere. He'll get hold of some small trifle about a man, and blab, blab, he'll publish all over the place in a way that's intolerable; or he'll go and tell So-and-so something about you, and he'll come and tell you something about So-and-so, in order that he may set you both by the ears, and then step in between you as mediator. 3. If you think I'm not telling you the truth, observe this fact; not only has he no friend, but he's in great luck if he's spoken of without being abused. 4. Ah! his father and mother must have been a bad lot to have been the parents of a fellow so odious and contemptible.

1. 混帳 *'hun-chang*, literally, an account in confusion; a strong term of abuse implying some mischievousness.
2. 行子 *'hang-tzŭ*, literally, one of a class, a fellow; but used always in a bad sense.
3. 心眼 *hsin yen*, the eyes of the heart or mind, by which its intelligence is emitted; it, the heart, should be red.
4. 嘈說 *ch'ao shuo*, to chatter, to babble; intensified by *'hun*, preceding it. See DIAL. VIII, 81.
5. 不堪 *pu k'an*, not to tolerate, intolerable; construe, he *chang-yang*, promulges it to a degree that I *pu k'an*.
6. 傳 *ch'uan²*, to propagate reports; when read *ch'uan⁴*, a story. 7. 德 *tê²*, virtue, *tê-hsing*, virtuous conduct.

LESSON LXV.

Senior. I was coming home from the office just now, when, at some distance from me, I heard the noise of a large party on horseback. I looked hard as they came up to me, and I saw it was What's-his-name, our old neighbour; you know. Such a toilet and such a team, quite a case of "the sleek steed and the costly

PART VI. THE HUNDRED LESSONS. T'an Lun P'ien. LXIII-LXVI.

cloak," and the man himself well filled out both in face and person! He saw me, but he took no notice of me whatever; screwed his head back and looked up to the sky. At first I was going to call out to him to stop, and I would have made him well ashamed of himself; but, on second thoughts, I said to myself, "Pooh! What's the use? It isn't his recognition of me that would make me respectable. Who has got leisure to go into such a question with him? I am sure I've not." 2. Dear me! you must remember well enough, Sir, how he used to go on down in our neighbourhood three years ago. He was wretchedly poor; so poor that, as soon as he had his breakfast, he had to set to work to secure a dinner. Day after day he'd be roaming about as restless as a spirit; when he had nothing to eat, doing without; but trying everyone for a meal; very lucky if he managed to pick up any trifle of the commonest description. He'd come to my house at least two or three times a day, and if he didn't ask for one thing he would for another. I should like to know what there was belonging to me that he didn't taste; he made my chopsticks shine again, he ate with them so often. Well, one fine day he becomes a new man, with means of his own, and his antecedents all pass out of his head. Really, without presumption, I think we can afford to be quite indifferent about the bearing of such a beggar on horseback.

1. 轟 'hung, originally, a clatter of wheels; roar of thunder or of cannon; any loud clamour. Construe, there was a noise that came to be, was such, as if there were a large body of men, &c.
2. 裘 ch'iu², a certain long dress lined with fur, more commonly called p'i 'ngao, the words fei ma ch'ing ch'iu, sleek steed and light fur cloak, (the light fur being expensive,) are a classical passage somewhat shorn of its proportions, signifying a wealthy condition.   [call, &c.
3. 來著 lai-cho is auxiliary, observe, of yao, to be about to, not of hsiu ju, to insult; pi shih, at the time, I was going to
4. 游 yu², to roam; yu 'hun, a wandering spirit.
5. 希罕 hsi-'han, rare, shih-cho, if he picked up one straw, even that, a straw, was esteemed a rarity.
6. 筷 k'uai,⁴, the chopsticks, used as knife and fork by the Chinese.
7. 咂 tsa¹, to put in the mouth; to taste with the tongue.
8. 求不著人 ch'iu-pu-chao-jen, he no longer requests people, sc. to assist him; here, with money; it might mean with their talents, he is become independent.
9. 旦 tan⁴, properly, sunrise; yi tan, one day.
10. 景況 ching k'uang, circumstances; k'uang, amongst other meanings has, classically, that of to bestow; hence, the condition of things bestowed by heaven.
11. 擡 tai², to carry; properly, as two men carry anything on a pole between them; t'ai-chu, only figurative, of extolling another or one's self.

LESSON LXVI.

1. *Senior.* Well, of all bad memories in the world, I do think yours is the worst. What did I tell you the day before yesterday? On no account to let any mortal know anything about this business; notwithstanding which you have let it out. All the arrangements you and I have been privately concerting have been made public, and at this moment they are the talk of the town. If they get to the ears of these people, they'll feel shame first, then shame will turn to anger; and if, in their disgust at our proceedings, they commence operations against us, a nice mess we shall be in. There's a good scheme brought to nothing, and all your doing.
2. *Junior.* You're blaming me unjustly, Sir, I assure you. It's of no use entering into particulars, for, under existing circumstances, you wouldn't believe me, if I made my innocence as plain as words could make it; but God sees my heart, and time will show whether I have been talking or not. In the meantime I should say that, instead of feeling unkindly towards me before you know whether I am to blame or not, you had best pretend to be entirely ignorant of the publicity of this affair, and keep your eye on the movements of the other party. If they are not going to quarrel, they are not; if they are, you'll have time enough to reorganise your plans and be prepared for them.

1. 囑 chu², to enjoin on another one's equal or inferior; chu-fu, not so imperative as fên-fu, which is to command as a superior.   [figuratively.
2. 洩漏 hsieh lou; both characters mean to leak, and serve, singly, in their literal sense; the combination is only used
3. 羞惱 hsiu-nao, not used except with the rest of the phrase, hsiu will become nao, and both be turned into nu, rage.
4. 動起 tung ch'i, with lai, as an auxiliary, to set going, e.g. mischief; here, the hand and foot, to act against aggressively.
5. 總然 tsung-jan, admitting that; although I were fên-pien, to argue, [until there was] a teeth-clean-mouth-plain—'s [state of things]. Observe that the word ya-ch'ih, teeth, is used for talk, as ch'ih in LXIX, note 4; ch'ing-pai, plain and clear; were I to argue till my talk fully explained this case.
6. 道理 tao-li, here in the sense of theory, system, again make a theory; devise some other order of proceeding.

KEY TO THE TZŬ ERH CHI. **Colloquial Series.**

LESSON LXVII.

1. *Senior.* You are an excellent fellow, I know, with the best heart possible, but you are too blunt. When you know a man's faults, you give him no law at all; you will tell him plainly what you think. It is an act of friendship to correct one's friends' faults, but one should study the person to see whether advice will do good, before one gives it. It isn't right, surely, to tender advice to every one that comes under the denomination of friend, without reference to degrees of intimacy. Now in what you said to So-and-so, you meant well, I am sure, but it put him out very much. He stared with astonishment. "Ho, ho," thought he; "I must mind what I am about; he means mischief."

2. *Junior.* This is very salutary counsel of yours, Sir; it's no doubt the right medicine for my complaint. I have full faith in the prescription. I know as well as any one that this bluntness has always been a fault in my character. Something like this to-day turns up, my lips burn to speak, and out it comes. It's an old saying, that words addressed to a man who is not worthy of them, are words thrown away. I'll reform in earnest, at once; and if from this time forth, Sir, I commit myself by speaking when I ought to be silent, I'll give you leave to spit in my face.

1. 渣 *cha*¹, dregs, lees, here, impurity, unsoundness.
2. 規過 *kuei kuo*, to correct the fault of another; *kuei*, properly, a compass; *kuo*, transgression.
3. 親疏 *ch'in su*, near and far.
4. 不由的 *pu-yu-ti*, without one's allowing it, involuntarily; abbreviated from *pu-chin-pu-yu-ti*, not restraining, not allowing, independently of one's pleasure in the matter.
5. 與言 *yu yen*, to a person to speak; *pu k'o*, if it be not right to [such a person] to speak, *êrh*, and yet, one does speak to
6. 縱使 *tsung shih*, although, in no way differing from *tsung jan*, LXVI, 5. [him, &c.
7. 啐 *ts'ui*¹, to spit. 8. 沫 *mo*⁴, properly, scum; *t'u*, to spit; *t'u-mo*, spittle.
9. 領 *ling*³, properly, the neck; hence, to lead; from inclination of the head, (probably,) to receive; *ling-shou*, to receive, specially, if not solely, an injury, never used I believe, except when preceded as here by *kan hsin*.

LESSON LXVIII.

1. There is no better fellow than yourself, but it's too simple of you to keep on praising that friend of yours in the way you do. A scoundrel like that! What is there so wonderful about him? Why, you ought never to mention his name! 2. He's the kind of man that will agree to do anything so long as he has a favour to ask of you, but the moment his business is settled he turns on his heel, and forgets there is such a person as you in the world. 3. He was hard up last year, and he came to beg me to help him. No one asked him if he had anything to put down, but of his own accord he told me that he had got a nice book, "which," says he, "I'll send you to look at, if you like." 4. This was the promise he made me, but, when the loan was raised, not a word more did he say about the book. I waited a considerable time without any news of it, until one day we met, and then I asked him, "What about that book you promised me?" But instead of giving me any good reason for not sending it, on my putting the question to him in this way, face to face, he turned first red and then pale, and put me off with all sorts of excuses. 5. As for his book, a book is nothing so very curious. It didn't signify much whether he gave it me or not; but his gratuitous deception of one is simply disgusting in the extreme.

1. 稱讚 *ch'êng-tsan*, to praise, *tsan*, properly meaning to aid or support, should be distinguished from another *tsan*, of the same sense, which is simply this character written without the 149th Radical.
2. 吾 *wu*¹, a classical form of the pronoun of the first person; *chih wu*, more properly written with the 75th Radical, to the left of both characters, to make a defence, in speech, or action, where none ought to be made.

LESSON LXIX.

1. *Junior.* What motive you can have for so positively refusing to keep the present I have brought you, Sir, I really cannot make out. Do you treat me in this way because I came so late, or on some other ground? 2. As to the first, I have been in the habit of visiting here constantly, and I couldn't have done so unfriendly an act as to omit calling on your father or mother's birthday. What made me late was this, that I did not know in time that it was a birthday. If I had known it, I should of course have been here long ago. 3. I don't mean to say that my presence or absence would have made any material difference; still, had I been in

PART VI. THE HUNDRED LESSONS. T'an Lun P'ien. LXVII–LXX.

time, I might have been of use in helping you to do the honours, and as to my present, Sir, even supposing that your other friends and relations have brought things in such quantities that it is impossible to get through them all, and that the trifles I have brought are not worth mention, still they were brought to show that I have a certain sense of affectionate regard for your parents. 4. I don't presume to press your parents to eat my presents, but if they were just to taste them it would show a kindly feeling towards me, and this would make me quite contented; whereas, a positive refusal to receive them places me in a very disagreeable dilemma. It becomes as unpleasant for me to sit here as to go away.

1. 固 *ku*⁴, originally, fortifications; hence, adequate fortifications; hence, secure, impregnable; here, *ku tz'ŭ*, positively to decline.
2. 尚且 *shang ch'ieh*, a strong affirmative, *su-ch'ang*, all along, I, in very deed, have constantly come; [and this being so] on your parents' birth-day notwithstanding not to have come, &c.
3. 還少麼 *hai shao mo*, are they indeed few? [No]. 4. 掛齒 *kua ch'ih*, to hang on the teeth, *sc.* to speak of.
5. 嚐 *ch'ang*², to taste by eating or drinking.
6. 倒爲了難 *tao wei liao nan*; [whichever I might do, my intention either way being good,] you nevertheless make me a difficult course.

LESSON LXX.

1. *Junior.* Have you heard what they say, Sir? That *gourmand* of ours is utterly ruined, and in the greatest distress; all in rags like a mere beggar, and shivering away there under a quilt that is all in pieces.

2. *Senior.* I said he'd come to no good, the gallows-bird! Last year he underwent every species of suffering, and, if he had had any strength of mind, he would have turned over a new leaf. We know what the proverb says, "If the poor man chooses to be the rich man's mate, the mate will have no breeches to wear." This is quite true, and, accordingly, it behoved our friend to revise his tastes. What business had he to be fancying this wine or that dish, and to gad about precisely as if he was a rich man and a grand seigneur? I said at the time, "Wait till the winter, and then we shall see how he gets on." And now there he is, in the mess I predicted he would be.

3. *Junior.* Yes, Sir; I don't wonder at your being down on him; still, now that he is in this wretched condition, it won't do to look on and see him die outright; will it? The right thing, it appears to me, would be for us each to give a trifle, and make a subscription for him.

4 *Senior.* That is, you would give him pecuniary aid. I don't think that's a good suggestion. I'll tell you why. He is so constituted, as you must know, that the moment he got hold of the money there would be an end to it; not a fraction would he keep in hand. He'd spend the whole of it. No; I should say that if we were to buy him a suit of clothes, that would be of some use.

1. 饞 *ch'an*², to be an epicure; *ch'an-tsui*, to gluttonise, to be always eating.
2. 破敗 *p'o-pai*, to be ruined; of persons, or temples, without funds; not otherwise used.
3. 襤褸 *lan*² *-lu*⁴, tattered and torn; the two characters not used apart from each other.
4. 花子 *hua-tzŭ*, a beggar; *q. d.* *hao*⁴ *hua ch'ien chih tzŭ*, a fellow who has been fond of spending money.
5. 戰 *chan*⁴, properly, to fight in battle; here, and often, to tremble as from cold or fear.
6. 抖 *tou*³, to shake as you would a piece of paper to get the dust off it.
7. 披 *p'ei*¹, also *p'i*¹, to throw over one's person, to carry over one; carrying over his person a *p'o pei*, ragged coverlid.
8. 趁願 *ch'ên yüan*, to come in for the wishes, *sc.* the bad wishes, of some one; *kai ssŭ-ti*, the deserving to die; the two epithets are entirely separate.
9. 志氣 *chih ch'i*, resolution; had there only been to his share a fraction of resolution.
10. 伴的 *pan ti*, an associate, used verbally in the foregoing clause.
11. 回過味兒 *hui-kuo wei-êrh*, to profit by experience, the Chinese olive is said not to be tasted until after it is swallowed; its *wei*, flavour, then *hui-kuo-lai*, comes back.
12. 心腸 *hsin ch'ang*, heart and bowels; here, for the mind; a man in sorrow may be said to have no *hsin-ch'ang*, heart to do this or that.
13. 游玩 *yu-wan*, roaming about and amusing himself.
14. 上冬 *shang tung*, the beginning of winter, *shang-ch'iu*, the beginning of autumn; but *shang* is not so used with spring or summer.
15. 可當 *k'o tang*; the *k'o* would not be used here, if the position that he ought to die were affirmative.
16. 攢 *ts'uan*², to pile up together, *ts'uan-ts'ou*, to make up a heap or amount by contribution.
17. 一套 *i t'ao*, of good clothes, would mean no more than a *p'ao-tzŭ* and a *kua-tzŭ*; here, a whole suit of common garments.

KEY TO THE TZŬ ERH CHI. Colloquial Series.

LESSON LXXI.

1. *Senior.* How is it I have been so long without a sight of you? You manage to be running here and there and everywhere. Why can't you come to my house when you have a little time to spare?

2. *Junior.* I have been coming to pay you a visit for some time past, but I became mixed up in an affair that didn't concern me in the least, and I got so entangled in it, that, latterly, I have never had a moment to myself from morning to night. I have not been able to get away before to-day, and I should not have got away to-day if I hadn't told them what wasn't the case. I said I had business of importance, which was an untruth, and they have just let me go in consequence.

3. *Senior.* Well, you have come at the right moment; I was just feeling very low. You'll be able to give me a little of your company, I hope, so as to let us have a day's chat together. We'll have a quiet dinner, and then you can go. I'll not order anything additional.

4. *Junior.* But, really, it makes me uncomfortable to be turning the house upside down gratuitously whenever I come here. That's the reason I don't come much oftener.

5. *Senior.* Don't talk as if you were such a stranger, pray. When did the coolness commence between us? Another time, if a certain number of days were to elapse without a visit from you, I should get something ready, and send you a formal invitation; but what we have here is not worth talking about, so don't refuse it. Besides, I have eaten everything that you had to give me at your house, and if you are going to act so disloyally by me, it will be a plain proof that you want me not to go there any more.

1. 奔 *pên*¹, to run, when read *pên*⁴, it may stand alone, colloquially, for to go; as *pên*¹ʳ, it forms part of various combinations; *pên-po*, literally, to run as waves, to go hurrying about.
2. 摘 *chai*², so read only in this combination, properly, *chai*¹, EXERC. XII, 2, to take off, as one's cap, fruit on a tree, &c.; *chai-t'o*, to take one's self off, withdraw one's self.
3. 放了 *fang liao*, let me go, released me.
4. 騷 *sao*¹, originally, to stir, set in motion; to fidget actively or passively; *sao-jao*, to fidget a person, put him to trouble; *sao jên*, a man of troubles; elegantly, a poet; *q. d.* one who vents his *sao*, sorrows, in verse.
5. 外道 *wai tao*, reasoning on the basis of one's being an outsider, why should you thus regard yourself as an outsider?
6. 實誠 *shih-ch'êng*, truthful, reliable; *pu shih-ch'êng*, is the falsehood of politeness; it might, here, almost be rendered *ceremoniously*.

LESSON LXXII.

1. *Junior.* Oh! here you are at last, Sir. I have been waiting for you a long time. A few minutes more and I would have been in bed.

2. *Senior.* Well; what made us so late was this: we were just starting for your house when, to our horror, a fellow, who is the greatest bore in the world, presented himself, and set to work talking; din, din, on he went without stopping; all about nothing, too; first one trifle and then another; there was no end to it. If I had had nothing else to attend to, I shouldn't have objected to more or less of a yarn; I should have let him spin it out; but I feared that you would begin to feel uncomfortable at our non-appearance, so I was obliged to stop him by telling him that we were busy to-day, and must put off the rest of it till to-morrow. If it hadn't been for him we should have been seated here ever so long ago.

3. *Junior.* Oh! don't imagine that you are late; you have arrived in the very nick of time. Here! Who is outside there? Be quick and lay the table; the gentlemen must be hungry; and look sharp with whatever you have got to bring in.

4. *Senior.* No, no, Sir; pray don't give any such orders. A slice of meat, quite plain, will do very well. There is no occasion for all these dishes. You are not going to treat us as if we were strangers, surely?

6. *Junior.* Nay, what little there is here is only by way of showing my desire to be hospitable. There's nothing much worth offering you. But do eat something with your rice, Sir.

5. *Senior.* We don't require pressing with such a display before us, I can assure you. We are not waiting to be asked, and we shan't lay down our chopsticks till we can eat no more.

7. *Junior.* In that case I've nothing more to say; that's treating me as if you really loved me.

1. 死肉 *ssŭ jou*, dead flesh, a fellow without animation; unexpectedly there happened to present himself a certain *ssŭ jou*, who provokes people's disgust.
2. 刺 *tz'ŭ*⁴, properly, to pick with a point. 3. 休 *hsiu*¹, to rest; to cease; *tz'ŭ tz'ŭ pu hsiu*, the worry of incessant talking.
4. 絮 *hsu*⁴, gossamer, the down of the willow; the quality of cotton, &c., which may be drawn out to an indefinite length.

PART VI. THE HUNDRED LESSONS. T'an Lun P'ien. LXXI-LXXIV.

5. 叨 *tao*¹, colloquially, to talk; properly read *t'ao*¹, to receive, be the subject of, as kindness, mercy; *hsü-t'ao*¹, much talk; a long yarn.
6. 等急 *têng chi*, to be made impatient by waiting.
7. 坐煩 *tso fan*, seated a long time; *fan*, not here indicating fatigue either in one's self or one's host.
8. 副 *p'ien*⁴, to slice; *pai jou*, meat boiled without salt or seasoning.
9. 蔬 *su*¹, properly, wild vegetables; *ts'ai su*, food, dishes, in general, when a compliment to the *cuisine* is intended.
10. 當客 *tang k'o*, representing strangers; do you taking us act towards us as strangers; or, merging *pa* in *wo-mên*, as the object of the verb *tai*, do you treat us as strangers.
11. 就著 *chiu-cho*, literally, moving on to, proceeding to; adding something to the plain rice which he is already eating.
12. 盛 *shêng*⁴, a state of prosperity or affluence.
13. 設 *shê*⁴, properly, to place in order, to array; *shêng shê*, to put out in great abundance; used only, as here, of dishes; there is no occasion *kuo jang*, to exceed in invitations to eat and drink; there is an over-display of dishes, &c.
14. 我兄弟 *wo hsiung-ti*, me, your younger brother.

LESSON LXXIII.

1. *Junior.* Where are you from, Sir, may I ask?
2. *Senior.* I have been to visit a relation of mine who lives down yonder. Won't you step into my house and sit down, Sir?
3. *Junior.* Do you reside in this neighbourhood, Sir?
4. *Senior.* Yes; in this house. I moved here not long ago.
5. *Junior.* Oh! indeed, Sir. Then we are not so very far from each other. If I had been aware that you lived here, I should have called before. Go on, Sir, pray; I'll follow you, if you please.
6. *Senior.* What, in my own house? Who ever heard of such a thing? Now, please take the upper seat.
7. *Junior.* Thank you, I am very well where I am.
8. *Senior.* But if you sit where you are sitting, what place am I to take?
9. *Junior.* I have got a seat, thank you; and a seat with a back to it.
10. *Senior.* Here! Bring a light.
11. *Junior.* Not for me, thank you, Sir. I can't smoke; I have a sore mouth.
12. *Senior.* Well, then, bring some tea.
13. *Junior.* Drink first, then, pray.
14. *Senior.* After you, Sir. Boy, go and see what there is in the kitchen, and bring whatever is ready first.
15. *Junior.* No, indeed, Sir, do not put yourself to so much trouble. I have still got to go somewhere else.
16. *Senior.* But it's only whatever is ready; nothing is being prepared for you. Do try and eat a little of anything you please.
17. *Junior.* Not just now, thank you, Sir; but we are old acquaintances, you know; and now that I have found out where you live, I'll come another time and spend the day with you. To-day I really have not the time, so I'll say good-bye.

1. 來著 *lai-cho*, coming; having been to what place are you coming?
2. 順便 *shun pien*, elliptical for *shun-cho ni-ti pien tao*, your halt being an incident *shun*, in accordance with *pien tao*, the way most convenient to you; *shun pien*, cannot be applied to a course of action, or otherwise than here.
3. 上坐 *shang tso*, sit in the upper seat; generally to the left of the host, though, in some cases the arrangement of the room makes the right seat, as farthest from the door, or from the outer wall, the place of honour.
4. 靠頭 *k'ao t'ou*, something to lean against when one is seated; not necessarily the back of a chair.
5. 瘡 *ch'uang*¹, generally, a large boil or ulcer; a *k'ou ch'uang* may be any pimple in the mouth.
6. 將就 *chiang-chiu*, make an effort, sc. although the food is not good, to eat it.

LESSON LXXIV.

1. *Senior.* You were out very late yesterday; whose house were you at?
2. *Junior.* I went to pay a visit to a friend of ours. He lives close to the west wall of the city, an

KEY TO THE TZŬ ERH CHI. Colloquial Series.

immense way from this; and then he made me stay and eat a bit of dinner with him; so that, altogether, it was rather late before I got home.

3. *Senior.* I had something of importance that I wanted to talk to you about, and I sent several times to ask you to look in, but your servants said you had left home in the cart, without saying where you were going to. "Well," I said, "he doesn't visit a great deal; he'll only have gone to see some one in our small circle, and he'll be certain to come here afterwards;" but no such thing. I waited till sunset, but you never came, and, thought I to myself, I might just as well not have waited at all.

4. *Junior.* I was out, Sir. I had started long before your messenger came to look for me, and when I got home, and my servants told me you had been sending for me three or four times, I would have come to you at once, but it was very late to be disturbing you; and, besides, I was afraid the street gates would be shut; so I waited till to-day, and here I am.

1. 圈兒內 *ch'üan -'rh nei*, within the circle, *sc.* of our friends.
2. 小子們 *hsiao-tzŭ-mên*, the servants, not the sons of the house.
3. 柵欄 *cha⁴-lan²*, a wooden-barrier or gateway at the end of a street, closed at night; *cha* is properly the upright poles, which form this, *lan*, the transverse beams that connect the poles; *lan-tzŭ* is becoming the term for an outlaws' stockade.

LESSON LXXV.

1. Wasn't it to visit your cemetery that you left town the day before yesterday?
2. It was.
3. How is it that you only got back to-day?
4. Our cemetery is so far off that you can't go and return in a day. You have to stay there a couple of nights. I started the day before yesterday, the moment the city gates were open, and I travelled all day; but it was night before I reached the place. I offered my meat and drink offerings yesterday, passed the second night there, and commenced my journey home with the dawn this morning; but though I didn't venture to halt, except for a mouthful of lunch, I only got back here just as the gates were being closed for the night.
5. Ay, they may say what they like about the preferableness of cemeteries that lie a good way off, but, if one's posterity have not wherewithal, they won't find it so easy to pay their visits there three times a year.
6. They will not, indeed. We had a cemetery very near the city, but as there was no room for any more graves in it, we engaged the geomancers to look at some ground for us, and we laid out ours where it now is, because they said it was a good spot for one. It *is* a long way off, to be sure; still, the long and the short of it is that we must manage to get to our cemetery somehow or other; like rich people, if we have money, or like poor people, if we have none; and supposing our circumstances were so narrow as to put a cart beyond our means, we could always reach the cemetery and pour our cup of wine to the dead if we would but walk there. As to what a man's descendants will do by him, that depends entirely upon their own dispositions. If they are good-for-nothing fellows, whose regard for their ancestors is so slight that they can't pay the usual visits to his tomb because it lies some distance off, it by no means follows that they would burn a piece of paper money to him, were the family grave-yard ever so near.

1. 莊子 *chuang tzŭ*, a small village; as we say, the country; observe *lai-cho*, as in LESSON LXXIII, shewing that the person addressed is returning.
2. 當天 *tang t'ien*, in one day; read *tang⁴*, but with the meaning of *tang¹*; so read apparently because *tang jih*, when it has the same meaning is so read, whereas when the latter is read *tang¹ jih*, it means, on the day when such a thing occurred.
3. 頂城門兒 *ting ch'êng mên-'rh*, as though I had *ting*, run my head, against the gate before it was opened.
4. 供 *kung⁴*, see EXERC. XXXVIII, 15; here in the sense of laying out a sacrifice; read *kung¹*, it means the evidence or admission of a criminal or a witness.
5. 打尖 *ta chien*, to eat any short meal when travelling. See *chien*, EXERC. XXX, 21; its employment here cannot be [explained].
6. 塋 *ying²*, a grave-yard.
7. 風水 *fêng-shui*, wind and water; a term for the condition of a locality geomantically considered; *k'an fêng-shui ti*, a geomancer.
8. 紙錢 *chih ch'ien*, the paper money, shaped like ingots, which is burned to the dead.

PART VI. THE HUNDRED LESSONS. T'an Lün P'ien. LXXIV–LXXVII.

LESSON LXXVI.

1. Which of their family is it that is dead? I was passing their house three days ago, and I observed that they were all in mourning. It was my day at the office, so I hadn't time to make any inquiries; but I have just heard that a younger brother, or cousin of their father, is dead. Is it his brother?
2. It is; his own brother.
3. Have you paid your visit of condolence?
4. Yes; they were reading the service of the dead yesterday, and I was there the whole day.
5. Do you know when he is to be buried?
6. I hear about the end of the moon.
7. Whereabouts is their cemetery?
8. Close by ours.
9. Oh, dear! That's a long way off; I should say at least forty li, if not fifty. The next time you call, you can tell our friend for me how sorry I am to hear of his loss, and that I shall pay him a visit to condole with him in person as soon as I am off duty. And pray, whatever you do, let me know when they are going to bury his uncle; for, if it is not in my power to accompany the coffin to the cemetery, I shall certainly go with it outside the city. There has never been much intercouse between the nephew and myself, but whenever we do meet, we are very cordial. And, besides, all the world should be friends; so if I do go the whole length in testifying my sympathy with him on the occasion of so serious a loss, I don't apprehend that people will say that I am running after him.

1. 不在 *pu tsai*, not to be, to be dead.
2. 穿孝 *ch'uan hsiao*, to be in mourning; to be wearing clothes in token of *hsiao*, filial piety, or, in a more extended sense, family affection.
3. 該班 *kai pan*, to come to one's turn of duty according to the rollster; see *pan*, EXERC. XVI, 12.
4. 喪 *sang*^{1}, to die; death; to be distinguished from *sang*^{4}, to do mortal, or, irreparable damage to; see LESSON LII, 4; *tiao*, literally, to hang up, *sc.* one's contribution of paper money; see above, LESSON LXXV, 8; *tiao sang*, to mourn with the bereaved.
5. 殯 *pin*^{4}, to carry a coffin to the grave; *ch'u pin* is the funeral as the act of the family; *sung pin* may be the same, or it may be the attendance of friends at the funeral.
6. 道惱 *tao nao*, condolence in case of death; *tao*, to tell, *sc.* my sympathy with your *nao*, trouble, sorrow; see below, *fan nao*, in the same sense.
7. 信兒 *hsin*^{n}-*'rh*, as we say a word of intimation; whether in writing or verbally.
8. 偺們 *tsa-mên*, cannot be made here to include the person spoken to.
9. 走動 *tsou-tung*, of any ordinary movement; going about; *tsou-pu-tung*, unable to move.

LESSON LXXVII.

1. I was at home when he came; and lying down. All of a sudden something woke me. I listened and heard a strange voice in the drawing-room. Who can this be, thought I, talking so loud? Oh! of course it's that bore What's-his name. I went into the room, and, at the first glance, I saw it was he sure enough. And there he sat as stiff as a post, and talked and talked, first of this and then of that; his tongue never stopped from the moment he came in. And he staid such a time; two dinners might have been served while he was there. It was getting dark before he went away. 2. It really is too bad that a man should come to your house and sit there talking the whole day, whether he has got anything to say or not; and it is not only that this fellow makes your head ache with his exhaustive chatter about all manner of dirty trifles that have been talked of till they are stale, but he has got another detestable trick of laying hands on everything. When he is coming to call, everything good, bad, or indifferent, has to be put out of his sight. You musn't let him set eyes on anything; if you do, he asks no questions, but he just snaps it up, and away he goes with it. 3. No one has ever been able to say a good word for him since he was born; and is it to be pretended that such men, who are but beasts within, in whom all principle is annihilated, are to have the monopoly of whatever it strikes them will be to their advantage?

KEY TO THE TZŬ ERH CHI. Colloquial Series.

1. 挺 *t'ing*³, of persons or things, to stick up stiffly.   2. 黃昏 *'huang-'hun*, twilight of the evening only.
3. 穀 *ku*, properly, any kind of grain; *ku-tzŭ*, used generally of rice with the husk on; *ch'ên*, that is stale, and, here, spoiling; *lan chih-ma*, damaged sesame.
4. 餿 *sou*¹, rotten rice; to rot like rice; things, that were as stale rice and damaged sesame, that people have *chiang-chiu*, curiously discussed, until they were *sou*. Observe that all between *pa* and *shih-ch'ing*, is attributive of the latter.
5. 聽得 *t'ing tê*; [a person] listening arrives at the condition of a person whose head is quite aching, &c.
6. 惡 *nu*⁴, to hate; to be distinguished from the same character read *o* or *wo*, EXERC. XXXIX, 21; *k'o-wu*, odious, detestable.
7. 撈摸 *lao-mo*, properly, of taking things out of the water, generally, of picking up things.
8. 說頭 *shuo t'ou*, a point, or trait, of which one can speak favorably; he, *chê i pei-tzŭ*, this whole life-time of his, has never had that merit.
9. 雜碎 *tsa sui*, properly, miscellaneous fragments; the offal of sheep and pigs.

LESSON LXXVIII.

1. What is the meaning of this? Don't you perceive what a bore you must be, always asking for anything out of the common way that you happen to see in people's possession? It's positively disreputable. After one has let you have things, too, ever so many times, because one didn't know how to refuse. Why can't you be satisfied? Why must you go on insisting on having everything that belongs to a man? 2. But worse than this, to be angry because you can't get it! Presents are a matter of favour; if people won't make presents, they commit no sin; and what right have you, therefore, to lose your temper with those that don't give what they want? Suppose that it was something of yours that some one or other took a liking to, mightn't you have a liking for it as well? And how would you feel if your wishes were not consulted at all, and the whole concern was carried off bodily? 3. I gave way to you yesterday, because I knew what an ill tempered fellow you are; but no one else would have done so. Now ponder my words well, and mend your ways without loss of time. 4. If you were a man of no means, it would be another affair; but that is not your case; and when you have wherewithal to feed and clothe yourself, what can make you so eager to lay hands on every small thing going? I wonder you are not afraid of being talked about as a man that can't see a thing belonging to another without begging for it.

1. 絮煩 *hsü fan*, the annoyance occasioned by trouble repeatedly given.   2. 本分 *pên fên*, one's proper duty.
3. 摔搭 *shuai-ta*, to fling things about; *shih hsing-tzŭ*, giving vent to temper; *shuai-ta jên*, to shew one's anger against a person by throwing things about.
4. 行子 *'hang-tzŭ*, slightly abusive, as above, in LESSON LXIV, 2.
5. 眼皮子淺 *yen p'i-tzŭ ch'ien*, the eyelid of no thickness; so that whatever is seen is thought worth having.

LESSON LXXIX.

1. "If you don't study in your youth," says the ancient proverb, "what will you do when you grow old?" The moral of which is, that all men ought to study with diligence, and that no man should be idle. But, of all people, it behoves the Bannerman to be diligent. For, whereas any man, no matter who, that achieves by application the power of doing something for himself, may be looked on as provided for,—to those who study so hard as to rise to the highest standard of qualifications, an official career is *a fortiori*, a certainty. 2. Now, to attain this point is more the duty of the Bannerman than of any one else; because he has to trouble himself neither about his food nor his clothing. He is exempt from agricultural labour, coolie labour, and mechanical labour. He has nothing to do but eat the rations given him by the State, without stirring from his place. And if, with all these privileges, he does not set to work in his youth to study hard, what qualities will he acquire that will enable him to exert himself in the service of his lord and master? Or what return will he make to heaven for bringing him into the world and keeping him in it?

1. 藝 *i*⁴, properly, ability; *shou-i*, handicraft.
2. 努 *nu*³, to exert one's self; *nu-li*, with all one's might; *ch'in hsio*, to be diligent in learning.
3. 以著 *i-cho*; the *i* in the sense of, to employ.

PART VI. THE HUNDRED LESSONS. T'an Lun P'ien. LXXVII-LXXXI.

LESSON LXXX.

1. What is properly meant by the expression, "well-doing" is the observance of those principles in conformity with which it is man's duty to live, namely, duteousness, subordination, loyalty, and truth. It is not only those who go sacrificing to spirits and Buddhas, or giving alms to the priests of Tao or Fo, that are to be accounted well doers. A man may be a vicious man, and if so, he may repair bridges, or mend roads, as much as he pleases, but will that give him absolution? Not at all; neither is it in the power of the very Buddhas and spirits themselves to bestow happiness upon him. 2. All that going to heaven if you fast, and going somewhere else if you eat meat, is mere talk got up by the priests of the Buddhist and Taoist sects to enable them to put bread in their mouths. It is not all to be taken for gospel. If they did not terrify people with this tremendous story and that tremendous story, how would they swindle them out of their money? And if they were obliged to confine themselves strictly to what Buddhism enjoins, to shut the gates of the temples, and stay quietly within doors, devoutly reading out their sacred books, never going abroad to convert the elect of Buddha, they would have neither food to eat nor clothes to put on; and then what would they do? Could they live upon air?

1. 悌 $t'i^4$, duty to elder brothers and seniors, as $hsiao$ is to parents.
2. 齋 $chai$, reverent, respectful; here, to shew respect to Buddha, by subsidising his priests. See note on DIALOGUE VII, 10; also below 4 and 8.
3. 揭了 $chieh\ liao$, loosen, absolve him of his $tsui$-ngo, iniquities.
4. 喫齋 $ch'ih\ chai$, to fast, the same as $ch'ih\ su$, DIALOGUE VIII, 33, the opposite of '$hun\ ts'ai$.
5. 獄 yu^4, classically, a prison; $ti\ yu$, the hell of the Buddhists; $t'ien\ t'ang$, their paradise.
6. 借端 $chieh\ tuan$, to borrow a kind or form of things; to make something a plea for.
7. 餬 'hu^1, only used in '$hu\ k'ou$, to plaster the mouth, sc. with a little food, not more than will enable one to live.
8. 持 $ch'ih^2$, to grasp in the hand, $ch'ih\ chai$, maintain a reverent heart and bearing, to be devout.
9. 化緣 '$hua\ yuan$, the begging of Buddhist priests, whose ostensible avocation is to 'hua, convert, those who $yu\ yuan$, those whose lot it is, sc. to repay the kindness done them by the priest now asking alms, when both were in a former existence

LESSON LXXXI.

1. *Junior.* I've come for the express purpose of asking your advice, Sir, in a matter that interests me. It's a thing that might be attended with certain consequences to myself, perhaps, were I to do it; but, on the other hand, it would be a great pity, now that I've gone as far as I have gone, to leave it undone. It's not in reason to let an advantage that is ready to drop into your mouth go away to other people who have no claim to it; but what with objections to doing it, and objections to not doing it, I am fairly in a dilemma, and I want you to tell me what line you think will preserve me perfectly harmless in the transaction.
2. *Senior.* Your course is clear enough. There's nothing to prevent you making your mind up, surely. Let the thing alone, and it will be all the better for you. How are you to keep people's mouths shut if you don't? And it's when the thing comes to be well talked about that you will find yourself in a difficulty. It's but little good you'll get out of it, and that little is neither more nor less than the first growth of future trouble. Whatever advantage may belong to it, there is, without doubt, disadvantage; and it will be too late to repent when you come to grief. My advice to you is not to hesitate. Make up your mind positively *not* to do the thing, and have no more to say to it. If you continue undecided, if you can't give up the idea, you'll be like the man who not only gets no rice into his sack, but loses his sack to boot. You'll incur all the disgrace that attaches to a discreditable affair.

1. 顯 $hsien^3$, brightness; visibility; this thing is plainly visible and easy to be seen.
2. 那幾 $na\ ts'ai$, elliptical for na-$ko\ shih$-'hou, at that time; $ts'ai$, then, &c.
3. 拉扯住了 la-$ch'é\ chu$-$liao$, to keep back from moving onward, where circumstances are the cause; were the cause a person, the verb would be $la\ chu$. The construction is here passive; $q.\ d.$ if, delaying and doubting without intermission, you let yourself be held fast.
4. 打不成米 ta-pu-$ch'êng\ mi;$ the verb ta is here a verb of action of which one object is mi, rice, and the other $k'ou$-tai, the bag, understood; $ch'êng$ is the auxiliary meaning little else than $tê$ or $liao$ would mean.
5. 醜 $ch'ou^3$, ugliness of the face; here, figuratively, of moral deformity.

KEY TO THE TZŬ ERH CHI. Colloquial Series.

LESSON LXXXII.

1. *Junior.* There is something I want to ask you to do for me, Sir, but I feel some delicacy in addressing you on the subject; I have asked so many favours of you. Still, if I don't apply to you, there is no one else who can manage the matter for me, and I am therefore come to trouble you once more.
2. *Senior.* Isn't it that affair in which you want Chang's assistance?
3. *Junior.* It is. How came you to know that, Sir?
4. *Senior.* Your son was speaking to me about it this morning, and I went over there at breakfast-time, but, as luck would have it, Chang was out. Towards noon, I went again; but, as I entered the court, I heard a noise of talking and laughing in the drawing-room. So I went up the steps, and quietly put my tongue to the window-paper, and on looking through the hole I had made, I saw a room full of people, one helping the other to wine, and the other returning the compliment; and the whole company eating and drinking, and as merry as possible. At first I thought I would go in; but there were a great number of the guests who were strangers to me, and it struck me that they would be dreadfully put out at my obliging them all to get up from their wine to receive me; so I withdrew. The servants saw me and wanted to announce me, but I made signs to them not to do so. Don't you disturb yourself, however. I'll arrange it all with him comfortably the first thing to-morrow morning.

1. 瑣 *so*[3], properly, fragments of precious stones; hence, things small, trifles; *fan-so*, to give trouble to.
2. 纏交晌午 *ts'ai chiao shang wu*, just as [the *ssŭ* period, nine to eleven,] was joining the *wu* period, [eleven to one].
3. 階 *chieh*[1], a flight of stone or brick steps; in *t'ai chieh*, the word *t'ai*, terrace, does not modify the meaning.
4. 攪在一處 *chiao tsai i ch'u*, literally, stirred up together.
5. 冲散 *ch'ung san*; if I by *ch'ung*, breaking in, were to make them *san*, disperse, quit their places.
6. 得人意兒 *tê jên i-êrh*, to please people; *kuai*, as before, an intensive; monstrously to displease.

LESSON LXXXIII.

1. It wasn't of my own motion that I took charge of the affair for him, I am sure. I am a quiet stay-at-home sort of man, and I don't know where he found out that I knew the person he wanted; but he came to me again and again about him. "I rely entirely upon you, Sir," said he, and begged that I would be so good as to say a word for him. He never let me out of his sight, in short. 2. Well, as you very well know, I've always been a soft-hearted fellow, and when I saw a man in this kind of strait, imploring me on his knees to assist him, I hadn't the face to send him home discontented; and, as nothing I advanced would induce him to leave me alone, I undertook the commission for him. 3. So I spoke to my friend So-and-so about his affair, but I found that he was not, as I had hoped, alone in the case, and he declined to engage himself to me, as he said there were too many parties to be consulted. At first I was going to enter into particulars, and press the matter farther, but I thought to myself I had best say no more about it. To judge from appearances, the thing is not to be brought about, and what right have I to insist on anyone's undertaking it, *nolens volens*? 4. So I went back and told my principal what had occurred, and, instead of thanking me for the trouble I had taken, he turned round and abused me as a marplot, and scowled at me so that I really felt as if I had no hope left. If I had known what was to come of it, I certainly should not have spoken at all. What object could I have had in speaking?

1. 跪 *kuei*[4], to kneel.
2. 推托不開 *t'ui-t'o-pu-k'ai*, though I *t'ui*, put forward excuses, *t'o-pu-k'ai*, I could not get myself away from him, *t'o* should be written with the 130th Radical.
3. 不承望 *pu ch'êng-wang*, contrary to the hope I had entertained; *ch'êng-wang*, recipient of hope, is not found except with *pu* preceding it.
4. 掣 *ch'ê*[4], to pull towards one; *ch'ê chou*, to hold back by the arm.
5. 挽 *wan*[3], colloquially, to force round, as the ends of a bow; *wan-'hui*, to force back from a direction already taken.
6. 壓派 *ya p'ai*, literally, with pressure to require; *p'ai*, being used in the sense of official requisition.
7. 允 *yun*, to sanction, give assent to; *ying-yun*, to promise assent, agree to a proposition.
8. 撩 *liao*[4], to let down; a hanging screen, for instance; *liao*[1], to close up such a screen; it is here, of course, *liao*[4].
9. 圖 *t'u*, used before as a map or plan; here, a verb; to contemplate, or plan.

PART VI. THE HUNDRED LESSONS. **T'an Lun P'ien.** LXXXII–LXXXIV.

LESSON LXXXIV.

1. I did think that I should have had no difficulty in arranging that affair of yours with him; but instead of that, he proved so utterly impracticable, the wretch, that it gave me a great deal of trouble before I could manage it. 2. When I told him what had passed between you and me in conversation on the subject, his countenance fell at once, and he told me I was talking nonsense. This made my blood rise directly. If that's to be the order of the day, thought I, so be it; and I felt every inclination to say something sharp to him in return. 3. But then I reflected and reasoned with myself. It would be a mistake, I said, to lose my temper with him; I am here about the business of friends, not on my own account; and if he and I fall out, it will be to the loss of other people's time and pains; besides which, after all, what will it cost me to give in to him a little? 4. So I let him run on finding fault till he was tired, taking all he had to give, without allowing a syllable to escape me; and I sat on and on, watching him and humouring him, until by degrees I got so far as to press my request on him earnestly, and he then and there assented. 5. Now, if I had been a little hasty, you see, your affair would never have been settled.

1. 一遍 *i-pien*, one time; here untranslateable in our idiom.
2. 惹他 *jê t'a*, to provoke him a provocation.
3. 爲的 *wei ti*, the cause, that which is the *wei*⁴, because of.
4. 容讓 *jung jang*, to give way to; *jung*, properly, capable of containing; used singly as to allow, to let, a person speak or act.
5. 數落 *shu-lo*, literally, to run down the whole score; used only as here of moderate vituperation; *wo shu-lo t'a i tun*, as we say, I told him all I thought about his conduct.

LESSON LXXXV.

1. *Host.* May I ask to what I am indebted for the pleasure of this visit, Sir?
2. *Visitor.* Well, as our good luck has brought you and myself together in this world, we are come to beg you to let us have your daughter in marriage. My son here is not at all superior, I admit, to the rest of his kind, either in mind or person, nor does he possess any extraordinary accomplishments; but, on the other hand, he neither drinks nor plays, nor does he ever visit those haunts of dissipation where men lose their wits; he has never been astray. And now, gentlemen, if you don't consider him unworthy your goodwill, I shall ask you to be so kind as to tell him so. (*To his son.*) Step forward, and let us prefer our request with our heads to the ground.
3. *Host.* Stop, gentlemen! (*To all the company.*) Pray be seated, everybody, and hear what I have got to say. We are all kinsmen here, it is true; be our degree what it may, all of the same flesh and blood; there is no one present who is not known to everyone else. But what I have to say is this: Marriages, we know, are made in heaven quite independently of man; and parents, however great the affection with which they regard their children, can do no more than hope they may be matched in a manner that will satisfy their own anxiety to do their utmost for their offspring. Still, as my old people have never seen your son, I had better present him; and, on the other part, my ladies can have my little girl brought out for them to see.
4. *Visitor.* Certainly, Sir, you are quite right. Please go in and inform your ladies, and take my boy in for them to see. It will not be too late for him to make his *kotow*, when all parties are agreed.

1. 吾兄 *wu hsiung*, my brother; see above, LESSON LXVIII, 2.
2. 見教 *chien chiao*, to bestow instruction; the word *chien* is found in the sense of conferring, bestowing, in various complimentary phrases used in letters.
3. 有緣 *yu yuan*, see LESSON LXXX, 9.
4. 求親 *ch'iu ch'in*, to ask for [the daughter of the person addressed] as a wife for one's son, younger brother, or other [junior.
5. 超 *ch'ao*¹, literally, to overleap; *ch'ao ch'un*, to rise above the crowd.
6. 迷 *mi*², to lose, stray off, the road; *mi-'hu*, to cause to stray and make unsteady, used specially of libertinism; the expression *ch'u-ch'u-êrh*, places one goes to, can be used in any connexion.
7. 棄 *ch'i*⁴, to abandon; *ch'i-hsien*, to leave a person unnoticed because he is not to one's taste; not used of things.
8. 叩 *k'ou*⁴, to knock the head, *k'ou ch'iu*, to ask a favour on one's knees.
9. 挼 *yeh*⁴, properly, to hold up by the arm; *k'u pa*, anxiously drawing out; *k'u yeh*, anxiously helping along, *sc.* the incidents that shall conduce to the children's happiness.

47

KEY TO THE TZŬ ERH CHI. Colloquial Series.

LESSON LXXXVI.

1. *Visitor.* Are not these clothes being made for your daughter's intended?
2. *Host.* Yes.
3. *Visitor.* And what are all these people about?
4. *Host.* They are tailors that have been called in for the job.
5. *Visitor.* Dear! dear! but have you forgotten our old ways then? Why, in former days, all the girls in the house could make clothes. If the question was the making up of a cotton *ao*, for instance, all hands took a part in laying the wadding and fitting the lining; and when this had been turned, one would be stitching the overlap, another would be laying the chalk line, and another closing the seam of the arm-hole, and another binding the collar. If there was a cuff to hem, it would be hemmed; if there was a button to be put on, it was put on; and in a day or two, at the most, the work was done. Even the caps were made in the house. People would have sneered at you if you had hired a tailor to make one, or if you had gone to the expense of buying one.
6. *Host.* What you say is quite correct, Sir. Still you only know one part of the story, and not the other. In the first place, is there no difference between the style of the past time and that of the present? In the next, the wedding-day is well in sight; we have but ten days left, all told; and though we are not giving ourselves a moment's rest, and the tailors are working night and day, it's a question now whether the clothes will be ready in time or not. If we were to hold on, *coute que coute*, to the old usage, why we should be like the soldier who comes on the parade-ground all in good time, and contrives notwithstanding to be late for parade. It would never do for us to let things be behindhand, surely, when we knew right well how time was flying.

1. 壻 *hsu⁴*, the husband of one's daughter; colloquially, he is always so-and-so's *nu-hsu*, but when asking the wife's parents about him, you call him *ling hsu*.
2. 以 *i*; a somewhat classical construction; 是 being used pretty much as *pa* before the object of *lun*.
3. 襟 *chin¹*, the overlap of the Chinese dress which buttons on the right breast and side.
4. 謄 *t'ang⁴*, the line made on the dress in chalk or ink, to guide the tailor in stitching.
5. 煞 *sha¹*, properly the same as *sha*, to kill; sometimes used as '*hên*, very; here, to close the seam of the *ko-chih-wo*, the arm-pit, not used of any other part of the dress.
6. 領條 *ling t'iao*, the strip of stuff that binds the neck of a garment.
7. 沿 *yen²*, properly, the shore of sea, lake, or river; hence, along the edge of; here, of hemming the edge of the cuff slightly doubled back.
8. 見笑 *chien hsiao*, to laugh at; see *chien*, LESSON LXXXV, 1; people might *chien hsiao* in their hearts; here, without laughing outright, they laugh through the nose, sneer.
9. 掐 *ch'ia¹*, to nip between finger and thumb.
10. 旗杆 *ch'i-kan*, flag-staff, staff of the colours; to be on the drill-ground and miss drill, *sc.* by falling asleep there, after being at the trouble of rising early in order to attend.
11. 成事 *ch'êng shih*, to complete the matter in hand, *sc.* as it ought to be completed; *ch'êng shên-mo shih*, how far would it be right, if *ta chêng-cho*, widely opening, the eyes, we were *tan-wu*, to make a mess of the business.

LESSON LXXXVII.

1. *Junior.* Where does this son stand in the family, Sir?
2. *Senior.* He is the Benjamin of the party; the child of my old age.
3. *Junior.* Has he had the small-pox?
4. *Senior.* He had it last year.
5. *Junior.* And do all these boys come one after the other?
6. *Senior.* One after the other, without a break. There were nine born, and there are nine there alive.
7. *Junior.* Is it possible? Well, Sir, in sober earnest I must say that your good lady is a clever mother and an experienced nurse; quite a *tzŭ-sun niang-niang*. You're a fortunate man, indeed.
8. *Senior.* Fortunate! I must have sinned in a previous existence, I think. The elder children are a little more bearable, but the chatter of these younger ones makes a din that gives me the headache.
9. *Junior.* Well, we're all alike in this world. Folks that have plenty of children and grandchildren are always discontented because the number is so large, while others, like myself, who have but few, are always wishing to have more, without being able to have them. It's a hard matter for heaven to satisfy both parties.
10. *Senior.* If your little girl had lived, how far would she have got in her teens?

PART VI. THE HUNDRED LESSONS. T'an Lun P'ien. LXXXVI-LXXXIX.

11. *Junior.* She was in her seventh year when she died; she would be ten years old if she was alive now.
12. *Senior.* Ah! that was a nice child. The mention of her name even now makes me feel for you. She looked so different and talked so differently from other children. If she was brought in to see any one she stood so erect, and her manner was so quiet; and when she came forward to ask you how you were, it quite touched one to look at her. That little tongue of hers, too, could talk of anything. If she was asked a question on any subject, she would come out with a long story, just as if some one had taught it her, and not omit a word. A child like that is as good as any ten. Mine here are not worth the trouble of bringing up.

1. 出花 *ch'u 'hua*, to have the small-pox; literally, to put forth flowers, to blossom.
2. 挨肩 *ngai-chien*, standing shoulder to shoulder; in which sense it may be used literally; here, figuratively, in consecutive order.
3. 存了 *ts'un-liao*, there are preserved, there are alive.
4. 嫂 *sao³*, the wife of one's elder brother; *ta sao-tzŭ*, wife of one's eldest brother; the person addressed being complimentarily assumed to be this relative.
5. 吱 *chih¹*, with *cha*, a sound of chattering.
6. 老天爺 *lao t'ien-yeh*, the old lord of heaven, providence.
7. 沒得 *mei-tê*, she died, *lit.* was not, came to be not; generally read *mei-ti*.
8. 安詳 *ngan-hsiang*, may be used of demeanour that is *ngan-ching*, quiet, and *hsiang-hsi*, careful.
9. 可憐 *k'o-lien*; observe the construction; the *êrh* makes a substantive of *k'o-lien chien*, with tender feeling beholding, *q. d.* touched one as soon as one beheld her; *êrh*, a person, to look on whom moved one directly; *ti*, of that class was she.
10. 頂十個 *ting shih ko*, would be a substitute for ten; *ting*, in the sense of *ting-pu*, to replace.

LESSON LXXXVIII.

1. *Visitor.* It was really too good of you, when I had eaten of your morning sacrifice yesterday, to send your evening sacrifice to-day. Why did you?
2. *Host.* My dear Sir, not a word. It was my duty to present it, and I was just going to send to you to invite you to come over. But you know how all my people here are occupied. The pigs have to be killed and their insides made up, and all these things keep their hands so busy, that I had no one I could make a messenger of.
3. *Visitor.* Oh! I didn't wait for an invitation, for I know well enough that you have to attend to everything yourself, and that is why I engaged our friends here to come along with me and eat your *ta jou*. We did fear that we should be late; however, here we are in the nick of time. Now, gentlemen, we won't put our host to the trouble of attending to us individually, let us just sit down in a row, *seniores priores*, and begin.
4. *Host.* Let me beg you to eat, gentlemen. Put a little broth over the meat.
5. *Visitor.* Eh, Sir? What? Formalities on an occasion like this? Never was such a thing heard of amongst us Manchus before. The meat is your ancestors' dole, remember, and it is not in reason that your guests should require pressing to eat it. Friends and relatives who come for the purpose, should not either be received with ceremony when they arrive, nor accompanied to the door when they depart. This fashion you are introducing of pressing your visitors on such an occasion is quite out of order.

1. 背燈 *pei têng*, literally, behind the lamps, in the dark; used only with reference to sacrifices (offered by the Manchus only) after removing the lights. They *chi shên*, offer [pork] to the spirits, *sc.* of their ancestors, shortly after midnight. The other sacrifice, also of pork, is offered in the dark, about eight on the evening of the same day.
2. 大肉 *ta jou*, is the meat which has been offered in the *pei têng* sacrifice, and which, on the following day, friends are invited to eat.
3. 序齒 *hsu ch'ih*, in order of our teeth, that is, our ages.
4. 一溜 *i liu*, as a stream uninterrupted, the seniors not ceremoniously declining the upper seats.
5. 泡 *p'ao⁴*, properly, a bubble; here and elsewhere, to pour.
6. 克 *k'o¹*, classically, *k'o⁴*, to be able; here, without meaning, *k'o-shih*, being simply used to represent a Manchu word signifying bounty. More politely this *ta jou* is called 神餘 *shên yü*, the leavings of the ancestral spirits.

LESSON LXXXIX.

1. When we were in Manchuria we used to go out after game regularly every day, and one day that I was out, a roe-deer sprang out of the grass before me. I laid on with the whip immediately, and then I let

KEY TO THE TZŬ ERH CHI. **Colloquial Series.**

fly an arrow at him. It fell a little short, and by the time I got my hand behind me to draw out another, I could only just see his tail bobbing, and, in the twinkling of an eye, he was over the crest of the hill and breasting the hill next to it. I gave chase with all the speed I could muster, but he topped the hill and was off down the far slope of it.   2. Well, I kept my horse at it, and, the moment I got well up with the roe-deer, I let fly another arrow, but, this time, over his head. Strange to say, a deer that was coming cantering over the brow of the hill in my direction, stood right into my shot, and down he fell.   3. Such a throw is too good a joke, really; but, as they say, you get a thing always when you least expect it. I may as well keep the story to myself, however, for, if I were to tell it, people would think it was only a traveller's tale.

1. 關東 *kuan-tung*, the country east of the Shan 'Hai Kuan, the barrier which divides Manchuria from China Proper.
2. 尾巴 *i-pa*, the tail; the character *wei* is, in this combination, which is purely colloquial, pronounced *ı*.
3. 山前 *shan ch'ien*, the front, the opposite side, of the hill I was ascending; having passed this, the animal was *wang shang*, ascending, the next hill.
4. 鹿 *lu*, evidently not the same as the *p'ao*, though what other species of deer there is nothing to shew.

LESSON XC.

1. *Senior*. I find it very dull this spring weather, sitting at home all day idle; and I have nothing to do.
2. *Junior*. It is dull, indeed. I went out yesterday with a young brother of mine. He came in and invited me to go outside the walls with him for a stroll, and we went on till we came to a place that was all country, with a distant spring prospect that was really charming. Along the river banks the red peach-blossoms were looking so fresh, and the willow branches so green; all kinds of birds were calling pleasantly in the trees, and a gentle breeze blew the scent of the meadows against one's nostrils. Small craft were moving to and fro without ceasing on the water, and, on both sides of it, people were strolling about in parties of four or five. My brother and I followed a narrow winding path till we reached a spot where the wood was thick, and there all in one *tableau*, we saw before us a group of people, some playing the guitar, some singing, some selling tea and wine; and then, for refreshments, there were live fish and live shrimps to be had, and very cheap. We spent a full day enjoying ourselves. Don't take it ill of me, Sir, that I didn't ask you to accompany us. It wasn't that I wished to conceal our trip from you; but I feared that we might fall in with some one that would be disagreeable to you; so I didn't come to look for you.

1. 曠 *k'uang*⁴, properly, empty, vacant; hence, disused; *k'uang-yeh*, properly, desert and wild, but used of the country in general as distinct from the town.
2. 可愛 *k'o-ngai*; observe the construction; the prospect truly caused people *k'o*, to be justly able, *ngai*, to love it.
3. 桃 *t'ao*², the peach-tree.
4. 柳 *liu*³, the willow-tree.
5. 彈 *t'an*², to touch the strings of an instrument with the finger; to play on a stringed instrument.
6. 蝦 *hsia*¹, shrimps.

LESSON XCI.

1. The day before yesterday we made an excursion to the Western Hills, and I really may say that it was impossible to enjoy anything more. A ramble by day is pleasant enough we know, but it is even more delightful by night.   2. When we had had our dinners, we got into a boat, and, before very long, the moon rose as bright as day. We punted gently down the stream, and, as we came round a point in the hills, there lay a broad sheet of silver before us; sky and water so blended together that there was no saying which was which; hill and stream, too, in perfect repose.   3. We had punted the boat on to a spot where the reeds were thick, when, all of a sudden, the sound of a temple bell was heard, and as it came booming down the wind, one's heart felt as free as if all its cares had been washed away. In short we were in such a state of contentment, that I defy the gods themselves to be happier than we were. There we sat enjoying the thing more and more, and we drank the whole night long without either getting drunk or feeling sleepy.   4. It is but seldom in the course of one's life that one lights on such a moon and such weather; and when one does, it is a pity not to turn them to good account, is it not?

PART VI. THE HUNDRED LESSONS. **T'an Lun P'ien.** LXXXIX–XCIII.

1. 盡興 *chin hsing*, exhaustively pleasurable; *chin*, to exhaust; *hsing* for *kao hsing*, elevation of spirit. See *hao-liao hsing*, towards the end of the third paragraph of this Lesson.
2. 暢 *ch'ang*⁴, properly, to penetrate; to grow, increase; *ch'ang-k'uai*, the sensation of happiness belonging to freedom from care.
3. 撐 *ch'êng*¹, to keep off an assailant with the hand; with a boat, as here, to push with a pole, to punt; *ch'êng-p'o*, to burst, as a box over full.
4. 浩 *'hao*⁴, like a large sheet of water; *'hao-'hao*, sheet-like, *ju yin*, as silver.
5. 蘆葦 *lu*² *-wei*³, reeds, rushes; both may be used independently, as in *lu 'hua*, *wei 'hua*, the flower of such reeds; a reed is *i kên wei-tzŭ*.
6. 悠 *yu*¹, properly, mournful; also, distant, *yu-yu yang-yang*, mournfully spreading.
7. 慮 *lu*⁴, to bethink one, more especially of what is to come, to be anxious about, forethoughtful.
8. 皆 *chieh*¹, all; only used colloquially in some few combinations.
9. 出世 *ch'u shih*, not who have died, but who have left this world and become spirits.
10. 朗 *lang*³, bright.
11. 致 *chih*⁴, a word of many meanings; in books most commonly to cause, in which sense it occurs colloquially in the combination *i chih*, whereby was occasioned, the result of which was, hence, the cause, occasion; but, here, its sense is form, or appearance, *ching*, see LESSON LXV, 10, *ching-chih*, scenery, landscape.
12. 徒 *t'u*², originally, to walk on foot, also, empty; hence, *t'u jan*, in vain, to no purpose.
13. 度 *tu*⁴, to cross over, pass through; *hsu-tu*, vainly to pass; used humbly, elsewhere, in stating one's age; I have vainly passed so many years, here, *t'u jan hsu tu*, means to have passed by without availing one's self of.

LESSON XCII.

1. The day before yesterday we went out, a few of us, for a stroll, and, turn which way we would, we got into difficulty. First of all, as we left the city, we got off the right road, and made a round, I can't tell you where. However, by dint of asking here and inquiring there as we went along, we did hit the canal-lock. There we seated ourselves in a boat, and chatted and hobnobbed until we had dropped down to *Tung 'Hua Yuan*. Here we turned back, but by the time we reached the lock, the sun was well down.   2. So, as soon as dinner was over, I said to them all, "Gentlemen, we had better be off. The servants have all got to walk, and it's a long way home." Not a bit of it; nobody would stir; and there they sat on, talking and laughing, until, by-and-bye, they saw that it was close to sunset, and then they got on their horses and began to ride back as hard as they could.   3. By the time they reached the suburb, there was a slight glimmer of moonlight, and the people coming out of the city were all crying out, Make haste! and telling us that one leaf of the gate was shut to already. This made us more anxious than ever, and we laid on with the whip and pressed our horses up to the wall; but the rear of the party was shut out all the same.   4. It was certainly an expedition with a merry beginning and a sorrowful termination.

1. 受罪 *shou tsui*, literally, to receive punishment; here, to come to grief.
2. 放著 *fang-cho*, we let go our hold of *chêng-ching tao*, the proper or regular road.
3. 閘 *cha*², a lock in a canal, *cha-k'ou*, the points on the river bank at which the locks lie; *q.d.* their ports. See DIAL. VIII, 21.
4. 儘自 *chin-tzŭ*, not of the persons' will, but of their act; they sat on and on.
5. 恍惚 *huang*³ *-'hu*¹, properly, of indecision of mind, of which it is often used; but often, as here, of the struggling light of the sun and moon.
6. 加 *chia*¹, properly, to add to, but often employed, as here, for the verb *to use*.
7. 乘 *ch'êng*, literally, riding on, *hsing*, a merry, exalted, state of mind; *sao hsing*, having swept that state away.

LESSON XCIII.

1. *Visitor.* It's dreadfully hot. I suspect it's the very hottest day we have had this summer; there is not a breath of wind stirring. Everything in the house is so burning, it scorches one's hand to touch it, and the more cold water one drinks the thirstier one feels. I could see nothing else for it, so I took a bath, and after cooling myself a little while in the shade of the trees, I felt somewhat more at my ease. But you; what are you about? On a fiery day like this, when every one else is sitting stripped to the middle in dread of the heat, there you are seated writing, with your head down to the table. What sin did you commit before you were born? Do you intend to kill yourself?

KEY TO THE TZŬ ERH CHI. Colloquial Series.

2. *Host.* This is all very fine talk for idlers like you, who have no business to do, and who just take your ease from one year's end to the other. But what do you say to the pedlars, for instance, who, in order to earn a hundred cash or so to keep them alive, have to run about in all directions carrying great loads, with their backs bending under their weight, and their necks stretched out, crying their wares till the perspiration runs off them like rain? Are they as well off as I am here, writing at any pace that suits me, and with wherewithal to live upon? Besides, it is the rule, and it always has been, that the summer should be hot and the winter should be cold. Let it be as hot as it will, put up with it quietly, and perhaps you may light on a cool moment. As the proverb says, "It will be cool, if you only determine it shall be." But you won't escape the heat, if you let it put you out at all, remember.

1. 立夏 *li-hsia*, the commencement of summer, one of the twenty-four fortnightly terms, into which the Chinese year is divided.
2. 頭一 *t'ou-i;* construe, the number one hot of days, the hottest of days; had the speaker meant the first hot day we have had, he would have said, *t'ou i t'ien ts'ai jo*.
3. 光著 *kuang-cho*, bare, naked.
4. 暑 *shu*³, sun-heat; *chung*, to hit as a mark; *chung-shu*, to get a fever, suffer from heat.
5. 孽 *nieh*⁴, the earliest sprouts of any vegetation; *tsui nieh*, the punishment incurred, according to the Buddhists, for sin in a previous state of existence.
6. 吆喝 *yao*¹ *-'ho*⁴, not used apart; to cry wares, &c. in the street; also to call to a person to desist, or to go away.
7. 易 *yi*, or *i*, used in EXERC. XXXVI, 11, as easy; here, to change.

LESSON XCIV.

1. *Host.* Hallo! Where have you been to in such rain as this? Come in directly.
2. *Traveller.* I have been attending the funeral of a friend. The morning was dull, still, though it looked rather like rain at that time, the day was perfectly fine at noon; so I went. But, as we were on our way back, I saw the clouds begin little by little to gather, and in no time the whole sky was overcast. So I said to my people, I don't like the look of the weather; get on with you or we shall be caught in the rain. Well, as I was speaking, down it came with a rush, Sir. There wasn't much chance of shelter, as you may suppose, out there in the open country, and, as I couldn't get on my felt coat, or my waterproof, quick enough, I was wet through from head to foot.
3. *Host.* Never mind; change your clothes; I will give you some of mine to put on, and, as it's so late, you had better not go into the city till to-morrow. I have nothing much worth eating in this out-of-the-way corner; still, I have got some little pigs and chickens of our own rearing, and we'll kill one or two for your supper.
4. *Traveller.* Oh! no excuses, pray, on the score of my fare, Sir. I'm lucky enough, I'm sure, to have found so snug a billet to rest in. I don't see how I could have helped facing the rain otherwise.

1. 響 *hsiang*³, brightness; also, sound, in which sense, according to some authorities, it is here used with reference to the sound of the ground on a clear day; whether as bright or ringing, it is intensive of *ch'ing*, clear, fine.
2. 稠 *ch'ou*², thick, as grain growing close together. 3. 涮 *shua*¹, the sound of falling rain; it has no other meaning.
4. 氈 *chan*¹, felt, or any like fabric. 5. 樓 *ch'i*¹, to roost like birds; *ch'i shên*, to rest the body, set one's self down.
6. 冒著 *mao-cho*, running the head against; *'han p'a*, is it indeed probable, that I could have gone on without facing the rain.

LESSON XCV.

1. I got an awful frightening last night. I had had quite enough of this succession of dismal days. What with a leak here and damp there, there was not a place in the whole house one could lie down in without getting wet. 2. And then the mosquitoes, the bugs, and the fleas, together were so intolerable that there was no getting to sleep. There I lay tumbling and tossing about without having slept a wink until after morning bells. I then closed my eyes deliberately, and in the course of a little time I was dropping off, when, just as I was half asleep, I was roused by a tremendous crash to the north-west of the house, that sounded as if a mountain had collapsed, or the earth been rent asunder. I lay ever so long trembling with fear and my heart going pit-a-pat, until at last I opened my eyes, and seeing that nothing in the room had been injured, I sent out to ascertain what was the matter, and was told that it was the end wall of a neighbour's house that had come down, undermined by the rain. 3. Dear me! it's something beyond a sleeping-man's powers of endurance, an uproar like that.

PART VI. THE HUNDRED LESSONS. T'an Lun P'ien. XCIII–XCVII.

1. 厭 熟 *hsin shou*, it was no longer a novelty; observe *hsia tê*, raining it had attained to, had rained until, &c.
2. 蚊 *wên*², musquitoes, gnats; *ch'ou ch'ung*, stinking insects, sc. bugs.
3. 虼 蚤 *ko*⁴ *·tsao*³, fleas; *ko* is a character not recognised by the dictionaries; *tsao*, in books, is used alone.
4. 叮 *ting*¹, properly, of talk that bores one; worried me *tê*, to such a degree that, it was really hard to bear them.
5. 忍 了 *jên liao*, I bore it; *jên* is influenced by *ch'iang*; perforce I closed my eyes, and perforce I bore the annoyance a little while.
6. 崩 *pêng*¹, the sound of a mountain overthrown or collapsing; used classically of the death of an emperor. [while.
7. 响 *hsiang*³, to sound; properly written as in LESSON XCIV, 1, but with the 180th Radical under it instead of *hsiang*.
8. 陡 *tou*³, colloquially, of heights, precipitous, descending abruptly; *tou-jan*, suddenly.
9. 突 *t'u*, properly, to come upon unawares; to butt against; *t'u-t'u-ti*, knock, knock, as water bubbling up from a spring; here, of one's heart.
10. 山 牆 *shan ch'iang*, the hill-shaped wall, the gable of a house.
11. 震 *chên*⁴, the shock of a clap of thunder, or to shock like one; how *chiug-tê-ch'i*, could a man go through, the shock of such a sound.

LESSON XCVI.

1. Yesterday morning when I got up, it was so dark I thought the sun could not have risen yet. I stepped out into the court to look, and I saw that it was daylight, but that the sky was as black as pitch. However, I washed my hands and face, and I was going to start for the *yamên*, when it began to spit, and soon after I heard it pouring; so I sat down again, and I might have been seated time enough to drink a cup of tea, when there came a clap of thunder, followed by a fall of water just as if some one had upset a basin. I thought it was too violent a rain to last very long, and that I would wait a little, and start when it held up. But I was quite out; it rained all day and all night without stopping; nor was it till after breakfast this morning that the sun began to show himself a little. It's fine seasonable rain though, for all that. I should think the ground is well saturated everywhere. The autumn crops are certain to be fair.

1. 霹 *p'i*¹, the sound of a clap of thunder; not used alone.
2. 雷 *lei*², thunder; *p'i-lei*, combines the ideas of the suddenness and loudness of a clap of thunder.
3. 傾 *ch'ing*², to turn out the contents of anything by upsetting it; *ch'ing p'ên*, a bowl upset.

LESSON XCVII.

1. It was so cold the night before last that it woke me up, and I lay awake till morning. The moment it was light I jumped out of bed, and on opening the door to take a look, I found the whole place glittering white with snow. 2. About eleven o'clock, after I had breakfasted, it began to snow harder; the flakes grew larger and larger, and came fluttering wavily down. Said I to myself, "I've nothing to do. I wish a friend would drop in for a chat; how is this to be managed?" 3. To my great delight, just at that very moment, in came the servants and announced some visitors. I told them to put out something to eat and drink, and to light a pan of charcoal. Then I made haste and asked my friends to walk in, which they did. The wine and other things that were ready were brought in, and we sat sipping our liquor without hurrying ourselves, until by-and-bye we had the door-curtain rolled well up to see how things looked, and there before us was a superb snow-scene that beat anything one had ever beheld. The snow was falling thick in all directions; hill, stream, and woods, all white with it. The sight made us jollier than ever. We got out the chess-board and played two games, and after dinner, just as it was dusk, our party broke up.

1. 飄 *p'iao*¹, to whirl round as wind.
2. 颻 *yao*², the same as *p'iao*, unless combined with which it is not found.
3. 爐 *lung*², to prepare a stove; make a fire.
4. 簾 *lien*², a curtain or screen, properly of split bamboo, but also used of those composed of other materials.
5. 雅 *ya*³, of anything that is nice, refined; *ch'ing-ya*, may be said of scenery, of the interior of a house, &c.; the snow-scene, as compared with anything, was fine.
6. 紛 *fên*¹, in numbers and in confusion.
7. 棋 盤 *ch'i p'an*, would be a chess board; *i p'an ch'i*, a set of chessmen; *hsia-liao i p'an*, played one game.

KEY TO THE TZŬ ERH CHI. **Colloquial Series.**

LESSON XCVIII.

1. Yesterday we were all at the *yamên*, and it was a fine clear day without a breath of wind. All of a sudden, the sun began to look gloomy, and I said to the rest of them, "I don't like the look of the weather; we are going to have a blow, and we had best be off." They all thought so too, and we broke up accordingly. 2. I had just reached home when the storm began in earnest. The way in which the blast roared through the trees was something awful, and this continued until after midnight, when the wind lulled a little. 3. But as I was coming here this morning I remarked that every one I met was doubled up with the cold. People were all hissing and blowing, and running to keep themselves warm. 4. As for me I got on pretty well at first, for I had my back to the wind; but when I came to breast it, the cold set my cheeks and my whole face tingling as if they had been pricked with needles. My fingers grew so stiff that I couldn't hold my whip; and my very spittle became ice before it could reach the ground, and broke in pieces as it fell. 5. Never did anybody in all his life see such cold.

1. 慘 淡 *ts'an tan*, of weather, gloomy; *ts'an*, of the sky, sad; *tan*, of the sun's rays, weak.
2. 吸 *hsi*¹, the sound of drawing the breath in, *'ha*, here, the sound of the breath emitted.
3. 攣 *lien*⁴, of the fingers stiffening; *chu-lien*, so stiff that they could not *chu*, keep their hold of anything.
4. 跌 碎 *tieh-sui*, broke in pieces as it fell.

LESSON XCIX.

1. Man stands highest of all created beings, as being possessed of reason. If he did not know good from evil, if he could not understand the rule of right, wherein would he differ from the beasts? 2. Well, in the relations of friends, the right rule is that each should treat the other with proper respect, is it not? That I should show a certain deference to you, and you to me? 3. Now, this fellow, ever since he has arrived this time, has been bullying and over-bearing on all occasions; giving people whatever bad language came into his head. Whether he thinks this clever, or what else may be the meaning of his conduct, I can't say; but just look at the man with that ill-favoured phiz of his and his large paunch; and to think that a genius like that has the pretension to imagine himself a man of education, is enough to make one's flesh creep. Then his voice is more like a dog's bark than anything else; it disgusts people so that they can't bear to hear him speak. 4. If he had any of the proper sentiments a man ought to have, he would feel how unpopular his way of talking makes him; but, no, not a bit of it, he bears himself as if it made everybody like him, and he was all the more contented in consequence. I can't understand it. 5. His father was always a good enough kind of man when he was alive. What sin could he have committed before he was born, to breed such a good-for-nothing as this? However, there's nothing before him now; his father expended all the luck of the family. He has come to the end of his tether, and as for rising any higher, as he expects, I should like to know how he is to compass it.

1. 畜 *ch'u*⁴, originally, to breed or rear; domestic animals; *ch'u-shêng*, animals, not being wild animals; here, the beasts of the [field.
2. 豪 *'hao*², among other meanings, eminent by prowess, heroic; here, in a bad sense.
3. 橫 *'hêng*⁴, see *'hêng*², EXERC. XL, 12; here, morally what *'hêng* is materially; *'hao-'hêng*, the qualities of a bully.
4. 信 著 *hsin-cho*, trusting to; *q. d.* leaving it to his mouth, *'hun ma*, at random to abuse, people.
5. 嘴 巴 *tsui-pa*, properly, the cheeks; *tsui-pa ku-tzŭ*, the jaw-bones; here used for the whole face, that face being ill-looking.
6. 臌 *ku*³, to bulge out, as paper, a wall, &c.; here, of the person.
7. 傻 *sha*³, properly, a sharp-fellow; but colloquially, always the reverse.
8. 肉 麻 *jou ma*, the flesh creeping; *ma*, elliptically representing *ma mu*, hemp-seed and wood, used for inanimate matter; hence, the affection of a foot asleep, or a palsied limb which is *ma mu*.
9. 腆 *t'ien*³, thick, substantial, here, of the skin of the face; brazening it out, he *pu chih ch'ih*, is insensible to shame.
10. 興 頭 *hsing-t'ou*, happiness, contentedness; *hsing*, as in *kao-hsing*, LESSON XCI, 1; a man's *hsing-t'ou* may be *'hao*, or *pu-'hao*; that is, he may be contented or discontented.
11. 福 分 *fu fên*, the amount of happiness allotted [his family], his father *hsiang chin*, enjoyed to exhaustion.
12. 結 果 *chieh kuo*, he has formed into fruit; *q. d.* he has done blooming, he has come to the end of his career.
13. 陞 騰 *shêng-t'êng*, to rise; *sc.* as an official.

54

PART VI. THE HUNDRED LESSONS. T'an Lun P'ien. XCXVIII-C.

LESSON C.

1. What do you mean by leading such a life as this? All you do of a day is to fill your belly, and then to take up your guitar, or your lute, and go on strumming upon it for no purpose that I can make out. Do you propose to make yourself famous by your guitar playing, or are you going to get your bread by it? 2. We have the luck to be Manchus, and as such we have Government rice to eat, and Government money monthly to spend. Our quarters, from the roof that covers our families to the ground that is under our feet, are all our master's. We owe him some return then; and when a man, while he neglects the acquisition of things right and proper for him to learn, and displays no zeal in the discharge of his duty, devotes himself heart and soul to such an accomplishment as this guitar-playing, he is a disgrace to the name of Manchu. Surely it would be better worth your while to be studying than expending all the best powers of your mind on a subject of this sort. 3. Recollect that the proverb says, "It is as much the mission of man to rise as it is the property of water to descend;" and remember that, however great proficiency you may achieve on the guitar, you won't escape the repute of being a dirty low-caste individual. Will your ability to play the guitar avail you as a qualification when you come to be pitted against other competitors for office, pray? 4. Certainly not; and if I am not speaking the truth, perhaps you'll name some one high in rank or office who owes his first appointment to his skill on the guitar, will you?

1. 琵琶 *p'i*² -*p'a*¹, a certain stringed instrument.
2. 絃 *hsien*², also a musical instrument; *t'an*, to play, either on it, or on the *p'i-p'a*; see LESSON XC, 5.
3. 頭頂 *t'ou-ting*, what my head rises to, *sc* my roof, *chiao tz'ŭ*, what my foot treads, *sc*. my floor.
4. 鑽著 *tsuan-cho*, burrowing with, *sc*. the mind.
5. 玷 *tien*⁴, a blemish, as on a jewel.
6. 污 *wu*¹, foul; *pei-wu*, mean and dirty.
7. 出身 *ch'u shên*, to commence an official career.

END OF KEY TO PART VI.

PART VII. THE TONE EXERCISES. Lien-hsi Yen Shan P'ing-Tsê Pien.

The following Part, as described by its Chinese title, is *pien*, a compilation, *lien-hsi*, for practice in, *p'ing-tsê*, the tone system, *lit*, the smooth and the deflected tones in vogue, in the metropolitan department of *Shun-t'ien Fu*, classically distinguished as *Yen Shan*. It will be seen that page 219 repeats, in the same order, but, for practice sake, without the orthography, the table of characters given on pages 8 – 11 of Part I, as representing the Sounds of the Dialect. Let these be denominated, for the moment, Sound Index characters. In the succeeding pages of the part before us will be found a Chinese text in columns headed each one by a Sound Index character, having immediately below it a note of its meaning in Chinese; below this note, a series of four places, some occupied by characters, some blank, which represent the Tone Classes, or changes of tone to which each Syllabic Sound is liable, and may therefore be called the Tone Scale; and below the Tone Scale, a corresponding series of short exercises in the Tones. The Sound Indices are ranged from left to right in their original numerical order, but if the student be at any time at fault, his search will be farther guided by the numbers placed under every fifth character, which refer him to the Sound Table in Part I.

The note explaining the sense of the Sound Index is composed in accordance with a Chinese method of illustration which cannot be too soon taken into account; I have enlarged upon its importance in the Preface. And now as regards the Tone Scale: where the *yin*, sound, represented by the Sound Index, is common to *tzŭ*, written words, in all the four tones, the Tone Scale exhibits four characters, of which the Sound Index is one, placed in the order of the Tones; the *shang p'ing* taking the upper place in the series, the *hsia p'ing*, the second, and so on. Where no *tzŭ* is to be found under a particular tone, the interruption of the series is marked by a circle. If the student listen carefully to the teacher reading the Tone Scale of one Syllable after another, he will not be long, unless his ear is unusually defective, in catching the chime of the Tones, and, this once caught, he will soon habituate himself to determine the Tone of any *tzŭ* that he may hear pronounced for the first time.

The short exercises which follow the Tone Scale, are composed of the words given in the Scale, combined each with one or more such words as they most ordinarily accompany. The text of these is repeated in the Key with orthography and tone marks, and a careful translation. As the combination given in the explanatory Chinese note appended to each Sound Index, is itself always one of the exercises, its meaning must be looked for amongst the translations of these.

It is scarcely requisite that anything more should be said as to the manner of using these exercises or upon their utility. Different ears are differently accommodated, and it will appear to some that the law and practice of the Tones is more satisfactorily understood from the study of examples of greater length, and unrestricted by the regular sequence here observed. Nothing can be simpler in such a case than to convert any number of short sentences out of Parts III, IV, or V, more particularly the last, into tone exercises, with the aid of a native speaker. Without the assistance of the latter, acquisition of the Tones is a pure impossibility.

The Tone Scale has been made to include the entire Sound Table within its limits, for the express purpose of enabling the student to test for himself the influence of Tone upon the independent Syllabic Sound. From the notes in the order of the Finals appended to these observations, he will perceive that this modification is often such as almost if not fully to justify us in representing the syllabic change effected by the Tone as a distinct Syllabic Sound; but that our alphabet is hardly equal to the emergency, this distinction would have been attempted in the Peking Syllabary. It remains to direct attention to certain departures from the rule prescribed by the Tone Scale, to which the Syllabic Sound is subject when it is not independent, but connected with other Sounds, whether as part of dissyllable, or of a longer combination.

To take the last first. The student will recall the few words said about Rhythm in page 7 of Part I. Now let him turn to the Chinese text of Part VI, and get his teacher to enunciate rapidly the words *t'ou i tsung-'rh-yao-chin-ti shih-ch'ing*, the first and foremost of essentials, at the foot of the first column, or the words *ko-ch'u-'rh-ko-ch'u-'rh-ti hsiang-t'an*, particular dialect, in the second column; or let him take *'huang-'huang-'rh chang-lo chang-lo*, to lend a hand every now and then, (Part V, Section iii, 2,) or *kên chih-ti shih-ti chê-mo ch'ing-ch'iao*, as light and little bulky as paper, (Section iv, 4). He will see, if he watch the speaker's voice carefully, that, even though he may be unable to declare that this or that syllable has quite passed to a new place in the Tone Scale, the syllables first uttered are not uttered with the full Tone belonging to them as

KEY TO THE TZŬ ERH CHI. Colloquial Series.

independent syllables. This need not alarm him. Tone is to the Chinese monosyllable pretty much what Quantity is to the individual syllable in Latin. As we shall presently see, its primitive or natural conditions are so affected by position, that change of position will, in some cases, produce entire change of Tone. But, rhythmically, in long combinations such as I have instanced, and especially in attributive and adverbial constructions, there is a modulation of the voice that is not to be defined by the Tone Scale, and which nothing but practice can teach; just as rules of prosody will carry us only a certain length in Latin. It is impossible that such words as *Constantīnŏpŏlĭtānus*, *mĕmŏrābĭlĭă*, *văgābūndŭs*, should have been articulated without a rhythmical emphasis more or less at variance with the apparent prescriptions of prosody. The prosody of our own vowels is the sport of circumstances, still the fluctuation in the value of the vowels in *analysis* and *analytical*, *meteorology* and *meteorological*, is somewhat analogous to that which we are here considering.

In the matter of just accentuation, therefore, the memory will be greatly relieved, if the language be treated, whenever construction will admit of it, as polysyllabic. The individual Syllabic Sound should be ticketed, so to speak, by its Tone, as the syllable in a Latin word is by its quantity, and that it may not be forgotten, the Syllabary should be frequently consulted; but, in speaking, the student may safely endeavour to reproduce any sound that forms part of a more than a dissyllabic combination, rather with reference to correct rhythmical emphasis of the whole polysyllable, than to strict accordance with the tone-quantity of its component parts.

A change of meaning in the *tzŭ*, monosyllabic word, in some cases involves a change of the *yin*, syllabic sound, in some, the *yin* is retained but the Tone changes. In dissyllabic combinations, where the two words combined belong, as independent syllables, to the same Tone Class, the tone of the first or second is disturbed; in some cases slightly, in some so much as to authorise the relegation of the word to a Tone Class not properly its own. The following combinations read aloud will shew to what extent the Tone in different places of the Scale will be affected under the conditions adverted to.

1. 山西 shan¹ hsi¹ west of the hills, (the province so named)
   西山 hsi¹ shan¹ the western hills
   當差 tang¹ ch‘ai¹ to be employed officially
   珍珠 chên¹ chu¹ pearls

2. 湖南 'hu² nan² south of the lake, (the province so named.)
   南湖 nan² 'hu² the southern lake
   衙門 ya² mên² a public office
   銀錢 yin² ch‘ien² money in general

3. 起早 ch‘i³ tsao³ early in the morning
   洗臉 hsi³ lien³ to wash the face
   小馬 hsiao³ ma³ a small horse
   馬小 ma³ hsiao³ the horse is small

4. 日月 jih⁴ yueh⁴ days and moons
   數目 shu⁴ mu⁴ a number
   算計 suan⁴ chi⁴ to reckon.
   志向 chih⁴ hsiang⁴ ambition

Under the 1st Tone, I consider the voice to fall in the second syllable in *Shan Hsi*, but to be lower on *hsi* than on *shan* in *Hsi Shan*; to rise on the second syllable of *tang-ch‘ai*, and to fall on the second in *chên chu*. Under the 2nd Tone, the abruptness with which the syllable closes is to me much more apparent in the last syllable than in the first. But the native teachers will not admit, in either case, that the Tone is modified. Under the 3rd, the change is more remarkable; the first syllable is changed nearly if not quite to the 2nd Tone; still, there is a manifest limitation proper to particular vowels. If you make a native repeat hsiao³ ma³, ma³ hsiao³, a certain number of times, you will perceive that the voice rises and falls as if the words were accented hsiáo mā, mā hsiào. Where three words are joined, as in *wu³ tou³ mi³*, five bushels of rice, the last is the only one which is sounded with a full 3rd Tone; in *tsao³ ch‘i³ hsi³ lien³*, to wash the face in the morning, the Tone of *ch‘i* certainly differs from that of *tsao*, but *lien* is the only word of the four that preserves the full 3rd Tone. Under the 4th Tone, the voice descends in the second syllable, but not so pronouncedly as under the 3rd Tone. Different examples will shew that this inflection, again, is more evident with some vowels than with others; but double the suan⁴ in suan-chi, and you will still find the second *suan* in *suan-suan*, to reckon, lower in key than the first, although the difference detected does not transfer the syllable to any other of the four Tones in the Scale; and it is only of these four that a native speaker conceives our dialect capable.

The words *tzŭ, erh*, appended to nouns, *ti*, following both nouns and verbs, and *liao* corrupted to *la* and *lo*, also after verbs, but more frequently at the end of a sentence, cannot be allowed, while in this enclitic relation to other words, to belong to any Class in the Tone Scale; but, when not enclitics, they reassert their rights; as in *tzŭ³ sun¹*, posterity, *erh² ma³*, a stallion, *ti² ch‘io⁴*, positively, *liao³ shih⁴*, to finish an affair. The word *cho²* when enclitic becomes *cho⁴*.

PART VII. THE TONE EXERCISES. Lien-hsi Yen Shàn P'ing-Tsê Pien.

a.—Under the 1st tone, the *shang-p'ing*, the *a* is sounded somewhat as in *ant*, *yarn*, *mast*, very slowly pronounced. Under the 2d, the *hsia-p'ing*, shorter and sharper, as in *artful*, *architect*. Under the 3d, the *shang*, the *a*, commencing as under the *shang-p'ing*, gradually descends and then suddenly rises; the vowels in the words *aha! papa*, with the italicised consonants dropped, give some idea of the effect of this tone on the terminal *a*. Under the 4th tone, the *ch'u*, the vowel sound begins on a higher key than under the *shang-p'ing*, and descends immediately, not protracted, but *diminuendo*; as it were, A-A-A.

ai.—Under the 1st tone, the two vowels in *ai* are pronounced in nearly equal time; the latter if anything quicker than the other. Under the 2d, the *i* prevails, as when a speaker ejaculates *ay?* implying surprise and doubt. In the 3d, it is on *a* that the voice descends, and on *i* that it remounts; the vowel sound produced somewhat resembling that in *careen*. In the 4th tone, the voice dwells on the *a*; the latter part of the diphthong being, if I may use the expression, enclitic; as though it were written *áa-y*.

an.—The remarks on *a* are generally applicable to this final, except that, in the 2d tone, the inflection of the vowel is more apparent; if indeed the vowel itself does not become a diphthong.

ao.—In this final the *a* and *o* are uttered in the 1st tone, as in *ai*, with a slight degree more prolongation of the *a* than of the *o*. Under the 2d tone, *ao* is almost *áu*, or *áoo*; indeed in the words *ao* or *ngao*, it is nearly *ou* in *loud*. Under the 3d tone, as the voice rises on the *o*, that vowel becomes nearly *au*, *aw*, in *caul*, *brawl*. Under the 4th tone, the *a* claims again the longer utterance, the *o* figuring but enclitically, as it were *aa..ŏ*.

eh.—The only syllable in which this final is found is *yeh*. In the 1st tone it might be written *ieh*, and, as in the case of *ai*, *ao*, the voice is evenly distributed over both parts of the diphthong; but, in the 2d, the *y* is an undoubted consonant, and the syllable, simply *ye* in *yet*. In the 3d, there is the double vowel sound noticed before, commencing as though the sound to be uttered were *yea*, but rising suddenly to the sound of the *e* in *yet*. In the 4th tone, the sound is a prolonged declining *yea*. It might be otherwise expressed by Y-E-E-E

ê or o.—It is under the 2d tone that the *ê* approaches the *o* in *lot*, *top*. In the rest it is nearer the vowel sound of *learn*, *sir*, *earth*, *terse*. In the 3d and 4th tones, the reduplication of the vowel sound is apparent; as if *lê*, for instance, were written *léê*, *lê-ê-ê*.

ên.—The vowel is reduplicated in the 3d and 4th tones. Try to intone the word *upper*, in the key of the 3d and 4th tones, and then drop the consonants; the *u-ê* remaining give a fair idea of the vowel sound required.

erh.—There is properly no *shang-p'ing* tone in this sound, but, as will be seen in many instances, the vowel sound of *êrh*, when placed in enclitic relation to a word preceding it, is absorbed more or less in the vowel sound of that word. The tone is also modified. It was called by the compiler of the Syllabary a *shang p'ing*, in preference to any other tone, although he allowed that, in strictness, the *êrh*, with its new sound, did not belong to any one of the four classes. In my opinion, the fusion modifies the tone, not only of the *êrh* itself, but also of the word to which it is attached.

i.—The independent sound *i*, is frequently also *yi*, but the *y* is not so apparent, if it appear at all, in the *shang p'ing*, as in the other tones. The student must beware of shortening the *i* of the *hsia-p'ing* into *ih*. The vowel preserves its length, the difference between its sound in the 1st and 2d tones being faintly represented by that in *cheer* and *peep*. In the 3d, the *i* is inflected, rising as if *ee-ih*; in the 4th, as if *ee..e.e*.

ia.—In the 1st tone, the *i* is distinct though not so prominent as the *a*. In the 2d, the *a* is rather more prominent; *chia*², sounding *chya*. In the 3d, *chia*³, sounds *cheeah*; in the *chia*⁴, is almost *chéyaa*.

iang.—The remarks on *ia* apply equally to *iang*; but in the syllables *liang*, *niang*, the *i* in the 1st, 3d, and 4th tones, is often much nearer *ey*. In the 2d tones, it is almost *y* consonantal, *lyang*², *nyang*².

iao.—The remarks on *ao*, *ia*, and *iang*, apply to the effect of tone on this final. In the 1st, 3d, and 4th, tones, especially in the syllables *liao*, *niao*, the *i* becomes almost *ey*; in the 2nd, it is *y*, the *ao* becoming a sound between *aoo* and *ow*.

ieh.—As in *ia*, in the 1st tone, the first vowel and the second are articulated distinctly one from the other, and with nearly equal stress. In the 2d tone, the *i* becomes *y*, and in 3d and 4th, nearly *ey*. Thus the changes in *ch'ieh* might be expressed thus:— *ch'iyeh*, *ch'yeh*, *ch'eyeh*, *ch'éyeh*. In *lieh*, *mieh*, *nieh*, in all except the 2d tone, usage seems very capricious; the same native sounding *i* at one time as *ee*, and at another as *ey*.

ien.—The remarks regarding the vowel *i* in *ieh* apply equally to the *i* in *ien*. The *en* is nearly as uncertain as the *an* in *uan*, frequently becoming *an*, under the 3d, and yet more frequently under the 4th tone.

ih.—The difference between the *i* in the 1st, and that in the 2d tone, is faintly represented by that between the same vowels in *children* and *chip*. In the other two it is inflected as in *a*, *ê*, &c.; beginning like the *ee* in *cheek*, and rising suddenly to the *i* in *ill*, then descending gradually in the 4th. Drop the consonants in the word *limit*, and prolong the utterance of the latter vowel to form some idea of the sound of the final *ih*⁴.

in.—As in *ih*. Take the vowel sound in *thin*, *thick*, as approaching those under the 1st and 2d tones and unite the vowel sounds in the first two syllables of *initial*, for the 3d, and of *incident* for the 4th, tone.

io.—When preceeded by *hs* and *l*, this final is, in Peking, as often *uo*, or *ueh*, as *io*; after *n* more rarely. Under the 3d tone, *lio* is pronounced *li-ó*, under the 4th, *nio* is rather *nyó-ó-ó*.

iu.—In the 1st tone the two sounds *ee* and *oo*, of which *iu* is compounded, are distinct and even, as in *ai*, *aó*, *ia*. In the 2d, the *iu* is nearly *yew*, but shorter; as though written *yeuh*. In the 3d, the voice descends on the *ee*, to rise sharply on the *ooh*, and in the 4th, dwells on the *ee*, and breaks off on the *oo* in a lower key.

KEY TO THE TZŬ ERH CHI. Colloquial Series.

iung.—This syllable is only found in the 1st and 2d tones. The vowel *i* is not so distinct as in *ia*, *ieh*; in the 1st tone and in the 2d, *i* is nearly *y*; read *hsiung* ², almost *syung*. The *u*, or *oo*, sound inclines to *ó* in *home*, in the 1st, but is *oo* in the 2d tone, and pronounced short as if the final *g* were nearly a *k*, or a French nasal.

o.—In the 1st tone the *o* is nearly as in *roll*; in the 2nd, it is shorter as in *shot*; a slight reduplication of the vowel sound following, somewhat as if it were *oóh*. In the 3d tone, a second vowel is also perceptible, but rather resembling *á*. In the 4th, the change of vowel is very slightly felt, the dominant sound being *o*, which is prolonged *diminuendo*. In the single *o*, or *ngo*, the nasal pronunciation of it, much as it modifies the vowel sound, does not affect the tone.

ou.—In the 1st tone, *ou* is much as in *round*; in the 2d, shortened as in *lout*, but with a certain inflexion as though it were *owoo*, or *owuh*. This is more clear in the 3d and 4th tone, which might be expressed *où-óo* ³, *oŭ-oo* ⁴.

ü—In the 1st tone the *ü* as in the French *pureté*; in the second, as in the French *tut*, *salut*. In the 3d and 4th, the reduplication and inflection of the vowel noticed in *a*, *i*, *o*, is perceptible, as though *u*³ were *ü-uh*, and *u*⁴, *ü - u - - u*.

üan.—This presents the same difficulties as *ien*, so far as the vowel *a* is concerned. The *a* of the 1st tone, pronounced sometimes broad as in the syllables ending in *an*, is flattened sometimes to the *a* in *mat*, and sometimes modified so as to be nearly the *e* in *then*; *uen* is the orthography of Morrison and others. The native who was my guide, whatever might be his pronunciation under the 1st, made little difference under the 2d, uttering the *an* as in the English *can*, *mantle*. In the 3d, the uncertainty between *a* and *e* is greater than in the 4th tone, which prefers the *a*. In both, the vowels are distinguished much as in *ia*, *ieh*, &c.; as it were *uan* ³, *uaan* ⁴.

ueh.—In the 1st tone, the voice pauses evenly on *u* and *eh*, which last vowel is pronounced as in *sentry*; in the 2d, *eh* is as in *set*, and is much clearer than the *u*. In the 3d, the *eh* of the 1st tone is prolonged, the *u* shortened; in the 4th, the *u* is more prominent to the ear, and the stress of the voice is laid upon it, but the *eh* is very prolonged.

ün.—The *u*¹ is the French *une*; in *un*² the vowel sound resembles that in *lutte*, slightly inflected, as if an *i* very faint, and rapidly pronounced, intervened between *u* and *n*. In *un*³, and *un*⁴, there is the reduplication of the vowel before noticed.

u.—The *u*¹ resembles *oo* in *coon*; the *u*², *oo* in *cook*. In *u*³, *u*⁴, the vowel is reduplicated like *a*, *i*, *o*, above; *u*³, as if *ù-üh*; *u*⁴, as *ŭ-uh*, or *oo-ooh*.

ua.—In the 1st tone, the *ua*, is certainly nearly *óá*; in the 2d, the *o* almost disappears, becoming *oo*, *u*, or *w*; in the 3d, it is again apparent, prominence being given to the *a*, or *ah*, which is very short; in the 4th, it seems to depend on the initial consonants which vowel shall be sounded; *shua* ⁴ sounds *shóaa*, but *hua* ⁴ is *'hiaa*.

uai.—What applies to *ua* is more or less true of *uai*, so far as the *u* is concerned; but, in the 1st tone, the division is between *u* and the diphthong *ai*; in the 2d, *u* is consonantal and *ai* shortened; in the 3d, the voice descends on *u* and rises sharp on *a*; to which *i* is enclitic; in the 4th, the voice rises on the *u*, and dies away on the *ai*, dwelling more on the first vowel. In the 1st, 3d, and 4th tones, *u* might often be *o*, and in the 2nd, *w*.

uan.—The division of the vowel sounds is as in *ua*. In the 3d tone, the final is almost *ówán*; in the 4th, *óan*, like *awn*, in *awning*, or *ohn*, in the German *ohne*.

uei.—In the 1st tone, the vowel sounds are nearly *oowei*; in the 2d, *wey*; in the 3d *oò-w.é.i*; in the 4th, *óo-w.e.i*; the *i* leaning enclitically on the *e*. The *u* in all four tones in *kuei* is nearer *w* than in '*hui*.

uên, un.—The double vowel might be written for all four tones, but is more remarkable in the 3d, and 4th. In the 1st, the *u*, or *oo*, sound is dominant, prolonged as in *pool*, *moon*; in the 2d, the *u* is nearly the vowel in *put*, *foot*. But, in the 3d tone, the vowel sounds are well divided, as if *oo-ún* or *ú-én*; and, in the 4th, as if *óo-ün* or *ú-ên*, the latter part declining gradually as if *ù-é-n*.

ui.—As observed under *uei* there is a difference between that final and *ui*. This is most perceptible in the syllable '*hui*, and under the 2d tone; in others, *ui* is nearly if not quite *uei*. The syllable *chui* might otherwise be written *chóó-ēy* ¹, *chooy* ², *choo-éy* ³, *chóo-ey* ⁴. The same native will be found to pronounce this differently at different times.

un.—In the 1st tone there is a perceptible inflection of the vowel, but slighter than in *huên*, *kuên*. In the 2d, it is nearly the *un* in the Italian *punto*, pronounced quickly; though a certain reduplication is still to be perceived. In the 3d and 4th tones, this inflection is acted on by the tones as in *an* and other finals noticed before.

ung.—The remarks on *un* apply generally to *ung*; but in the 2d tone, the inflection of the vowel is less apparent. The *g* final is faint in the same tone. Indeed *ung* ² is something between the final sounds of the French *long* and *longue*. The sound is rather *u* than *ó*, in *yung*.

uo.—The three syllables to which I have assigned this final in the Syllabary, are '*huo*, *kuo*, *shuo*. I must admit that it is only in the last that the *u* asserts itself as a vowel; in the rest it has the power of *w*. In *shuo*, the tones might be expressed thus; *shûóh* ¹, *shwòh* ², *shuó* ³, *shu-óh* ⁴.

ü.—The difficulty here is in representing the vowel sound; this determined, the inflections of it by the tone resemble those in the other final vowels. The word *sy-rup*, with the italicised consonants struck out, might represent *szü* ¹; such, *szü* ²; the 3d, and 4th might be otherwise written *szü-üh*, *szü-ü-h*; but our alphabet aids us less in this than in any sound in the Table.

There remain unnoticed a few finals, the tone-rules affecting which do not differ from those already laid down for others. Those under *an* suffice for *ang* and *êng*, under *ai* for *ei*, under *eh* for *en*, under *ih* and *in* for *ing*, under *ueh* for *uo*, and under *ua* and *uan*, for *uang*.

PART VII. THE TONE EXERCISES. *a — ch'ai.*

The larger characters and numbers to the left of the page correspond with those in the Sound Table prefixed to the Tone Exercises, and are followed by a general explanation of their meaning. The examples in smaller type, which are, in fact, a repetition of the Exercises, are literally translated.

阿 *a*, a particle sometimes affirmative, sometimes interjectional; as the last, partly interrogative.
1.
- 是阿 *shih⁴ a¹*, ... It is so indeed.
- 阿甚麼 *a³ shên² mo²*, ... Ha! What?
- 阿哥 *a⁴ ko¹*, ... (the Manchu *agê*,) elder brother. The sons of a reigning emperor are called *ako*; the eldest being *ta ako*, the second *êrh ako*, and so on.

愛 *ai*, ⁿᵍ*ai*, to love.
2.
- 哀求 *ai¹ ch'iu²*, ... To implore, cry to in tribulation.
- 塵埃 *ch'ên² ngai²*, ... Dust.
- 高矮 *kao¹ ngai³*, ... Tall and short; of things, high and low.
- 愛惜 *ai⁴ hsi¹*, ... To love.

安 *an*, ⁿᵍ*an*, peace; comfort; health; well-being.
3.
- 平安 *p'ing² an¹*, ... Peace, freedom from trouble.
- 俺們 *an³ mên¹*, ... A provincial form of the pronoun *we*.
- 河岸 *'ho² ngan⁴*, ... The bank or shore of a river.

昂 *ang*, ⁿᵍ*ang*, high; rising.
4.
- 低昂 *ti¹ ang¹*, ... Low and high.
- 昂貴 *ang² kuei⁴*, ... High in price.

傲 *ao*, ⁿᵍ*ao*, to boil, (not used alone in speaking.)
5.
- 熬菜 *ao¹ ts'ai¹*, ... To boil meat, vegetables, &c.
- 熬夜 *ao² yeh⁴*, ... To work at night, burn midnight oil.
- 綿襖 *mien² ao³*, ... A quilted (*lit.* cotton) *ao*, article of dress worn by both sexes; it may be long or short.
- 狂傲 *k'uang² ao⁴*, ... Conceited and supercilious; arrogant.

乍 *cha*, suddenly, unexpectedly.
6.
- 渣滓 *cha¹ tzŭ³*, ... Dregs; leavings of things eaten or drunk.
- 劄文 *cha² wên²*, ... A despatch to an inferior.
- 一拃 *yi⁴ cha³*, ... A span.
- 乍見 *cha⁴ chien⁴*, ... To see, or meet, unexpectedly.

茶 *ch'a*, tea.
7.
- 叉手 *ch'a¹ shou³*, ... The two hands clasped together.
- 茶酒 *ch'a² chiu³*, ... Tea and wine; said of a meal prepared for guests.
- 扠腰 *ch'a³ yao¹*, ... To place the hands on the hips; stand akimbo.
- 樹杈 *shu⁴ ch'a⁴*, ... The fork formed by a bough at the point it branches off from the stem.

窄 *chai*, narrow.
8.
- 齋戒 *chai¹ chieh⁴*, ... Fasting and purification.
- 住宅 *chu⁴ chai²*, ... [speaking of another's] a residence.
- 寬窄 *k'uan¹ chai³*, ... Broad and narrow; the breadth of.
- 欠債 *ch'ien⁴ chai⁴*, ... To be in debt.

柴 *ch'ai*, fuel; being wood, weeds, or any similar firing.
9.
- 拆毀 *ch'ai¹ 'hui³*, ... To demolish, as houses, furniture, &c.
- 柴炭 *ch'ai² t'an⁴*, ... Wood and charcoal.
- 樣冊子 *yang⁴ ch'ai³ tzŭ⁴*, . . . A book of patterns, such as milliners use.

斬 *chan*, to decapitate; the *chan* in *chan chiao*, [capital punishment by] beheading or strangling.
10. Observe that *chan*, standing by itself, is read *chan*³, but, being followed by *chiao*³, a word in the third tone, becomes *chan*². In the example of the third tone, therefore, *chan*³, the Numerative of lamps, has been substituted for it.

沾染 *chan*¹ *jan*³, ... Steeped in, saturated with; hence, morally, contaminated.
一盞燈 *yi*⁴ *chan*³ *têng*¹, . . . A lamp.
驛站 *yi*⁴ *chan*⁴, ... Government post stations, courier offices.

產 *ch'an*, to produce, as females, the earth, &c.
11. 攙雜 *ch'an*¹ *tsa*², ... To mix up, so that the component parts are undistinguishable; said of fluids or solids; also used figuratively.
嘴饞 *tsui*³ *ch'an*², ... Gluttonous.
產業 *ch'an*³ *yeh*⁴, ... An estate; property producing an income.
懺悔 *ch'an*⁴ *'hui*³, ... To reform, *neut.*; literally, to reform and see the error of one's ways.

章 *chang*, a rule; a law.
12. 章程 *chang*¹ *ch'êng*², ... Regulations.
生長 *shêng*¹ *chang*³, ... To be born and to grow up.
帳目 *chang*⁴ *mu*⁴, ... Bills; debts.

唱 *ch'ang*, to sing.
13. 娼妓 *ch'ang*¹ *chi*⁴, ... A prostitute.
長短 *ch'ang*² *tuan*³, ... Long and short; length.
木廠 *mu*⁴ *ch'ang*³, ... A woodyard.
歌唱 *ko*¹ *ch'ang*⁴, ... To sing.

兆 *chao*, a presage.
14. 招呼 *chao*¹ *'hu*¹, ... To hail, call to.
着急 *chao*² *chi*², ... Eager, in a good sense; also, over-eager.
察找 *ch'a*² *chao*³, ... To make search for.
先兆 *hsien*¹ *chao*⁴, ... A presage, an omen.

吵 *ch'ao*, the wrangle (of two or of more).
15. 吵嚷 *ch'ao*¹ *jang*³, ... Noise of loud voices.
窩巢 *wo*¹ *ch'ao*², ... Nest of birds; lair of beasts; den of thieves.
煎炒 *chien*¹ *ch'ao*³, ... To fry in oil, fat, &c.
錢鈔 *ch'ien*² *ch'ao*⁴, ... Cash and paper; or, a cash-note, but this is oftener called a *ch'ien-p'iao*.

這 *chê*, the pronoun *this*.
16. 遮掩 *chê*¹ *yen*³, ... To screen, as another's faults.
摺奏 *chê*² *ts'ou*⁴, ... To report to the Throne in a *chê*, memorial.
再者 *tsai*⁴ *chê*³, ... Again (in argument); farther; what is more, &c.
這個 *chê*⁴ *ko*⁴, ... This one.

車 *ch'ê*, a cart, carriage, &c.
17. 車馬 *ch'ê*¹ *ma*³, ... Carts and horses.
拉扯 *la*¹ *ch'ê*³, ... To drag.
裁撤 *ts'ai*² *ch'ê*⁴, ... To do away with; dismiss part of an establishment; abrogate a law, &c.

這 *chei*, this.
18. 這塊兒 *chei*⁴ *k'uai*⁴ *êrh*, . . Here, in this place; *chei* is simply short for *chê yi*, this one. Observe *k'uai êrh*, pronounced *k'uairh*⁴.

眞 *chên*, true.
19. 眞假 *chên*¹ *chia*³, ... True and false; the truth of anything.
枕頭 *chên*³ *t'ou*², ... A pillow; *lit.* to pillow the head.
地震 *ti*⁴ *chên*⁴, ... An earthquake.

PART VII. THE TONE EXERCISES. chan – ch'iang.

臣 ch'ên, a public servant in his relation to the sovereign; not applied, except historically, to any
20.   but the higher officers of state.
  嗔怪 ch'ên¹ kuai⁴, ... To rebuke sternly, censure gravely, either to the face or behind the back.
  君臣 chun¹ ch'ên², ... Sovereign and minister.
  砢磣 k'o¹ ch'ên³, ... Hideous; very unsightly; of persons or things.
  趁著 ch'ên⁴ cho⁴, ... Taking advantage of; sc. circumstances, opportunity, &c.

正 chêng, upright.
21. 正月 chêng¹ yüeh⁴, ... The first moon of the year (chêng¹).
  整齊 chêng³ ch'i², ... Regular; in symmetrical order.
  正邪 chêng⁴ hsieh², ... Of lines, roads, &c. straight and diverging; hence, figuratively, moral
           and depraved, orthodox and heterodox.

成 ch'êng, accomplishment as opposed to failure.
22. 稱呼 ch'êng¹ 'hu¹, ... To address a person, or speak of one (by such or such a term of respect).
  成敗 ch'êng² pai⁴, ... Accomplishment or failure.
  懲辦 ch'êng³ pan⁴, ... To punish, punishment of, crime.
  斗秤 tou³ ch'êng⁴, ... Measures and weights; lit. pecks and steel-yards.

吉 chi, of good omen.
23. 雞犬 chi¹ ch'uan³, ... Poultry and dogs; e.g. none left in a country that has been devastated;
           the place of them to be shunned by a compounder of medicines, because his operations should be conducted in quiet.
  吉凶 chi² hsiung¹, ... Auspicious and inauspicious.
  自己 tzŭ⁴ chi³, ... One's self.
  記載 chi⁴ tsai⁴, ... To put on record in a history, essay, &c.

奇 ch'i, strange.
24. 七八 ch'i¹ pa¹, ... Seven, eight.
  奇怪 ch'i² kuai⁴, ... Strange, curious; how strange.
  起初 ch'i³ ch'u¹, ... At the beginning.
  氣血 ch'i⁴ hsueh³, ... The constitution; lit. breath and blood.

家 chia, a house; home; the family.
25. 住家 chu⁴ chia¹, ... To live at home.
  夾帶 chia² tai⁴, ... To carry privily; lit. under the arm.
  盔甲 k'uei¹ chia³, ... Casque and coat of mail; armour.
  價錢 chia⁴ ch'ien², ... The price of.

恰 ch'ia, to coincide with exactly.
26. 掐花 ch'ia¹ 'hua¹, ... To pick a flower off its stem.
  卡子 ch'ia³ tzŭ³, ... A custom's barrier; also, the clasp of a belt.
  恰巧 ch'ia⁴ ch'iao³, ... In the nick of time; in exact coincidence.

楷 ch'iai, (also k'ai,) the stalk of grass.
27. 楷書 ch'iai³ shu¹, ... The written character in which despatches are copied; say, round-hand.

江 chiang, a river; rather of large streams than small.
28. 大江 ta⁴ chiang¹, ... The great river, sc. the Yang-tzŭ.
  講究 chiang³ chiu⁴, ... To look into curiously, minutely, fastidiously, particularly; hence, in
           some cases, the result of such care; e.g. if one chiang-chiu, is particular, about one's room, one's room is chiang-chiu.
  匠人 chiang⁴ jên², ... A workman, an artisan.

搶 ch'iang, to carry off with violence.
29. 腔調 ch'iang¹ tiao⁴, ... Sound in accord; in tune, whether of speaking or singing; also, figuratively, of things.
  牆壁 ch'iang² pi⁴, ... Properly, a partition wall, but used of any wall of a house.
  搶奪 ch'iang³ to², ... To rob, or steal.
  戧木 ch'iang⁴ mu⁴, ... Wooden supports, scaffolding.

KEY TO THE TZŬ ERH CHI. Colloquial Series.

交 *chiao*, to interchange.
30.
- 交代 *chiao¹ tai⁴*, ... To hand over to a successor in office; also, to give orders to a servant or subordinate.
- 嚼過 *chiao² kuo⁴*, ... One's bread, literally, to eat, = the *food*, needed to enable one *to pass* one's days, = to live.
- 手腳 *shou³ chiao³*, ... Hand and foot. Observe *shou*³ becomes nearly *shou*² before *chiao*³.
- 叫喊 *chiao⁴ han³*, ... To call out loud; to call to a person.

巧 *ch'iao*, cunning; but also, clever, of men; ingenious, of things.
31.
- 敲打 *ch'iao¹ ta³*, ... To beat as drums, gongs, &c.; to knock at a door.
- 橋梁 *ch'iao² liang²*, ... A bridge; *lit*. bridge beams.
- 巧妙 *ch'iao³ miao⁴*, ... Of men, clever; of inventions, ingenious.
- 俏皮 *ch'iao⁴ p'i²*, ... Of women only, well-looking, also, well-dressed; used *fig*. of fair words that cover censorious allusions.

街 *chieh*, a street.
32.
- 街道 *chieh¹ tao⁴*, ... Public ways.
- 完結 *wan² chieh²*, ... To complete; completed.
- 解開 *chieh³ k'ai¹*, ... To untie; to explain. Cf. *solvere*.
- 借貸 *chieh⁴ tai⁴*, ... To borrow.

且 *ch'ieh*, moreover.
33.
- 切肉 *ch'ieh¹ jou⁴*, ... To slice meat, cutting vertically.
- 茄子 *ch'ieh² tzŭ³*, ... (Amongst other things,) the brinjal, or egg-plant.
- 況且 *k'uang⁴ ch'ieh³*, ... Moreover, farther.
- 姬妾 *chi¹ ch'ieh⁴*, ... Concubines. In speaking of one alone, *ch'ieh* would be used without *chi*.

見 *chien*, to perceive.
34.
- 奸臣 *chien¹ ch'ên²*, ... A traitorous, or disloyal minister.
- 裁減 *ts'ai² chien³*, ... To diminish number or quantity.
- 見面 *chien⁴ mien⁴*, ... To have an interview with; during a *tête-à-tête*.

欠 *ch'ien*, to owe; to be deficient in.
35.
- 千萬 *ch'ien¹ wan⁴*, ... A thousand myriads, = any number.
- 錢財 *ch'ien² ts'ai²*, ... Money, wealth.
- 深淺 *shên¹ ch'ien³*, ... Deep and shallow; the depth of.
- 該欠 *kai¹ ch'ien⁴*, ... To owe.

知 *chih*, to know.
36.
- 知道 *chih¹ tao⁴*, ... To know.
- 值班 *chih² pan¹*, ... To be on duty in one's turn.
- 指頭 *chih³ t'ou²*, ... A finger.
- 志向 *chih⁴ hsiang⁴*, ... Ambition, *lit*. direction or aim of one's resolution.

尺 *ch'ih*, the Chinese foot, = about 14 inches English.
37.
- 紅赤赤 *'hung² ch'ih¹ ch'ih¹*, ... Red as red can be.
- 遲誤 *ch'ih² wu⁴*, ... To fail, or ruin, by unpunctuality.
- 尺寸 *ch'ih³ ts'un⁴*, ... Feet and inches; the length of.
- 翅膀 *ch'ih⁴ pang³*, ... A bird's wings.

斤 *chin*, the Chinese pound.
38.
- 斤兩 *chin¹ liang³*, ... Pound and ounce; see Note, PART III, page 84.
- 錦繡 *chin³ hsiu⁴*, ... Embroidery, in gold, silk, &c.
- 遠近 *yuan³ chin⁴*, ... Far and near, distance.

親 *ch'in*, nearly related or allied.
39.
- 親戚 *ch'in¹ ch'i⁴*, ... One's relatives, in general.
- 勤儉 *ch'in² chien³*, ... Industrious and frugal.
- 寢食 *ch'in³ shih²*, ... Sleep and food, part of a proverb in which anxiety of mind is said to interfere with both rest and appetite.
- 狗嗆 *kou³ ch'in⁴*, ... The dog is vomiting, a dog's vomit.

PART VII. THE TONE EXERCISES. *chiao — ch'ou.*

井 *ching*, a well.
40.   眼睛 *yen³ ching¹*, ... The eyes; *lit.* the pupil of the eye.
    井泉 *ching³ ch'üan²*, ... Wells and springs; but, with *shui*, the water of either or both, as distinguished from river water.
    安靜 *an¹ ching⁴*, ... Quiet, tranquil; said of the mind, of a scene, of a state of things.

輕 *ch'ing*, light, as opposed to heavy.
41.   輕重 *ch'ing¹ chung⁴*, ... Light and heavy (morally or materially); also, the weight of things; value of character, counsels, &c.
    陰晴 *yin¹ ch'ing²*, ... (Of the sky,) clouded or fine; rainy or fine; the weather.
    請安 *ch'ing³ an¹*, ... To enquire after the health of; hence, a form of salutation.
    慶弔 *ch'ing⁴ tiao⁴*, ... Congratulations and condolences.

角 *chio*, a horn.
42.   角色 *chio² shê⁴*, ... The particular business in which a man is engaged, class he belongs to. You ask, what is his *chio shê?* The word *shê*, here meaning class, description.

卻 *ch'io*, to stop abruptly. Observe the other form of this character in the example below.
43.   推卻 *t'ui¹ ch'io⁴*, ... To decline; to refuse.

酒 *chiu*, Chinese wine or spirit in general.
44.   究辦 *chiu¹ pan⁴*, ... To enquire into and punish an offence.
    酒肉 *chiu³ jou⁴*, ... Wine and meat; the dinner one gives one's friends. Such a man is not a *chiu-jou* friend, *sc.* not in one's intimacy, or, not one with whom one would be intimate.
    救護 *chiu⁴ 'hu⁴*, ... To succour, as people in poverty, danger, &c.

秋 *ch'iu*, autumn.
45.   春秋 *ch'un¹ ch'iu¹*, . . Spring and autumn; the title of a certain historical work attributed to Confucius.
    央求 *yang¹ ch'iu²*, . . . To beseech; *yang* intensifies *ch'iu*, but is not so strong as *ai*; which see above.
    飯糗了 *fan⁴ ch'iu³ liao³*, . . . The rice is [boiled to] gruel. The *hao* becomes in fact *lo*; nearly *lo⁴*.

窘 *chiung*, straitened; of space or fortune.
46.   窘迫 *chiung³ p'o⁴*, ... Hard pressed, by circumstances, want of means, &c.

窮 *ch'iung*, extremity; the farthest verge.
47.   貧窮 *p'in² ch'iung²*, ... Very poor; poverty.

卓 *cho*, a table.
48.   桌凳 *cho¹ têng⁴*, . . Tables and stools or benches; generic of any furniture an upholsterer would supply.
    清濁 *ch'ing¹ cho²*, ... Clear and muddy; hence, perspicuity and obscurity.

綽 *ch'o*, roomy; hence, comfortable.
49.   擉礆 *ch'o¹ p'êng⁴*, ... To poke and to bump against; hence, collision in general.
    寬綽 *k'uan¹ ch'o⁴*, ... In easy circumstances.

晝 *chou*, day, as distinguished from night.
50.   週圍 *chou¹ wei²*, ... Surrounding; all round.
    車軸 *ch'ê¹ chou²*, ... The axle-tree.
    臂肘 *pei⁴ chou³*, ... The arm, *lit.* the upper and lower parts of the arm.
    晝夜 *chou⁴ yeh⁴*, ... Day and night.

抽 *ch'ou*, to draw towards one.
51.   抽查 *ch'ou¹ ch'a²*, ... To examine one article of a lot.
    綢緞 *ch'ou² tuan⁴*, ... Silk and satin; silk manufactures.
    醜俊 *ch'ou³ chün⁴*, ... Ugly and fair.
    香臭 *hsiang¹ ch'ou⁴*, ... Good smells and bad.

KEY TO THE TZŬ ERH CHI. **Colloquial Series.**

句 *chü*, a short clause.
52.
  居處 *chu¹ ch'u³*, ... A dwelling-place; one's abode. Note *ch'u*, in this sense, properly, *ch'u⁴*. See below, Ex. 62.
  賭局 *tu³ chü²*, ... A gambling-table.
  保舉 *pao² chü³*, ... To recommend for promotion. Note *pao*, properly, *pao³*, but *pao²* before *chü³*.
  句段 *chü⁴ tuan⁴*, ... Clauses and sentences; *q. d.* such or such a piece of writing will **not** make them, = is not constructed so as to make sense.

取 *ch'ü*, to take, as opposed to presenting.
53.
  冤屈 *yüan¹ ch'ü¹*, ... Wronged, oppressed.
  溝洫 *kou¹ ch'ü²*, ... Ditches and gutters; drains in general.
  取送 *ch'ü³ sung⁴*, ... To take and to present.
  來去 *lai² ch'ü⁴*, ... Coming and going.

捐 *chüan*, to contribute in aid of the necessities of the government.
54.
  捐納 *chüan¹ na⁴*, ... To contribute, as above; *lit.* to contribute and present.
  舒拳 *shu¹ chüan³*, ... Open, as the hand, and closed, as the fist.
  家眷 *chia¹ chüan⁴*, ... One's family; said of one's wife alone, or of wife and children.

全 *ch'üan*, complete.
55.
  圈點 *ch'üan¹ tien³*, ... Circles and points; the former marking the sentence, the latter, the clauses in the sentence; or, to punctuate with circles. See any page in PART III of this Series.
  齊全 *ch'i² ch'üan²*, ... Completeness; *lit.* in regular order and complete.
  犬吠 *ch'üan³ fei⁴*, ... A dog's bark; the dog barks.
  勸戒 *ch'üan⁴ chieh⁴*, ... To warn; *lit.* to counsel and warn against, *sc.* a vice, or bad habit.

絕 *chüeh*, to cut off.
56.
  噘嘴 *chüeh¹ tsui³*, ... To protrude the lips, to pout.
  斷絕 *tuan⁴ chüeh²*, ... To cut off.
  馬撩橛子 *ma³ liao⁴ chüeh³ tzŭ*, A horse's kick; *liao*, meaning to lift. Note *tzŭ* enclitic and its tone [consequently ill-defined.
  倔喪 *chüeh⁴ sang⁴*, ... Churlish.

缺 *ch'üeh*, vacant, deficient.
57.
  補缺 *pu³ ch'üeh¹*, ... To fill up a vacancy.
  瘸腿 *ch'üeh² t'ui³*, ... Lame.
  確然 *ch'üeh⁴ jan²*, ... Positively so.

君 *chün*, the sovereign.
58.
  君王 *chün¹ wang²*, ... The sovereign; *wang*, being used in its ancient and classical sense.
  菌子 *chün³ tzŭ*, ... Rice with the husk on. Note *tzŭ* enclitic.
  俊秀 *chün⁴ hsiu⁴*, ... Fine, of person or talents.

羣 *ch'ün*, properly, a drove or flock; also, a party of persons.
59.
  成羣 *ch'êng² ch'ün²*, ... To make a group or party.

爵 *chüo*, nobility, high position.
60.
  爵位 *chüo² wei⁴*, ... Position, where the person spoken of is of somewhat high rank.

卻 *ch'üo*, see above 43, *ch'io*.
61.

主 *chu*, lord; master; host.
62.
  猪羊 *chu¹ yang²*, ... Pigs and sheep; farming stock.
  竹子 *chu² tzŭ*, ... The bamboo. Note *tzŭ* enclitic.
  賓主 *pin¹ chu³*, ... Guest and host.
  住處 *chu⁴ ch'u⁴*, ... One's abiding place, residence.

PART VII. THE TONE EXERCISES. *chü – ch'ui.*

出 *ch'u*, to go forth or out of.
63.
- 出外 *ch'u¹ wai⁴*, ... To leave home for a place at a certain distance.
- 廚房 *ch'u² fang²*, ... A kitchen.
- 處分 *ch'u³ fên⁴*, ... The punishment of official delinquency; *ch'u³*, to regulate; hence, to punish an official, *sc.* by fine or disgrace.
- 住處 *chu⁴ ch'u⁴*, ... One's abiding place.

抓 *chua*, to clap the hand, paw, claw, upon.
64.
- 抓破 *chua¹ p'o⁴*, ... To tear by clapping the hand, &c. upon.
- 雞爪子 *chi¹ chua³ tzǔ*, . . A fowl's claw.

欻 *ch'ua*, any whistling sound produced by the rapid movement of something through the air.
65.
- 欻一聲 *ch'ua¹ i⁴ shêng¹*, . . There was a whiz, a whirr, or any sudden sound.

拽 *chuai*, properly, to draw, or drag, towards one.
66.
- 拽泥 *chuai¹ ni²*, ... To fling mud at; how *chuai¹*, comes to mean *fling* is not explained.
- 鴨跩 *ya¹ chuai³*, ... A duck waddles; or, the waddle of a duck.
- 拉拽 *la¹ chuai⁴*, ... To drag or draw, a person, thing, or animal.

揣 *ch'uai*, to feel with the fingers.
67.
- 懷揣 *'huai² ch'uai¹*, . . To stick [a thing] in the breast of one's garment; [a thing] stuck in the breast
- 揣摩 *ch'uai³ mo¹*, ... To feel for, with the hand; or, *fig.* of a person speculating, to guess.
- 蹲踹 *têng¹ ch'uai⁴*, ... To kick a succession of short kicks.

專 *chuan*, special, individual.
68.
- 專門 *chuan¹ mên²*, ... *Lit.* the only entrance; one particular pursuit, or, devotion to one pursuit.
- 轉移 *chuan³ yi²*, ... Transfer of things from place to place; of cases, *sc.* by correspondence between coordinate jurisdictions.
- 經傳 *ching¹ chuan⁴*, ... The ancient classics of China and the commentary, *lit.* the tradition.

穿 *ch'uan*, to bore through; hence, to get into one's clothes.
69.
- 穿戴 *ch'uan¹ tai⁴*, ... What one wears on the body, and carries on one's head; apparel.
- 車船 *ch'ê¹ ch'uan²*, ... Carts and junks; carriage by land and water.
- 痰喘 *t'an² ch'uan³*, ... An asthmatic affection; *t'an*, the phlegm, the effort to expectorate which produces the *ch'uan*.
- 串通 *ch'uan⁴ t'ung¹*, ... In collusion with.

壯 *chuang*, stout, hearty.
70.
- 裝載 *chuang¹ tsai⁴*, ... To load, put into; to contain.
- 粗裝 *ts'u¹ chuang³*, ... Bulky; or, simply, of large dimensions.
- 壯健 *chuang⁴ chien⁴*, ... Robust.

牀 *ch'uang*, a bed.
71.
- 牕戶 *ch'uang¹ hu⁴*, ... A window. Observe that this *ch'uang¹* is properly written without the 65th Radical; the vulgar form, as here, with it.
- 牀鋪 *ch'uang² p'u⁴*, ... Bed and bedding.
- 闖入 *ch'uang³ ju⁴*, ... To burst one's way into.
- 創始 *ch'uang⁴ shih³*, ... To found, invent, originate.

追 *chui*, to pursue.
72.
- 追趕 *chui¹ kan³*, ... To overtake.
- 廢墜 *fei⁴ chui⁴*, ... To go to rack and ruin.

吹 *ch'ui*, to blow with the breath.
73.
- 吹打 *ch'ui¹ ta³*, ... Beating drums and playing on wind instruments.
- 垂手 *ch'ui² shou³*, ... To let the hands hang down; hands so hanging.

KEY TO THE TZŬ ERH CHI. Colloquial Series.

准 chun, to authorise.
74. 准駁 chun³ po², ... Approval and disapproval.

春 ch'un, spring.
75. 春夏 ch'un¹ hsia⁴, ... Spring and summer.
純厚 ch'un² 'hou⁴, ... Morally sound; sincere.
蠢笨 ch'un³ pên⁴, ... Loutish and stupid. See PART III, EXERC. XXI, 8, 9.

中 chung, central; inner.
76. 中外 chung¹ wai⁴, . . . Within and without; in the capital and the provinces; native and foreigner.
腫疼 chung³ t'êng², ... Swollen and painful.
輕重 ch'ing¹ chung⁴, ... Light and heavy; the weight of.

充 ch'ung, to represent; to act as.
77. 充當 ch'ung¹ tang¹, ... Representing, filling the place of.
虫蟻 ch'ung² yi³ or i³, ... Creeping things; *lit.* reptiles and ants.
寵愛 ch'ung³ ai⁴, ... To make a favorite of.
鐵銃 t'ieh³ ch'ung⁴, ... A petard; small iron ordnance without a carriage.

擉 ch'uo, to strike with a point.
78. 擉撐 ch'uo¹ p'êng⁴, ... Collision in general; *lit.* blow with the point and laterally.

額 ê, a limit as of number or quantity.
79. 太阿 t'ai⁴ ê¹, ... Ah! wondrous! The name of a sword in history.
頟數 ê² shu⁴, ... A fixed number.
爾我 êrh² ê³, ... You and I (the ancient pronunciation of *wo*, I, being *ⁿgo* or *ⁿgê*.)
善惡 shan¹ ê⁴, ... Virtuous and vicious.

恩 ên, ⁿgên, favor.
80. 恩典 ên¹ tien³, ... Grace; *lit.* law or rule of grace; originally, grace of the sovereign.
揞倒 ên⁴ tao³, ... To keep [a man] down on the ground by force.

哼 êng, a sound; humph!
81. 哼阿 êng¹ a¹, ... To hem and to haw.

兒 êrh, a son.
82. 兒女 êrh² nü³, ... Sons and daughters.
耳朵 êrh³ to⁴, ... The ear.
二三 êrh⁴ san¹, ... Two or three.

法 fa, a means.
83. 發遣 fa¹ ch'ien³, ... To send into exile.
法子 fa² tzŭ, ... Means, plans, resources.
頭髮 t'ou² fa³, ... The hair of the head.
佛法 fo² fa⁴, ... The code of Buddha.

反 fan, to turn back or over.
84. 翻騰 fan¹ t'êng², ... Topsy-turvy.
煩惱 fan² nao³, ... Distressed in mind.
反倒 fan³ tao⁴, ... Upset, turned over.
喫飯 ch'ih¹ fan⁴, ... To eat rice; generally, to eat any meal.

方 fang, square.
85. 方圓 fang¹ yüan², ... Square and round.
房屋 fang² wu¹, ... House and rooms; the house [is clean, is dirty, &c.]
訪查 fang³ ch'a², ... To make enquiry into.
放肆 fang⁴ ssŭ⁴, ... To give way to violence, evil passions; to commit disorderly acts.

PART VII. THE TONE EXERCISES. *chun – 'hang.*

非 *fei*, the wrong as opposed to the right.
86.
    是非 *shih⁴ fei¹*, ... Right and wrong; also, tittle-tattle, scandal.
    肥瘦 *fei² shou⁴*, ... Fat and lean.
    賊匪 *tsei² fei³*, ... Banditti, rebels, &c.
    使費 *shih³ fei⁴*, ... Expenses, *sc.* in the way of fees, &c. which one has no right to pay.

分 *fên*, to divide.
87.
    分開 *fên¹ k'ai¹*, ... To divide into shares, portions, &c.
    墳墓 *fên² mu⁴*, ... A grave; a grave-yard.
    脂粉 *chih¹ fên³*, ... Red pigment and white; cosmetics in general.
    職分 *chih² fên⁴*, ... The duties of one's office.

風 *fêng*, wind.
88.
    風雨 *fêng¹ yü³*, ... Wind and rain.
    裁縫 *ts'ai² fêng²*, ... A tailor; *lit.* to cut and to sew.
    供奉 *kung⁴ fêng⁴*, ... Make tender of [service], *sc.* in the palace; said of the attendance of high officers on the sovereign; anciently, and still politely, to offer, present, a thing.

佛 *fo*, Buddha.
89.
    佛老 *fo² lao³*, ... Buddha and Lao Chün; the latter, the founder of the Tao sect.

否 *fou*, not so.
90.
    浮沉 *fou² ch'ên²*, ... Floating and sinking.
    然否 *jan² fou³*, ... Whether so or not.
    埠口 *fou⁴ k'ou³*, ... Any port on sea or river.

夫 *fu*, a man, a husband.
91.
    夫妻 *fu¹ ch'i¹*, ... Husband and wife.
    扶持 *fu² ch'ih²*, ... To hold one's self up by, *e. g.* a staff; *fu*, to hold up, as by the arm, *ch'ih*, to grasp in the hand.
    斧鉞 *fu³ yueh⁴*, ... Axes.
    父母 *fu⁴ mu³*, ... Father and mother.

哈 *'ha*, the sound ha.
92.
    哈哈笑 *'ha¹ 'ha¹ hsiao⁴*, . . . To laugh heartily.
    蝦蟆 *'ha² mo⁴*, ... A frog.
    哈吧 *'ha³ pa¹*, ... The chin.
    哈什馬 *'ha⁴ shên² ma³*, . . . Certain pastry eaten in Peking; also, dried frogs, or some such eatable, brought from Manchuria.

害 *'hai*, grave injury, moral or material.
93.
    咳聲 *'hai¹ shêng¹*, ... The exclamation *'hai!*
    孩子 *'hai² tzŭ*, ... A child.
    江海 *chiang¹ 'hai³*, ... The waters; *lit.* rivers and seas.
    利害 *li⁴ 'hai⁴*, ... A strong intensive, used more commonly of evil things than good. See EXERC. XVI, *ex.* 7.

寒 *'han*, cold.
94.
    顢頇 *man¹ 'han¹*, ... Dilatorily, undecidedly; the two characters are not used apart.
    寒涼 *'han² liang²*, ... Cold.
    叫喊 *chiao⁴ 'han³*, ... To call to; to call out.
    滿漢 *man³ 'han⁴*, ... Manchus and Chinese.

砰 *'hang*, to beat the ground preparatory to building a wall.
95.
    打砰 *ta³ 'hang¹*, ... (See above, *'hang.*)
    各行 *ko⁴ 'hang²*, ... Every trade.
    項圈 *'hang⁴ ch'üan¹*, ... The playthings hung round a child's neck; *'hang*, properly, the neck, but not colloquially used in northern mandarin.

KEY TO THE TZŬ ERH CHI. **Colloquial Series.**

好 'hao, good; to love, be addicted to, in the habit of.
96.
蒿草 'hao¹ ts'ao³, ... Jungle.
絲毫 ssŭ¹ 'hao², ... The floss of silk, a particle of any kind, very common with a negative; q. d. not a particle.
好不好 'hao³ pu⁴ 'hao³, . . . Is it well (or good) or not? (Commonly implying that it is.)
好喜 'hao⁴ hsi³, ... To be addicted to [any pursuit, good or evil].

黑 'hê, 'hei, black.
97.
黑白 'hei¹ pai², ... Black and white; used also figuratively as with us; q. d. he can't tell black from white, = good from bad.
黑豆 'hei³ tou⁴, ... Black beans; black pulse.

很 'hên, originally, wilful, litigious, but commonly a strong intensive; often written with the 94th
98.   [Radical.
傷痕 shang¹ 'hên², ... The scar of a wound.
好得很 'hao³ tê² 'hên³, . . . Exceedingly good.
恨怨 'hên⁴ yüan⁴, ... Animosity; 'hên, properly, wrath that one feels, yüan, that one vents.

恆 'hêng, constant, enduring.
99.
哼哈 'hêng¹ 'ha¹, or êng¹ a¹, . . To hum and to haw.
恆久 'hêng² chiu³, ... Enduring for ever.
兇橫 hsiung¹ hêng⁴, ... Ferocious, brutal.

河 'ho, a river.
100.
喫喝 ch'ih¹ 'ho¹, ... To eat and drink.
江河 chiang¹ 'ho², ... Rivers, in general.
賀喜 'ho⁴ hsi³, ... To congratulate.

後 'hou, after, in time or place.
101.
鹵鹹 'hou¹ hsien², ... Briny salt; salt in the extreme.
公侯 kung¹ 'hou², ... The two first titles of the ancient five orders of national, as distinct from imperial, nobility; kung, generally translated duke, 'hou, marquis.
牛吼 niu² 'hou³, ... The lowing of oxen; 'hou, also, the roar of a lion.
前後 ch'ien² 'hou⁴, ... Before and behind, in time or place.

戶 'hu, sudden.
102.
忽然 'hu¹ jan², ... Of a sudden.
茶壺 ch'a² 'hu², ... A tea-pot.
龍虎榜 lung² 'hu² pang³, . . . Dragon and tiger affiche; the list published of graduates, who obtain degrees as licentiates or doctors. Note 'hu, properly 'hu³, but 'hu² before pang³.
戶口 'hu⁴ k'ou³, ... A family; population; lit. the mouths in a house.

花 'hua, flowers.
103.
花草 'hua¹ ts'ao³, ... Flowers and grass, or herbs; vegetation.
泥滑 ni² 'hua², ... The mud is slippery.
話敗人 'hua³ pai⁴ jên², . . . To speak ill of a person behind his back, whether your censure be merited or not.
說話 shuo¹ 'hua⁴, ... To speak, talk; also, spoken language.

壞 'huai, to injure seriously, to destroy.
104.
懷想 'huai² hsiang³, ... To think, cherish a thought.
損壞 sun³ 'huai⁴, ... To spoil, be spoiled, more or less; said of things.

換 'huan, to exchange.
105.
歡喜 'huan¹ hsi³, ... To rejoice; to delight in.
連環 lien² 'huan², ... Several rounds [of musketry, or artillery]; also, of the involution of circles in a pattern, q. d. ring on ring.
鬆緩 sung¹ 'huan³, ... Slackened, as zeal, industry.
更換 kêng¹ 'huan⁴, ... To change; most commonly of employés; not menials.

PART VII. THE TONE EXERCISES. ‘hao – hsiao.

黃 ‘huang, yellow.
106. 荒亂 ‘huang¹ luan⁴, ... Wild disorder; e.g. that occasioned by a bad year, by brigandage, &c.
　　青黃 ch‘ing¹ ‘huang², ... Green and yellow; said of ripening corn.
　　撒謊 sa¹ ‘huang³, ... To tell lies.
　　一晃兒 yi² ‘huang⁴ ’rh, . . . A flash; its duration, = a moment. Note erh enclitic; pronounce huaⁿrh.

回 ‘hui, to turn back.
107. 石灰 shih² ‘hui¹, ... Lime.
　　回去 ‘hui² ch‘ü⁴, ... To go back.
　　後悔 ‘hou⁴ ‘hui³, ... To repent.
　　賄賂 ‘hui⁴ lu⁴, ... Bribes.

混 ‘huên, ‘hun, mingled in confusion.
108. 昏暗 ‘hun¹ an⁴, ... Dark, as a cloudy day; obscure, of a man's meaning.
　　鬼魂 kuei³ ‘hun², ... The spirit of man after death.
　　渾厚 ‘hun³ ‘hou⁴, ... Lit. stupidly honest; that will not see another's faults.
　　混亂 ‘huên⁴ luan⁴, ... In great confusion; of things tumbled together; also, fig. of the state of a country.

紅 ‘hung, red.
109. 烘烤 ‘hung¹ k‘ao³, ... To heat before the fire.
　　紅綠 ‘hung² lü⁴, ... Red and green; as trees in blossom.
　　欺哄 ch‘i¹ ‘hung³, ... To deceive by telling falsehoods.
　　煉汞 lien⁴ ‘hung⁴, ... To smelt quicksilver; but fig. of the preparation by the Taoist priests of drugs that are to prolong life.

火 ‘huo, fire.
110. 剮口子 ‘huo¹ k‘ou³ tzŭ, ... The space between the fingers, or any like indentation on the body.
　　死活 ssŭ³ ‘huo², ... Dead or alive; whether he will live or not [one cannot tell].
　　水火 shui² ‘huo³, ... Water and fire; a poor man has these, = these and nothing beside; they are said to be wu ch‘ing, unnatural, unreasonable, in cases of flood or fire. Note shui³ changed to shui².
　　貨物 ‘huo⁴ wu⁴, ... Merchandise.

西 hsi, west.
111. 東西 tung¹ hsi¹, ... East and west; a thing.
　　酒席 chiu³ hsi², ... A dinner (to guests).
　　喜歡 hsi³ ‘huan¹, ... To like, be pleased with.
　　粗細 ts‘u¹ hsi⁴, ... Coarse and fine; the quality of any thing coarse or fine.

夏 hsia, summer.
112. 瞎子 hsia¹ tzŭ, ... A blind man.
　　雲霞 yun² hsia², ... Cloud and mist.
　　春夏 ch‘un¹ hsia⁴, ... Spring and summer.

向 hsiang, towards; in the direction of.
113. 香臭 hsiang¹ ch‘ou⁴, ... Fragrance and stench.
　　詳細 hsiang² hsi⁴, ... Minutely, detailedly.
　　思想 ssŭ¹ hsiang³, ... To think; bethink you!
　　方向 fang¹ hsiang⁴, ... Direction taken or to be taken.

小 hsiao, small.
114. 消減 hsiao¹ chien³, ... To diminish; fall off.
　　學徒 hsiao² t‘u², ... An apprentice.
　　大小 ta⁴ hsiao³, ... Great and small; the size of.
　　談笑 t‘an² hsiao⁴, ... To chat and laugh.

些 hsieh, few, little of.
115. 些微 hsieh¹ wei¹, ... A trifle; in a small degree.
    靴鞵 hsüeh¹ hsieh², ... Boots and shoes; hsieh, commonly written 鞋.
    氣血 ch'i⁴ hsieh³, ... Constitution; lit. breath and blood.
    謝恩 hsieh⁴ ên¹, ... To thank for favor shewn.

先 hsien, before in time.
116. 先後 hsien¹ 'hou⁴, ... Before and after.
    清閒 ch'ing¹ hsien², ... Tranquil; undisturbed by cares, noise, &c.
    危險 wei² hsien³, ... Dangerous.
    限期 hsien⁴ ch'i¹, ... A given date; a limited period.

心 hsin, the heart; also, the mind.
117. 心性 hsin¹ hsing⁴, ... The nature of the heart or mind; its character, morally.
    尋東西 hsin² tung¹ hsi¹, ... To look for a thing.
    書信 shu¹ hsin⁴, ... A note or letter.

姓 hsing, family name, surname.
118. 星宿 'hsing¹ hsü⁴, ... The stars; lit. star-constellation.
    行為 hsing² wei², ... Conduct; actions.
    睡醒 shui⁴ hsing³, ... Asleep or awake, also, to wake up.
    姓名 hsing⁴ ming², ... Surname and name.

學 hsio, to learn.
119. 學問 hsio² wên⁴, ... Acquired knowledge, learning; lit. learning and asking.

修 hsiu, to repair; to prepare.
120. 修理 hsiu¹ li³, ... To put in order, e.g. mechanism, roads, &c.
    糟朽 tsao¹ hsiu³, ... Rotten.
    領袖 ling³ hsiu⁴, ... Collar and cuff, or sleeve; also, fig. for the best hand, the managing man.

兄 hsiung, elder brother.
121. 兄弟 hsiung¹ ti⁴, ... Elders and juniors in a family.
    狗熊 kou³ hsiung,² . . . . . A dog-bear; a bear said to devour the dog; numbers are shown about Peking.

須 hsü, necessary; must.
122. 必須 pi⁴ hsü¹, ... Must; is sure to.
    徐圖 hsü² t'u², ... To take time in devising; to deliberate.
    應許 ying¹ hsü³, ... To promise.
    接續 chieh¹ hsü⁴, ... In connection with the foregoing; lit. receiving, taking up, and continuing.

喧 hsüan, hsüen, the uproar of a crowd.
123. 喧嚷 hsüen¹ jang³, ... Clamour of many voices.
    懸掛 hsüan² kua⁴, ... To be suspended; as a hanging lamp, a sign-board.
    揀選 chien² hsüen³, ... To select [officials for promotion]. Note chien³ changed to chien².
    候選 'hou⁴ hsüen⁴, ... [Of officials] awaiting selection.

雪 hsüeh, snow.
124. 靴鞵 hsüeh¹ hsieh², ... Boots and shoes. See hsieh².
    穴道 hsüeh² tao⁴, ... In anatomy, the space between the joints; the points at which, in acupuncture, the needle is introduced; applied in geomancy to the features of ground.
    雨雪 yü² hsüeh³, ... Rain and snow. Note yü³ changed to yü².
    鑽穴 tsuan¹ hsüeh⁴, ... To excavate, as a mine; of wild beasts, to dig a den to lie in.

PART VII. THE TONE EXERCISES. *hsieh – jou.*

巡 *hsün*, to go rounds.
125. 薰蒸 *hsün¹ chêng¹*, ... Of steamy vapour [after rain, off a fen, &c.]
  巡察 *hsün² ch'a²*, ... To go rounds, as a watch, a cruiser, &c.
  營汛 *ying² hsün⁴*, ... A military post; collectively, the military in a particular locality; *lit.* battalions, or cantonments and minor stations.

學 *hsüo*, (also as above, *hsio*; also *hsüeh*;) to learn.
126. 學生 *hsüo² shêng¹*, ... A pupil; a student.

衣 *i*, or *yi*, clothes.
127. 衣裳 *i¹ shang¹*, ... Clothes in general; originally, *i*, of the upper clothing, *shang*, of the lower.
  一個 *i² ko⁴*, ... One. See Note on Numeratives, EXERC. I.
  尾巴 *i³ pa¹*, ... The tail of beasts, fish, &c. Note *i³*, properly *wei³*.
  容易 *yung² i⁴*, ... Easy.

染 *jan*, to dye.
128. 然否 *jan² fou³*, ... Is it thus or not? also, Whether it be so or not [is uncertain].
  沾染 *chan¹ jan³*, ... Thoroughly saturated with; deep dyed in; [used literally, but also, *fig.* of vicious habits.]

嚷 *jang*, to talk too loud; to be noisy.
129. 嚷嚷 *jang¹ jang¹*, ... To blab; to let out secrets. *Obs.* the second *jang*, becomes nearly *jang⁴*.
  瓤子 *jang² tzŭ*, ... The inside of a melon, pulp, seeds, and juice.
  嚷鬧 *jang³ nao⁴*, ... To quarrel, have altercation with a man, make a row, as one man or many.
  謙讓 *ch'ien¹ jang⁴*, ... To decline anything offered one; to decline praise as unworthy of it.

繞 *jao*, to wind round, *act. and neut.*
130. 饒裕 *jao² yu⁴*, ... Affluence; *lit.* plenty to eat and more.
  圍繞 *wei² jao³*, ... To enwreath, wrap round; also, *fig.* of a siege.
  繞住 *jao⁴ chu⁴*, ... To deprive of the power of movement by tying; also, *fig.* of affairs. Cf. complication, hand-tied.

熱 *jê*, or *jo*, hot.
131. 冷熱 *lêng³ jo⁴*, ... Cold and hot; cold and heat; temperature.

人 *jên*, man.
132. 人物 *jên² wu⁴*, ... Men and all other created things; also, mankind.
  容忍 *yung² jên³*, ... Forbearing, tolerant.
  責任 *tsê² jên⁴*, ... Responsibility; *lit.* the blame-bearing, the blame-trust.

扔 *jêng*, to throw from one.
133. 扔棄 *jêng¹ ch'i⁴*, ... To fling away as useless.

日 *jih*, the sun; the day.
134. 日月 *jih⁴ yüeh⁴*, ... Sun and moon; also, days and months.

若 *jo*, if.
135. 若論 *jo⁴ lun⁴*, ... If it be argued; also, if one is speaking of —, = as regards, with reference to.

肉 *jou*, meat, flesh.
136. 揉的一聲 *jou¹ ti¹ i⁴ shêng¹*, . . There was a sudden whirr, or any like sound, not loud; *jou*, properly, to rub between the hands.
  剛柔 *kang¹ jou²*, ... Hard and soft; morally, firm and yielding.
  骨肉 *ku³ jou⁴*, ... Bone and flesh; also, *fig.* of near relationship.

KEY TO THE TZŬ ERH CHI. **Colloquial Series.**

如 *ju*, if; like as; also, in accordance with.
137. 如貼 *ju¹ t'ieh¹*, ... Of management of private affairs, satisfactory; also, of health, good.
   如若 *ju² jo⁴*, ... If.
   强入 *ch'iang³ ju³*, ... To force wares on a buyer; force one's things into a house. Note *ch'iang³* nearly *ch'iang²*, before *ju³*. In PART V, SEC. II, 50, it is, properly, *ch'iang²*.
   出入 *ch'u¹ ju⁴*, ... To go out and come in; hence, expenditure and revenue; also, in sentences, *ch'u*, lenient, *ju*, severe.

輭 *juan*, soft.
138. 軟弱 *juan³ jo⁴*, ... Soft and weakly; feeble.

瑞 *jui*, blessings; prosperity.
139. 花蘂 *'hua¹ jui³*, ... Petals of a flower.
   祥瑞 *hsiang² jui⁴*, ... Prosperous condition, *sc.* of a state.

潤 *jun*, moistened.
140. 潤澤 *jun⁴ tsê⁴*, ... [Of weather,] soft, slightly damp.

榮 *jung*, anciently, the beauty of flowers, plants, &c. as distinguished from that of trees.
141. 榮耀 *jung² yao⁴*, ... Brilliant, *e.g.* as a cortege, &c.; oftener used of externals, but also o virtue, ability, &c.
   氄毛 *jung³ mao²*, ... Down of birds' feathers; the shorter hair of camels, &c.

嘎 *ka*, the *ca* in cachinnation.
142. 嘎嘎的笑 *ka¹ ka¹ ti¹ hsiao⁴*, . A roar of laughter.
   打嘎兒 *ta³ ka² 'rh*, . . . To spin, *lit.* strike, a pegtop.
   嘎雜子 *ka³ tsa² tzŭ*, . . A cross-grained fellow; not sympathetic.
   雞嘎嘎蛋兒 *chi¹ ka⁴ ka⁴ tan⁴-rh*, Cry of a hen laying.

卡 *k'a*, or *ch'ia*, a post in a pass.
143. 卡倫 *k'a¹ lun²*, ... An inland customs station.

改 *kai*, to change.
144. 該當 *kai¹ tang¹*, ... Ought rightly to be.
   改變 *kai³ pien⁴*, ... To change, *sc.* laws, fashions, &c. for good or evil.
   大概 *ta⁴ kai⁴*, ... A general outline; generally; probably.

開 *k'ai*, to open.
145. 開閉 *k'ai¹ pi⁴*, ... Open or closed, *sc.* a gate, a shop, &c.
   慷慨 *k'ang³ k'ai³*, . . . Liberal, large-hearted. Note *kang³* nearly *kang²*, before *k'ai³*.

甘 *kan*, sweet.
146. 甘苦 *kan¹ k'u³*, ... Sweet and bitter.
   追趕 *chui¹ kan³*, ... To overtake.
   才幹 *ts'ai² kan⁴*, ... Abilities.

看 *k'an*, to see; to look at.
147. 看守 *k'an¹ shou³*, ... To keep guard over.
   刀砍 *tao¹ k'an³*, ... To strike with a sword.
   看見 *k'an⁴ chien⁴*, . . . To see.

剛 *kang*, hard, hardness; also, firm.
148. 剛纔 *kang¹ ts'ai²*, ... Just now; just then. It is thought by some that this character is corruptly used for 將 *chiang*.
   土堈子 *t'u³ kang³ tzŭ*, . . A rise in the level of ground. Note *t'u³* nearly *t'u²*, before *kang³*.
   擡杠 *t'ai² kang⁴*, ... A pole to carry things on, two men supporting each an end.

PART VII. THE TONE EXERCISES. *ju – k'o*.

炕 *k'ang*, a stove-bed.
149. 康健 *k'ang¹ chien⁴*, ... At ease in mind and in vigorous health.
　　 扛擡 *k'ang² t'ai²*, ... To carry as luggage, with poles between two men; or, generally, of porterage.
　　 不抗不卑的 *pu⁴ k'ang³ pu⁴ pei⁴ ti*, Neither overweening nor cringing.
　　 火炕 *'huo³ k'ang⁴*, ... The stove-bed of brick used in the north of China.

告 *kao*, to tell to.
150. 高低 *kao¹ ti¹*, ... High and low; the height of; also, of persons, difference of degree, or ability.
　　 稿案 *kao³ an⁴*, ... Official papers; the correspondence, archives, of an office.
　　 告訴 *kao⁴ su⁴*, ... To inform, tell to; *su*, alone, is, properly, to complain.

考 *k'ao*, to examine, as candidates for degree, for employment in clerkships, &c.
151. 尻骨 *k'ao¹ ku³*, ... The *os coxendicis*.
　　 考察 *k'ao³ ch'a²*, ... To examine, search, as tide-waiters, &c.
　　 依靠 *i¹ k'ao⁴*, ... To depend on, as a friend on a friend, or a subordinate on a superior authority.

給 *kei*, properly, *chi*, to give; hence, *to* and *for*.
152. 放給 *fang⁴ kei³*, ... To issue, as grain, money, clothes, &c. to the poor, pay to troops, &c.

刻 *k'ei*, properly, *k'ê*, to engrave, only pronounced as here, in *k'ei-sou*.
153. 刻搜 *k'ei¹ sou¹*, ... To annoy, act vexatiously to.

根 *kên*, root.
154. 根本 *kên¹ pên³*, ... The very beginning, *fons et origo*; the cradle of a race, the family of a man, the origin of a case; *kên*, properly, the root of a tree below, *pên*, above, the soil.
　　 鬥限 *tou¹ kên²*, ... The "chaff" of mountebanks, strolling story-tellers, &c.
　　 艮卦 *kên⁴ kua⁴*, ... The symbol or diagram *kên*, the seventh of the *pa kua*, eight diagrams, which may be called the categorical indices of Chinese philosophy; *kên*, generally indicative of immobility, stable.

肯 *k'ên*, to wish; to choose.
155. 肯不肯 *k'ên³ pu⁴ k'ên³*, ... Will you . . . . ? *lit.* will you or won't you, but, in effect, not so strong.
　　 一掯子 *i² k'ên⁴ tzŭ*, ... A bundle of anything that one requires both hands to hold.

更 *kêng*, more; to change.
156. 更改 *kêng¹ kai³*, ... To change, alter.
　　 道埂子 *tao⁴ kêng³ tzŭ*, ... Any foot-path left by the side of a road that is flooded, or otherwise
　　 更多 *kêng⁴ to¹*, ... More; a greater number, or quantity.　　　　 [obstructed.

坑 *k'êng*, a hollow, ditch, pit.
157. 坑坎 *k'êng¹ k'an³*, ... A dip in a road.

各 *ko, kê*, each, every.
158. 哥哥 *ko¹ ko¹*, ... Elder brother.
　　 影格 *ying³ ko²*, ... Copy slips; *ying*, a shadow, hence, an appearance, *ko*, here, in the sense of lines laid down for guidance. The Chinese copy-slip is in columns of characters separated by lines, and which the student traces through a sheet of paper laid over the copy-slip.
　　 各自各兒 *ko⁴ tzŭ⁴ ko³-'rh*, . . By one's self.
　　 幾個 *chi³ ko⁴*, ... Some, a certain number.

可 *k'o, k'ê*, to be right, to be able; with adjectives and in attributive constructions, much what the
159.　　 termination *bilis* is in Latin.
　　 可惜了兒 *k'o¹ hsi¹ liao³-'rh*, . . Alas! or, lamentable; *lit.* that can be pitied, that it is right to pity.
　　 可否 *k'o² fou³*, ... Is it right or not? Is it practicable or not? Whether right or not. Note that *k'o* is properly *k'o³*. See PART III, EXERC. VI, 12.
　　 饑渴 *chi¹ k'o³*, ... Hunger and thirst.
　　 賓客 *pin¹ k'o⁴*, ... , A guest.

KEY TO THE TZŬ ERH CHI. Colloquial Series.

狗 *kou*, a dog.
160. 溝洫 *kou¹ ch'ü²*, ... Ditches; *kou*, large and artificial; *ch'ü*, small water-ways; generally, the drains of a city.
    小狗兒的 *hsiao³ kou²-'rh ti¹*, . . You young dog!—to a child (not abusive).
    猪狗 *chu¹ kou³*, ... Pigs and dogs, said of dirty people; also *lit.* = domestic animals in general.
    足彀 *tsu² kou⁴*, ... Sufficient.

口 *k'ou*, the mouth.
161. 摳破了 *k'ou¹ p'o⁴ liao³*, . . . To work a hole through with the finger nail. Note *liao* euclitic, nearly *lo⁴*.
    口舌 *k'ou³ shê²*, ... Altercation.
    叩頭 *k'ou⁴ t'ou²*, ... To knock the head on the ground; to kotow.

古 *ku*, ancient.
162. 料估 *liao⁴ ku¹*, ... To estimate; as cost, amount of materials.
    骨頭 *ku² t'ou⁴*, ... A bone, one's bones; observe *ku*, properly *ku³*, here *ku²* ; *t'ou*, properly *t'ou²*, here *t'ou⁴*.
    古今 *ku³ chin¹*, ... Ancient and modern; in past times and at present.
    堅固 *chien¹ ku⁴*, ... Stable, sound, strong; as a city-wall, a ship, &c.

苦 *k'u*, bitter.
163. 窟窿 *k'u¹ lung¹*, ... A hole.
    甜苦 *t'ien² k'u³*, ... Sweet and bitter; also *fig.* of one's lot in life.
    褲子 *k'u⁴ tzŭ*, ... Trowsers.

瓜 *kua*, gourd.
164. 瓜果 *kua¹ kuo³*, ... Gourds and fruit; collective of such productions.
    多寡 *to¹ kua³*, ... Many and few; how many? the number of.
    懸掛 *hsüan² kua⁴*, ... To suspend, be suspended, in space.

跨 *k'ua*, to bestride.
165. 誇獎 *k'ua¹ chiang³*, ... To praise, one's self or another.
    侉子 *k'ua³ tzŭ*, ... A person remarkable for country accent, unfashionable dress, &c.
    跨馬 *k'ua⁴ ma³*, ... To ride with both legs on the same side.

怪 *kuai*, singular; strange; monstrous.
166. 乖張 *kuai¹ chang¹*, . . Of a person with ways of his own; one who does not get on well with others.
    拐騙 *kuai³ p'ien⁴*, ... To do one out of anything; to beguile as kidnappers children, slaves, &c.
    怪道 *kuai⁴ tao⁴*, ... Strange! *lit.* strange to say; of breaches of etiquette, eccentricities, &c.

快 *k'uai*, quick.
167. 搔痒痒 *k'uai² yang³ yang²*, . . To scratch an itching. Note that *k'uai*, properly *k'uai²*, becomes nearly *k'uai¹* before *yang³*, but the second *yang*, nearly *yang²*.
    快慢 *k'uai⁴ man⁴*, ... Quick and slow; the speed of.

官 *kuan*, an official.
168. 官員 *kuan¹ yuan²*, ... An official; *yüan*, meaning the same thing as *kuan*.
    管理 *kuan³ li³*, ... To manage, take care of. Note *kuan³* nearly *kuan²*, before *li³*.
    習慣 *hsi² kuan⁴*, ... To be practised in, expert at; well used to.

寬 *k'uan*, wide, roomy.
169. 寬窄 *k'uan¹ chai³*, ... Wide and narrow; the breadth of.
    款項 *k'uan³ hsiang⁴*, ... Larger and smaller items; expenditure.

光 *kuang*, lustre, brightness.
170. 光明 *kuang¹ ming²*, ... Bright, intelligent.
    廣大 *kuang³ ta⁴*, ... Extensive.
    遊逛 *yu² kuang⁴*, ... To stroll, exercise; to travel as a tourist.

PART VII. THE TONE EXERCISES. *kou – lai*.

況 *k'uang*, moreover.
171. 誆騙 *k'uang¹ p'ien⁴*, ... To humbug.
     狂妄 *k'uang² wang⁴*, ... Arrogant and wrong doing; said of persons in high station.
     況且 *k'uang⁴ ch'ieh³*, ... Moreover; in addition.

規 *kuei*, a pair of compasses.
172. 規矩 *kuei¹ chü⁴*, ... Proper custom or conduct; *lit.* compasses and rule.
     詭詐 *kuei³ cha⁴*, ... Artful, deceitful.
     富貴 *fu⁴ kuei⁴*, ... Rich; *lit.* rich and honorable.

愧 *k'uei*, to be ashamed.
173. 虧欠 *k'uei¹ ch'ien⁴*, ... To be in debt.
     揆守 *k'uei² shou³*, ... The master-mind in a business, the best hand; *ellipt.* for 揆度 *k'uei-to*, to measure, 守分 *shou fên*, to do one's duty.
     傀儡 *k'uei³ lei³*, ... An ill-looking person, *lit.* an ugly doll. Note *k'uei³* nearly *k'uei²* before *lei³*.
     慚愧 *ts'an² k'uei⁴*, ... Remorse.

棍 *kuên*, or *kun*, a staff.
174. 翻滾 *fan¹ kuên³*, ... Topsy-turvy, like things in a pot of boiling water.
     棍子棒子 *kuên⁴ tzŭ pang⁴ tzŭ*, . Sticks and staves, such as children might use in play, or ruffians in a fray.

困 *k'uên*, or *k'un*, one of the eight *kua*; see *kên*.
175. 坤道 *k'uên¹ tao⁴*, ... Female, earth, moon, as distinct from male, heaven, sun, &c.
     閨閫 *k'uei¹ k'uên³*, . Whatever belongs to woman; used often like our phrase *the sex*; also, as feminineness.
     乏困 *fa² k'uên⁴*, ... Tired and sleepy.

工 *kung*, labour.
176. 工夫 *kung¹ fu¹*, ... Labour; also, the time it occupies; hence, leisure.
     金礦 *chin¹ kung³*, ... Gold mines.
     通共 *t'ung¹ kung⁴*, ... The whole of any thing or number.

孔 *k'ung*, hollow.
177. 空虛 *k'ung¹ hsü¹*, ... Cleaned out.
     面孔 *mien⁴ k'ung³*, ... The cavities of the face; eyes, ears, nostrils, &c.
     閒空 *hsien² k'ung⁴*, ... With nothing to do.

果 *kuo*, fruit.
178. 飯鍋 *fan⁴ kuo¹*, ... A pan to cook rice in.
     國家 *kuo² chia¹*, ... The state; *lit.* state-family.
     結果 *chieh² kuo³*, ... The fruit is formed; also, *fig.* of a result; also, *ne plus ultra*,
     過去 *kuo⁴ ch'ü⁴*, ... To pass by.

闊 *k'uo*, wide.
179. 寬闊 *k'uan¹ k'uo⁴*, ... Extensive; *e.g.* as a country.

拉 *la*, to draw, or drag.
180. 拉扯 *la¹ ch'ê³*, ... To drag, *sc.* a person; also, *fig.* to implicate; also, of the relationship of some one with one's relation; *q.d.* such a person dragged into relationship.
     邋遢 *la² t'a⁴*, ... Slovenly in dress; in business, the opposite of 俐羅 *li lo*, prompt, decided.
     蝲蝲蛄 *la³ la³ ku³*, ... The mole cricket. Observe the second *la³*, before *ku³*, nearly *la²*; the first *la* consequently remains *la³*.
     蠟燭 *la⁴ chu²*, ... Wax candle.

來 *lai*, to come.
181. 來去 *lai² ch'ü⁴*, ... To come and go.
     倚賴 *i³ lai⁴*, ... To rely on; specially of self-reliance in a bad sense.

懶 *lan*, idle.
182. 鬤鬆 *lan¹ san¹*, ... Dawdling; *lit.* of hair dishevelled.
    貪婪 *t'an¹ lan²*, ... Covetous.
    懶惰 *lan³ to⁴*, ... Idle.
    燦爛 *ts'an³ lan⁴*, ... Properly, bright, as fire-light; variegated in colour.

浪 *lang*, a wave.
183. 檳榔 *ping¹ lang¹*, ... The betel, or areca-nut.
    狼虎 *lang² hu³*, ... Wolves and tigers; *fig.* of ravenous appetite or gluttony; also, of temerity.
    光朗 *kuang¹ lang³*, ... Bright, unblemished; *e.g.* as fine jeweller's work.
    波浪 *po¹ lang⁴*, ... Waves.

老 *lao*, old.
184. 打撈 *ta³ lao¹*, ... To fish up, or try to fish up, out of water, whether person or thing, visible or invisible.
    勞苦 *lao² k'u³*, ... Fatigue, bodily rather than mental.
    老幼 *lao³ yu⁴*, ... Old and young.
    旱潦 *'han⁴ lao⁴*, ... Drought and inundation.

勒 *lê*, originally, a bit; it has other meanings, but is not used colloquially, except in combination
185.   with a verb, as here.
    勒索 *lê¹ so⁴*, ... To "squeeze," extort anything from.
    歡樂 *'huan¹ lê⁴*, ... To rejoice, make merry, as a large party together.

累 *léi*, or *lei*, to entangle, embarrass.
186. 勒死 *lei¹ ssŭ³*, ... To strangle.
    雷電 *lei² tien⁴*, ... Thunder and lightning.
    累次 *lei³ tz'ŭ⁴*, ... Time after time.
    族類 *tsu² lei⁴*, ... One's relatives; *q. d.* the whole tribe.

冷 *lêng*, cold.
187. 稜角 *lêng² chio⁴*, ... Literally, edge and corner; *fig.* for extremity, *q.d.* nothing to lay hold of.
    冷熱 *lêng³ jo⁴*, ... Cold and hot; temperature.
    發愣 *fa¹ lêng⁴*, ... To be absent; to stare idiotlike.

立 *li*, to stand upright.
188. 玻璃 *po¹ li¹*, ... Glass.
    分離 *fên¹ li²*, ... Separated as members of a family dispersed.
    禮貌 *li³ mao⁴*, ... Politeness, manners.
    站立 *chan⁴ li⁴*, ... To stand up, as persons; to stand well, as a building, a business.

倆 *lia*, vulgar for *liang*, two.
189. 倆三 *lia³ sa¹*, ... Two or three.

兩 *liang*, the Chinese ounce.
190. 商量 *shang¹ liang¹*, ... To consult together.
    涼熱 *liang² jo⁴*, ... Cool and hot.
    斤兩 *chin¹ liang³*, ... Catties and ounces.
    原諒 *yuan² liang⁴*, ... To pardon.

了 *liao*, to end, complete.
191. 無聊 *wu² liao²*, ... In despair; *lit.* without resource.
    了斷 *liao³ tuan⁴*, ... To decide definitively, as a case in court; the decision of a case.
    料理 *liao⁴ li³*, ... To manage, attend to, as business in a shop, household affairs.

PART VII. THE TONE EXERCISES. *lan – lüeh.*

裂 *lieh*, arrayed in order.
192. 罷咧 *pa⁴ lieh¹*, ... An interjection, common, at the end of a sentence; = that's all about it.
     瞎咧咧 *hsia¹ lieh² lieh²*, . . . Gibberish of small children; in grown up people, romancing.
     咧嘴 *lieh³ tsui³*, ... To draw down the corners of the mouth in a way indicative of contempt or hostility. Note *lieh* nearly *lieh²*.
     擺列 *pai³ lieh⁴*, ... To array at given distances, *e. g.* a rank of soldiers.

連 *lien*, to unite.
193. 接連 *chieh¹ lien¹*, . . . United, as what follows with what precedes. Oftener pronounced *chieh¹ lien²*.
     憐恤 *lien² hsü⁴*, ... To compassionate.
     臉面 *lien³ mien⁴*, ... The face.
     練習 *lien⁴ hsi⁰,²*. . . . . . To practise; practised in.

林 *lin*, a forest or grove.
194. 樹林子 *shu⁴ lin² tzŭ*, ... A forest.
     房檁 *fang² lin³*, ... The cross-beams of a roof.
     租賃 *tsu¹ lin⁴*, ... To hire [a room, or house].

另 *ling*, additional.
195. 零碎 *ling² sui⁴*, ... Fragments; odds and ends.
     領袖 *ling³ hsiu⁴*, ... See *hsiu⁴*.
     另外 *ling⁴ wai⁴*, ... Separately, additionally.

略 *lio*, originally, to lay out ground, *e.g.* in fields. See *lüeh, lio.*
196. 謀略 *mou² lio⁴*, ... Strategical combinations; plan of a campaign.

留 *liu*, to detain; keep.
197. 一遛兒 *i⁴ liu¹ 'rh*, ... The act of gliding past, as when a person wants to pass unnoticed. Observe the *êrh*, absorbed.
     收留 *shou¹ liu²*, ... To take in, give hospitality to, a person, for a certain length of time.
     楊柳 *yang² liu³*, ... The willow.
     五六 *wu³ liu⁴*, ... Five or six.

駱 *lo*, a mule.
198. 擄起袖子 *lo¹ ch'i³ hsiu⁴ tzŭ*, . To tuck up the sleeves. Observe *ch'iang lo*, to carry off people or property, properly, *ch'ang³ lo³*, but, when combined, *ch'iang² -lo³*.
     騾馬 *lo² ma³*, ... Mules and horses.
     裸身 *lo³ shên¹*, ... Stark-naked.
     駱駝 *lo⁴ t'o²*, ... A camel.

陋 *lou*, mean, in spirit or appearance; used only in combination.
199. 摟衣裳 *lou¹ i¹ shang¹*, ... To hold up the skirts of one's long dress.
     樓房 *lou² fang²*, ... A house with an upper story.
     酒簍 *chiu³ lou³*, . . Wine baskets; large wicker bottles lined with oiled paper. Note *chiu²* nearly *chiu³*.
     鄙陋 *pi³ lou⁴*, ... Mean-spirited, vulgar-minded; ungentlemanlike in conduct.

律 *lü*, an ass. *laws*.
200. 驢馬 *lü² ma³*, ... Asses and horses.
     屢次 *lü³ tz'ŭ⁴*, ... Several times; repeatedly.
     律例 *lü⁴ li⁴*, ... Statutes and minor enactments.

戀 *lüan*, affection for one's family, birth-place, &c.
201. 依戀 *i¹ luan⁴* or *lüen⁴*, ... To cling affectionately to family, home, friends, &c.

略 *lüeh*, see *lio*; it is hard to say when this character is pronounced *lüeh* and when *lio*:
202. 忽略 *hu¹ lüeh⁴*, ... From carelessness, from indifference —.

KEY TO THE TZŬ ERH CHI. **Colloquial Series.**

掄 *lün*, to whirl round.
203. 混掄 ʻ*huên*⁴ *lün*¹, ... Whirling madly round, *sc.* a staff or the like.
　　人倫 *jên*² *lün*², ... The five relations, *sc.* of prince to minister, father to son, husband to wife, brother to brother, and friend to friend. See *lun.*
　　渾圇著 ʻ*huên*³ *lün*³ *cho*, ... In the lump; of speaking inexactly; of buying wholesale; of wholesale massacre; *lün*, a mass or large number of anything. Observe *huên*³ nearly ʻ*hun*² before *lün*³.
　　講論 *chiang*³ *lün*⁴, ... To talk of; be speaking of.

略 *liio*, See *lio* and *lüeh*.
204. 大略 *ta*⁴ *liio*⁴, ... General outline.

路 *lu*, a road.
205. 嘟嚕 *tu*¹ *lu*¹, ... A bunch of grapes, cash, fish, &c.; a sound like *turrh*, of common occurrence in Mongolian; hence, applied to thick guttural speech of any man.
　　爐灶 *lu*² *tsao*⁴, ... A kitchen fire.
　　船櫓 *ch'uan*² *lu*³, ... The stern-paddle of a junk.
　　道路 *tao*⁴ *lu*⁴, ... Roads and ways.

亂 *luan*, confused, disorderly.
206. 雜亂 *tsa*² *luan*⁴, ... Of things jumbled together.

論 *lun*, to speak of, discuss a matter.
207. 車輪 *ch'ê*¹ *lun*², ... The wheel of a cart.
　　囫圇 ʻ*hu*² *lun*³, ... In the gross, without distinction of quality; of bolting down a fruit *whole*.
　　沒論 *mei*² *lun*⁴, ... Not to speak of = setting apart, something already spoken of.

龍 *lung*, the dragon.
208. 窟窿 *k'u*¹ *lung*¹, ... A hole.
　　龍虎榜 *lung*² ʻ*hu*³ *pang*³, . . . The published list of passed graduates; *lit.* the roll, or placard, of dragons and tigers. See note on ʻ*hu*³.
　　瓦隴 *wa*³ *lung*³, ... The lines or furrows between the tiles of a roof. Note *wa*³ nearly *wa*².
　　胡弄局 ʻ*hu*² *lung*⁴ *chü*², . . . Of any thing or affair which *seems* all right, but has been so made or managed as to be worthless; ʻ*hu lung*, to take in by words or deeds; *chü*, properly, a chessboard.

馬 *ma*, the horse. Observe *ma*, properly *ma*³, in *ma p'i*³ nearly *ma*².
209. 爹媽 *tieh*¹ *ma*¹, ... Daddy and mammy.
　　麻木 *ma*² *mu*⁴, ... Numb, as a foot asleep, a paralytic limb.
　　馬鞍 *ma*³ *ngan*¹, ... A saddle.
　　打罵 *ta*³ *ma*⁴, ... Blows and curses, or abuse.

買 *mai*, to buy.
210. 葬埋 *tsang*⁴ *mai*², ... To bury, of the dead only.
　　收買 *shou*¹ *mai*³, ... To buy things brought to one for sale.
　　發賣 *fa*¹ *mai*⁴, ... For sale; to sell or expose to sale.

慢 *man*, slow.
211. 顢頇 *man*¹ ʻ*han*¹, ... Dilatory, the opposite of 簡决 *chien chüeh*, to decide promptly, summarily.
　　隱瞞 *yin*³ *man*², ... Close, as the opposite of talkative, outspoken.
　　豐滿 *fêng*¹ *man*³, ... Abundant, *sc.* as a dinner; *fêng tsu*, plentiful, as a year.
　　快慢 *k'uai*⁴ *man*⁴, ... Quick and slow; the speed of.

忙 *mang*, hurried, hasty.
212. 白茫茫 *pai*² *mang*¹ *mang*¹, . . . The brightness of a large sheet of water. Cf. ʻ*hao* ʻ*hao*, LESSON XCI, 2.
　　急忙 *chi*² *mang*², ... Haste (not hurry); without loss of time.
　　鹵莽 *lu*³ *mang*³, ... In a rough-and-tumble style; applied by an ancient philosopher to his own carelessness as a farmer. Observe *lu*³, nearly *lu*², before *mang*³.

80

PART VII. THE TONE EXERCISES. *liin – miu*.

毛 *mao*, hair.
213. 貓狗 *mao¹ kou³*, ... Cats and dogs; in such phrases as What a noise they make, &c.
　　　羽毛 *yü³ mao²*, ... Feathers; *lit.* feathers and hair.
　　　卯刻 *mao³ k'ê⁴*, ... The fourth of the twelve two-hour periods of the Chinese day; say 5 to 7 a.m.
　　　相貌 *hsiang⁴ mao⁴*, ... Appearance of the face; the countenance.

美 *mei*, beautiful; of woman's beauty.
214. 煤炭 *mei² t'an⁴*, ... Coal and charcoal.
　　　美貌 *mei³ mao⁴*, ... Handsome countenance [of a woman].
　　　愚昧 *yu² mei⁴*, ... Stupid; used of one's own humble opinion.

門 *mên*, a gate, a door.
215. 捫搎 *mên¹ sun¹*, ... Caressing fondly a child, a pet, a bijou; *mên*, to press the hand on; *sun*, to move it, smoothing or patting the object.
　　　門扇 *mên² shan⁴*, ... The leaf of a door.
　　　憂悶 *yu¹ mên⁴*, ... Sad; *yu*, grief; *mên*, joylessness.

夢 *mêng*, a dream.
216. 懵懂 *mêng¹ tung³*, ... Thick-headed; *mêng-mêng-tung-tung* also used.
　　　結盟 *chieh² mêng²*, ... To bind one's self by an oath, to heaven or to man.
　　　勇猛 *yung³ mêng³*, ... Ardour in fight, in study, &c. Note *yung³* nearly *yung²* before *mêng³*.
　　　睡夢 *shui⁴ mêng⁴*, ... To dream.

米 *mi*, rice with the husk off.
217. 眯睡眼 *mi¹ fêng² yen³*, . . Eyes nearly closed by nature.
　　　迷惑 *mi² 'huo⁴*, ... Blindness of a vicious mind; all abroad, as a person who has lost his way.
　　　米糧 *mi³ liang²*, ... Food in general; as we say, bread.
　　　機密 *chi¹ mi⁴*, ... Close, in word or deed.

苗 *miao*, the young blade of corn, &c.
218. 喵喵的貓叫 *miao¹ miao¹ ti¹ mao¹ chiao⁴*, The mewing of cats.
　　　禾苗 *'ho² miao²*, ... The young blade of corn.
　　　藐小 *miao³ hsiao³*, ... Small, of insignificant dimension; used contemptuously or not. Observe *miao³* nearly *miao²*, because followed by *hsiao³*.
　　　廟宇 *miao⁴ yü³*, ... Temples in general.

滅 *mieh*, to extinguish.
219. 咩咩的羊叫 *mieh¹ mieh¹ ti¹ yang² chiao⁴*, The baa-ing of sheep.
　　　滅火 *mieh⁴ 'huo³*, ... To extinguish a light or a fire.

面 *mien*, the face.
220. 綿花 *mien² 'hua¹*, ... Cotton.
　　　勉力 *mien³ li⁴*, ... To exert oneself.
　　　臉面 *lien³ mien⁴*, ... The face.

民 *min*, the people, as distinct from the government.
221. 民人 *min² jên²*, ... The people; or, one of the people, as distinct from the Bannermen.
　　　憐憫 *lien² min³*, ... To feel pity; *lien hsü* (see *lien⁴*), is to shew it.

名 *ming*, a name.
222. 姓名 *hsing⁴ ming²*, ... Name and surname.
　　　性命 *hsing⁴ ming⁴*, ... Life; as in the phrase, cases of life and death, &c.

謬 *miu*, perverse.
223. 謬妄 *miu⁴ wang⁴*, ... To ruin by perversity.

KEY TO THE TZŬ ERH CHI. **Colloquial Series.**

末 *mo*, the end or tip.
224. 揣摩 *ch'uai³ mo¹*, ... To conjecture.
    甚麼 *shên² mo²*, ... What?
    塗抹 *t'u² mo³*, ... To blot out a character; also used, modestly, of one's own performances with pen or pencil.
    始末 *shih³ mo⁴*, ... From beginning to end [of a story].

謀 *mou*, to plot a plan.
225. 圖謀 *t'u² mou²*, ... To lay plans, for good or for evil.
    某人 *mou³ jên²*, ... A certain man; so-and-so.

木 *mu*, a tree.
226. 模樣 *mu² yang⁴*, ... Style, appearance; of men or things; *mu²*, alone, a mould.
    父母 *fu⁴ mu³*, ... Father and mother.
    草木 *ts'ao³ mu⁴*, ... Plants and trees; the vegetable kingdom.

那 *na*, the demonstrative pronoun *that*.
227. 在這兒那 *tsai⁴ ché⁴ 'rh na¹*, . . Here; in this place. Note *na*, simply an expletive.
    拏賊 *na² tsei²*, ... To seize a thief.
    那個 *na³ ko⁴*, ... Which one? Which?
    那裏 *na⁴ li⁴*, ... That place; there. Note *li³* in *li-t'ou*; but in *na⁴-li*, There, nearly *li⁴*, also in *na³-li*, Where? the latter *na* consequently remaining *na³*.

奶 *nai*, milk.
228. 牛奶 *niu² nai³*, ... Cow's milk.
    耐時 *nai⁴ shih²*, ... Putting up with the fortunes of the hour.

男 *nan*, the male; man.
229. 喃喃囈語 *nan¹ nan¹ i⁴ yü³*, . . The babbling of a person in a dream.
    男婦 *nan² fu⁴*, ... Men and women; politely said of persons of both sexes suffering by any general calamity.
    災難 *tsai¹ nan⁴*, ... Calamity. Note *nan*, difficult, read *nan²*.

囊 *nang*, a bag or purse.
230. 嘟囔 *tu¹ nang¹*, ... To mumble, talk indistinctly; to babble as a baby.
    囊袋 *nang² tai⁴*, ... A money-bag or purse hung from the waist.
    攮了一刀子 *nang³ liao i⁴ tao¹ tzŭ*, To have run a knife into [a man]. Note *liao* enclitic.
    齉鼻子 *nang⁴ pi² tzŭ*, ... Applied to the sound of a voice, a nasal twang.

鬧 *nao*, properly, noise of voices; very commonly, to be angry; also, of things that should not
231.   happen, to happen; as we say, war, plague, or less matters, *broke out*.
    撓着 *nao¹ cho*, ... Fingering, fiddling with.
    鐃鈸 *nao² pa⁴*, ... Cymbals, great and small.
    煩惱 *fan² nao³*, ... In great trouble.
    熱鬧 *jo⁴ nao⁴*, ... Noisy, bustling, as a fair, a street, &c.

內 *nei*, inside.
232. 內外 *nei⁴ wai⁴*, ... Within and without; inner and outer; native and foreigner.

嫩 *nên*, tender, as meat, as young sprouts; the bones and flesh of a young child are *nên*.
233. 老嫩 *lao³ nên⁴*, ... Tough and tender; of meat, young plants.

能 *nêng*, to be able.
234. 才能 *ts'ai² nêng²*, ... Capacity, ability.

你 *ni*, thou.
235. 泥土 *ni² t'u³*, ... Dirt, as on a travel-soiled dress, in an unclean room, &c.
    擬議 *ni³ i⁴*, ... To suggest, propose for deliberation.
    藏匿 *ts'ang² ni⁴*, ... To hide (active and neuter) with evil intent.

PART VII. THE TONE EXERCISES. *mo — niio.*

娘 *niang*, a mother; in the plural, women.
236.
爹娘 *tieh¹ niang²*, ... Daddy and mammy.
蘊釀 *yun⁴ niang⁴*, ... Taking time, not hurrying; *yün⁴*, secret, kept hid, *q.d.* for a long time; *niang⁴*, to ferment as wine.

鳥 *niao*, a bird.
237.
喵喵的貓叫 *niao¹ niao¹ ti¹ mao¹ chiao⁴*, Cats' mewing.
鳥獸 *niao³ shou⁴*, ... Birds and beasts.
屎尿 *shih³ niao⁴*, ... Filth; *lit.* dung and urine.

揑 *nieh*, to work with the fingers.
238.
捏弄 *nieh¹ nung⁴*, ... To mould as clay; to knead as dough.
呆獃 *nieh² tai¹*, ... Loutish, stupid in appearance.
罪孽 *tsui⁴ nieh⁴*, ... The retribution of sin done in a previous existence, = ill-fortune.

念 *nien*, to think of, to remember; also, to read.
239.
拈花 *nien¹ 'hua¹*, ... To pick flowers.
年月 *nien² yueh⁴*, ... Years and months.
捻匪 *nien³ fei³*, ... The Nien Fei, *lit.* Filchers, a banditti who infest the borders of Shan Tung and Ho Nan. Observe the *nien³* nearly *nien²*, because followed by *fei³*.
念誦 *nien⁴ sung⁴*, ... To recite, as the Buddhist priest his books.

您 *nin*, a polite form of the second person. See PART III, EXERC. XXV, 1.
240.
您納 *nin² na⁴*, ... The same as *nin*.

甯 *ning*, tranquillity. This character was properly written 寧, but being the second in Mien Ning,
241.
the name of the Emperor, the style of whose reign was Tao Kuang, was altered as the law requires.
安甯 *an¹ ning²*, ... In a state of peace.
擰壞 *ning³ huai⁴*, ... To spoil by fiddling with; as the works of a watch, a lock, &c.
佞口 *ning⁴ k'ou³*, ... A specious glib talker; *lit.* an eloquent mouth, = a smooth tongue.

虐 *nio*, tyrannical.
242.
暴虐 *pao⁴ nio⁴*, ... Passionate and tyrannical; tyranny.

牛 *niu*, the ox.
243.
妞兒 *niu¹ 'rh*, ... One's little girl.
牛馬 *niu² ma³*, ... Oxen and horses; one's cattle.
鈕扣 *niu³ k'ou⁴*, ... Buttons of a Chinese dress.
拗不過來 *niu⁴ pu¹ kuo⁴ lai²*, . There is no bringing him round or over.

挪 *no*, to move from one place to another.
244.
挪移 *no² i²*, ... To shift one's residence; of officials, to misapply public money.
懦弱 *no⁴ jo⁴*, ... Imbecile, of no ability.

耨 *nou*, to weed.
245.
耕耨 *këng¹ nou⁴*, ... To till and to weed; agricultural operations.

女 *nü*, woman.
246.
男女 *nan² nü³*, ... Male and female; man and woman; husband and wife.

虐 *niieh*, see *nio*.
247.

虐 *niio*, see *nio*.
248.

KEY TO THE TZŬ ERH CHI. Colloquial Series.

奴 *nu*, a slave; when alone, not applied to women.
249. 奴僕 *nu² p'u⁴*, ... A slave; one's slaves in general; also, one's servants.
　　 努力 *nu³ li⁴*, ... To exert one's self.
　　 喜怒 *hsi³ nu⁴*, ... Temper 不常 *pu ch'ang*, uneven.

暖 *nuan*, also *nan*, warm; as weather, clothes, room, &c.
250. 暖和 *nuan³ 'huo⁴*, ... Warm; also read *nuan³ ho²*, *nan³ ho²*.

嫩 *nun*, see *nên*.
251. 老嫩 *lao³ nun⁴*, ... See *nên⁴*.

濃 *nung*, of liquids, thick; especially with reference to colours.
252. 濃淡 *nung² tan⁴*, ... (Of colours) deep and faint.
　　 擺弄 *pai³ nung⁴*, ... To busy one's self about, as one's garden, &c.; also, to meddle with, fiddle with.

訛 *o*, ⁿᵍ*o*, to deceive [people].
253. 哦一聲 *o¹ i⁴ shêng¹*, ... To give an *o* of assent.
　　 訛錯 *o² ts'o⁴*, ... Error, in reporting, copying, &c.
　　 善惡 *shan⁴ o⁴*, ... Virtue and vice; the virtuous and the vicious.

偶 *ou*, ⁿᵍ*ou*, properly, an image; hence, of times concurring; accidentally.
254. 毆打 *ou¹ ta³*, ... To beat.
　　 偶然 *ou³ jan²*, ... Accidentally; *q. d.* it occurred thus.
　　 嘔氣 *ou⁴ ch'i⁴*, ... To provoke a man to anger by one's words; *lit.* to spit [that which causes] wrath.

罷 *pa*, to cause to cease.
255. 八九 *pa¹ chiu³*, ... Eight or nine.
　　 提拔 *t'i² pa²*, ... To prefer one man to another.
　　 把持 *pa³ ch'ih²*, ... To engross power, business; there is another expression for usurpation of high authority.
　　 罷了 *pa⁴ liao*, ... It is ended; or, that is all about it. Note *liao* enclitic.

怕 *p'a*, to fear.
256. 琵琶 *p'i² p'a¹*, ... A musical instrument with four strings.
　　 扒桿兒 *p'a² kan¹-'rh*, ... To climb up a mast or pole.
　　 恐怕 *k'ung³ p'a⁴*, ... To fear.

拜 *pai*, to salute; hence, to visit.
257. 掰開 *pai¹ k'ai¹*, ... To break open with the two hands; as an apple, &c.
　　 黑白 *'hei¹ pai²*, ... Black and white; see *'hei*.
　　 千百 *ch'ien¹ pai³*, ... One thousand one hundred; a thousand and more [years].
　　 拜客 *pai⁴ k'o⁴*, ... To visit a person; the paying of visits.

派 *p'ai*, to distribute; hence, very commonly, to send on a mission or errand.
258. 拍打 *p'ai¹ ta³*, ... To tap with the hand, somewhat hard; *e. g.* a box, to see whether it is full or empty; a dress, to shake the dust out of it.
　　 木牌 *mu⁴ p'ai²*, ... A raft.
　　 一屁股瓠下 *i² p'i⁴ ku³ p'ai³ hsia⁴*, Popped himself down; said of an ill-bred person who takes a seat uninvited. Note *ku³* not *ku²*, though followed by *p'ai³*.
　　 分派 *fên¹ p'ai⁴*, ... To send in different directions; to apportion duties to different persons.

半 *pan*, the half.
259. 輪班 *lun² pan¹*, ... To serve in turn. See *pan*, PART III, EXERC.
　　 板片 *pan³ p'ien⁴*, ... Small boards or pieces of wood; *e. g.* the blocks cut for Chinese printing.
　　 整半 *chêng³ pan⁴*, ... The whole and the half.

PART VII. THE TONE EXERCISES. *nu – pêng*.

盼 *p'an*, to look for anxiously.
260. 高攀 *kao¹ p'an¹*, ... (Modestly,) I have the honour of his acquaintance; *p'an*, in the sense of drawing towards one, *e.g.* a branch one wants to break off; *kao p'an*, I draw to me the lofty [branch]
    盤查 *p'an² ch'a²*, ... To search, as the guard at a gate, customs' barrier, &c.; *p'an²*, a bowl, or bath, a receptacle; why used in *p'an ch'a*, is not explained.
    盼望 *p'an⁴ wang⁴*, . . . To look for, hope for; *so*, the coming of a person, a better state of things, &c.

幫 *pang*, to help.
261. 幫助 *pang¹ chu⁴*, ... To help.
    綑綁 *k'uên³ pang³*, . . To bind with cords;—men, animals, boxes, &c. Note *k'uên³* nearly *k'un²* before *pang³*.
    毀謗 *'hui³ pang⁴*, ... To backbite, ruin by censure deserved or undeserved.

旁 *p'ang*, the side of the person, a house, &c.
262. 胖腫 *p'ang¹ chung³*, ... Swollen as the body, a limb, a finger.
    旁邊 *p'ang² pien¹*, ... The side, by the side of.
    吹唪 *ch'ui¹ p'ang³*, ... To brag of one's talents, fortune, &c.
    胖瘦 *p'ang⁴ shou⁴*, . . . Fat and lean; *p'ang tzŭ*, a corpulent person.

包 *pao*, to wrap up; to envelope; hence, to enclose, enclosed.
263. 包裹 *pao¹ kuo³*, ... To wrap up; *pao*, singly, to wrap as in paper, in a cloth, &c.; *kuo*, to tie round, as the head with a handkerchief; the dissyllable *pao kuo*, might be used of the former act, but of the latter, *kuo* alone.
    厚薄 *'hou³ pao²*, ... Thick and thin; morally, of feelings, of intimacy.
    保護 *pao³ 'hu⁴*, ... To succour; to take care of person or property, one's own or another's.
    懷抱 *'huai² pao⁴*, ... To carry in the bosom as a child, an article; also, *fig.* of the mind, of its powers; of gratitude, not of anger, &c.

跑 *p'ao*, to run.
264. 拋棄 *p'ao¹ ch'i⁴*, ... To fling away anything that is worn out, useless; also, money, goods.
    袍袴 *p'ao² kua⁴*, ... *P'ao*, the long under-garments, *kua*, the long outer garment.
    跑脫 *p'ao³ t'o¹*, ... To run off, as a prisoner, a dog, &c.
    槍礮 *ch'iang¹ p'ao⁴*, ... Small-arms and artillery.

北 *pei*, the north.
265. 背負 *pei¹ fu⁴*, ... To carry on the back, as a child, a bundle.
    南北 *nan² pei³*, ... South and north.
    向背 *hsiang⁴ pei⁴*, ... Front and rear, of the person, a house; of things, where we speak of *face*, such as a clock, &c.

陪 *p'ei*, to bear company, be mate to.
266. 披衣 *p'ei¹ i¹*, ... To throw one's clothes on or over one, not buttoning, tying, &c.
    陪伴 *p'ei² pan⁴*, ... To be a comrade to, to bear one company.
    配偶 *p'ei⁴ ou³*, ... To be mate to, well-mated; said of a well-matched married couple.

本 *pên*, the root of a tree above the ground. See *kên*.
267. 奔忙 *pên¹ mang²*, ... Running about in haste; as a man much occupied.
    根本 *kên¹ pên³*, ... See *kên*.
    投奔 *t'ou² pên⁴*, ... To fly to a person or place for refuge.

盆 *p'ên*, a bowl or basin.
268. 噴水 *p'ên¹ shui³*, ... To spurt water out of the mouth, as over a floor to lay the dust, over materials in certain tailoring operations, &c.
    盆礶 *p'ên² kuan⁴*, . . . Earthenware; *lit.* bowls and jars; *kuan*, also, when of wood, meaning bucket.
    噴香 *p'ên⁴ hsiang¹*, ... To smell agreeably, as flowers, savoury dishes.

迸 *pêng*, to jump, or leap.
269. 繃鼓 *pêng¹ ku³*, ... To fasten tight [the drum-head of] a drum; *pêng*, used of any similar tightening with cords, thongs, &c.
    迸跳 *pêng⁴ t'iao⁴*, ... To jump about as a flea, a dog, &c.

KEY TO THE TZŬ ERH CHI. **Colloquial Series.**

朋 p'êng, a friend; properly, from circumstances.
270. 割烹 ko¹ p'êng¹, ... Of eating, *the fare;* literally, *ko*, to cut up the meat, *p'êng*, to fry it: politely, the *ko p'êng*, was good or was not good.
朋友 p'êng² yu³, ... Friends. See EXERC. XXIV, 16.
手捧 shou³ p'êng³, ... To hold up in the palms of the two hands joined together. Note *shou³* nearly *shou³*.
碰破 p'êng⁴ p'o⁴, ... To break by violent contact with; collision.

必 pi, necessary; must.
271. 逼迫 pi¹ p'o⁴, ... To press hard, duly or unduly; oftener, the latter.
口鼻 k'ou³ pi², ... Features, face, *lit.* mouth and nose [well or ill-looking].
筆墨 pi³ mo⁴, ... Pencils and ink; also, *fig.* composition, literary merit.
務必 wu⁴ pi⁴, ... Must positively; is sure to.

皮 p'i, skin, hide.
272. 批評 p'i¹ p'ing², ... To criticise, canvass the merits of character, composition, &c.
皮毛 p'i² mao², ... The hair or fur of an animal.
鄙俚 p'i³ li³, ... Vulgar, coarse, the opposite of 文雅 *wên ya*, well-mannered. Note *p'i³* nearly *p'i²* before *li³*.
屁股 p'i⁴ ku³, ... The buttocks; the breech.

表 piao, the outside; hence, to make manifest; hence, a watch.
273. 標文書 piao¹ wên² shu¹, . . To date and punctuate an official document [with red ink].
表裏 piao³ li³, ... Outside and inside, outer garment and its lining. Note *piao³* nearly *piao²*, before *li³*.
鰾膠 piao⁴ chiao¹, ... Glue made from fishes' entrails.

票 p'iao, originally, a gleam of fire; *wên p'iao*, a warrant, or summons.
274. 漂沒 p'iao¹ mo⁴, ... Of a ship or any thing tossing about in water; *q. d.* now floating, now unseen.
嫖賭 p'iao² tu³, ... Addicted to women and play; profligacy in general.
漂布 p'iao³ pu⁴, ... To bleach linen.
錢票子 ch'ien² p'iao⁴ tzŭ, . . A cash note. Note *tzŭ* enclitic.

別 pieh, to separate; different.
275. 憋悶 pieh¹ mên⁴, ... Sad, as a person under restraint of mind or body.
分別 fên¹ pieh², ... To distinguish, the distinction of, one from another.
彆嘴 pieh³ tsui³, ... To pout the lips; *pieh*, literally, stiff as a bow that will not bend. Note *pieh³* nearly *pieh²*, before *tsui³*.
彆拗 pieh⁴ niu⁴, ... Stiff-necked, not to be brought round, *pieh⁴ = pieh³*.

撇 p'ieh, to sweep or brush aside with the hand; *fig.* of changing the subject in conversation.
276. 撆開 p'ieh¹ k'ai¹, ... (See the line above.) This character is only another form of that in the example of *p'ieh³*.
撇了 p'ieh³ liao, ... To have rejected, put away, a friend, anything. Note *liao³* enclitic, and read as *la* or *lo*; *p'ieh³*, consequently, still *p'ieh³*.

扁 pien, flat.
277. 邊沿 pien¹ yen², ... Along a river-bank, or the sea-shore; only used where there is water.
圓扁 yüan² pien³, ... Round and flat.
方便 fang¹ pien⁴, ... Convenient.

片 p'ien, a piece, as of wood, paper, &c.; a clause as distinct from a sentence.
278. 偏正 p'ien¹ chêng⁴, ... Slanting and upright; *fig.* partial and impartial.
便宜 p'ien² i⁴, ... Cheap. See PART III, EXERC. XIII. Note *i⁴* properly *i²*.
諞拉 p'ien³ la¹, ... To brag; to parade one's talents, feats, wealth, position, &c.
片段 p'ien⁴ tuan⁴, ... *Lit.* clauses and sentences, but = phraseology or composition which is connected and complete. See PART VI, LESSON II, 2.

PART VII. THE TONE EXERCISES. p'êng – sa.

賓 *pin*, a guest.
279.
- 賓主 *pin¹ chu³*, ... Guest and host.
- 殯葬 *pin⁴ tsang⁴*, ... To bury; a funeral; *pin*, to carry and escort the coffin; *tsang*, to inter it.

貧 *p'in*, poor.
280.
- 拼命 *p'in¹ ming⁴*, ... To expose one's life recklessly; *lit*. to fling it away.
- 貧窮 *p'in² ch'iung²*, ... See *ch'iung*.
- 品級 *p'in³ chi²*, ... Official grade; *lit*. class and step.
- 牝牡 *p'in⁴ mou³*, ... (Politely,) the male and female of animals; *mou ma*, a stallion; *p'in niu*, a cow.

兵 *ping*, a soldier.
281.
- 兵丁 *ping¹ ting¹*, ... A soldier; *ting*, properly, an adult male, a male aged sixteen.
- 稟報 *ping³ pao⁴*, ... To report or state to a superior; *ping*, ordinarily rendered-petition; *pao*, to announce, give notice of.
- 疾病 *chi² ping⁴*, ... (Politely,) in a bad way, in very bad health.

憑 *p'ing*, to lean against, rely on; hence, at the pleasure of.
282.
- 砰磅 *p'ing¹ p'ang¹*, ... Of a crashing noise of any sort; *e. g.* of a man in a rage, a house falling, &c.
- 憑據 *p'ing² chü⁴*, ... Proof; *q. d.* what one leans on and takes hold of.
- 聘嫁 *p'ing⁴ chia⁴*, ... To marry one's daughter; *lit*. betrothal and [woman's] marriage.

波 *po*, a wave of sea water or fresh.
283.
- 水波 *shui³ po¹*, ... The ripple of water.
- 淮駁 *chun³ po²*, ... To authorise or disapprove a transaction, or proposition, officially.
- 播米 *po³ mi³*, ... To winnow or cleanse rice, as in a *po-chi*. Note *po³* nearly *po²*.
- 簸箕 *po⁴ chi⁴*, ... A shallow wicker scoop in which dust or dirt may be gathered, grain winnowed, &c.; it is some three inches high at the back, with sides sloping down to the front.

破 *p'o*, to break by collision, by letting fall.
284.
- 土坡 *t'u³ p'o¹*, ... A mound, or hillock, of earth, natural or artificial.
- 婆娘 *p'o² niang²*, ... Women.
- 簍籮 *p'o³ lo¹*, ... A shallow wicker basket; *e. g.* such as in the north carters feed their teams out of.
- 破碎 *p'o⁴ sui⁴*, ... Smashed to pieces.

不 *pou*, this pronunciation of *pu¹*, not, is only used in poetry.
285.

剖 *p'ou*, to rip open.
286.
- 掊剋 *p'ou¹ k'o⁴*, ... Only colloquial in the quotation 掊剋在位 *p'ou k'o tsai wei*, he is a grasping official; [Shu Ching.]
- 剖開 *p'ou³ k'ai¹*, ... To rip open a melon or any large fruit. The limitation in PART III, EXERC. XXXV, *ex*. 25, is incorrect.

不 *pu*, not, no.
287.
- 我不 *wo³ pu¹*, ... I say no!
- 不是 *pu² shih⁴*, ... Not to be so; not to be right; hence, a fault.
- 補缺 *pu³ ch'üeh¹*, ... To fill a vacancy.
- 不可 *pu⁴ k'o³*, ... It is not admissible; [I, you, he,] ought not.

普 *p'u*, universal. Note the formation of the character; *q. d.* all-pervading as the sun's rays.
288.
- 鋪蓋 *p'u¹ kai⁴*, ... One's bedding.
- 葡萄 *p'u² t'ao²*, ... Grapes.
- 普遍 *p'u³ pien⁴*, ... In all parts, or all sides.
- 鋪子 *p'u⁴ tzŭ*, ... A shop; very commonly written 舖. Note *tzŭ* enclitic.

灑 *sa*, to sprinkle.
289.
- 撒手 *sa¹ shou³*, ... To loosen the hand, let go; also, *fig.* of relaxing efforts.
- 一眼瞧著 *i⁴ yen³ sa² chao²*, . The eye suddenly lit on [some thing or person long sought].
- 洒掃 *sa³ sao³*, ... To sprinkle with water and sweep [a floor, &c.]. Note *sa³*, nearly *sa²*, before *sao³*.

KEY TO THE TZŬ ERH CHI. Colloquial Series.

賽 sai, to rival, pit one's self or another against.
290. 腮頰 sai¹ chia⁴, ... The cheeks.
賭賽 tu³ sai⁴, ... To compete with; to race; to bet.

散 san, to disperse.
291. 三四 san¹ ssŭ⁴, ... Three or four.
傘蓋 san³ kai⁴, ... An umbrella; specially, the red umbrella borne before officials.
散放 san⁴ fang⁴, . To distribute, as alms, food to the poor, to prisoners; pay to troops, small employés, &c.

桑 sang, the mulberry tree.
292. 桑梓 sang¹ tzŭ³, ... The mulberry and the tzŭ (a sort of cedar? Williams); the trees planted where a village was founded; hence, the home of one's fathers.
嗓子 sang³ tzŭ, ... The throat. Note tzŭ enclitic.
喪氣 sang⁴ ch'i⁴, ... Ill-omened; to be down-hearted because of an ominous occurrence.

掃 sao, to sweep.
293. 騷擾 sao¹ jao³, ... To harass, as an oppressor the people, troops a country.
掃地 sao³ ti⁴, ... To sweep the ground.
掃興 sao⁴ hsing⁴, ... Lit. swept away pleasure, happiness; a reverse of fortune.

嗇 sê, to love inordinately, to covet.
294. 嘶嘶的叫狗 sê¹ sê¹ ti¹ chiao⁴ kou³, The sound ss! ss! to a dog.
吝嗇 lin⁴ sê⁴, ... Niggardly.

森 sên, properly, dense as foliage; hence used intensively.
295. 森嚴 sên¹ yen², ... Very severe.

僧 sêng, a Buddhist priest.
296. 僧道 sêng¹ tao⁴, ... A priest, Buddhist and Taoist. See PART III, EXERC. XXXIII.

索 so, originally, a rope.
297. 調唆 t'iao² so¹, . . . To egg on, instigate, specially to quarrels, litigation; t'iao in the sense of mixing up.
鎖上 so³ shang⁴, ... To lock as a door, a box, &c.
追溯 chui¹ so⁴, ... Lit. to pursue up stream, to look back to past occurrences.

搜 sou, to search, as a guard, police, &c.
298. 搜察 sou¹ ch'a², ... To search and examine.
老叟 lao³ sou³, ... Reverend Sir; (classical). Note lao³ nearly lao².
咳嗽 k'ê² sou⁴, ... To cough.

素 su, properly, simple, unadorned.
299. 蘇州 su¹ chou¹, ... Su-chou (Soochow), the prefecture of that name, in which stands the eastern capital of the province of Chiang Su.
迅速 hsün⁴ su², ... In great haste; as fast as possible.
平素 p'ing² su⁴, ... Heretofore; lit. even and blank, here applied to past time uninterrupted.

算 suan, to reckon.
300. 酸的鹹的 suan¹ ti¹ hsien² ti¹, . . Sour and salt; suan hsien used fig. in speaking of ability or inability to distinguish between good and evil, &c. Cf. our word taste.
算計 suan⁴ chi⁴, ... To reckon up; also, to calculate an issue, &c.

碎 sui, broken, in fragments.
301. 雖然 sui¹ jan², ... Although.
跟隨 kên¹ sui², ... Following [a person].
骨髓 ku³ sui³, ... The marrow of the bones. Note ku³ nearly ku² before sui³.
零碎 ling² sui⁴, ... Fragmentary; miscellaneous; odds and ends.

88

PART VII. THE TONE EXERCISES. *sai – shêng.*

孫 *sun,* a grandson.
302. 子孫 *tzŭ³ sun¹,* . . . . . . Sons and grandsons; also, posterity in general.
    損益 *sun³ yi⁴,* . . . . . . Injury and advantage; the relative advantages of; also, modification, as of laws, usages, &c.

送 *sung,* to accompany, as a visitor to the door.
303. 松樹 *sung¹ shu⁴,* . . . . . The fir tree.
    毛骨悚然 *mao² ku³ sung³ jan²,* . Horror-struck; *lit.* hair and bones shuddering. Note that the tone of *ku³* is hardly modified, if at all, though followed by *sung³*.
    迎送 *ying² sung⁴,* . . . . . To welcome [the coming] and to speed [the parting guest].

殺 *sha,* to kill.
304. 殺死 *sha¹ ssŭ³,* . . . . . . To kill, *sc.* human beings; of animals use *sha* alone.
    蠢傻 *ch'ih¹ sha³,* . . . . . A stupid loutish looking person.
    拏剪子剹一點 *na² chien³ tzŭ sha⁴ i⁴ tien³,* To give a snip with scissors.

曬 *shai,* the action of the sun's rays.
305. 篩子 *shai¹ tzŭ,* . . . . . . A sieve.
    顏色 *yen² shai³,* . . . . . . Colour.
    曬乾 *shai⁴ kan¹,* . . . . . . To dry, or be dried, by exposure to the sun.

山 *shan,* a mountain.
306. 山川 *shan¹ ch'uan¹,* . . . . Hills and streams.
    雷閃 *lei² shan³,* . . . . . . The lightning is flashing, or, a flash of lightning.
    善惡 *shan⁴ o⁴,* . . . . See *ê, o.*

賞 *shang,* to bestow.
307. 商量 *shang¹ liang¹,* . . . . . To consult with a person.
    晌午 *shang² wu³,* . . . . . Noon. Note *shang,* properly *shang³,* but *shang²* before *wu³.*
    賞賜 *shang³ tz'ŭ⁴,* . . . . . To confer on, bestow on.
    上下 *shang⁴ hsia⁴,* . . . . . Above and below; also, nearly, thereabouts.

少 *shao,* few.
308. 火燒 *'huo³ shao¹,* . . . . . Burned by fire.
    刀勺 *tao¹ shao²,* . . . . . . Knives and spoons; kitchen hardware in general.
    多少 *to¹ shao³,* . . . . . . How many? also, *to¹ shao⁴,* a good number, or, what a number!
    老少 *lao³ shao⁴,* . . . . . . Old and young.

舌 *shê,* the tongue.
309. 賒欠 *shê¹ ch'ien⁴,* . . . . . To owe; debt.
    唇舌 *ch'un² shê²,* . . . . . Lips and tongue; after *fei,* to expend, = much discussion.
    棄捨 *ch'i⁴ shê³,* . . . . . . To abandon, a house, a thing; discard an acquaintance.
    射箭 *shê⁴ chien⁴,* . . . . . To shoot arrows.

身 *shên,* the body.
310. 身體 *shên¹ t'i³,* . . . . . . The body; used in certain phrases only, as more polite than *shên-tzŭ.*
    神仙 *shên² hsien¹,* . . . . . Spirits and fairies; the latter being *shên* of a lower order.
    審問 *shên³ wên⁴,* . . . . . To examine, as parties, witnesses, in a case civil or criminal.
    謹慎 *chin³ shên⁴,* . . . . . Cautious, *sc.* in word and deed.

生 *shêng,* to bear as children; to be born.
311. 生長 *shêng¹ chang³,* . . . . Born and bred.
    繩子 *shêng² tzŭ,* . . . . . A cord.
    各省 *ko⁴ shêng³,* . . . . . Every province.
    賸下 *shêng⁴ hsia⁴,* . . . . . There remains [a balance, a surplus, remnant, &c.].

事 *shih*, affairs; an affair.

312. 失落 *shih¹ lo⁴*, ... Lost; of a thing, not a person.
    九十 *chiu³ shih²*, ... Ninety; also, nine or ten.
    使喚 *shih³ 'huan⁴*, ... To employ a servant; to be employed as one.
    事情 *shih⁴ ch'ing²*, . . . Affairs; an affair. Note *ch'ing*, properly *ch'ing*, but modified almost to *ch'ing¹*.

手 *shou*, the hand.

313. 收拾 *shou¹ shih²*, ... To mend, put to rights; also, referring to a person, to serve him out; *shou*, to put away, *shih*, to pick up.
    生熟 *shêng¹ shou²*, ... Raw and ripe, as fruits, &c.; of wild tribes, savage and reclaimed.
    手足 *shou³ tsu²*, ... Hand and foot, = united as brothers.
    禽獸 *ch'in² shou⁴*, ... Wild birds and wild beasts.

書 *shu*, a book or writing.

314. 詩書 *shih⁴ shu¹*, ... The Shu Ching, Canon of History, and the Shih Ching, Canon of Poetry, commonly known as the Book of Odes.
    贖罪 *shu² tsui⁴*, ... To redeem, pay ransom for, a crime.
    數錢 *shu³ ch'ien²*, ... To count cash.
    數目 *shu⁴ mu⁴*, ... The numbers; the number of.

刷 *shua*, to brush.

315. 刷洗 *shua¹ hsi³*, ... To brush and wash [boots].
    耍笑 *shua³ hsiao⁴*, ... ,, To banter.

衰 *shuai*, to wear out, decay.

316. 衰敗 *shuai¹ pai⁴*, ... ,, Downcome; to be ruined.
    摔東西 *shuai³ tung¹ hsi¹*, . . To switch or flip away a thing.
    草率 *ts'ao³ shuai⁴*, ... ,, Carelessly [executed]; *shuai*, in the sense of going with the current.

拴 *shuan*, to tie up.

317. 拴捆 *shuan¹ k'uên³*, ... To bind; *shuan*, alone, meaning with one cord or few; *k'uên*, with many.
    涮洗 *shuan⁴ hsi³*, ... To rinse.

雙 *shuang*, a pair.

318. 成雙 *ch'êng² shuang¹*, ... To make pairs, or a pair.
    爽快 *shuang³ k'uai⁴*, ... Brisk, frank.
    雙生 *shuang⁴ shêng¹*, ... Twins.

水 *shui*, water.

319. 誰人 *shui² jên²*, ... What person?
    山水 *shan¹ shui³*, ... Scenery.
    睡覺 *shui⁴ chiao⁴*, ... To sleep.

順 *shun*, obedient, that which follows the stream.

320. 順當 *shun⁴ tang⁴*, ... Right, as rule requires.

說 *shuo*, to speak.

321. 說話 *shuo¹ 'hua⁴*, ... To speak.
    朔望 *shuo⁴ wang⁴ (shuo⁴ or so⁴)*, . The first and the fifteenth of the Chinese moon.

絲 *ssu*, silk.

322. 絲線 *ssŭ¹ hsien⁴*, ... A silken thread, threads of silk.
    死生 *ssŭ³ shêng¹*, ... Dead or live; *e. g.* is he dead or alive? Life and death [are as Heaven decrees'].
    四五 *ssŭ⁴ wu³*, ... ,, Four or five.

PART VII. THE TONE EXERCISES. *shih – t'ao.*

大 *ta*, great.
323. 答應 *ta¹ ying⁴*, ... To reply in the affirmative; to assent.
  搭救 *ta² chiu⁴*, ... To help; *ta*, in the sense of hooking arm to arm.
  毆打 *ou³ ta³*, ... To assault, to beat violently, with the hand, or with weapons. Note *ou³* nearly *ou²*.
  大小 *ta⁴ hsiao³*, ... Great and small; hence, size, extent, degree of.

他 *t'a*, he.
324. 他人 *t'a¹ jên²*, ... A third person.
  佛塔 *fo² t'a³*, ... A Buddhist pagoda.
  牀榻 *ch'uang² t'a⁴*, . . A bed-stead; *t'a*, used politely, in the same sense, alone, as we use *couch* for *bed*.

歹 *tai*, bad.
325. 獃呆 *tai¹ nieh²*, ... See *nieh*.
  好歹 *'hao³ tai³*, ... Good and bad; the quality of. Note *'hao³* nearly *'hao²*.
  交代 *chiao¹ tai⁴*, ... See *chiao*.

太 *t'ai*, too much.
326. 孕胎 *yun⁴ t'ai¹*, ... To be pregnant; *yün*, to carry in the womb, *t'ai*, the fœtus.
  扛擡 *k'ang² t'ai²*, ... See *k'ang*.
  太甚 *t'ai⁴ shên³*, ... Too greatly.

單 *tan*, single; odd as distinct from even.
327. 單雙 *tan¹ shuang¹*, ... Single and in pairs; odd and even.
  膽子大 *tan³ tzŭ ta⁴*, . . . Courageous; *lit*. large of liver. Note *tzŭ* enclitic, *tan³* unchanged.
  雞蛋 *chi¹ tan⁴*, ... A hen's egg.

炭 *t'an*, charcoal.
328. 貪贓 *t'an¹ tsang¹*, ... Grasping, said of officials.
  談論 *t'an² lun⁴*, ... To converse, chat.
  平坦 *p'ing² t'an³*, ... Level, as a road or way.
  柴炭 *ch'ai² t'an⁴*, ... Fuel (wood, grass, &c.) and charcoal.

當 *tang*, right.
329. 應當 *ying¹ tang¹*, ... Is properly, ought to [be or do].
  攩住 *tang³ chu⁴*, ... To stop by barring the way.
  典當 *tien³ tang⁴*, ... To pawn; *tien*, in this combination, provisional proprietorship; *tang*, to stand for, to represent.

湯 *t'ang*, broth, soup.
330. 喝湯 *'ho¹ t'ang¹*, ... To drink soup.
  白糖 *pai² t'ang²*, ... White sugar.
  矖臥 *t'ang³ wo⁴*, ... To lie down and sleep.
  燙手 *t'ang⁴ shou³*, ... To scald the hand.

道 *tao*, a way; the right way.
331. 刀槍 *tao¹ ch'iang¹*, ... Swords and muskets (matchlocks).
  搗線 *tao² hsien⁴*, ... To reel silk.
  顛倒 *tien¹ tao³*, ... Hind part before; upside down.
  道理 *tao⁴ li³*, ... Right principles; the rationale of; also, a system of religion or philosophy. Note *li* alone, *li³*, but, here, nearly *li⁴*; in other compounds, clearly *li³*.

逃 *t'ao*, to flee.
332. 叨恩 *t'ao¹ ngên¹*, ... To receive bounty or a favour; *lit*. eat bounty.
  逃跑 *t'ao² p'ao³*, ... To fly, as a slave, a prisoner, &c.
  討要 *t'ao³ yao³*, ... To demand, press for, whether with a claim or without.
  圈套 *ch'üan¹ t'ao⁴*, ... A snare, a trap; also used figuratively.

得 *tê*, to obtain; to succeed in.
333. 話叨叨 *'hua⁴ tê¹ tê¹*, ... Prosy talk. Note the second *tê* in *tê-tê* nearly *tê⁴*, although, properly, *tê¹*.
得'失 *tê² shih¹*, ... To gain and to lose; success and ill-success; the possible out-turn of.

特 *t'ê*, special.
334. 忐忑 *t'an³ t'ê¹*, ... Infirm of purpose; little used, and said to be corrupt for 憚怵 *t'an t'u*.
特意 *t'ê⁴ i⁴*, ... A special purpose; on purpose, intentionally.

得' *tei*, corrupt for *tê yao*, must be, or must have.
335. 小鑼兒鏑鏑的聲兒 *hsiao³ lo² 'rh tei¹ tei¹ ti¹ shêng¹ 'rh*, The sound emitted by a small gong when
必得 *pi⁴ tei³*, ... Must positively. [struck.

等 *têng*, a class; a place in a series; to wait.
336. 燈燭 *têng¹ chu²*, . . The lights; *lit.* lanterns and candles, or the candle or light in the lantern.
等候 *têng³ 'hou⁴*, ... To wait awhile.
馬鐙 *ma³ têng⁴*, ... Stirrups.

疼 *t'êng*, sore, painful; also, tender.
337. 鼕鼕的鼓聲兒 *t'êng¹ t'êng¹ ti¹ ku³ shêng¹ 'rh*, The sound of a tom-tom.
疼痛 *t'êng² t'ung⁴*, ... In pain.
板櫈 *pan³ t'êng⁴*, ... A wooden bench (long and low).

的 *ti*, see PART III, EXERC. II; also Note, page 104.
338. 我的 *wo³ ti¹*, ... Mine.
仇敵 *ch'ou² ti²*, ... An enemy; *ch'ou*, feud; *ti*, to stand before as a rival, antagonist, &c.
到底 *tao⁴ ti³*, ... To the bottom; at last; also, objectively, after all.
天地 *t'ien¹ ti⁴*, ... Heaven and Earth; as we say, Nature.

替 *t'i*, to take the place of; instead of.
339. 樓梯 *lou² t'i¹*, ... A staircase to an upper story.
提拔 *t'i² pa²*, ... To select a person by preference.
體量 *t'i³ liang⁴*, ... To shew consideration to.
替工 *t'i⁴ kung¹*, ... To do another's work for him.

弔 *tiao*, to hang.
340. 貂皮 *tiao¹ p'i²*, ... Sable; marten's fur.
弔死 *tiao⁴ ssŭ³*, ... To put to death by hanging, one's self or another person.

挑 *t'iao*, to pick out.
341. 挑選 *t'iao¹ hsüan³*, ... To select, pick and choose.
條陳 *t'iao² ch'ên²*, ... To present a memorial or report in sections to the Throne.
挑着 *t'iao² cho*, ... Holding up on the point of anything.
跳躍 *t'iao⁴ yao⁴*, ... To frisk about, as a dog, horse, &c.; used of great physical activity in a man.

疊 *tieh*, a fold; to fold.
342. 爹娘 *tieh¹ niang²*, ... Father and mother.
重疊 *ch'ung² tieh²*, ... Repeatedly. Note *ch'ung²*; but *chung*, heavy, *chung⁴*.

貼 *t'ieh*, properly, to stick, as a placard on a wall; the thing so stuck.
343. 體貼 *t'i³ t'ieh¹*, ... To humour, to accommodate.
銅鐵 *t'ung² t'ieh³*, ... Copper and iron.
牙帖 *ya² t'ieh⁴*, . . . Licences to firms being members of a guild; *ya*, properly, a tooth; *q.d.* one of a set.

PART VII. THE TONE EXERCISES. *tê – tu.*

店 *tien*, a shop; an inn.
344. 掂量 *tien¹ liang⁴*, ... To weigh; of things or matters.
　　 圈點 *ch'üan¹ tien³*, ... See *ch'üan*.
　　 客店 *k'o⁴ tien⁴*, ... An inn.

天 *t'ien*, heaven.
345. 天地 *t'ien¹ ti⁴*, ... See *ti⁴*.
　　 莊田 *chuang¹ t'ien²*, ... Farmhouse and land; farms.
　　 拏舌頭餂 *na² shê² t'ou² t'ien³*, . To touch with the tip of the tongue.
　　 掭筆 *t'ien⁴ pi³*, ... To work the pencil [on the ink-slab], when about to write.

定 *ting*, to fix, make stationary; to establish.
346. 釘子 *ting¹ tzŭ*, ... A nail.
　　 頂戴 *ting³ tai⁴*, ... See *tai⁴*.
　　 定規 *ting⁴ kuei¹*, . . To lay down rules, settle an order of proceeding; *lit.* to plant [a leg of the] compasses.

聽 *t'ing*, to hear.
347. 聽見 *t'ing¹ chien⁴*, ... To hear, *q. d.* hearing to perceive.
　　 停止 *t'ing² chih³*, ... To cease, or cause to cease.
　　 樹梃 *shu⁴ t'ing³*, ... The bough of a tree, larger than a *shu chih*, bough or twig.
　　 聽其自然 *t'ing⁴ ch'i² tzŭ⁴ jan²*, . Let [him, it] have [his, its] own way.

丢 *tiu*, to lose.
348. 丢失 *tiu¹ shih¹*, ... To lose, as a child stolen or strayed, an animal, or any thing inanimate.
　　 呀嗳 *ya⁴ tiu³*, ... A derisive exclamation addressed to a person who has failed in something; *q. d.* oh! you clever fellow.

多 *to*, many.
349. 多少 *to¹ shao³*, ... See *shao³*.
　　 搶奪 *ch'iang³ to²*, ... See *ch'iang³*.
　　 花朶兒 *'hua¹ to³ 'rh*, ... A bud.
　　 懶惰 *lan³ to⁴*, ... See *lan³*.

妥 *t'o*, secure, sound.
350. 託情 *t'o¹ ch'ing²*, ... To appeal to the feelings, *sc.* of a person who has to decide for or against one; the appeal may be direct or through another. The phrase is used only where one's cause is bad, or without much hope.
　　 駱駝 *lo⁴ t'o²*, ... See *lo⁴*.
　　 妥當 *t'o³ tang⁴*, ... (Of proceedings) satisfactory, secure.
　　 唾沫 *t'o⁴ mo⁴*, ... To spit; *mo*, spittle; *t'o*, also *t'u⁴*, to spit (saliva only).

豆 *tou*, pulse in general.
351. 兜底子 *tou¹ ti³ tzŭ*, ... *Fig.* from beginning to end [of an affair]; the *tou-tzŭ* is, specially, the receptacle of sacking in which a Chinese mason carries mortar; a similar receptacle may be formed of the flap of a garment or the like; *tou ti-tzŭ*, from the bottom of such a receptacle.
　　 升斗 *shêng¹ tou³*, ... *Shêng*, the Chinese pint, dry measure; *tou* = ten *shêng* (Williams).
　　 綠豆 *lü⁴ tou⁴*, ... Green beans, as distinguished from black.

頭 *t'ou*, the head.
352. 偷盜 *t'ou¹ tao⁴*, ... To steal; theft.
　　 頭臉 *t'ou² lien³*, ... The head; *lit.* the head and face.
　　 透澈 *t'ou⁴ ch'ê⁴*, ... To penetrate thoroughly, as having thorough knowledge of any subject; also, to be very intelligent.

妬 *tu*, jealous.
353. 督撫 *tu¹ fu³*, ... *Tu* for *tsung-tu*, governor-general; *fu* for *hsün-fu*, governor of a province.
　　 毒害 *tu² hai⁴*, ... To poison.
　　 賭博 *tu³ po⁴*, ... To gamble.
　　 嫉妬 *chi⁴ tu⁴*, ... Jealous, envious; also, transitively, to envy.

KEY TO THE TZŬ ERH CHI. Colloquial Series.

土 *t'u*, earth, clay.
354. 禿子 *t'u¹ tzŭ*, ... A bald man.
　　 塗抹 *t'u² mo³*, ... To efface, as writing.
　　 塵土 *ch'ên² t'u³*, ... Dust.
　　 唾沫 *t'u⁴ mo⁴*, ... See *t'o⁴*.

短 *tuan*, short.
355. 端正 *tuan¹ chêng⁴*, ... Upright, as things duly placed; also, moral rectitude.
　　 長短 *ch'ang² tuan³*, ... Long and short; the length of; also, a man's merits and defects, but, especially, his defects.
　　 斷絕 *tuan⁴ chüeh²*, ... To cut off, as with a knife; also used figuratively.

團 *t'uan*, a ball or lump.
356. 團圓 *t'uan² yuan²*, ... Round as a ball; united, all in a body, as a family.

對 *tui*, opposite to.
357. 堆積 *tui¹ chi⁴*, ... To pile together, accumulate.
　　 對面 *tui⁴ mien⁴*, ... Opposite to.

退 *t'ui*, to retire.
258. 推諉 *t'ui¹ wei³*, ... To put one's work on another, lay one's fault to another's charge.
　　 腿快 *t'ui³ k'uai⁴*, ... Fast legs; a good walker.
　　 進退 *chin⁴ t'ui⁴*, ... To advance and retire, [equally difficult; a dilemma].

敦 *tun*, properly, substantial.
359. 敦厚 *tun¹ 'hou⁴*, ... Honest; sincere; staunch.
　　 打盹兒 *ta³ tun³-'rh*, . . To wink from sleepiness. Note *ta* nearly *ta²* before *tun³*; *erh* absorbed in *tu-rh*.
　　 遲鈍 *ch'ih² tun⁴*, ... Slow in thought or action; *tun*, properly, blunt, as a knife.

吞 *t'un*, to swallow; to bolt.
360. 吞吞吐吐 *t'un¹ t'un¹ t'u³ t'u³*, . Of a man who will tell but half his story; *t'u*, being to spit out (anything). Note the first *t'u* nearly *t'u²*.
　　 屯田 *t'un² t'ien²*, ... Lands granted to soldiers; military colonies.
　　 褪手 *t'un⁴ shou³*, ... To draw the hands into the sleeves, as the Chinese do for warmth's sake.

冬 *tung*, winter.
361. 冬夏 *tung¹ hsia⁴*, ... Winter and summer.
　　 懂得 *tung³ tê²*, ... To understand.
　　 動靜 *tung⁴ ching⁴*, ... To be stirring; a movement; *lit.* to stir stillness.

同 *t'ung*, the same, together with.
362. 通達 *t'ung¹ ta²*, ... To permeate as the power of nature; to penetrate, as the will or intelligence of the sovereign; also, of great intelligence in general.
　　 會同 *'hui⁴ t'ung²*, ... United with, in association with.
　　 統帥 *t'ung³ shuai⁴*, . A generalissimo; in modern times, one holding unusually large power, civil and military.
　　 疼痛 *t'êng² t'ung⁴*, ... In great pain.

雜 *tsa*, miscellaneous.
363. 腌臢 *a¹ tsa¹*, ... Dirty.
　　 雜亂 *tsa² luan⁴*, ... An omnium-gatherum; confusion.
　　 咱的 *tsa³ ti¹*, ... Why? why so?

擦 *ts'a*, to rub clean.
364. 擦抹 *ts'a¹ mo³*, ... To rub and wipe, as with a cloth.

PART VII. THE TONE EXERCISES. *t'u – ts'ên.*

在 *tsai*, to be; to be in or at.
365. 栽種 *tsai¹ chung⁴*, ... To plant. Note *chung⁴*, to plant; *chung³*, a sort.
    宰殺 *tsai³ sha¹*, ... To kill animals.
    在家 *tsai⁴ chia¹*, ... To be at home.

才 *ts'ai*, ability.
366. 猜想 *ts'ai¹ hsiang³*, . . . To imagine, conjecture.
    才幹 *ts'ai² kan⁴*, ... Ability.
    雲彩 *yün² ts'ai³*, ... Clouds; *lit.* cloud colours.
    菜飯 *ts'ai⁴ fan⁴*, ... Victuals; *lit.* the rice and other viands.

賛 *tsan*, properly, to aid with counsel.
367. 簪子 *tsan¹ tzŭ*, ... Women's head-gear.
    偺們 *tsan²-mên¹*, ... We, more commonly pronounced *tsa-mên*. See PART III, EXERC. II, 4.
    儹錢 *tsan³ ch'ien²*, ... To be putting away money.
    參贊 *ts'an¹ tsan⁴*, ... An official title; see PART III, EXERC. XIX, *ex.* 2.

慚 *ts'an*, properly, shame as from being disgraced.
368. 參考 *ts'an¹ k'ao³*, ... To compare authorities.
    慚愧 *ts'an² k'uei⁴*, ... Shame, felt at one's own wrong doing.
    悽慘 *ch'i¹ ts'an³*, ... Misery.
    儳頭 *ts'an⁴ t'ou²*, ... Blockhead, ninny; properly, a man without confidence in himself.

葬 *tsang*, to bury.
369. 貪賍 *t'an¹ tsang¹*, ... To covet, as a grasping official; *tsang*, in the sense of presents.
    階們 *tsang²-mên¹*, ... We; the same as *tsan-mên*, or *tsa-mên*.
    葬埋 *tsang⁴ mai²*, ... To bury [a corpse].

倉 *ts'ang*, a granary.
370. 倉庫 *ts'ang¹ k'u⁴*, ... The granaries and money vaults [of a jurisdiction].
    瞞藏 *man² ts'ang²*, ... Dishonest concealment [of person or thing].

早 *tsao*, early.
371. 週遭 *chou¹ tsao¹*, ... All round; *q. d.* at every point encountering, or encountered.
    穿鑿 *ch'uan¹ tsao²*, . . . *Lit.* to bore [as through stone], and to cut with a chisel; *fig.* to start questions in the course of an enquiry.
    來得早 *lai² tê² tsao³*, . . . To have come early. Note *tê* enclitic; the tone hence modified.
    造化 *tsao⁴ 'hua⁴*, ... To create, as the deity; also, substantively, the luck born with a man.

草 *ts'ao*, plants; specially, grass.
372. 操練 *ts'ao¹ lien⁴*, ... To drill; to be drilled.
    馬槽 *ma³ ts'ao²*, . . A manger; in the north of China made of wood and moveable; also, made of brick.
    草木 *ts'ao³ mu⁴*, ... See *mu⁴*.

則 *tsê*, then; consequently.
373. 則例 *tsê² li⁴*, ... Laws, regulations; *tsê*, here meaning rule, law.

策 *ts'ê*, a plan; a means.
374. 計策 *chi⁴ ts'ê⁴*, ... Ordinarily, any plan; in military matters, strategy.

賊 *tsei*, a thief, robber, any one in arms against the government.
375. 賊匪 *tsei² fei³*, ... Brigands, outlaws.

怎 *tsên*, an interrogative particle.
376. 怎麽 *tsên³-mo²*, ... How? why? what?

參 *ts'ên*, uneven, irregular.
377. 參差 *ts'ên¹ tz'ŭ¹*, ... Uneven; *e. g.* as foliage, herbage, &c.; used of inconsequence in action.

KEY TO THE TZŬ ERH CHI. **Colloquial Series.**

增 *tsêng*, to add to.
378. 增減 *tsêng¹ chien³*, ... To increase and diminish; modification.
    怎麼 *tsêng³-mo²*, ... What? why?
    餽贈 *k'uei⁴ tsêng⁴*, ... To present, as food or anything, to friends.

層 *ts'êng*, a layer; story of a house; a step in a series.
379. 𧆛一聲上了房 *ts'êng¹ i⁴ shêng¹ shang⁴ liao³ fang²*, One jump (lit. the sound of one jump) and he was up on the house. Note *liao* enclitic, hence nearly *la*, its tone also modified.
    層次 *ts'êng² tz'ŭ⁴*, ... Regular order.
    蹭蹬 *ts'êng⁴ têng⁴*, ... Said in pity for a person who is unlucky, always failing through no fault of his own; *ts'êng*, of feet that drag in walking; *têng*, of inability to move; *q.d.* one that can never get on.

作 *tso*, to make; to do; in which senses it is alway *tso⁴*, whether singly or compounded.
380. 作房 *tso¹ fang²*, ... The work-shop; the shop where things are *made*, not *sold*.
    昨日 *tso² jih⁴*, ... Yesterday.
    左右 *tso³ yu⁴*, ... Right and left; in the neighbourhood of a place; in the company of a superior, specially the sovereign.
    坐臥 *tso⁴ wo⁴*, ... *Lit.* sitting and lying down, = in all positions; not generally used except when followed by *pu an*, uncomfortable.

錯 *ts'o*, error.
381. 揉搓 *jou² ts'o¹*, ... To rub between two hands.
    矬子 *ts'o² tzŭ*, ... A dwarf.
    錯失 *ts'o⁴ shih¹*, ... Error, mistake, in business, copying, &c.; *shih*, here meaning to fail or miss.

走 *tsou*, to move; to walk.
382. 行走 *hsing² tsou³*, ... Of the subordinates, *to be employed in* a public department.
    奏事 *tsou⁴ shih⁴*, ... To represent a matter to the Throne.

湊 *ts'ou*, to collect, or be collected together.
383. 湊合 *ts'ou⁴ 'ho²*, . . Of persons assembled in one place, or enterprise; of funds contributed by a number.

祖 *tsu*, a grand-father.
384. 租賃 *tsu¹ lin⁴*, ... See *lin⁴*.
    手足 *shou³ tsu²*, ... See *shou³*.
    祖宗 *tsu³ tsung¹*, ... One's ancestors.

粗 *ts'u*, coarse.
385. 粗細 *ts'u¹ hsi⁴*, ... See *hsi⁴*.
    喫醋 *ch'ih¹ ts'u⁴*, ... Words of envy, or jealousy; specially, in a woman's mouth; *lit.* to eat vinegar.

攥 *tsuan*, to grip in the hand.
386. 鑽幹 *tsuan¹ kan⁴*, ... To strive hard after an object; *tsuan*, to bore, perforate; often, in a bad sense, to strive to compass by intrigue.
    纂修 *tsuan³ hsiu¹*, ... To revise, recompile, a work, a code; *tsuan*, properly, to collect together; specially, materials available.
    攥住 *tsuan⁴ chu⁴*, ... To grasp in the hand, *sc.* anything that is moveable, and that the fingers can nearly close round.

竄 *ts'uan*, to burrow, as rats, mice, &c.
387. 馬驤 *ma³ ts'uan¹*, ... A horse's starting, forward or aside.
    攢湊 *ts'uan² ts'ou⁴*, ... To make up a set of things, or a sum of money, by picking here and borrowing there.
    逃竄 *t'ao² ts'uan⁴*, ... [Said pompously of rebels or any enemy] flying from one place and finding their way to another.

PART VII. THE TONE EXERCISES. *tsêng — wan*.

嘴 *tsui*, the lips.
388. 一堆 *i⁴ tsui¹*, ... A pile of fruit; a group of men.
　　 嘴脣 *tsui³ ch'un²*, ... The lips; the mouth.
　　 犯罪 *fan⁴ tsui⁴*, ... , To transgress; *lt*. run foul of punishment.

催 *ts'ui*, to urge.
389. 催逼 *ts'ui¹ pi¹*, ... To press with great earnestness, (whether justly or not).
　　 隨他去 *ts'ui² t'a¹ ch'ü⁴*, . . . Let him go if, or as, he likes.
　　 萃集 *ts'ui⁴ chi⁴*, ... A large assemblage of able or virtuous persons, of good things.

尊 *tsun*, honored.
390. 尊重 *tsun¹ chung⁴*, ... To esteem, shew esteem for.
　　 撙節 *tsun³ chieh²*, . . . To economise; *orig*. a classical expression; *lt*. to walk in, = to practise, moderation.

寸 *ts'un*, an inch.
391. 村莊 *ts'un¹ chuang¹*, ... A village.
　　 存亡 *ts'un² wang²*, ... Dead and living; *e.g.* father *ts'un*, mother *wang*, &c.
　　 忖量 *ts'un³ liang⁴*, ... To think over, reflect on.
　　 尺寸 *ch'ih³ ts'un⁴*, ... See *ch'ih* ³.

崇 *tsung*, a kind or sort; also, a collective.
392. 大宗 *ta⁴ tsung¹*, ... The larger proportion.
　　 總名 *tsung³ ming²*, ... A general designation.
　　 縱容 *tsung⁴ yung²* or *jung²*, . . To leave too free; to tolerate license.

蔥 *ts'ung*, onions.
393. 蔥蒜 *ts'ung¹ suan⁴*, ... Onions and garlic.
　　 依從 *i¹ ts'ung²*, ... According to, *sc*. a man's own view, his advice, &c.

子 *tzŭ*, a son.
394. 資格 *tzŭ¹ ko²*, ... Length of service; *tzŭ*, goods, means; here, pay; *ko*, the columns of a register; *q. d.* the time one has been borne on the books.
　　 子孫 *tzŭ³ sun¹*, ... Sons and grandsons.
　　 寫字 *hsieh³ tzŭ⁴*, ... To write.

次 *tz'ŭ*, a time or turn.
395. 齜著牙兒笑 *tz'ŭ¹ cho ya² 'rh hsiao⁴*, To grin, to shew the teeth as one laughs.
　　 磁器 *tz'ŭ² ch'i⁴*, ... Porcelain; finer earthenware, as distinct from *wa* ³.
　　 彼此 *pi³ tz'ŭ³*, ... 'This and that; you and I; any two parties, as regards their relation to
　　 次序 *tz'ŭ⁴ hsü⁴*, ... Regular order.　　　　[each other. Note *pi* ³ nearly *pi* ².

瓦 *wa*, a tile; pottery.
396. 刨挖 *p'ao² wa¹*, ... To dig up or out.
　　 娃娃 *wa² wa²*, ... Little children; babies.
　　 甎瓦 *chuan¹ wa³*, ... Bricks and tiles.
　　 鞋襪 *hsieh² wa⁴*, ... Shoes and stockings.

外 *wai*, outside.
397. 歪正 *wai¹ chêng⁴*, ... Slanting and perpendicular.
　　 舀水 *wai³ shui³*, ... To bale out water. Note *wai* ³ nearly *wai* ².
　　 內外 *nei⁴ wai⁴*, ... , . Within and without; also, native and foreign.

完 *wan*, terminated.
398. 水灣兒 *shui³ wan¹-'rh*, ... A bay.
　　 完全 *wan² ch'üan²*, ... Completed; in a state of completeness.
　　 早晚 *tsao² wan³*, ... Early and late; sooner or later. Note *tsao* ³ nearly *tsao* ².
　　 千萬 *ch'ien¹ wan⁴*, ... Thousand myriad, ten millions; *fig*. any number.

往 *wang*, to go; hence, towards, to.
399. 汪洋 *wang¹ yang²*, ... Vast expanse of water.
     王公 *wang² kung¹*, ... Princes and dukes.
     來往 *lai² wang³*, ... To come and to go; intercourse.
     忘記 *wang⁴ chi⁴*, ... To forget.

為 *wei*, read *wei²*, to do; to be; but read *wei⁴*, because of.
400. 微弱 *wei¹ jo⁴*, ... Sickly, feeble; as men, plants, &c.
     行為 *hsing² wei²*, ... Actions, conduct.
     委員 *wei³ yüan²*, ... To depute an officer; the officer deputed.
     爵位 *chuo² wei⁴*, ... See *chuo²*.

文 *wên*, ornament; literary culture.
401. 溫和 *wên¹ 'huo⁴* or *'ho²*, . . . Warm.
     文武 *wên² wu³*, ... Civil and military; *wên* = educated.
     安穩 *an¹ wên³*, ... Steady, as things that stand firm; sound, of recovered health.
     問答 *wên⁴ ta¹*, ... Question and answer.

翁 *wêng*, an aged man.
402. 老翁 *lao³ wêng¹*, ... The old man, used respectfully of the father of the person addressed.
     水甕 *shui³ wêng⁴*, ... A large water ewer.

我 *wo*, the pronoun I.
403. 窩巢 *wo¹ ch'ao²*, ... See *ch'ao²*.
     你我 *ni³ wo³*, ... You and I. Note *ni³* nearly *ni²*.
     坐臥 *tso⁴ wo⁴*, ... See *tso⁴*.

武 *wu*, military.
404. 房屋 *fang² wu¹* or *u¹*, . . . Buildings, tenements.
     有無 *yu³ wu²*, ... Possessing or not; existing or not.
     文武 *wên² wu³*, ... See *wên²*.
     萬物 *wan⁴ wu⁴*, ... The myriad things; all things in creation.

牙 *ya*, a tooth.
405. 丫頭 *ya¹ t'ou²*, ... A servant-girl; *ya*, properly of the tuft of hair on either side of the head.
     牙齒 *ya² ch'ih³*, ... The teeth.
     文雅 *wên² ya³*, ... Polite; well-bred; specially with reference to one's language.
     壓倒 *ya⁴ tao³*, ... To keep pressed down with a weight.

涯 *yai*, properly, the edge of water.
406. 天涯 *t'ien¹ yai²*, ... The horizon.

羊 *yang*, sheep.
407. 央求 *yang¹ ch'iu²*, ... To apply to for help; *lit.* invitingly beg.
     牛羊 *niu² yang²*, ... Sheep and oxen.
     養活 *yang³ 'huo²*, ... To support persons; to rear, as animals, fish, plants, &c.
     各樣 *ko⁴ yang⁴*, ... Every kind.

要 *yao*, to want; to will; to be about to.
408. 腰腿 *yao¹ t'ui³*, ... The back, *lit.* the loins, and the legs; *t'ui* more commonly written 腿.
     遙遠 *yao² yüan³*, ... Very distant.
     咬一口 *yao³ i⁴ k'ou³*, . . . To give a bite to.
     討要 *t'ao³ yao⁴*, ... To demand.

PART VII. THE TONE EXERCISES. *wang – yün.*

夜 *yeh,* the night.
409. 噎住 *yeh¹ chu⁴,* . . . . . . To stick fast, to have something so stuck fast, in the throat.
　　老爺 *lao³ yeh²,* . . . . . . Sir; a gentleman, *lit.* old gentleman; *lao-yeh-'rh,* a popular name for the sun.
　　野地 *yeh³ ti⁴,* . . . . . . Uncultivated or uninhabited ground.
　　半夜 *pan⁴ yeh⁴,* . . . . . . Midnight, half the night.

言 *yen,* words.
410. 喫煙 *ch'ih¹ yen¹,* . . . . . . To smoke.
　　言語 *yen² yu³,* . . . . . . Words, sayings; oral language.
　　眼睛 *yen³ ching¹,* . . . . . . See *ching¹.*
　　河沿兒 *'ho² yen⁴-'rh,* . . . . The bank of a river; along the bank.

益 *yi,* advantage; addition to.
411. 作揖 *tso¹ yi¹,* . . . . . . To make a certain Chinese salutation.
　　益處 *yi² ch'u⁴,* . . . . . . Advantage. Note *yi²*; elsewhere, always *yi⁴.*
　　易經 *yi⁴ ching¹,* . . . . . . The Yi Ching, Book of Permutations, said to be the oldest of Chinese classical works.

音 *yin,* sound.
412. 聲音 *shêng¹ yin¹,* . . . . . . Sounds of any kind.
　　金銀 *chin¹ yin²,* . . . . . . Gold and silver.
　　勾引 *kou¹ yin³,* . . . . . . To inveigle; to entice into any evil.
　　用印 *yung⁴ yin⁴,* . . . . . . To use the seal; to seal officially.

迎 *ying,* to welcome.
413. 應該 *ying¹ kai¹,* . . . . . . Ought to.
　　迎接 *ying² chieh¹,* . . . . . . To receive as a guest.
　　沒影兒 *mei² ying³-'rh,* . . . . There is no sign, *lit.* no shadow, of such or such a thing.
　　報應 *pao⁴ ying⁴,* . . . . . . To recompense, as Heaven.

約 *yo,* to engage; an engagement, treaty, &c.
414. 約會 *yo¹ 'hui⁴,* . . . . . . To make an appointment with.
　　音樂 *yin¹ yo⁴,* . . . . . . Musical instruments in general.

魚 *yü,* fish.
415. 愚濁 *yü¹ cho²* or *chuo²,* . . . Muddled, stupid; *cho,* turbid.
　　魚蝦 *yu² hsia¹,* . . . . . . Fish in general; *lit.* fish or shell-fish.
　　風雨 *fêng¹ yu³,* . . . . . . See *fêng¹.*
　　預備 *yu⁴ pei⁴,* . . . . . . Ready; to make ready.

原 *yüan,* properly, in the beginning.
416. 冤屈 *yüan¹ ch'ü¹,* . . . . . . To be wronged, by unjust deed or word.
　　原來 *yuan² lai²,* . . . . . . In the first instance; in fact.
　　遠近 *yüan³ chin⁴,* . . . . . . See *chin⁴.*
　　願意 *yuan⁴ i⁴,* . . . . . . To wish.

月 *yüeh,* the moon.
417. 子曰 *tzŭ³ yüeh¹,* . . . . . . "The philosopher said." These words precede the sayings of Confucius, Mencius, and others, recorded in the classics of China.
　　乾噍 *kan¹ yüeh²,* . . . . . . To munch one's food dry, having none but poor fare and nothing to drink with it.
　　年月 *nien² yueh⁴,* . . . . . . Years and moons; lapse of time.

雲 *yün,* cloud.
418. 頭暈 *t'ou² yün¹,* . . . . . . The head giddy.
　　雲彩 *yun² ts'ai³,* . . . . . . Clouds.
　　應允 *ying¹ yün³,* . . . . . . To consent to.
　　氣運 *ch'i⁴ yün⁴,* . . . . . . Luck; of the state's prosperity; *yün ch'i* of a person's luck.

KEY TO THE TZŬ ERH CHI. Colloquial Series.

有 *yu*, to be, to have; possession, existence.
419. 憂愁 *yu¹ ch'ou²*, ... Sad (in heart and countenance).
    香油 *hsiang¹ yu²*, ... Oil that is not lamp-oil; any oil used in the kitchen.
    有無 *yu³ wu²*, ... See *wu²*.
    左右 *tso³ yu⁴*, ... See *tso³*.

用 *yung*, to use.
420. 平庸 *p'ing² yung¹*, ... Commonplace; *p'ing*, even, = not above the level; *yung*, here, unintelligent.
    容易 *yung² i⁴*, ... See *i⁴*.
    永遠 *yung³ yüan³*, ... For ever. Note *yung³* nearly *yung⁴*.
    使用 *shih³ yung⁴*, ... To employ.

END OF KEY TO PART VII.

PART VIII. CHAPTER ON THE PARTS OF SPEECH. Yen-Yü Li Lüo.

[The history of this so-called Chapter on the Parts of Speech will have been read in the Preface. As is there stated, a Chinese in no way connected with its compilation has christened it the Yen-Yu Li Luo, say, Summary of the Laws of Phraseology. The text almost tells its own story throughout; where it is unequal to the occasion, the translation and notes will supply the deficiency.

The student will observe that *tzŭ*, which we generally translate *character*, is here translated *word*; the *pi 'hua*, or pen-strokes, which compose the *tzŭ*, written forms of words, being fairly renderd *characters*, as that term is applied to the alphabetic elements of writing in other languages. He has been warned not to look for a Grammar in the Chapter, whatever its title, but, for convenience of reference, its contents have been arranged in the order usually allotted by English grammarians to our Parts of Speech and the subdivisions proper to these larger categories. They will consequently be found distributed under the following heads:

I. INTRODUCTORY OBSERVATIONS.
II. THE NOUN AND ARTICLE.
III. THE CHINESE NUMERATIVE NOUN.
IV. NUMBER.
V. CASE.
VI. GENDER.
VII. THE ADJECTIVE AND ITS DEGREES OF COMPARISON.
VIII. THE PRONOUN (PERSONAL, RELATIVE, POSSESSIVE, DEMONSTRATIVE, DISTRIBUTIVE, INDEFINITE).
IX. THE VERB (AS MODIFIED BY TENSE, MOOD, AND VOICE).
X. THE ADVERB (OF TIME, PLACE, NUMBER, &c).
XI. THE PREPOSITION.
XII. THE CONJUNCTION.
XIII. THE INTERJECTION].

I. INTRODUCTORY OBSERVATIONS.

1. It seems to give your countrymen a good deal of trouble to acquire our language, Sir. What is the difficulty?
2. There are several difficulties; difficulties of pronunciation, difficulties with the individual words, and, greater still, difficulties of composition.
3. Yet all foreigners seem to learn each other's languages with tolerable facility. Is Chinese so entirely different from all foreign languages?
4. No language in the world is absolutely without something in common with its fellow languages of course. The character of the expressions by which any man gives utterance to his thought will be sure to vary greatly according to circumstances. A phrase may be directly affirmative of existence or non-existence, or it may be interrogative, imperative, optative, or interjectional. When we say, for instance, This man is dead, That man is not dead, there is a direct affirmation of existence or non-existence. Is that man dead? is interrogative. Kill that man, is imperative. Would that that man were well! is optative. Alas! That man is dead, is interjectional. Do you understand my meaning, Sir?
5. Perfectly. The law you are speaking of may be regarded as a general law which affects all language written or spoken, one to which Chinese and foreigners from natural community of sentiment conform.
6. Just so. Now to come to the difficulty with single words; it is one peculiar to the Chinese written language. For the formation of words in writing, every other nation that possesses a literature, has a given number of characters (*lit.* pen-strokes), each with a sound of its own; and the combination of a certain number of these not only produces a word in form, but also serves the purpose of establishing its sound.

4. *Obs.* 1. character of expression; *shên ch'i*, see above Dial. X, gait, air, attitude. *Obs.* 2. interjectional; *ching-ya*, properly, to start with fright and astonishment. *Obs.* 3. my meaning; *pi i*, humble, lowly, meaning.
5. community of sentiment; more literally, It is li, the reasonable consequence, of *tzŭ jan hsiang t'ung*, the natural identity, of man's feelings in every nation.
6. peculiar; *tu i*, isolated strangeness. Note its enforcement by the addition of *wei*, only, before '*han wên*.

KEY TO THE TZŬ ERH CHI. Colloquial Series.

7. There is a certain resemblance between this and the Manchu method of writing. But, in Chinese, although the language is otherwise written, the words are formed of eight particular strokes which are called *tzŭ mu*, the mothers of the written words. Will not these be the same as your letters, Sir?
8. The application of the two differs widely. Chinese words, it is true, are written with eight particular strokes; but, though each of these has a sound of its own, the sound of any word they may go to form, has no reference whatever to the sounds of the strokes.

    We will write for instance the word *shih* (ten), one of the numerals. This is formed of one horizontal and one perpendicular stroke. The horizontal stroke is properly called *yi*, the perpendicular stroke, *kuên*; the two combined in writing produce the word *shih*. It will be at once apparent that their business is exclusively with its form, and that they have nothing whatever to do with its sound. This, [the impossibility of learning the sound of a word from the strokes employed to write it,] is regarded by foreigners as a very great difficulty in the study of written Chinese.
9. How do foreigners succeed in establishing the sound of one of their words in writing?
10. In this way. Foreign nations have for the purpose some twenty odd characters, the principle of combining which so as to form words it does not take very long to learn, and, this once learnt, the sound of any word one meets with can be determined; whereas, in a Chinese written word, there is no positive criterion of its sound. If it has not been met with in reading, its sound cannot be known; the word must be looked out, and when it has been found, there is nothing to guarantee the reader against forgetting its sound when he sees it again.
11. That is true enough. We Chinese are in no fear of forgetting the words, because we learn them as single words when we are young children.
12. Exactly; but we foreigners, not having committed Chinese books to memory, cannot of course fail to encounter the difficulty I describe with single words, when we read Chinese, and our difficulties are immeasurably greater when we come to combine words in composition.
13. I have understood that foreign composition is a somewhat simpler matter than ours.
14. Yes; because in foreign languages, considered with reference to composition in them, the single words are each referred to a particular category, and for the formation of these into sentences there are works which set forth the rules of construction so clearly that they may be comprehended at a glance. There are no works of this sort in Chinese for the positive definition of the laws of composition. A writer constructs his sentences according to his recollection of the manner in which words are combined in the texts he has read, and, his sentence constructed, he is enabled to link his sentences together in longer pieces of composition. The single words in Chinese are classified generally in two grand categories, as *hsü tzŭ*, empty or unsubstantial words, and *shih tzŭ*, solid or substantial words; but I have never arrived at a thorough understanding of the distinction, though I have looked carefully into the question over and over again.

9. succeed; *lit.* what good method have they?
10. *Obs.* 1. can be determined; *ting-tê-chun*, fixing attain, = fix with, accuracy; note that the combination makes the verb to define, determine &c., and that, although it contains the potential auxiliary *tê* within it, it is reinforced by *k'o t*. *Obs.* 2. whereas, on the other hand; *chih*, to come to [another question, namely,] *jo*, if. *Obs.* 3. no criterion; *lit.* there is not a place [at which a person] can *chun*, decide as by standard, [that such a sound] is the assumed sound.
11. learn them when young; *tsung*, from = at, the time when we are little fellows, we *hsien*, first, = before we go any further, *jên*, recognise, read, single characters.
14. texts he has read; he remembers the *tzŭ yang*, phraseology, *chi tsai*, recorded and inserted, in books. Note *chi*, to remember, and *chi*, to record.

PART VIII. ON THE PARTS OF SPEECH. **Yen-Yü Li Lüo.** I.

15. The denomination *shih tzŭ*, substantial words, is generic of all words that have a regular, (or, *bonâ fide*) signification; and these are subdivided again according as they may be employed into *ssŭ tzŭ*, dead words, and *'huo tzŭ*, live words.

It is not so easy to define the precise characteristics of the *hsü tzŭ*. For example, in the sentence *ni pu yao ch'ien mo* (Don't you want money? or, Won't you have money?) the word *mo* has no regular, [say, translateable,] meaning. It is used simply to shew that the sentence is interrogative. It is a *hsü tzŭ,* an unsubstantial word. Of the remaining words in the sentence, *pu*, not, has a substantive meaning, and yet, in Chinese, it is accounted a *hsu tzŭ*. The words *ni*, thou, *yao*, to want, and *ch'ien*, money, are all *shih tzŭ*, substantial words. Distinguished as *ssŭ tzŭ*, dead words, and *'huo tzŭ*, live words, *ni* and *ch'ien* are dead words, and *yao* is a live word.

The word *yao*, again, which we have just spoken of as a live word, and which, in the passage before us, *is* a live word, may be used as a dead word elsewhere. For instance, in the phrase *ch'i yao tsai su*, The essential is despatch, the words, *yao* and *su* are unquestionably dead words. Is there no live word then, you will say, in the sentence? Yes, to be sure; the word *tsai*, is, or, is in, is a live word. If you go farther and ask which words are substantial and which unsubstantial, the answer is that the two words *ch'i* and *tsai*, though each possesses a regular meaning, are, in this phrase, accounted unsubstantial words.

16. It is evident, then, that the denominations *hsü tzŭ* and *shih tzŭ* are quite capable of being interchanged, one for the other, as circumstances may require.

17. Perfectly capable; to such an extent that some people go the length of saying that every word is half a dead word and half a live word.

18. The limitations of our language are somewhat more inflexible. The terms in it have not the convertibility of terms in Chinese. But now, to come to the English language, let us for the moment separate [its grammar into] two grand divisions, the single words of the language and the laws of sentences. In the one division the single words are referred each to one of nine categories (the Parts of Speech); the other gives the rules by which single words are made into sentences, and sentences into longer sections of composition.

19. Is the distinction that we observe in Chinese essays between the *ku*, pairs of sentences even in length, and *tuan*, odd sentences, at all the same as the *chü fa*, laws of sentences, of which you have been speaking?

15. *Obs.* 1. interrogative; lit. that the *k'ou chi*, the air or tone of the sentence, is *ting-wên ti*, interrogating. The verb *ting*⁴, properly, to fix; here implying that the speaker knows what answer he must receive, q. d. You want money, don't you? *Obs* 2 of the remaining words; note the construction; the remain-ing some ones among. *Obs*. 3. the word *yao* again; *jan-'rh*, but; *jan*, thus, this is so, *erh*, and yet ...... *Obs*. 4. is a live word; *ku jan*, certainly, positively; very commonly used where an admission is made on the one part to emphasise an objection on the other, q. d. it *is* so here, no doubt, but &c.

16. quite capable; note the construction: — *ta yu*, they possess in a great degree *li*, a principle, qualified by all that intervenes between *yu* and *li*, viz. the according-to-time-and-circumstance-able-to-inter-change principle. The verb *t'ung* in *pien-t'ung*, has the force of both *per* and *trans* in similar Latin compounds.

17. to such an extent; *shên*, in extreme degree, to such a degree as *chih*, to arrive at this, that there are people &c.

18. limitations; *hsien*, to mark bounds; *chih*, originally, to cut; laws; to govern; *hsien-chih*, the laws limiting are somewhat *ssŭ*, dead, inflexible.

19. *Obs.* 1. essays; *wên-chang* is used generically of all elegant composition ancient or modern, but, specially, of the essays required at modern examinations for degree. *Obs*. 2. the *ku* are the members, literally, the thighs, of a *p'ien* of *wên-chang*, a piece of elegant composition; they must be in pairs and of equal length. *Obs*. 3. the *tuan* are single paragraphs of from 60 to 120 words. An essay may be all of *tuan*, or may have *tuan* between any two pairs of *ku*, or at longer intervals.

KEY TO THE TZŬ ERH CHI. **Colloquial Series.**

20. Not the same. The *chü fa* of Chinese composition merely regard the relative proportions of sentences. Our theory is this; — It is essential to the constitution of a sentence that it contain *kang*, a subject, and *mu*, a predicate. The person, thing, transaction, condition, spoken of, is the subject; the qualifications of the subject, as that it is right or wrong, existent or non-existent, active or passive, form its predicate. It is hence evident that that in which there are nothing but *ssŭ tzŭ*, without any *'huo tzŭ*, cannot well be regarded at a sentence. If, for instance, we were merely to say Man, Rain, Horse, without adding a *'huo tzŭ* to these three words, we should have the head of a sentence without the tail, neither more nor less; words so spoken could not be considered as being language with a meaning; and the same, it is self-evident, holds good of the exclusive employment in any case of *'huo tzŭ* without *ssŭ tzŭ*. The sentences, The man is good, It rains, Is the horse fast? are sentences, because their intelligibility is complete.

Then, as to subject and predicate, in the first of these sentences the word *jên*, man, is the subject, and the words which treat of his qualities are the predicate. In the second sentence, Rain is falling (*Anglicè* It rains,) *yü*, rain, is the subject, and the word that treats of its falling or not falling, is the predicate. In the third *ma*, horse, is the subject, and the words treating of the horse's rate of speed are the predicate.

II. THE NOUN AND THE ARTICLE.

21. The distinction of the *kang* from the *mu* is not wholly ignored in Chinese composition, but I have never heard before of the distribution of words into nine categories that you speak of.
22. Possibly not, Sir. In Chinese the words are not assigned in this way to particular categories. In English, all such denominations as person, thing, transaction, circumstances, are in the categorical classification of the language entitled nouns, *ming-mu*. The words Man, Book, Illness, Year, for example are all *ming-mu*, nouns.

When a noun occurs in English, whether written or spoken, there is often prefixed to it another word to shew whether it has been the subject of a former proposition or not. In Chinese no words are specifically distinguished as performing this function; still, when occasion demands, there is a method of discriminating between definiteness and indefiniteness.

When we hear it said, for instance, *yu ko jên lai, yu i ko jên lai*, A person is come, we know that the person spoken of has not been spoken of before, and that in the mind of the speaker there is an indefiniteness [as to the individuality of the person in question]. But if a speaker were to say, *na ko jên lai liao*, The person, that person, is come, the hearer would know that the person come was the person who had been earlier mentioned. By means of the limitation thus clearly laid down by the speaker, there is a positive indication [of the fact].
23. Our words *na* and *chê*, properly speaking, are employed to distinguish between *this* and *that*.

20. *Obs.* 1. subject and predicate; *kang*, properly, the drag-rope of a net; the chief consideration with reference to the relations of life, subjects of writing, as we say, *the worthier*. *Obs.* 2. *mu*, the eye, used in the sense of subdivision, or section. Cf. *chang-mu*, accounts, *mu-lu*, an index. *Obs.* 3 self-evident; *pu tai yen i*, one does not wait for words to tell one; *i*, a classical expletive found only at the end of sentences.
22. *Obs.* 1. categorical classification; the fixed rule dividing the categories of words. *Obs.* 2 nouns; *ming*, name; *mu*, still in the sense of subordinate divisions, *q. d.* name and index. It is scarcely necessary to observe that although no violence is done to the real meaning of the combination *ming-mu* by translating it *nomina*, the Chinese do not apply the term to any word as a grammatical distinction. *Obs.* 3 an indefiniteness; *mang*, a waste of waters, *wu ting hsiang*, no certain direction. *Obs.* 4. But if a speaker; *shê*, to place, *ponere*; *jo*, if. Cf. the Portuguese, *posto que*, and our *sup-pose*.
23. Our words; note the *hsieh* acting as a plural affix to *chê*, which, however, so far as Chinese grammar is concerned, might with equal propriety stand either alone, or be followed by *ko*.

PART VIII. ON THE PARTS OF SPEECH. **Yen-Yü Li Lüo.** II-III.

24. That is perfectly true; I shall return to that use of them by-and-bye; but in the phrase *na ko jên,* given in paragraph 22, the *na* employed is not *that* as distinguished from *this,* [not the demonstrative pronoun], but serves, in short, to shew that the proposition is not indefinite; [in other words, it is the definite article].
25. The Chinese word *ch'i* would seem on some occasions, but not as a rule, to correspond to the English definite article.
26. You are right. In the phrase *ch'i yü ti,* The remaining ones, the word *ch'i* shews definitively that all besides certain [things or persons] already excluded, are included [in the proposition of the speaker]. The *ch'i* in the phrase *ch'i yao tsai t'zŭ,* The essential is this, again, serves specially to indicate *the* important point [in a proposition]. But take the following:— *hsiang-shih na-ko jên, ch'i hsin pu k'o wên,* With a man like that, there is no telling what is passing in his mind (*lit.* no questioning his heart,) the *ch'i* is simply to be construed as *t'a,* he, his.

Nouns may be used both in English and Chinese without any præpositive word; *e. g.* Man is the most intelligent of all created beings; Gold is heavier than Silver. In these two sentences, Man, Gold, Silver, are generic denominations, and as such can be used without any article; and so with proper names,

III. THE CHINESE NUMERATIVE NOUN.

27. Chinese nouns, on the other hand, have the following peculiarity. Whenever a noun, person or thing, occurs in Chinese, there may be prefixed to it an associate (or attendant) noun, between which and itself there is, with reference to form or use, an affinity. In the sentences *i ko jên, i wei kuan, i p'i ma, i chih ch'uan,* the words *ko, wei, p'i,* and *chih,* are the nouns attendant on *jên,* man, *kuan,* officer, *ma,* horse, and *ch'uan,* ship. These attendant nouns are not exclusively prefixes of the nouns they accompany; they sometimes follow them. In speaking, for instance, of horses or ships collectively, we may say, *ma-p'i,* horses, *ch'uan-chih,* shipping.
28. And where a noun has just occurred, the attendant noun may be used as a substitute for it; as in the following case:— Suppose a person to have been buying cattle and to say to me, *mai liao niu,* I was buying cattle, yesterday. I ask him, *to-shao chih,* how many head, did you buy? He answers, I bought *shih chi chih,* some ten head. In this instance *niu,* cattle, is the noun proper, and *chih,* the attendant noun. The attendant noun being substituted for the noun proper, the repetition of the latter becomes unnecessary.
29. The attendant noun is also occasionally substituted for the noun proper, in Chinese which is not colloquial,

24. *Obs.* 1. perfectly true; *tsŭ-jan,* self existent = a matter of course; *k'o,* properly or permissibly; something as in our phrase, It *may be* stated as an axiom, that &c. See 26, *na k'o pu ts'o.* *Obs.* 2. I shall return; the *ch'ieh,* elliptical for *chan-ch'ieh,* for the present; *lit.* that for the present wait, [until] hereafter again I speak. *Obs.* 3. the *na* employed; *chuan,* special, particular, = *the* word employed. Note *ch'ieh,* on the contrary, at the head of the last clause of the sentence, rendered in English by the disjunctive *but* at the beginning of the first.
26. English and Chinese; *ht.* in the language of both nations there are places = instances [in which the words described] *k'o ch'u,* may go, absent themselves, be dispensed with.
27. *Obs.* 1. peculiarity; *chuan shu,* specially belonging to, a particular property. *Obs.* 2. ships collectively; *ta shu,* as we say, a number of men, ships &c.; *ta,* as in *ta chia, ta kai.*
29. not colloquial; it should farther have been observed that the Numerative also precedes its noun in the written, pretty much as in the oral, language.

KEY TO THE TZŬ ERH CHI. **Colloquial Series.**

30. To conclude, the true function of the attendant noun is, apparently, to distinguish the generic from the specific (or the general from the particular). The nouns *t'ien*, being *'huang t'ien*, Heaven, or *t'u*, being *'hou t'u*, Earth, are general designations incapable of subdivision into minor denominations; they have consequently no attendant nouns associated with them. Where the general designation [applies to what] is capable of subdivision into parts or items, the attendant noun is of use in numeration, in that it represents the item as distinguished from the total.

31. [These attendant nouns, therefore, will be spoken of henceforth as Numeratives,] and a list is now given for the use of the student of all the Numeratives in connection with the nouns to which they are attached.

(THE NUMERATIVES ARRANGED IN ALPHABETICAL ORDER.)

盞 *chan*³. 1. [Numerative of lamps; *e.g.*] Bring a lamp; I want to read. 2. [Not of lanterns; *e.g.*] the *têng-lung* is the lantern one uses when one is walking. 3. The word *chan-tzŭ* is also synonymous with *wan-tzŭ*, a cup. You may say *yi chan ch'a*, for a cup of tea, or *yi wan ch'a*, with equal propriety.

張 *chang*¹ acts as the Numerative of all such words as Table, Chair, Bed, Stool, Bow, Paper, Loom, Net, as being things which shew a certain broadness.

陣 *chên*⁴, [Numerative of showers, gales, outbreaks, &c., *e.g.*] a heavy fall of rain, a gale of wind, an uproar, uproarious discussion, of a certain duration. The word *chên* means, properly, to fight an action, and is used as a Numerative with reference to the suddenness which is the condition [of the occurrences in question]. It implies, say, such eagerness to arrive that [the person or event] cannot wait.

乘 *ch'êng*². 1. *ch'êng* is, properly, to mount, as a horse, to get on, as a cart, or to board a ship. 2. It is occasionally the Numerative of *chiao*, sedan-chair, but *ting* is more common.

劑 *chi*⁴, a dose. A *chi* of medicine is a draught composed of a number of drugs. When a number of drugs are made up into pills, the composition is spoken of as *yi liao yo*.

架 *chia*⁴, [literally, a frame; you say,] a piece of ordnance, a single hawk or falcon, a clock, a single tie-beam, (wall-plate). Of the tie-beam, you say, speaking of two, *liang chia*; but you may also say *i tui*, a pair.

30. *Obs.* 1. To conclude; *tsung chih*, in sum. Construe thus:— In sum, if we carefully investigate the true use of the attendant word, it would seem intended distinctly to separate the *tsung lei*, general denomination, and the *chuan hsiang*, individual item: for instance, *t'ien*, as in *'huang-t'ien*, and *t'u*, as in *'hou t'u*, are denominations which are *lei*, generalities, without *hsiang*, items; how should they have attendant nouns? But in the case of those *tsung ming*, comprehensive terms, in which *lei*, the generality, or total, can be divided into *hsiang*, the particular, or item, if it be necessary to enumerate so many *hsiang* of a *lei*, it is in that case convenient to make a *hsi mu*, particularising index, of the attendant noun. *Obs.* 2. Heaven, Earth; *'huang t'ien*, sovereign heaven, *'hou t'u*, queen, or empress, earth; the twin powers of nature. Cf. Cœlus, father of Saturn, and Tellus; also, **ge anassa**, queen earth; see Sir John Davis on Funeral Rites, in The Chinese, Chapter viii.

chang. 1. all such words; note the *so yu* supported by *chê hsieh tzŭ* at the end of the clause. 2. which shew a certain broadness; note the literal meaning:—It is because its form slightly possesses a width-fashion. Cf. our vulgar *wide-like*.

chi. a draught; *lit.* made into a broth to be drunk.

PART VIII. ON THE PARTS OF SPEECH. **Yen-Yü Li Lüo.** III.

間 *chien*¹. 1. *chien* is the space between four wooden pillars. It is consequently the Numerative of House, Room, &c.; but we must be careful how we use it. 2. For instance, when a person says, I have bought *i ko fang-tzŭ*, he means that he has bought a whole *so*, or a whole *ch'u*, a set of premises, comprising *shu chien fang-tzŭ*, several buildings. Were he to say, *na ko fang-tzŭ 'hao*, (that is a good house,) the expression would be understood to apply to all premises inside the outer, *lit.* the great, gate. 3. If you asked a man, How many *chien* are there in that house, *na ko fang-tzŭ*, and he were to reply, Some thirty *chien*, he would be speaking of all the apartments into which the house is capable of being subdivided, [all the spaces defined by four wooden pillars,] without reference to their dimensions. 4. In the palaces of Chinese princes and dukes, there is generally on the north side, in rear of the rest, a building with an upper and lower story, each of which is subdivided into five or seven *chien*. Referring to its divisions, when you are outside, you say it is a *fang-tzŭ* of five or seven *chien*; if you are inside the house, you say there are *wu ch'i chien u-tzŭ*, five or seven rooms, [as the case may be]. 5. In the following, We two live in *i ko u*, the speaker means that there are a number of *chien* in communication with one another, and that there is but one door for ingress or egress. If he were to say, We two live in *i chien u-tzŭ*, he would mean, We occupy the same apartment, there being a door of the building besides [the door of the room]. 6. When you ask, How many *chien* are there in this *liu* of *fang-tzŭ*, you are asking the number of houses in the row.

件 *chien*⁴, [originally, to divide; to enumerate,] is the only Numerative of articles of clothing. With such nouns as affairs, utensils, despatches, &c., to which it acts as Numerative, it may be exchanged for other Numeratives.

隻 *chih*¹, [properly, half a pair,] is the Numerative of Fowl, Duck, Goose, Tiger, Ship, Box, and like words; also, of Shoe, Boot, Arm, Hand, Foot, Eye, all of which being things that make 雙 *shuang*, pairs, *chih* is employed to shew that a half pair is meant. Of a *shuang* of shoes, for instance, you say that one *chih* has been lost.

枝 *chih*¹, is the Numerative of *chih*, the branch of a tree; *i chih 'hua*, a stalk of flowers, is used where a number of flower-blossoms are growing on the same stem. You may use *chih* with *pi*, a pencil, and *ti*, a flute, but *kuan*, a tube, is more common. Observe that there is a difference between *chih* and *chih-tzŭ*. You may say a *chih-tzŭ*, column, of troops or volunteers.

軸 *chou*², [properly, the nave of a wheel]. The expression *i chou 'hua 'rh*, signifies a scroll mounted. The word *chou* is used with reference to the two knobs of the roller which shew themselves at the lower end of the scroll. For the same reason the *kao-fêng*, patents according rank to the parents or ancestors of an official, (be they living or dead,) are spoken of as being so many *chou* in number.

*chien*¹. 2. all premises; note *t'ung* supported by *tou*, all: the great gate; *i ko ta mên*, the one great gate, *q. d.* the sole great entrance. 3. *Obs.* 1. all the apartments; construe, He does not distinguish great from small; *an ko chien*, he lays the hand on, *sc.* counts, each apartment, *erh*, and, speaks. Observe that *an* amongst other meanings, = *chü*, to hold in the hand; both *an* and *chu* being commonly rendered according to; *q. d.* by what I have hold of, I infer. Note a similar construction of *erh shuo* under the next Numerative; also of *erh lun*, under *l*. *Obs.* 2. princes and dukes; the *wang*, Princes, are the two highest classes of Manchu and Mongolian nobles; the *kung*, Dukes, the fifth and sixth; the *beilé* and *beutsé*, third and fourth classes, are also included in the generic term *wang kung*. The latter term, *kung*, has been, from ancient times, the first of five orders of rank, to a certain extent hereditary, accorded to Chinese; but the *fu*, palace, is distinctively the residence of the *wang kuug*.

chou. is used with reference; note the construction; *ku tz'ŭ ts'ai shuo*, because of this therefore [do men] say it, being placed at the end of the clause. The *kao-fêng* are, literally, mandates conferring rank; *kao*, intimation of superior to inferior; *fêng*, properly, fief, hence rank. Note that *kao-fêng* is, more properly, to confer such rank; the patent is *kao-ming*.

KEY TO THE TZŬ ERH CHI. Colloquial Series.

句 *chü*⁴, is the Numerative of language, oral or written.

卷 *chüan*³, [a Numerative of Book, Document, &c.;] you may use it with *ts'ê-tzŭ*, a roll, or return, or with *shu*, a book; but *pên* is more common with both.

炷 *chu*⁴, [properly, the wick of a lamp;] the Numerative of joss-stick; a number of *chu*, sticks or rods of joss-stick, held together by a paper band, are called a *ku*, a limb, and five *ku*, a *fêng*, [say,] packet.

處 *ch'u*⁴, place, is synonymous with *ti-fang*, a certain extent of space. When you say that you have bought *i ch'u fang-tzŭ*, a house, you include all premises within the boundary walls. You might say the same of a single building which has no boundary walls.

串 *ch'uan*⁴, [a string of things strung together, as] pearls, priests' beads, court beads. A string of priests' beads, or court beads, may also be spoken of as a *kua*⁴ of beads. The Numerative of Bead, as a single bead, is *k'o*.

樁 *chuang*¹, piles, wooden stakes covered by the ground. It is used in the spoken language with *shih ch'ing*, an affair, where the object of the speaker is to speak specially of one matter amongst a number. It is a means of particularising. The Numerative *chien*⁴ is much more common with *shih-ch'ing*.

牀 *ch'uang*², a bed, is used with Coverlid, Mattrass, Carpet.

方 *fang*¹, square, Numerative of Brick and Stone [in regular stacks].

封 *fêng*¹, [originally, a fief; later, a seal; hence, to seal up]. It acts as the Numerative of Letter and like words. It means, properly, to keep concealed. This is why it is used with *shu tzŭ*, *shu hsin*, letters.

幅 *fu*⁴, [a strip, Numerative of Paper,] is not the same as *chang*; it rather approaches *t'iao*; still, the difference of width [respectively indicated by the two words] is not so very great. A *fu*, sheet, of note-paper, is a *chang* of note-paper. Speaking of *pu*, Cloth, you may say a *fu*, length, of cloth, or you may number lengths of Silk by the *fu*; it being understood that both sides of the piece are uncut.

副 *fu*⁴, [a Numerative of certain things in pairs; originally, to divide in two; hence,] used always with reference to sets in pairs, as a pair of *tui-tzŭ*, (scrolls with verses, mottoes, upon them); a set of ear-rings.

桿 *kan*³, [a bough, Numerative of] *ch'iang*, [whether translated as] Musket or single-pointed Spear; of *ch'êng*, Steel-yard; of *ch'a*, three-pointed Spear. It has reference in all these cases to form. If the *ch'iang* be a *ch'ang-ch'iang*, *sc.* spear, not musket, it is equally correct to use *t'iao* as the Numerative; but *t'iao* cannot be used with *ch'iang* as musket, or with the other nouns mentioned.

chü. language oral or written; note the difference between 'hua wên, as here rendered, and wên 'hua, which means the talk of well-bred, educated, persons.

chüan. *t'sê-tzŭ*, roll or return, *sc.* of persons, such as a muster roll, a census return &c.; *t'sê* also read *ch'ai*; see Tone Exercises.

ch'uan. court-beads, the neck-lace worn in full dress by civilians of the fifth and higher grades; by military men of the fourth and higher grades; *ch'uan* is Numerative of Necklace &c.

fang. like *to*, regular in form, as opposed to *tui*, an irregular heap. The Numerative of single Bricks &c. is *k'uai* a piece.

fêng. to keep concealed; note the construction; *lit.* because this word properly has the meaning of to wrap up [so that there shall be] non-appearance. Note the polysyllable *pao-tsang-pu-lao-tï*, formed by *ti* into an attributive of *li*.

fu. 1. not so very great; note the construction *k'uan-chai*, the width of. 2. uncut; both sides are *chih chiu*, woven completely; *chiu* in the sense of *ch'êng-chiu*, entire; but the meaning of the whole, what is stated in the text; the word *fu* enumerates the shorter lengths into which a piece of cloth or silk torn or cut crosswise is divided.

PART VIII. ON THE PARTS OF SPEECH. Yen-Yü Li Lüo. III.

根 *kên*¹, [properly, a root below the ground,] is the Numerative of Mast, Flag-staff, Staff or Pole, Bamboo Pole, Lamp-wick, Felled-timber, Hair of the head [or body], Hair of the beard, and similar nouns; always having reference to form. With *kuên-tzŭ*, a staff or porter's pole, it is as correct to use *t'iao* as *kên*.

個 *ko*⁴, [anciently, besides other meanings, an individual,] used in a great many different positions, but more constantly in such phrases as *chê ko jên*, this man, *chê ko li*, this sense, principle, theory, *che ko tung-hsi*, this thing. With other nouns it may or may not be employed.

棵 *k'o*¹, is never employed but as the Numerative of Tree.

顆 *k'o*¹ [originally, a small head, hence the unit of small round things;] used with Pearl, Head decapitated; in both cases with reference to form. Any round thing can in general be numbered by *k'o*.

口 *k'ou*³. 1. [the mouth;] you may use it with Cooking-pan, Bell, Sword, Water-pot; of so many Persons. But though it does act as Numerative to all these nouns, there is a distinction to be observed regarding its use with Persons. Females spoken of separately are *k'ou*; of a number of men, you say so many *ming*, names, or so many *ko*, individuals. 2. The word *tao* with *k'ou*, means weapon, *sc.* a sword. You may also say *i pa tao* for a sword; also, for the pork-butcher's knife. 3. The bell described as *i k'ou chung* is that hung in temples. It has no tongue, and has to be struck to make it sound.

股 *ku*³, [properly, the under part of the thigh; one of the Numeratives of Road;] with *tao*, a road or way, *ku = t'iao*; in more polished conversation *ku* is found with *lu*, a road.

塊 *k'uai*⁴, a bit, or piece; you may use it with Dollar, Ink-cake, Brick, Door-slab (*pien*³); but it is very comprehensive. *Ex.* Take *a* dollar and buy *a* carpet; or, [some one] bought *a* carpet with *a* dollar.

管 *kuan*³, a tube, Numerative of things that present a certain length to the grasp, and are hollow within; for instance, Pencil, Flute, Clarinet; in all which cases, however, it may be exchanged for *chih* (Numerative of Branch, Stalk, &c.)

綑 *k'uên*³, [properly, to bind in a bundle,] used with Fire-wood as faggot, Straw, &c. as bundle, Onions, as bunch; meaning always that some of the article spoken of is bound up.

粒 *li*⁴, [properly a grain of rice,] used, as having reference to the form of the article, with Rice, or with Pill.

領 *ling*³, [properly, the neck,] used only with *hsi-tzŭ*, Mat, and *wei pao*, Rush-screen.

面 *mien*⁴, a face, is Numerative of Gong, Drum, Flag or Banner, Mirror [of glass or metal].

把 *pa*³. 1. [properly, to grasp in the hand.] All articles that have a *pa*⁴-*'rh*, handle that the hand can lay hold of, are enumerated as so many *pa*³. 2. All such nouns, for instance, as Tea-pot, Knife, Slice (kitchen utensil,) Fork, Fan, Lock, take *pa*. 3. With *i-tzŭ*, chair, you may use *pa* or *chang*.

ko. may or may not; *lit.* when otherwise [men] use the word *ko*, all [such use of it] is '*huó yung*, conditional use.
k'ou. 2. butcher's knife; *t'u*², originally, to flay; to kill; '*hu*, a person; *t'u 'hu*, the slayer *sc.* of pigs. 3. tongue; *to*⁴, clapper of a bell; described in an ancient commentary as the *mu shê*, wooden tongue, of *chin k'ou*, the metal mouth.
ling. rush screen; *wei*, the bulrush; *pao*², a coarse screen made of the bulrush.
pa. slice; the *ch'an* is a flat plate of tin or iron with a long handle, used to take things fried out of the pan.

KEY TO THE TZŬ ERH CHI. Colloquial Series.

包 *pao*¹, [properly, to wrap,] is Numerative of all articles that can be made into packages; such, for instance, as Sugar, Opium.

本 *pên*³, [properly, the lower trunk of a tree,] is used with *shu*, Book, *chang*, Accounts. With *shu* you may use *chüan*, chapter, but not with *chang*.

匹 *p'i*³, [anciently, amongst other meanings, the unit of horses;] the only Numerative of *ma*, Horse; with Ass and Mule you may also use *t'ou*, head, and under certain conditions *ko*, which is the invariable Numerative of Camel.

疋 *p'i*³, [originally written as *p'i* (Numerative of Horse), forty Chinese feet;] sole Numerative of Silk Piece-goods, Satin, Damask, Law, Gauze, Cotton Fabrics. It is properly applied only where nothing has been cut off; [as we say, *the* piece].

篇 *p'ien*¹: 1. [originally, before the invention of paper, a bamboo writing tablet;] Numerative of *wên-chang*, the essay in measured prose, *fu*, the essay in rhyming prose, and *lun*, the essay in four paragraphs; each of these terms signifying a piece of composition. 2. The question, How many *p'ien* are there in this book? has reference to the number of sheets = leaves; the *p'ien* here has a different sense from the *p'ien* used of a piece of composition.

鋪 *p'u*¹, to spread out, is used with no noun but *kang*, Stove-bed; with *ch'uang*, Bed, you always use *chang*. The *p'u*⁴ in *p'u-tien*, Shop, though syllabically the same, has a different tone.

所 *so*³, a place; *i so fang-tzŭ*, a house, is the same as *i ch'u fang-tzŭ*, both referring to the whole range of buildings within the entrance gate.

扇 *shan*⁴. 1. *shan* is, properly, an article used to drive away the heat, and give oneself air, [a fan]; on account of its resemblance to which a door is called *shan*. 2. That house has not got all its doors yet; there are four or five still wanting.

首 *shou*⁴, [originally, the head; hence, a beginning; here, a stanza;] is only used with Poetry, q. d. as a word marking the beginning and ending of the lines [*lit*. sentences, *sc.* that make a stanza]. The writer makes any number of stanzas according to the subject of his verse, and the number of lines in each stanza varies; it may be four, eight, twelve, or at the most sixteen. The stanzas are not necessarily of an even number. One may with equal propriety make a poem of four or five stanzas, or of some score.

檯 *t'ai*². 1. *t'ai* is properly to carry, as two or more persons by united action. At a funeral, the bier may have as many as sixty-four *t'ai*, bearers; [hence, applied to the thing borne, the Numerative of presents sent]. 2. The smallest wedding-trousseau consists of eight *t'ai*. If the family be wealthy, there may be as many as a hundred. 3. Whenever presents are sent to any one, the *t'ai* are in pairs.

pao. Obs. 1. packages; note the construction: — Whatsoever be things that [man] can wrap up out of sight, [speaking of these] all, can [one] use *pao* to act as the attendant word. Observe that the subject of both verbs *shou-ko* and *yung* is in reality *jên* understood. In Latin *fan* = *cumque*, in *quæcumque*, the *quæ* being represented by *ti* which stands for *things*; *shou* = *in* in *involno*, the words *ch'i-lai* = the inflection of the passive participle in *dus*, or the verbal adjective termination in *bilis*. Coin a word and the sentence would run *Quæcumque sint involubilia*. *Obs*. 2. opium; *yen t'u*, smoke-clay, so called from the colour and form of the balls in which the drug is imported.

shan. drive away heat; *ch'ü*¹, properly, to drive away wild animals; to drive away *shu*, heat, and *chao fêng*, invite air.

shou. the writer, *shih-chia*, the verse man, the poet, *k'an t'i*, looking to what is propounded, = *t'i-mu*, his subject, *sui tso*, proceeds to make, verse stanzas many or few. Note the force of *mu* in *t'i mu*.

PART VIII. ON THE PARTS OF SPEECH. Yen-Yü Li Lüo. III.

擔 tan⁴. 1. *tan* is a load such as one man carries over his shoulder on a porter's pole. 2. The phrase *t'a t'iao-cho i tan ch'ai-'huo*, he is carrying a load of fuel, means that the person spoken of bears the *pien-tan*, the flat pole, or his shoulder, and that fuel is borne at the two ends of the pole. 3. If the fuel borne be but a single faggot or parcel, it would be borne on a *kun-tzŭ*, a staff or stake, [not on a *pien tan*, and the said staff] would be *k'ang* [not *t'iao*] on the shoulder.

刀 tao¹, a knife; only used with Paper; a *tao* of paper being a quantity of sheets laid flat one upon the other; employed apparently with reference to the effort required to cut through a quantity of paper so placed.

道 tao⁴. 1. a road, *tao* is used always in the sense of *t'iao*, a strip, with River, Bridge, Wall, Wound, Imperial Decree. 2. The bridge outside the Front Gate of the capital is a *san tao ch'iao*, a triple bridge.

套 t'ao⁴. 1. [properly, an outer casing, wrapper; now, among other senses, a book-wrapper]. *i t'ao shu* means a number of books in one wrapper. One *t'ao* may be the whole of a work, or a work may be divided into several *t'ao*. 2. *i t'ao i-shang*, a suit of clothes is a *p'ao*, the long inner garment, and a *kua*, the somewhat shorter outer garment; you *ch'uan*, put on the *p'ao* underneath, and you *t'ao*, slip over it, the *kua*.

條 t'iao², [properly a twig;] it is common with Silk, as a single thread; Cord, as a single string; Sash, Girdle, Lock, Dog, Rainbow, Sense, (q. d. the sense or principle of a thing;) Street, Road. You may use *t'iao* with *'ho* a river, but also *tao*; and with *pei*, a coverlid; but *ch'uang*, a bed, is also Numerative of *pei*.

貼 t'ieh¹, [properly to stick on,] is not used as a Numerative except with Plaster, sc. cataplasm. With Gold-leaf, *chang* is oftener used than *t'ieh*.

頂 ting³, the crown of the head, is Numerative of Chair, Cap.

朶 to³, a bud; as a Numerative, only used with Flower. The common word for the bud of the unopened flower is *ku-to*.

梁 to⁴, [anciently, an antichamber; also, a target; here as stack,] Numerative of Wood, Brick, piled in regular order.

頭 t'ou², the head, used with Ox, Mule, Ass. It is equally correct to use *ko* with these nouns. Sheep are numbered by *chih*, not by *t'ou*.

堵 tu³, [anciently, a wall of 50 feet long,] is Numerative of Wall; *tu* or *tao*.

堆 tui¹, is like *to⁴*, a heap; but *to* applies to things regularly stacked, *tui*, to what is piled in confusion. Like *to* it is used with Wood, Brick; also with Earth and like things.

頓 tun⁴, [originally, to bow the head to the ground; subsequently, a turn or time; hence, a meal;] Numerative of Meal, Flogging; as though implying a certain fulness or completeness.

座 tso⁴, [properly, the standing part of a bed; any seat; a stand for vases, &c.] used with Mountain, Tomb, Temple, Pagoda.

tao. triple bridge, a bridge of three roads side by side.

*to*³. bud; the *ku*¹ in *ku-to* has no meaning.

*to*⁴. regular order; note the construction; one *to* wood, one *to* bricks, [men] saying effect [this proposition, that] there is *pai*, an array, *tê*, effecting, *ch'i* in regular order, *chêng*, composing; = the two expressions mean wood and bricks placed in regular order.

tui. like things; *têng lei*; fellow-class kinds, things homogeneous.

111

KEY TO THE TZŬ ERH CHI. Colloquial Series.

尊 *tsun*[1], [properly, that which is respected, specially as ruler or father;] you use it with *p'ao* cannon, but you also use *wei*[4] and *chia*.

尾 *wei*[3], a tail, Numerative of Fish; *t'iao* may also be used with fish.

位 *wei*[4], The character *wei* means the proper position of any person or thing, whether standing up or seated. Colloquially, it is used as in the following examples: Three officials of the rank of *ta-jên*; a single cannon; some visitors; and so on.

文 *wên*[2]. 1. [originally, streaks of any kind; later, writing, composition]. The word *wên* is Numerative of nothing but copper cash. 2. A single cash is commonly spoken of as *i ko ta ch'ien*. Were you to ask How many cash, *chi wên ch'ien*, does such a thing cost? the answer would be *chi ko ta ch'ien*, So many cash. 3. The use of the word in this capacity is found to date from the Chou Dynasty, when cash were first coined with an inscription upon them.

眼 *yen*[3], the eye, is used as Numerative of Well.

IV. NUMBER; SINGULAR AND PLURAL.

32. Proceeding next to the consideration of the Numbers of Nouns, the difference between the Singular and the Plural, we find that the Chinese language has a large variety of forms by which the one number is distinguished from the other. In some cases, the noun itself without the addition of a numeral will act as a noun of number; in some, plurality is represented by the reduplication of the noun; in some, such words as the following are employed:—

chung, all, a multitude;	*chüin*, all; specially, both;
to, many;	*ch'üan*, the whole, entire;
to[1] *shao*[3], how many?	*ta chia*, all the persons;
to[1] *shao*[4], a large number;	*chu*, all;
'hao hsieh ko, a good many;	*fan*, all whatever;
tou, all;	*têng*, a class or sort.

Lastly, where the number of a noun has to be stated numerically, the numeral may precede or it may follow the noun.

tsun. respected; cannon are had in special respect, and under certain circumstances are sacrificed to. See note on *wei*.

wei. three officials; in German, French, Italian, and other languages, indeed, through more rarely, in English, the appellative of respect is tacked somewhat in this way to certain nouns, but appositively, not numeratively; *e.g.* their lord-ships, the commissioners; *messieurs les deputés, &c.* The French might translate *chê i wei p'ao* by *monsieur le-dit canon*.

wên[2]. were you to ask, &c., = Did you use *wên* in your question, *ko* would be used in the answer, were the cash three, four, or any number. 3. *Obs.* 1. Chou Dynasty; the last of the three long dynasties which preceded our era, overthrown about B.C. 200 by the prince who suppressed his brother fendatories, and made himself emperor of all China. *Obs.* 2. first coined; construe thus:— if wo ask the origin [of the usage], it is one that commenced at the time that the Chou Dynasty coining cash thereon added *wên tzŭ*, written words.

32. *Obs.* 1. next; *tsai*, in the second place. *Obs.* 2. variety of forms; *pien 'huan*, more properly, interchanges. *Obs.* 3. noun of number; *lit.* there are [cases,] *ti*, in which, the noun proper, without adding to it phrases of number, is enabled *tang yung*, to do the service of, number words. *Obs.* 4. precede or follow. there are cases in which you place the number-word above, there are some in which you first mention the noun, and then add the number-word.

PART VIII. ON THE PARTS OF SPEECH. Yen-Yü Li Lüo. IV.-V.

33. Take the following examples:
    I hear *chung jên*, all men, every one, say, that '*hên to*, very many, a great number of people, people are come.
34. How many are there? There are '*hao hsieh ko*, a good number.
35. What kind of people are they *(tou)*? They are *chün*, all, people of perfectly good character.
36. Why have they *ch'üan*, all, come, or, come in a body? They have *ta chia*, all, public business, which they beg *chu wei*, you gentlemen, to manage for them?
37. There is a clue [to be found in] *fan shih*, all affairs. These men, *jên têng*, of course returned at once.
38. In the phrase, a number of people are come, *to shao* may be used in the sense *hsü to*; [that is, if *shao* be read *shao*⁴].
39. In the phrase *yu jên lai*, you cannot be sure whether one person is come or more. It may be employed where two people are come, or three; of more than three, the common phrase would be *yu chi ko jên*.
40. When you say '*hao hsieh ko jên*, a good few, you mean that the number of persons is tolerably large; such that you cannot tell at a glance how many there are. [each other.
41. The people, *na hsieh jên-mên*, in that house, (the members of that family,) are on very bad terms with
42. Unless the speaker is alluding to persons, the word *mên* is not employed.
43. The words *niu yang*, in the phrase *t'a lai ti shih mai niu yang*, (He is come to sell oxen and sheep,) must not be construed as meaning a single *niu* or a single *yang*.
44. In *chê chien fang-tzŭ*, one *chien* only is meant, but *chê fang tzŭ* means that there is a number of *chien*, apartments, greater or less in the house. [See the Numerative *chien*].
45. [The following example illustrates a variety of plural formations]. There are some people come. How many? Four. What are they come about, these people? They have brought some horses here. Who is going to buy the horses? They are not all going to be bought; one may be possibly. I don't much care to buy horses.

V. Case.

46. The English noun has three distinct modes of use assigned it, which are variously applied according to circumstances. As no such distinctions exist in Chinese, we shall here make shift with a series of three places, the order of which the reader will find illustrated in the four paragraphs following, if he will have the goodness to look at them.

35. they; *tou* evidently pluralising the subject, otherwise untranslateable. — good character; *liang shan*, virtuous, good citizens, the opposite of *hsiung ngo*, violent and vicious.
36. you gentlemen; *chu wei*, all [your] worships.
37. all affairs; see farther on the compound relative *fan*; these men, *jên têng*, man class, = more than one.
38. number of people; *hsü*, originally to listen to, to permit; in ancient texts also found with *chi*; as *chi hsü*, how many?
40. *Obs* 1. tolerably large; *chiao*, to compare, here, and often, = rather. *Obs*. 2. tell; *lit.* as if at one glance you cannot reckon clearly
41. bad terms; observe *pu* before '*ho-mu*, = un in unfriendly, *dis* in disagreeable; so *t'ai pu-ya*, very ill-bred or discourteous.
42. It should be noted that *mên* may make the plural of most personal nouns, and all personal pronouns You may say *na hsieh jên-mên*, those people, *ta-jên-mên*, their excellencies, *k'ê-shang-mên*, the merchants; but it is used generally if not always where the noun is preceded by a demonstrative pronoun or the definite article. The nouns *yeh-mên* and *niang-'rh-mên*, are used both as singular and plural; *ni-mên-ti yeh-jên-mên tou san-liao mo?* Have all your gentlemen left the office? *yu ko niang-'rh-mên lai*, there is a woman come. The syllable *mên* becomes *mê* or *mo* in *chê-mo-cho*, *na-mo-cho*, the *cho* being probably corrupt for *chê*, the classical relative.
45. going to be bought; construe, It is not [the case that] all must [some one] buy; buy one head [some one] indeed may.
46. *Obs*. 1. three distinct modes; *lit* the English in the use of nouns define three forms. *Obs.* 2 variously applied; according to circumstances, *kai-'huan*, interchanged *Obs* 3 make shift; *ch'uan-ch'ieh*, provisionally, we shall *fên ch'u*, make or invent a division into, *san têng*, three classes or gradations The reader will bear in mind the history of our word *case*. The nominative of the noun being the perpendicular, the cases were the divergences, the *fallings* away from it; thus, properly speaking, the nominative is not a case at all; but, as it is, in all inflected languages, the first of the series of forms so styled, it has here been made the first of the three classes between which and the cases an analogy has been attempted. *Obs*. 4. have the goodness; *lit* please look at the four paragraphs below; *chiu shih*, in that case [you will find them] to be *p'ang-yang*, examples, of the division into three *têng*, places in a series.

KEY TO THE TZŬ ERH CHI. **Colloquial Series.**

1. [The Nominative, as answering the question Who, What, Which.]
47. Who smashed, or, Who is it that has smashed, the tea-cup? That small child smashed it.
48. Who was it that wrote these words? That man Chang wrote them.
49. Which is the most intelligent of animals? The Dog.

2. [The Objective, as answering the question Whom, What, Which.]
50. Whom is that small boy beating? He is beating the little girl.
51. What is that woodman doing there? He is cutting boughs off trees.

3. [The Possessive, as answering the question Whose, or of What.]
52. Whose was that book that he has lost? It was that book of mine.
53. Had you not made him a present of that book of yours? No; it was only lent him.
54. Well then, ask him for that book of his to replace yours. His is not the same as mine.
55. What day did you lend it him? I lent it him the day before yesterday.
56. Why did you lend it him? He met me in the street carrying the book, and asked me to lend it him, but I refused.
57. If you refused, how come he by it? When I said I wouldn't let him have it, he snatched it out of my hand, and said he would return it in a couple of days.
58. Oh! this was abominable really. You had better not associate with him any more.

4. [The following shew the three Cases.]
59. According to English grammar, in the sentence, The outlaws have burned my parents' house, the word *tsei-fei*, Outlaws, is the first place in the series, (the Nominative Case), *fang-tzŭ*, House, is the second, (the Objective Case), and *lao jên chia*, Parents, the third, (the Possessive Case).
60. This is shewn if you put the following questions:— Who set fire to anything? The outlaws. What did they burn. A house. Whose house was it? My parents' house.
61. In a word, in every case, the noun representing the agent is in the first place of this series, the noun representing that which is acted on, is in the second, and the noun representing the possessor, in the third.

47. who smashed; *tsa*², to smash by throwing down or letting fall. Note the construction, which might be transposed, as *tsa-tê na ch'a-wan shih shui*. The *tê* in speech would as often as not be *ti*; it is best to treat it as a verb auxiliary of the verb immediately preceding it, and so with *tê* in *hsieh-tê* in the two following examples, whether you construe thus, Who is it that wrote these words, or, Whose writing are these words; the latter idiom giving force to *shih*, as the verb substantive, the subject of which is then the word *tzŭ*, which in the former we treat as the object.
48. that man Chang; note the *na-ko jên* following *hsing Chang ti*, the surnamed Chang one; were the sentence to begin *shih na-ko hsing Chang ti*, it would still end as in the text.
49. animals; *chu-shêng*, the brute; also used, as with us, of people, as a term of abuse; *chu*, read *hsü*, to rear; *liu chu*, the six *chu*, are horses, oxen, sheep, poultry, dogs, and pigs.
51. woodman; *ch'iao fu*, the man who *ch'iao*², collects fuel, is *k'an shu chih-tzŭ*, cutting tree boughs.
52. whose was that book; *tê* would be generally pronounced *ti*, = one, or, that which; *q d*. the lost one is whose book? The correct analysis of the construction is probably this. *tiu*, to lose, *tiu tê*, loss achieved, lost; [some one] *tiu tê*, has lost [a book; that book] is whose book. The *ti* in *shui ti*, clearly = *tê*, to obtain, possess; the who possessed, possessed by whom, whose, book. Compare the answer, It was that I-possessed book, that book belonging to me, = of mine.
53. made a present; *ni* before *na pên shu* acts as the possessive pronoun, not as the subject of *sung*, before which it would be quite correct to introduce another *ni*.— only lent; so translated to give due emphasis to the denial; note two *ti*, both = *tê*, and both acting as our participial inflections in *given* from *give*, *lent* from *lend*.
57. came he by it; how achieved, the having taken it away; treat *na-liao ch'u*, = *abstraho*, and *tê* as giving the force of the inflection *abstraxi*; compare the use of the auxiliaries *avoir* and *avere* in parallel constructions. — snatched it; *ta*, from; he from my hand within, violently, *lit* unyieldingly, tore it away.
58. associate; *ch'uan*, to go through as a string through things strung; *'huan*, to exchange; *ch'uan-'huan*, intimate relations.
59. grammar; *shuo fa* is commonly rendered phrase, mode of expression.
60. shewn; *lit*. how can [one] see it? For instance &c.
61. agent, *hsing ti*, the one that acts; acted on, subjected, *shou ti*, the one that receives; possessor, *kuei-wei ti*, the one to whom [the property] belongs; *kuei*, to return; compare *re-vert*.

PART VIII. ON THE PARTS OF SPEECH. Yen-Yü Li Lüo. V-VI-VII.

VI. Gender.

62. The sexes of the human race are distinguished as *nan*, man, and *nü*, woman; those of the brute creation, as *kung*, male, and *mu*, mother. No inanimate thing has gender. Mountain, water, wood, and stone, are all considered inanimate things.
63. [Sex is distinguished sometimes by particular designations, sometimes not; *e.g.*] Are that man and that woman sitting there, husband and wife? No; a brother, and a sister younger than he is.
64. I have bought seven chickens, of which two are cocks, and five, hens.
65. The male of horses is *erh ma*, stallion, the female, *k'o ma*, mare.
66. The bull is, colloquially, *kung niu*, the cow, *mu niu*.

VII. The Adjective and its degrees of comparison.

67. For the qualifying and classifying [in the order of their qualities] such of the *ming-mu* as are *shih-tzŭ*, nouns substantive, other words must be added to them. The substantive is as it were the principal, the word added to qualify and describe its degree, the auxiliary, (its adjective).
68. The word Good, for instance, means nothing by itself; it leaves you nowhere. You must add Person or Thing to it, and then it will serve the purpose of qualification.
69. For instance, in the phrases, This is a good man, This man is good, the word Good serves to characterise, or describe, the man.
70. In This paper is white, That paper is red, the words White and Red specify different kinds of paper.
71. In the phrases Coarse paper and Fine paper, This paper is coarse, That paper is fine, the words Coarse and Fine distinguish the one paper from the other as differing in degree of fineness or coarseness.

Degrees of Comparison. 72. There is, farther, a gradation of increase and decrease to be observed in the employment of the adjective, which the following section will explain.

73. He is intelligent. You are more intelligent. You are more intelligent than he. He is the most intelligent of all these people. He is more intelligent than those people. He is more intelligent than any one. He is the most intelligent man in the world.
74. That is impracticable. That is more impracticable. That is more impracticable still. Of [all] these methods the most impracticable is that.
75. The highest roof in Peking is that of the Emperor's palace.
76. He has more money than I, (or, His fortune is larger than mine).

62. has gender; *yin*, the female principle of nature, *yang*, the male; note the term *ssŭ wu*, used either alone or with *tung-hsi*.
66. the bull; *p'ang*, properly, a piebald ox or cow; not used colloquially.
67. *Obs.* 1. qualifying; *fên hsiang*, dividing into sorts, *ting têng*, determining ranks. *Obs.* 2. auxiliary; *fu chu*, to stand by and assist, as a minister his sovereign; *fu³*, properly the jaw or cheek; hence, the wood which keeps the wheel in its place.
68. nowhere; *cho-lo*, bottom found in sounding, definite whereabouts of anything. You say that an affair has *cho-lo* when it is satisfactorily disposed of.
69. characterise; *li* does the service of distinguishing the sort or quality.
72. gradation; *ts'êng-tz'ŭ*, literally, succession of layers.
73. in the world; *lit.* under heaven.
74. more impracticable; you might transpose *kêng* and *shih*, or introduce *shih* before *tsai*; but you could not say *tsai shih tso-pu-lai-ti*.

KEY to the TZŬ ERH CHI. **Colloquial Series.**

77. My abilities are not to be compared to his.
78. He is taller than I, (or I am shorter than he).
79. Which of those two speaks the better mandarin? Li is rather the better speaker of the two.
80. Who is the most learned of these three? Also Li.

VIII. The Pronoun.

Personal Pronouns. 81. The word by which a man designates himself when he is talking, is *wo*, I, me; The word by which I designate any one that I am addressing in conversation, is *ni*, Thou, thee; any person besides you and myself, is *p'ang jên*, a third party, and if you and I allude to him in conversation with each other, we designate him *t'a*.
82. The plural of the personal pronoun is *wo-mên*, we; *tsa-mên*, we two, or, all of us concerned; *ni-mên*, ye; *t'a-mên*, they.
83. The word *t'a* may be used in speaking of brutes in Chinese, but it cannot be applied to inanimate things.
84. Speaking of the dog, he said, *t'a*, he, is a good watch-dog. If you were to ask, Is that table taken away, the person addressed would reply, *na kuo lai liao*; he could not say, *na* T'A *kuo lai liao*.

Relative Pronouns. 85. 1. The man whom I went to see was not at home. 2. Whom did you go to see? 3. He is a teacher who used to teach me mandarin. 4. What is his name? 5. Chang. 6. Is it the Chang who lives in Tiger-skin Lane. 7. What lane did you say? 8. I said Tiger-skin Lane; the lane fourth from the south end of Great East Street, on the west side. 9. That is not the lane in which Chang lives; he lives outside the walls. 10. Whom is he teaching at present? 11. He is teaching two people, both of them my relations. 12. What is he teaching them? 13. He is instructing the elder in official correspondence, the younger in the Four Books. 14. Which of the two has made the more way? 15. I think the younger is abler than the elder. 16. What are you reading now yourself, Sir? 17. The book that you gave me last year.

77. not to be compared; *pi-pu-ch'i*, cannot rise to a level with, his abilities.
78. taller-shorter; his *shên-liang*4, his body-measure, stature.
80. most learned; construe thus. [*jo lun*, if we consider] these three men's *hsio-wên*, learning, which is strong. Note the adjective *ch'iang*, here *strongest*, because the comparison is of more than two; in the foregoing sentence, *stronger*, because two only are compared.
81. addressing; note the construction: — I to *shui*, whom, whomsoever, = any one, am speaking; [my] *ch'êng shui*, designation of any one is *ni*. Observe that the relation of these indefinite relatives to their antecedents, as also that of the correlative conjunctions, is constantly represented in Chinese, as here, by reduplication, especially of verbs or pronouns; *e.g. ni yao to-shao, k'o i na to-shao*, You can take whatever number you want, or, as many as you want; the strict analysis being, you want many or few, you can take many or few; *shih jên shih wu*, Be it person, be it thing = whether person or thing, *sui chao sui yung*, as you come upon them, so make use of them; *sui*, to follow, here and commonly, according to. Cf. *sequor, secundum*.
84. good watch-dog; note *lai*, auxiliary, following *kou*, the object of *t'i ch'i*, and *cho* as a participial inflection; *q. d.* he, being in the act of speaking of the dog, said, He knows how to guard the house. Observe that, in the foregoing sentence, *t'i-chi-lai* is not followed by *cho*.
85. 3. who used; note the position of the Numerative, which with *yi*, one, = the article *a*, not before, but after, the words which are formed by *ti = tê* into an attributive of the noun; *lit* [the man] is formerly-teach-me-mandarin-ing one teacher: — *kuan 'hua*, the spoken language of government. 7. what lane; *lit.* say again what lane it was. 8. fourth from the south end; *lit* it is that lane [described by all the words between *tsai*, to be, or, to be in or at, and *ti* or *tê*, which, as we should say, inflects *tsai*. Construe, It] is the-be-great-east-street-south-end-road-west-side-number-four-lane-*ing*, that lane. 12. What is he teaching them; *lit.* he teaches them what *kung k'o*, tasks; *kung*, labour, *k'o*, originally, examination. 13. correspondence; *wên-shu*, official documentary style, as distinguished from *wên-chang*, elegant composition: — the Four Books, viz. Ta Hsio, the Study for Adults, Chung Yung, The Mean, Lun Yu, the Dicta of Confucius, Mêng Tzŭ, [the Doctrines of] Mencius. 14. made the more way; *chien chang*, perceptible improvement; *q. d.* [men] *chien*, see, [him] *chang*, growing.

PART VIII. ON THE PARTS OF SPEECH. Yen-Yü Li Lüo. VIII.

86. You use the pronoun *shui*, who, only of persons; *shên-mo* and *na³-ko*, whether speaking of persons or things. *e.g.*
87. Who, *shui*, was it that told you to come? *shên-mo jên*, what person was it, &c.; *na-ko jên*, what person was it, &c.
88. What are you come for? I am come for the tea-cup. What are you doing here? I am putting the room to rights.
89. You may say *ni ai-hsi shih na ko*, which do you like, either of persons or things.
90. What is it that he is engaged upon over there? He has not told me what it is.
91. What he really wants is this.

Compound Relative Pronouns. 92. 1. Whosoever breaks the law must be tried and punished. 2. Any persons breaking the law, be they who they may, must be tried and punished. 3. Whosoever is deserving of reward, I shall be sure to reward.

93. 1. Those brigands are very ferocious; they kill every one they fall in with. 2. Whoever goes into the interior must take out a passport. 3. That story is false; it is not to be believed, be the teller who he may. 4. Whoever is recommended by him is promoted and rewarded. 5. Whatever he desires me to take in hand, I must take in hand. 6. Did I not tell you to bring over whatever books there were there? 7. Certainly; and are there any that I have not brought over? 8. There is a volume in the press that you have left behind.

Possessive Pronouns. 94. 1. Is he not your father? 2. No; he is my elder brother. 3. Indeed! What is his age? 4. He is upwards of twenty years older than I, (or, His age is greater than mine by more than twenty years). 5. Is that book yours, or did you borrow it? 6. It is my own. 7. Ha! It is the one you commissioned Chang to buy for you, is it not? 8. No, it is one that I bought myself. 9. Are you going to take a walk in the Tung 'Hua Yuan to-day? 10. No, I can't; I am on duty to-day. 11. Wouldn't it do if I were to take your duty for you? 12. I am much obliged to you, but I must do the thing myself. 13. What is the difference between your doing it and any one else's doing it? 14. In the first place, I am the responsible person, (or, it is my duty,) and besides, if I did not see to it myself, I should be sure to lay myself open to being found fault with by my superiors. 15. Who would tell them? 16. They wouldn't need to be told; they would find it out themselves.

86. you use; remember that *na*, when interrogative, is *na³*, when demonstrative, *na⁴*.
87. who was it that; note that in these three sentences *ti* is as often used as *tê*.
92. 1. whosoever breaks the law; *so yu*, whosoever or whatsoever there be; *so*, originally, place, position *q.d.* the position is this, *yu*, there are law transgress-ing [persons;] *tsung* all, *tei*, [man] must, try and punish. 2. be they who they may; *wu lun* [the agent, here, government,] does not discuss who it is that has broken the law, [the person who has broken the law, having broken it,] *chiu*, in consequence, must [the government] try and punish.
93. 1. fall in with; [let them] meet whom [they will] all they slay. 2. pass-port; *chih*, to grasp in the hand, *chao*, that which shews, a testimony; *chih-chao* is generic of various documents of the kind which are *ch'ü*, taken out. Understand *ti jên* after *nei ti*, the interior, all persons that enter &c. Note that *nei ti* is also one expression for China as distinguished from *wai kuo*, foreign countries. 3. be the teller; *p'ing*, as before, at the option of; let who will tell it, all ought [man] not to believe. 4. recommended; construe: Leave it to him to recommend [persons; those persons] are *shui*, any persons; all obtain promotion and reward. 7. are there any; *lit.* still are there I-have-not-brought-over ones?
94. 7. buy for you; note *kei ni* = what we call the dative case; *ti*, relative, representing *jên*, man, and *shu*, book; — Is it the-one-that you commissioned him-that-is surnamed Chang to buy for you? 8. myself; *wo pên jên*, and above with *ti*, as my own. 10. I can't; *pu hsing*, elliptical for *wo pu nêng hsing*. 11. take your duty; construe, [If you] commit to me instead of you to *tang*, bear, would it be well or not? 12. much obliged; *fei hsin*, as before; note *tei = tê yao*, it becomes, or is become necessary; it is certainly necessary that I myself *pan-tê*, should despatch, *ti*, that which [is the business of my *ch'ai-shih*]. You might construe, The business is such that I must &c. 13. what difference; *i yang*, one and the same fashion; Cf. uni-form; *lit.* you individually = you yourself, transact, your own transacting, *'hai*, compared with, another man's transacting, there is what non-uniformity? 14. lay myself open; *lit.* I should certainly invite my superiors' *t'iao-ch'ih*, reproof; *t'iao*, to pick out, *sc.* one's fault, *ch'ih⁴*, to blame. Note *ko-tzŭ-ko-'rh* and *tzŭ-chi-ko-'rh* = self.

KEY TO THE TZŬ ERH CHI. Colloquial Series.

Demonstrative Pronouns. 95. 1. Which of these two horses is the better? 2. In my opinion this is a good horse, and that is a bad one. 3. Which is the better bank of that river? 4. There is some scenery on that side; this side is somewhat barren. 5. Have you bought all these oxen? 6. I have bought those three dun cows; these black ones are his purchase. 7. What do you want to do with these things of mine? 8. They are not all yours. 9. Which of them is not mine? 10. This is not yours. 11. Very good; then I can do without that one; leave those.

Distributive Pronouns. 96. 1. Every member of the official establishment of the state has got his own duties. 2. Those two men have each his own way of going to work. 3. In gambling, every player puts up his own stake. 4. Neither of those propositions is a good one. 5. Two people gave him advice that day, and had he attended to either, he might have saved his life; unfortunately, he attended to neither. 6. He asked me whether I wanted to take the house on a long lease or a short one; I told him either would do. 7. It does not signify which of you two copies this paper; either will do. 8. They two go home three times a month, one being allowed to go on each occasion. 9. There will probably be something to do to-morrow, and so one of you two must remain here; it doesn't signify which; either will do. 10. The other day, he got drunk, and struck every one he met. 11. You say that these banditti all wear red turbans, don't you? 12. Whether they all wear them or not, I can't say, but every one that I saw had a red turban on. 13. Which of these two people do you like the better? 14. I do not like either of them. 15. When you come in here, you men, you must every one of you have on a belt ticket. 16. Which do you think the better of these two? 17. Either is as good as the other. 18. Which of these two jade things will you have. 19. They are both good; if I am to take one, the one is as good as the other.

Indefinite Pronouns. 97. 1. Which of those porcelain things does he want to buy? 2. He wants to buy them all. 3. Which article is it that you want to buy? 4. I do not want to buy any. 5. Are you in the right, or is he? 6. Every body says that I am. 7. The disorder has broken out very seriously in his family; they have all died of it but himself. 8. Any one could understand that. 9. Why doesn't he get some one to give him an opinion about that? 10. There is no one competent. 11. What? In an affair of this kind any one could; but they say that he is a selfwilled man, and will not take any one's advice but his own. 12. He is greatly to be pitied; nobody takes an interest in him, and it isn't only that people in general don't take an interest in him, but there are some people who hate him very much. 13. Could you say how many? 14. How many do you suppose? 15. I make out five. 16. I believe that there are a great many more. 17. Did any one tell you? 18. Yes; some one did tell me that in a certain family there are several people who dislike him much.

95. 4. barren; 'huang, either without wood, or uncultivated. 7. things of mine, note wo without ti, yet, by position, = the possessive. 11. do without; the k'o before pu-yao diminishes the directness of the affirmation; q. d. those, be it, I do not claim.
96. 3. his stake; chu, the direction of the fancy; in gambling, the stake by which one backs what one fancies; hsia chu, to put down one's stake. 5. gave him advice; for him, or to him, put forth a chu-i, opinion; — attended to either; t'ing, had he listened to shui ti, that which was the opinion of whichever he would, tou, both ways, could he &c. 10. struck every one; yu chien jên, [when] he happened to meet persons, chiu, thereupon, he struck. Cf. the Latin cunque, or cumque, originally quumque, our ever, generalising time, and hence, events. 11. red turbans; note that tou pluralises tsei; did you not say that those brigands all are round the head swathing red cloth? Note also ko ko, every one, each one; those that I saw were each swathing red cloth ones. 15. belt-ticket; yao p'ai, the badge hung in the girdle; tai, specially, to wear as a girdle, but freely used as to carry, to load. 18. two jade things; jade things of two kinds, differing in form, quality, or otherwise; — take one; lun i ko, if it be a question of one, na³ i ko, any one, shih tê, is good, will do.
97. 7. the disorder; note na⁴ ko, that disorder spoken of before, therefore translated the disorder. 10. no one competent; there is no one able t'i, vicariously, ta-suan, to make calculation. 11. self-willed; chüh, holding tenaciously, niu, twisting. 12. take an interest in; kuan, to look after. — people in general; hi, there is a certain number of people, = ever so many.

PART VIII. ON THE PARTS OF SPEECH. **Yen-Yü Li Lüo.** VIII-IX.

98. 1. Here, I say, how much coal have you bought here? 2. Eight piculs altogether. 3. Why did you buy so much? 4. You said that I was to buy a large quantity. 5. I said a large quantity, but I did not want as much as this. 6. If you don't want so much, you can sell some of it to somebody else. 7. How many cash did you pay a catty? 8. I paid four *tiao* a picul for it. 9. What a price! What shop did you buy it at? 10. At the T'ai Hsing in P'ing-an Street. 11. If it was so dear there, why didn't you go somewhere else? 12. There is no other coal-store in this neighbourhood. 13. What? Why, the other day, when I was in P'ing-an Street, I saw ever so many coal-stores. 14. There are some some way off, but they have all an understanding with each other. 15. But even if they have, you might beat them down; they don't all mean to patronise each other to such an extent as each to stand out for exactly what the other takes. And the coal doesn't look very good either; its' all nonsense asking four *tiao* a picul for such coal as this. 16. If I recollect right, last year, this kind of coal was something dearer. 17. Anyhow, I don't want such a quantity as this; I needn't take the whole of it. You just put out so much of it and sell it to some one else. 18. If you don't want the whole of it, how much do you want? 19. It will do if you keep three or four piculs. 20. And will you pay that price for it? 21. Yes, I will give you the money another day.

IX. THE VERB AS MODIFIED BY MOOD, TENSE, AND VOICE.

99. Words that predicate being, doing, suffering, whether of person or thing, are in English referred to one of the nine categories before mentioned; [that of the Verb to wit]. No such line being drawn in Chinese, and the invention of an equivalent [for the word Verb] presenting some difficulty, we shall take on us to employ the term '*huo tzŭ*, live words, which, though incomplete, is unobjectionable, and we shall endeavour, with the reader's permission, to shew by examples the analogies and contrasts of the '*huo tzŭ*, as employed under different conditions in both languages.

100. Were a Chinese to say, *ma p'ao, niao fei, ch'ung p'a, yü yu,* these sentences, uttered thus consecutively, must be taken to signify, that, as a species, the horse gallops, the bird flies, the reptile creeps, the fish swims.

98. 1. bought here; *chê ko mei*; how much of this coal have you been buying? 3. did you pay; note the construction; *shih*, to be, untranslateable in our idiom; *q. d.* you are in the position of having bought it for how much? 8. four *tiao*; originally, a *liang*, tael, ounce of silver, = 1,000 copper cash Peking currency; 1 *tiao* = 500 such cash; now, the tael is worth ten *tiao*. The proper cash has not been coined for some years, and its place is taken by a very base ten-cash piece, really worth about two cash 12. in this neighbourhood; *lit.* [if you go] from this to *tso chin*, what is on the left side and near; *tso* elliptical for *tso yu*, right and left. 14. understanding; *t'ung ch'i*, intercommunicating, cooperating, spirit; used also of a third party's mediating or communicating between two persons. 15. patronise; *ch'ên⁴*, properly, that which is worn next the skin; used as, to deal with, the custom of a customer. Construe. — They cannot, here-[a-man]-wanting-so-much-there-[a-man]-must-also-want-so-much — [wise], all be of a mutually patronising intention. The two clauses beginning *che-'rh* and *na-'rh*, together make a long adverbial construction, *q. d.* on the You don't sell I don't sell principle. Note *shih* where we should expect *yu*, to have; you may say *wo shih chê-ko i-ssŭ*, I am of this opinion. 16. recollect right; I seem to remember. 18. put out; *po*, set aside, very common of extraordinary application of government funds; *chi ch'êng*, properly, some tenths.

99. *Obs.* 1. predicate; *i*, to put forward as a proposition, *chi*, reaching to, touching. Construe, In English whether in the case of person or thing, *so-yu — tzŭ yang*, whatever words there be of the kind that *i-chi*, treat of, *wei*, being, *tso*, doing, *shou*, receiving &c. *Obs.* 2. equivalent; *lit.* it is comparatively hard *ch'uang-ch'u*, to invent, a special term. *Obs.* 3. incomplete; *lit.* though you cannot regard it as one altogether corresponding, the provisional employment of it is still in no way improper. *Obs.* 4. different conditions; *jang wo*, allow me; *mien-ch'iang*, to make an effort; also used modestly of what one can do; *tso ko pang-yang*, to give an example of the *hsiang-tui*, corresponding, and *hsiang-fan*, contrasting places, in the verb as the two notions *sui yung*, according to circumstances employ it.

KEY TO THE TZŬ ERH CHI. **Colloquial Series.**

101. Should you happen to hear a man say *ma p'ao*, you would in that case infer that he was speaking of some particular horse as being in the act of gallopping. It is much more usual, however, under these circumstances, to say *na-ko ma p'ao*.
102. The sentences *t'a nien shu, wo hsieh tzŭ*, I study, he writes, may mean either that we two are at this moment respectively engaged in studying and writing, or that these are habitually our respective tasks.
103. To the question, Are you two men both asleep there, the answer being, I am awake, but he is asleep, it is equally correct to reply in any one of the following forms:
    t'a shui; wo hsing-cho:
    t'a shui-chiao; wo hsing-cho:
    t'a shih shui-chiao; wo hsing-cho, or, *wo shih hsing cho.*
104. These are mainly examples of the verb as predicating being, [the verb substantive]. We shall postpone consideration of the verb as active and passive until we have said something about the six modes (Moods) in which the English verb may be used.

The Indicative Mood. 105. For instance, in the sentences *wo ai t'a*, I like him, *ni k'ên pu k'ên*, Will you not? the words *ai* and *k'ên* respectively shew that what is meant is a direct unconditional assertion and a direct unconditional question.

The Conditional Mood. 106. Were I to say, If he comes, I shall be sure to see him, my words would imply an uncertainty whether he was really coming.

The Potential Mood. 107. The sentence, He may (or, can) act as a teacher, may mean, either that he is competent to be a teacher, or that he can be a teacher if he pleases.

The Imperative Mood. 108. When you use the single word *lai*, Come, to any one, you command him to come; so, *tsou pa*, Go! *p'ao ch'ü*, Be off!

The Infinitive Mood. 109. In the sentence *t'a ai k'an shu*, He likes to study, *ai*, Like, and *k'an*, Behold, are both verbs; but *ai*, being governed by *t'a*, He, is according to English grammar in the indicative mood, while *k'an*, which has no word in particular to govern it, is regarded as general or indefinite. There is a manifest difference, for instance, between the [construction of] the *k'an* in *k'an shu 'hao*, It is good to study, *k'an shu shih ko 'hao shih*, It is a good thing to study, where it applies generally to all persons whatsoever, and that of the *k'an* in *t'a k'an shu*, He studies, where a particular person is indicated as the student.

The Participle. 110. 1. Besides the five modifications here more or less explained, to which the English verb is liable, there remains a sixth which it is rather more troublesome to deal with. 2. In the following:—

105. direct unconditional; *lit.* the words *ai* and *k'ên* respectively *tang*, represent, the *i-ssŭ*, purpose, of plainly indicating and definitively establishing direct assertion and direct interrogation. Strictly, they do not; it is shewn by the context.
106. really coming; *shih fou*, is it or is it not = whether, *chun*, with the certainty of a standard, *lai*, he will come.
107. if he likes; note the *yuan-i* put into what we call the Conditional Mood, by the *ts'ai* following it.
109. *Obs.* 1. *ai* being governed; *chi*, since, *shu*, is, т▲ *tzŭ so chu*, that which the word *t'a* governs; but *shu* very commonly means belonging to, subordinate to, in the jurisdiction of. *Obs.* 2. manifest difference; note the construction; the first proposition regarding *k'an*, being *yu*, compared with, the second, (in which *ti* represents *k'an*), the difference of the two *shuo-fa*, forms of expression, [a person] *i chien*, giving one glance at, will be thereon able to understand; — *hao*, to comprehend, *jan*, the so being.
110. 1. more or less explained; although the five *pien-'huan*, transformations, have been *luo*, in outline, summarily, *shuo ming-pai*, explained, *shêng*, remaining, there is one, comparatively somewhat difficult. 2. *was sick; tang shih*, at the time [referred to] :— this emperor, *na*, that = the :— most favored; *ch'ung* 3, to love, favor, as heaven the emperor, as the emperor a subject. The 'Han Ti, emperor of the 'Han, referred to, is Hsien Ti, about A.D. 220 :— conspired *mou*, planned, *p'an* 4, rebellion . — shell ; *cha* 4, a character unauthorised by the dictionaries, made up of *'huo*, fire, and *cha*,

PART VIII. ON THE PARTS OF SPEECH. Yen-Yü Li Lüo. IX.

Chang's best beloved child was sick;
The minister most favored by this emperor of the 'Han, conspired against him;
When the shell exploded, the soldiers standing up were wounded, those lying down escaped;
My rheumatism is so bad that I am never comfortable, standing, sitting, or lying down;
A state in disorder resembles a tottering wall;
the forms *t'êng-ai-ti*, tenderly loved, *ch'ung-ti*, favored, *chan-cho*, standing up, *t'ang-cho*, lying down, *tsò-cho*, sitting or seated, *yao-t'ang-hsia*, about to lie down, [here = falling,] when translated into English, will all be ranged under the sixth mood, or modification of the verb. 3. The use of the words *ti* and *cho* appears to be this; the addition of them to the verb, whether of being or doing, helps it to bring out a secondary meaning in support of that primarily indicated by it; they are intended to shew that the condition of whatever is, or is done, is one either of now being, of having been, or of being about to be.

The Tenses. 111. Whether it regard existence or action, there are in all but three places in the order of Time, viz. the Past, the Future, and the Present. These are its three grand divisions, in which, at the same time, there are subordinate distinctions to be observed.

112. The grand divisions are exemplified generally in the following: — I went to the *yamên* yesterday; I am reading to-day; to-morrow I shall rest.

113. The following will give some idea of the subordinate distinctions. **1.** Have you written that despatch? I am writing it. **2.** Have you bought that book? I have bought it. **3.** When he came in the morning, I was eating my breakfast; when he returned in the evening I had gone out. **4.** When will you come to me? Shall I come to-morrow at noon? No; at noon I shall be going to the *yamên*; but don't be uneasy; I shall have settled that affair for you before we meet again. **5.** I am writing (or, I have written) to Peking to tell them to ship all my books for this place. I have been writing too, all the morning. **6.** The day after to-morrow, I shall have been studying that book three months, and I shall have finished the eighth volume this evening. **7.** You must apply, you know. But I do apply. When you were buying a horse, why didn't you look out for a good one. I did look out for a good one, but I couldn't find one.

suddenly; *cha p'ao*, a shell, *cha k'ai*, to explode: — rheumatism; *lit.* bones sore; construe, My bones *na-mo*, being thus, as they are, are truly of a soreness; recumbent, standing, sitting, all ways am I not at ease. — tottering; *lit.* a wall about to lie down. Note that in these examples, wherever *tr* has been made to represent participial inflection, it might, in English, with equal if not greater propriety be construed as the relative; the child that Chang most loved; the minister that the 'Han Ti most favored &c. 3. secondary meaning; *lit.* If we carefully examine into the true use of *ti* and *cho*, it appears that the [sense] that the verb, whether it treat of action or existence, indicates when standing by itself, is the *chêng i*, proper or primary sense; add *ti* or *cho*, and they *p'ei-ch'u*, by their alliance bring out, *p'ang i*, a by-standing, =, secondary, sense; they are for the purpose of *pu-tsu*, complementing, *chuan-chih*, demonstration, that the matter [spoken of] is in the *hsing-shih*, formal condition, either of actually being, actually having been, or actually about to be. Note *k'o*, admissibly, coupled with 'huo, either, or; *chêng tsai*, actually in the condition specified. The term *chêng-i*, often means the plain, proper, sense of a particular word or passage; with *p'ang-i* it is used with reference to Chinese composition much as we use subject and predicate. Say, A ship carries passengers, says a Chinese; ship is the *kang* (see above 20), what is here said of her is the *mu*; that the ship is a ship, is the *chêng-i*; that she carries passengers, is the *p'ang-i*.

111. Past; *i*, to end, to cease, *ching* to pass through; — Future; *lit.* that which is not yet; *wei*, is also used as a simple negative; as in *wei-pi*, it does not follow, is not certain; — Present; that which is under the eye.

113. subordinate distinctions; the simple English grammar which I have more or less followed, describes the tenses illustrated in example 112 as the Main Tenses, and subdivides these in the order of the examples given in 130; viz.

    1. am writing, Present Incomplete;
    2. have bought, Present Complete;
    3. was eating, Past Incomplete; had gone, Past Complete;
    4. shall be going, Future Incomplete; shall have settled, Future Complete;
    5. have been writing, Progressive Form of Present Complete;
    6. shall have been studying, Progressive Form of Future Complete;
    7. do apply, Present Emphatic; did look out, Past Emphatic.

KEY TO THE TZŬ ERH CHI. **Colloquial Series.**

Dialogue shewing the construction of the Active Verb in most of its Moods and Tenses.
114. 1. What are you sitting looking at upstairs there? 2. At a man that there is over there. 3. What is he doing? 4. Beating something. 5. Do you know the man? 6. No, I never saw him before. 7. How long have you been sitting up there looking at him? 8. Not very long. 9. I think you are mistaken; nobody is beating anything. 10. No, I am not mistaken; I am still looking at him. 11. I think you are mistaken though, and that there is no one there at all. 12. What do you mean by no one at all? I was looking at him (or, I saw him,) when I first said I was, and I am still looking at him (or, I see him still). 13. Had you seen him before I put my first question to you? 14. Yes, long before. 15. You said just now that you had not been sitting here long. 16. And what I said was the truth. 17. I shall go and see if there is any man that you are looking at. 18. Very good; when you get to the spot you will be able to tell whether there is or not. 19. Can you wait till I come back. 20. If you are back soon I shall be still sitting here. 21. Have you got nothing to do? 22. Yes I have; but I shall be sure to have done it all by the time you return. 23. If the man is there when I get there, I'll apologise when I come back again. 24. I shall have been laughing at you for at least three days before you find out the truth. 25. How do you mean laughing at me three days before I find it out? 26. I say that it will be at least three days before you can satisfy yourself. 27. How can I possibly have to wait three days if I go to look immediately? 28. If you were to go to look this instant, you would be too late all the same. 29. How is that possible if you can still see the man? 30. If I were to say that he was still there, I shouldn't be speaking the truth. 31. Haven't you been saying all this time that you were looking at him? 32. I might have been looking at him when I said so, but it doesn't follow that you could overtake him now. 33. You mean that he is gone, don't you. 34. If I do, can you contradict me? 35. It doesn't matter whether I can or not; when you saw him moving you might have told me. 36. If you had come upstairs, you might have seen him yourself. 37. You would not let me come up then; will you let me now? 38. You can either come up, or go after the man, as you please. 39. What would be the good of my going after him; I might be chasing him all the morning without finding him. 40. There, there; don't be angry. 41. I am not angry, but I don't believe what you say. 42. Now, don't go on in that way; supposing that I was trying to take you in when I spoke before, I am speaking the truth now. 43. You have been taking me in all this time. 44. And supposing I have, what harm? 45. Well, in one word, do you think I could catch him up now? 46. You could easily have caught him up had you gone when I first told you to go. 47. If I had gone then, its not so certain that I should have taken the same road as he. 48. Well, don't go at all, if you're so full of objections. 49. Am I to go? 50. No; you couldn't find the man, for you don't know him. I shall go home. 51. Well, before you go, now I'm up here, shew me what

114. 12. Construe,—At the time I first spoke, seeing was seeing; now still is it the fact that there is seeing. 14. long before; note *chiu* isolating and emphasising *tsao*. 22. by the time you return; *tao pu liao*, [time] will not have reached your return; I then shall have for certain concluded my business. 24. To prevent any confusion, the reader should understand that the person seen by the speaker sitting upstairs, has moved from where he was when the conversation began, but is still in sight:— shall have been laughing; *chih-pu-chi*, see Part VI, XXXIV, 3; construe·— I await your *k'an-ming*, seeing clearly, completely; at the least I, before [you do], have three days laughter not ended, = shall have been laughing and shall still be laughing. 26. satisfy yourself; *wên ming*, enquire so as to ascertain; *ming* as in *ch'a ming*, *k'an ming*, completing the act implied. 30. *chiao*; compare Part VI, II, 4; q. d. Were any cause to make me say he is still at that place, &c. 31. looking at him; construe: All this time have you not been holding *chêng-shih-k'an-cho-ti* language, the language of one who was actually beholding. 32. I might have; *tang shih*, at the time, *chêng k'an cho*, [though I were]. actually behold — ing, *wei pi*, it does not follow that now [you] are still able to overtake [him]. 38. as you please; *lit.* You follow your liking to come up, your liking to look for the man, both are correct. 42. supposing; *ta-liang-cho*, calculating, estimating; a northern idiom. 48. full of objections; *chiao ch'ing*, of a self-willed nature that takes a line of its own.

PART VIII. ON THE PARTS OF SPEECH. Yen-Yü Li Lüo. IX.

direction he took. **52.** It doesn't signify whether I shew you or not; he can't be back again for the next three days. **53.** Where will he be for the next three days? **54.** He is gone to superintend something they are doing at the family cemetery. **55.** You said you didn't know the man; how do you know that he is repairing his cemetery? **56.** I did not recognise him at first, but I saw afterwards that it was Wang Li. **57.** What was Wang Li doing here beating any one? **58.** I didn't say that he was beating any one. **59.** Was he beating a horse then? **60.** No, he was beating a mule. **61.** How could I have caught him up if he was on a mule. **62.** He was not riding the mule; he was leading it. **63.** You do nothing but make a fool of me; I shan't ask you any more questions. **64.** I like that; it is you who are suspicious; but don't ask any more if you don't like.

Examples of the Passive Verb. **115.** The foregoing dialogue was intended to illustrate the use of the Verb in English, but as it contains comparatively but few instances of the Passive Verb, it is proposed to make good this deficiency in the following examples.

116. The sentence, Parents bring up children, predicates of parents that they are the agents of an act. In Children are brought up by parents, children are the object of an act.

117. The words *ni ta wo*, You beat me, distinguish you as the agent; in *wo pei ni ta*, I am beaten by you, *lit.* suffer your beating, I am the object or recipient. And in Chinese there are various ways of producing the latter construction.

118. 1. *E. g.* 1. That man is certainly to be pitied. He used to be Wang *ta-jên*'s gate-keeper some time ago, and in that capacity he was falsely accused of taking presents and saying nothing about it; for which he was severely beaten and discharged. 2. As he was returning to his native place he fell in with some robbers, was carried off into the mountains, and not only stripped of everything, but so terribly injured, that he must have died, had he not been picked up by a cart that was passing that way. 3. When he got to his own village, he found that the whole country had been recently overrun by banditti, that his father had been burnt out, and everything belonging to him destroyed. 4. His wife, who had come from a well-to-do family, had been deserted by her sons when the troubles broke out, and when he applied to her friends to see what they could do for him, although they had money,

---

54. superintend; *chien*, to enquire into, assume direction of. **59.** beating a horse then; *'han,'* a strong disjunctive; q. d. as he was not beating a man, was he then beating a horse. Note the addition of *lai-cho* and *cho* in 59, 61 and 62, and their omission in 57, 58, and 60, although the inflection of our verb is nearly uniform. **64.** suspicious; you *ko-tzŭ-ko-'rh*, your own self, raise doubts.

115. deficiency; *lit.* we now *ta-suan*, contemplate, adding a few phrases, *pu tsu*, to supply a *ko-chŭ*, form illustrative of, *shou ti*, the passive, [as opposed to *hsing ti*, the active].

117. latter construction; *lit.* the *li*, sense, being that of receiving something, when this is treated of in Chinese, the *tzŭ-yen*, phrases, are not only one. The grammarian describes such constructions as *is building*, or *is being* built, as the Passive Incomplete. It will be seen in the following examples, what the Chinese Passive, except where it is rendered by *chiao*, to cause, the precise operation of which is obscure, is produced by the employment of certain verbs signifying to receive, perceive, or suffer; all of them active verbs to which that which we regard as the verb changing to the passive voice, in reality, becomes the object.

118. Literally. 1. That man certainly may [men] pity. Formerly, at Wang *ta-jên's* acting as gate-keeper, *pei*, he was the subject of, men's wrong; [they] said [he] privily took money; because of this, he suffered beating very severely; then [his master] taking him discharged [him]. 2. He returning to his village went; on the road fell foul of robbers; [they] taking him carry [him] into the mountains; not only everything did they steal away clean; also received he wounds very serious; was it not that a cart by that place passed, that there were people who taking him lifted him up, he with complete certainty must have died. 3. He returning to his own village, then knew that the locality inhabited by him recently all had been the subject of robbers' disturbance; his father's house [they] had also burned; all property whatsoever [they] had also destroyed. 4. His wife was originally a virgin in a family, the proprietors of wealth; at the time the robbers appeared, [she] *chiao*, was the subject of, her sons' abandoning [her] and running away. The man seeking found out his father-in-law's family; asked them on his behalf to calculate a little; they, although they had money,

KEY TO THE TZŬ ERH CHI. Colloquial Series.

he was told that trade had been bad, and that they had lost too much to be able assist him in any way. **5.** Now just imagine what a case it was; he began with being falsely accused; was abused and beaten; then, besides being robbed and wounded, he finds his house utterly cleaned out; and, to wind up, after being victimised to this extent, he is made fun of by his wife's relations. Was there ever such a case of misery?

X. THE ADVERB, OF TIME, PLACE, NUMBER, DEGREE, &C.

Adverbs of Time. 119. 1. Will that man be here to-day, do you think? I don't think he will; he may come to-morrow. **2.** Why didn't he come yesterday? He did come yesterday, but he was late. **3.** Why should he have been later than you? My business at the *yamên* is over sooner than his. **4.** Did he come before I went out? No, Sir; after you had gone out. **5.** You tell him to come to-morrow the moment his business at the office over. I don't think I can; I shan't see him before he is here to-morrow. **6.** How do you mean? Wouldn't you see him if you were to go to the *yamên* directly? No, I should be sure to miss him; he would certainly have left the *yamên* before I arrived. **7.** Where does he live now? In the lane that I used to live in. **8.** When do you mean you used to live there? At the time you first came to Peking, Sir. **9.** That is a long time back. Yes; it's ten years ago, isn't it? Indeed it soon will be ten years. **10.** Didn't you come to Peking the first time in the suite of Wang *ta-jên*? No; that was the third time I came. **11.** How many times have you been to Peking altogether? Five times in all; the first time I came with my father, who was then alive. **12.** When was it that your father came to Peking? In the 23rd year of Tao Kuang. **13.** And when did he go home again? After three or four months' stay. **14.** And your second visit? That was two years later; I was sent up here by my father on business. **15.** I remember the occasion very well; you didn't stay very long that time. No; I had been in Peking but a few days, when I was recalled by a pressing letter from home. **16.** Yes? It was to tell you that your father was very ill, I think? No. My younger brother had been so badly hurt that he was not expected to live. **17.** Is your brother still alive? Oh yes; he recovered after

answering said, Our trade has of late been very bad; in every thing have we suffered (*ht.* eaten) loss; it is ten thousand times (= infinitely) difficult to help you. **5.** Bethink you; in the first instance, *chiao*, he suffered, men's false accusation; endured beating, endured reviling; afterwards it was that the robbers robbed and he received wounds; in addition, utterly was there not *so yu*, that which is, = anything, in his house; he in his single person having received all this hardship, still *chien hsiao*, feels the laughter, is ridiculed, *chiao*, by, his wife's family. Resembling a person's receiving this kind of misery, heretofore has there been a case?

Note *chiao*⁴, which is not to be explained except in one of two ways: — either it is corruptly used for *chiao*, otherwise *chio*, to perceive, which however is only read *chiao*⁴ in *shui-chiao*, to sleep; or it is *to cause*, and must be governed by an impersonal agent understood. This last construction might stand in *chiao erh-tzŭ jêng hsia*, was abandoned by her sons, (*q. d.* something made her sons abandon her,) but will not explain the *chiao* in *chiao t'a nu-jên chia li chien hsiao*; for the subject of *chien*, to see, perceive, be sensible of, is at once pronounced by Chinese to be *t'a* understood. Practically, it is in general simplest to ignore the etymological claims of *chiao*, and to translate it as *by*. It is noteworthy that *shou*, to receive, originally, meant to give; *ai*, to endure, *orig.* to strike; *pei*, to suffer, be the subject of, *orig.* a coverlid, thence to cover, to affect.

119. **1.** do you think; *k'o i*, is it possible that. **3.** business over; note *san*, properly, the dispersion of a number, thence, as below in 5, applied to the individual in a number, of employés: — is over; that is, habitually; *ch'ang shih na-mo-cho*, always it is thus. **5.** don't think; I fear it is not to be done; — shan't see him; note the *ts'ai* reinforced by the final clause, I cannot see him sooner, which is in reality redundant. **9.** indeed; *yuan shih*, it is certainly the fact that indeed quickly [will be] ten years ended. **11.** how many; note the *chi tz'ŭ*, how many times, between the verb *chin-kuo*, have entered, and *ching*, the capital, its object. **12.** alive then; *hsien fu*, my late father, a phrase we seldom use; note that the speaker so designates his father throughout. **14.** sent up by; note the construction; *shih*, [it, the occasion you ask about] was — all that follows; notice the position of *yu shih* after *wo*, me, and the *lai* at the close, which shews that the speaker is speaking in the place to which he had been sent. **17.** a while; *man-man-ti*, slowly, one of the commonest

PART VIII. ON THE PARTS OF SPEECH. Yen-Yü Li Lüo. X.

a while. **18.** If my memory serves me, your father was ill at the time? Yes, he was; I heard of his illness on my way down, and he died a few days after I got home. **19.** And that was the reason why you were so long without coming to Peking again? Of course; I couldn't leave home while I was in mourning for him. I came up after my mourning was over, and it was then that I accompanied Wang *ta-jên*. **20.** Is Wang *ta-jên* still in Peking? He is away on duty at present, but he will be back in a few days. **21.** I hear that you purpose leaving Peking yourself, Sir, shortly? Yes; I shall be off presently; I shall go home as soon as my term of service here is over.

Adverbs of Place. 120 **1.** Where is that man from? From T'ung-chou. **2.** Which is farthest from Peking, T'ung-chou or Chang-chia Wan? Reckoning from the Ch'i-'hua Mên, T'ung-chou is somewhat the nearer. **3.** Have you been there? Where do you mean? **4.** I meant to T'ung-chou. I have never been to T'ung-chou; I have been once at Chang-chia Wan. **5.** How come you to have been at Chang-chia Wan and not at T'ung-chou? I was coming from T'ien-ching by water, and that was what brought me to Chang-chia Wan. **6.** Oh, then you are not a Peking man? No I am not. **7.** And what is your country, Sir? I am a Chiang Su man. **8.** And from which prefecture? My native place is Su-chou. **9.** Do you know the Sungs who live inside the east gate of Su-chou? I suspect you mean outside the east gate. **10.** I am not quite sure whether they live inside or outside; the Sung I mean used to be in the Censorate. To be sure; I have been at his house often enough. **11.** Wasn't it the year before last that he returned home? I don't remember exactly; he has been back and forward so often, one time with another. **12.** What time was it that he came to such grief on the road? Oh, that time! That was the year before last; a relative of mine was with him. **13.** He fell in with some robbers in Ta-ming Fu, didn't he? Not robbers; they were braves that had mutinied. **14.** Did he meet them, or was he pursued by them? Neither; he heard that there was trouble on the high road, so he turned off by a branch road in a southerly direction. **15.** Well then, how was it that he didn't contrive to keep out of their way? So far from keeping out of their way, he went right in amongst them. **16.** Was he in a cart or riding? In a cart; and when he got to a certain spot, he found the mutineers in his front and in his rear, so that he could neither advance nor retreat. **17.** I was told that they fired upon him too? No, they didn't fire. **18.** How came he to be so badly hurt then? Well, in this way: he and my relative were both in the same cart, my relative sitting on the left side, and the Censor Sung on the right. The braves came to rifle the cart, and, crowding in upon it from the left, threw it over on its side. The two passengers went with it, and my relative being above and the Censor below, the Censor got badly bruised. **19.** Dear me! How was it that after going so far, the braves didn't take their lives?

expressions for presently, gradually; *'hao*³ *hao*, got well **18.** ill at the time; note *lai-cho* shewing continuance in the state specified, not its commencement. **19.** so long; [this] *shih*, was, *so i*, the reason why, *hsü chiu*, very long, &c.: — in mourning; *ting yu*, specially, the mourning of an official for his parents; *ting*, solitary, *q. d.* orphan, *yu*, sorrow: mourning over; *man fu*, having completed my *fu*; the *fu* in *i-fu*, clothes, here mourning apparel.

120. **2.** the *ch'i 'hua mên*; popular name for the *ch'ao-yang mên*, the great east gate of Peking. **8.** native place; *chi*², originally, a tablet; hence, a record, specially of registration; *pên chi*, the place to which I am registered as belonging. **10.** Censorate; *yu-shih*, literally, imperial historiographer, an ancient title now given to the members of the *tu-ch'a yuan*, all-examining court, which we style the Censorate — often enough; *'hao hsieh t'ang*, the word *t'ang*⁴, otherwise *tang*⁴, here = *hsing*, to go **11.** back and forward; treat *shih-ch'ang-tê* (or *ti*) as the adverb continually, constantly, &c. **13.** braves; *hsiang yung*, village or country braves, — mutinied, *pien*, to turn, change. **14.** pursued by them; note *chiao*; did [something] cause them to overtake him — branch road, *lit* he going by a *cha tao*, forked road, slanting south went. **15.** so far from it; *fan tao*, on the reverse, he went into their presence. **18.** the Censor, Sung *tu lao-yeh*, the *tu* representing *tu-ch'a yuan*; — crowding in, *yung*³, originally, to carry in the bosom; to surround, to follow as a crowd, to hustle; from the left side crowding came — threw it over; *chi*³, to press on, to push; *chi tê* pushed it so that the result effected was that it *'hêng t'ang hsia*, crosswise lay down — badly bruised; *shuai*¹, to give a shock to, as a blow or a fall; the Censor, by reason of the *shuai*, was *shang*, hurt, severely. **19.** the braves, *pu yao*, did not insist on their lives; —

KEY to the TZŬ ERH CHI. Colloquial Series.

It was all luck that they escaped. **20.** What kind providence came to their rescue? Well, as the braves were dragging their baggage out of the cart, their servants, who were all mounted, came up from behind, and the braves, not knowing what to make of the sound of the horses' feet, were panic-struck, and fled in all directions.

Adverbs of Number. 121. **1.** How many times have you been to the Temple of Kuan Ti? I have been thrice to the door, but I have only gone in once. **2.** Why didn't you go in the second time after having been in the first? Before I got in the first time, I paid the priests' fee. **3.** And wouldn't they take their fee the second time? They wanted it, but I said that I had paid the time before because it was my first time of coming, and that this time I should not pay. **4.** But when they wouldn't let you in the second time, why should you have gone a third? Some one said that the priests and I had misunderstood each other the second time, and recommended me to try again. **5.** And what said the priests on this third occasion? Why, they were even more impracticable than the time before; they said in so many words that it was quite impossible I should come in. **6.** On what grounds? In the first place, because it was a government temple; in the second, because the superior was not at home; and thirdly, because, said they, you didn't give any thing the last time you came, Sir. **7.** But, when they took this line, didn't you say any thing about feeing them? I did, but they said that even if I were to give three times as much as I did on the first occasion, they could not undertake to let me in.

Adverbs of Degree. 122. **1.** This is very good; that is very much the reverse. **2.** He does not write well; his brother writes very well. **3.** He praises you very highly. **4.** He was highly flattered by your invitation to dinner the other day. **5.** That affair to the north of Peking incensed the emperor extremely. **6.** You were excessively angry about a thing of no importance, and then you said what was very discourteous. **7.** That man's stupidity is beyond everything; he understands nothing that's said to him. **8.** When will [the tailor] bring me that thing? It was nearly finished last night, and I think they will be sure to have quite done it by this time. **9.** That house was nearly finished last month, and now it is quite ready. **10.** I have been such a time without studying, that I have almost forgotten the T'ung Chien. The 'Han Shu I have quite forgotten. **11.** As for those two men, Chang and Li, that I met to-day, I hardly know Chang, and I don't know Li at all. **12.** Those hills used

all luck; *chiao hsing*; see Part IV, Dial. IX, 41. 20. kind providence; what *chiu hsing*, star of rescue, divine intervention: — came up from behind; *ht.* those followers of theirs, riding beasts overtaking came; the braves heard the sound of horses gallopping; knew not what it was; all in the four directions in dismay dispersed.

121. 1. Kuan Ti, a hero of the 'Han Dynasty, since deified and worshipped as the god of war. 2. priest's fee; *hsiang ch'ien*, money to buy incense. 4. wouldn't let; *pu chiao*, not to cause; often, as here, to refuse permission; also, to prohibit. — gone a third; note the *yu* before *ch'u*; why must you a third time again go. 5. more impracticable; they still more liked not to consider the question; they plainly said, [that I] *tuan*, positively, could not go in. 6. superior; *tang-chia-ti*, the manager; in a family, or a religious house, what the *chang-kuei-ti* is in a shop; *tang*¹ in the sense of filling a post. 7. undertake to; *sc.* without the superior's permission, they could not *ying-hsu*, promise me, admittance.

122. 3. praises; *tsan*⁴, to speak of, to speak well of, to note; *tsan mei*, to note the goodness of. 4. highly flattered; *ht.* he much *chio*, felt, *t'i mien*, the respectability, honor, *sc.* that your invitation conferred on him. 5. incensed extremely; *ht* the emperor's wrath *chi-liao* culminated 6. very discourteous; *t'ai shang ya hao*, extremely, or too greatly, offended against *ya*, good breeding. 8. nearly finished; *tê liao*, so used of any thing that is in hand: — think they will be sure; *liao*, in the sense of to calculate; *liao-ku*, to conjecture. Except it be used in what we call the imperative mood, *liao ku* seems always to have *cho* affixed to it. Treat it here adverbially; Probably [by] this time *chun*, for certain, it is finished. 9. quite ready; *chin*, now, emphasised by *ts'ai* following it; *ch'uan*, completely, have [the builders] finished it. 10. quite forgotten; note 'Han Shu, (thé History of the 'Han Dynasty,) emphasised by *so* which we generally render by the relative. Were a similar construction required in Chinese not colloquial, the classical relative *chê* would supply the place of *so*; but a Chinese would regard *chê* as linked with *'Han Shu*, whereas *so*, although not exactly linked with *ch'uan*, is certainly uttered as belonging to the lower part of the clause. 12. so little care; *t'ai*, too

PART VIII. ON THE PARTS OF SPEECH. **Yen-Yü Li Lüo.** X-XI.

to be covered thick with wood, but the people have taken so little care of it, that there is now hardly any. **13.** Those are all good men, and Li is the best of them. **14.** He doesn't want to have to do with any of those people, and least of all with Liu. **15.** He punished them all severely, but Wang more severely than any of them. **16.** He called on me to-day, principally for the purpose of presenting his son to me. **17.** Did not you say so yesterday? I did. **18.** Wasn't this what you said yesterday? Yes, to be sure, that was what I said. **19.** Isn't this a good plan? No. Isn't it your plan? Not at all. Well, which of these two is the better? We can have a talk about this one; the other is utterly impracticable. **20.** Have you found those two men? I found out Li's house, but he was not at home; as for Chang, there is no such person. **21.** It is blowing terribly. **22.** The stars are beautifully bright this evening. **23.** The snow is excessively deep. **24.** That tea *is* spoiled, but not all spoiled; there is some of it that it will do to use. **25.** That teacher does not teach well. **26.** He sings very well. **27.** I am a little tired.

Miscellaneous Adverbial Constructions. 123. 1. Where is the child? He's nowhere but in the house; he can't be anywhere else. **2.** I know all about the thing; when he did it, where he did it, why he did it, and how he did it. **3.** The moment he heard about the thing, he went off. **4.** He has been a long time ailing, and he is not well yet. **5.** He is quite cured of his old complaint, (or, of the complaint he used to suffer from). **6.** He has only been here a few days this time. **7.** He has been over here once in the last few days. **8.** The roof was blown clean off, just as he left the house. **9.** The morning was clear, but all of a sudden the sky clouded over. **10.** I get up every morning at day break. **11.** I couldn't bring the boxes, because it was impossible to get them packed in time. **12.** Those gentlemen started too late to get out of the city. **13.** His wages are five taels a month. **14.** He had a narrow escape of being cashiered. **15.** That servant was pretty near being discharged. **16.** I go out for a walk every day. **17.** He is always very glad to see us when we go to call on him. **18.** In his action with the outlaws he got the worst of it. **19.** He took a good deal of pains in the matter, but without any result. **20.** That place was once very thickly peopled; it is sadly bare now. **21.** It's a long way, but, at the pace I go, I shall soon be there.

XI. THE PREPOSITION.

124. 1. A man appeared above (or over) the wall. **2.** He is leaning against the wall. **3.** I saw that knot of men at the time, and Chang was not among them. **4.** The intimacy between them is of very long standing. **5.** I went to see him but he was not at home; so I left word that I would come again before sunset. **6.** They put a log across the path and I caught my foot in it and came down.

much, *pu chao-ying*, not attend to. **14.** have to do with; *sc* as employés; *yao*, in the sense of to require the services of; hence, *pu yao*, to discharge, a servant or subordinate. **15.** more severely; *p'ien*¹, leaning to a side; hence, partial, special; *p'ien chung*, special gravity or severity. **16.** principally; *chung ti*, the weighty matter; by position = weightiest. **18.** to be sure; *yüan shih*, in very truth it was. **22.** beautifully bright; are very bright [so that man] *k'o*, may properly, *hsi*, rejoice.

123. 1. nowhere but; note *tso yu*; *q d.* [seek him] to the right, [seek him] to the left; *tsung*, in sum, *pu kuo*, he is not beyond, *shih tsai chia*, being in the house. **10.** every morning; *'huang*³, properly, a hanging curtain; here used as implying uncertainty (swinging to and fro?) *q d* as a rule I get up, but sometimes I do not &c. **11.** packed in time; note *pu liao*, could not, inserted between *tai* and *lai*, the whole clause being the subject of the verb *shih*; [the cause of] my inability to bring the boxes was [that the person or persons packing them] s *shih*, in the one moment, *shou-shih*, packed, *pu chi*, not arriving, did not complete, *sc.* at the *same* moment that I departed. **12.** too late; *kan*, [though] hastening, could not get out of the city. **14.** cashiered; *'huai kuan*, *q.d.* to ruin one's official position; he *ch'a-i-tien*, wanted but little, = a little more and he would. **20.** sadly bare; *hsiao*¹, properly a plant (according to Dr. Williams, rue); applied descriptively to mournful sights or sounds; *hsiao-t'iao*, forlorn, desolate.

124. 4. intimacy; *chiao ch'ing*, reciprocation of [friendly] sentiments; the days of this state of things are *shên*, deep, many. The passage is translated in this way merely to bring in the position *between*; various other English idioms would of course be equally correct. **6.** caught my foot; *pan*, properly, to wrap round and so to embarrass; *lit.* they taking a log

KEY TO THE TZŬ ERH CHI. Colloquial Series.

7. He met with a very serious accident on his journey. 8. Isn't there a garden behind the house? 9. There is a temple on the hill, and some houses in a hollow at the back of the hill. 10. We went past the Tung 'Hua Mên. 11. Did you go into the garden? 12. We went right through it. 13. Yesterday it was very hot throughout the whole day. 14. I have heard nothing about the matter we discussed that day, since we parted. 15. The boats going up stream are tracked against the current. 16. He brought his horse out of the stable, jumped upon him, and rode off. 17. I walked round the 'Huang Ch'êng yesterday. 18. He was going away from me when first I saw him, and then he faced about and came towards where I was. 19. The man ran across the field, and by the foot-path towards the road. 20. Chang *lao yeh* is off to 'Han-k'ou. Is he going by land or by water? He goes up the River in a steamer. How long will he take? Seven days. I thought a steamer could run from Shanghai to 'Han-k'ou in four days? So she can; but this one has cargo to deliver and take in at all the ports along the line.

XII. THE CONJUNCTION.

125. 1. He came to the *ya-mên*, although it was raining so hard. 2. The winter this year is not very cold, nor yet very damp. 3. Not only the boys went to see what was going on, that day, but the girls too. 4. His idea is that people can make out what he writes whether he has written it carefully or otherwise. 5. I shall go at any rate, whether you go or not. 6. Both he and I were wounded. 7. I feel pretty sure that you'll like it when you have tried it. 8. Do it either way; either will answer. 9. Say quick, east or west; which is it to be? 10. This is not merely pleasant, but useful as well.

XIII. THE INTERJECTION.

126. 1. Sudden sensations may find utterance in expressions which differ according as the feeling expressed is one of admiration, delight, pity, dislike, astonishment, or desire.
2. For instance: — Indeed! Before you have been learning three months, to speak so correctly! 3. Ah! Is it possible that, after so many years of suffering, you should have no feeling for the suffering of others? 4. Odious man! He has not only wasted time doing nothing, but what he has done is done so badly. 5. Poor fellow! To be so near his promotion, and to be cashiered for a thing

of wood, *'hêng,* put it crosswise on the road; [it] caught me, [and by catching caused me] a fall. 7. serious accident; *hsien,* dangerous; note the curious idiom; he encountered *'hên li 'hai ti,* or *tê,* that which was so *li 'hai,* that it became, *i ko hsien,* a danger. See *li 'hai* above in many places. 9. a hollow; *tung*4. 12. right through; *tu* giving activity to *ch'uan,* to pierce through, as to many other verbs; *q. d.* by way of the interior we penetrated through. 16. jumped upon him; *p'ien,* to get on a horse; also written with the Radical on the other side; in the form here used, often meaning to cheat. 17. the 'Huang Ch'êng; the Imperial Enclosure, a wall some six miles long surrounding the emperor's palace at Peking. 18. faced about; then he turned his face and I saw him = he seemed to, come towards my part; technically, we only say face about of a person who is standing still. 19. towards the road; *pên*1, to run; here read *pên*4, towards. The latter is a use of the word not authorised by the dictionaries. 20. along the line; *yen,* properly, down the tide; used as along, a road, an edge &c.

125. 5. whether you go; *pu kuan,* I regard not, it matters not to me. 8. do it; the *ch'u* is not to be taken as *go,* but simply as auxiliary of *pan.* 10. merely pleasant; *ching,* only, *k'ung,* emptily, *hsi-'huan,* [that which people] delight in.

126. 1. sudden sensations; the subject of the whole sentence is *shên ch'i;* the two first clauses are made pendent by *chiu.* Construe thus. — language proceeding from the lips, when there is *ching-ya,* sudden emotion, in the heart, — *chiu,* in such case, [the *shên ch'i,* spirit of the expression] *shih,* will be, *ko têng shên-ch'i pu-t'ung,* different kinds of spirit. Observe that *ko têng* pluralises *shên-ch'i,* at the same time that *ko,* each, is preferentially used as it were to disjoin the several feelings specified, *q. d.* whether of admiration, or delight &c. Note admiration, *t'an*4, properly, to sigh; dislike, *tsêng*1 *wu*4, to hate; astonishment, *hsiang pu tao,* unexpected, *ching,* to be startled. 2. wasted time; *pai* vainly, *tan-wu,* to delay and mismanage; not only this, but there have *nao,* presented themselves, several faults. 5. so near; note the

PART VIII. ON THE PARTS OF SPEECH. **Yen-Yü Li Lüo.** XI-XIV.

of so little importance. **6.** Ah! Your foreign contrivances are really most ingenious. **7.** Wang *lao-yeh* greatly admired those verses you wrote the other day. He kept on exclaiming, Beautiful! **8.** Astonishing! That a man should prefer a bad thing when he might have a good thing! It's utterly unreasonable. **9.** May Chang *lao-yeh* soon be well of his wound, and he will come to our rescue. I hear that he is well again. Indeed? That's good. And what is more, they say that he may be here the day after to-morrow. The day after to-morrow? May it be so!

force of *tou*; also that *t'a* is the subject of *shêng*; that of *ko*, to cashier, literally to strip, is emperor, or government, understood. **6.** contrivances; *chi*, a spring, *chi ch'i*, things moving by springs:— ingenious; *ch'iao*, cunning, *miao*, abstruse, minute, fine. **7.** greatly admired; *tsan miao* praised as fine. — kept on exclaiming; *hen 'hu*¹, repeatedly cried out. **8.** prefer; *lit.* he *fang-cho*, putting down q. d. not touching, the good thing, *pu yao*, rejects or declines it, *p'ien yao*, preferentially demands, the bad thing; is there such a principle, such reasoning, as this? **9.** That's good; *'hao chi*, the height of good: — may it be so; *pa pu tê*, one can't lay hold of it, it is too good to be true.

SUPPLEMENT. (XIV)

127. 1. Come here! **2.** *cha* (or *dja*). **3.** Bring some water. **4.** Do you want cold water or hot water, Sir. **5.** I want some cold water for my bath and some warm water to wash my face. **6.** There is warm water in the basin; but I'm afraid that it's of no use putting water in the bath, for it leaks. **7.** Be quick and get it mended. Have you brushed my clothes yet? **8.** Oh yes; the clothes have been brushed some time; the boots as well. **9.** Where on earth have you put the towel and the soap? **10.** The soap is on the shelf of the washhand-stand; the towel is hanging on the horse.
128. 1. Your baggage is come, Sir. **2.** Oh, very good. Have you counted the boxes? **3.** I have. There are twenty-four packages altogether. **4.** How can there be such number? I think some of them must belong to some one else. **5.** Do you remember how many packages you had, Sir? **6.** There are three portmanteaus, one wooden box, my bedding, and two small parcels; seven things in all.

127. 1. *lai*, come. **2.** *cha* or *dja*, a sound uttered to shew that a servant hears himself called. **3.** *na*, to take hold of: *shui*, water: *na-lai* to bring; but the object must be between the two verbs; you cannot say *na-lai shui*, for Bring water, though you may say *shui na-lai*, for I have brought the water, or the water is here. **4.** *lao-yeh*, Sir, a gentleman: *yao*, to want: *ti*, here, that which, = that which [you] want, Sir, *shih*, is [it] *lang shui*, cold water, [or] *shih*, is it, *k'ai shui*, boiling water; *k'ai*, literally to open. **5.** *hsi-tsao*, to bathe: *wên shui*, warm water: *hsi*, to wash. *lien*, the face. **6.** *p'ên*, a basin or tub: *li*, a place; within: *lien-p'ên li*, in the basin. *yu*, to be, or have; here, there is: *na*, the, that: *tsao-p'ên*, bathing tub: *lou*, to leak: *shih lou-ti*, is leaking: *p'a*, to fear, to doubt. *pu*, not. *nêng*, to be able: *tao*, to upset; hence, of water, to pour. — I fear that water cannot [to any purpose] be poured into the bath. **7.** *k'uai*, quick: *chiao*, to call, command, cause: *jên*, a man: *shou-shih*, to mend, *sc.* the bath. *pa*, to cease, cause to cease; here, a particle = that's all about it: *wo*, I; here, by position, of me: *i-shang*, clothes *wo na i-shang*, those clothes of mine, my clothes: *ni*, thou: *ch'ou-ta*, to dust; *ch'ou*, properly to draw, *ta*, to beat: *liao*, to finish, here marking past time; *ch'ou ta liao*, have dusted: *mo* or *mu*, not; *mo-yu*, have not; affirmatively, or, as here, interrogatively. **8.** *tsao*, early *i*, to stop, finished: *tsao-i*, some time since: *hsueh*, boots· *tzŭ*, a son; here, as very commonly with other nouns, appended to *hsueh*. *yeh*, also: *shua*, to brush. **9.** *tsêng-mo*, pronounced *tsêmmo*, how? what? — *ni*, a particle sometimes affirmative, sometimes, as here, interrogative: *shou*, hand, arm. *chin*, towel, napkin: *shou-chin*, towel· *i-tzŭ*, soap· *'han*, still; here disjunctive, = *but* where is the soap put. *ko*, to put: *tsai*, at or in *na li*, what place, where. **10.** *t'i*, a lower shelf or ledge: *pan*, a plank, board: *erh*, a son, appended like *tzŭ* to many nouns; when it follows *n* or *ng*, the full sound of these consonants is supressed; *pan-erh*, becomes *paⁿ-rh*, the *a* being slightly nasalised: *t'i-paⁿ-rh*, here, the lower shelf of the washhand-stand: *shang*, above; when following a noun as here, upon; the soap is on the shelf. *chia-tzŭ*, a frame or stand: *kua*, to hang: *cho*, a word of several uses, here auxiliary of *kua*, = *in the act of* hanging
128. 1. *ti*, here a possessive affix; *lao-yeh-ti*, the gentleman—'s = your; *hsing-li*, travelling baggage. **2.** *a*, an exclamation: *'hên*, very: *'hao*, good. *hsiang*, box, chest: *shu*, to count: *kuo*, to pass; here an auxiliary; *shu-kuo-liao*, have [you] counted. **3.** *ta*, large, great: *hsiao*, small: *t'ung*, to penetrate; hence, thorough; *ta*, together with, including all; *t'ung-kung*, the whole number. *erh*, two: *shih*, ten: *ssŭ*, four: *chien*, articles, items of a number of things, here rendered packages, because the things spoken of are baggage. **4.** *hsieh*, a few, a plurality: *na-li*, whence = how. *na-mo*, thus, that; how are there so many? *tou*, all; *p'a*, I fear, *pu-shih*, it is not [the case that] all are mine. **5.** *chi*, how many: *chih*, individual items of certain classes of things; here, of boxes: *chi*, to remember: *tê*, to obtain, attain to, succeed in; a most important auxiliary verb. Construe; — gentleman's (= your) boxes *to shao*, many few (= how many) pieces, succeed in remembering, not succeed &c.? **6.** *p'i*, skin, leather, fur; *p'i-hsiang*, leather portmanteau *yi* or *i*, one· *mu*, wood: *'han*, here, also: *p'u*, to spread; *kai*, to cover; *p'u-kai*, bedding. *ling*, isolated, fragmentary; *sui*, broken; *ling-sui*, odds and ends of: *pao*, to make into a bundle; a bundle or parcel: *chien*, an item of several classes of things *tsung*, to comprehend, comprehensive; *tsung-kung*, altogether: *ch'i*, seven: *yang*, kind, sorts, *yang-erh*, read *yang-'rh*. Construe; — There are fragmentary parcels

KEY TO THE TZŬ ERH CHI. Colloquial Series.

7. Will you step out and see which are your things, Sir. 8. Very good. How much have I to pay for the carts? 9. The fare from T'ien-ching is always five dollars for large carts, and three dollars for small carts. 10. They can wait a bit; I'll pay them as soon as I have squared my account with the other gentlemen.

129. 1. Where can I buy the things I want for my room? 2. Do you wan't more than you have got in your room, Sir? 3. These things are not mine; they are only lent me. 4. I can get chairs and tables for you from the shop, Sir. 5. And I want a book-case to put my books in. 6. There are no bookcases ready made. You must get the carpenter to make one. Do you want a washhand-stand and bed as well, Sir? 7. You must buy me a washhand-stand; I have brought a bed-stead with me. 8. Where is the bed put, Sir? 9. In the long wooden box; it's an iron bed-stead. 10. I'll go and get a carpenter to open it. 11. And there are some clothes of mine that must be washed. 12. I have told the washerman, and he'll be here presently.

130. 1. Do you burn oil or candle, Sir? 2. I have brought a lamp with me, and some packets of candles as well. 3. Which will you burn to-day, Sir? 4. It's so late you can light a candle for to-night;

two items; in all, seven sorts. 7. *ch'ing*, to request; pray! please! *ch'u*, to go out; *ch'ü*, to go; *ch'u-ch'ü*, to go out: *k'an*, to see; *k'an-k'an*, to take a look: *na-ko*, which; differently accented from *na-ko*, that: see which are *lao-yeh-ti*, yours, Sir. 8. *chiu*, a word of various uses; here = then, in that case: *shih*, here, to be right: *hao*, pronounced almost *la* or *lo*, is here an expletive; *chiu shih la*; in that case it is right: *ch'ê*, a cart: *ch'ien*, here, money; *na ch'ê chien ni*, that cart-money, eh? = how about the fare? 9. *hsiang*, towards, in the direction of; *hsiang-lai*, hitherto: *t'ien*, heaven; *ching*, a ford; *T'ien-ching*, the department and city we call Tien-tsin; *wu*, five: *k'uai*, a piece of anything; following a number and before *ch'ien*, as here, a popular expression for dollars. Construe:— Hitherto [from] Tien-tsin the large carts that come, all are five dollars. *san*, three. 10. *têng*, here, to wait *'hu*, to meet; here, a short time; with *êrh* pronounced *'hu-rh*: *t'ung*, with, *na hsieh*, those, q. d. those gentlemen we know of, the other gentlemen: *suan*, to reckon; *ch'ing*, clean; *suan-ch'ing*, to close accounts; also, to complete arrangements, engagements: *kei*, to give: *t'a*, he, they. Construe: Wait a while; [when] I with the gentlemen have reckoned clean, [I will] give them [their money].

129. 1. *u* or *wu*, a room: *chia-'huo*, utensils in general; here, furniture: *na-'rh*, interrogatively, where: *mai*, to buy. Construe:—The furniture that [I want] in my room, to what place shall [I, or, the buyers] go to buy? 2. *chê*, this, the; *chê-hsieh*, these: *kou*, enough; *yung*, to use; *kou-yung*, sufficient: *ti*, here, ones. Construe:— In your room Sir these = Are these that are in your room, still not sufficient ones, eh? 3. *ko*, an item of various classes of things; *chê-ko*, this one, these ones: *chieh*, to lend or to borrow: *tou shih chieh ti*, they are all lent ones, or borrowed ones. 4. *chiu shih*, then is it = in that case: *cho*, table: *i*, chair· *k'o-i*, here, can: *kei*, here, for: *p'u-tzŭ*, a shop; *p'u* is written as in *p'u-kai*, but differently accented. Observe *ch'u*, to go, at the end of the sentence. Construe:—In that case those tables and chairs — such things as tables and chairs, I can for *lao yeh*, = you, in the shop buy go, = buy them at a shop, get them from a shop. 5. *shu*, book; *shu-chia-tzŭ*, book-stand: *chuang*, to put into, to contain. 6. *mei*, used corruptly for *mo yu*, not to be, there is not: *hsien*, at the present time; *ch'êng*, to complete, completed; *hsien-ch'êng-ti*, ready made ones: *tei*, corruptly used for *tê-yao*, must require: *chiang*, an artisan of any kind; *mu-chiang*, wood workman, carpenter: *tso*, to make, to do: *ch'uang*, bed-stead: *yao pu yao*, want not want, = do you want? 7. *tai*, a sash, hence to lead; *tai-lai*, to bring with one; [as to the] bed-stead, there is one that I have brought. 9. *t'ieh*, iron; *t'ieh-ti*, of iron, an iron one. *ch'ang*, long; in the long wooden box, *chuang-cho*, contained; the *cho*-indicating participially that the thing spoken of is in such a state, = contain— ed in, pack — ed in. 10. *chao*, to seek; *pa*, to lay the hand on; *t'a*, it; (see page 116, *ex*. 84, where it is erroneously stated that *t'a* cannot be used of inanimate things;) *ta-k'ai*, to strike open, to open. In English we merge *pa* in the object; *pa t'a ta-k'ai* means simply, to open it. 11. *'han*, here, moreover, also; *'han ya*, also is it the fact that, my clothes being *tsang*, dirty, *tei hsi*, [some one] must wash. 12. *ching*, to pass through; *i-ching*, before verbs, marks past time: *kao*, to announce, declare; *su*, to tell, to complain; *kao-su*, to tell to. Were the object not expressed but understood, the phrase would run *wo i-ching kao-su-liao*, I have told [the person in question]; here, the object *hsi-i-shang-ti*, the-washing-clothes-one, = washerman, being expressed, observe that it comes between *kao-su* and *liao*: *k'uai*, quick; *k'o-i k'uai lai*, he can, it is possible for him, quickly to come.

130. 1. *tien*, a point; here to light: *yu*, oil: *têng*, lamp: *la*, wax. 2. *chan*, used with lamps &c., as the item of a number; *yi chan yu têng*, one oil lamp. Construe: [As to] that which I have brought, there is an oil lamp; also are there some packets of wax. 4. *chin*, present time; *chin erh*, pronounced *chirh*, to-day: *'hei*, black, dark; *k'uai 'hei*, it will soon be dark: *ming*, bright; with day, the morrow; with year, next year; *ming-erh*, pronounced *min-rh*, to-morrow: *tsai*, then,

PART VIII. ON THE PARTS OF SPEECH. Yen-Yü Li Lüo. XIV.

buy some oil to-morrow. 5. The cold weather is coming on, Sir; don't you mean to put down a carpet? 6. Yes I must have a carpet down. How about coal and charcoal? 7. The charcoal is the cook's affair; the gentlemen get their coal in together. 8. That back window lets in the wind terribly. Is there no way of stopping it? 9. The windows here are all papered up in the winter. 10. Then paste up the back window to-morrow; I won't have the front windows pasted.

131. 1. Your teacher is here, Sir. 2. Ask him to come in. Bring tea. *(To teacher)* Good morning, Sir. Take a seat. 3. *(Teacher)* Be seated pray. 4. There are some things in those phrases I was reading yesterday that I don't understand. 5. Where is your difficulty, Sir? 6. I can't find this word. 7. That is an unauthorised word. It's not in the dictionary. 8. And this one then? 9. That is *luan?* 10. And what is its Radical? 11. Its Radical is *yi* (the 5th Radical); under what Radical did you look for it? 12. I looked for it under *chao* (the 87th Radical). 13. That was a mistake. Do you know what the meaning of *luan* is? 14. I think I have met the word once before, but I'm not sure. Will you be so good as to tell me what word it is usually coupled with, Sir? 15. It forms part of a number of expressions. There is *tsa-luan, fan-luan, 'huang-luan, 'hun-luan, jao-luan, chih luan.* 16. Stop a moment! What do all these mean? 17. The proper meaning of *luan* is, in

in the second place; here emphasising the time; *mi ⁿ-rh,* to-morrow, *tsai,* then, buy oil. 5. *ju,* as; *ju-chin,* now; *t'ien,* here the weather: *lêng,* cold: *tɩ,* ground; *hsia,* below, down; *tɩ-hsia,* on the ground; *u-li tɩ-hsia,* on the floor of the room: *chan,* felt; *chan-tzŭ,* a carpet. 6. Observe the construction: a carpet is that which must be *p'u,* spread; *q. d.* a carpet, yes, one must be spread: *shao,* to burn; *'huo,* fire; *shao 'huo,* to make a fire, or keep up a fire: *mei,* coal; *t'an,* charcoal; *mei-t'an,* fuel of this kind in general. 7. *ch'u,* to cook; *ch'u-tzŭ,* a cook: *kuan,* to attend to, take charge of: *mên,* a plural particle; *lao-yeh,* gentleman, *lao-yeh-mên,* gentlemen: *'ho,* to unite; *'hu,* a comrade; *ho ho 'rh,* to combine as comrades, associate together for a purpose; the gentlemen associated buy coal. 8. *'hou,* behind; *t'ou,* head, end; *'hou t'ou,* the back of, behind: *ch'uang,* a window; *'hu,* a door; *ch'uang-'hu,* a window: *t'ou,* to penetrate thoroughly: *fêng,* wind. *h,* sharp; *'hai,* hurtful; *li-'hai,* a strong intensive; *q. d.* [through] that window at the back the penetrating wind *tê,* achieves, *li-'hai,* severity, excess: *tang,* to bar the way; *chu,* to reside, to stay; added to many verbs to complete their sense, as here; *tang-chu,* to stop effectually: *fa,* law, method; *fa-tzŭ,* means; is there no good means of completely stopping [the wind]? 9. *tz'ŭ,* this; *tzŭ p,* in this place: *tung,* winter: *na,* to lay hold of: *chih,* paper: *'hu,* to paste paper on; the *shang* merely completes the action of the verb. Observe *na chih,* taking paper, before the active verb *'hu-shang,* is construed like *pa t'a* in 129, 10, and *pa na 'hou-t'ou-tɩ* in the following example. 10. *chê-mo-cho:* thus: *ch'ien,* before in time or place; *ch'ien-t'ou-tɩ,* the front ones: *yung,* to use, utility; *pu yung,* it is useless, you need not.

131. 1. *hsien,* before, in time; *shêng,* to be born; *hsien-shêng,* elder-born, the designation by which teachers are addressed or spoken of. 2. *ch'ɩng,* here, invite him, = ask him to come in: *ch'a,* tea: *tso,* to sit. 3. The teacher repeats the same form of courtesy. 4. *'hua,* oral language; *t'iao,* a slip of anything; here, parts of columns of Chinese characters; *'hua-t'iao-tzŭ,* detached sentences, specially such as are given as examples of the spoken language: *ch'u,* a place; *yu ch'u,* there are some passages: *tung,* to understand; *pu-tung-tê,* [I] can't understand, not to be understood. 5. *nan,* difficulty; *nan ch'u,* difficult place, difficulty: *nɩn na,* you Sir; a polite expression: *shuo,* to speak; *shuo i shuo,* say a say; tell me. 6. *tzŭ* the written form of a word; what we commonly call the Chinese character; this character I *chao pu-chao,* seeking do not get hold of, cannot find; *chao-tê-chao* would be, have succeeded in finding. 7. *su,* common, vulgar; with *tzŭ* it simply means that the word is not classical: *tien,* law, rule; *tzŭ-tien,* dictionary, *q. d.* word-code. 8. [That being so,] then this one? 9. *luan,* disturbed, disordered. 10. *kuei,* to return to, revert to; *pu,* a class; *shou,* head; *pu-shou,* class-head, the term by which the 214 characters called by us the Radicals are distinguished, being those under which as keys or indices all the other characters in the language are ranged. Observe *han shih,* still is it, here, disjunctive = Well, but it *kuei,* reverts to, which class-head? 11. *pên,* here, properly, really: *yi,* a symbolical character, 5th of the Radicals. Construe:—The class-head properly is *yɩ;* that which you have been seeking, Sir, is what class-head?. 12. *chao,* claws, the 87th Radical. 13. *ts'o,* to err; error: *i,* thought, wish; *ssŭ,* to think; *i-ssŭ,* of persons, intention; of words, acts, signification. *pai* or *po,* white; *mɩng-pai,* to be clear, to see clear. 14. *fang-fu,* to resemble, to seem; I, it seems, remember; *chien,* to see; *chien-kuo,* to have seen: *tz'ŭ,* a turn or time: *yeh,* also: *tɩng,* to fix; fixed; here, certain; also not certain = but I am not sure: *ch'ang,* constant, ordinary: *shuo,* to speak; *hen,* to join to or with. Construe:— *ch'ang-shuo* commonly speaking *tɩ,* ones = persons, joining it to what word speak. 15. *yen,* the eye; *tzŭ-yen,* a phrase, of two or more words: *to,* several, many. See below. 16. *ai,* an exclamation; *man,* slow; *man-man-tɩ,* gently. Observe *tzŭ-yen 'rh,* pluralised by *hsieh* and *tou.*

KEY TO THE TZŬ ERH CHI. Colloquial Series.

confusion, not in regular order. Things are *tsa-luan* if they are tumbled in confusion. You say of affairs too that they are *tsa-luan wu chang*, without system or order. A serious outbreak of brigands (or outlaws) is *fan luan*. When the crops have failed, and the people are driven to robbery for lack of food and clothing, that is *'huang-luan* (bread riots, famine disturbances). A family is *'hun-luan* when it is without *kuei-chü*, discipline, or order. "There is *'hun-luan* in the world," is said when disorder prevails throughout the whole empire. A place is said to be *jao-luan*, disturbed, by brigands, when vagabonds of that description harry any locality with fire and sword. The phrase *chih luan wu ch'ang*, means that the empire may be at one moment perfectly tranquil and at another in great disorder. **18.** Thank you. And now which is the commonest of all these phrases? **19.** The commonest I should say is *tsa luan*. It may applied to any kind of thing. **20.** Very good; then henceforward when I see *luan* I shall remember that it is the *luan* in *tsa-luan*.

17. *chêng*, to complete, be completed; *ch'i*, regular, in even order; *chêng-ch'i*, regular, orderly.
tung, east; *hsi*, west; *tung-hsi*, any material thing:
pu, to arrange; *chih*, to place; *pu-chih*, to arrange in proper order:
tsa, miscellaneous, higgledy-piggledy; *tsa-luan* is said of things that are not *pu-chih*.
pan, to manage, administer; *shih*, affairs:
wu, not to be, not to possess; *chang*, a rule, settled form:
chih, here of the same force as *ti*.
tsei, robbers, any persons in arms against government; *fei*, law-breakers, outlaws; *tsei-fei*, brigands, bad characters:
nao, to break out, said of anything happening which ought not to happen:
fan, to turn front to rear, upside down &c.; *fan-luan*, subversion of order:
nien, the year; *sui*, the year, specially of one's age; *nien-sui*, the year, specially with reference to its harvest; as we say good or bad years:
shou, to ingather; *shou-ch'êng*, that which is ingathered, the harvest:
pai, one hundred; *hsing*, a tribe, the surname of a tribe; *pai-hsing* or *po-hsing*, the Chinese; any *plebs* as distinguished from their officials:
ch'ih, to eat; *ch'uan*, to pierce through; to put on clothes; *ch'ih-ch'uan*, food and raiment:
ko, each, every:

ch'iang, to rob; *to*, to steal; *ch'iang-to*, to rob; robbery in general. Construe: — The year has no harvest; the people have not food and clothing; in every place [they] commit robbery; that is *'huang-luan*. The word *'huang* means desert, uncultivated:
kuei, compasses; *chu*, rule; *kuei-chu*, proper rule of conduct. *'hun*, turbid, confused:
shih, the world, a generation; *chieh*, bounds; *shih-chieh*, the world:
p'u, universal; *p'u-t'ien-hsia*, all under heaven, = the whole empire
chi, the highest ridge; extreme in degree
jao, to molest, disturb, as brigands a population.
lei, a class kind; *tsei-lei*, brigand-kind = brigands.
mou, any, certain; *mou ch'u*, a certain place, *sha*, kill. Construe — *jao-luan*, means that *na*, those, = such or such, brigands laying hand on any locality's people, if it be not that they slay, then it is that they burn.
chih, to keep in order; *chih luan*, order and disorder in a state. *chu*, a phrase or sentence.
shih, time, a time; *yu shih*, there are times, = sometimes.
t'ai, very much, too much; *p'ing*, smooth; undisturbed; *t'ai p'ing*, universal tranquillity.
ta luan, great disorder, universal disorder.
nêng, to be able; ability.
i-ssŭ, as before, meaning, signification. Construe: — The phrase *chih luan wu ch'ang* is of the empire-sometimes-all-tranquil-sometimes-greatly-disturbed-all (= both)-can-not (= neither-can-be)-fixed-for-certain — 's meaning.

18. *ling*, here to receive; *chiao*, to teach; *ling chiao*, I have received instruction; a common form of Thank you for the information you have given me *li-t'ou*, inner side, inside; *tsui*, very, most; *tsui ch'ang yung ti*, the one [men] most commonly use. **19.** *sui*, to follow, hence, to accord with; *sui ch'ang*, constantly; here, by position = most constantly; the one [men] most commonly use, *p'a*, I fear, = I imagine, is &c.; *pa*, to stop; here, an expletive. **20.** *ti*, bottom; *ti-hsia*, down below; when applied, as here, to time, henceforward.

END OF KEY TO PART VIII.

CORRECTIONS AND ADDITIONS IN THE *COLLOQUIAL SERIES* OF THE TZŬ ERH CHI,

AND IN THE APPENDICES, KEY, SYLLABARY, AND WRITING EXERCISES, ACCOMPANYING IT.

I.—ERRORS IN THE TEXT OF THE TZŬ ERH CHI.

PART I.

Page 7,   Line 21,   for tolerable   read a tolerable.

PART II.

" 14,   Line 3,   for 73rd, the moon,   read 74th, the moon.
" 15,   "   3,   "   27 h'an   " 27 'han.
" 18, observe Radical 95, yuan, formerly read *hsuan*; its sound having been changed because it formed part of an emperor's name.
" 18, Radical 118,   for chü   read chu.
" 21,   "   192,   " luxurious   " luxuriant.
" 30, Line 5,   " milet   " millet.
" 30,   "   16,   " hsiang-niu p'i   " hsiang niu p'i.

PART III.

Page 40,   for 凉 read 涼
" 42,   " 凉 " 涼
" 46,   " 貫 " 貴
" 52, Col. 6, " 槍 " 鎗
" 53, " 2, " 肱 " 胡
" 54, " 2, " 嚷 " 嚷
" 55, " 2, " 寗 " 寧
" 60, " 2, " 斟 " 斟
" 60, " 2, " 石 " 石
" 62, " 5, " 夫 " 失

Page 65, Col. 6, 12, for 畫 read 畫
" 68, " 2, " 慌 " 慌
" 68, " 2, " 諕 " 諕

N.B.—The following words, being new, should have been explained in the Single Words of Exercises 34 and 36.

Page 65, ex. 18 離 li^2, to separate from.
" 65, " 19 戚 $ch'i^4$, properly, mournful, combined with *ch'in*, related to, relations.
" 67, " 19 櫃 $kuei^4$, a standing press.

PART IV.

Is without Errors except in the Punctuation.

133

TZŬ ERH CHI. Colloquial Series.

PART V.

Page	118,	ex.	2,	for 俏 read 修	Page	124,	ex.	14, for 嗚 read 嗚
,,	121,	,,	40,	,, 氷 ,, 冰	,,	125,	,,	13, ,, 愰 ,, 愰
,,	123,	,,	26,	,, 怺 ,, 怺	,,	127,	,,	9, 11, ,, 緯 ,, 緯
,,	124,	,,	11,	,, 畫 ,, 畫	,,	128,	,,	23, ,, 怺 ,, 怺
					,,	171		

PART VI.

Page	137,	Col.	1,	for 涼 read 涼*	Page	194,	Col.	7, for 鎗 ,, 槍
,,	167,	,,	6,	,, 窗 ,, 寧	,,	208,	,,	7, ,, 鎗 ,, 槍
,,	178,	,,	7,	,, 得 ,, 得				

PART VII.

Page	219,	Sound	50,	for 畫 read 畫	Page	219,	Sound	353, for 肚 read 姤
,,	222,	Col.	50,	,, 圕週 ,, 週圕	,,	223,	Col.	75, line 6, ,, 夏 ,, 春
,,	229,	,,	185,	,, 累雷 ,, 勒雷	,,	232,	,,	238, ,, 10 ,, 孳字 ,, 孼本
,,	230,	,,	203,	,, 論䏻 ,, 論䐉	,,	240,		,, 本漂 ,, 字標
,,	230,	,,	211,	,, 夬 ,, 央	,,	234,	,,	274, ,, 詩 ,, 書
,,	241,	,,	407,	,, ○ ,, 黑	,,	236,	,,	314, ,, 6, ,,
,,	224,	,,	97,	,, 黑 ,, ○				

PART VIII.

Page 207, Col. 2, Sentence 84, should begin at 棍

II.—APPENDICES.

Page	3,	Column	5,	for 訢 read 訢	Page	12,	Les.	13, for 枚 read 枚
,,	5,		17,	,, 建 ,, 健	,,	13,	,,	33, ,, 裏 ,, 裏
,,	11,	Sec.	15,	,, 束 ,, 束	,,	13,	,,	57, ,, 裏 ,, 裏
,,	12,	Les.	2,	,, 傳 ,, 傳	,,	14,	,,	71, ,, 奔 ,, 奔

* Note that 涼 and 涼 are both read *liang*². The two characters are the same in sound, tone, and meaning; but *liang* is 涼 in 涼熱, *liang-jo*, cool and hot, and 涼 in 涼薄, *liang-po*, literally, cool and thin, a figure for lukewarmness in the cause of virtue, partial depravity.

CORRECTIONS AND ADDITIONS.

III.—ERRORS IN THE TEXT AND NOTES OF THE KEY.

PART III.

Page	30,		for	惜	read 撒
,,	38,		,,	脖	,, 脖
,,	41,		,,	s.c.	,, sc.
,,	69, Single Words	11,	,,	when even	,, still, even.
,,	71, Words Combined	17,	,,	expressien	,, expression.
,,	73, Single Words	12,	,,	yŭan	,, yùan,
,,	81, Words Combined	19,	,,	pen	,, pên.
,,	93, Exerc. XIX		,,	Ex. 10 Obs. 2	,, Ex. 9. Obs.

PART IV.

Page	121, 10, note		for	tzu	read tzŭ.
,,	128, 35, ,,		,,	Fu-shing	,, Fu-hsing.
,,	135, ex. 19, (at the end)	supply		It's an excellent idea.	
,,	139, 74, note		for	enterrupted	,, interrupted.
,,	140, ex. 77,		,,	Book of Odes	,, Chung Yung ; (see Preface page i.)

PART V.

Page 141, 22, note, compare with page 148, 26; the latter is correct.

,,	160, 16, ,,	for	wives', babble,	read wives ; babble,
,,	162, 10, ,,	,,	divinity ; he	,, divinity who.
,,	163, 35, ,,	,,	tu⁴	,, t'u⁴.
,,	167, 8, ,,	,,	Sec. XII	,, Les. XII.
,,	173, 6, ,,	,,	begining	,, beginning.
,,	171				

PART VI.

Page	1, Les. ii	Para. 2 line 4,	for	thing, I do	read thing I do.
,,	3, ,, v	note 5,	,,	hsuing	,, hsiung.
,,	3, ,, ,,	,, 10,	,,	shi	,, shih.
,,	6, ,, x	,, 4,	,,	come	,, comes.
,,	8, ,, xiii	,, 8,	,,	k'o-t'ui	,, ko-t'ui.
,,	9, ,, xv	line 5,	,,	well	,, will.
,,	13, ,, xxi	note 3,	,,	c'hi	,, ch'i.
,,	16, ,, xxvii	,, 4,	,,	手歇	,, 歇手
,,	17, ,, xxix	,, 3,	,,	fen	,, fên.
,,	18, ,, xxx	,, 10,	,,	chian	,, chiang.
,,	25, ,, xliii	,, 6,	,,	s.c.	,, sc.
,,	37, ,, lxvi	,, 6,	,,	system,	,, system ;
,,	40, ,, lxxii	,, 2,	,,	pick	,, prick.
,,	43, ,, lxxvi Para. 9,		,,	intercouse	,, intercourse.
,,	45, ,, lxxx	note 3,	,,	掬	,, 解

TZŬ ERH CHI. Colloquial Series.

PART VII.

Page 63,   for 正邪 *chêng⁴ hsieh²*, read 邪正 *hsieh chêng*.
" 67, Les. 71,   " *hu*   " *'hu*.
" 69, " 94,   " 凉   " 涼
" 75, " 149,   " *k'ang³*,   " *k'ang⁴*. This example stood originally *k'ang³ k'ai*, (see *k'ai*,) but was changed on account of the inflection of the Tone noticed in the translation of those words. There is no other instance of *k'ang³* in the colloquial.
" 75, " 151,   " os coxendicis   read os coccygis.
" 76, " 161,   " euclitic   " enclitic.
" 79, " 200,   " *lu*, an ass   " *lu*, statutes.
" 84, " 259,   " EXERC.   " EXERC. XVI, 12.
" 88, " 297, *after* rope *add* See *lê*.
" 93, " 353,   *for* 肚   " 妒
" 100, " 420,   " nearly *yung⁴*,   " nearly *yung²*.

PART VIII.

Page 101, line 6,   *for* renderd *read* rendered.
" 103, *ex.* 15, *note*, " *k'ou-chi* " *k'ou-ch'i*.
" 107, line 22,   *after* Numeratives *supply* 2. It is correct, for instance to speak of an affair as *i chuang shih-ch'ing*, of a number of utensils, &c., as *chi yang chia-'huo*, or of despatches as *chi t'ao wên shu*.
" 109,   *after* ling *supply* 輛 *liang⁴*, Numerative of carts, carriages, having two wheels.
" 112, "   *under* IV, NUMBER, notice that with the exception of *têng*, the Collectives by which plurality is as often shewn as in any other way, have been by mistake omitted. Mr. Edkins's Grammar, 2nd Edition, page 139, gives a good list of Collectives, some of which, however, I have treated as Numeratives.
" 112,   *note, for* feudatories,   *read* feudatories.
" 115, *ex.* 69, "   " does the service &c.,   " with reference to his *p'in*, character, quality, *p'ing²*, pronounces a criticism.
" 116, compare 83, 84, with 129, *note* 10, page 130.
" 116, *ex.* 84, *for* he said   *read* you may say.
" 117, " 93, " is promoted   " must be promoted.
" 117, " 93, " There is a volume &c., " You have left behind the volume in the press.
" 117, " 92, *note*, 2, *for wu lun* should follow Government.
" 121, " 113, " " given in 130, *read* given in 113.
" 123, " 117, " " as the verb   " as the subject of the verb.
" 127, " 123, " 1, *add*   The word '*huang* ought possibly to be written with the 61st Radical. It would then mean unsettled in mind.
" 130, line 5,   *for* wan't   " want.

CORRECTIONS AND ADDITIONS.

IV.—ERRORS IN THE PEKING SYLLABARY.

Page 3, sound 353, for 肚 read 妒
" 32, head line " chang – chêng " chang – ch'êng.
" 65, " jang – ju " jan – ju.
" index " 哼 165 " 跨 165
" 83, head line " mi – mın " mi – mo.
" 91, " pa – p'ang " pa – p'ên.
" 99, " su – sung " su – shai.
" 111, index " 肚 353 " 妒 353

Note that 丸 綂 芃 under the 2nd Tone of the 105th Syllable, should be under the 2nd Tone of the 398th.

" 酷 under the 1st Tone of 163rd Syllable, should be under the 4th Tone.

V.—ERRORS IN THE WRITING EXERCISES.

Page 8, Radicals 83 乞, and 84 氏, have been transposed.

VI.—ERRORS IN PUNCTUATION IN THE TZŬ ERH CHI.

1.—Add a point below the following characters.

PART III.

Exerc.		ex.		Character		Exerc.		ex.		Character	
	3,	"	30,	"	5.		9,	"	4,	"	2.
"	4,	"	14,	"	35.	"	9,	"	5,	"	11.
"	5,	"	12,	"	11.	"	9,	"	6,	"	23.
"	5,	"	18,	"	6.	"	9,	"	6,	"	33.
"	5,	"	20,	"	12.	"	10,	"	15,	"	23.
"	5,	"	20,	"	23.	"	11,	"	7,	"	10.
"	6,	"	7,	"	8.	"	11,	"	11,	"	5.
"	6,	"	9,	"	22.	"	12,	"	12,	"	8.
"	7,	"	16,	"	2.	"	12,	"	13,	"	16.
"	7,	"	16,	"	9.	"	12,	"	14,	"	6.
"	8,	"	8,	"	12.	"	12,	"	17,	"	5.
"	8,	"	15,	"	5.	"	13,	"	11,	"	5.
"	8,	"	16,	"	2.	"	13,	"	12,	"	2.
"	8,	"	18,	"	2.	"	13,	"	12,	"	12.
"	8,	"	18,	"	8.	"	13,	"	20,	"	4.
"	8,	"	19,	"	5.	"	14,	"	12,	"	12.

[Continued on next page.

TZŬ ERH CHI. **Colloquial Series.**

Exerc.	14,	ex.	13,	Character	宜
,,	15,	,,	8,	,,	5.
,,	15,	,,	8,	,,	18.
,,	15,	,,	8,	,,	23.
,,	15,	,,	8,	,,	44.
,,	15,	,,	9,	,,	26.
,,	15,	,,	11,	,,	35.
,,	15,	,,	13,	,,	4.
,,	16,	,,	9,	,,	2.
,,	16,	,,	10,	,,	20.
,,	16,	,,	10,	,,	35.
,,	16,	,,	10,	,,	56.
,,	16,	,,	13,	,,	8.
,,	16,	,,	15,	,,	3.
,,	16,	,,	15,	,,	13.
,,	16,	,,	16,	,,	9.
,,	16,	,,	17,	,,	35.
,,	17,	,,	12,	,,	20.
,,	18,	,,	6,	,,	12.
,,	18,	,,	7,	,,	2.
,,	18,	,,	8,	,,	6.
,,	18,	,,	9,	,,	3.
,,	18,	,,	12,	,,	7.
,,	18,	,,	13,	,,	4.
,,	18,	,,	14,	,,	4.
,,	18,	,,	17,	,,	12.
,,	19,	,,	12,	,,	23.

Exerc.	19,	ex.	18,	Character	10.
,,	19,	,,	18,	,,	42.
,,	21,	,,	11,	,,	4.
,,	21,	,,	12,	,,	6.
,,	22,	,,	12,	,,	4.
,,	22,	,,	19,	,,	5.
,,	23,	,,	10,	,,	57.
,,	26,	,,	17,	,,	35.
,,	26,	,,	21,	,,	2.
,,	27,	,,	15,	,,	30.
,,	29,	,,	3,	,,	4.
,,	29,	,,	14,	,,	7.
,,	29,	,,	17,	,,	5.
,,	30,	,,	8,	,,	18.
,,	30,	,,	12,	,,	6.
,,	32,	,,	16,	,,	14.
,,	32,	,,	19,	,,	2.
,,	32,	,,	19,	,,	7.
,,	33,	,,	15,	,,	5.
,,	34,	,,	9,	,,	2.
,,	34,	,,	17,	,,	2.
,,	35,	,,	18,	,,	4.
,,	35,	,,	22,	,,	6.
,,	36,	,,	18,	,,	15.
,,	36,	,,	18,	,,	44.
,,	37,	,,	15,	,,	19.
,,	37,	,,	18,	,,	43.

PART IV,

N.B.—Count the columns from the right of the page.

Page	76,	Col.	2,	Character	7.
,,	76,	,,	4,	,,	1.
,,	76,	,,	6,	,,	音
,,	77,	,,	6,	,,	字
,,	77,	,,	9,	,,	15.
,,	78,	,,	2,	,,	6.
,,	79,	,,	12,	,,	2.
,,	82,	,,	3,	,,	21.
,,	82,	,,	4,	,,	3.
,,	85,	,,	2,	,,	3.
,,	85,	,,	4,	,,	1.
,,	85,	,,	6,	,,	3.
,,	85,	,,	7,	,,	19.

Page	86,	Column	6,	Character	11.
,,	89,	,,	9,	,,	是
,,	91,	Sentence	15,	,,	2.
,,	91,	,,	27,	,,	5.
,,	91,	,,	28,	,,	4.
,,	91,	,,	35,	,,	3.
,,	92,	Column	4,	,,	話
,,	93,	,,	10,	,,	9.
,,	94,	Sentence	16,	,,	6.
,,	94,	Column	9,	,,	7.
,,	95,	Sentence	10,	,,	3.
,,	105,	Column	2,	,,	4.
,,	105,	,,	6,	,,	5.

[*Continued on next page.*

CORRECTIONS AND ADDITIONS.

Page	105,	*Column*	7,	*Character*	1.	*Page*	97,	*Column*	7,	*Character*	15.
,,	109,	*Sentence*	4,	,,	1.	,,	98,	,,	4,	,,	3.
,,	109,	,,	9,	,,	4.	,,	98,	*Sentence*	28,	,,	8.
,,	109,	,,	15,	,,	8.	,,	99,	*Column*	1,	,,	4.
,,	109,	,,	24,	,,	3.	,,	99,	,,	7,	,,	15.
,,	109,	,,	26,	,,	5.	,,	99,	*Sentence*	3,	,,	10.
,,	97,	*Column*	3,	,,	7.	,,	99,	,,	11,	,,	5.
,,	97,	,,	4,	,,	10.	,,	100,	*Column*	7,	,,	12.
,,	97,	*Sentence*	43,	,,	4.	,,	100,	*Sentence*	76,	,,	15.
,,	97,	,,	45,	,,	7.	,,	101,	,,	40,	,,	7.
,,	97,	*Column*	7,	,,	1.	,,	102,	,,	19,	,,	4.

PART VIII.

Page 265, Col. 6, Character

2.—Remove the point below the following character.

PART III.

Exerc. 18, ex. 6, Character 16.

N.B.—Revise the Punctuation in Part III of the Key by the Table of Errata in the same Part given on pages 137 – 138.

"早期北京话珍本典籍校释与研究"丛书总目录

早期北京话珍稀文献集成

（一）日本北京话教科书汇编

《燕京妇语》等八种　　　　　　四声联珠
华语跬步　　　　　　　　　　　官话指南·改订官话指南
亚细亚言语集　　　　　　　　　京华事略·北京纪闻
北京风土编·北京事情·北京风俗问答
伊苏普喻言·今古奇观·搜奇新编

（二）朝鲜日据时期汉语会话书汇编

改正增补汉语独学　　　　　　　修正独习汉语指南
高等官话华语精选　　　　　　　官话华语教范
速修汉语自通　　　　　　　　　无先生速修中国语自通
速修汉语大成　　　　　　　　　官话标准：短期速修中国语自通
中语大全　　　　　　　　　　　"内鲜满"最速成中国语自通

（三）西人北京话教科书汇编

寻津录　　　　　　　　　　　　北京话语音读本
语言自迩集　　　　　　　　　　语言自迩集（第二版）
官话类编　　　　　　　　　　　言语声片
华语入门　　　　　　　　　　　华英文义津逮
汉语口语初级读本·北京儿歌　　汉英北京官话词汇
北京官话：汉语初阶

（四）清代满汉合璧文献萃编

清文启蒙　　　　　　　　　清话问答四十条
一百条・清语易言　　　　　清文指要
续编兼汉清文指要　　　　　庸言知旨
满汉成语对待　　　　　　　清文接字・字法举一歌
重刻清文虚字指南编

（五）清代官话正音文献

正音撮要　　　　　　　　　正音咀华

（六）十全福

（七）清末民初京味儿小说书系

新鲜滋味　　　　　　　　　过新年
小额　　　　　　　　　　　北京
春阿氏　　　　　　　　　　花鞋成老
评讲聊斋　　　　　　　　　讲演聊斋

（八）清末民初京味儿时评书系

益世余谭——民国初年北京生活百态
益世余墨——民国初年北京生活百态

早期北京话研究书系

早期北京话语法研究
早期北京话语法演变专题研究
早期北京话语气词研究
晚清民国时期南北官话语法差异研究
基于清后期至民国初期北京话文献语料的个案研究
高本汉《北京话语音读本》整理与研究
北京话语音演变研究
文化语言学视域下的北京地名研究
语言自迩集——19世纪中期的北京话（第二版）
清末民初北京话语词汇释